U.S. Army
Warrant Officers

TURNER PUBLISHING COMPANY
Publishers of America's History
412 Broadway, P.O. Box 3101
Paducah, KY 42002-3101
502-443-0121

U.S. Army Warrant Officers Association Staff:
CW5 Raymond A. Bell, President
CW5 Richard M. Scalzo, Sr., Vice President
CW5 John E. Lucius, Secretary
CW3 Alice V. Reid, Treasurer
CW4 (Ret) Don Hess, Executive Vice President

Copyright® 1996 Turner Publishing Company
All Rights Reserved.

Turner Publishing Company Staff:
Chief Editor: Robert J. Martin

Library of Congress Catalog Card No. 95-60321
ISBN: 1-56311-185-3
Limited Edition. Printed in the U.S.A.
Additional copies available from Turner Publishing Company

This book or any part thereof may not be reproduced without the written consent of
Turner Publishing Company. This publication was compiled using available information.
The Publisher regrets it cannot assume liability for errors or omissions.

Photo on cover and title page: The Quiet Professional *by Don Stivers in commemoration*
of 75 years of sacrifice and service by the Warrant Officers Corps.

Warrant Officer Eagle

Every warrant officer, regardless of specialty or component wears the warrant officer eagle. The warrant officer eagle was approved by the chief of staff, Army on 20 November 1920 and was adapted from the great seal of the United States, representing America. In conjunction with the Arrows, which symbolize the military arts and sciences, it is representative of the American soldier. The

surrounding wreath is the traditional symbol of victory or special achievement.

As a whole, the warrant officer eagle is truly representative of the warrant officer corps, for what is a warrant officer if not an American soldier who has achieved special qualifications in the military arts and sciences.

Table of Contents

Dedication

I am the Army Warrant Officer

My story is a proud one-worthy of being told—of an obscure and simplistic beginning. A story laced with words such as professionalism, pride, reliability, integrity, dedication, perseverance, courage, competence and technical expertise. A story that continues to grow in stature--a story without end. Rather, a future of proportions limited only by the parameters of imagination and innovation.

I was conceived of civilian parentage in 1886. My parents were the Army Headquarters Clerk and Field Clerk. It took some years for the Judge Advocate General to determine that my parents held military status. An act in 1918 established the Army Mine Planters Service where I was given my first titles of Master, Mate, Chief Engineer and Assistant Engineer of the Coast Artillery Vessels. In effect, I had three grades established for Masters, First and Second Mates. I was given an officer's uniform and my own distinctive insignia. By 1920, my technical expertise had been recognized and I was authorized to be appointed in clerical, administrative and band-leading activities. I was expanded to an Armywide authorization of 1,120. I had started to mature.

In 1922, my growth was restricted when my total authorization was reduced to only 500, plus the band-master and 40 mine planters. My rank was restricted to only one grade except in the mine planters. It was not until the 1940s, with a few exceptions in 1936, that I regained my momentum lost in the early 1920s.

An act in 1941 was the most significant legislation since my birth. The act authorized two grades: Chief Warrant Officer and Warrant Officer Junior Grade. Flight pay was authorized for duties involving aerial flight. The act also provided that I might be assigned to such duties as may be prescribed by the Secretary of War, and further, that I could be empowered to administer oaths for all military administration. I gained much stature and was destined for more rapid growth. By 1942, an examination was developed to allow me to expand further to some 40 occupational areas. In 1944, the first woman was appointed to my ranks.

Following World War II, my numbers were reduced along with the rest of the Army. I was limited to approximately 12,400 spaces. There was a surplus of warrant officers as a whole, but also several critical shortages in some hard-skilled areas. Between 1953 and 1957, the Department of the Army conducted a searching analysis of my program to determine my total contributions and my destiny.

The result of the Army's study reaffirmed a need for my services and my continuation. The study gave me the definition that stood for nearly 30 years: I am a highly skilled technician who is provided to fill those positions above the enlisted level which are too specialized in scope to permit the effective development and continued utilization of broadly trained, branch qualified commissioned officers."

A new warrant officer program was announced in 1960. During 1966 to 1969, I was further scrutinized for career development, additional pay, Regular Army appointments, below the zone promotions and civilian schooling. By the early to middle 1970s, it was determined that I would have a Senior Warrant Officer Course, training at the basic, intermediate and advanced levels- civilian schooling opportunities were to abound.

In 1984 I was again placed on the examination table. This time I received the most comprehensive analysis ever performed in my history. The Total Warrant Officer Study Group, commissioned by the Army Chief of Staff, determined what the future holds for me. The study reaffirmed the Army's continued need for my services and presented the Chief of Staff with a plan on how the future warrant officer force is to be accessed, trained, utilized, promoted and separated. Finally, after 68 years, I had my own institutional personnel management system. I am better trained, progressively utilized and given the opportunity to serve a full 30 years as a warrant officer. Congress has established another pay grade to fill an incentive gap between CW4 and retirement. For the first time in my history, I feel comfortable with the outlook of my future.

On 8 November 1985, a significant event took place that corrected a long-standing discrepancy between the Army and the other services' warrant officers. Public Law 99-145 was signed by the President and allowed for commissioning of all services' warrant officers at permanent grade W2. Previously, only the Navy, Marine Corps and Coast Guard warrant officers received commissions. I am now at the level of prestige enjoyed for many years by warrant officers in my sister services.

The years have seen my active participation in shaping policies and programs that affect my destiny. I have my own career manager at Department of the Army who understands my uniqueness. I gained voting rights in the 1970s on promotion and selection boards. I have expanded to over 70 occupational specialties and have survived many combat missions. I have flown aircraft on the front line, sailed ships of supplies, doctored, administered, spoken, written, advised, assisted, commanded, maintained and been an integral part of every aspect of our great Army. I have provided the cohesion for many a unit.

I am the Army Warrant Officer.

(The above article, author unknown, briefly portrays the Army warrant officer from inception to present. Warrant officers had been the Army's technical experts for over 77 years).

4

Acknowledgments

Don Hess
Executive Vice President USAWOA

Since June 1920, the U.S. Army has been well served by a small group of quietly professional individuals known as "warrant officers." From the original small group of the "dough-boy" era who dealt with mine sweeping and harness and horses, today's warrant officers epitomize professionalism in a diverse range of technical specialties spanning the entire range of sophisticated equipment essential to the modern Army. They hold the Army's institutional knowledge and are the masters of today's technological frontier serving as leaders, trainers, and maintainers of the systems and soldiers entrusted to their care. They continue to quietly and carefully build on the reputation of professional excellence established by the warrant officers of years past.

This book represents an attempt by the U.S. Army Warrant Officers Association to provide, in one publication, a synopsis of the Army Warrant Officer Corps from its inception through 1995, the 75th anniversary of the Corps as we know it today.

The reader will find this book includes coverage of the Warrant Officer Corps and the Warrant Officers Association for several reasons. First, prior to the early 1960s the Warrant Officer Corps received little or no attention from the Army. Career management for warrant officers was either non existent or fragmented as it suffered from centralized or decentralized management depending on the disjointed Army policies in effect at various times in history. As a result, appointment, assignment, promotion, utilization and training of warrant officers was inconsistent and resulted in great confusion about the role of the warrant officer.

Second, as a result of this confusion, concerned warrant officers, from their beginning, organized warrant officer associations. Through the years the associations addressed the professional concerns for this unique group of officers who felt they needed an organization dedicated exclusively to the interests of warrant officers.

Finally, the story of the Warrant Officer Corps is incomplete without including the role of the Association which has been a conduit in presenting these professional concerns to the Army leadership. The efforts of the Warrant Officers Association, although few in numbers, resulted in professional concerns being introduced, studied and implemented by the Army leadership. Since the early 70s the Army leadership has encouraged the Association's active participation in warrant officer issues and supported the Association's meetings with speakers at the highest Army level. The Association is grateful for their support.

This book is a labor of love. Other warrant officers, to numerous to mention, contributed their time, talent, experience and photographs to make this book possible. We especially owe a debt of gratitude to Turner's Mr. Bob Martin whose expertise and assistance were invaluable to us.

DON HESS,
CW4, USA, Retired
Executive Vice President, USAWOA

Publisher's Message

Dave Turner, President
Turner Publishing Company

The United States Army Warrant Officer Corps celebrated 75 years of proud service to our Nation in 1995. It is my privilege to publish their story which deservedly takes its place in the annals of distinguished military history. From humble beginnings of civilian lineage in 1886 with the Army Headquarters Clerk and Field Clerk ranks through the years in Army Mine Planters Service in 1918, fulfilling the highly technical military of occupational specialties in WWII, Korea, Vietnam, and the Gulf War, the Army Warrant Officer has answered the call and stood strong to make the U.S. Army successful in every endeavor.

I wish to thank CW4 (Ret) Don Hess, Executive Vice President of the United States Army Warrant Officers Association for his tireless effort in helping write and compile the manuscript as well as many of the historic photographs contained in this volume. Likewise, I thank the more than 500 U.S. Army Warrant officers and their families for submitting their personal vignettes and photographs for inclusion. This is your history and I hope it will be a keepsake which will remind you of the hard work and sacrifice that are necessary to keep America the land of the free and the home of the brave.

Sincerely yours,

Dave Turner
President

U.S. Army
Warrant Officers'
History

First National Convention of the USAWOA, Ft McPherson, GA, 11-13 Aug. 1921.

The Warrant Officer Story

The Warrant Officer Story brings to members of the United States Army Warrant Officers Association and to other warrant officers who wish to learn of it, a facet of our nation's history which has never been fully told.

This history is an earnest desire to tell the story of the thousands of men and women who have served the Corps, or may in the future serve in old and new ways to help keep the nation secure.

The story begins in the aftermath of World War I, and includes the trials, tribulations, and triumphs of a relatively small group of men and women who served in the Corps.

The Warrant Officer Story is told in two sections. Section one is the story of the Warrant Officer Corps. Section two is the story of the Warrant Officers Association which had its early beginnings immediately after the inception of the Corps.

The History of the Army Warrant Officer

The Beginning (1916 - 1940)

In the U. S. Army, the warrant officer lineage can be traced back to the Headquarters Clerks of 1896, later designated Army Field Clerks. However the first Army use of the words "warrant officer" occurred on 20 July 1918 when an Act of Congress established the Army Mine Planter Service as part of the Coast Artillery Corps and appointed in it warrant officers to serve as masters, mates, chief engineers, and assistant engineers of each vessel. This act established three grades for warrant officers - master, first mate and second mate, and corresponding grades for marine engineers. A separate section on the evolution of the Mine Planter Service is included in Chapter XII.)

Although the Army rank of warrant officer first appeared in the Mine Planter Service in 1918, the subsequent creation of the rank for the Army as a whole was authorized on June 4, 1920. The principle idea was that such officers should perform clerical and administrative duties which, during World War I, had been performed by Army Field clerks (formerly headquarters clerks) and Field Clerks, Quartermaster Corps (formerly Clerks, Quartermaster Corps) thereby rendering unnecessary the continued services of such Clerks. This historical interrelations of Army warrant officers and field clerks deserves special attention because their employment in the Army affected and was affected by the creation and evolution of the rank of warrant officer.

The work of the Army Field Clerks and Field Clerks, Quartermaster Corps, in World War I was officially considered to be "of the greatest importance" in connection with the organization of the Army and the administration of its affairs and the need for specialized personnel in the Army to handle its clerical work. This concern was expressed by the War Department on May 19, 1920 in an appeal addressed by the Secretary of War on that date to the Senate Committee on Military Affairs, requesting the inclusion in H.R. 12775, then before Congress, of a section authorizing the appointment of warrant officers outside the Army Mine Planter Service. The statement was made in this communication that the primary purposes of creating the office of warrant officer for the Army as a whole, as understood by the War Department, would be those of rendering more economical and efficient the administra-

tion of the larger tactical units in the field by furnishing a class of officers who would be able to perform many of the subaltern duties otherwise performed by commissioned officers at division, corps and Army headquarters. Another purpose for creating the office of warrant officer would be to provide the means of recognizing the services of those enlisted men who had served creditably as commissioned officers in World War I, but, who, because of a lack of educational qualifications, were ineligible for appointment to commissioned grades in the Regular Army. It was also pointed out that the creation of the rank of warrant officer for the Army as a whole would afford a means of eliminating from the Army in the field the Army Field Clerks and Field Clerks, Quartermaster Corps, who, "because of their lack of qualifications for or authority to command, have always occupied an anomalous position in the Army in the field." It was suggested that those clerks who had the necessary military qualifications for service in the field could be appointed warrant officers.

While the War Department had the view expressed above, it is evident that the Congress, in enacting the legislation creating the warrant officer grade (other than Army Mine Planter Service), had in mind improvement of the situation of career enlisted men by providing a higher grade and better status to which they could be appointed after long and faithful service. In defense of the legislation, Mr. Wadsworth stated on the floor of the Senate:

"This provision is for the very purpose of giving better treatment to veteran non-commissioned officers of the Regular Army, the old sergeants and quartermaster sergeants, and men of that high grade and type. This provision is for the very purpose of taking better care of them and giving them a better status. An enlisted man, having served 25 years in the Regular service and reached the grade of top sergeant, has reached the age, probably, of 60 years. He cannot become a second lieutenant because the average age of second lieutenant in the Army is only about 27 or 28." (Page 5695, Congressional Record, April 7, 1920.)

On June 4, 1920, H.R. 12755 was approved and included the section (4a) which had been requested by the War Department. It authorized a maximum of 1,120 warrant officers in addition to those who had been authorized for the Army Mine Planter Service by the Act of July 9, 1918, and subsequent related acts. The 1120 authorized positions were to be filled by former officers who had served honorably in World War I, enlisted men with at least 10 years service with 5 years service if they had served in World War I; Army Field Clerks, Pay Clerks, Quartermaster Corps, and Band Leaders. In 1922 the ceiling for warrant officers had been lowered to 600, exclusive of 40 Mine Planter Service warrant officers and also of Band Leaders. In 1926 Congress passed a law which gave Field Clerks the rank and pay of warrant officers because they did not transfer in the numbers anticipated.

War Department General Orders, No. 65, October 29, 1920, published regulations concerning the appointment and assignment of warrant officers, providing, among other things, that they should not be permanently appointed in branches, but of the Army at large, and that they would be assigned to tactical units, departments, corps, area headquarters, etc., for clerical, administrative and supply duties. By the terms of War Department General Orders, No. 71, December 1, 1920, warrant officers were exempted from the jurisdiction of special courts martial. War Department Circular No. 384, November 16, 1920, prescribed the uniform to be worn by warrant officers. (A separate article on the history

of the warrant officer uniform and insignia, by CW4 John "Mike" Yates is printed in Chapter VI.)

Between 1922 and 1935, except for Band Leaders and members of the Mine Planter Service, no appointments to the warrant ranks were made. There was only one pay grade from 1920 to 1941, except in the Mine Planter Service (as previously mentioned).

Army figures show that the strength varied over the years. From 963 in 1922 it rose gradually to 1263 in 1927, dropping back to 731 in 1941. However, in spite of losses due to death and retirement, between 1936 and 1937 the number did increase from 784 to 794. The reason was that in 1936 examinations were given and a list of eligibles was established from which to appoint individuals to refill vacancies in the Warrant Officer Corps.

Even in 1936 the Army was uncertain about what an Army warrant officer was and whether there was a place for the warrant officer in the Army's personnel structure. Although it had given the rank to such specialists as band leaders, marine engineers and field and pay clerks, it had also used the rank and the Corps as a reward for former commissioned officers who no longer met the officer educational requirements, and as a reward for enlisted personnel with long service. In a report to the Military Affairs Committee of the House of Representatives the Army stated: "For the future, then, the grade provides a suitable reward for outstanding noncommissioned officer who are too old to be commissioned and who otherwise could look forward to no further advancement."

"In the Army there are organizational needs for only two general classes of personnel, namely, officers and enlisted men.

"Thus, primarily to reward those outstanding noncommissioned officers, there has been created an office or position (warrant officer grade) not demanded by organizational needs, but which is justifiable, even though the position does not fit readily into the military system."

In 1939, this was still the official Army staff position, as a memorandum from the G-1 to the chief of staff shows: " .... The warrant officer grade has been used as a means of rewarding enlisted men of long service and special qualifications rather than to fill essential military personnel requirements .... Increase in the authorized strength of warrant officers is not contemplated upon mobilization except as to requirements for bandleaders." The total strength of the Warrant Officer Corps decreased until 1942 because of the large numbers of warrant officers who were being transferred to commissioned status during that period.

Expansion (1941 - 1947)

In 1941 the second truly important piece of legislation affecting Army warrant officers was passed. An Act of August 1941, amplified by an Executive Order in November of that year, provided that warrant officers could be assigned duties as prescribed by the Secretary of the Army and that when such duties necessarily included those normally performed by a commissioned officer, the warrant officer would be vested with all the powers usually exercised by commissioned officers in the performance of such duties. The Act of 1941 also established two warrant officer grades, Chief Warrant Officer and Warrant Officer Junior Grade, and authorized flight pay for those whose duties involved aerial flight.

During World War II, there was no clear policy on warrant officers within the Army. Appointment, assignment, promotion, utilization and training of warrant officers were decentralized to major commands with little supervision from the War Department General Staff. Thousands of warrant officers were appointed but there are no exact figures on the numbers made. These warrant officers served in some forty occupational areas during that war. In January, 1944 the appointment of women as warrant officers was authorized, and by the end of the war there were forty-two female warrant officers on active duty. (A separate chapter is included on the evolution of female warrant officers.)

Consolidation (1948 - 1956)

After World War II, appointment of warrant officers ceased. But in 1948 and into 1949 a series of competitive examinations was given which led to the appointment of about 6000 Regular Army warrant officers, 4500 were appointed in 1948, an additional 1500 in 1949. This long-range warrant officer career plan, began in 1948, provided for Army TOEs to be redrafted to provide a number of positions especially for warrant officers. This concept of incentive, rather than reward, was to be a capstone rank into which enlisted personnel could advance. However, this change resulted in mixed utilization so that, in practice, warrant officers became largely interchangeable with junior commissioned officers or senior enlisted personnel. The Korean War forced abandonment of this program late in 1950.

The *Career Compensation Act of 1949* provided two new pay rates for warrant officers. The designations of Warrant Officer Junior Grade and Chief Warrant Officer were retained, but the grade of Chief Warrant Officer was provided with pay rates W2, W3 and W4. In the *Warrant Officer Personnel Act of 1954*, these three pay rates became grades and the Warrant Officer Junior grade, became Warrant Officer.

In 1951, centralized control of Army warrant officer appointments was given back to major commanders, repeating the pattern of World War II. The result was the appointment of about 14,000 temporary warrant officers in some 60 different military of occupational specialties (MOS) most of which were the same as MOSs for commissioned officers. In 1952, this appointment program was brought to a halt because of budgetary limitations. Also, for budgetary purposes, warrant officers were counted as commissioned officers. With Congress closely scrutinizing the officer structure, the Army decided that spaces taken by warrant officers took away spaces that could be better employed for commissioned officers. A Defense Department sponsored committee recommended that the warrant officer be eliminated from all services in favor of a limited duty officer program. The Army refused to concur in this program, and instead, pressed for a *Warrant Officer Personnel Act* which was passed.

The end of the Korean War brought cuts in Army personnel strength and warrant officers were not exempt. A 20 percent reduction in strength was ordered and a 30 percent cut in requirements. Although warrant officers were used extensively in the Korean War, it had become apparent that the use of the warrant officer grade as either a reward or an incentive was inadequate. Needed as a basis for the Warrant Officer Corps was a new concept consistent with functional Army requirements. A Study Group was formed in 1953 and their recommendations approved in February 1954. That study recommended a further study which was begun in April 1954, and completed in October. From October, 1954 to January 1957, the recommendations of the second study were reviewed, coordinated and modified.

Revitalization (1957 - 1975)

"The Future of the Warrant Officer"

In January, 1957, the Army issued an approved concept and policy for the warrant officer based on the above study, which is quoted in part below:

"1. The warrant officer continues to have a definite place in the Army's personnel structure in spite of anxiety in some quarters that the Army may have little need for the Warrant Officer in the future.

"2. An increasing requirement for personnel to operate and maintain mechanical, electrical, and electronic equipment provides a firm future for the Warrant Officer. These jobs in which continuity of both assignment and requirement options must be filled by personnel who possess a high degree of technical skill acquired through extensive training. Because of the extension of the Warrant Officers into the technical areas, a gradual reduction of Warrant Officer spaces in the administrative and supply areas will evolve.

"3. The Warrant Officer, under the Army's present concept, is a highly skilled technician who is provided to fill those positions above the enlisted level which are too specialized in scope to permit the effective utilization of broadly trained, branch-qualified commissioned officers. Warrant Officers will be utilized only to fill bona fide organizational requirements and will not be considered as a category of personnel established as a reward or incentive for either enlisted personnel or former commissioned officers."

The Army finally developed a clear and concise definition of a warrant officer : An officer appointed by warrant by the Secretary of the Army to perform specialized or technical middle management functions above the enlisted level, to specialized for commissioned officer, and technical as opposed to tactical."

The Army adopted a "two phase" program to carry out its concept. Phase I consisted, essentially, of a forced attrition program to bring the warrant officer corps down to 10,500 men, and Phase II, the retraining or reclassifying of those who held unwanted MOS into needed fields, retiring non-regulars at 20 years service, but keeping Regulars who could not be reclassified or retrained until they had completed 30 years service or until they retired voluntarily, whichever came first.

Although Phase I was essentially completed in March, 1959, a full three years ahead of schedule, the Regular Army issue remained. There were 3294 Regular Army warrant officers, but only 1373 were serving on active duty as warrant officers. The balance were serving as commissioned officers, and, although experience indicated that few would ever serve as warrant officers, space had to be kept to permit this if they so desired.

In 1960, the Army ordered its new warrant officer program implemented. It published its new MOS manual for warrant officers, outlined utilization policies, criteria for selection of warrant officer positions, and instructions for conversion to the warrant officer MOS system. Although the warrant officer program was vastly improved it did not standardize personnel policy among the various monitoring branches which assigned warrant officers and it failed to reinstate a Regular Army Warrant Officer appointment program.

In 1966, as part of a continuing effort to improve operation of the new concept, another Warrant Officer study group was formed at Department of the Army. This study was to develop a formal Warrant Officer Career Program that would be responsive to future Army requirements while concurrently offering enough career opportunities to attract high quality personnel.

The Study Group examined all aspects of the Warrant Officer Corps, made a number of recommendations in areas such as pay, promotion, utilization, and education. As a result of these recommendations various actions were initiated over the next 6 years to provide more attractive career opportunities for warrant officers. Below the zone selection for promotion grade CW3 and CW4 were implemented in 1967. The Regular Army program was reopened to warrant officer applicants in 1968 after have been closed for 20 years, and subsequent changes reduced service eligibility criteria and simplified application procedures. Since 1970 the military education available to warrant officers has been remarkably expanded. Previously, there was no formal progressive military schooling program for warrant officers. By the end of 1972, a tri-level education system had been established which provided formal training at the basic or entry level for warrant officers in 59 occupational specialties at the intermediate or mid-career level for 53 specialties and at the advanced level for 27 specialties. In 1973, the three levels of training were redesignated from basic, intermediate, and advanced, to entry, advanced and senior, respectively. Simultaneously, as the result of successful testing of the concept, the Warrant Officer Senior Course (WOSC) was established to provide all warrant officers with access to the highest level of professional education.

In 1973, DA began to implement a plan to close the gaps in the warrant officer military education system by directing the expansion or modification of existing advanced (formerly intermediate) courses to accommodate all warrant officer specialties. Civil schooling opportunities also increased during this period. The educational goal for warrant officers was upgraded from a two-year college equivalency to attainment of an associate degree. Warrant officers, for the first time, were authorized entry into fully funded civil school programs. As a means of aiding progression toward goal achievement, cooperative degree programs began to be established in the colleges and universities near the installations conducting the warrant officer career course in order to provide students in the military establishment the opportunity of completing the requirements for MOS related associate degrees while in attendance at their career courses. In conjunction with increased educational opportunities, duty positions requiring warrant officers with master's degrees were validated for the first time by the Army Education Requirements Board (AERB). As a means of forecasting and controlling their assignment and training opportunities, warrant officers were incorporated into the HQ DA Projected Requisitioning Authority (PRA) a management tool long used for commissioned officers but not applied to warrant officers until 1975. By the close of 1975, the Army's capability for professionally developing the Warrant Officer Corps had been significantly expanded, and warrant officers in the modern program were being offered developmental opportunities that their predecessors never had available.

The years following inception of the Warrant Officer Career Program saw increasing warrant officer participation in the development of policies and programs. To lend greater visibility to the program and to serve as a contact point for warrant officer plans, a Warrant Officer Plans Section, headed by a warrant officer, CW4 John "Mike" Yates, was assigned to the Officer Personnel Management Directorate of the US Army Military Personnel Center (MILPERCEN). CW4 Yates was replaced by CW4 Richard Sauer. The early efforts and results of these two professionals laid the groundwork for the future warrant officer program management.

Later, these functions were moved to the Warrant Officer Professional Development Branch in the newly formed Warrant Officer Division of the Officer Personnel Management Directorate of MILPERCEN. Opportunities for professional development were enhanced by the formation of the Warrant Officer Division. The Division was organized in 1975 based on the recommendations contained in a 1972 study pertaining to the reorganization of the Office of Personnel Operations, the forerunner of MILPERCEN. The Warrant Officer Division was organized to manage all warrant officers not members of the special branches (MC, MSC, VC and JAGC). This formation was concurrent with the change in commissioned officer management philosophy from that of management by branch (e.g., Infantry, Engineer, Ordnance) to that of management by grade (e.g., COL, LTC, MAJ, and company grades. Previously, the Army warrant officer force career management had been transferred from one agency to another throughout the course of this century. In 1920, warrant officers were appointed in the Army-at-large to assignments in various headquarters and tactical units. In 1941, AR 610-5, Warrant Officer General Provision, specified The Adjutant General as the assignment agency for the warrant officer in accordance with the recommendations of the Chiefs of the Arms and Services concerned. In April 1960, based on an approved 1957 study, the management and assignment of warrant officers was transferred to the branches and remained there until 1965 when the Aviation Warrant Officer Branch, Office of Personnel Operations, was created to manage all aviation warrant officers. For the first time since the inception of the Warrant Officer Corps the mission of assigning, managing and professionally developing warrant officers (less the special branches) provided a centralized and recognizable coordination point for warrant officers. Warrant Officer career managers are assigned to the Warrant Officer Division (WOD), by branch specialty, to manage individual warrant officer careers. Career managers, in coordination with the Personnel Actions and Professional Development branches within WOD, tend to all career needs for the personnel they manage. Career managers are responsible for implementing military personnel management policies, programs and systems; assigning individuals to fill valid requirements; programming military and civilian schooling for warrant officers based on Army requirements; and providing individual counseling on career needs and development. In 1983, two warrant officer positions were established in the offices of the Deputy Chiefs of Staff for Personnel (DCSPER) and Plans and Operations (DCSOPS) to provide warrant officer perspective to the highest level of warrant officer program management. CW4 Richard Sauer was the initial officer assigned to DCSPER and CW4 John Morrison was assigned to DCSOPS. These professional warrant officers brought the warrant officer perspective to the highest level of warrant officer program management and by their performance ensured that the increasing technological complexity of the modern Army dictated a need for a corps of highly qualified warrant officers to fill those positions at the management level. *(More detailed information on the Warrant Officer Division, DCSPER and DCSOPS, including a listing of key personnel who have managed and established the policies affecting the Warrant Officer Corps since the inception of the Warrant Officer Career Program in 1975 is published in Chapter XIV.)*

Image Interpretation Technician (962A). Warrant Officers serving at the Washington Navy Yard, DC, 1973. Back row: Al Stoneking, Don Hopkins, Graham Murray, Harry Rettke (deceased). Middle row: Danny Fite, Paul Richard, Jim Brown, Ron Peterson, Hank King. Front row: Bob Matsunaga (deceased), Ted Armstrong, Col. Ardovin, Wayne Simpson, Mr. Gibson (deceased). (Courtesy of Paul B. Richard)

Total Force (1976-1984)

Recognizing the need for qualified, highly trained individuals available to rapidly expand the active Warrant Officer Corps in time of emergency and to meet other Army requirements, Reserve Component warrant officers not on active duty and National Guard warrant officers are integrated into the Army's professional development program. In 1978, the Officer Personnel Management System (OPMS) - USAR was established under the provisions of AR 140-10. Personnel Management Officers (PMO located at ARPERCEN in St. Louis, MO, provide counseling and assistance in career planning and training for each officer. The PMO's primary function is to keep those warrant officers for whom he or she is responsible, active in attaining or maintaining MOS qualification in accordance with mobilization requirements. (A separate chapter on the Reserve Component warrant officer is included as Chapter VIII.)

Total Warrant Officer System (1984-1987)

The greatest change in the history of the Warrant Officer Corps began quite informally. On a quiet Saturday morning in 1983, at the Warrant Officer Division, MILPERCEN, a visionary division chief, his professional development chief, and a small group of senior warrant officer career managers, met to discuss the future of the Warrant Officer Corps. From this small beginning evolved the Total Warrant Officer Study (TWOS) which was chartered by the Chief of Staff Army (CSA) in September 1984. TWOS was the first Department of the Army-level comprehensive study of warrant officer management across the Total Army. Essentially, TWOS was to answer the following questions, "What are warrant officers doing now?", "What should warrant officers be doing in the future," and "What is the definition of a warrant officer?" Based on the charter and assumptions that were developed, the TWOS Group developed this mission statement "Examine the role and utilization, professional development, management, compensation programs, policies and procedures, and recommend changes where the effect would enhance combat readiness for the Total Army." (Because of the importance of this document to the Warrant Officer Corps, the entire Executive Summary of the TWOS is published in Chapter XIII.)

Commissioning of Warrant Officers (1986)

While the TWOS was in progress another significant legislative event occurred in 1986 with the change in Title 10 of the US Code, the law governing treatment of military personnel. This law authorized the commissioning of warrant officers in all the services and recognized the warrant officer as a full fledged officer with all the rights and authority of a commissioned officer. It also standardized the procedures and policies among the Armed Forces on the utilization and treatment of warrant officers.

Under this law Regular Army warrant officers will be commissioned by the President upon promotion to Chief Warrant Officer. An other-than-Regular Army (OTRA) warrant officer will be commissioned as permanent Chief Warrant Officer by the Secretary of the Army. Temporary promotions under the Army of the United States system have no effect on commissioning. Warrant officers in grade WO1 will continue to be appointed, not commissioned, by the Secretary of the Army. There is no legal distinction between Presidential and Secretarial appointments. New policy provisions pertaining to commissioned warrant officers were approved in May 1987 by the Deputy Chief of Staff for Personnel. Warrant officers will continue to be assigned to warrant officer positions in the primary or additional military occupational specialties. The main effect of commissioning is on the powers of a commissioned warrant officer. The commissioned warrant officer is authorized to:

- Order enlisted soldiers into arrest or confinement.

- Administer an oath of enlistment or reenlistment.

- Administer various oaths in performance of duties when acting as an adjutant, assigned as a military personnel officer, or specifically designated by other Army regulations.

- Sit on courts of inquiry or be detailed as a general staff officer or inspector general.

- In the grade of CW3 or higher, when appointed by a general court-martial convening authority, act as a summary court-martial officer to try criminal offenses, conduct inquests or dispose of personal effects.

- In the grade of CW4, when appointed by a general court-martial convening authority (except a warrant officer possessing 713A) as an investi-

Image Interpretation Technician (962A). Warrant Officers assigned to USAINTC, Ft. Meade, MD, 1976. Back row: Al Stoneking, Graham Murray, Walt Enderlein, Bob Ralston, Ken Taylor, Harry Rettke (deceased), Don Young. Front row: Danny Fite, Don Hopkins, Hank King, Paul Richard, Ron Peterson. (Courtesy of Paul B. Richard)

1st Warrant Officer Company with TAC Officers and candidates. (Courtesy of Bruce W. Ohnesarge.)

CW5 Helton being promoted. (Courtesy of Bruce W. Ohnesarge.)

gating officer under the provisions of Article 32, USMJ).

These and other powers of the warrant officer are defined in AR 611-112, *Manual of Warrant Officer Military Occupational Specialties.*

Meanwhile, the TWOS completed their work and submitted their recommendations to the Chief of Staff Army. The TWOS group did their work well as evidenced by the approval of most of their specific recommendations by the Chief of Staff, Army. As a result, significant changes occurred which resulted in the adoption of the Total Warrant

Officer System. A cornerstone of the system was a new definition for warrant officers:

"An officer appointed by warrant by the Secretary of the Army based on a sound level of technical and tactical competence. The warrant officer is the highly specialized expert and trainer who, by gaining progressive levels of expertise and leadership, operates, maintains, administers, and manages the Army's equipment, support activities, or technical systems for an entire career."

Warrant Officer Management Act (WOMA)

With this definition as the cornerstone, the Army began to develop a Warrant Officer Management System. The passage of the Warrant Officer Management Act (WOMA) on 5 December 1991 gave the Army the legislative tools to establish a personnel management system for warrant officers which included:

- The creation of grade Chief Warrant Officer Five (CW5).

- A single promotion system. Before WOMA, warrant officers were under a dual promotion system (temporary - Army of the United States (AUS) and permanent - Regular Army (RA).

- Selective early retirement. A strength management provision that allows the Army to control the size of the retirement eligible force.

- Regular promotions below the zone (BZ) for CW4 and CW5 only. Before WOMA, BZ promo-

tions were authorized for grades CW3 and CW4. WOMA does not allow BZ promotions for CW3 as did the previous policy.

- Selective continuation in grade. A provision that allows the Army to selectively continue, in grade, warrant officers who are nonselect for promotion to the next higher grade but are required for a shortage MOS.

- RA warrant officers to sit on RA boards. Before the passage of WOMA, warrant officers were not allowed to be a member on any RA selection board.

- The Army to equalize action of two-time non-select separation procedures. This provision aligns warrant officers with the commissioned officer force in terms of the time allowed to be separated for reasons of a second-time non-select for promotion to the next higher grade.

WOMA became the foundation for the current Warrant Officer Personnel Management System which included the following major tenants in addition to those established by WOMA:

Position Coding

The most significant policy change to warrant officer management was to code positions on personnel authorization documents by rank. Position coding by rank was the catalyst for the restructure of the Warrant Officer Corps to include recruiting, utilization, training and professional development. For the first time the Army used documented requirements as the frame of reference for decisions about warrant officer actions. Before rank coding of positions, the MOS primarily determined the assignment of a warrant officer without regard to rank, experience and skills. Positions have been coded to reflect a rank to be used by the requisition authority and assignment managers at all levels. Rank coding allows warrant officers to be assigned to progressively more challenging duties during their careers and provides commanders with the right individual with the right training and experience to perform duties at different levels of responsibility.

Management by Warrant Officer Service

Under the 1992 Warrant Officer Management Act (WOMA) warrant officers are managed by years of Active Federal Warrant Officer Service (AFWOS) versus years of Active Federal Service (AFS). Warrant officer management begins at appointment as a warrant officer, however, seniority for pay and retirement is based on total years of AFS.

Each warrant officer has the opportunity to serve a full 30 years as a warrant officer or until reaching mandatory retirement at age 62, whichever occurs first. Warrant officer management is by year group (YG); the YG is the fiscal year (FY) in which appointed. YG management allows each warrant officer equal consideration for assignments, promotions, and schooling with others of similar experience and years of AFWOS.

Revised Education System

Another major tenet of the Warrant Officer Management System was a revised Warrant Officer Education System (WOES). Under this system warrant officers are trained for utilization at each of the four career levels (WO1/CW2, CW3, CW4 and CW5). As a part of WOES the Warrant Officer Technical and Tactical Certification Course (WOTTCC) was renamed the Warrant Officer Basic Course (WOBC) and the Senior Warrant Officer Training Course (SWOTC) was renamed the Warrant Officer Advanced Course (WOAC). Training for both the WOBC and WOAC is done at that the basic branch level. The Warrant Officer Staff Course (WOSC), for those selected for promotion to CW4 is conducted by the Warrant Officer Career Center (WOCC) at Fort Rucker, Alabama. The Master Warrant Officer Training Course (MWOTC) was renamed the Warrant Officer Senior Staff Course (WOSSC) and is also conducted by the WOCC.

The Warrant Officer Management System today includes the above tenets along with the provisions of WOMA mentioned above.

Warrant Officer Leader Development Action Plan (WOLDAP)

On 2 May 1992, the Office, Deputy Chief of Staff for Operations (ODCSOPS) activated the Leader Development Decision Network (LDDN) for formulating a Warrant Officers Leader Development Plan (WOLDP), applicable to both Active Component (AC) and Reserve Component (RC), to ensure the Army's total warrant officer personnel management and training systems produce competent and confident warrant officer leaders. The WOLDAP was formulated through a series of workshops with representatives from the Army staff, Major Army Commands (MACOMs), and selected other agencies concerned with warrant officer leader development. Also, each branch proponent contributed to the development process.

On 18 February 1992, the Chief of Staff Army (CSA) approved for implementation, the following recommendations of the WOLDAP study group:

- Establish warrant officer life cycle models for each MOS.
- Review, update, revise, and standardize the Warrant Officer Training System.
- Implement standardized selection criteria and accession goals for 8 years AFS with 12 years AFS accession cap.
- Conditional appointment to WO1 upon completion of WOCS.
- Establish by grade position coding for WO1/CW2; CW3; CW4 and CW5. Identify Army and Branch MOS immaterial warrant officer positions and pinpoint assignments for CW5s.
- Establish a warrant officer training institution to be executive agent for all warrant officer common core training and to conduct the WOCS, WOSC and WOSSC.
- Improve RC warrant officer recruiting with recruiter assets, better coordination between components, and RC command emphasis.
- Institutionalize and market understanding of warrant officer roles, duties and responsibilities.
- Raise civilian education goals to professionals the warrant officer force: obtain associate degree by career point (CW3), and bachelor degree by CW4. Identify more Army Education Requirements System (AERS) positions.
- Retain warrant officer insignia and centralized management.
- Establish State Military Academies for WOCS at selected regional sites and a credit to AC standard.
- Establish a limited warrant officer MOS system, similar to officer MOS II, for warrant officers through grade CW4.

As the Warrant Officer Corps celebrates 75 years of service to the Army in 1995, the role of today's warrant officer is drastically different from his or her predecessor. From the original small group of the "dough-boy" era who dealt with mine sweeping and harness and horses, today's warrant officers epitomize professionalism in a diverse range of technical specialties

Mass swearing-in of Warrant Officer candidates to WO1. (Courtesy of Bruce W. Ohnesarge.)

spanning the entire range of sophisticated equipment essential to the modern Army. They hold the Army's institutional knowledge and are the masters of today's technological frontier serving as leaders, trainers, and maintainers of the systems and soldiers entrusted to their care. They continue to build on the reputation of professional excellence established by the warrant officers of years past.

The Army is committed to full implementation of a professional warrant officer career program which results in warrant officers who start younger, serve longer, are better educated, and have better leadership skills; warrant officers who are the product of centrally managed training by a warrant officer institution; warrant officers who are professionally developed and have the right training for positions at all levels, including senior experienced warrant officers for critical jobs; and warrant officers in the Reserve Components who are available to support readiness.

From a past in which warrant officers have faithfully, successfully, bravely, and often brilliantly served their country as technicians, the future can be even more professionally rewarding as they serve as officers, leaders, soldiers and technicians. *(For more information on specific activities see the separate chapters on the following subjects: Reserve Components, WO Division, WO Insignia, WO Recruiting, Female WO, "Firsts: in the Corps")*

Reserve Components

by CW5 David P. Welsh

Introduction

On 5 October 1981, John O. Marsh, Jr., Secretary of the Army, stated "When I talk about the total force concept, I mean just that. This is a three legged stool, whereby the Active Army, the National Guard, and the Reserve are coequal partners. This nation is equally dependent upon each of the legs. The reliance of the Total Army on the Reserve Component continues to grow and the future will challenge the Total Army's ability to meet demands across the entire spectrum of conflict. "Therefore, the Reserve Component warrant officer must be fully prepared for combat prior to mobilization. In order to be fully prepared, they must possess and be proficient in the skills required to execute their defined roles of leader, trainer, operator, maintainer, or manager. This expanded role clearly recognizes the importance of the Reserve Component warrant officer as part of our deterrent force."

BG Goodbarry and CW5 Helton cutting the ribbon to dedicate the Warrant Officer Career Center (WOCC) at Ft. Rucker, AL on Oct. 1, 1992. (Courtesy of Bruce W. Ohnesarge.)

Currently, more than half of the Army's deployable forces are in the Reserve Components. As of the end of fiscal year 1995 there were 7,261 male and 270 female warrant officers in the Army National Guard (ARNG) with some 4,015 aviators and the balance in technical MOS. In the Army Reserve (USAR), there were 5,596 male and 403 female warrant officers with 1,949 aviators and the balance in technical MOS. The federal mission of the ARNG has evolved into one of providing combat forces for expansion of the Army during contingency operations and mobilization. Conversely, the predominant USAR mission is to provide combat support (CS) and combat service support CSS units and elements for contingency operations and during mobilization. In addition, the USAR contains a pool of individuals to provide Individual Mobilization Augmentees to the expand active Army, JCS, DoD and joint activity staffs for sustained operation during contingencies and/or mobilization. The USAR manpower pool also provides Individual Ready Reservists (IRR) and retirees for recall during the various phases of mobilization.

The Army will require the deployment of Reserve Component units and individuals during

WO Candidates being sworn-in as WO1s in the Regular Army. (Courtesy of Bruce W. Ohnesarge.)

most future contingency operations in the future. Total Army force planning is no longer a concept, it is integral to contingency plan execution.

Army National Guard Background

The Army National Guard has more than 2,600 units in about 3,600 communities across the nation and in its territories. These units train at more than 3,000 armories and operate about 930 maintenance shops, 115 aviation facilities and 71 major training sites, which support their efforts. This network of support facilities includes traditional training sites at Camp Shelby, Miss., Fort Bragg, N.C., Camp Dodge, Iowa, and Fort Dix, N.J. A field medical training site in Panama maintains and restores medical equipment used by medical units deploying to Central and South America. Other medical training sites are at Camp Shelby and Fort Indiantown Gap, Pa.

Today, almost one half the Army's combat units and more than a third of its overall strength are found within the Guard. About 398 Army National Guard units and more than 62,000 Guardsmen supported Operations Desert Shield and Desert Storm. Of these, more than 37,000 deployed to Southwest Asia, 3,400 went to Europe and almost 6,000 were stationed in the United States in case of need. The beginning of 1996 once again finds the Army National Guard answering the call to the colors with some 21 units /mobilized under Presidential Selected Reserve Call-up (PSRC) for Operation JOINT ENDEAVOR in support of the Implementing Force (IFOR) operations in Bosnia as this history goes to press.

In 1993, Army National Guard personnel numbers declined, as did the active military establishment. Reaching peak strength of 457,000 in 1989, the Guard reduced to about 431,000 in 1992, and is projected to drop to 367,000 by fiscal year 1999.

Army Reserve Background

The Army Reserve traces its origin to 1908, when Congress authorized the establishment of a medical reserve corps that could be ordered to active duty to support the Army. In 1912 Congress authorized an Army Reserve of trained citizen-soldiers, and in 1916 the National Defense Act created the Officer Reserve Corps and the Enlisted Reserve Corps. Once established, the Army Reserve immediately became a valuable resource to the Army. More than 160,000 served on active duty during World War I and more than 200,000 served in World War II, often

providing much-needed leadership to a rapidly expanding Army.

More than 240,500 Army Reservists were activated for the Korean War, with 14 battalions, 40 companies and a large number of individuals going to Korea. In 1961 almost 69,000 USAR soldiers were activated for the Berlin Crisis. During the Vietnam War, Army Reservists were again activated, with 35 units serving in Vietnam. Since then, Army Reservists have been activated to serve in Grenada, Panama, Southwest Asia, Somalia and Haiti. Of these, the activation for Operation Desert Shield/Desert Storm was the largest, with approximately 85,000 being activated and 40,000 serving in Southwest Asia. Among these were approximately 20,000 IRRs, who filled vacancies in units or performed other specialized duty. During those operations, Army Reservists provided transportation, medical, civil affairs, postal, engineer, military police, maintenance and many other kinds of support. As this history goes to press, the Army Reserve is once again answering the "call to the colors" under Presidential Selected Reserve Callup (PSRC) with over 50 units and well over 2,000 USAR soldiers (includes individual volunteers and Individual Mobilization Augmentees (IMA)) mobilized for Operation Joint Endeavor in support of NATO Implementing Force (IFOR) in Bosnia.

The U. S. Army Reserve is the active Army's federal reserve force. It is made up of highly trained and ready-to-go combat support and combat service support forces that can move on short notice to give the active Army the resources it needs to deploy overseas and to sustain combat troops during wartime, contingencies or other operations. It is the Army's main source of transportation, medical, logistical and other units, and it is the Army's only source of trained individual soldiers to augment headquarters staffs and fill vacancies in units.

The Army Reserve consists of the Selected Reserve (troop program units and individual mobilization augmentees), the Individual Ready Reserve (IRR) and the Retired Reserve, totaling more than 1,000,000 reservists, upon whom the President can call when needed. The drawdown of the Selected Reserve will achieve an end strength of 208,000 soldiers by 1998.

Environment

Compared to the Active Component the Reserve Component warrant officer's environment is unique. The typical Reserve Component warrant officer is fundamentally a citizen soldier. The role

of the citizen soldier can be traced to pre-Revolutionary days and every major war or mobilization since. In the civilian community they may be professionals in their field but, as a citizen soldier they must be professionals, trained and ready to mobilize at a moment's notice. The primary mission of the Reserve Component warrant officer is to prepare for wartime missions, to be able to meet the mobilization mission of the Total Army and to fight in combat. The ARNG warrant officer has an additional state mission; to be prepared to execute the orders of state authorities, when required, to protect and preserve life, peace, property, order, and public safety. Except during periods of Federal mobilization, state governors retain control of the ARNG.

Warrant Officer Insignia

Although there was little change in the management of the Warrant Officer Corps from its inception until its revitalization in 1957, the same cannot be said for the insignia and uniform worn by warrant officers through the years. Unlike the commissioned officer insignia which has remained constant from the beginning of our Army, the warrant officer insignia was subject to continuing modification at the hands of the Department of the Army.

On 15 December 1972 the current insignia of rank for warrant officers was adopted amid much controversy on the part of warrant officers. We are indebted to CW4 (Retired) John "Mike" Yates for the following historical information on the warrant officer insignia and uniform. His research was done while assigned to the Professional Development Branch, Military Personnel Center, DA, and published in the US Army Warrant Officers Association NEWSLINER in 1973.

A Short Introduction to the History of Human Fallibility
by CW4 (Ret) John "Mike" Yates

Since adoption of our new warrant officer insignia on 15 December 1972 the winds of controversy have swirled in various quarters. Some welcome the change and think the new bars look better than the old. Some oppose the change on the hallowed grounds of tradition. Some were offended because they weren't consulted prior to the change. Some have been subjected to jocular epithets such as "Mortician Technician," "Licorice Lieutenant," and "Black Panther." In any case, arguments have been adduced, justifications cited, tempers ruffled, and patience tested to no constructive end. The change has been made and it is irrevocable, at least for the time being.

Now it may be true, as alleged, that these new insignia permit easier identification of our ranks, but I have yet to be addressed as "Chief Warrant Officer Three." No indeed! My bosses continue to call me "Chief," a title to which my American Indian wife firmly believes I am not entitled. The point here is that from WO1 to CW4 our mode of address has been and continues to be relatively constant. The weight of opposition, then, seems to hinge upon the amended color of our insignia.

Having thus become interested in this question of color, I began an exodus out of the present into available historical documents to determine the extent to which our tradition has been violated by the switch from brown to black. (From this point on, I will italicize each color mentioned to help serve as points of reference.) The result of this journey was a surprising confirmation of human fallibility. This latest change was not the first revision of color imposed upon the Warrant Officer

Corps, nor the second, nor even the third. In one form or another we have been associated with and identified by a total of 8 different colors throughout our history. Where, then, lies tradition? The Corps will be celebrating its 55th birthday this July (1973), and 8 colors in 55 years produces an average of only 6.875 years per color: hardly enough time to build a main battle tank, much less a tradition. Here is a record of the excursion.

As is well-known by all faithful readers of Chapter 2, DA Pamphlet 600-11, the predecessor of the warrant officer was the Army Field Clerk and the Field Clerk, Quartermaster Corps, both of whom were authorized by the Act of August 1916. After their authorization, however, there was some controversy over their status. They were initially considered civilians, but eventually the Judge Advocate General determined that they had military status. This question having been settled, the War Department issued, on 29 December 1917, Change 1 to Special Regulations No. 41, paragraph 4 of which recognized this newly-won military status by prescribing a uniform for these personnel in the following words:

> Army Field Clerks, and Field Clerks, Quartermaster Corps, will wear the same uniform as officers, omitting all insignia of rank and the *brown* braid on the cuff of the service coat. Cord for service hat to be of *silver* and *black* silk intermixed.

It is in some respects unfortunate that the uniform regulations of today are not nearly as concise as this one. Nevertheless, those who have read this far will have been struck by three salient points:

a. The color *brown* was part of the commissioned officer's uniform;

b. This *brown* part of the uniform was specifically omitted from the uniform prescribed for the new, third category of personnel; and

c. *Silver* and *black* were the first colors used to identify and distinguish those personnel who were later to evolve into the Warrant Officer Corps.

It was not until the Appropriations Act of 9 July 1918 that the rank and grade of warrant officer, per se, was created. This act, published by the War Department in Bulletin No. 43, 22 July 1918, established:

> in the Coast Artillery Corps of the Regular Army a service to be known as the Army Mine Planter Service, which shall consist, for each mine planter in the service of the United States, of one master, one first mate, one second mate, one chief engineer, and one assistant engineer, who shall be warrant officers appointed by and holding their offices at the discretion of the Secretary of War.

Although no rank or precedence was established among these warrant officers, the act, in effect, created five grades inasmuch as a different level of annual pay was authorized for each of the five positions: "Masters, $1,800; first mates, $1,320; second mates, $972; chief engineers, $1,700; assistant engineers, $1,200."

The question of rank and insignia apparently caused some problems at Headquarters, for 18 months elapsed before insignia were announced for the newly created Warrant Officer Corps. We should note here that their original uniform was *blue*, but in a memorandum dated 25 November 1919 The Adjutant General was advised that "the Secretary of War directs that ... the issue of *blue* uniforms and *black* shoes is no longer authorized and the olive drab uniform as at present prescribed for the army will be issued in lieu thereof."

Insignia for shirt (1921). Left above: Commissioned officers; Right above: Warrant officers; Below: Enlisted personnel.

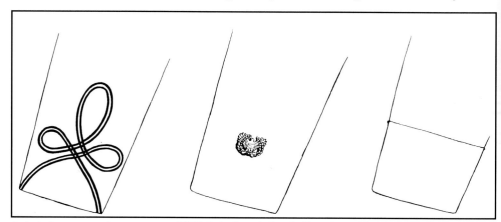

Insignia for overcoat sleeves, pattern of 1921. Left: Commissioned officers (captain), 1/8-inch black braid. center: Warrant officers, bronze, one inch high. Right: Enlisted men.

Shortly thereafter, in War Department Circular No. 25, 17 January 1920, a three-step sleeve-band system was established which, along with two descriptive devices, created distinctive insignia for each of the five job specialties. On the service coat and overcoat, the following insignia were to be worn:

a. *Masters and Chief Engineers*: "Four parallel bands of *brown* braid, 1/2 inch wide on each sleeve, 1/2 inch apart, the bottom parallel to, and 3 inches above, the edge of the sleeve.

b. *First Mates and Assistant Engineers:* Three bands of *brown* braid.

c. *Second Mates*: Two bands of *brown* braid.

d. In addition to the bands of braid, masters and mates were to wear an embroidered *brown* foul anchor" while the engineering personnel were to wear a "*brown* embroidered, three-bladed propeller" centered on each sleeve and placed 1/4 inch above the upper band.

The first official insignia of rank for the Warrant Officer Corps were *brown*! Possibly so. But we must pause here to recognize the fact that this same circular goes on to specify that:

> when the white uniform is worn the insignia of rank will be similar to that prescribed ... except that bands, anchors, and propellers will be or white.

As an amateur historian, I would be disposed to say that the precedent for wearing the first official color cannot be determined. It could have been either *brown* or *white*, depending upon whether that first warrant officer, putting on his first uniform under the first insignia system, chose to don his service uniform or his white uniform. The point here is that neither color had as yet been designated as a "branch" color.

The ink had barely dried on Circular No. 25

Insignia for collar (1918) for warrant officers.

when warrant officers in fields other than the Army Mine Planter Service were authorized by Act of Congress—Amendments to the National Defense Act—Articles of War, 4 June 1920. It is noteworthy that Section 4a in Chapter I of this act specifically provided for the appointment of Army Field Clerks and Field Clerks, Quartermaster Corps, as warrant officers. The provisions of this act were implemented in War Department Bulletin No. 25, 9 June 1920, and, predictably, the uniform question was again stirred up. The extent of the debate can be inferred from a memorandum dated 6 November 1920 which advised the Chief of Staff:

> "Now that the status of the recently authorized warrant officers has been determined ... the uniform should be settled."

If you keep in mind the fact that no rank or grade structure had as yet been authorized (other than the implied grades based on the job specialties in the Mine Planter Service), you will better understand the next section of the memorandum, which states:

> "The uniform for warrant officers, Mine Planter Service, was established last January in Circular 25, and it is suggested

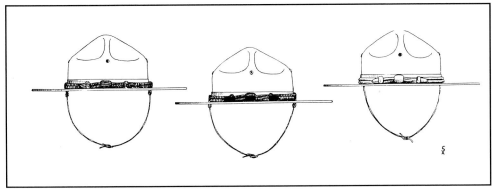

Service hats (ca. 1921) with prescribed hat cords: commissioned officers, (L) (black and gold); warrant officers, (C) (silver and black); and enlisted men, (R) (yellow). Both commissioned and warrant officers' hats are fitted with adjustable leather chin straps, while enlisted man's pattern is equipped with strings to be tied under the chin, as first issued in 1912. Most enlisted men purchased leather straps for their hats. Drawn from specimens in the author's collection.

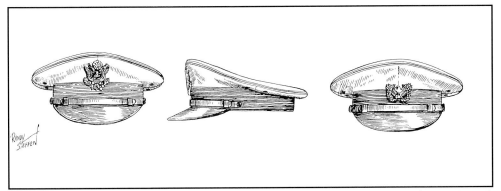

Service cap for commissioned officers, warrant officers and contract surgeons, 1921 pattern. (L) is the commissioned officer's cap; (R) is the warrant officers cap. It is made of olive-drab woolen material with a band of olive-drab mohair braid. Visor and chin strap are russet leather. Drawn from a specimen in the author's collection.

that that be taken as a precedent so that all warrant officers will wear the uniform of officers with the change in hat cord, the omission of the sleeve braid and the omission of rank insignia.

Ten days later, the War Department issued Circular No. 364, dated 16 November 1920, entitled "Uniform for Warrant Officers," which stated:

Warrant officers of the Army will wear the uniform prescribed for officers with the following changes and modifications:

1. No insignia of rank will be worn.
2. The braid on the sleeve will be omitted.

Warrant officers who served as commissioned officers during The World War are authorized to wear a braid of *forest green* on the sleeve.

3. The hat cord will be *silver* and *black* silk intermixed, with *black* acorns and keeper.

As was the case with the uniform of the field clerks, we find here that again the color *brown* (in the form of braid on the sleeve), rather than being assigned the function of warrant officer identification, has been specifically excluded from the warrant officer's uniform, while a new color, *green*, now makes its appearance for the purpose of identifying a particular category of warrant officers. Applicable to all, however, are the *silver* and *black* hat cords which we first saw announced in 1917 as part of the field clerks' uniform.

Up until now, we still have neither a warrant officer insignia nor a generally applicable rank structure for which insignia of rank could be devised. By 20 November 1920, however, we learn from a memorandum that the Chief of Staff had approved "for all warrant officers, an eagle stand-

ing on a bundle of arrows, all enclosed in a wreath," and this new insignia was included in War Department Circular No. 72, 16 March 1921, which again prescribed for warrant officers hat cords of *silver* and *black*.

A little less than two months later, in a memorandum dated 12 May 1921, the Quartermaster General was advised that the plaster model of the warrant officer insignia approved by the Secretary of the War has been executed by the sculptor Anthony de Francisci under the direction of the Fine Arts Commission, and from correspondence dated 24 June 1921 we learn that the United States Mint made the master hubs for the insignia. So now, finally, we have the warrant officer insignia—that famous and sometimes controversial "eagle rising"—a badge of distinction to be worn proudly by all warrant officers, setting them apart from both commissioned and enlisted as a separate, third category of personnel. But wait! Let's glance at the instructions which implemented the wear of this new insignia.

AR 600-35, 14 October 1921, is the uniform regulation which directs wear of the newly born eagle, and there he is, in paragraph 13b(2)(z):

"An eagle, rising, standing on a bundle of 2 arrows, all enclosed in a wreath, device to be 1 inch in height."

The first thing we notice, however, is that this remarkable eagle comes in two colors: for warrant officers wearing the service uniform, the regulation requires "insignia to be in dull *bronze*," but for those wearing the white uniform, it states: "Insignia.—Same except to be in *gold* or gilt metal." Well, that's all right. Warrant officers have always been the most flexible group in the Army. But little did they realize the degree to which this AR would flex them. For reading further, we find that instead of using the new insignia to identify all warrant officers as a corps, the regulation implemented

various exceptions which, in effect, split the Warrant Officer Corps up into four subgroups, each of which was identified by different insignia. Are you ready for such diversity? Here they are:

a. Group 1 (Army Field Clerks): "Two crossed pens, 1 inch in height, with the insignia of the Adjutant General's Department, 3/8 inch in height, in the lower angle."

b. Group 2 (Field Clerks, Quartermaster Corps): "Two crossed pens, 1 inch in height, with the insignia of the Quartermaster Corps, 3/8 inch in height, in the lower angle."

c. Group 3 (Army Mine Planter Service): The previously described bands of brown or white braid, plus anchor or propeller, as appropriate.

d. Group 4 (all other warrant officers): The previously described "eagle rising," plus, when wearing the white mess jacket, "Four bands of white braid ... on each sleeve." Here, it is interesting to note that in terms of implied grade, warrant officers in general were equated with the Mine Planter Service master or chief engineer.

Before passing onward, it is worth observing that this regulation closes with paragraph "45. Colors of branches," in which, although a branch color is assigned to such diverse elements as the Bureau of Insular Affairs, the Militia Bureau, and the Detached Enlisted Men's List, no color is assigned to the Warrant Officer Corps.

Five years passed before the next change of insignia, and this was not so much a change as a consolidation. If you remember the act of 4 June 1920 which authorized warrant officers other than Mine Planter Service, you will be interested to know that among its provisions was a statement that there would be no more appointments as Army Field Clerks or Field Clerks, Quartermaster Corps. Since then, presumably, attrition eliminated these two categories. In any case, the new uniform regulation, AR 600-35, 31 December 1926, omits any mention of them. The insignia specifications for the remaining two groups of warrant officers remained identical to those in the previous regulation. There was, however, a revision of our eagle's description into its final, and current, form. Paragraph 16b(2)(aa) states: "Warrant officers.—An eagle, rising with wings displayed standing on a bundle of 2 arrows, all inclosed in a wreath." Did you catch that change? The rising Eagle now has his wings displayed, and the insignia remains the same to this day. A total of 8 years, 5 months, and 23 days had passed from inception of the Warrant Officer Corps to finalization of its heraldic device and description, and the remaining 46 years give us a sufficient period on which to found a claim that our eagle truly represents a tradition. And if wt base the starting date on the earliest record of design approval (i.e., 20 November 1920) instead of final heraldic description, then the tradition stretches back over 52 years. It is appropriate, then, to interject a personal word of caution to those who advocate killing the "eagle rising" for the purpose of donning career branch insignia: be careful of that which you wish to cast away; it is one of our few links to a turbulent past.

The warrant officer uniform now remained stable for almost ten years. Then a significant change occurred in a context which made its announcement surprising. Near the end of this ten-year period of stability, the Army decided to adopt a new blue uniform. Regulations for acquisition and wear of the new uniform were issued as an interim change to the 31 December 1926 regulation via War Department Circular No. 66, 15 October 1936. In describing the ornamentation of various articles of this new uniform, the circular continually mentions "color of the arm or service" in connection with warrant officers. For examples:

a. Paragraph 2b discusses the full dress belt,

and subparagraph (4)(b) states: "Other officers, warrant officers, and contract surgeons Four-vellum gold lace … with three silk stripes … of the first-named color of the arm or service.

b. Paragraph 2j, in discussing the blue dress cap, states in subparagraph (5)(b): "Other officers, warrant officers, and contract surgeons A band of grosgrain silk of the first-named color of the arm or service, with a band of two-vellum gold lace.

c. Paragraph 2p(2)(b) gives the following specifications for the shoulder loops: "Other officers, warrant officers, and contract surgeons. The upper surface of shoulder loop to be covered with facing cloth of the first-named color of the arm or service."

d. Trimming of the blue dress trousers is given in paragraph 2r(3)(b) as follows: "Other officers, warrant officers, and contract surgeons a stripe of facing cloth of the first-named color of the arm or service, welted at the edges."

As a point of passing interest, we note that after the big play that sleeve stripes received in previous warrant officer uniforms, this circular's instructions on the new blue dress coat state, in

paragraph 2e(6)(c): "Warrant officers.—Without stripe." But let's return to the point. We know that until now no "branch" (i.e., arm or service) color has been specified for warrant officers. So what is this circular talking about? Aha! There it is— another interim change. Paragraph 2s states:

"Colors of arms or services.—As prescribed by paragraph 49, AR 600-35, with the following added:

v. Warrant officers, brown."

Here is the birth of our branch color, an occurrence preceded by over 18 years of prenatal activity and, thus, postponed into our own generation. I find myself wondering how the warrant officers of 1936 responded to this announcement. Were they shocked, amazed, pleased, or outraged? Did they, perhaps, have to put up with jokes somewhat cruder than "Licorice Lieutenant"? Apparently, I'm not the only one who wondered about this strange turn of events. A later memorandum on the subject stated in part:

"No explanation as to why this color was chosen could be located."

We might assume, as did the writer of the

memorandum, that the selection of *brown* was based on the precedent of the *brown* braid on the sleeve of the service uniform of warrant officers in the Army Mine Planter Service, but this assumption overlooks the fact that not once, but several times thereafter, *brown* was specifically excluded from warrant officer uniforms because its inclusion would fail to make the distinction sought inasmuch as *brown* braid was a part of the commissioned officer's uniform.

The writer goes on to point out that *silver* and *black* had at least an equal, if not a higher claim to precedence, but again he offers no explanation for the choice of brown. We are Left with the impression that the choice was a hurried and arbitrary attempt associated with adoption of the new blue uniform.

Whatever untold tales underlie that choice, we have still not reached the end of the journey, for there are still no warrant officer grades nor insignia of rank. All warrant officers received the same pay and allowances with the exception of the differential authorized for the five job specialties in the Mine Planter Service. It was not until 21 August 1941 that the Warrant Officer Corps was provided with a grade structure. In Chapter 384 of Public Law 230, the 77th Congress created two grades of warrant officer: chief warrant officer (CWO) and warrant officer, junior grade (WOJG), and authorized up to 40% of the Corps to be appointed in the grade of CWO. Another note of passing interest is that Section 5 of this chapter authorized warrant officers to retire after 15 years of active service, but we won't venture in that direction now.

Instead, let us consider the fact that the Army now had a problem: how would CWOs be distinguished from WOJGs? On 4 September 1942 the answer was published in Change 1 to AR 600-35 dated 10 November 1941, paragraph 25 of which describes insignia of grade:

"c. Warrant officers other than of the Army Mine Planter Service.

(1) Chief warrant officer— One gold bar 3/8 inch in width and 1 inch in length, with rounded ends, having a brown enameled top and a longitudinal center of gold 1/8 inch in width

(2) Warrant officer (junior grade)— One gold bar 3/8 inch in width and 1 inch in length, with rounded ends, having a brown enameled top and a latitudinal center of gold 1/8 inch in width."

Two months later, another change was made in order to identify aviation warrant officers, then called flight officers. War Department Circular 366, 7 November 1942, announced that flight officer bars were the same as those for WOJG, as shown above, except that the enamel would be of *blue* instead of *brown*. Throughout this period of change, the warrant officers of the Army Mine Planter Service remained unaffected, so that as of 7 November 1942 the Army had set apart three subgroups of warrant officers within the Warrant Officer Corps, each of which was distinctively identified by means of grade insignia:

a. Group 1 (Army Mine Planter Service): Sleeve braid, anchors and propellers, as previously explained.

b. Group 2 (Flight Officers): WOJG bar with *blue* enamel.

c. Group 3 (all other warrant officers): Brown enameled insignia as described above.

The next 5 months and 22 days passed uneventfully as the flight officers pinned on their new insignia and flew, bombarded, or navigated their ways through the wild blue yonder. But this peaceful interlude was interrupted by the crash of the single greatest change ever made in the policy

The new service uniforms, pattern of 1926. (L) Enlisted man, corporal, 2nd Cav., wears a peak-lapel-collar coat and new-pattern breeches. Leather leggings are higher than the 1917 pattern and lacing studs are closer together. A strip of leather around the tops, a continuation of the facing, identifies them as privately purchased and custom-made. Insignia on his sleeves indicate service of 12 months in France during World War I with 3 enlistments or 9 years. (Left arm) Single chevron on lower part of right sleeve shows receiving a single wound during the war. (C) Warrant officer, officer's service coat without braid on sleeves. Regulation prescribed the same uniforms for warrant officers, contract surgeons and commissioned officers. Instead of Model 1921 officer's belt, warrant officer wears a 1 3/4 inch wide russet one with brass center-bar buckle. This warrant officer was wounded twice during his year and one-half overseas. (R) Captain, 2nd Cav., Model 1921 officer's belt and new service uniform with insignia as per AR 600-40 (1926). Sleeve markings indicate wounded once during 18 months service in France. All 3 wear authorized decoration and service ribbons and expert marksman badges with qualification bars.

CW4 Joe Howell, Recruiting Command briefs warrant prospective warrant officer candidates on the requirements to become a warrant officer.

governing warrant officer insignia. On 29 April 1943 the War Department published Change 16 to AR 600-40, and "By Order of the Secretary of War" the rising eagle was executed. The order of execution prescribed that instead of wearing the warrant officer eagle insignia, all warrant officers would wear the "insignia indicating arm, service, bureau, etc." to include the "Branch Unassigned" insignia if necessary.

Someone, however, had underestimated the power of that eagle, for less than three months later he rose like a phoenix to nestle again upon the breasts of the Warrant Officer Corps. On 20 July 1943 two publications were issued by the War Department to resuscitate the eagle and restore him to duty: Change 25, AR 600-35, and Change 28, AR 600-40. The break in service lasted exactly 82 days. It was a close call.

Following this resurrection, no further changes were announced until 1947, and this announcement took the precaution of giving a future effective date, ten months in advance. In Circular No. 118, 9 May 1947, the War Department stated that it was seeking legislation to authorize four grades of warrant officers in the Army, to be effective on or about 1 March 1948. These grades were listed in the categories of: Chief Warrant Officer, Senior Warrant Officer, Warrant Officer First Class, and Warrant Officer.

No color was specified for these insignia, but it would be interesting to know whether they were *brown* and *gold, black* and *silver,* or some other combination.⁻

On 15 September 1947, the Quartermaster General submitted to the Director of Personnel and Administration strike samples of these insignia, and on 28 November 1947 they were approved. During the process, however, the titles for the designs were changed to: Chief Warrant Officer (4 bars); Warrant Officer, First Class (3 bars); Warrant Officer, Second Class (2 bars); and Warrant Officer, Third Class (1 bar). It was further stated in this correspondence that implementation of the action would be deferred until legislation was secured setting up the new grade. The War Department proceeded to prepare for the expansion by announcing in paragraph 6, Circular No. 1, 1 January 1948:

> "a. It is planned to establish four grades of warrant officers, with the following titles, and with pay and all allowances substantially corresponding to the first four pay periods of commissioned officers:

(1) Chief warrant officer.
(2) Warrant officer, first class.
(3) Warrant officer, second class.
(4) Warrant officer, third class.

Apparently, there was considerable delay in obtaining the legislation required to implement this plan, but that is a guess. Whatever the reasons may have been, these designs and grade titles were never implemented. The question of insignia color is, therefore, moot.

About two years after these plans were laid, Section 201(a) of the Career Compensation Act, dated 12 October 1949, did in fact provide four separate pay grades for warrant officers, but it also caused the Corps to enter into a rather anomalous period which lasted more than six years. To understand this eccentricity, you must first realize that the Career Compensation Act did not specify the manner in which warrant officers would advance in grade, nor did the law establish the distribution of warrant officers among the four pay grades. Next, you must also understand that the term "warrant officer" as given in the United States Code, Title 37, Chapter I, paragraph 231c, meant a commissioned warrant officer, warrant officer, and flight officer, as well as master, chief engineer, first mate, assistant engineer, and second assistant engineer of the Army Mine Planter Service. In summary, these two laws recognized four pay grades among eight categories of warrant officers, interspersed with five implied grades. However, by 1951 the flight officer and the Army Mine Planter Service were no longer provided for in Army Special Regulations (SR 600-60-1, 26 October 1951). The Department of the Air Force was established 17 September 1947 and the Army Mine Planter Service, as such, no longer existed in the Army. The combined result was that warrant officer titles and insignia of rank remained the same throughout this period: Chief Warrant Officer and Warrant Officer (Junior Grade). It may be a little puzzling to appreciate the fact that during this time only two rank insignia were used to identify warrant officers in four different pay grades, but we have an analogous situation even today, We still have four pay grades, of course, but only two titles: Chief Warrant Officer and Warrant Officer.

Improvements in the Warrant Officer Corps began in 1954. Public Law 379-83d Congress, 29 May 1954, revised certain laws relating to warrant officers, and provided a statutory career plan which was similar in many respects to that in effect for commissioned officers. This act was promulgated

in War Department Bulletin No. 4, 11 June 1954. As part of this new career plan, the Department of Defense organized a committee to recommend unified insignia for warrant officers of all the military services, Records indicate that in considering designs for the insignia, the committee directed attention to such factors as morale, historical background, symbolic significance, distinctiveness, simplicity, and production problems. After reviewing the committee's report, the Assistant Secretary of Defense advised the Assistant Secretary of the Army, on 17 August 1954, of the concurrence by the other military services in the proposed designs. The Quartermaster General was so advised on 24 August 1954, and he began the process of acquiring production samples.

On 14 October 1955 the Assistant Chief of Staff, G-1, advised the Quartermaster General that the samples of the Army warrant officer insignia were approved and that a worldwide message should be dispatched advising the field the insignia was authorized for wear upon receipt.

From that date until 15 December 1972, a period of slightly more than 17 years, these "unified" insignia were in effect. The change was made a part of the Army uniform regulation, AR 670-5, on 20 September 1956. The other services adopted the same design, but each used a different color of enamel: Air Force-medium blue; Navy-dark blue; Marine Corps scarlet; Coast Guard (since 16 August 1960)-dark blue.

It is true that these 17 years constitute the longest period of time without change of insignia that the Warrant Officer Corps has ever had. Yet it is not even the length of a full career. It is an astonishing fact that at no time in the history of the Corps has a warrant officer served an entire career under the same set of insignia. From among those now serving who received their warrants between 15-31 December 1972, may be one who will set this precedent when he retires on 1 January 1993 (for the purpose of this projection, I am defining a full career as 20 years of active warrant officer service). To permit the possibility of achieving this precedent, those of us now serving, as well as those who follow, must strongly support our new insignia against any future change. Predictably, there will be some proposals advanced within the next 20 years to change our insignia again, but if we can hold onto the current insignia that long we will, at last, have the opportunity to establish a tradition. Even if the grade structure is eventually expanded by adding W5 and W6, there would be no need to revise the present insignia for grades W1 through W4. And this returns us to our point of entry into the maze, i.e., color.

I have finally drawn a conclusion based on the following facts:

a. 29 December 1917: Upon determination that the predecessors of the Warrant Officer Corps (the Army Field Clerks and Field Clerks, Quartermaster Corps) held military status, the part of the prescribed uniform which set them apart as a separate class of personnel was the *silver* a id *black* hat cord.

b. 9 July 1918: When the warrant officer rank, as such, was created and established in the Army Mine Planter Service, specialized insignia were authorized which did not include *silver* and *black*. These colors, however, continued in service without interruption, for it wasn't until 4 June 1920 that further appointment of Field Clerks was prohibited.

c. 4 June 1920: Warrant officers in fields other than the Army Mine Planter Service were authorized, and the uniform regulations for them specified a hat cord of *silver* and *black*. These colors have remained in use for the purpose of warrant officer identification ever since.

d. Today: The only current uniform item, insignia, or color which today's warrant officer can trace back to its origin in an uninterrupted chain is his *silver* and *black* hat cord. The new insignia of rank pick up these colors and transmit them to our shoulders.

My conclusion, then, is this: The change of insignia which we underwent on 15 December 1972 was a good move. Instead of breaking tradition, it launched us back into a tradition about which we had forgotten. *Silver* and *black* have always been our colors, and it was the switch to brown in 1936 that violated the tradition. In terms of their color, today's insignia can be worn with the pride of many years' service which encompass the entire history of the Warrant Officer Corps. Instead of complaining about the change, we should welcome it. And then we should proceed to the next step: obtaining an official redesignation of our "branch" color from the newcomer, brown, to that good old reliable, silver and black intermixed.

Here, introduction ends and history begins.

Warrant Officer Recruiting

Background

The US Army Recruiting Command (USAREC) assumed the responsibility for warrant officer recruiting on 1 January 1987. Prior to this date, the mission of recruiting warrant officers had not been tasked to any agency as Army policy. Unlike the commissioned officer force, which is supported by military academies, Reserve Officer Training Corps (ROTC), and Officer Candidate School (OCS); and the enlisted force, supported by USAREC and the Worldwide Reenlistment Network, warrant officers did not have either a proactive system or any agency tasked with the responsibility for recruiting. Due to the lack of a lead agency, Warrant Officer Division, (WOD) USAMILPERCEN, assumed the mission of proactive warrant officer recruiting for fiscal year (FY) 83-84 only. Traditionally, policy for annual procurement of warrant officers depended upon a voluntary system developed in WOD, MILPERCEN, and had been announced annually in DA Circular 601-85-X (Officer Personnel, Warrant Officer Procurement). Beginning in 1979, applications for warrant officer appointment steadily declined. The active Army warrant officer accession goal for FY 83 was 1250. MILPERCEN received 1320 applications, of which 687 were selected for appointment. As selection rates for warrant officer accessions traditionally were between 40 and 50 percent of applications submitted, a minimum of 3000 applications were required in the proper MOS to select for appointment the required 1500. To reduce shortfalls, WOD initiated recruiting programs such as Project 10,000. To attract qualified applicants, the MILPERCEN Recruiting Team placed advertisements in branch and professional magazines. Also, MILPERCEN, with DCSPER guidance, effected temporary policy changes in appointments (E7 and above direct appointment to W2). However, these past attempts did not sufficiently meet Army needs.

In FY 83, field commanders expressed concern, through readiness reports and direct communication with MILPERCEN, about the effect warrant officer shortages were having on fielding and maintaining the numerous high-tech systems being introduced into the Army. The Commander, MILPERCEN, aware of the declining numbers of applications and the concerns of the field commanders, took positive action to correct the problem.

At that time three specific actions were taken by the Army to enhance MILPERCEN ability to recruit warrant officers.

(1) Army policy was changed 1 October 1983 to permit soldiers in grades E-7 through E-9 to be directly appointed to CW2. This initiative provided monetary incentive and lessened the time in service for a warrant officer to be considered for promotion to CW3. However, this policy was not sufficient to meet the warrant officer recruiting goal in FY 84, and was canceled 1 October 1985. The policy failure only served to highlight the problem of insufficient numbers of personnel applying for warrant officer appointment.

(2) In August 1983, at the direction of the DCSPER, WOD formed a special DA Warrant Officer Recruiting Team. The team consisted of a warrant officer from each proponent having warrant officer shortages and members of the WOD. The team was to recruit worldwide to meet large accession goals. Although the recruiting team was successful, it was not a systematic solution to the problem. Recruiting teams caused considerable disruption of field unit activities and the recruiting cost for fielding a team was an unfinanced requirement and was not practical to be repeated each year to fill requirements.

(3) Project 10,000 was a WOD recruiting initiative utilizing the Enlisted Personnel Management Division (EPMD) Enlisted Master File (EMF), which contains data on all enlisted soldiers. Project 10,000 is used to proactively solicit warrant officer applications from qualified NCO with warrant officer potential. As a result, letters are forwarded to each soldier's commander requesting a favorable command endorsement on the soldier's application for warrant officer.

How Other Services Recruit Warrant Officers

Warrant officer recruiting in the Marine Corps, Navy and Coast Guard, like the Army, uses a service circular announcing vacancies in order to solicit applications for WO appointment. Unlike the Army, the other services receive far more qualified applications than there are positions available. However, it must be pointed out that the other services have much smaller WO requirements than does the Army, while the percentage of enlisted populations are similar.

There are other recruiting similarities among the other services. Other services access warrant officers from the in-service enlisted force. Standards for selection are also very competitive.

There are also dissimilarities in the other services' warrant officer program. The Army warrant officer cannot progress to Limited Duty Officers (LDO) as in the Navy. The Army demands more than technical competence from its warrant officers. Army warrant officers are also expected to be trainers, leaders and managers. Also, Army warrant officers are accessed from enlisted status at earlier career points.

Current Warrant Officer Recruiting

Headquarters, United States Army Recruiting Command (USAREC) is responsible for recruiting warrant officers from the enlisted ranks. Department of the Army determines the USAAREC warrant officer accession mission based on the needs of the Army, authorization documents, and the availability of class seats. USREC establishes Warrant Officer Recruiting Teams to travel world-wide to conduct information briefings to soldiers interested in the Warrant Officer Program. Soldiers are invited to attend these briefings. If a soldier is interested and meets the requirements an application is submitted to USAREC through the servicing Military Personnel Office (MILPO).

The next major step in the application process

involves the proponent responsible for the warrant officer specialty applied for. The proponent reviews each application to ensure that all the prerequisites established by the proponent have been met. This check also determines if the applicant has the sufficient training and experience in the specialty to be competitive as a warrant officer applicant.

HQ USAREC then organizes a DA selection board to review and select the best qualified soldiers based on the whole person concept. The results of the selection board are released by world-wide message to all MILPOS. Those selected are scheduled by WOD for attendance to the Warrant Officer Candidate School (WOCS) at Fort Rucker, AL.

Class dates are scheduled by Warrant Officer Accessions Branch at DA. Upon completion of WOCS the newly appointed warrant officers will attend the Warrant Officer Basic Course (WOBC).

The current warrant officer selection process is a far cry from the direct appointment system in which individuals completed their applications, went before a field board with a warrant officer representative, and waited to hear from the respective career management branch.

Female Warrant Officers

Background:

Research in this subject is difficult as few records and statistics are available. However, there is evidence that the first appointments of women as warrant officers occurred during the latter period of World War II. Available records indicate that March 1944 was the date of initial accession of women into the Warrant Officer Corps. Before then there existed a question as to whether or not women soldiers could be appointed warrant officers if they held positions which, for a man, carried the grade. Legislation concerning the Womens' Army Corps (WAC) did not mention the matter, and on this basis The Judge Advocate General ruled that appointment of women was illegal because the law did not specify that it was legal. The question was brought to the War Department's attention by several major commanders who wished to appoint to warrant officer grade the women who were filling warrant officer positions. It was then that The Judge Advocate General was overruled. The Department of the Army G-1 held that such appointment was legal under the general authority to admit women to full army status, and the Chief of Staff upheld this opinion. At the end of World War II, 42 women were in the Warrant Officer Corps, but thereafter appointments virtually ceased. (Reference: The Women's Army Corps, United States Army in World War II Special Studies, Office of the Chief of Military History, P. 577).

1968-1975

The population of women warrant officers during this period ranged from 23 in 1968 to 46 in 1979. The women warrant officers of 1968 were assigned to the following branches: AG 8; MI: 9; MP: 2; QM: 2; and SC:2: From 1968 to 1975 the quantity of women warrant officers remained stable throughout this period. These data reflect within the Warrant Officer Corps a symptom of change that is typical both of the Army at large and of society as a whole, i.e., expanding opportunity for employment of women. The following points highlight the experience of that decade:

Sociological Inhibition. About 50 percent of all warrant officer MOS are of maintenance specialties which, historically, have not been attractive to women. Also, social conditioning frequently discouraged women from entering these specialties. Such conditioning resulted in informal constraints that not only prevented women from entering the "hard skill" enlisted occupations that feed many of the warrant officer specialties. This conditioning also tended to encourage their entry into traditional "soft skill" occupational areas such as administration, supply or personnel. For most of this period only 5 of the 14 warrant officer control branches accounted for the entire female population, predominantly in the following MOS: 711A-Personnel Technician (AG); 971A-Counterintelligence Technician (MI); 951A-Criminal Investigator (MP); 761A-Unit Supply Technician (QM); and 721A-Cryptographic Technician (SC).

Qualification Criteria. During this period, the most important prerequisites for appointment in most warrant officer specialties (other than aviation) were technical competence and supervisory experience. Because of this, the primary target of the warrant officer accession program was the active enlisted base at the noncommissioned officer grade level. Within the enlisted career programs, with "stovepiped" MOS tracks, it is at the SSG or SFC level that individuals first acquire supervisory experience which bridges the several MOS in a career field. Consequently, even if there had been a large female population in the lower grades, they would not have possessed the qualifications needed for a warrant officer appointment. Throughout this period, the total female enlisted population was small and the quantity of NCO personnel was a small fraction of the total (e.g., of the 26,328 enlisted women on active duty in mid-FY 1974, only 669 were in rank SSG, or 2.5 percent of the total). Combining this with the fact that not all enlisted MOS are feeders for warrant officer specialties it can be seen that there were very few women in the zones from which warrant officers could be drawn. All these factors served to keep the female warrant officer numbers at a low level.

1975-1978

In August 1972 the Army approved a plan for expanding the role of women. Follow-on actions significantly increased the size of the enlisted base, however, with few exceptions, it still took 6-10 years to grow a qualified warrant officer appointee. Thus, the major benefits to the Warrant Officer Corps of enlisted female expansion were projected to be seen in the FY 78-82 time frame. An indication of these benefits was initially seen in the sharp rise in the population of women warrant officers which began in 1975 and resulted in the number of female warrant officers more than doubling by 1978. This rising population of female warrant officers was the result of three special factors:

1. Source of increase. Increases in the total number in women warrant officers was primarily attributable to opportunities made available to women in just two specialties, Aviation and Medical Corps. The Aviation Branch accessed 11 female warrant officers and the Medical Corps 8 in branches that previous had no female members. These two branches alone contributed 79 percent of the increase that occurred between 1975 and 1978.

The aviation increase resulted from a decision in FY 73 by the Chief of Staff, Army to authorize aviation training for women. The first female warrant officer candidate entered this 10 month training program in FY 74, and the first woman to complete the training was appointed a warrant officer in FY 75. Since then, the population of women warrant officer aviators has been increasing each year. Because this is the only specialty in which warrant officers are expected to be "hands on" equipment operators, it is the only field that is amenable to direct recruiting for warrant officer candidate training as an enlistment option. Therefore, the enlisted female expansion contributed

directly to the aviation element of the warrant officer increase, because there was no need to "grow" NCOs in appropriate feeder MOS before recruiting/selecting individuals for warrant officer flight training.

The Medical Corps increase resulted from an increase in the Physician's Assistant specialty, MOS 911A. This warrant officer specialty was established in FY 72. Appointment in this specialty required completion of a 2-year warrant officer candidate course, so the first output of warrant officers was not seen until FY 74. Because clinical medical experience was a prerequisite for entry into this program, the Army drew warrant officer candidates primarily from enlisted assets. Therefore, the enlisted female expansion did not contribute to the Medical Corps element. Instead, women already in the Army's medical specialties were given access to this previously unavailable career field opportunity for warrant officer appointment.

2. Expansion of Specialties. The second factor leading to the increase in the rising population of women warrant officers was the expansion of women into specialties previously excluded. Prior to 1975 only 36 percent of the warrant officer specialties (32 of 90) opened to women. With the lifting of many of these exclusions, 80 percent (72 of 90) warrant officer specialties were now open to women. Further evolution resulted with the revision of the warrant officer MOS structure, revised in 1977, which created a warrant officer MOS structure of 59 specialties of which 85 percent (50 of 59) were open to women. A later revision opened up 97 percent (57 of 59) of warrant officer specialties for the appointment of women warrant officers.

3. Nontraditional Specialties. The third factor leading to the increase in the rising population of women warrant officers was the appointment in nontraditional specialties. With the elimination of MOS exclusions, women received appointments in specialties which previously had zero female membership. Not only were more women applying for warrant officer appointments, but they were able to apply in a wider range of specialties than at any time in the past.

Present

In 1995, the woman warrant officer population continues to attract high quality candidates from the enlisted female population on active duty and in the reserve forces. The female warrant officer population is 616 of the total active duty warrant officer strength of 12338. In the reserve forces the female warrant officer strength is 673 from a reserve forces warrant officer strength of 12857.

Unlike both the enlisted and commissioned officer accession programs, which primarily draw from civilian markets, the warrant officer program relies heavily on the active Army enlisted base. Except for the aviation specialty, which is a "hands-on" function, prior military experience is an important requisite to warrant officer appointment and performance. Consequently, there has been little input to the warrant officer ranks directly from the civilian market except for the aviation candidate enlistment option. Therefore, the expansion of the female enlisted force on active duty and in the reserve components continues to provide a strong base from which female warrant officers can be drawn.

Total Warrant Officer System (TWOS)

Recommendations and Decisions

1. The Total Warrant Officer Study (TWOS) started to develop a management system for warrant officers, eventually to be called the Total

Warrant Officer System (TWOS), with the premise that the current management program was not adequate to develop the future warrant officer force, The TWOS Charter asked two essential questions

"Can and should adjustments be made to OPMS to adequately accommodate the warrant officer force?"

"Can and should a warrant officer personnel management system be developed which possesses the tools needed to properly manage the force?"

A strategic goal was inferred and established from the charter: "To develop a formal warrant officer management system or prove that it can't or shouldn't be done."

The premise and charter questions caused TWOS to conduct an extensive analysis of both past and current warrant officer management programs to identify and incorporate strengths and eliminate weaknesses in driving toward the strategic goal.

2. During the TWOS decision briefing, the CSA approved warrant officer management in terms of warrant officer service and position coding of manning documents by rank groups to reflect the three levels of warrant officer skill and experience, The CSA also approved the submission of a legislative package to: authorize grade W5; provide for selective career extension similar to "selective early retirement" (applies only to commissioned officers); and to establish a single active duty list (ADL) for promotions with regular Army integration at promotion to W3.

3. Additional issues briefed to the CSA under the umbrella of a "30 Year Warrant Officer Career plan will be coordinated with appropriate ARSTAF agencies or MACOMs for feasibility analysis. Some issues identified to date are: warrant officer recruiting; a warrant officer objective force model; and revision of the Warrant Officer Training System (WOTS).

Background

1. The Army has never had a requirements-based, institutionalized career management system for the warrant officer. At best, past career management of warrant officers has been a mixture of Army policies and law, ill-defined concepts, and fluctuating management procedures,

2. The Army warrant officer force career management has been transferred from one agency to another throughout the course of this century. In 1920, warrant officers were appointed in the Army-at-large to assignments in various headquarters and tactical units. In 1941, AR 610-5, Warrant Officer General Provision, specified The Adjutant General as the assignment agency for the warrant officer in accordance with the recommendations of the Chiefs of the Arms and Services concerned. In April 1960, based on an approved 1957 study, the management and assignment of warrant officers was transferred to the branches and remained there until 1965 when the Aviation Warrant Officer Branch, Office of Personnel Operations, was created to manage all aviation warrant officers. In 1975, warrant officer management, less the special branches (MC, MSC, VC, and JAGC) was centralized under Warrant Officer Division, Officer Personnel Management Directorate, US Army Personnel Center (MILPERCEN) and remains there today.

3. Every major study or restudy since 1964 has addressed, or was directed to review, the issue of a full 30 year career program for the warrant officer. No study had addressed the lack of institutionalized management in a total system context. Rather, each study attempted to rationalize programs, redefine role and utilization policies, and provide incentives

BG Goodbarry and CW5 Helton unveil the new Warrant Officers Career Center Emblem. (Courtesy of Bruce W. Ohnesarge)

CW4 George Gonsalves receiving the guid-on as the first ever Commander of the 1st WO Co., that trains the Warrant Officer Candidates. (Courtesy of Bruce E. Ohnesarge)

as antidotes for problems caused by the lack of a requirements based system.

4. The TWOS concluded that the current program evolved because the WO force is small compared to the total Army. Its management procedures are unclear, constantly changing and subject to improvisation, The reason for lack of an institutionalized management system is the current policy that permits any warrant officer to serve in any position within a MOS, regardless of grade. Stated another way, the current program is not requirements-based in terms of training, utilization, and rank.

5. The TWOS also concluded that while there are strengths in the current personnel management program identified weaknesses prevent career force development and management required for the warrant officer in the complex future Army. TWOS addressed personnel management in the context of the tenets of the OPMS as outlined in DA PAM 600-3, keeping in mind that OPMS, the Enlisted Personnel Management System (EPMS), and the Defense Officer Personnel Act (DOPMA) do not apply to the warrant officer. The TWOS established the following objectives for a future WO management system:

"Provide the Army the ability to maximize return on investment through training, utilization, continuity, and career progression. Increase competency and productivity, thus enhancing combat

readiness. Motivate toward extended service, Reduce turbulence in the training base."

Total Warrant Officer Study

EXECUTIVE SUMMARY

The Department of the Army Total Warrant Officer Study (TWOS) Group was chartered by the Chief of Staff, Army (CSA) in September 1984. This was the first Department of the Army-level comprehensive study of warrant officer management across the Total Army. Essentially, TWOS was required to answer the following questions, "What are warrant officers doing now?", "What should warrant officers be doing in the future," and "What is the definition of a warrant officer?" Based on the charter and several assumptions that were developed, the TWOS Group developed this mission statement "Examine the role and utilization, professional development, management, compensation programs, policies and procedures, and recommend changes where the effect would enhance combat readiness for the Total Army,"

The TWOS accomplished this mission through review of current systems, analysis of programs, surveys sent to warrant officers and commissioned officers, proponent workshops, warrant officer steering groups, and general officer advisory groups. The TWOS Group briefed findings and recommen-

dations to the CSA on 24 June 1985. During this briefing, the CSA approved a new definition of an Army Warrant Officer, the coding of personnel authorization documents by rank groups to reflect three levels of warrant officer utilization, and the management of warrant officers in terms of warrant officer service which will provide an opportunity for 30 years service as a warrant officer. The CSA also approved submission of a legislative package that includes provisions for creation of warrant officer grade W5, a single promotion system with mandatory integration into the Regular Army concurrent with promotion to W3, and a provision for Selective Career Extension (a program similar to Selective Early Retirement for commissioned officers).

One of the most significant of these actions was the development of a new warrant officer definition, While the existing definitions exclusively keyed on technical competence, the new definition requires warrant officer appointments to be based on a sound level of technical and tactical competence. The definition formalizes the warrant officer's role as a trainer and leader, and requires that the Army professionally develop warrant officers for assignment in positions that are progressively challenging and difficult. This progressive development system proposed by TWOS is structured around three skill levels compatible with the new graded coding system on personnel authorization documents, Warrant officer positions on authorization documents are not graded under the current manning system. This allows the assignment of any warrant officer, W1 through W4, to any position authorized by his Military Occupational Specialty (MOS), The new system will fill warrant officer positions with warrants who have the requisite training and experience essential to the position. The system will be able to do this by coding personnel authorization documents by three rank groups: Warrant Officer (W1-W2), Senior Warrant Officer (W3-W4), and Master Warrant Officer (W5), thereby establishing three utilization levels. The proposal for grade W5 stemmed from analysis which revealed these three distinct levels of warrant officer utilization, TWOS determined from the analysis that the three levels result, not only from the completion of required training, but that they are also experientially driven, The Master Warrant Officer level positions require a very senior warrant officer who has been developed over a period of twenty years of warrant officer service to become a true branch technical integrator. In order for the Army to recognize and benefit from the third level, (Master Warrant Officer), an additional grade is required. Grade W5 will also enhance the retention goals for retirement eligible master warrant officers by providing increased compensation. The new grade of W5 will require congressional approval, During the interim period, and in the event that grade WS is not approved, selected W4 will receive the Master Warrant Officer designation and be assigned to Master Warrant Officer Positions. The position grading system will ensure that the levels of warrant officer rank and experience are spread throughout the force. It will ensure the proper mix of warrant officers at every echelon of the Army. This does not mean that position grading will correspond with the echelon of a unit organization. Position grading will correspond with the skill requirements of a given position, It will allow the Army to build a requirements based warrant officer training system, The essence of the warrant officer role will remain at the war fighting level,

Training will occur in three phases during the warrant officers' career to allow maximum utilization at each level and provide the experience needed before advancement to the next utilization level.

The TWOS concept of warrant officer training will change the current warrant officer training system by requiring certification at each training level. Entry level training is already well established. However, additional programs are required for proponents who lack entry level' training or whose entry level training is inadequate. Initiatives have already been undertaken by Training and Doctrine Command to standardize the advanced level (to be renamed senior level) warrant officer training. The Warrant Officer Senior Course will require major revision and will evolve into Master Warrant Officer Training. The major difference will be a break from the traditional general subjects course to a course that addresses MOS and branch-oriented, specific instruction. This course will provide selected warrant officers with the branch-related training needed to become technical integrators. The TWOS also recommended that the use of existing courses not currently available to warrant officers be considered during the training development process to maximize the use of training resources.

The TWOS Group recognized that management changes must accompany changes in training and force composition. Management by years of Warrant Officer Service rather than by years of Active Federal Service will simplify what has become a very complex process with regard to schooling, assignments, promotions, and other personnel management procedures. This policy, similar to the one used for commissioned officers, means that when enlisted soldiers receive an appointment as a warrant officer, their personnel management clock is reset to zero" while retaining seniority for pay and retirement. It will also allow the Army to manage warrant officers in terms of year groups and will establish a new career plan that provides the opportunity for warrant officers to stay on active duty for 30 years as a warrant officer or until the mandatory retirement age of 62, Another issue which will serve as a corollary to the 30 Year Career Plan is the Regular Army Integration Program. Under the program, Reserve warrant officers on active duty who are selected for promotion to W3 must accept an appointment in the Regular Army or request release from active duty. The program is similar in concept to the provision of the Defense Officer Personnel Management Act (DOPMA) that provides for automatic integration of commissioned officers selected for promotion to major, The integration program will allow Reserve warrant officers to integrate into the Regular Army at the W3 promotion point,

The TWOS Group also recommended that the Army develop an aggressive recruiting program to sustain the warrant officer force, There has never been an institutionalized recruiting program for the entire force. The current system relies on voluntary application of enlisted soldiers, This has often left the Army short of required numbers of warrant officers, A proactive recruiting program will not only sustain the force in numbers required, but will provide the quality required as well.

The TWOS Group considered many compensation issues which pertain to warrant officers. The only recommendation was that the Army develop a pay scale for W5 if Congress approves the grade. However, the TWOS suggested that the compensation issues should be revisited following full implementation of the Total Warrant Officer System. The thrust of this review would be to determine if additional compensation measures are required to attract and retain warrant officers in the right numbers and with the right skills,

The TWOS Group considered the Reserve Components in every aspect of the study. However, the inherent constraints placed on members in the Reserve Components may require some adjustment in how the Army applies TWOS recommen-

CW5 Helton addressing distinguished visitors after the ribbon cutting and dedication of the WOCC. (Courtesy of Bruce W. Ohnesarge)

dations in the Reserve Components. Work will continue throughout the implementation phase with the Army Reserve and Army National Guard in order to achieve the desired results.

Warrant officers have been, and will continue to be, the Army's technical experts. The development of the Total Warrant Officer System (TWOS) is essential if the Army is to fully capitalize on warrant officer expertise. Full implementation of the recommendations by this study group will require the total cooperation of all agencies involved with the management and utilization of Army warrant officers.

Evolution of the Aviation Warrant Officers (AWO)

Editors note: The above was extracted from the fourth edition of the Army Aviation Personnel Plan.

The establishment of the Air Force as a separate armed service and the demobilization of the armed forces after World War II created serious shortages of aviators in Army Ground Forces. Organic Army Aviation was cut to its pre-World War II level just when the Army was trying to increase organic aviation. With the arrival of new helicopters, the Army needed more helicopter pilots but congressionally imposed commissioned officer strength levels prevented pilot expansion. The Army requested authority to establish the Flight Officer/Warrant Officer program. This proposal was rejected because the Army already had three groups of personnel—enlisted, warrant officer and commissioned officer. As a fall back position, the Department of the Army (DA) decided that the grade of flight officer was in reality a warrant officer (WO) grade with a restriction to the WO junior grade rank.

This proposal envisioned a WO pilot who would spend an entire military career in the aviation field, much like the concept of today's Aviation Warrant Officer (AWO). Because there was no Aviation Branch for commissioned officers or enlisted soldiers, the WO pilot would provide the continuity needed in Army Aviation. The Army felt that the WO pilot would ensure stability and expertise that was often diminished or lost completely due to commissioned officer rotation in and out of aviation assignments. Commissioned officers were required to maintain their branch expertise to get promoted. With WO pilots staying in avia-

tion flying assignments throughout their careers, aviation would gain the stability needed to maintain combat effectiveness.

The officers involved with Army Aviation had great plans for the use of the WO pilot. The Department of the Army policy for the proposed WO pilot limited them to the operation of aircraft on administrative type missions only. So despite the tremendous World War II record of flight officer/warrant officer aviators, when a mission involved transporting field grade staff officers or required technical or tactical responsibilities the aircraft was piloted by a commissioned officer.

Army leaders were certain that Army Aviation would benefit in many ways from the WO pilot program, in spite of restrictive policies. First, the WO pilot could become the capstone of the enlisted maintenance career; second, commissioned officer pilot shortages could be filled by WO pilots; third, WO pilots could carry a large portion of the commissioned officer aviator additional duties, thus allowing commissioned officers more freedom and greater involvement in command duties; and fourth it would cost less to pay WO pilots than commissioned officer pilots. With the number of Pilot positions required, the Army envisioned all aviator positions from second lieutenant through captain being converted to WO pilot positions.

In late 1949 the WO pilot proposal was approved. Army leaders decided that the WO helicopter pilot MOS should be made available to qualified enlisted soldiers and to qualified civilian personnel. Although the Artillery School at Fort Sill trained officers and enlisted personnel in advanced aviation skills, the Transportation Corps was designated as the proponent agency for aviation WO MOS, with the Air Force still responsible for Army aviator flight training.

Meanwhile, the Adjutant General decided that inclusion of the helicopter pilot in the aircraft maintenance career field was inappropriate. The Army staff agreed there was no apparent relationship between aircraft maintenance and the knowledge and skills necessary to fly helicopters. It was decided that technical knowledge in mechanics was not a prerequisite for helicopter pilot training since no other service used aircraft mechanic technical knowledge as a prerequisite for pilot training. The WO MOS code was designated "1066." Regardless of what aircraft a WO pilot was qualified in, there was only one MOS. The news spread quickly and the Army began receiving applications from across the spectrum of enlisted career fields.

The first WO candidate class to train in helicopters was the Army Helicopter Pilot Course, Class 51A. The class started training in April 1951 with 28 students and graduated 25 students in December 1951. When students initially began training, they were told that after 12 months in grade as a WO they would receive commissions

Sign in front of HQTRS, 92nd AVN Co., Quinhon, Vietnam, June 1966. (Photo by B. Liggenstoffer)

62nd AVN Co., possibly at Marble Mountain, DaNang, Vietnam (Royal Coachmen), 1971. (Photo by B. Liggenstoffer)

CW4 George Gonsalves addressing distinguished guests, TAC officers and candidates at dedication of Warrant Officer Career Center. (Courtesy of Bruce W. Ohnesarge.)

Recovery of crashed YO-3A near Long Than, Vietnam, August 1971. (Photo by B. Liggenstoffer)

similar to flight officers in the Army Air Forces. But after 39 months in grade, none of the WOs received nor was offered a commission. In fact, they were all still WO1s, none had been promoted to CW2. It wasn't until 1955 that WOs started being promoted. Flight pay remained another inequity, and it wasn't until 23 years later, in 1974, that WO pilots received flight pay equal to commissioned officer pilots.

The transportation helicopter table of organization and equipment (TOE), TD 55-57T, was published in 1950 with positions that called for WO helicopter pilots. Each company had 21 H-19 Sikorsky, 12-place helicopters (nicknamed "Chickasaw"). Five of these helicopter transportation companies were slated for duty in Korea. Of the five, only two reached Korea before the end of the war, the 6th and 13th. They both departed for Korea on 7 December 1952 and were the first Army helicopter companies in combat.

These first WO helicopter pilots played an important role in the early development of Army Aviation. Newly rated WO pilots evacuated wounded soldiers, directed artillery strikes, and transported troops and supplies throughout the Korean battlefield.

Aviation WOs, although few in number, proved their worth to the Army. It appeared that the heli-

copter and the WO pilot were here to stay. No one then could envision the role WO helicopter pilots would ultimately play in the evolution of Army Aviation.

After the Korean War, the Army Aviation School moved from Fort Sill to Camp Rucker, Alabama in the latter part of 1954. With the increased emphasis on helicopter training, the rotary wing training section was elevated to a department level status equal in status to fixed wing training. The first helicopter class began training with 6 commissioned officers, 2 warrant officers, and 17 warrant officer candidates (WOCs) and graduated on 30 April 1955.

In the mid-1950s, Army Aviation began to reorganize and expand. Camp Rucker was redesignated Fort Rucker effective 13 October 1955. The Department of Defense (DOD) directed the Army to assume all Army Aviation training and in April 1956 transferred Welters Air Force Base Texas, to the Army. The Army redesignated the base to Camp Wolters. It became the primary helicopter school for the Army, receiving the first class of WOCs in November 1956. Fort Rucker then became the Army advanced helicopter school. From 1953 to 1957 an in-depth analysis was completed to determine whether the AWO Corps should be continued and what, if any, its future role should be. These studies determined that WOs should remain an integral part of Army Aviation. However, much like today, due to budget cuts and WO strength caps, WO appointments were reduced. Warrant officer Pilot training was suspended in 1959 after only 1,100 WO pilots had been trained.

In 1961 Army Aviation deployed its first helicopter and fixed wing units to Vietnam. In 1963 WO Pilot training was resumed with an input of 720 WOCs.

The mid-1960s saw a dramatic period of growth for AWOs. Aviation WO strength swelled from approximately 2,960 in 1966 to more than 12,000 by 1970. No one envisioned the impact that WO aviators would have on the conduct of the war in Vietnam, nor the impact Vietnam would have on Army Aviation.

In 1962 the Army began an in-depth study and test of the tactical airmobility of organic Army ground forces. These tests proved the airmobility concept and the necessity and value of WO pilots. As a result of these tests, the 11th Air Assault was formed. On 1 July 1965, it became the 1st Cavalry Division (Airmobile) and deployed to Vietnam in August. As more combat units deployed to Vietnam, aviation became more visible and its role in combat was apparent. Warrant officer aviators flew through the heaviest concentrations of enemy fire in the Vietnam War and were involved in every aspect of combat operations. Helicopters became the symbol of the Vietnam war, and helicopter pilots were among the first to be killed in the war and among the last to leave. The combat attrition rate for AWO Pilots was 20 times that of United States Air Force (USAF), United States Navy (USN), and United States Marine Corps (USMC) aviators. This was in large part due to the intense loyalty these aviators shared and the leadership role played by many AWOs. An AWO would land to rescue a downed aircrew regardless of the circumstances, weather conditions, or enemy firepower. This had a profound positive effect on Army aviator morale.

Aviation warrant officers did more than just fly in Vietnam; they performed as aviation section leaders, platoon leaders, operations officers, and liaison officers. A few WOs even commanded companies for brief periods. Despite their tremendous success as combat leaders in Vietnam, AWOs were often on the receiving end of some strange local policies. In Korea in 1969, some commanders specifically forbade any AWO from being an aircraft commander in their unit. Uniform policies were mixed as well. Aviation warrant officers were forbidden to wear flight jackets and had to wear field jackets to keep warm while flying. Aviation warrant officer instructor pilots at Fort Wolters, Texas, were issued Nomex flight suits only after all other instructors and officer students had received theirs. Supplies of flight suits from this new material were limited; so, priorities for issue were based on rank not on mission. Forming the Aviation Branch in the early eighties helped eliminate many of these inequities.

The early '70s saw a reduction in force (RIF) and reduced AWO accessions. The field Army officially left Vietnam in March 1973. As a direct result of the heat seeking missile threat faced in Vietnam in 1972 and 1973, the tactics of Army Aviation. Nap-of-the-earth flying became the tactic of the period and by the late seventies night vision goggles were also being used. A key event also occurred during this period. In 1974 as a result of a congressional committee recommendation AWOs received flight pay equalization with commissioned aviators.

Modernized aircraft began flowing into the inventory beginning with the UH-60 Blackhawk. A fateful personnel decision was made in conjunction with fielding the Blackhawk. Army policy sent new, inexperienced aviators through Blackhawk transition. When this policy was coupled with an aircraft transition of only 15 hours and a few manufacturer design flaws, the overall accident rate for Army Aviation skyrocketed. This led to a series of messages by General Thurman, then Army Vice Chief of Staff. These messages required the Aviation Branch to institutionalize a process that directly involved the chain of command in the mission briefing and crew selection process.

In the early '80s, the AH-64 Apache and the modernized CH-47D Chinook began to arrive. The Apache initially required significant factory support. Intensive management overcame problems and the aircraft distinguished itself in two subsequent wars.

From 1981 through 1987, AWO accessions were curtailed to allow more non-rated WOs to be accessed. This was necessary because active duty WO budget end strength (BES) was, and is, constrained below the level necessary to fill documented, modified tables of equipment (MTOE) and tables of distribution and allowances (TDA), positions.

On 12 April 1983, Aviation became a branch. Commissioned officers and enlisted soldiers were designated to wear the branch insignia. A request was submitted to the Army leadership to authorize aviation warrant officers to bear the Aviation branch insignia as an exception to the regulation which requires all warrant officers to wear the warrant officer insignia in lieu of the branch insignia. The request was denied. Aviation warrant officers have been centrally managed since 1965, first in the Warrant Officer Aviation Branch and since 1975 by the Warrant Officer Division, Total Army Personnel Command. Centralized management insures the integrity of the Warrant officer Corps by assigning, managing and professionally developing warrant officers, regardless of specialty.

Since 1954 aviation warrant officers provided the tactical and technical continuity for ground forces aviation for nearly 30 years. The wearing of branch insignia versus the warrant officer insignia remains a controversial issue among many aviation warrant officers.

In 1984, the Chief of Staff chartered the Total Warrant Officer Study (TWOS) to redefine current and future roles, and training requirements, for WOs to meet the Army and individual needs. The

Warrant officers in front of U-6A Beaver at Saigon, Vietnam, Nov. 1971. MI Liasion pilots. (L) unidentified, (R) Gary Kennedy. (Photo by B. Liggenstoffer)

Army Lockheed YO-3A, homebase at LongThan North, July 1971. Ten of these aircraft flew low level night surveillance. Attached to Airplane Co., OV-1 Mohawk. (Photo by B. Liggenstoffer)

CSA approved the TWOS results in June 1985. The TWOS took a close look at how, when, where, and why the Army trains WOs. As a result of the findings, many changes occurred in the way the Army accesses, trains, and manages WOs. The TWOS career program included the establishment of the branch immaterial Warrant Officer Candidate Course (WOCC), the development of the common core Senior Warrant Officer Training Course (SWOTC), and the implementation of the Master Warrant Officer Training Course (MWOTC). All of these Warrant Officer Training System (WOTS) courses were established at the United States Army Aviation Center (USAAVNC) by the fall of 1988.

The TWOS also recommended that legislation (Warrant Officer Management Act) be submitted to Congress to create the rank of CW5, a single promotion system, provisions for a selective early retirement process, and management by years of WO service.

The master warrant officer (MWO) program was instituted to select, train, and identify CW4s who would occupy master warrant (MW) positions until the Warrant Officer Management Act (WOMA) legislation was passed by Congress.

A new WO definition under TWOS finally recognized the leadership roles and responsibilities that AWOs had been filling since 1942.

The TWOS also required that all WO positions be stratified into three levels of responsibili-

ties. These levels were "WO" for WO1 and CW2, "SW" for CW3 and CW4, and "MW4 for CW5. Even with AWO positions stratified into three levels, WO1s and CW4s were still interchangeable for utilization purposes. Army Regulation 614-100 allows AWOs to be utilized in the next lower rank group. This meant that a SW with the rank of CW4 could be used in the next lower rank group of WO.

In 1986 all Aviation Branch AWO positions were coded as WO, SW, or MW. This initial coding effort was flawed from the outset by artificial constraints. The Aviation Branch was not allowed to establish MW positions where they were needed but was forced to code only existing, one-deep positions as MW. This resulted in the majority of MW positions being coded for aviation safety officers with the remaining MW positions being spread from company to corps level. Another artificial constraint was the number of MW positions allocated to the Aviation Branch. With a MW position cap of 3.4 percent, the branch was limited to 235 MW positions. To support the warfighting requirements of the branch, 347 MW positions were needed. To fix this dysfunctional rank coding problem would take the next 6 years.

During the mid-'80s, aviation units were transitioning to the Army of Excellence (AOE). This revised structure proved to have lasting adverse impact on the maintainability and sustainability of the branch. Maintainer positions were reduced by approximately 33 percent while aircraft were reduced by only 9 percent. What had previously been called a platoon was now called a company, still commanded by a captain. What previously had been called a company and commanded by a major was now called a battalion and commanded by a lieutenant colonel.

In 1986 the Enlisted Aviator Study (EAS) was completed. The results of this study concluded that creating an enlisted aviator was possible but not desirable. The leadership role of AWOs encompassed nearly all flight training, maintenance test flights, safety, and operations. To eliminate the AWO would have been a large step backward in maintaining the warfighting capability of the Aviation Branch.

In the spring of 1987, the Aviation Branch Personnel Proponency began to actively participate in controlling new accessions and all flight training seats for the branch. This resulted in increased AWO accessions in fiscal years (FYs) 1988, 1989, and 1990 and reduced aviation commissioned officer (ACO) accessions.

A policy change was implemented by Major General Parker, then Aviation Branch Chief, that called for "training to requirements." This new policy had several ramifications. Since there were no instructor pilot positions for ACOs except at the USAAVNC, all HQDA instructor pilot training seats for ACOs were eliminated. The fixed wing selection board process for AWOs was validated as a viable process but flawed in execution. Senior AWOs, highly qualified in advanced helicopters, were being selected for fixed wing training. Not only did an understrength MOS lose a highly competent operator, trainer, or maintainer, but the aviator found himself senior in rank yet junior in experience in the fixed wing community. By the early nineties the fixed wing aviator population had reached an inverse career field make-up of 53 percent in the rank of CW4, 37 percent in the rank of CW3, and 10 percent in the rank of CW2.

By 1988, authorizations for AWO aviators were rapidly outdistancing the branch's ability to train. The HQDA staff determined that too many AWO aviator positions had been documented. The Deputy Chief of Staff for Operations (DCSOPS) removed 142 AWO positions labeled as "overstructure."

Operation "Prime Chance" saw Army Aviation in the unparalleled role of protecting the USN in the Persian Gulf. Flying armed and updated versions of the venerable OH-58 scout of Vietnam fame, AWOs sought out and attacked enemy vessels engaged in mining international waterways.

In 1989 the Army began reducing authorizations through a process called Quicksilver. Quicksilver I and II removed 1,209 AWO positions from the Active Component (AC).

In December 1989 the world learned that Army Aviation owned the night. Operation "Just Cause" saw Army Aviation take its place as a full member of the combat arms community. In a brief but complex aviation based operation, United States forces, led by Army Aviation, successfully liberated Panama from the dictatorship of Manuel Noriega.

In August of 1990 President Bush ordered United States Forces into Saudi-Arabia to establish a defensive posture against Iraq. Operation "Desert Shield" was in response to the Iraqi occupation of Kuwait. The military buildup continued throughout the Fall and Winter of 1990. One of the AWO personnel problems highlighted by this mobilization was the shortage of AWOs in the aggregate, and Chinook and Blackhawk qualified AWOs in specific. The shortage of AWOs in the aggregate was a direct result of WO BES constrained to a level below documented MTOE and TDA requirements. The shortage of Chinook and Blackhawk pilots was the direct result of the United States Army Training and Doctrine Command (TRADOC) training budget decrements imposed in FYs 88, 89, and 90, exacerbated by worldwide fleet groundings for both aircraft types.

The Army civilian and military leadership learned that there is no short-term readiness risk when underfunding AWO aviator accessions, it is all long-term risk. Concentrated efforts by TRADOC and the USAAVNC were unable to make any progress on producing more Chinook and Blackhawk pilots until three months after the war ended in March of 1991.

In January 1991 the air war against Iraq began. The following month a 4-day ground war ensued. This ground war phase began when Army Aviation attack aircraft destroyed a radar site deep inside the borders of Iraq at 0200 in the morning. The majority of those attack cockpits were filled by AWOs.

If there had ever been any doubt before, Desert

WO James D. Robbins, Saudi Arabia. (Courtesy of James D. Robbins)

Cam Rahn Bay base OPS, Vietnam, December 1971. (Photo by B. Liggenstoffer)

Army PV-2s at Cam Rahn Bay, Vietnam, December 1971. (Photo by B. Liggenstoffer)

Shield and Desert Storm had showcased the three primary tenets of the Aviation Branch—deployability, versatility, and lethality. This brief war again confirmed the combat leader role of AWOs. These soldier-officer-aviators were at the forefront of both operations and led many combat sorties into enemy held territory.

Special operations AWOs assumed a key role in a mission that is the doctrinal province of the USAF. Search and rescue of downed Aviation (SOA) aircrews is an Air Force mission, but the Special Operations, (Aviation (SOA) AWOs were better trained and equipped. Many aircrews owe their lives to the bravery of these aviators who successfully completed dangerous rescue missions. Aviation non-rated maintenance officers excelled in directing the repair and maintenance of aircraft under exceptionally harsh environmental conditions.

While Operations Desert Shield and Desert Storm were in progress, HQDA planners were proceeding with plans to down size the Army. With the fall of the Berlin wall in 1989 and the subsequent breakup of the Union of the Soviet Socialist Republic, the armed forces of the United States were charged with reducing the military structure and associated expenses.

One target of this reduction effort was AWOs. With documented AWO requirements of about 7,200 and an actual inventory of 6,900, HQDA initially planned to selectively retire approximately 300 AWOs in FY 92.

Despite the lessons learned in operations Desert Shield and Desert Storm about the long-term adverse combat readiness impact of underfunding the AWO BES, the AWO BES for FYs 91 and 92 was reduced below documented MTOE and TDA requirements levels.

In the Fall of 1991, the President of the United States signed the Warrant Officer Management Act (WOMA) into law with an effective date of 1 February 1992. A DOD report on the WOMA stated technical expertise is still important, but no longer enough. Warrant officers, regardless of rank or specialty, also have to be proficient in basic tactical and leadership skills. In a fast moving combat environment, WOs could find themselves the senior leader in an isolated island of conflict. Their knowledge of tactics and ability to understand the commander's strategy could spell the difference between survival or destruction. Their use of independent judgment and their ability to act quickly could decide the outcome of the battle. This doctrinal change now places heavy demands on WOs' technical, tactical, and leadership abilities. They must be prepared to handle contingencies, to include assuming command, if isolated from commissioned officer leadership.

The WOMA enacted key provisions of the TWOS by establishing the rank of CW5, a single promotion system, provisions for selectively retiring regular Army (RA) WOs, and managing warrant officers by year group, based on years of warrant officer service (WOS). Unfortunately, there was no WOMA implementation team formed to convert this law into Army regulation.

Some senior HQDA officers wanted to schedule a WO selective early retirement board (SERB) because the enlisted and commissioned officers (both groups were overstrength) were going through the SERB process. This was despite the fact that the AWO aviator inventory would be under the BES limit by the end of FY 92. Although there was no WO SERB nor RIF in FY 92, a WO SERB was tentatively scheduled for October of 1992.

In February 1992 the Chief of Staff of the Army, General Sullivan, signed the Warrant Officer Leader Development Action Plan (WOLDAP). The WOLDAP required that all AWO positions be stratified into four levels—WO, W3, W4, And W5; that appointment to WO-1 occur after WOCC; changed civilian education goals; that WO common core training be established as a USAAVNC tenant element under the direct control of TRADOC, required pinpoint assignment of CW5s; and disapproved the Aviation Branch request for AWOs to wear their branch insignia.

The WOLDAP proved to be the solution for the continuing problem of AWO misutilization. Warrant officers were no longer interchangeable by MOS and grade; just as with commissioned officers, rank and date of rank had precedence in occupying duty positions. For many, this was a new way of doing business.

Full implementation required that three major problems had to be overcome. First, the rank coding table had to be stratified into four vertical levels of AWO utilization; second, commanders at all levels had to understand that business as usual with regards to AWO utilization had changed, rank became a primary factor in AWO utilization; and third, AWOs had to learn the new system. For example, if a newly assigned CW4 safety officer arrives at the assigned battalion and the current battalion safety officer is a CW3, the CW4 should occupy the battalion safety position and the CW3 should go to a line company.

The TWOS, WOMA, and WOLDAP combined to change the accession, training, utilization, promotion, and assignment of Aviation warrant officers. Warrant Officer Division, PERSCOM, has begun to assign AWOs based on rank and MOS.

Installation assignments officers and S-1s must assign AWOs to positions based on rank and aircraft skills.

Warrant officer aviators have come a long way. Over the years warrant officers have more than proven themselves to be the backbone of Army Aviation. Without WOs, aviation branch maintenance, operations, training, and safety would cease.

Evolution of the Marine Warrant Officers
by CW5 Lynn D. Ridley

The history of the Marine warrant officer dates back to the beginning of the Army Warrant Officer Corps. Unfortunately, most documented history is lost. Valuable sources of information such as vessel logbooks were only retained five years and then destroyed. Much of what follows is information gained from interviews with former marine warrant officers, including members of the old Mine Planters Service.

While warrants to act as paymasters and quartermaster clerks had been used in the Army for sometime, the rank and grade of warrant officer was not created until an Act of Congress in July 1918 established the Mine Planter Service in the Coast Artillery Corps. The act authorized the appointment of warrant officers to serve as masters, mates, chief engineers, and assistant engineers on vessels operated by the Mine Planter Service.

The annual pay of these warrants ranged from $1,800 for masters to $972 for second mates. Initially, they wore navy blue uniforms but in 1920 the Secretary of War prescribed an olive green uniform with distinctive sleeve insignia of a series of brown stripes to denote rank. Masters wore four subdued brown stripes with a brown anchor, chief engineers wore four brown stripes with a brown propeller, down to two brown stripes for mates and assistant engineers.

In 1919 there were 37 warrant officers in the Mine Planter Service. By 1921 that number had grown to 88, and then a Congressional Act of 1922 reduced the total authorization to 40 warrant officers. The authorization remained at 40 until 1942 when Congress fixed the authorization at six warrant officers for each planter in service or under construction. By the close of 1942 the number of warrants had grown to 62.

During World War II, 16 new planters ships were constructed and conducted operations in the waters off the Philippines, South America, Central America, and the United States. Two planters were lost during the war—the *Planter Frank* was torpedoed in 1942 near Maul, Hawaii; and the *Harrison* was captured by the Japanese in the Philippines. The vessel was used by the Japanese Imperial Navy until it was finally sunk by U.S. aircraft at Yokouska in 1945.

The Mine Planter Service was discontinued in 1948. Members of the service were incorporated into the Transportation Corps in 1949, and the vessels were taken over by the Navy, or in some cases by the Coast Guard for use as buoy tenders.

When the Transportation Corps was formed in July 1942, six new harborcraft companies were formed in Charleston, South Carolina. Soon after, the first Transportation warrant officer was appointed as "Marine Master." Initially, each of the six units were authorized five warrants, two deck officers, two engineer officers, and one crane master. These warrants are not to be confused with the Mine Planter warrants who at this time were still serving with the Coast Artillery Corps. Later, the Mine Planter warrants would merge with the Transportation Corps.

1st C-12AQC taught by the US Army at USAAVNC, Ft. Rucker, AL, Oct. 91- Nov. 91, C-12 AQC 92-1 (1st Class) (L to R) CW2 N.M. Qualantone, CW4 Bud Liggenstoffer (instructor) and CW4 R.S. Johnson. (Photo by B. Liggenstoffer)

In 1944, three of the new units deployed to the Pacific and three to Europe. By this time the authorization for warrant officers had grown from five in each unit to ten. The units and assigned warrant officer served with distinction throughout the remainder of the war.

After World War II, the Transportation Corps moved to Fort Eustis and following construction of the main pier in 1947, the harbor craft arrived. Training for marine warrant officers was established during this period with the creation of the harborcraft deck and engine officer courses in 1949. (These were comprehensive courses lasting almost six months. They continued to be taught until 1983 when they were redesignated the marine warrant officer pre-appointment course. The in 1985, as a result of the Total Warrant Officer Study, they were again redesignated, becoming the marine warrant officer technical and tactical training courses, but the content of the courses has remained virtually unchanged since 1949. Good navigation is still good navigation!)

The Army watercraft inventory continued to grow during the 1950s. By 1959 there were some 3,500 vessels of all types, but warrant officer strengths remained fairly constant at approximately 110. Many of these vessels were small craft with enlisted coxswains, and it was not uncommon to find commissioned officers as vessel masters on large watercraft. This practice, which started in World War II, continued until about 1953 when warrant officers assumed the duties.

Marine warrant officers served in the Korean War at the port of Inchon and Puson, and operated cargo vessels in both coastwise an ocean service in the Pacific.

In the mid 1960s, the strength of the Marine Warrant Officer Corps began to expand during the Vietnam build up. With 131 warrants in 1963, the number became 432 by 1968. As in previous conflicts, marine warrant officers served with distinction throughout the entire Vietnam theater of operations. In the early 1970s the strength fell to 220, and by the early 1980s the number was down to 148 and projected to drop even further. In 1983 the Transportation Center initiated action to reverse the downward trend in marine warrant officer strengths.

The result was a new draft of AR 56-9, Watercraft, that outlined a warrant officer candidate program as opposed to direct appointment of marine warrant officers. At this time the harborcraft deck and engine officer courses, which had been conducted since 1949, continued. The problem was that these courses conducted officer training, but were not officer producing. Noncommissioned officers attended the training, but then simply returned to their units as NCOs. The AR 56-9 change required an application for warrant officer be approved prior to course attendance. Successful completion of the course would result in an appointment as a marine warrant officer.

The marine warrant officer preappointment course was again altered in 1985 as a result of the Total Warrant Officer Study which eliminated direct appointment for all warrant officer specialties and created mandatory candidate training. The Total Warrant Officer Study also gave the mission of recruiting warrant officers to the U.S. Army Recruiting Command. This opened up additional markets to assess potential marine warrant officers.

Today, the marine warrant officer strengths are healthy and fully support the worldwide readiness of the Transportation Corps. In fact, our on-hand number slightly exceeds our authorized number for the first time in over 20 years.

The marine warrant officer specialty is the oldest warrant officer specialty in the Army. Ma-rine warrant officers served in World War II, Korea, Vietnam, the Mayaguez Incident, Grenada, Panama, and in Operations Desert Shield/Storm. These men and women excelled through combat, force structure changes, equipment redesigns, and mission changes. Through it all, the marine warrant officer has always responded when called and served with honor and distinction.

As I researched this article, I had the pleasure of interviewing "Captain Mike" Trivella, the first warrant officer appointed as a marine warrant after the Transportation Corps was founded in 1942. Captain Mike recounted the story that shortly after he had been appointed, he had to take an official photograph. Later, his commanding officer made him retake the photograph after it was discovered that he had worn Transportation Corps brass instead of the warrant officer "SquashBug" which had been in use since 1921. Today, almost 50 years later, the Army is still wrestling with whether or not warrant officers should wear branch insignia.

The more things change, the more they remain the same.

Warrant Officer Qualifications at a Glance

During the evolution of the marine warrant officer, a variety of methods have been used to demonstrate marine qualifications. The current dual system of certification and licensing was established in 1982.

A U.S. Coast Guard license has always been recognized as proof of qualification, and in fact was required for appointment as a Mine Planter warrant officer. (A Coast Guard license was not required for appointment in the newly formed Transportation Corps in 1942.)

Since the Mine Planters Service was abolished in 1948, several licensing methods have been employed. These include a Transportation Corps Letter of Competency and a Transportation Corps Letter of License established in 1965 when AR 611-8, Marine Personnel Licensing and Utilization of Marine Service Books, was published.

In 1971, AR 56-9, Watercraft, superseded AR 611-8 and required Army personnel to possess an Army license which would be awarded upon successful completion of an appropriate course, or upon completion of a written examination. AR 56-9 has been revised many times, but still remains the Bible for marine qualifications.

CW5 Ridley was the Marine Warrant Proponency Officer in the Office of the Chief of Transportation, Fort Eustis. Virginia; he is now assigned to the CASCOM, Fort Eustis, Virginia.

Health Services Maintenance Technicians (MOS 670A)

The genesis of medical equipment maintenance in the U.S. Army was an inevitable consequence following the acquisition of the first piece of sophisticated medical instrumentation. However, it did not gain the status of a specialized function until World War II when a flood of new technical equipment came into the hospital system. Prior to World War II a typical 1939 era post or station hospital consolidated its maintenance functions into the supply organization. Actual maintenance requirements were coordinated with the on-post ordnance, engineer, and signal shops. The repair of highly technical items of equipment such as x-ray systems and electrocardiograph machines was predominately accomplished by contracts with civilian medical equipment technicians. However, the draft took its toll on these technicians and compounded maintenance support problems.

When World War II began, maintenance problems quickly intensified and by the end of 1942 the need for an organized medical maintenance program within the Medical Department became increasingly evident. In April 1943, The Surgeon General announced a policy concerning maintenance of medical equipment. This policy set the wheels in motion to create a "Medical Department Maintenance Program." Because the newly created program had a serious lack of technically qualified officers in August 1943, The Surgeon General directed that 10 Medical Administrative Corps officers be selected to attend the newly established Maintenance and Repair Course at the St. Louis Medical Depot. Upon graduation, these commissioned officers were awarded the MOS of 4890-Medical Equipment Maintenance Officer. They filled assignments in The Surgeon General's Office, staffed depot shops, and served as field liaison officers. By the end of 1944, 56 officers had graduated from the school in St. Louis and 5 officers had been awarded the MOS based on their prior training in civilian life. By V-J Day the feedback from the field indicated that the Medical Department Maintenance program was effective and had gained enthusiastic acceptance at all levels of the Medical Department. The program was so successful that postwar evaluations recommended its peacetime continuance.

In 1918 warrant officers were first authorized in the U.S. Army. Their role quickly expanded, and by 1946 they held 40 different commissioned officer MOSs. However, the MOS of 4890, Medical Equipment Maintenance Officer was still held exclusively by commissioned officers. During this period of time, warrant officers within the Medical Department were primarily utilized in two MOSs: 4490-Medical Supply Officer and 350B-Field Medical Assistant.

The practice of warrants officers holding the same MOS as commissioned officers caused contradictions in the assignment process. Further, the policy of decentralized warrant officer appointments by the major commands, based on a concept that each major commander knew his own needs, resulted in inconsistent utilization practices and uncertain concepts of the warrant officer's role and function. To better define and improve the utilization of warrant officers, The Department of the Army between 1953 and 1957, conducted an extensive analysis to determine if the Warrant Officer Corps should be continued; and, if so, its future role and purpose.

This analysis resulted in a completely new warrant officer concept and the basis for our present warrant officer program. A resultant policy change eliminated the two existing Medical Service Corps warrant officer specialties because they held the same titles as commissioned officers. The new warrant officer role was defined as that of a highly skilled technician. In 1959 the Medical Department submitted a proposal for 366 Medical Service Corps warrant officer positions in five different fields: clinical laboratory, dental laboratory, optical laboratory, medical equipment repair, and sanitation. Only the medical equipment repair technician was adopted and the MOS 202A-Biomedical Equipment Repair Technician joined the Medical Service Corps in 1961. By 1964, 96 Biomedical Equipment Repair Technician warrant officers were on active duty in the Medical Service Corps.

The role of the Biomedical Equipment Repair Technician remained relatively unchanged until 1988, when a decision was made to replace the 210A-Utilities Operation and Maintenance Technicians- in TOE units with a Biomedical Equipment Repair Technician thereby expanding their role within the TOE structure. Also a decision was made to change the title and number designation to better describe the expanded role and to move the number designation in-line with the 67 numerical series commissioned Medical Service Corps officers. The new and existing MOS and title are 670A, Health Services Maintenance Technician. *Portions of this document were extracted from The MSC History Book Ginn, Richard V.N., Col., MS. and the Medical Department, United States Army. Medical Supply in World War 1l, Office of The Surgeon General 1968.*

Warrant Officer Career Management

Early Years

The Army warrant officer force career management has been transferred from one agency to another throughout the course of this century. In 1920, warrant officers were appointed in the Army-at-large to assignments in various headquarters and tactical units.

In 1941, AR 610-5, Warrant Officer General Provision, specified The Adjutant General as the assignment agency for the warrant officer in accordance with the recommendations of the Chiefs of the Arms and Services concerned. In April 1960, based on an approved 1957 study, the management and assignment of warrant officers was transferred to the career branches except for Aviation warrant officers, who were managed by the Transportation Branch. Driven by increased aviator requirements during the Vietnam conflict, a decision was made in 1965 to manage

---

Warrant Officer Division

Division Chiefs
COL Robert Joyce	1975
COL Roy Shirley	1976
COL Robert L. Travis	1977
COL Arthur Bills	1979
COL George Morgan	1980
COL Paul Wenzel	1982
COL Willis R. Bunting	1984
COL Joel Hinson	1985
COL Billy Miller	1988
COL Mike Mosely	1989
COL Gerald Crews	1990
COL Richard L. Crampton	1995

Deputy Division Chiefs
CW5 Butch Davis	1993
CW5 Tom Story	1994

Professional Development Branch Chiefs
CW4 Lloyd Washer	1975
CW4 Dick Sauer	1979
CW4 David Helton	1984
CW4 Dennis Jinks	1986
CW4 John Dougherty	1987
CW4 "Butch" Davis	1988
CW4 Joel Voisine	1990
CW4 Robert Bucksath	1993

Professional Development Branch Members
CW3 Alex Fletcher	1980
CW2 Don Woodruff	1980
CW4 Robert Woods	1975
WO1 Billy Laubach	1981
CW3 Robert Gratkkowski	1985
CW3 George Sullivan	1986
CW2 Rick Cruz	1986
CW3 Mike McClane	1986
CW2 Jeannete Johnson	1982
CW4 Kenneth Johnson	1980
CW4 Ellis Walker	1974
CW3 Peggy Davis	1994
CW4 Dave Boyer	1995
CW4 Joe Pearson	1994
CW4 Kerri Workman	1995
CW4 Rick Romano	1994
CW4 Stan Freeman	1984
CW2 Ernie Vera	
CW3 Nash Montgomery	1994
CW3 Jackie Offerman	

Personnel Actions Branch Chiefs (Later consolidated with Professional Development Branch)
CW4 Rick Nelson	1978
CW4 John Valaer	1974
CW4 Al DeLucia	1985

Personnel Actions Branch Members
CW3 William Helm	
WO1 Alice Reid	
CW4 Gladys Skinner	
CW3 Don Zerbe	
CW4 Tom Mihara	1980
CW2 Randy Blackburn	1994

Aviation Branch Chiefs
CW4 Lee Komich	
CW4 David Helton	
CW4 Grant South	
CW4 Tom Story	1986
CW4 Bill Sanders	
CW4 John Kissell	
CW4 Harry Arthur	
CW4 David Helton	
CW5 Darrell Pope	1993
CW5 Chuck Angle	1995

Aviation Branch Members
CW4 Chuck Hawk	1976
CW4 William Hines	1976
CW4 Tom Keene	1976
CW4 Lee Komich	1978
CW4 James Hall	1981
CW4 Joe King	1979
CW4 James Newhouse	1978
CW4 Chris Vermillion	1981
CW4 Clark Ward	1978
CW4 Grant South	1982
CW4 Euel Henry	1983
CW4 William J Clark	
CW4 Timothy Cline	
CW4 Rick Pickard	
CW4 Will Stuckey	1975
CW4 Curt Oldroyd	
Cwr Tim McGee	
CW4 Meade Roberts	
CW4 Paul Ashley	
CW4 Larry Morgan	
CW4 Dick Carroll	1977
CW4 Charles Sturtevant	1977
CW4 Ted Hall	1981
CW4 Al Salinas	
CW3 Dave Prewitt	1993
CW4 Gil Robertson	
CW5 John Lucius	
CW5 Dough Guertson	1994
CW4 Sandra Beebe	
CW4 Joe Pearson	
CW4 George Gonsalves	
CW4 Loren Ashley	

Tech Services Branch Chiefs
CW4 Tom Grice	1992
CW4 Frank Baker	1979
CW4 Bill Fisher	1988
CW4 Don Needles	1989
CW4 Joyn McQuire	
CW5 Chris Winch	1995
CW5 Curtis Adkins	

Adjutant General Corps
CW4 Jim Duprist	1976
CW4 Billy Bishop	1978
CW4 John Barbonus	1979
CW4 Morris "Mo" Broome	1981
CW4 Joe Edmunson	1983
CW4 John Reid	1986
CW4 Joe Burgess	1993
CW3 Tom Sutterfield	1995

Engineer Branch
CW4 Ed Wall	1980
CW4 Alex Fletcher	1978

CW4 Fred Norman	1982
CW4 Ed Cole	1983
CW4 Frank Russell	1976
CW4 Keith Carter	1975
CW4 Ellis Walker	1974
CW4 Gene Derby	1976
CW4 Frank Washburn	

Weapons Maintenance/Air Defense
CW4 Frank Baker	1979
CW4 Rodney Pendleton	1982
CW4 John Watson	1982
CW4 Charles Osbourn	
CW4 Paul Plancon	
CW4 Murray Woods	
CW4 Charles Bush	1976
CW5 Rufus Montgomery	
CW4 Pat Francis	1989
CW4 Bob Bucksath	
CW4 John Clancey	1994

Quartermaster Branch
CW4 Walter Kessecker	1975
CW4 Daryl Giddings	1976
CW4 William Mullins	1982
CW4 Homer Johns	
CW4 Hilliard Haynes	
CW4 Les Craig	
CW4 Rufus Montgomery	

Military Police Branch
CW4 Dick Greaves	1976
CW4 Fred Meine	1982
CW4 Mike Ebert	
CW4 Don Needles	
CW4 John McQuire	

Military Intelligence Branch
CW4 Ralph Ochs	1975
CW4 Edward Mooney	1981
CW4 Maceo Boston	
CW4 Walter Johnson	
CW4 Robert McInnis	
CW4 William Hines	
CW4 Roger Bostic	
CW4 Lloyd Thyen	
CW4 Jerry Walters	1995

Ordnance Branch
CW4 Don Bullen	1975
CW4 Ted Reno	1979
CW4 Fred Norman	1982
CW4 Rich Catello	
CW4 Tom Grice	
CW4 Lynn Yarboro	

Signal Branch
CW4 William Draper	1975
CW4 "Wes" Mott	1976
CW4 Roland E. Bennett	1977
CW4 Hank Rilely	1979
CW4 John Watson	
CW4 Ralph Bowden	
CW4 Tony Wilkins	
CW4 Bruce Gardener	
CW4 Rick Coombe	1995

aviation warrant officers separately and a Warrant Officer Aviation Branch was formed in the Office of Personnel Operations.

Based on the recommendations contained in a 1972 study pertaining to the reorganization of the Office of Personnel Operations, the forerunner of MILPERCEN, the Warrant Officer Division was organized to manage all warrant officers who were not members of the Special Branches. This formation was concurrent with the change in commissioned officer management philosophy from that of management by branch (e.g., Infantry, Engineer, Ordnance) to that of management by grade (e.g., COL LTC, MAJ, and company grades) In 1980, MILPERCEN again reorganized to facilitate the implementation of the revised Officer Personnel Management System (OPMS). This reorganization changed the management focus from that of grade to branch/functional area ad created the Combat Arms, Combat Support Arms and Combat Service Support Arms Divisions within Officer Personnel Management Directorate, MILPERCEN. These divisions have the dual mission of making worldwide assignments against valid requirements for commissioned officers. Since warrant officers were not covered by OPMS, this 1980 reorganization did not affect the Warrant Officer Division which continued to centrally manage warrant officers.

The issue of what agency should have the mission of assigning, managing and professionally developing warrant officers is periodically studied for possible integration into the individual career branches for centralized coordination.

Warrant Officer Division (1975)

The listing of key personnel who have managed the careers of warrant officers since the inception of the Warrant Officer Division in 1975 is on page 27. The list is not complete because records are not available for the entire period.

The Warrant Officer Association Story
The Beginning 1920-1943

Historical documents tell us that the first Warrant Officers Association in the Army was organized at Fort McPherson, GA, in March 1921. It didn't take long after the appointment of warrant officers in 1920, in other than the Mine Planters Service, for the warrant officers to believe they were not being properly recognized as officers.

The first National convention of the Warrant Officers Association United States Army was held at Fort McPherson, GA on 11-13 August 1921. At the time of the first National convention the Association consisted of seven local councils, which with the membership at large, totaled a membership of 276. There is no record of the activities of the first National Convention.

The Constitution and By-laws of the Association were approved. The Preamble of the Constitution stated:

We, the undersigned Warrant Officers of the United States Army, having formed an association for the furtherance of the best interests of the service and of our grade, announce the objects of our Association as follows:

To foster a spirit of patriotism and devotion to duty among our members commensurate with the high ideals of the service.

- To promote a spirit of true comradeship among warrant officers.

- Through the example set by our members, to maintain the morale of the service.

- To uphold the dignity, and command the respect which is ours.

Washington, DC, the National Executive Council of the Warrant Officers Association of the United States of America, 1957-1959.

Arlington, VA, the brain trust of the Warrant Officers Association of the United States of Army in 1959. Left to right: CWO Murray McKenzie, treasurer; CWO Ted Bentley, secretary; CWO Paul King, president; CWO Grant Acker, vice president.

- To disseminate professional information among warrant officers.

- To promote the social welfare of our members.

Elected at the first national convention were: President: E. I. Sharp; Second Vice President W. E. Lunsford; Trustees: Albert Fiess; G. P. Stone; Perry B. Jackson. Other officers are not known.

The second National Convention was held on 9-11 May 1922 at Ft. McPherson, GA. The convention was opened with addresses by Major General John L. Hines, commanding the Eighth Corps area, Brig Gen E. M. Lewis, commanding the Second Division, Brig Gen William R. Smith, commanding Fort Sam Houston, COL B. B. Buck, commanding the Ninetieth Division, Organized Reserves, and COL Selah R. H. Tomkins, commanding Camp Stanley, TX.

General Hines offered some excellent advice when he urged the Association to abstain from mixing in politics. He stated that in his opinion, it was most unfortunate that the law provided for assignment of warrant officers to duties of a clerical nature only. However, he thought that any steps taken to alter this condition should be taken through proper military channels. Our friends would soon cease to be our friends if we tried to work through politics.

President E. I. Sharp reported that the aggregate membership had steadily increased to a total of 786 members. Available records indicated that 1228 warrant officers had been appointed, exclusive of those in the Mine Planters Service, but including band leaders. He recommended that no further recruiting of members be instituted since all

eligibles had been invited to join and had elected not to do so. The warrant officers of the Mine Planters Service had also been invited but declined because they had their own organization.

President Sharp reported that the publication and circulation of a monthly periodical had been initiated and the results were flattering. Other publications included a directory of warrant officers. In their campaign to increase the pay of warrant officers they were often confronted by the inquiry: "Who are you and why?" National legislators and others displayed a lack of knowledge on warrant officers as to whether we were needed in the Army; whether we merited the position we held; what our superiors thought of us and of the compensation awarded for our services. As a result, a booklet entitled Warrant Officers United States Army ,was published. (Copy available in the National office.)

At the second National Convention the delegates adopted the following resolutions:

- To take steps with a view to establishing the headquarters of the Association in Washington, DC

- To use every legitimate effort to enhance the value of our grade in the eyes of the War Department and our military supervisors, and to create a situation which will cause the elimination of the restricted nature of the duties now assigned to warrant officers.

- To apprehend and vigorously combat any and all activities which tend to discredit the capabilities and qualifications of warrant officers.

Elected at the second National Convention

were President: E. I Sharp; Vice President M. Surrerus; Directors: Hugo May, William H. Gage, John H. Worfred and Wallace C. Welch.

Early records also indicate that the Constitution and by-laws of the Association were revised and amended on 6 April 1927 to include the following Code of the Warrant Officers Association which would be read by the presiding officer immediately upon convening all official meetings and again before adjournment.

Washington, DC, the Warrant Officers Association of the United States of America met in August 1959 to reorganize the Association to include all services.

Fort Myer, VA, Representative Joel Broyhill, R-VA, addresses a Warrant Officer Association dinner on 30 March 1960 in Patton Hall. President Paul King is at left.

Code of the Warrant Officers Association, US Army (1922)

1. Each member of this Association should regard fellow members as friends and brothers.

2. He should conduct himself at all times in a manner reflecting credit upon and inspiring confidence in himself and all warrant officers of the Army.

3. He should strive to promote friendliness and sociability among brother members and their families, and also among non-members and their families.

4. He should be ever alert for opportunity to render service in time of need; to assist in every way possible brother members overtaken by misfortune, and to offer comfort and sympathy in bereavement.

5. He should never speak disparagingly of brother members, nor discuss the shortcomings of another member except in a spirit of kindness and with a sense of constructive criticism.

6. He should strive to attain, and aid other members to attain a higher professional efficiency.

7. He should never take action prejudicial to military discipline, nor which might reflect discredit or dishonor upon himself or the warrant grade.

8. He should encourage and assist the most intelligent, capable, and worthy enlisted men of the service to become warrant officers whenever vacancies occur.

These early warrant officers attempted to improve their status by seeking, in the face of the Army's chronic reluctance to endorse such measures, the passage of broadening Federal legislation. Despite their efforts to correct disparities in pay and inadequacy of allowances, assignment to technical duties, and other improvements in the warrant officer program, little progress was made until the pressures of the national emergency leading to World War II. (These improvements have been highlighted in Section 1 of this book). It seems ironic that the improvements came about at the time the Association was disbanding because of the requirements of World War II. At its peak, the Association had 25 local councils and about 1400 members both active and retired warrant officers.

A New Start (1957-1971)

In Germany in 1957, Army warrant officers felt the need to establish an association. A similar need was felt in the Far East. In 1958 a move was made to consolidate the two separate associations with the Air Force Warrant Officers Association which had been formed in 1955. The intent was to establish a national headquarters in Washington, DC. The Air Force Warrant Officers Association, because of a USAF directive that members of that service should not join any organization devoted to the welfare of only one segment of the Air Force, decided not to merge and eventually dissolved. The separate associations, less the Air Force Warrant Officers Association merged to form the Warrant Officers Association of the United States of America (WOAUSA), which resulted in the national Warrant Officers Association being resurrected again in late 1959.

The success of the WOAUSA was limited for a number of reasons. The loss of Air Force warrant officers cut into their numbers. Also, the Navy was struggling with its concept of warrant officers and limited duty officers and had proposed a five year program of non-appointment of warrant officers to evaluate the effect on the two programs which were in direct competition for appointment of qualified enlisted members. The Navy concluded that warrant officers were still needed and that all future

WO1 Louis R. Rocco

CW2 Frederick E. Ferguson, AVN. (Photo by Oscar E. Porter, Courtesy of US Army)

CWO3 Michael J. Novosel. (Photo by Oscar E. Porter, Courtesy of US Army)

CW4 (Ret.) Howard P. Melvin
Quartermaster Hall of Fame

CW4 (Ret.) Stephen N. Chobanian
QM Hall of Fame

CW4 (Ret.) John A. Ward
Quartermaster Hall of Fame

CW4 (Ret.) Daryl W. Giddings
Quartermaster Hall of Fame

CW4 George Gratchen
Quartermaster Hall of Fame

CW4 Ted Reno
Quartermaster Hall of Fame

The President of the United States of America, authorized by Act of Congress, March 3, 1863, has awarded in the name of The Congress the Medal of Honor to

WARRANT OFFICER LOUIS R. ROCCO

UNITED STATES ARMY

For conspicuous gallantry and intrepidity in action at the risk of life above and beyond the call of duty:

Warrant Officer (then Sergeant First Class) Louis R. Rocco, United States Military Assistance Command, Vietnam, Advisory Team 162, distinguished himself on 24 May 1970, northeast of Katum, Republic of Vietnam, when he volunteered to accompany a medical evacuation team on an urgent mission to evacuate eight critically wounded Army of the Republic of Vietnam personnel. As the helicopter approached the landing zone, it became the target for intense enemy automatic weapons fire. Disregarding his own safety, Warrant Officer Rocco identified and placed accurate suppressive fire on the enemy positions as the aircraft descended toward the landing zone. Sustaining major damage from the enemy fire, the aircraft was forced to crash land, causing Warrant Officer Rocco to sustain a fractured wrist and hip and a severely bruised back. Ignoring his injuries, he extracted the survivors from the burning wreckage, sustaining burns to his own body. Despite intense enemy fire, Warrant Officer Rocco carried each unconscious man across approximately twenty meters of exposed terrain to the Army of the Republic of Vietnam perimeter. On each trip, his severely burned hands and broken wrist caused excruciating pain, but the lives of the unconscious crash survivors were more important than his personal discomfort, and he continued his rescue efforts. Once inside the friendly position, Warrant Officer Rocco helped administer first aid to his wounded comrades until his wounds and burns caused him to collapse and lose consciousness. His bravery under fire and intense devotion to duty were directly responsible for saving three of his fellow soldiers from certain death. His unparalleled bravery in the face of enemy fire, his complete disregard for his own pain and injuries, and his performance were far above and beyond the call of duty and were in keeping with the highest traditions of self-sacrifice and courage of the military service.

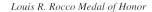

Louis R. Rocco Medal of Honor

The President of the United States of America, authorized by Act of Congress, March 3, 1863, has awarded in the name of The Congress the Medal of Honor to

CHIEF WARRANT OFFICER FREDERICK E. FERGUSON

UNITED STATES ARMY

For conspicuous gallantry and intrepidity in action at the risk of life above and beyond the call of duty:

Chief Warrant Officer Frederick E. Ferguson, United States Army, distinguished himself by conspicuous gallantry and intrepidity while serving with Company C, 227th Aviation Battalion, 1st Cavalry Division (Airmobile) at Hue, Republic of Vietnam. On 31 January 1968, Chief Warrant Officer Ferguson, commander of a resupply helicopter, monitoring an emergency call from wounded passengers and crewmen of a downed helicopter, under heavy attack within the enemy controlled city of Hue, unhesitatingly volunteered to attempt evacuation. Despite warning for all aircraft to stay clear of the area due to heavy anti-aircraft fire, Chief Warrant Officer Ferguson began a low-level flight at maximum airspeed along the Perfume River toward the tiny, isolated South Vietnamese Army compound in which the crash survivors had taken refuge. Coolly and skillfully maintaining his course in the face of intense, short range fire from enemy occupied buildings and boats, he displayed superior flying skill and tenacity of purpose by landing his aircraft in an extremely confined area in a blinding dust cloud under heavy mortar and small arms fire. Although the helicopter was severely damaged by mortar fragments during the loading of the wounded, Chief Warrant Officer Ferguson disregarded the damage and, taking off through the continuing hail of mortar fire, he flew his crippled aircraft on the return route through the rain of fire that he had experienced earlier and safely returned his wounded passengers to friendly control. Chief Warrant Officer Ferguson's extraordinary gallantry, determination and intrepidity saved the lives of five of his comrades. His action are in the highest traditions of the military service and reflect great credit on him and the United States Army.

Frederick E. Ferguson Medal of Honor

The President of the United States of America, authorized by Act of Congress, March 3, 1863, has awarded in the name of The Congress the Medal of Honor to

CHIEF WARRANT OFFICER MICHAEL J. NOVOSEL

UNITED STATES ARMY

For conspicuous gallantry and intrepidity in action at the risk of life above and beyond the call of duty:

Chief Warrant Officer Michael J. Novosel, 82d Medical Detachment, 45th Medical Company, 68th Medical Group, distinguished himself on October 2, 1969 while serving as commander of a medical evacuation helicopter in Kiem Tuong Province, Republic of Vietnam. He unhesitatingly maneuvered his helicopter into a heavily fortified and defended enemy training area where a group of wounded Vietnamese soldiers were pinned down by a large enemy force. Flying without gunship or other cover and exposed to intense machine gun fire, Chief Warrant Officer Novosel was able to locate and rescue a wounded soldier. Since all communications with the beleaguered troops had been lost, he repeatedly circled the battle area, flying at low level under continuous heavy fire, to attract the attention of the scattered friendly troops. This display of courage visibly raised their morale, as they recognized this as a signal to assemble for evacuation. On six occasions he and his crew were forced out of the battle area by the intense enemy fire, only to circle and return from another direction to land and extract additional troops. Near the end of the mission, a wounded soldier was spotted close to an enemy bunker. Fully realizing that he would attract a hail of enemy fire, Chief Warrant Officer Novosel nevertheless attempted the extraction by hovering the helicopter backward. As the man was pulled on board, enemy automatic weapons opened fire at close range, damaged the aircraft and wounded Chief Warrant Officer Novosel. He momentarily lost control of the aircraft, but quickly recovered and departed under the withering fire. In all, 15 extremely hazardous extractions were performed in order to remove wounded personnel. As a direct result of his selfless conduct, the lives of 29 soldiers were saved. The conspicuous gallantry and extraordinary heroism displayed by Chief Warrant Officer Novosel were an inspiration to his comrades in arms and reflect great credit on him, his unit, and the United States Army.

Michael J. Novosel Medal of Honor

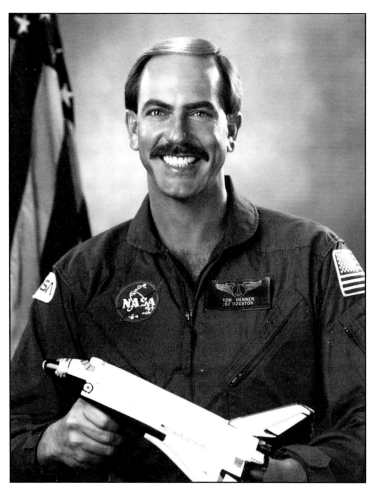

Astronaut Tom Hennen, first WO in space.

appointments to the limited duty officer program should be from the warrant officer ranks. This experiment by the Navy may have caused a reluctance of many Navy warrant officers to become members of the Warrant Officers Association. Finally, the uncertainty of Army warrant officers about their future status also appears to have caused some hesitancy among Army warrant officers about joining the Association

Overriding all these factors was the negative attitude of both service headquarters and of local commanders toward the formation of a separate association for warrant officers. This attitude had a strong effect on the ability of interested WOA members to form or maintain chapters. As a result, the Warrant Officers Association dropped in membership from a high of almost 2000 in 1959 to a low of less than 400 in early 1963.

Following the national meeting in 1959 which merged the separate warrant officer associations into a national organization, there is no record of another meeting of the Warrant Officers Association of the United States of America, although some local chapters continued to meet for social and local interests.

United States Army Warrant Officers Association

1972-1973

The genesis of the current worldwide association for Army warrant officers was an idea generated in Indianapolis, Indiana, in July 1972 when forty-two Adjutant General warrant officers met informally for fun, camaraderie, and the opportunity to exchange professional concerns with each other. After considerable discussion on the role of the warrant officer of that time period it was determined that this small group should take on the task of organizing a warrant officers association. Dues were established at $5.00 per year and the group elected Don Hess, Washington DC, as Chairman, Pro Temp, Joe Cheatum, Indianapolis, IN, as Vice Chair; Charles Austin, Secretary, and Paul Lieber, Treasurer, both from the Washington area to simplify administration. Numerous meetings were held in the Pentagon by warrant officers from the Washington area to explore the requirements for establishing a warrant officers association. The original by-laws of the previous warrant officers associations were obtained and examined. The new by-laws were developed using the original bylaws as guidelines and revising as necessary. The By-laws state the following objectives:

1. To foster a spirit of patriotism and devotion to duty among our members commensurate with the high ideals of the Army and our position therein.

2. To recommend programs for the improvement of the Army.

3. To promote the technical and social welfare of our members.

4. To promote a spirit of true comradeship among our members.

The next step was to announce in Army Times the formation of a Warrant Officers Association and to open a post office box to receive applications. The response was immediately overwhelming. Unlike earlier warrant officer associations the current Association found the Army leadership supportive of their goals. The South Post, Fort Myer, VA had several vacant offices and the newly formed association was provided with an empty office at no cost. With a donated typewriter, mimeograph machine and volunteer help the Association officers began to correspond with warrant officers around the world and to establish guidelines for the operation of local chapters. During this

Alexandria, VA. The newly elected permanent officers of the USAWOA were installed by CW04, Archie Yanno (R), President of the US Coast Guard Warrant Officers Association on July 12, 1973. (L to R): Paul Lieber, treasurer; Dale Swafford, secretary; Robert Hamilton, vice president and Don Hess, president.

Alexandria, VA. CW4 John "Mike" Yates, Professional Development Branch, MILPERCEN, DA, was the author of DA Pamphlet 600-11, Warrant Officer Professioanl Development, 1972.

Alexandria, VA. MG Sidney Berry, Chief, Military Personnel Center, addressed the first membership meeting of the USAWOA on July 12, 1973.

time period Secretary Charles Austin retired and moved from the Washington area. CW4 Dale Swafford volunteered to assume the secretarial duties and was instrumental in setting up office procedures to handle the mail. The isolated location of the office, coupled with the dwindling population within the South Post area, resulted in a decision to move the office to the basement of the home of Don Hess to provide better supervision and more timely response to the numerous requests received for Association information. Part time administrative help carried on the office administration with limited supervision because the national officers were volunteers with full time military duties.

The first publication was a Warrant Officer pamphlet issued in September 1972 which outlined the Association objectives as stated above. It also reiterated a basic philosophy of working within the system to build a reputation as a professional association dedicated to recommending improvements in the Army and the Warrant Officer Corps, and to disseminating professional information to members. Within the first six months, membership rose from 42 to over 2000 thanks to the efforts of warrant officers in the field who recruited fellow warrant officers and organized chapters at most

Alexandria, VA. Al Cox, President, European Region, addressed the USAWOA members, 1973 Convention.

major installations. The first stateside recognized chapter of the USAWOA was Ft. Bragg which was chartered on 25 October 1972.

During this formative period extensive coordination was being conducted with the newly formed European Warrant Officers Association organized by CW4 George Gratchen in Mannheim Germany, which resulted in a merger of these two associations.

Annual Convention 1973

The first Annual Convention was held from 9-12 July 1973 at the Holiday Inn, Alexandria, VA, adjacent to the Hoffman Building. 16 chapters from Europe, 19 chapters from CONUS and other areas, and 57 members at large were present which represented 1698 warrant officers. This was the first formal meeting of the Association since the initial meeting in Indianapolis, IN in June 1972 which originally established the USAWOA.

Since the officers elected at Indianapolis, IN were pro-temp officers, the delegates elected new officers for the coming year: President Don Hess, Vice President, Bob Hamilton, Secretary Dale Swafford, and Treasurer, Paul Lieber, The newly elected officers were installed by CW4 Archie Yanno, President of the Coast Guard Warrant Officers Association.

Guest speakers at the first meeting included COL William Louisell, ODCSPER, who spoke on the Army Warrant Officer Career Program; COL Ted Crozier, Chief, Aviation Warrant Officer Branch, discussed the Warrant Officer Civilian and Military Education Program; and MG Sidney Berry, Chief, Military Personnel Center who stated that true professionalism will lead to the kind of recognition and representation we all desire. General Berry attended an afternoon session and he stated: "I learned more about warrant officers in my three hour visit to your meeting than in my three years as commander at MILPERCEN."

Major items of business were the ratification of the Constitution and the acceptance of the By-laws; the unanimous approval of the proposed increase in the annual dues from $5.00 to $10.00, effective 1 September 1973, and the establishment of charter membership for members on the roles from 1972 until 31 July 1973, the date of the first annual meeting.

The various resolutions dealt with USAWOA urging vigorous action be initiated to:
- Correct the existing disparity in flight pay.
- Adjust the inequities between commissioned/warrant officer pay and allowances, billeting assignments and fees assessed by the CHAMPUS program.
- Authorize concurrent travel for CW4s and CW3s on the promotion list.
- Authorize appropriate equivalent quarters, BOQ and family for CW4s and CW3s on the promotion list.
- Resolve travel differences and disparities between DA civilian and military personnel authorizations.
- Require warrant officers to wear the insignia of the Warrant Officer Corps at all times when in uniform.
- Reinstate the basic branch scarf for warrant officers and require wear whenever branch scarves are required as part of the uniform dress.
- Integrate an educational program on the role of the warrant officer in all phases of commissioned and enlisted training.
- Poll the majority of the Warrant Officer Corps prior to changes to warrant officer rank or branch insignia.
- Implement a warrant officer career program for all warrant officer career fields
- Establish a USAWOA sponsorship program for all warrant officers
- Identify and solicit USAWOA membership of newly appointed warrant officers and notify the gaining command of arrival.

The USAWOA grew rapidly as shown by the number of chapters officially recognized at the Annual Meeting. (The chapters were recognized as charter chapters and entitled to the designation as "Silver Chapters" provided they maintained continued active status as a chapter. The European Region chapters, formerly chapters of the European Warrant Officers Association, were formally recognized as USAWOA chapters with the merger of the two associations.)
- Anchorage Chapter, Ft Richardson, AL
  27 Oct 1972
- Arizona Chapter, Ft Huachuca, AZ
  Nov 1972
- Ft Benning Chapter, GA
  3 May 1973
- Ft Bragg Chapter, NC
  25 Oct 1972
- Canal Zone Chapter, Panama
  7 Feb 1973
- Garden State Chapter, Ft Dix, NJ
  7 Jun 1973
- Golden Gate Chapter, San Francisco, CA
  9 Feb 1973
- Ft Gordon Chapter, GA
  30 Nov 1972
- James P Ervin, Jr. Chapter, Ft Greely, AL
  31 Nov 1972
- Fort Hood Chapter, TX
  11 Oct 1972

Alexandria, VA. Col. Ted Crozier, Chief Aviation Warrant Officer Branch, addressed the members and guests at the 1974 banquet.

Alexandria, VA. The first Board of Directors (BOD) meeting of the USAWOA was held on Jan. 24, 1974 at the Hoffman Bldg. The BOD consisted of all active chapters recognized by the national headquarters. The wall map indicated the location of the chapters.

Alexandria, VA. Newly elected officers of USAWOA for 1974 were (L to R): Don Moore, treasurer; Dale Swafford, secretary; Neil McLeod, vice president and Robert Hamilton, president. The officers were installed by outgoing president Don Hess on July 13, 1974.

- Fort Meade Chapter, MD

- Monterey Bay Chapter, Fort Ord, CA
  25 Jan 1973
- Last Dozen Chapter, Ft Riley, KS
  13 Apr 1973
- Northeast Chapter, Ft Monmouth, NJ
  12 May 1973
- Northwest Chapter, Ft Lewis, WA
  20 Feb 1973
- Okinawa Chapter, Okinawa
  23 May 1973
- Pikes Peak Chapter, Colorado Springs, CO
  10 Apr 1973
- Raleigh Chapter, Raleigh, NC
  22 May 1973
- Ft Rucker Chapter, AL
  10 Dec 1972
- Vint Hill Farms Chapter, Warrenton, VA
  22 Mar 1973
- South Florida Chapter, Homestead AFB, FL

- Sooner Plains Chapter, Ft Sill, OK
  2 Aug 1973
- Hampton Roads Chapter, Ft Eustis, VA

- Gold Coast Chapter, Miami, FL
  25 Jul 1973
- Redstone Arsenal Chapter, AL
  1 Aug 1973
- Ken-Tenn Chapter, Ft Campbell, KY
  15 Aug 1973
- Albany Chapter, Albany, NY
- European Region
  12 Jul 1973
- Allied Command Europe Chapter (ACE)
  SHAPE   12 Jul 1973
- Berlin Chapter
  12 Jul 1973
- Frankfurt Chapter
  12 Jul 1973
- Hanau Chapter
  12 Jul 1973
- Karlshrue Chapter
  12 Jul 1973
- Nahe Valley Chapter (Baumholder)
  12 Jul 1973
- New Ulm Chapter
  12 Jul 1973
- Nord Bayern Chapter (Nurnburg)
  12 Jul 1973
- Pisa Chapter
  12 Jul 1973
- Pirmasens Chapter
  12 Jul 1973
- Rhein Neckar Chapter (Manheim)
  12 Jul 1973
- Rheinland Pfalz Chapter (Kaiserlsatern)
  12 Jul 1973
- Schweinfurt Chapter
  12 Jul 1973
- Stuttgart Chapter
  12 Jul 1973
- Sud Bayern Chapter (Augsburg)
  12 Jul 1973
- Vicenza Chapter
  12 Jul 1973
- Heilbronn Chapter
  12 Jul 1973

So the official birth of the Association took place with great expectations. The attitude of the warrant officers who traveled from near and far to sound the note of professionalism was outstanding as was the attitude of the members of the Department of Army guest speakers and their support staff as they welcomed us aboard. The meeting closed with a well attended dinner dance and an optimistic spirit.

1974

First Board of Directors Meeting

The first semi-annual Board of Directors (BOD) meeting was held on 28 January 1974 at the Hoffman Building in Alexandria, VA. At that time the presidents of the chapters constituted the national Board of Directors. The first BOD meeting truly was a working session, beginning at 0915 hours and adjourning at 2130 hours. At this historic meeting the financial and administrative status of the association was covered with approval of the financial statement; a proposed budget; completion of income tax requirements; and approval of our nonprofit status by the IRS. A bank proposal from Chase Manhattan Bank for warrant officers in Europe was presented by European Region President Al Cox and approved by the BOD. COL (Ret) Robert Morris, Director of the Military Department of University Bank of Maryland (Unibank) outlined the benefits of banking with Unibank.

In other business the BOD instructed the national officers to:
- Pursue advertising in the monthly newsletter to help defray the cost of printing and mailing our publication
- Take necessary action to incorporate the national association.
- Take necessary action to employ an executive vice president to conduct the administrative affairs of our Association.
- Officially go on record as supporting total equalization of flight pay.
- Establish a life membership program.

- Request DA conduct a study on the problem of short turnaround time presently being experienced by warrant officers in specific MOSs.

The directors heard a presentation by BG Forrest, Director, Officer Personnel, MILPERCEN in which he discussed warrant officer professional development improvements to include the establishment of the Warrant Officer Senior Course

Alexandria, VA. Secretary of the Army, Howard "Bo" Calloway addresses the Second Annual Convention of the USAWOA on July 12, 1974.

Alexandria, VA. President Bob Hamilton addresses the Second Annual USAWOA Convention in 1974.

European Region. Attendees at the Second Annual Convention of the European Region, USAWOA met May 1-4, 1974.

Alexandria, VA. CW4 Richard Sauer, followed CW4 "Mike" Yates as the driving force behind early WO professional development before the formation of the Warrant Officer Division in MILPERCEN, 1974.

(WOSC) for selected senior warrant officers; Warrant Officer Advanced Courses (WOAC) for all warrant officers; cooperative degree programs at each school that conducts warrant officer career courses to provide opportunities for warrant officers to achieve civil education goals; replacement of the Long Range Active Duty Program (LRADP) with a Managed Tenure Program; appointment of warrant officers to serve on AUS promotion and other boards; and improvement of communication between DA and the warrant officer in the field by designating a section for warrant officers in branch newsletters and adding WOA chapters to branch newsletter mailing lists; more warrant officer information provided to Army Times, and service journals; improving the warrant officer appointment process; and revising the warrant officer career planning pamphlet to include more comprehensive guidance.

General Forrest reiterated the Army's strong commitment to the Warrant Officer Corps now and in the future.

The European Region was ably represented at the BOD meeting by ER President Al Cox and CW4 George Gratchen, the founder of the European Warrant Officers Association. The unique problems facing the warrant officers in Europe were addressed with General Forrest and led to personal interviews with several Officer Personnel Directorate branch chiefs to discuss these problems.

The following members represented their chapters at our first Board of Directors meeting:
- CW4 Howard Rappold, Arizona Chapter
- CW2 Allen Todd, Ft Bragg Chapter
- CW3 Carl A Hallada, Canal Zone Chapter
- CW2 Dave Colwell, Ft Gordon Chapter
- CW3 Stan Becker, Hampton Roads Chapter
- CW4 Mike Dimeglio, Ft Meade Chapter
- CW3 James Dawkins, Northwest Chapter
- CW2 Ralph Milward, Okinawa Chapter
- CW3 Roy McBee, Pikes Peak Chapter
- CW4 Melvin LaPointe, Redstone Arsenal Chap.
- CW3 David Helton, Ft Rucker Chapter
- CW3 Dave Pridgeon, Southern Florida Chapter
- CW3 Ralph Blair, Vint Hill Farms Chapter
- CW4 Bryon Smith, Tidewater Chapter
- CW2 Ernest Spann, Leon G Bonfield Chapter
- CW4 Lloyd Washer, Potomac Chapter
- CW2 Dale Fransten, Lord Fairfax Chapter
- CW4 Ken Snyder, Aberdeen Edgewood Chap.
- CW3 Al Cox, European Region (17 chapters)
- CW4 George Gratchen, Rhein Neckar Chapter
- Other chapters were represented by proxies to the national officers.

1974 Annual Convention

The second annual Convention was again held at the Holiday Inn, Alexandria, VA from 9 - July 1974 with CW3 Al Cox as the appointed convention chairman calling the delegates to order at 0900. 50 chapters were represented by delegates or by proxy through delegates. The minutes of the first annual meeting were read and approved. The finance report for the period 1 January through 30 June 1974 was presented and accepted.

The keynote speaker was the Honorable Howard "Bo" Calloway, Secretary of the Army who praised the Warrant Officer Corps for its professionalism and urged the Corps to help the Army in the transformation from a draft to a volunteer Army environment. Other speakers included COL Ted Crozier, Chief Warrant Officer Aviation Branch, MILPERCEN who briefed on the warrant officer candidate school and the warrant officer senior course. Robert B. Laurents, Senior Legislative Counsel, National Association for Uniformed Services (NAUS) explained how private associations function within the legislative process. Congressman Sam Stratton (D-NY) a member of the House Armed Services Committee, discussed flight pay, regular pay, retirement and promotion of military personnel. He credited USAWOA for alerting his subcommittee to the discrepancies within the proposed flight pay bill and invited the Association officers to attend the subcommittee hearings to ensure the warrant officer views are considered along with enlisted and commissioned officers.

The delegates considered 52 resolutions and after lengthy discussion and vote, various resolutions dealt with USAWOA urging vigorous action be initiated to:
- Authorize Cat I concurrent travel for CW4s and CW3s on the promotion list.
- Eliminate the surcharge payment for officers and warrant officers utilizing military dining facilities
- Retain the current policy and monetary payment for accrued leave.
- Authorize "Responsibility Pay" for commissioned and warrant officers serving in a higher grade.
- Authorize a special monetary duty allowance for all assigned vessel crewmembers for performing sea duty.
- Include warrant officers in the OPD team that visits overseas and CONUS installations each year.
- Assign a chief warrant officer in the office, Chief, Army Reserve to monitor warrant officer actions.
- Adopt an expansion of our region system to allow for worldwide region representation.
- Advertise, interview and employ an executive vice president to administer the Association.
- Other resolutions dealt with policies pertaining to drug abuse, amnesty, rehabilitation programs, savings programs, social security integration, and other miscellaneous areas.

The membership voted to elect the following officers for the coming year: President Bob Hamilton; Vice President Neil McLeod; Secretary Dale Swafford and Treasurer Don Moore. Outgoing President Don Hess administered the oath of office to the newly elected national officers.

Major General Harold Moore, Commanding General, MILPERCEN addressed the members and spouses at the banquet. He covered a wide variety of warrant officer actions which had become policy during the past year and stated that positive action would continue to benefit warrant officers in the future.

The second annual USAWOA Convention ended with the delegates departing with a feeling of

accomplishment, greater unity, strength and understanding. The following chapters listed below were represented by their elected delegates or by proxy:
- Arizona Chapter — 56
- Crater Chapter (VA) — 13
- Ft Bragg Chapter (NC) — 144
- Ft Benning Chapter (GA) — 56
- Garden State Chapter (NJ) — 22
- Golden Gate Chapter (CA) — 12
- Hampton Roads Chapter (VA) — 45
- Last Dozen Chapter (KS) — 17
- Ft Meade Chapter (MD) — 42
- Monterey Bay Chapter (CA) — 45
- Northeastern Chapter (NJ) — 29
- Northwest Chapter (WA) — 50
- Pikes Peak Chapter (CO) — 75
- Redstone Chapter (AL) — 47
- Aviation Ctr Chapter (AL) — 68
- Sho-Me Chapter (MO) — 29
- Vint Hill Farms Chapter(VA) — 32
- Bonifield Chapter (GA) — 18
- Ft Gordon Chapter (GA) — 35
- Lord Fairfax Chapter (VA) — 48
- Derby Chapter (KY) — 79
- Northern Lights Chap (AK) — 26
- Raleigh Chapter (NC) — 26
- Aberdeen Chapter (MD) — 21
- Hanau Chapter (Ger) — 110
- Rhine Neckar Chap (Ger) — 73
- European Region (23 Chap) — 860

During the remainder of 1974 the Association worked to build a professional reputation among the Army Staff and the DoD and to improve the image of the Corps. Issues included: appointing warrant officers as voting members on the AUS promotion boards; a commitment from the various branches to devote a section of their branch newsletters exclusively to warrant officer matters; a commendation by members of Congress for our efforts to increase the flight pay of warrant officer aviators under the Aviation Career Incentive act of 1974.

At the post and community level the involvement of local chapters in community activities brought them the respect and pride of their commanders. Involvement in the Scouting, Little League and ADYA programs and assistance to various charitable organizations raised the visibility and the esteem of the Warrant Officers Association among the various military communities.

On 7 November 1974 the Association was approved for incorporation in the State of Virginia which completed the legal requirements for our Association to be recognized as a professional organization. The Board of Directors and the membership directed that the constitution and by-laws of our Association be amended to comply with the Virginia incorporation requirements

1975

As we entered 1975 the Council of Presidents (COP) met on 13 January at Fort Myer, VA, Twenty five members were present which included four members from the European Region. The articles of incorporation were explained and a summary of administrative actions taken were presented.

The COP was addressed by BG Mundie, Chief of Officer Professional Development, DA, and Sergeant Major of the Army Leon Van Autreve who covered various professional development actions affecting the Warrant Officer Corps and the Army.

A major action by the COP was the hiring of Don Hess as the first National Executive Secretary effective 1 April 1975. Don served as the first President of the Association and had been acting as the chief administrative officer of the Association since its inception. The COP bestowed a lifetime membership on Don and George Gratchen, the founder of the European Region, for their dedication and devotion to the USAWOA.

In April 1975 the USAWOA was accepted for membership in the Council of Military Organizations, (COMO) a consortium of major military associations working together to present a united front in its efforts with congressional leaders. This action granted USAWOA access to the knowledge and experience of the full time legislative representatives from such influential associations as The Retired Officers Association (TROA), Association of the US Army (AUSA), Reserve Officers Association (ROA), Noncommissioned Officers Association (NCO) and others. (A complete listing of COMO and The Military Coalition are listed in a separate chapter on legislative activities.)

In May 1975 one of the most significant actions affecting the Warrant Officer Corps took place with the formation of a Warrant Officer Division in MILPERCEN. A chapter on the Warrant Officer Division is included in this history and is mentioned here only to point out that this consolidation of the various career branches within OPD under a single Division Chief resulted in the Association having a single point of contact to address professional concerns rather than dealing with numerous Branch Chiefs whose population was largely commissioned officers with a small number of warrant officers. The first Warrant Officer Division Chief, COL Robert Joyce was extremely receptive to our Association and agreed to provide a monthly column for our NEWSLINER. Succeeding Division Chief's have kept up this tradition.

1975 Annual Meeting

The first Annual Meeting of the Members. USAWOA, Inc. was held at the Sheraton Inn Washington/Northeast, New Carrollton, MD from 7 to 9 July 1975, hosted by the national office. This Annual Meeting was different from the two previous Annual Conventions because the Articles of Incorporation specified that each individual member must be given the right to vote, either in person or by written and signed proxy to another member attending the meetings. Prior to this meeting, the delegate system enabled chapter officers to cast a vote for members within their chapter. Also, because of the incorporation in the state of Virginia, chapter charters were reissued to all existing chapters based on the official recognition by the state.

A quorum was present for the Annual Meeting, the Council of President's meeting and the Board of Directors Meeting.

Guest speakers included Acting Secretary of the Army Norman Augustine, LTG Harold Moore, Army Deputy Chief of Staff for Personnel (DCSPER) ; LTG Fred Kornet, Deputy Chief of Staff for Logistics (DCSLOG); BG John H. Johns, Director, Human Resources Development, DCSPER; LTC Lenderman, Acting Chief, Warrant Officer Division (WOD) and warrant officer members of the WOD. Also speaking was CW4 John "Mike" Yates, Chief, Warrant Officer Plans Section. Also, the National officers and directors reported on their areas of responsibility.

The Members elected CW3 Alfred E. Cox, as president, CW2 Cletus McKeown as Vice President, Frank Stamey as Secretary, and Carl Hess as Treasurer. Directors elected were Albert M. Holcombe, Charles Linderman, Don Desjardins, Robert Hutchinson, Barry Farris and Jimmy Gray.

After detailed discussion the members voted to:
- Support a change to AR 670-5 authorizing warrant officers to wear the trefoil and sleeve band on the mess uniform jackets.
- Approved the printing of the warrant officer code of ethics on the reverse side of the membership cared.

- Support S433 to change the name of the Medal of Honor to the "Congressional Medal of Honor."
- Oppose any legislation providing amnesty to deserters and draft evaders.
- Approve the recognition of distinguished and honor graduates of the Warrant Officer Advanced and Senior Courses by awarding Academic Certificates of Achievement
- Support the extension of the Food Stamp Program to eligible personnel and dependents serving in overseas areas.
- Support a legislative proposal to change the waiting period for collection of survivor benefits to coincide with the one year waiting period for civil servant employees.
- Support the discontinuance of Article 15 punishment in individual OMPF.
- Support a change to discontinue the reduced retired pay portion of military retired pay when the spouse dies.
- Support a change to regulation to permit an individual who is selected for mandatory retirement and who is in the primary zone for promotion to be retained on active duty until the results of the selection board are announced; and if selected, to be allowed to remain on active duty long enough to retire at the higher grade.
- Approved the initiation of a program to select a USAWOA Warrant Officer of the Year.
- Support a policy of chapter participation in funeral services of deceased warrant officers.
- Support a policy for DA to permit personal reviews of OMP files by mail.

The banquet speaker was BG (Ret) Eugene M. Lynch, who spoke on the development of the warrant officer program through the years and the role of the warrant officer in the future. A special guest was CWO (Ret) Chester Maxim, 86, a resident of the Soldiers and Airman's Home, who was appointed as a warrant officer in the Mine Planters Service in 1920.

Fayetteville, NC. MG John Forrest, ODCSPER, DA, addresses warrant officers and guests, 1976 banquet.

Fayetteville, NC. Col. Roy Shirley, Chief, Warrant Officer Division, DA, explains the formation of the Warrant Officer Division during the 1976 Annual Meeting.

Fayetteville, NC. Ft. Bragg Silver Chapter Pres. Don Talbott welcomes members and guests to the 1976 Annual Meeting banquet, celebrating 200 years of military service to our country.

Colorado Springs, CO. General Chappie James, USAF, addresses warrant officers and guests at the 1977 annual meeting on July 9, 1977.

Colorado Springs, CO. Col. Robert Travis, Chief, Warrant Officer Div., discusses warrant officer actions at the Department of the Army level at the 1977 Annual Meeting.

1976

The 1976 Council of President's/Board of Directors meeting was held 5-7 January 1976 at Fort Myer, VA. Eight of the 9 directors were present along with the elected officers and the National Executive Secretary. 10 chapter presidents were on hand and 22 proxies were provided by chapters. Three representatives from the European region and other members-at-large were also present.

MG Gard, Commander, MILPERCEN, addressed the strength of the Army, the promotion outlook, the Managed Tenure Program and Senior Course and warrant officer career management. COL Robert M. Joyce, Chief Warrant Officer Division, spoke on the implementation of the new Warrant Officer Division, MILPERCEN.

CW4 George Gratchen, Chairman of the Finance Committee, reported that over $6,000 had been donated to Project SOFA. Phase II of Project SOFA is the development of a contingency fund of $10,000.

The most significant action to be approved was a complete revision of the Association dues structure effective 1 April 1976 to include:
-    Elimination of Chapter dues. Prior to this action members in different locations were faced with different amounts of dues to join the Association because each chapter established local dues based on the activities of the chapter. As members transferred from one chapter to another they were faced with paying additional local dues at the new chapter. Also many members were joining the national association, and not joining a local chapter because of the different dues structure, personalities or other reasons.
-   Rebate of dues to chapters. To soften the financial impact on the elimination of local chapter dues, a national rebate of $5.00 per member, per year was approved for payment to the nearest chapter for accounting and administrative purposes for all members thus eliminating a member-at-large category and providing a standard dues structure for our Association.
-   Multi-Year Membership Plan: A plan was approved to allow members to enroll or renew for 3 or 5 years at a substantially reduced cost. Effective 1 April 1976 the dues were established as 1 year membership $24.00; 3 year membership $60.00 and 5 year membership $90.00.
-   A special Bicentennial Lifetime Membership for $200 was approved effective from Jan 1976 to 9 July 1976. After that date life membership fee was established as $350.00.

Other business included selecting Fort Bragg, NC as the host chapter for the 1976 Annual Meeting; the establishment of Associate and Honorary memberships to those persons not otherwise eligible for regular membership; and the sanction of wives auxiliaries to be chartered at the local level.

The Association monthly publication, NEWSLINER, took on a new look in April 1976 in a newspaper tabloid style in lieu of the newsletter style. The newsletter format was limited to 12 pages and was mailed first class. The Association applied for and obtained a second class permit from the post office which significantly decreased the mailing costs. At the same time a contract with a printer for a newspaper format allowed for more information and less turnaround time. As the newspaper format became more familiar the office staff assumed the responsibility for pasting up the NEWSLINER which further cut the cost.

1976 Annual Meeting

The second Annual Meeting of the Members was held on 7-9 July 1976 at Fayetteville, NC, hosted by the Fort Bragg Chapter. A quorum was present for the Annual Meeting, the Council of Presidents and the Board of Directors Meeting. Elected to national office were Cletus McKeown, President; Neil McLeod, Vice President; Frank Stamey, Secretary, and Carl Anderson, Treasurer. Elected to the Board of Directors were: Alfred E. Cox; Lee Anderson, Eastwood B. Gregory; William Trennum; Harold Garwood, Robert Scott, and John (Mike) Yates.

BG Jack Mackmull welcomed the members to Ft Bragg; LTC Ray Hawthorne presented a detailed briefing on the Defense Officer Personnel Management System and its impact on the warrant officer program. COL Roy Shirley, Chief Warrant Officer Division discussed the organization of the Warrant Officer Division and the warrant officer program; and MG John Forrest, ODCSPER, delivered the banquet address to the members and their spouses. Reports were given by the national officers and directors in their respective areas of responsibility.

1977

1977 opened with the Council of President's/ Board of Directors meeting on 10-12 January 1977 at Fort Myer, VA to chart the course of the Association. A quorum of Directors and chapters were represented. Addresses were delivered by LTG George Sammet, Jr., Deputy Commanding General, Materiel Development, US Army Materiel Development and Readiness Command; COL Roy Shirley, Chief Warrant Officer Division; Mrs. Jeanne Allnatt, European Region Auxiliaries Coordinator, and other officers from the Association.

During the meeting the officers voted to:
-   Terminate Project SOFA and transfer assets to the USAWOA operating account.
-   Approve a proposed budget for the coming year.
-   Approve a life insurance policy of $100,000 on the Executive Vice President with USAWOA as beneficiary to insure transition in the event of the death of the Executive Vice President.
-   Approve the Pikes Peak Chapter as the host for the 1977 Annual Meeting.

1977 Annual Meeting

The third Annual Meeting of the Members was held in Colorado Springs, CO on 6-9 July 1977. CW3 Cletus McKeown became the first individual to be re-elected to the office of President; CW4 Frank Stamey was elected as Vice President; CW4 Charles E Dunn as Secretary; and CW4 Harlow Paul as Treasurer. Three new Directors were elected for a two year term. CW4 (Ret) Albert M. Holcombe as Director of Legislation; CW4 William R, Head, Fort Gordon, GA, as Director of Public Relations; and CW3 Franklin A. G. Burbee, Germany, as Director of Plans and Programs. They joined the other directors serving the second year of their term: CW4 George C. Gratchen, Director of Membership; CW2 Harold W. Garwood, Director of Finance; and CW4 Robert D. Scott, Director of Administration.

Members were addressed by General Daniel James, Jr., USAF, Commander in Chief, NORAD, on the role of the military in today's society; MG John Forrest, Commanding General, 4th Infantry Division, Ft Carson, CO on his reflections of the volunteer army; COL Robert Travis, Chief Warrant Officer Division, on warrant officer actions at the DA level; LTC James W. Searcy, MILPERCEN Action Officer, on the proposed enlisted aviator concept; Mrs. Carol Clemmons, National Coordinator for the Warrant Officer Wives Auxiliary, on the progress at various chapter locations; and the national officers on the status of the Association.

In major items of business the officers voted to:
- Select San Antonio, TX, as the site for the 1978 annual meeting with the Lone Star Chapter as the host.
- Oppose the adoption in any form of the enlisted aviator program.
- Support the distribution of food stamps to overseas area.
- Support modification to the reserve component retirement eligibility policy .
- Support the retention of full medical, dental and optical care for retired military personnel.
- Support the modification of the Tax Reform Act to enable servicemen stationed overseas to qualify for the Earned Income credit.
- Support the increase in Readjustment Pay from $15,000 to $30,000 for those involuntarily separated from the Service.
- Support the extension of charter flight privileges to retired service members.
- Support the publication of warrant officer promotion board statistical analysis.
- Oppose awarding blanket veterans benefits to those individuals receiving upgraded discharge; and that decisions be made on a case by case basis.
- Support the extension of the Hot Lunch Program to all DoD controlled schools.

During the year the Association accomplished several of its goals including:

The formation of a national Warrant Officer Association Auxiliary under the guidance of Mrs. Carol Clemmons.

Providing educational information to the American Council on Education (ACE) to grant college credits to warrant officers for their demonstrated performance in their MOS's.

Persuading the editor of the Officers Guide to include more warrant officer information in their book, and as a result, the 39th edition of the Officers Guide included, for the first time, comprehensive information about the unique role of the warrant officer.

Although many positive actions were taking place, 1977 was a crucial year for the Association. A drop in membership to a low of 2,000 and a nonrenewal rate of almost 75% resulted in the national office ending the year in poor financial straits. The national officers addressed this issue boldly, and presented several options to the 1978 BOD/COP meeting to alleviate these problems.

1978

The 1978 Council of President's /Board of Director's meeting was held on 23 January 1978 at Fort Myer, VA with opening remarks by General John R Guthrie, Commander, US Army Material Development and Readiness Command. General Guthrie solicited the comments of warrant officers on the various systems being developed by AMC.

San Antonio, TX. Pres. Frank Stamey, Vice Pres. Robert D. Scott, and Director Eastwood "Bill" Gregory are installed as 1978 national officers by Executive Vice Pres. Don Hess.

San Antonio, TX. LTG William B. Caldwell, III, Commander, 5th U.S. Army, addressed the members and guests at the 1978 Annual Meeting on Aug. 11, 1978.

COL Robert Travis, Chief, Warrant Officer Division, discussed a decade of progress in the Warrant Officer Corps and the Association's contributions during the past 5 years.

BOD members present were: Cletus McKeown, President; Frank Stamey, Vice President, Al Cox, Past President, Charles Dunn, Secretary, Al Holcombe,, George Gratchen, and Don Joyce. Other attendees were Bill Gregory, 2d Vice President, and Don Hess, Executive Vice President. 32 chapters were represented in person or by proxy for the COP.

Reports were also presented by Association national officers and directors including an in-depth Management Committee Report by Bob Scott; a Dues Report by Jay Garwood, Director of Finance and Budget; the National Wives Auxiliary Steering Committee Report by Carol Clemons; and a comprehensive Financial Statement from July - December 1977.

In other actions the BOD directed that:
- The dues of $24 be retained for all warrant officers on active duty, and reduced to $12 for warrant officers not on active duty. The breakout of dues were set at $18.00 to the operating fund; $5,00 to chapter rebates; and $1.00 to the Regions for administrative support for members.
- The Executive Committee enter into a membership services contract with a reliable company and

institute a membership campaign utilizing the services of this company.
- A credit card payment system be established for regular and lifetime dues.

As the year progressed aggressive and outstanding recruiting efforts by positive-thinking members of the Association at all levels, resulted in the payment of the outstanding obligations and an increase in membership. The rebates to chapters were paid on time and were the largest amount since the Association was formed. New chapters were formed and interest was once again on the rise.

1978 Annual Meeting

The fourth Annual Meeting of the Members was held in San Antonio TX, on 7-11 August 1978 co-hosted by the Lone Star Chapter in San Antonio, and the Fort Hood Chapter, Killeen, TX. Elected to national office were CW4 Frank Stamey, President; Robert D. Scott, Vice President; CW4 Charles E. Dunn, Secretary; and CW4 Harlow Paul, Treasurer. Elected to the Board of Directors were: CW3 Alfred E Cox; CW3 Eastwood (Bill) Gregory; and CW4 William Barton.

Guest speakers included COL George Rogers, Deputy Post Commander, Ft Sam Houston; COL Robert L. Travis, Chief, Warrant Officer Division, and LTG William B. Caldwell, III, Commander,

5th US Army. The membership also heard presentations by the national officers on the state of the association to include the financial status; a proposed budget for 1979; a membership report; status of the 1977 resolutions; and the status of the 1978 proposed resolutions.

LTG John R. McGiffert, Director of the Army Staff, addresses the membership at the 1979 Annual Meeting in Alexandria, VA.

At the Annual Meeting action was voted on to:
- Add the national Vice President and the European Region President as voting members of the Board of Directors.
- Restructure the directors primary responsibility to their respective regions, rather than to functional areas of responsibility.
- Provide funds for immediate implementation of automation of the membership files and records.
- Purchase of a distinctive WOA ring for sale to the members.
- Increase the frequency of the NEWSLINER from monthly to bi-monthly (twice a month) effective in January 1979
- Select the Lord Fairfax Chapter (Washington-Virginia area) to host the 1979 Annual Meeting in the Washington area.

During 1978 the Association developed sound administrative procedures which were published in a Chapter Operations Manual to standardize our chapter operations. Also developed and approved were By-laws, National Headquarters Financial and Administrative Management Manual; National Board of Directors Operations and Semi-Annual Meeting Procedures Manual and Annual Meeting of the Members Operations Manual. These manuals provided clear, concise, professional guidance to current and future leaders at the chapter, region and national levels. Special credit was given to Robert Scott for his dedication to the administration of our Association. The directors also established a voting process to remain in session by mail

to allow them to react to pressing business between the BOD meetings and the Annual Meeting.

1979

The 1979 Board of Directors Meeting was held on 15-17 January 1979 at Fort Myer, VA with 10 of the 11 directors present and 27 chapters represented in person or by proxy. In addition to reports by the national officers and directors, COL Arthur Bills, newly appointed Chief of Warrant Officer Division, MILPERCEN briefed on current warrant officer actions within Warrant Officer Division. CW4 Richard Sauer, Chief, Warrant Officer Professional Development Division, MILPERCEN, briefed on the programs and advancements in the entire Warrant Officer Corps. Jim Seabron, International Group Plans (IGP) reported on the details to implement a membership services agreement. Mr. Ed Kormendi, Brick Mill Studios, Wilton, NH presented a fund raising proposal for Christmas and all purpose cards to be mailed to our membership. In other major actions the BOD voted to:
- Approve a one year membership extension to any member who recruits 10 or more members within a 30 day period.
- Approve an increase in rent and utilities for the national officer from $175 to $200 per month.
- Accept Past-President Cletus McKeown's resignation from the EXCOM due to his PCS to Fort Bragg, NC
- Require written approval of the national headquarters for the sale or use of any material bearing the USAWOA trademarked logo.
- Approve the position on equalization of commissioned/warrant officer flight pay.
- Terminate the Insurance Agent of Record status with the European Region by Mr. Tony Delisa because of the contract signed with IGP to provide a membership services program.

1979 Annual Meeting

The fifth Annual Meeting of the Members was held on 12-16 August at the Charter House Motel, Alexandria, VA,. hosted by the Lord Fairfax Chapter. Guest speakers included LTG John R. McGiffert, Director of the Army Staff; who was the banquet speaker; MG James L. Kelly, Commanding General, USA Army Engineer Center, the keynote speaker, A MILPERCEN panel of COL Arthur Bills, Chief, Warrant Officer Division, CW4 Dick Sauer, Professional Development Directorate, and CW4 Arthur Kilpatrick, MOS Evaluation Branch, briefed the members on the ongoing warrant officer programs within MILPERCEN. LTC David Carothers, Action Officer, Director of Military Personnel Management, ODCSPER, briefed on the warrant officer strength and management policies with ODCSPER and LTC Jerry Witherspoon Chief, Compensation and Entitlements Team, ODCSPER, presented a briefing on the proposed new military retirement system. BG Carl H. McNair, Jr. presented a briefing on the warrant officer aviation picture to equalize flight pay for warrant officers. MAJ Mel Smith, Evaluations Systems Office, MILPERCEN, presented a very comprehensive briefing on the new officer efficiency report. Ms. Nancy Taylor, International Group Plans (IGP) presented an informative briefing on the CHAMPUS supplement and other benefits available to our members.

In addition to the above, the membership heard presentations by the national officers on the state of the association. Major items of business included action to:
- Support increase in military pay equally with

Alexandria, VA. Board of Directors met on Jan. 15-17, 1979 to chart the Warrant Officer Association's course for the coming year.

Col. Arthur Bills, Chief, Warrant Officer Division, addresses the Council of Presidents/Board of Directors during the Annual Meeting, Aug. 12-16, 1979.

wage increase guidelines proposed for the private sector.
- Change the BOD/COP semi-annual meeting to April of each year and the Annual Meeting to October.
- Increase membership services to include travel, lodging and other buying services discounts.
- Support the retired officer recall program.
- Support the revitalization of the selective service system.
- Support reduction of the ever-widening gap in base pay between 01 to 04 and W1 to W4 with equal years of service.
- Reduce the frequency of the NEWSLINER to monthly, from twice monthly publication.

The members re-elected the following officers to lead the association in the coming year. President Frank Stamey; and Vice President Robert D Scott; Ronald J. Whalen was elected as Secretary and Charles Dunn was elected as Treasurer.

Elected to the Board of Directors were John P Ritter, Germany; Robert O'Day, San Antonio, TX; Don Joyce, Hampton, VA.

1980

The 1980 Semi-Annual Chapter Presidents/ Board of Directors meeting was held on 21-23 April 1980 at the Charter House Motel in Alexandria, VA. Thirty-six chapters were represented in person or by proxy. Eight directors were present. Directors absent because of duty commitments were Cletus McKeown, Past President; Ron Adams, Region 1, and Al Cox (who was present on 23 April).

COL Arthur Bills, Chief, Warrant Officer Division, presented the keynote address. Other speakers were Jim Seabron, International Group Plans, who updated the members on the status of our insurance program and membership development. Bill Sheppard, representing Gull Associates, discussed possible memorabilia items available to our members. The national officers and directors reported on their areas of responsibility.

In major items of business during the meetings the officers voted to:
- Continue the current dialogue with officials at all levels to ensure that the pay proposals previously recommended be implemented.
- Direct the Executive Committee to conduct a feasibility study on the need, duties, costs, etc., of an additional full time staff member to assist the national office in administration, editorial duties and legislative requirements, and that the study be presented at the 1980 Annual Meeting.
- Reject the opening of regular membership to warrant officers of other services (Associate membership is currently available under the by-laws.)
- Continue the practice of maintaining inactive chapters on a stand-by status for possible reactivation.
- Reject the selling of USAWOA membership mailing list to USAA.
- Direct the Executive Committee to analyze and update bookkeeping procedures for more efficient presentation to the members.
- Direct the Executive Committee to aggressively pursue funds management policies pertaining to a savings/investment program.
- Direct the Executive Committee to review and report on our multiple-year membership programs and make recommendations at the Annual Meeting.
- Direct the Executive Committee to review our fund raising activities and enter into agreements, when feasible to replace the Greeting Card program.

1980 Annual Meeting of the Members

The sixth Annual Meeting of the Members was held on 14-17 October 1980 at the Charter House in Alexandria, VA. A quorum was present for the Annual Meeting, Council of Presidents and Board of Directors meetings. The guest speakers included the Army's first team, The Chief of Staff, General Meyer, the Deputy Chief of Staff for Personnel, LTG Yerks, The Chief, Army Reserve, MG William R. Berkman and those in the nuts and bolts business of warrant officers including MAJ Mike

Alexandria, VA. LTG Maxwell Thurman, Army DCSPER, addressed the members and guests at the 1981 Annual Meeting.

Alexandria, VA. Gen. Myer, Chief of Staff, US Army, adresses warrant officers and guests during the 1980 Annual Meeting, Oct. 14, 1980.

Alexandria, VA. Col. George Morgan, Chief, Warrant Officer Division, addresses warrant officers, 1980

Alexandria, VA. LTG Gen. Robert Yerks, Army DCSPER, installs the newly elected national officers on Oct. 17, 1980. (L to R): LTG Yerks; Pres. Robert Scott; V.P. Ronald J. Whalen; Treas. James T. Luttrell; Director Donald R. Joyce; Secretary Gordon Koch and Director Jack Ritter.

Borland on aviation issues, COL George Morgan, Chief, Warrant Officer Division, PERSCOM; and CW4 Richard Sauer, ODCSPER.

Elected Officers were: President Robert D. Scott; Vice President Ronald J. Whalen; Secretary Gordon Koch, and Treasurer James T Luttrell, Jr. Directors elected were George Eby, Region 1; Edward Kolosvary, Region 2; Barry Farris, Region 3; Edward Fitting, Region 4; Jack Ritter, Region 5; and Don Joyce, Region 6. The officers were installed by our guest speaker, LTG Yerks, Army Deputy Chief of Staff for Personnel.

The members took action to:
- Support equalization of flight Pay.
- Support the establishment of a Warrant Officer Orientation Course
- Support the expansion of Warrant Officer advanced courses to all MOS
- Support the Warrant Officer Senior Course as a permanent part of warrant officer education.
- Support the incorporation of a warrant officer information program in commissioned officer service schools.
- Support an increase in warrant officer quarters allowance.
- Support assignment of field grade housing to CW4s.
- Support automatic concurrent travel for CW4s.

Ft. Campbell, KY. Col. Paul Wenzel, Chief, Warrant Officer Division, DA, addresses the membership at the 1982 Annual Meeting.

- Support an increase in Variable Housing Allowance (VHA)
- Support the designation of key warrant officer positions on manning documents.
- Support the increase in warrant officer pay.
Position papers on the above actions were presented to the Army DCSPER and many of these actions were addressed favorably for the first time.

1981

The 1981 Council of Presidents/Board of Directors meeting was held on 22-24 April 1981 at Fort Myer, VA. 38 chapters were represented in person or by proxy and eight directors were present. Directors absent because of duty commitments were Jack Ritter, Region 5, Barry Farris, Region 3 and Ed Kolosvary, Region 2. A quorum of chapter presidents and directors was confirmed. The keynote address was given by COL George Morgan, Chief, Warrant Officer Division. The members also hosted a luncheon with the Council of Military Organizations (COMO) and heard first hand of the on-going legislative activities in support of the military community.

National officers and directors presented reports in their areas of interest.

As a result of the reports, briefings and discussion, action was taken to:
- Approve the Imperial 400 Motor Inn in Alexandria as the site of the 1981 Annual Meeting.
- Approve the elimination of the three and five year membership options because of lack of participation.
- Rejected 82 specific motions related to the by-laws and other administrative manuals, however, the Executive Committee (EXCOM) was directed to consider the changes on an individual basis and present their recommendations to the directors by mail.
- CW4 Holcombe was presented a USAWOA Certificate of Achievement (our highest award) in appreciation for his outstanding research and recommendations on our administrative publications.
- Direct that a motion be presented at the Annual Meeting to change the frequency of the Annual Meeting from once a year to once every two years with BOD/COP meetings as needed, but at least every six months.
- Direct that a motion be presented at the Annual Meeting to change the term of national officers from one year to two years with no more than two consecutive terms in the same office. The cycle would start with the election and Annual Meeting in October 1982.

- Direct the EXCOM to review and adjust the NEWSLINER advertising rates as needed.
- Direct that the EXCOM track the warrant officer pay proposals through DoD and Congress.

The meeting was closed out with a philosophical discussion on the role of the Association in dealing with controversial positions. As a professional Association we resolved to take a strong stand on issues and present them in a professional manner when we are confident we represent the views of the Warrant Officer Corps.

1981 Annual Meeting of the Members

The 7th Annual Meeting of the Members was held on 20-23 October 1981 at the Imperial Motor Inn in Alexandria, VA. A quorum was confirmed for the Annual Meeting, Council of Presidents and Board of Directors meetings.

COL George Morgan, Chief, Warrant Officer Division delivered the keynote address. Other speakers were LTC Douglas Thorp, Deputy Chief, Warrant Officer Division, CW3 Al Fletcher, and CW4 Ken Johnson, Professional Development Branch, WOD. LTG Maxwell Thurman, newly appointed Army Deputy Chief of Staff for Personnel was the speaker.

Proposals were presented by TELEFORCE Associates and INTELFORCE Associates to provide potential employment service for USAWOA members. A status report was received from Bob Hunt, Account Executive from Consumers United Insurance Company on the number of USAWOA members participating in the insurance program. A proposal to provide leased or purchased automobiles at a substantial savings was presented. Also, a representative from the VFW solicited the Association's support on the goals and objectives of the VFW.

National officers and directors reported on the activities in their areas of responsibility including the status of the warrant officer Auxiliaries from National Coordinator Linda Pinault.

After review of all the information presented, the members voted to:
- Approve the changes to the Articles of Incorporation which changed the classes of membership and the number of directors for the Association.
- Select the Ken-Tenn Chapter as the host for the 1982 Annual Meeting.
- Direct that TRADOC be advised that more hands-on training should be re-instituted in service schools to reinforce the learning through self pace.
- Support the extension of the expiration date of the Vietnam Era G.I. Bill Educational Benefits Program to 10 years beyond the date of separation from active military service of Vietnam veterans.
- Support a change to the current limits on reimbursement for loss/damage of household goods and hold baggage from $15,000 to actual replacement value.
- Support implementation of a system to provide more timely payment of costs incurred for health and medical care received under the CHAMPUS program.
Other proposals were referred to the Executive Committee for further research on:
- Single Promotion system.
- Pay inadequacies for warrant officers.
- Free Intra-Command mail for overseas locations.
- Warrant officer recognition.
- Limited Duty Officer concept.

Re-elected officers at the Annual Meeting were: President Robert D. Scott; Vice President Ronald J. Whalen; Secretary Gordon Koch and Treasurer James T. Luttrell, Jr. Reelected to the Board of Directors were John P. Ritter, Region 5 and Edward R Fitting, Region 4. Newly elected to the Board of Directors were Lynn A. Freund, Re-

Ft. Campbell, KY. BG Gerald H. Betke, ADC, 101st ABN Div., installed the newly elected officers at the 1982 Annual Meeting. (L to R): Vincent Pinault, director; Albert M. Holcombe, director; Gordon Koch, vice president; Ronald J. Whalen, president and Alfred E. Cox, director.

Linda Pinault, European Region Auxiliary Coordinator, updates the members on the auxiliary status in Europe at the 1984 Annual Meeting.

Ft. Belvoir, VA. LTC(P) Richard Gornto, Chief, Total Warrant Officer Study (TWOS) briefed the membership on the status of the new study at the 1984 Annual Meeting.

Ft. Belvoir, VA. COL Willis R. Bunting, Chief, Warrant Officer Division, installs the 1984 national officers at the 1984 Annual Meeting. (L to R) President Carl Burnett; Secretary James T. Luttrell, Director Albert M. Holcombe, Director Carl Newhart; Director Percy Butler; Director Don Desjardins.

gion 1; George G. Fairfax, Region 2; Victor D Dunham, Region 3; and James C. Pujo, Region 6. The elected officers were installed by LTG Maxwell Thurman, Army Deputy Chief of Staff for Personnel, who was the banquet speaker.

1982

The 1982 Board of Director's Meeting was held on 5-6 April 1982 at Fort Myer, VA. 21 chapters were represented in person or by proxy and eight directors were present. Directors absent due to duty commitments were Jack Ritter, Region 5; Vic Dunham, Region 3; and Past President Frank Stamey. A quorum of directors was present. A quorum of chapter representatives was not present.

The keynote address was delivered by COL George Morgan, Chief, Warrant Officer Division who spoke on the activities of the Division.

The national officers and directors reported on their respective activities. Director Jim Pujo reported on the status of the job placement program. A major emotional issue which surfaced was the 14% pay raise given to all officers as opposed to the 19% pay raise given to the NCO Corps. This "targeted" pay raise hurt the procurement and retention of warrant officers. The USAWOA also participated in a Joint Seminar on warrant officer pay conducted by the personnel and compensation people of each service.

The BOD/COP voted to:
- Hold the 1982 Annual Meeting at Fort Campbell KY on 3-6 October hosted by the Ken-Tenn Chapter.
- Reject a Corporate membership program.
- Approve the production of a memorabilia brochure.
- Approve a change in the rebate criteria to expedite the processing of renewal applications.

1982 Annual Meeting

The 8th Annual Meeting of the Members was held on 3-6 October at Fort Campbell, KY. A quorum was present for the Annual Meeting, Council of Presidents and Board of Directors meetings. The keynote address was given by COL (P) William H Harrison, Chief of Staff, Fort Campbell. Also speaking were MG Billy Wellman, The Adjutant General, KY National Guard and MG Wallace, Adjutant General, Tennessee National Guard who spoke on the role of the reserve forces in the One Army concept. COL Paul Wentzel, Chief, Warrant Officer Division, and his team briefed on the activities of the Division. Individual counseling of members was conducted by the WOD assignment man-

agers. The national officers and directors reported on their activities including Linda Pinault, Spouses Auxiliary and Director Jim Pujo on membership services.

Elected Officers were: President Ronald J. Whalen; Vice President Gordon Koch, Secretary James Luttrell; and Treasurer Walter Purkoski; Region 1 Director Len Detwiler; Region 2 Director Albert Holcombe; Region 3 Director Vincent Pinault; Region 4 Director Alfred E Cox; Region 5 Director Percy Butler; and Region 6 Director Cletus McKeown. The officers were installed by BG Gerald H. Betke, ADC, 101st Airborne Division.

In major items of business action was taken to:
- Encourage DA to emphasize to all installations and major commands that proper warrant officer assignments are essential to professional development.
- Express the concern that officer BAS should as a minimum equate to the actual dining facility charges.
- Continue to support the warrant officer pay equalization program.
- Recommend that the initial clothing allowance authorization upon appointment be changed to authorize an allowance which is consistent with the actual cost of clothing.
- Vigorously defend the current retirement pay system.
- Oppose any legislation which would treat retirement pay as property in divorce settlements.
- Support extension of the current GI Bill.
- Support the recognition of US Army warrant officers as officers in NATO countries.
- Terminate our job placement service with INTELFORCE because of the lack of contract fulfillment on their part.

1983

The 1983 Semi-Annual Chapter Presidents/ Board of Director's meeting was held on 28 February - 1 March 1983 at Fort Myer, VA. 38 chapters were represented in person or by proxy and nine Directors were present. Director Al Cox from Region 4 was not present because of TDY and Director Vincent Pinault, from Region 3 was not present because of duty commitments. A quorum was present. The keynote address was delivered by Major Larry Armbright, Deputy Chief, Warrant Officer Division, assisted by CW4 Ken Johnson. Reports were rendered by the national officers in their respective areas.

In major items of business action was taken to:
- Approve the selection of the Washington area as the location for the 1984 Annual Meeting.
- Continue the life membership program.
- Initiate a recruiting incentive to be worked out by the Executive Committee.
- Retain the USAWOA Ring Program as a separate memorabilia account.

1983 Annual Meeting of the Members

The 9th Annual Meeting of the Members was held on 1-3 August 1983 at Fort Myer, VA. Over 1400 members were represented either in person or by proxy. All the national officers were present except for Region 3 Director Vincent Pinault. Also absent was Linda Pinault, Warrant Officer Auxiliary Coordinator. All the officers submitted their reports which were published in the NEWSLINER.

Major items of business included approval of proposals directing USAWOA to:
- Express concerns to DA to retain the management of aviation warrant officers under the control of the WOD.
- Support an incentive pay program for enlisted personnel based on demonstrated skills.

- Support a change to AR 630-5 granting service members 10 days as non-chargeable leave under emergency considerations.
- Support a change to AR 55-71 to authorize all personnel in career status to ship POV's to and from CONUS regardless of place of purchase or manufacture.
- Support the efforts by the DoD and US Postal Service to provide for eliminating the postage requirements for letters and packages that are handled internally by the military in overseas locations.
- Direct that all future Association income generated from undesignated contributions be designated to the Lifetime Reserve Fund until such time as the Reserve Fund is equal to the Lifetime Members Liability.
- Support reimbursement of the cost of military moves in line with the Federal civilian work force.
- Continue awarding a one year free membership to the Distinguished Graduate of the Warrant Officer Senior Course.
- Continue to offer a reduced warrant officer candidate membership.
- Review the advertising rates as raise as necessary to defray the expense of producing and mailing the NEWSLINER.
- Require all BOD members to declare in writing their intent to attend the Annual Meeting and that their names be included on the USAWOA proxy form.

The membership disapproved the following proposals to:
- Support the establishment of CW5 and CW6.
- Increase the membership dues for retired warrant officers.
- Terminate the Lifetime Membership Program effective 1 October 1983.

1984

The 1984 Semi-Annual Council of President's/ Board of Director's meeting was held on 12-13 March 1984 at Fort Myer, VA. Thirty-eight chapters were represented in person or by proxy and a quorum of chapters was confirmed. Ten directors were present and a quorum of directors was confirmed. COL Willis R Bunting, Chief, Warrant Officer Division was the keynote speaker. He was accompanied by CW4 Lloyd Washer, CW4 Ken Johnson, Warrant Officer Action Officer, ODCSPER; CW4 Chuck Hawk, Warrant Officer Action Officer, ODCSOPS, and CW3 Tom Simonian, Warrant Officer Coordinator, OPMS Study Group, ODCSPER. Reports were presented by all the national officers.

The following major items of business were approved:
- Support action to provide for warrant officers assigned to a long tour area to attend their advanced course on a TDY and return basis.
- Add key senior commanders to the NEWSLINER mailing list.
- Prepare a USAWOA briefing suitable for any audience for use by chapters in briefing commanders and other individuals on the role of today's warrant officers.
- Support amendment to the Title 38 to eliminate forfeiture of a portion of retired pay when receiving VA disability compensation.
- Accept a request by the Lord Fairfax Chapter to host the Annual Meeting in October 1984 in the Washington area.
- Permit chapters chartered in the first year of the existence of the Association to include the designation "Silver" in their chapter.
- Accept a proposal to request the membership to vote on a dues increase at the upcoming Annual Meeting.

1984 Annual Meeting

The 10th Annual Meeting of the Members was held on 14-16 October 1984 at The John S Mosby Reserve Center at Fort Belvoir, VA. Over 1700 members were represented in person or by proxy and 55 of our active chapters were represented. Nine of the 11 directors were present. The keynote address was given by COL Peter Sterns, Deputy Installation Commander, Fort Belvoir. A major presentation was given by LTC (P) Ronald E Gornto, Chief of the newly appointed Total Warrant Officer Study (TWOS).

The national officers and directors briefed the members on their activities during the past year. Linda Pinault, Warrant Officer Auxiliary Coordinator also presented her report. The banquet address was given by COL Willis R Bunting, Chief, Warrant Officer Division, who also installed the newly elected national officers: President Carl Burnett; Vice President; Lynn Freund; Secretary James T. Luttrell; Albert M. Holcombe; Region 2, Vincent Pinault; Region 3; Carl D Newhart; Region 4; Percy D Butler, Region 5; and Don G. Desjardins, Region 6.

A major issue was the increase of dues, which had not been raised since 1976. The increase was a difficult decision, however, no other alternative such as decreasing the frequency of the NEWSLINER was acceptable to the membership.

Alexandria, VA. COL Bernard Quick, Project Officer, Total Warrant Officer System, addresses the 1986 BOD meeting on April 7, 1986.

Ft. Carson, CO. COL Joel Hinson, Chief, Warrant Officer Div., heads a panel discussing current WO actions at the 1986 Annual Meeting. (L to R): CW4 Nicholas DiGiralamo, NG; CW2 Linda Carpenter, ARPERCEN; COL Hinson; CW4 Dennis Jinks, Chief, Professional Development Branch, WO Div.; CW4 David Helton, ODCSPER; and CW4 Tom Simonian, TWOS Action Officer.

Wildhorn Ranch, CO. COL Joel Hinson, Chief, Warrant Officer Division, installs the newly elected national officers on Oct. 10, 1986. (L to R): COL Hinson; President Dennis Jinks; Vice Pres. Stephen Murphy; Treas. Harvey Prenedeville; Director James Wilson and Director Carl Newhart.

Herndon, VA. CW4 (Ret) George Gratchen, Father of the European Warrant Officers Association, visits the national office to keep abreast of activities, 1986.

Ft. Belvoir, VA. COL Billy Miller, Chief, WO Div., addresses the Council of Presidents/BOD on March 15, 1988.

Ft. Rucker, AL. COL Joel H. Hinson, Chief, WO Div., PERSCOM, DA, addresses the 1987 USAWOA Annual Meeting.

Ft. Rucker, AL. USAWOA Pres. Dennis Jinks presents a Certificate of Appreciation to MG Ellis Parker (R) for his address to the 1987 Annual Meeting banquet.

The new dues structure effective 1 January 1985 was: Active Duty Members: $36.00; Reserve and National Guard members: $36.00; Retired members: $24.00; Lifetime Members (one time) $500.00; Associate: $36.00. Regions would receive a 1.00 rebate and chapters would receive rebates of $5.00 for active duty members and $3.00 for retired members, payable quarterly.

1985

The 1985 Semi-Annual Council of President's/Board of Director's meeting was held on 11-12 March 1985 at The John S Mosby US Army Reserve Center, Fort Belvoir, VA. Forty one chapters were represented in person or by proxy and a quorum of chapter presidents was confirmed. Eleven directors were present and a quorum of directors was confirmed. Immediate Past President Gordon Koch was absent due to duty commitments.

The keynote address was given by LTC

Larry Armbright, Acting Chief, Warrant Officer Division. He was accompanied by CW4 David Helton, Chief Professional Development Branch. WOD. A comprehensive briefing on the Total Warrant Officer Study (TWOS) was given by CW4 Dennis Jinks, a member of the study group. National officers and directors presented reports on their respective activities.

The officers voted to:
- Pursue a new CHAMPUS insurance supplement to replace the terminated insurance agreement.
- Increase the publicity on the Building Fund drive by adding individual inserts in the NEWSLINER.
- Offer a quality calendar to members of the Association as a fund raiser in lieu of greeting and Christmas card programs. Proceeds to be applied to the Building Fund.
- Accept the offer of the Lord Fairfax Chapter to host the 1985 Annual Meeting to be held 23-25 September 1985.
- Reject the elimination of the 1986 Semi-Annual Meeting because of the need to evaluate the TWOS and other ongoing programs.

1985 Annual Meeting

The 11th Annual Meeting of the Members was held on 23-25 September 1985 at the John S. Mosby Reserve Center at Fort Belvoir, VA, hosted by the Lord Fairfax Chapter. Over 1200 members were represented either in person or by proxy and 52 of our 63 active chapters were represented. A quorum was present for the Annual Meeting, the COP and BOD.

Presentations were made by LTC (P) Joel H. Hinson, Chief, Warrant Officer Division, assisted by CW4 Dennis Jinks, Chief, Professional Development Branch, Warrant Officer Division, MILPERCEN. The members also heard presentation from CW4 Bob Sidaway, Army Reserve Personnel center, St. Louis, MO. A major presentation was given by the Total Warrant Officer Study (TWOS) representatives (CW3 Carl Burnett and CW4 Tom Simonian). Our keynote speaker was MG William G. O'Lesky, Office of the Deputy Chief of Staff for Personnel.

After detailed discussion the members voted to:
- Support the POW/MIA issue as a top priority for full accounting of Americans still missing from any military conflicts and repatriation of the remains of those who died serving our nation.
- Direct that a page in the NEWSLINER be dedicated to showing specifically the status of individual contributions to the Building Fund.
- Approve a Building Fund Corporate Donation Program.
- Approve a recruiting campaign directed toward warrant officer candidates.
- Approve Corporate member category at nat'l level.

1986

The 1986 Semi-Annual Board of Director's/Council of President's meeting was held on 7-8 April 1986 at Fort Myer, VA and Cameron Station, VA. 32 chapters were represented in person or by proxy and a quorum of presidents was confirmed. Ten directors were present and a quorum of directors was confirmed. Directors Gordon Koch and Len Detwiler were not present because of duty commitments.

The keynote address was given by COL Burnet R. Quick, Officer System Implementation Team, MILPERCEN, who provided an overview of the ongoing evaluation of the officer corps. He was assisted by CW4 Tom Simonian.

Also addressing the association leaders were COL Joel H. Hinson, Chief Warrant Officer Division, CW4 Dennis Jinks, Chief, Professional De-

Other major business approved included proposals for USAWOA to:
- Support full pay compatibility with the first four commissioned grades.
- Establish a building fund to purchase a permanent residence for the national office.
- Explore and implement an optional allotment system or annual dues payment method.
- Appoint Assistant Vice President positions: Reserve Affairs; National Guard Affairs; and Retired Affairs.
- Endorse and support action by the National League of Families of American Prisoners and Missing in Southeast Asia for the accountability of these personnel.
- Consolidate warrant officer entry level courses at a single installation to achieve a consistent level of training for all entry level warrant officers.
- Establish a warrant officer proponent agency within TRADOC to direct and coordinate training and professional development of the Warrant Officer Corps.

velopment Branch, WOD, CW4 Tom Simonian, Total Warrant Officer Study (TWOS), and CW2 Gary Pohrmann, Office Chief of Army Reserve on Reserve aspects of TWOS.

The national officers and directors presented reports on their respective areas of interest. The members also heard reports from the Compensation Committee chaired by Bob Scott and the National Operations Committee, chaired by Ron Whalen. The BOD approved the appointment of Dennis Jinks as the National building Fund Coordinator to develop procedures to publicize the Building Fund. The Executive Committee was directed to take action to continue their educational efforts on the need for our current dues structure, and to publicize the awards program approved for chapter recruiting.

1986 Annual Meeting

The 12th Annual Meeting of the Members was held on 6-10 October 1986 at the Wildhorn Ranch, west of Colorado Springs, CO. sponsored by the Pikes Peak Chapter. Over 1100 members were represented either in person or by proxy and 40 chapters were represented in person or by proxy constituting a quorum for the Council of Presidents meeting. A quorum was also confirmed for the Board of Directors meeting.

Newly elected national officers were: Dennis Jinks, President; Len Detwiler, Vice President; Stephen Murphy, Secretary; Harvey D. Prendeville, Treasurer; Region 2 Director Robert Giffin; Region 3 Director Jimmy Carpenter; Region 4 Director Carl Newhart; Region 5 Director Leo Ott; and Region 6 Director James T. Luttrell.

The Professional Development Seminar was held at Fort Carson, CO. Speakers included COL Joel H. Hinson, Chief, Warrant Officer Division,; CW4 David Helton, ODCSPER Warrant Officer Staff Officer; CW4 Dennis Jinks, Chief, Professional Development Branch, Warrant Officer Division; CW4 Thomas Simonian, TWOS Action Officer; CW4 Nicholas DiGiralamo, Warrant Officer Action Officer, National Guard Bureau, and CW2 Linda Carpenter, Warrant Officer Action Officer, ARPERCEN.

After considering many items of business the members voted to:
- Approve the publication of continuing articles outlining the need for a permanent office facility for the national headquarters.
- Approve the establishment of an ad hoc committee to research the positive actions taken by the USAWOA and publish a pamphlet or brochure for membership recruiting.
- Explore the establishment of an automatic dues deduction procedures with a financial institution.
- Support the Warrant Officer Division as a separate entity responsible for career development of all warrant officers within MILPERCEN.
- Approve the establishment of an Auxiliary pilot program for warrant officer candidates at Ft Rucker, AL.
- Approve an amendment to the USAWOA By-laws requiring mandatory attendance at all called meetings of the Board of Directors and that two consecutive unexcused absences may result in disqualification from the BOD.
- Approve a recruiting and retention program for the next 12 months.
- Approve a policy statement in support of Auxiliaries.
- Oppose the erection of a monument in Arizona to honor Vietnam War protesters.
- Oppose the design of a Master Warrant Officer grade (CW5) which includes a five pointed star in the middle of a bar.
- Oppose the re-establishment of a DA field selection board for warrant officer candidates.

Heidelberg, Germany. Lynn Ridley, USA Recruiting Command, briefs the 1988 Annual Meeting audience on the efforts of USAREC to obtain the highest quality warrant officers into our ranks.

Heidelberg, Germany. European Region President Dave Adams briefs the members to the 1988 Annual Meeting.

Heidelberg, Germany. Behind the scenes. European Region Pres. David Adams (R) and his Annual Meeting planning committee are presented USAWOA Certificates of Appreciation for their great work in organizing the 1988 USAWOA Annual Meeting.

Niagara Falls, NY, COL Michael Mosely, Chief, Warrant Officer Division, addresses the members at the Annual Meeting on Oct. 5, 1989.

Albert M. Holcombe Memorial Award

Virginia Holcombe Memorial Award

1987

The 1987 Semi-Annual Council of Presidents/Board of Director's meeting was held on 2-3 March 1987 at Ft. Myer, VA. Thirty eight chapters were represented in person or by proxy and a quorum of presidents was confirmed. Eight directors were present and a Board of Directors quorum was confirmed. Vice President Len Detwiler, Secretary Steve Murphy, Jim Wilson, Director Region 1 and Bob Giffin, Director Region 2 were not present because of duty commitments.

The keynote address was given by COL Joel H. Hinson, Chief, Warrant Officer Division, MILPERCEN. Other presentations were given by CW4 David Helton, ODCSPER Action Officer on the commissioning of warrant officers; CW4 Kurt Porter, Aviation Weapons Systems Logistician, ODCSLOG on aviation safety; CW3 Carl Burnett on the Warrant Officer Study; CW4 Lloyd Washer, TRADOC, on warrant officer education and training; CW4 Dale Copley, TWOS representative from the USAR on warrant officer activities within the USAR; CW4 Nick DiGirolamo, USAWOA Assistant Vice President for National Guard Affairs on warrant officer activities within the National Guard. The national officers and directors briefed on their areas of responsibility.

After spirited discussion in study groups and on the floor the officers voted to:
- Approve a change to the national by-laws to permit chapters and regions to change their local by-laws to permit officers to serve for one or two year terms.
- Support the legislative action necessary to eliminate the discriminatory practice which requires disabled veterans to forfeit the amount of earned retirement pay which is equal to their disability compensation awarded by the VA.
- Approve the Aviation Center Chapter to host the 1987 Annual Meeting at Ft. Rucker, AL.

1987 Annual Meeting

The 13th Annual Meeting of the Members was held on 6-9 October 1987 at the Lake Lodge at Fort Rucker, AL. Over 1000 members were represented in person or by proxy and 42 chapters were represented. A quorum was present for the Annual Meeting, Council of President's and Board of Director's meetings.

The national officers and directors reported on their activities during the past year. Other speakers during the business meetings and at the Professional Development Seminar included: BG Rodney Wolfe, COL Joel H. Hinson, Chief, Warrant Officer Division, CW4 John Dougherty, Chief, Professional Development Branch, Warrant Officer Division; CW4 David Helton, ODCSPER Warrant Officer Action Officer; CW4 Thomas Simonian, TWOS Action Officer, CW4 John Morgan, Recruiting Command; CW4 David Welsh, OCAR on the AGR Program; CW4 Dale Copley on the USAR implementation of TWOS; CW3 Cecil Trawick, Army Reserve Personnel Center on the IRR/MIA program; CW4 Robert Griffin, Aviation Proponency, Ft Rucker; ;and CW4 Dennis Jinks from USAWOA. The banquet speaker was MG Ellis Parker.

The USAWOA national level awards were presented to the following chapters:

Hanau Silver - Highest Recruiting
Birmingham - Highest Retention
Heilbronn - Overall Best in Recruiting and Retention
Nord-Bayern - Donations
Karlsruhe - Donations
Rhein Neckar - Community Services
Heidelberg - Sustaining Programs
Pikes Peak - Building Fund Donations
During the Meetings action was taken to:
- Support formal training for those warrant officers undergoing reclassification.
- Approved a change in USAWOA Bylaws to require national officers to reside within 300 mile radius of the national office.
- Support legislation to include tuition assistance for warrant officers of the Selected Reserve serving on full time active duty.
- Support the establishment of a DoD joint commission to study the role, utilization and management of warrant officers within the DoD.
- Approve a change to USAWOA Bylaws to permit the establishment of Warrant Office Candidate (WOC) sub-chapters for installations providing technical and tactical certification training.
- Approve a proposal to change USAWOA Bylaws to eliminate dual regional voting officers.
- Approve a BOD voting process to provide regional vote on the BOD for each 500 regional members or fraction thereof.
- Approve the development of a Life Membership Payment system on a monthly basis.
- Approve a change in USAWOA By-laws to permit national directors to designate an elected region or chapter official from within their region to vote on their behalf at the BOD meetings.
- Express USAWOA concern over the legislative package which limits warrant officer service to 24 years unless selected for MW4/CW5.

1988

The 1988 Semi Annual Council of President's/Board of Director's meeting was held on 15 March at the John S Mosby Reserve Center, Fort Belvoir, VA. 30 chapters were present in person or by proxy and 12 directors were present. A quorum was confirmed for both meetings.

The keynote address was given by COL Billy J. Miller, Chief, Warrant Officer Division. Other speakers were CW4 John Dougherty on TWOS; Representatives from Pentagon Federal Credit Union (PFCU) presented the first USAWOA affinity cards to the Association directors.

After lengthy discussion the directors voted to:
- Support the establishment of a Chief Warrant Officer of the Army to provide warrant officer representation at the highest Army level.
- Direct a membership survey be developed to determine membership desires on recruiting, retention, program and products.
- Support the changing of procurement policies to allow members from other services to apply for appointment the Army Physician's Assistant Program.
- Approve purchase of a building or building site for national office prior to 1988 Annual Meeting.
- Approve the European Region as the site of the 1988 Annual Meeting, location to be determined by the European Region.

1988 Annual Meeting of the Members

The 14th Annual Meeting of the Members was held on 24-29 October in the Officers Club in Patrick Henry Village in Heidelberg, Germany. Over 1000 members were represented either in person or by proxy and 59 presidents were represented in person or by proxy at the Council of President's meeting. All directors were present for the BOD with the exception of Secretary Dale Copley and Region 3 Director Jimmy Carpenter who were absent because of duty commitments. A quorum was present for the Annual Meeting, the COP and the BOD. Presentations were made by the national officers and directors in their areas of responsibility.

Newly elected national officers and directors were: David P Welsh, President; Stephen J. Murphy, Vice President; CW4 Dale G. Copley, Secretary; Albert M. Holcombe, Director Region 2; Jimmy E. Carpenter, Director Region 3; Lynn A. Freund, Director, Region 5.

After detailed discussion the members voted to:
- Approve a report by the Building Committee to purchase an office for the National Headquarters.
- Support the design for a W5 insignia consisting of a bar of silver outline bordering a solid black inlay with a five point silver star in its center.
- Support Master Warrant Officers as senior raters for subordinate warrant officers within their chain of command.
- Support the establishment of a Mobile Maintenance Diagnostic Assistance Training Team (MMDATT) to provide in-unit maintenance assistance for the Abrams Tank and Bradley Infantry Fighting Vehicle.
- Support the Master Warrant Officer Training Course in the conduct of study projects in the areas

of Warrant Officer/civilian pay comparability and warrant officer specialty retention pay.
- Endorse the efforts of the Reserve Officers Association (ROA) WO Committee to support the TWOS.
- Support the amendment of Title 10 USC 2007 to authorize tuition assistance for reserve component warrant and AGR officers.

- Refer a draft Awards Manual to the Council of President's for further recommendation.
- Approve a budget for 1989.
- Support the feasibility of developing a slating process to pinpoint assignments of warrant officers designated as MW4.
- Approve publicizing the results of the voting of

Heidelberg, Germany. Officers show their support for the USAWOA Pentagon Federal Credit joint venture to provide affinity VISA cards for USAWOA members at the 1988 Annual Meeting.

Heidelberg, Germany. Over 800 warrant officers are present at the Professional Development Seminar during the 1988 Annual Meeting to hear the latest information from the Army leadership and the Association.

The oldest and the youngest. CW4 (Ret.) Albert M. Holcombe and WO1 Nelda Jane Murphy cut the ceremonial cake at the 1988 Annual Meeting.

Heidelberg, Germany, National Auxiliary Coordinator Linda Pinault (L), European Region Vice Pres. Carl Mueller and Shirley Rinehard coordinated an outstanding 1988 Annual Meeting

Ft. Leonard Wood, MO. CW4 Harrell "Pete" Reinhard received the first Warrant Officer of the Year award ever given by the Assoc. The award was announced at the 1989 Annual Meeting for his contributions in Germany and was presented by MG Daniel R. Schroeder, CG, Ft. Leonard Wood, MO upon Pete's arrival at the base.

Herndon, VA. April 1989. The official ribbon cutting of the new USAWOA office was conducted by the oldest member present, Albert M. Holcombe (L) and the youngest, David Adams as USAWOA Pres. Dave Welsh looks on.

Herndon, VA. USAWOA members pose for the cake cutting celebrating opening of the national office at the 1989 Board of Directors meeting in April 1989.

Herndon, VA. The Warrant Officer Seal hangs proudly in the window of the new USAWOA Headquarters. The eagle was donated by CW4 Edward Moody and his wife, who created the staind glass eagle.

- Defer a decision on the Annual Meeting site in Germany for the 1991 meeting.

The Professional Development Seminar was a great success, turning out over 800 warrant officers. Guest speakers included COL Billy Miller, Chief, Warrant Officer Division, PERSCOM; MG Robert L. Gordon, USAREUR Deputy Chief of Staff, Resource Management; CW4 Lynn Ridley, Recruiting Command; CW4 George Phillips, 1st PERSCOM; CW4 David Welsh, Office Chief of Army Reserves; Lynn Freud, Signal Proponency; and CW4 Dennis Jinks, USAWOA.

The first Annual Meeting held in Europe ended with a Warrant Officer Ball at the Heidelberg Officers Club. The guest speaker was the founder of the European Warrant Officers Association, CW4 George Gratchen who was instrumental in the merger of the European Warrant Officers Association with the USAWOA.

1989

The 1989 Council of Presidents/Semi-Annual Board of Director's meeting was held on 3-4 April at the new Association Headquarters in Herndon, VA. 37 Chapters were represented in person or by proxy. All Directors were present. A quorum was present for the COP and the BOD. Guest speakers were LTC David R. Quimby, Deputy Chief, Warrant Officer Division, (WOD) PERSCOM and CW4 John Dougherty, Chief Professional Development Branch, WOD.

National officers and directors presented briefings in their respective areas. A milestone was reached with the grand opening of the Newly purchased office suite. CW4 (Ret) Albert M. Holcombe, the oldest Director in age and length of USAWOA director service joined hands with CW3 David Adams, the youngest director in age and USAWOA director service to cut the ribbon which symbolically opened a new era for the Association. The Building Fund was originated in January 1985. As a result the Association raised $130,000 in donations toward the purchase of the national office. A loan of $20,000 was secured which will be paid off as soon as possible.

In other business the officers voted to:
- Support the sending of a PERSCOM Warrant Officer Division team to Europe on an annual basis to coincide with the European Region Annual Conv.

the Council of Presidents and Board of Directors to the membership.
- Approve establishing an Executive Committee to carry on the day to day operation of the Association.
- Approve USAWOA Certificates of Apprecia-

tion to 9 members of USAREC whose duties involve recruiting warrant officers.
- Approve the new National office as the site of the BOD/COP meeting in April 1989.
- Reject the creation of a special membership category for warrant officer candidates.

- Support a change in the computation of retired warrant officer to make it consistent with commissioned and enlisted personnel.
- Support a mandatory one hour block of training to NCOs to educate them on the warrant officer career opportunities.
- Approve a special category of Associate membership for warrant officer candidates.
- Approve a long range plan to more effectively market the Association to members and nonmembers.
- Approve draft auxiliary bylaws to be sent to chapters for review and comment.
- Approve the preparation of a ballot to determine the membership desires on opening Association membership to warrant officers of all the uniformed services.

1989 Annual Meeting

The 15th Annual Meeting of the Members was held on 1-6 October at the USAF Reserve Base in Niagara Falls, NY, hosted by the Niagara Frontier Chapter. Over 600 warrant officers were represented in person or by proxy at the Annual Meeting. A quorum was present for the Council of President's and Board of Directors meetings.

The keynote speaker was MG William F. Ward, Chief Army Reserve. Other speakers were COL (P) Thomas W. Sabo, DCG, 98th Div; COL Michael Mosely, Chief, Warrant Officer Division and MW4 Butch Davis Chief, Professional Development Branch, PERSCOM,; CW3 Carl Burnett, Structure Analyst, ODCSPER on WOMA legislation; CW4 Dave Welsh, OCAR, who briefed on TWOS applicability to Reserve Components; CW2 Mark Belsky, Tactical Officer, WOCS, Ft McCoy, WI; on the Warrant Officer Candidate Course; CW3 Randy Simmons from the US Army Recruiting Command, and Exec VP Don Hess spoke on the objectives of the USAWOA. During the business sessions the national officers and directors presented reports on their respective areas of responsibility.

A major item of business was a vote of 397 for and 326 against, by the membership to open the membership of the Association to warrant officers of all the uniformed services. This action would require a change in the USAWOA Article of Incorporation and President Welsh appointed CW4 (Ret) Bob Scott, our National Parliamentarian, to chair a committee to prepare changes to our Articles of Incorporation

A first for the Association was the award of the

Herndon, VA. In April 1990 the USAWOA celebrated the burning of the mortgage on the national office. L to r: European Region President Dave Adams, Past National President Dennis Jinks, Director Albert M. Holcombe, and President Dave Welsh.

Fort Belvoir, VA. COL Mike Mosely, Chief Warrant Officer Division, addressed members at the 1990 Annual Meeting Professional Development Seminar.

Herndon, VA. The national office staff prepare Christmas packages for the troops in Desert Storm/Shield. L to r: Linda Pascale and Marybeth Perelli. December 1990.

Arlington, VA. Past Presidents of the USAWOA at the 1990 Annual Meeting banquet at Fort Myer, VA. Front row, l to r: Frank Stamey, 1978-80; Alfred E. Cox, 1975-76; Don Hess, 1973-74. Back row, l to r: David P. Welsh, 1988-92; Dennis Jinks, 1986-88; Carl Burnett, 1984-86; and Robert D. Scott, 1980-82.

Virginia M. Holcombe Memorial Award for the National Spouse of the Year. This award was established to honor Virginia Holcombe, one of the first ladies of the USAWOA who passed away in 1988.

Reston, VA. The 1991 USAWOA Warrant Officer of the Year was awarded to CW4 Howard Lundin, an active Guard/Reserve warrant officer assigned to the Army Reserve Support Center, shown with his wife, Becky.

Virginia Holcombe exemplified the role of the auxiliary member as she led by deed and example. The memorial award not only honors and recognizes her for her endeavors but also serves as a goal for all auxiliary members, current and future, to strive to achieve.

Mrs. Carol L. Fierros, AZ Wives Auxiliary was the first recipient. The award was presented to Mrs. Fierros by CW4 (Ret) Albert M. Holcombe, husband of Virginia.

The first recipient of the Warrant officer of the Year Award was CW4 Harrel G. Rinehard for his contributions while serving with the Karlsruhe Chapter in Germany prior to his reassignment to Ft. Leonard Wood, MO. CW4 Rinehard was presented the award by MG Daniel R. Schroeder, Commanding General and Commandant of the US Army Engineer School, Ft. Leonard Wood, MO.

Chapter Awards were presented to:
- Lone Star - Best Retention
- Niagara Frontier - Best Recruiting
- Hanau - Highest Recruiting
- Lone Star - Best Overall Recruiting and Retention
- Rhein Neckar Silver - Building Fund Donations
- Karlsrue - Professional Development
- Rhein Neckar Silver - Community Donations
- Morning Calm - Community Service
- Rhein Neckar Silver - Community Service, Sustaining Programs

After detailed discussion the members voted to:
- Support equal entitlements for warrant officers in line with commissioned officer pay grades in such areas as weight allowances, housing entitlements, etc.
- Support the treatment of warrant officers of the US Forces as officers in line with appropriate commissioned officer pay grades.
- Approve a proposal to simplify the voting and publicity on actions at the COP meetings.
- Support the inclusion of warrant officers as Team Chiefs and members of Food Management Assistance Teams (FMAT)

1990

The 1990 Semi-Annual Board of Director's/ Council of President's meeting was held on 21-22 April in the Conference Room of our new national office. Fifty chapter presidents in person or by proxy, and all directors were present. A quorum was present for both meetings.

A celebration of the mortgage burning took place at the BOD meeting when after only 13 months the membership raised $20,000 to burn the mortgage the national office. The final donation for $300 was received from the Arizona Chapter Wives Auxiliary and presented by Region 2 Director Al Holcombe.

During the meeting action was taken to:
- Support the reinstatement of funds for warrant officers to obtain associate degrees.
- Support a constitutional amendment making it illegal to burn, mar, desecrate or destroy the US Flag as a form of protest.
- Approve a USAWOA scholarship program for dependents of Association members.
- Approve the inclusion of Auxiliary Bylaws in the Association Chapter Operations Manual.
- Approve a change in Council of President's meetings from semi-annually to annually in conjunction with the Annual Meeting.
- Approve the National Capitol Region as the host for the 1990 Annual Meeting at Fort Belvoir VA 21-26 October 1990.

1990 Annual Meeting of the Members

The 16th Annual Meeting of the Members was held on 21-26 October 1990 at Sosa Recreation Center on Fort Belvoir, VA, hosted by Region 6 with the majority of support coming from the Lord Fairfax Silver Chapter. The keynote address was given by COL Gerald P. Williams, Deputy Commander, Ft. Belvoir. Over 900 members were represented in person or by proxy and a quorum was present for the Annual Meeting, Council of Presidents and Board of Directors meetings.

Elected to serve the Association for the coming years were President Dave Welsh; Vice President Steven Murphy; Secretary B. J. Scott; Region 2 Director Albert M. Holcombe; Region 3 Director Carl Klomp; Region 4 Director David C. Adams; Region 5 Director Roy S. Raby, Jr. Region 6 President Howard Lundin and Region 1 President Roy Valiant were elected by their respective regions. Immediate Past President Dennis Jinks completes the Board of Directors. The national officers were installed by LTG Reno, Army Deputy Chief of Staff for Personnel, at the Installation and Awards Banquet.

The Association Annual awards were presented by LTG Reno to the following individuals:.
- CW3 Al Bamsch, Nord Bayern Chapter - The USAWOA Warrant Officer of the Year Award.
- Anne M. Rollinson, Mannheim, Germany - The Virginia M. Holcombe Memorial Award for National Spouse of the Year The Rollison's are presently assigned to Fort Drum, NY and Region Director Dave Adams will presented the award in a ceremony at Fort Drum.

The national chapter and region awards were presented to the following chapters:

Alexandria, VA. COL Michael Mosely (L), Chief, WO Div., accepts a warrant officer eagle plaque from USAWOA's Don Hess to be mounted at the entrance to the Warrant Officer Division.

Reston, VA. The 1991 Virginia M. Holcombe Memorial Spouse of the Year award was presented to Valerie Valiant for her work with the European Region where her husband, Roy, is the European Regional President.

- Pisa - Best Retention and Overall Best in Recruiting and Retention (two awards)
- Louisiana Purchase - Best Recruiting and Highest Recruiting (two awards)
- Aberdeen Edgwood - Professional Development
- Munich - Community Donations
- Ft Gordon - Community Service
- European Region - Community Service for Sustaining Programs
- Region 6 - Overall Best Region

After discussion both in study groups and on the floor, the members voted to:
- Approve the display of all past USAWOA presidents in an appropriate place within the national office.
- Approve the European Region as host of the 1991 Annual Meeting in Heidelberg, Germany 21-25 October 1991.
- Support the Veterans Against Drugs coalition formed to combat the drug epidemic.
- Approve the formulation of a marketing strategy to support the passage of WOMA.
- Support the designation of 1991 as the "Year of the Warrant Officer."
- Approve the updating of USAWOA briefing slides and recruiting supplement.
- Approve a USAWOA College Scholarship program to award $1000 scholarships to deserving children of USAWOA members.

1991

The 1991 Semi-Annual Board of Director's meeting was held on 26 April at the Association national officer in Herndon, VA. All directors were present except Past President Dennis Jinks who submitted a written report. The national officers presented reports in their respective areas of responsibility. A major issue was the impact of Desert Storm on the activities of the chapters. Region and chapter officers and members were among the over 40% of the active warrant officer force and over 22% of the reserve force who served in Desert Storm.

After lengthy discussion the directors voted to:
- Support 1991 as the Year of the Warrant Officer. (This proposal was deferred by the BOD because of Desert Storm.
- Support revision of the Dual Component Program to protect the retirement eligibility of warrant officers released from active duty prior to completion of 20 years of active federal service.
- Direct a letter be sent to the DCSPER requesting clarification on the proper lapel insignia and uniform accouterments for aviation warrant officers.
- Implement a mailgram publicity campaign to each representative and senator urging support of WOMA.
- Affirm the action taken by USAWOA to bring warrant officer pay to the attention of the 7th QRMC.
- Defer a final decision on Heidelberg as the site of the 1991 Annual Meeting pending information from European Region.
- Disapprove a proposal to provide Accidental Death and Dismemberment Membership Benefit due to prohibitive cost to the Association.
- Direct that a committee be formed to review the total organization of USAWOA to include Articles of Incorporation, by-laws, manuals and policies and report their findings at the 1991 Annual Meeting.

1991 Annual Meeting
The 17th Annual Meeting of the Members was held at the national office in Herndon., hosted by the national office on 22-24 October 1991. Over 1200 members were represented in person or by proxy and 34 presidents were represented at the

Heidelberg, Germany. COL Jerry Crews, Chief, Warrant Officer Division (L) and Roy Valiant, President, European Region, cut the ceremonial cake at the 1992 Annual Meeting banquet.

1992. Ft. Rucker, AL. CW5 David Helton (R) and Director, WO Career Center, and BG (P) Robert A. Goodbarry, Deputy Commander, Aviation Center, cut the ribbon officially opening the Warrant Officer Career Center.

Heidelberg, Germany. Ralph Smith (R) is presented his USAWOA Warrant Officer of the Year for 1992 from Pres. David P. Welsh during the 1992 Annual Meeting.

Heidelberg, Germany. CW4 Tom Piatti (R) is installed as national president by Immediate Past President CW4 David Welsh at the 1992 Annual Meeting.

Council of President's meeting. A quorum was present for the Annual Meeting, Council of Presidents and Board of Directors meetings.

Presentations were made by COL Gerald L. Crews, Chief, Warrant Officer Division, Total Army Personnel Command. The members also heard

presentations from the National officers reported on their various activities.

The Association annual awards were presented at the banquet at the Hidden Creek Country Club in Reston, VA. President Dave Welsh was the Master of Ceremonies and COL Gerald L. Crews was the banquet speaker and awards presenter. The Warrant Officer of the Year was CW4 Howard Lundin, an Active Guard/Reserve officer assigned to the Army Reserve Support Center in Rosslyn, VA. The Virginia M. Holcombe Memorial Award for National spouse of the Year award was present to Mrs. Valerie Valiant, wife of CW4 Roy A. Valiant from the Rhein Neckar Silver Chapter.

The Chapter awards were presented to:
- Stuttgart Silver Chapter - Best Retention and Overall Best in Recruiting and Retention (two awards
- Arizona Silver Chapter for Highest Recruiting and Best Recruiting (two awards)
- Louisiana Purchase Chapter - Professional development
- Munich Chapter - Community Donations and Community Service, Sustaining Programs
- Wuerzburg Chapter - Community Service
- Region 5 - Overall Best Region in Recruiting and Retention

After detailed discussion in study groups and on the floor the members voted to:
- Support the corrected retirement grade of CW4 to MW4 for those retired as MW4 (Automated personnel records do not recognize MW4).
- Support the inclusion of the date of commissioning in the Remarks column on warrant officer Record Briefs (ORBs).
- Support an across-the-board pay increase at the 24 year point for all ranks.
- Support the reversal of the WOMA legislation which excludes from consideration to CW5 those warrant officers who were retired and recalled to active duty without a break in service.
- Approve the Lifetime Trustee award to Past President Carl Burnett for his outstanding efforts in developing a comprehensive awards and marketing plan.

1992

The 1992 Semi-Annual Board of Director's meeting was held on 24 April at the National office. Vice President Tom Piatti and Region 3 Director Carl Klomp were excused. Roy Raby Director Region 3 recently resigned because of a personal commitment which did not leave him time to serve. A quorum was present.

The national officers reported on their activities. A major portion of business was:
- An interim report of the WOA 2000 Committee chaired by Rick Cornelius. This committee was charged with examining the current structure of the Board of Directors, the National Executive Committee; the Council of Presidents; chapters; Annual Meetings of the Members; various programs offered to our membership; NEWSLINER input and format; relationships with sister associations; USAWOA publications and recruitment and retention. The committee will make a final report to the Annual Meeting in 1992.
- A review and discussion of the finalized Warrant Officer Leader Development Action Plan.
- A review of an updated USAWOA brief complete with script and slides to be available to chapters or members.
- A review of our legislative activities including WOMA.

In other actions, the Board voted to:
- Accept the WOA 2000 Interim Report
- Approve an annual audit of our financial records.

1992 Annual Meeting

The 18th Annual Meeting of the Members was held on 26-30 October at Heidelberg, Germany, sponsored by the European Region. Over 1100 members were represented either in person or by proxy and 28 presidents were present for the Council of President's

CW2 Jeremiah G. Marshall, (left) the current commander of the Warrant Officer Candidate (WOC) Company of the Ordnance Center and School at Aberdeen PG, MD, stands proudly with past commanders of the WOC Company. L to r: Marshall, CW3 Wesley B. Davis, CW4 Troy A. Daugherty, MWO Thomas G. Grice and CW4 Norman D. Purdy. June 1992.

Alexandria, VA. CW3 Tom Hennen (left), Payload Specialist, STS-44 presents a plaque to the USAWOA which displays the US Army flag, and Crew patch which were flown aboard the Orbiter Atlantis, STS-44. The plaque also includes pictures of the Atlantis and their crew and a certificate to the USAWOA for support of the space program and professional representation of the Warrant Officer Corps. L to r: CW3 Hennen, CW3 John Hawker, Alternate Mission Payload Specialist; President Dave Welsh; VP Tom Piatti; and Clay Kelley.

Ft. Campbell, KY. Mrs. Willie Frank, widow of CW4 Ray Frank, KIA Somolia, cuts the Warrant Officer cake at the 1993 Annual Meeting assisted by CW3 Larry Hickerson.

Ft. Campbell, KY. CW4 Suzanne Curtis is presented the National President's Award at the 1993 Annual Meeting in recognition of her four years service as Chair, National Awards Committee. Presenting the award is MG Keene, Commanding general, Ft. Campbell, KY.

meeting and a quorum was present. A quorum was also present for the Board of Directors meeting. Excused for duty commitments were Region 5 Director Gene Newton, Region 2 Director Carl Burnett, and Region 5 Director Jimmy Carpenter.

Elected to National office were President Thomas A Piatti; Vice President Clay Kelley; Secretary B. J. Scott; Region 2 Director Carl Burnett; Region 3 Director Jimmy Carpenter; Region 4 Director Richard Scalzo; Region 5 Director Gene Newton; Region 6 Director Charles Dunn.

The Association annual awards were present to the following individuals:

Ralph Smith, Rhein Neckar Silver Chapter - Albert M. Holcombe Memorial Award for the Warrant Officer of the Year.

Louise Braman, Rhein Neckar Silver Chapter - Virginia M Holcombe Memorial Award for the Warrant Officer Spouse of the Year Award.

The Association chapter awards were presented to the following chapters:

Thousand Island - Best Retention
Bayern-Jura - Best Recruiting
Hanau Silver - Highest Recruiting
Nord Bayern Silver - Overall Best in Recruiting and Retention
North Texas - Professional Development
Munich - Community Donations and Community Service Sustaining Program (2 Awards)
Berlin - Community Service
Vint Hill Farms Station - Community Service

A major activity at the Annual Meeting was a Professional Development Seminar in which all warrant officers in Europe were invited. The highlight of the seminar was a presentation by COL Gerald Crews, Chief, Warrant Officer Division, PERSCOM, DA. Other speakers were COL John Fuller, Office of the DCSPER, USAREUR, who spoke on personnel policies in Europe, MW4 David P. Welsh, OCAR, DA, who addressed the latest issues from the Warrant Officer Leader Development Action Plan (WOLDAP). CW4 (Ret) Robert D. Scott, who addressed the leadership obligations of warrant officers to counsel enlisted personnel on financial matters; and USAWOA Executive Vice President Don Hess who briefed on the efforts of our Association to improve the Army and the Corps. In addition to the formal briefings, assignment managers from PERSCOM, DA conducted approximately 1000 personal interviews with warrant officers concerned about their future in the current drawdown environment.

During the meeting action was taken to:
- Approve a member-at-large category to permit members to elect to belong to a chapter or remain as a member-at-large.
- Approve a modification to the rebate system in conjunction with the member-at-large status.
- Direct that region directors prepare an annual budget request for their projected expenses.
- Reject the addition of monetary incentives to the USAWOA awards program.
- Approve the 1993 USAWOA budget.

During the meeting a memorial service was conducted for two friends of the Association who passed away in 1992. Lenore Quigley Hess, wife of Executive Vice President Don Hess was honored with a posthumous award of the Virginia M Holcombe Memorial Spouse of the Year Award. CW4 (Ret) Albert M. Holcombe, charter member and long time director was honored by naming our National Warrant Officer of the Year Award as the Albert M. Holcombe Memorial Warrant Officer of the Year Award. (See photo page 46)

1993

The 1993 Semi-Annual Board of Director's meeting was held on 24 April in Herndon, VA with 7 directors present. Absent were Region 2 Director Carl Burnett and Region 3 Director Jimmy Carpenter due to duty commitments. A quorum was present.

A special guest was COL Gerald Crews, Chief Warrant Officer Division, PERSCOM. Past President David Welsh was recognized by the Board with the Lifetime Trustee Award, the highest award of our Association.

In a major decision, the Board approved a change in the format for the NEWSLINER from a tabloid size newspaper to a booklet format similar to the annual ALMANAC. The board also addressed the automation needs of the national office and agreed to a long range plan to network the office computer system and upgrade our computer hardware. Other reports were presented by the national officers on the status of membership, property inventory, recruiting efforts, job placement; insurance; and the status of the Warrant Officer History Book.

COL Crews offered suggestions on how the Association could better market itself to the membership. A general discussion was held on how to improve the image of the Association to the members and to the Army.

1993 Annual Meeting

The 19th Annual Meeting of the Members was held on 26-30 October at Fort Campbell, KY, hosted by the Ken-Tenn Chapter. Over 1100 members were represented either in person or by

Ft. Campbell, KY. USAWOA displays the achievements of outstanding persons. Virginia M. Holcombe (L) in whose honor the USAWOA Spouse of the Year award is named; CW3 Tom Hennen, the first warrant officer to orbit the earth; and Albert M. Holcombe, in whose honor the USAWOA Warrant Officer of the Year award is named.

Ft. Stewart, GA. National officers of the USAWOA at the 1994 Annual Meeting. (L to R): VP Dick Scalzo; Treas. Alice Reid; Dir. Gene Perrino; Dir. Frank Meeks; Pres. Ray Bell; Dir. Mary Carter; Immediate Past-Pres. Tom Piatti; European Region Pres. Gerry Wentworth and Exec. VP Don Hess.

proxy and 32 presidents were represented at the Council of President's Meeting. At the Board of Director's meeting 7 directors were present. Excused directors were Gene Newton; Jimmy Carpenter and Carl Burnett because of duty commitments.

The Association annual awards were presented to the following individuals:

- CW2 Mitchell E. Saddler, Fort Bragg Silver Chapter received the Albert M. Holcombe Memorial Award for Warrant officer of the Year.
- Mrs. Wendy Y. Mathy from Europe was presented the Virginia M. Holcombe Memorial Award for Nation Spouse of the Year
- Aberdeen Edgewood Chapter - Best Retention Award

- Oberfaltz-Franken Chapter - Best Recruiting Award
- Fort Bragg Silver Chapter - Highest Recruiting Award
- Wuerzburg Chapter - Overall Best Chapter in Recruiting and Retention
- Augsburg - Professional Development
- Berlin Chapter - Community Affairs for Donations
- Nord Bayern Silver and Wuerzburg Chapters - Community Affairs for Services
- Augsburg Chapter - Community Affairs for Sustaining Programs

Over 400 warrant officers of all components, active duty, reserve components and retirees attended the Professional Development Seminar on 29 October. Presentations were given by MG Fred Vollrath, Director, Military Personnel Management, ODCSPER, DA; COL Gerald Crews, Chief, Warrant Officer Division, PERSCOM; CW5 Jack Lynch, National Guard Bureau; CW5 Dave Welsh, Office Chief of Army Reserve, DA; MW4 Curt Oldroyd, ODSCPER, DA; CW5 Jim Damron, Commandant, Warrant Officer Career Center, Fort Rucker, AL; and USAWOA President Tom Piatti and Executive Vice President Don Hess.

Assignment managers from PERSCOM, DA; Army Reserve and National Guard Bureau were on hand to provide personal interviews, counsel members and provide communications back to Reserve Component headquarters.

At the meeting action was taken to:
- Support technical amendments to extend the mandatory retirement of reserve commissioned warrant officers from age 60 to age 62.
- Support legislation to authorize tuition assistance for Reserve component warrant officers toward associate, baccalaureate and graduate level degrees.
- Support the recommendations of the 7th QRMC passed at the 1992 Annual Meeting.
- Support the continued funding of commissaries.
- Support the legislation to restore equity of COLA to the same schedule as federal retirees.
- Support a change in Army policy to permit AGR warrant officers to serve 20 years of Active Federal Warrant Officer Service.
- Support the continuation of full health benefits for all military retirees.

1994

The 1994 Semi-Annual Board of Director's meeting was held on 24 March at the Army National Guard Readiness Center with all directors present except Region 2 Director Carl Burnett and Region 3 Director Jimmy Carpenter who were excused. Region 5 Director Gene Newton resigned because of time constraints due to his civilian position. The Board unanimously appointed Gene Perrino, Ft. Stewart, GA (Victory Chapter) to fill the unexpired term of Gene Newton. The directors reported on their activities and the positive results from our members on the new-look NEWSLINER. Membership continues on the upswing both in active duty, reserve components, and retired warrant officers. Chapter interests remains high although many warrant officers are in a member-at-large status, particularly in areas where chapters are not active.

Major Items of business included a vote to:
- Approve an 800 toll free number for our members to contact the national officer.
- Approve the commissioning of a commemorative warrant officer painting by Don Stivers to celebrate 75 years of warrant officer service to our nation.

Ft. Stewart, GA. The National officers are installed by COL Richard A. Hack (center), DISCOM Commander, Ft. Stewart, GA. at the 1994 Annual Meeting. (L to R): Pres. Ray Bell; VP Dick Scalzo; Sec. John Lucius; European President Gerry Wentworth; COL Hack; Region Directors Mary Carter; Frank Meeks; Gene Perrino and Dave Welsh.

Ft. Stewart, GA. Director Mary Carter was selected as recipient of the Albert M. Holcombe Memorial Award as the 1994 USAWOA Warrant Officer of the Year.

Hinesville, GA. President Ray Bell (R) and Hinesville Mayor Allen Brown lay a wreath at the Hinesville Eternal Flame in commemoration of those who served during WWII.

A highly successful Professional Development Seminar was conducted on 25 March by the Lord Fairfax and Minuteman Chapters. Over 300 warrant officers of all components attended to hear LTG Thomas Carney, Army Deputy Chief of Staff for Personnel, provide an overview of America's Army and the effects of the drawdown on the Army and the Warrant Officer Corps. CW5 Jack Lynch, Warrant Officer Program Manager, Army National Guard updated the members of the National Guard and CW5 Dave Welsh, Warrant Officer Program Manager, Office, Chief of Army Reserve, covered the same areas for the USAR warrant officers. CW5 Jim Damron, Commandant, Warrant Officer Career Center, Ft Rucker, AL, described the total warrant officer education system from candidate courses to training for CW5s.

The seminar also included a TRADOC warrant officer representative and warrant officer members of the various proponents who briefed on the respective elements of their branches. CW5 Fred Meine, TRADOC briefed on the Warrant Officer Leader Development Action Plan (WOLDAP) and chaired a panel of USAR, ARNG, Career Center representatives and proponent officers from Signal, Ordnance, Transportation and OTJAG.

COL Gerald Crews, Chief, Warrant Officer Division, PERSCOM, closed out the day's activities with career information for all warrant officers and challenged them to set the example by their professionalism and personal appearance.

1994 Annual Meeting

The 20th Annual Meeting of the Members was held from 1 to 5 November at Fort Stewart, GA, home of the 24th Infantry Division.

Elected to National office were Raymond A Bell of Fairfax, VA; President; CW5 Richard M. Scalzo, Sr., of Laurel MD as Vice President; CW5 John Lucius of Springfield, VA as Secretary. Elected to the Board of Directors were Region 2 Director Mary Carter of Los Angeles, CA; Region 3 Director Franklin D Meeks of Sparta, WI; Region 4 Director George Rollinson of Theresa, NY; Region 5 Director Eugene L Perrino, Sr. of Ft Stewart GA; and Region 6 Director David P Welsh of Alexandria, VA. Also serving on the Board of Directors is Gerald Wentworth of Germany (elected by the European Region Membership) and Immediate Past President Tom Piatti of Fort Rucker, AL. Appointed to national officers were Assistant Vice President for Reserve Affairs Matthew A Wojdak, Jr. of Brighton, IL; Assistant Vice President for Intra-Service Liaison, Ray A Vaughn of Harrisburg, PA; and Chair of the WOA 2000 Committee Robert D Scott of Reston, VA. The directors were installed by COL Richard A Hack, DISCOM Commander, Fort Stewart, GA.

Guest Speakers during the Annual Meeting included COL Gerald Crews, Chief, Warrant Officer Division, PERSCOM, Department of the Army; CW4 Joe Howell, Recruiting Command; CW5 David Welsh, Program Manager, Office Chief of Army Reserve; and CW5 David Helton, Director, Warrant Officer Career Center, Fort Rucker, AL who was also the banquet speaker.

The Association annual awards were presented to the following individuals:
- The Albert Holcombe Memorial Award for Warrant Officer of the Year was presented to CW3 Mary Carter from the Southern California Chapter.
- The Virginia M Holcombe Memorial Award for National Spouse of the Year award was presented to Mrs. Angie Chambless from Germany.

The chapter awards were presented to:
- Niagara Frontier Chapter for Best Retention Award.

- Arlington Hall Minuteman Chapter for Best Recruiting Award and Highest Recruiting Awards.
- Statue of Liberty Chapter for Overall Best Chapter in Recruiting and Retention and for Professional Development Awards;

- Augsburg Chapter for Community Affairs for Donations Award;
- Rhein Neckar Silver Chapter for Community Affairs for Sustaining Programs Award.

Chapters activated since our last Annual Meet-

Arlington, VA. LTG Thomas Carney, Army DCSPER addresses the warrant officers at the Prof. Development Seminar hosted by the Arlington Hall Minuteman Chp. in March 1994

Arlington, VA. COL Gerald Crews, Chief, Warrant Officer Division, briefs warrant officers on current actions within the WO Division in March 1994.

Ft. Stewart, GA. USAWOA ladies support the 1994 Annual Meeting by selling USAWOA memorabilia during the breaks in business sessions. (L to R): Phyllis Scalzo; Rose Scott; Fran Bell and Pauline Hess.

Ft. Stewart, GA. CW4 (Ret.) Robert D. Scott, Chairman, WWII Commemoration Committee, presents 1994 President Tom Piatti with the official certificate of USAWOA's participation in the Army Commemoration celebration.

Ft. Rucker, AL. Don Stivers (L), noted military artist, unveils The Quiet Professional *during the celebration of the 75th Anniversary of the Warrant Officer Corps. Exec VP Don Hess, WOCC Director Dave Helton and Aviation Center Chapter Pres. Roy Doughtry look on. (June 1995)*

ing: Minnesota Chapter. Chapters re-activated: ACE Chapter in Belgium; Aloha Chapter in Hawaii; North Texas Chapter north of Dallas TX. Chapters de-activated: Berlin Chapter; Frankfurt Silver Chapter; St. Lewis Gateway Chapter.

In major Items of business the officers voted to:
- Reduce dues to $24 for newly appointed warrant officers for their first year of membership.
- Publish a membership survey in the upcoming Almanac to determine the desires of the membership in various areas.
- Forward the Association position on military compensation for warrant officers to the Director of the Quadrennial Review of Military Compensation for their analysis prior to forwarding their report to the President.
- Support the rescinding of the Dual Compensation Act to permit Regular Army warrant officers employed by all branches of the government to receive their full retirement pay entitlement.
- Select the Fort Bragg Silver Chapter to be the Host Chapter for the 1995 Annual meeting.

During 1994 the Department of Defense designated the USAWOA as a World War II Commemorative community. A Certificate of Designation was presented to President Tom Piatti in a ceremony at the Annual Meeting. The first activity was to designate the 1994 Annual Meeting in commemoration of the sacrifices of our armed forces and all those who served on the home front during W.W.II. The second event was a wreath laying ceremony at the eternal flame in Hinesville, GA with Mayor Allen Brown and incoming USAWOA President Ray Bell participating in this ceremony. Other events were programmed for 1995.

1995

The 1995 Semi-Annual Board of Director's meeting was held on 6 April 1995 at the National Guard headquarters in Arlington, VA with 8 directors present. Absent were Secretary John Lucius and Region 4 Director George Rollinson.

A review of the short range objectives of our Association included:
- A review of Association briefings, and other published material to ensure they reflect the most current information available to the Association.
- Tabulating responses to the membership survey published in the 1994 USAWOA Almanac.
- Increasing the participation of proponent agencies through the publications of MOS specific articles of professional information.
- Continuing our strong focus on recruiting and

Ft. Bragg, NC. The Albert M. Holcombe Memorial Award as USAWOA Warrant Officer of the Year was presented to Past Pres. Tom Piatti (L) for his efforts in Washington and at Ft. Rucker, AL. Presenting the award is Pres. Ray Bell. (Oct. 1995)

Ft. Rucker, AL. More than 300 warrant officers and guests from around the nation gathered on June 9, 1995 for the 75th Anniversary of the founding of the Warrant Officer Corps. The W4 Reunion Committee and the Aviation Center Chapter planned the celebration which included a picnic, dinner, dance and other activities.

Ft. Bragg, NC. COL Richard Crampton, Chief, WO Div., briefs warrant officers at the Professional Development seminar on Oct. 28, 1995.

Ft. Bragg, NC. LTG Theodore Stroup, Army DCSPER addresses the warrant officers at the Professional Development Seminar on Oct. 28, 1995.

Fayetteville, NC. Pres. Ray Bell and Fayetteville Mayor J. L. Dawkins lay a wreath in commemoration of the 50th Anniversary of World War II. (Oct. 1995)

retaining membership as we grow in numerical and professional strength.

- Maintaining professional contact with newly assigned key officials in leadership positions in DA, DoD and Congress to keep the key role of the warrant officer in today's Army.

Long range objectives include:

- Reviewing the duties and responsibilities of our elected officials.
- Reviewing our region boundaries as they are presently constituted.
- Increasing our visibility with other professional associations to project the professional image of the Army warrant officer in the military community at large.
- Enhancing our electronic voice mail capabilities to ensure more timely distribution of warrant officer information around the world.
- Providing video presentations of our Professional Development Seminars to those areas we have not been able to reach in the past.

The Board of Directors also analyzed the Association membership by component, branch, rank and career field to assist in developing a comprehensive plan to recruit and retain warrant officers; reviewed the office automation upgrade to include cost and current status; noted the positive impact of the 1-800-5-USAWOA toll free number which provides members and chapters with a timely method for reporting changes in membership status and chapter information; applauded the continuing improvement of the NEWSLINER and methods to keep the production costs down while expanding the areas of coverage; encouraged efforts in conjunction with the Military Coalition to keep the members informed on those legislative issues which impact on the military community, particularly in the critical areas of health care and COLA for military retirees.

Professional Development Seminar

A Professional Development Seminar was conducted at the Army National Guard Readiness Center in Arlington VA on 7 April 1995 designed to provide up-to-date information on warrant officer career and personnel policies for all components. LTG Theodore G. Stroup, Jr., Army Deputy Chief of Staff for Personnel, was the keynote speaker. Other speakers included CW5 Ken Bouchard, Warrant Officer Career Center, Fort Rucker, AL; CW4 Joe Howell, Recruiting Command; CW5 Curt

Herndon, VA. Bob and Rose Scott donate print #1000 of The Quiet Professional *to the national office.*

Ft. Bragg, NC. Silver Chapter Pres. Gary Bosworth (center) and Chapter VP Roscoe Leggs (R), present a print of The Quiet Professional *to Post Commander LTG Hugh Shelton after his speech to the 1995 Annual Meeting. (Oct. 1995)*

Oldroyd, Office of the Deputy Chief of Staff for Personnel; CW5 Bob McGinnis, Warrant Officer Division, PERSCOM, DA; CW5 Arbie McInnis, TRADOC; and COL (Ret) Gerald Crews, Job Placement Counselor, the Retired Officers Association; CW5 David P Welsh, Program Manager, for the Office Chief of Army Reserves; and CW5 Jack Lynch, Program Manager, Army National Guard. These knowledgeable individuals brought their expertise to over 170 warrant officers of all components who expressed their appreciation to the various speakers for their contributions to the all day seminar.

75th Anniversary Celebration

On 9 June the Aviation Center Chapter, Fort Rucker, hosted a 75th Anniversary celebration of the Warrant Officer Corps. Over 300 warrant officers were on hand for the weekend celebration. Members from Class 55-5, the first class of warrant officer helicopter pilots to graduate at Fort Rucker, class 56-12 and members of the Helicopter Square Dance Team were among those who returned to the site of their early training. Joining them were current members of the Warrant Officer Career Center, warrant officer candidates and other warrant officers from as far away as Germany. Tours of the Warrant Officer Hall of Fame, US Army Aviation Museum, and Warrant Officer Career Center were concluded. A dinner dance featured a brief history of our illustrious Corps, professional entertainment and an excellent band. A picnic at the Lake Lodge concluded the weekend celebration

Mr. Don Stivers, noted military artist, unveiled his original painting "The Quiet Professional" which commemorates 75 years of warrant officer service.

1995 Annual Meeting

The 20th Annual Meeting of the Members was held at the Holiday Inn, Bordeaux, in Fayetteville, NC from 24-28 October 1995, sponsored by the Fort Bragg Silver Chapter.

The Association National Awards were presented to the following individuals:
- CW4 Thomas A. Piatti, Career Center Chapter (Fort Rucker, AL) and CW3 (Ret) Richard C. Easingwood, Fort Bragg Silver Chapter received CW4 Albert M. Holcombe Memorial Awards for Warrant Officer of the Year.
- Christina S. Manzo, Oberfalz-Franken Chapter received the Virginia M. Holcombe Memorial Award for National Spouse of the Year.

The Annual Chapter Awards were presented to the following chapters:
- Niagara Frontier Chapter - Best Retention Award
- Minnesota Chapter - Best Recruiting Award
- Career Center Chapter (Fort Rucker) - Highest Recruiting Award
- Aloha Chapter (Hawaii) - Overall Best Chapter in Recruiting and Retention
- Arlington Hall Minuteman Chapter - Best Professional Development Award
- Rheinland Pfalz Chapter (Germany) - Community Affairs Award for Donations
- Greater Atlanta Chapter - Community Affairs Award for Services
- Rhein Neckar Silver Chapter - Community Affairs Award for Sustaining Programs

Professional Development Seminar

A Professional Development Seminar attracted over 300 warrant officers of all components. The keynote speaker was LTG Thomas G. Stroup, Jr, Army Deputy Chief of Staff for Personnel. Other speakers were COL Richard W. Crampton, Chief, Warrant Officer Division, PERSCOM, DA; CW4 Thomas A. Piatti, Warrant Officer Career Center, Fort Rucker, AL; CW4 Joe Howell, Recruiting Command; CW5 David P Welsh, Office Chief of Army Reserves; CW5 William Harrison, Commanche Project Officer; and CW4 (Ret) John Allnatt, on retired affairs. In addition to the formal presentations over 200 warrant officers of all components received career counseling from the as-

Ft. Bragg, NC. National Officers conducting the Annual Meeting business session. (L to R): Treas. Alice Reid; Prs. Ray Bell; VP Dick Scalzo and Sec. John Lucius. (Oct. 1995)

European Region Convention, 1974.

European Region 3rd Convention, 1975.

signment managers from Warrant Officer Division, PERSCOM, DA, and ARPERCEN, St. Louis, MO. The national officers also reported on their respective areas of responsibility.

In major items of business the officers voted to:
- Support the passage of S.69 which would permit military retirees 65 or older to retain CHAMPUS as a supplementary payer to Medicare.
- Direct the Executive Committee to study the benefits and cost of the Association health care supplemental insurance program to determine if a more competitive program is available for the membership.
- Support a technical amendment to legislation to authorize extension of National Guard and Army Reserve Warrant Officers to be retained until age 62 when they possess critical skill or for other extenuating circumstances at the discretion of the Service Secretary.
- Support a technical amendment to legislation to authorize tuition assistance for Reserve Component officers and warrant officers for funding towards associate, baccalaureate and graduate level degrees in line with the goals in the WOLDAP.
- Support a change in Army policy to permit AGR warrant officers to serve 20 years of Active Federal Warrant Officer Service.

The Annual Meeting closed with an formal ball and an address by LTG Hugh Shelton, Commanding General, XVIII Airborne Corps. His personal and professional respect for today's technical and tactical warrant officer leaders was evident in his remarks which have been echoed around our Army for the men and women who wear the eagles on their lapels.

European Warrant Officers Association

Early Beginnings 1971-73

The European Warrant Officers Association, (EWOA) a separate organization of concerned warrant officers was formed in Germany and held its organizational meeting on 9 October 1971. The first President of the European Region was CW4 George C. Gratchen who was known affectionately as the Father of the EWOA. George's vision for the Corps included an ex-

European Region 4th Convention, 1976.

Heidelberg, Germany. Delegates at the European Region Convention in 1978 listen to discussion from the floor.

Warrant Officers Convention, 1978.

European Region Convention, 1979.

Heidelberg, Germany. European Region officers in 1979. L to r: Treasurer Jim Wright, VP John Wilson, President Leo Ott, and Secretary Ray Bell.

amination of all areas of professional development for warrant officers from accessions, education, promotion, assignment, compensation and retirement. Initial efforts of the European Warrant Officers Association focused on:

- Developing a more proficient technically qualified warrant officer through attendance at military and civilian courses of instruction on a par with those available to commissioned and enlisted personnel;
- Obtaining equalization of flight, hazardous duty, and other special pays to recognize the contributions of the warrant officer;
- Seeking realignment of the basic pay scales to eliminate the inequities in the present pay system;
- Recognizing senior warrant officers by establishing field grade quarters for W4s and where the number of warrant officers justifies, separate warrant officer housing areas;
- Assigning additional duties commensurate with the rank and responsibilities of senior warrant officers.

George firmly believed that through the Association, warrant officers could work together and assist each other in accomplishing the mission of the US Army and reestablish the image of technical expertise, dedication, pride and professionalism with the members of the Corps. With the assistance of key warrant officers who identified potential chapters within Europe George traveled well over 20,000 miles in Germany and other countries in Europe to organize chapters, energize chapter officers, and encourage warrant officers to join the EWOA. Recognizing that the EWOA could address issues in Europe but did not have representation in the US George contacted the USAWOA with the purpose of merging the EWOA with the newly formed USAWOA in Washington, DC. After personal contact and review of similar objectives the EWOA merged with the USAWOA and became the European Region of USAWOA.

European Region, USAWOA

1974-Present

The European Region was the largest region within the Association and elected its own officers whose president served on the USAWOA

Heidelberg, Germany. Past Association leaders at the 1981 European Region Convention. L to r: George Gratchen, President, European WOA; Cletus M. McKeown, future national president; and Percy Butler, 1980 European Region President.

Germany, 1994. The Virginia Holcombe Memorial Award as USAWOA National Spouse of the Year was awarded to Mrs. Angie Chambless, for her efforts on behalf of the European Region. The award was presented in Europe by the European Region President.

Board of Directors. The chapters established within the European Region are listed below. The chapters that organized the European WOA were designated as Silver Chapters and are indicated with an *.

ACE
Ansbach
Augsberg
Bad Krueznach
Bamberg
Berlin
Darmstadt
Eifel Chapter
Frankfurt
Fulda/Wildfliken
Giessen
Goeppingen
*Hanau Silver Chapter
Heidelberg Chapter
Heilbronn
Illesheim
Karlsruhe
Main Tauber
Mainz-Wiesbaden
Munich
Nahe Valley
Neu-Ullm
Nord Deutchland
Nord Bayern
Oberpfalz-Franken
Pirmasens/Zweibrucken
Kaiserslautern
Pisa
*Rhein Neckar Silver
Schwaebisch-Gmuend
Schwaebisch-Hall
Stuttgart
Vicenza

1974-Present

CW3 Alfred E. Cox had assumed the presidency of the EWOA from George Gratchen and with the USAWOA merger became the first European Region President. His dedication to the Association was evidenced by his decision to withdraw an approved curtailment and request an extension to serve a full term as President, European Region. Al traveled throughout Germany "selling" USAWOA and developing leadership for the future of the Association by his dedication and personal sacrifice. During Al's term of office he was ably assisted by an outstanding group of chapter officers who continued to build on the foundation of the EWOA and the USAWOA.

Al was followed in office by the following officers of the European Region:

President	Vice Pres
1974 CW2 Jimmy Gray	CW4 George W. Eby
1975 CW4 Richard A. Dropik	CW4 Charles Dunn
1976 CW3 John Allnatt	CW3 Charles E. Yates
1977 CW3 James W. Hubers	CW3 William L. Fitzgerald
1978 CW4 George W. Eby	WO1 Richard R. James
1979 CW3 Leonard D. Ott	CW2 John T. Wilson
1980 CW3 Percy Butler	CW3 Joseph L Pisano
1981 CW3 James H. Wright	CW3 Leonard Detwiller
1982 CW2 Lynn Freund	CW2 Roger Ewing
1983 CW2 Lynn Freund	CW2 Billy Carter
1984 CW4 Dennis Jinks/	CW3 Ronald D. Bowman
CW2 Stanley A. Jones	
1985 CW3 James E. Wilson	CW2 Jose D. Montes
1986 CW4 Art Abrahamson	CW4 Robert A. Schulte
1987 CW4 Joseph A Wittstrom	CW4 Robert A. Schulte
1988 CW3 David C Adams	CW4 (Ret) Carl Mueller
1989 CW3 David C Adams	CW3 Roy Valiant
1990 CW4 Roy A Valiant	CW3 Albert Bamsch
1991 CW4 Roy A Valiant	CW2 Mark Varney

Manhein, Germany. Rhein Neckar chapter in one of their many Fests to assist the community.

Heidelberg, Germany. The largest group of warrant officers ever assembled (more than 800) were on hand to hear President Jinks and other speakers at the 1988 Annual Meeting Professional Development Seminar on Oct. 28, 1988.

Heidelberg, Germany. European Region officer in 1990. President Roy Valiant and Vice President Al Bamsch installed by Bob Schulte.

1992 CW4 Roy A. Valiant   CW2 Mark Varney
1993 CW4 Roy A. Valiant   CW2 Mark Varney
1994 CW2 Gerry Wentworth   CW3 (Ret) James E. Wilson
1995 CW5 John Parry   WO1 Paula A. Scherer

Community Affairs

The European Region plays an active role in the various communities by donating monies to the myriad of charities throughout the command. Each year over $50,000 is donated by the region and chapters. Many hours of off duty time was donated by Association warrant officers to make their communities a better place to live. Activities include selling food and drink at chapter booths, sponsoring bowling tournaments; organizing car washes, repairing and distributing toys, preparing holiday baskets for the needy; donating funds to child care centers, schools, orphanages, chapels, scouts, and other local charities; sponsoring fashion shows; and awarding scholarships to deserving students. These contributions to the various communities earn for the European Region warrant officers a reputation of caring and compassion throughout the Command.

Chapter Activities

For over 20 years chapter activities revolved around providing professional development information to their members. In addition to monthly chapter meetings the European Region sponsored an Annual Convention in Europe and the European Warrant Officer Ball. The Region holds monthly Council of President's (COP) meetings to discuss issues pertaining to the members of their chapter to include professional development matters on promotion, assignment, legislation and other pertinent information. Actions approved by the local chapters and the Council of Presidents result in many improvements in the local communities and the European Command as a whole. Proposals approved by the European Region affecting the entire Warrant Officer Corps are forwarded to the national office for voting by the entire membership at the Annual Meeting of the Members. Actions approved by the members at the Annual Meeting set the direction for the future of the Association.

Recognition

The Region established a quarterly awards program for the selection of a warrant officer, warrant officer spouse, and warrant officer family of the quarter. At the Annual Convention nominations were selected for the national Warrant Officer and Warrant Officer Spouse of the Year. The Region also established a scholarship program for high school seniors of members with a child graduation from DODDS High School.

Auxiliary Activities

During the history of the European Region the following chapters have benefited from chapter auxiliaries: Ansbach, Frankfurt, Hanau, Heidelberg, Karlsrule, Munich, Nord Bayern, Oberpfalz-Franken, Rhein Neckar, Schwabisch Hall, and Wuerzburg. These auxiliaries, as a separate entity, helped gain recognition for the USAWOA through their involvement, both singularly and with the chapter, in their respective communities. They planned and executed, within their community's guidelines, ways to earn money which was then distributed to various worthwhile areas of their community.

The collapse of the Berlin Wall and the Soviet Union brought with it the examination of our military forces. The drawdown of forces affected the European Command and the base closings resulted in personnel turmoil in Europe. Despite the drawdown the strength of the European Region remains strong through the consolidation of many chapters and the warrant officer's desire to maintain the camaraderie developed through the years.

From their beginning as an association for warrant officers in Europe to their merger as the European Region, USAWOA, members of the European Region continue to set the example for others to emulate. For most of the existence of the USAWOA the European Region was the largest in size and the strongest in activities. The camaraderie established in early years as the European Warrant Officers Association has been kept alive with the first reunion of the European Region WOA in 1994, followed up by another reunion in September 1995. Although no longer the largest region within

USAWOA, European Region maintains its unique role as the only active region within the Association and continues to provide excellent leadership at the local, region and national level.

A Proud Past and a Bright Future

In 1995 the Warrant Officers Association celebrated the Army Warrant Officer Corps' 75th anniversary. Warrant officers world wide - active, reserve, or retired - looked back with great pride to this important milestone in our history. It was a time to reflect on a proud heritage filled with record breaking achievement, heroic men and women, and patriotic service to our nation. It was also a time to focus on the bright and exciting future of the Army, the Corps, and the Association.

Heidelberg, Germany. Members enjoy the festivities at the 1992 European Region Banquet.

1972. Hanau, Germany. Early leaders of the Hanau Chapter and the European Region were (L to R) Al Cox and Jim Hubers.

U.S. Army
Warrant Officers'
Biographies

Editor's note: All members of the U.S. Warrant Officers Association were invited to write and submit biographies for inclusion in this publication. The following are from those who chose to participate. The biographies were printed as received, with only minor editing. The publisher regrets it cannot accept responsibility for omissions or inaccuracies within the following biographies.

First National Council, 1921.

GLEN EUGENE ADAMS, CW2, born June 2, 1960, Van Buran, AR. Entered Army 1978 as 12B combat engineer. At assignment with 8th Engrs at Ft Hood, he met and married Debra Ann Adams from Tulsa, OK. They have three children: Glen II, Jessica and Tiffany. Reclassified to 74F computer programmer in 1982 while stationed at 3rd Inf Div. After PCSing to Ft McPherson working in WWMCCS, received appointment as W01-251A data processing tech.

As new W01 was assigned to 2nd Armd Div (FWD), Garlstad, Germany 1989, and later transferred to USAREUR and worked as chief software tech, chief of operation branch, chief network tech and chief automation support team for OCDSINT.

Awards/Medals: Army Commendation w/5 OLCs, Army Achiev w/3 OLCs and Good Conduct w/3 OLCs.

Earned AS degree from City College of Chicago, BA degree from St Leo College and the Univ of New York, and is a graduate student with the Univ of Maryland. Currently WOA Heidelberg Chap president.

JAMES A. ALBRITTON, CW3, AUS (RET), born Aug 8, 1924, Sarasota, FL. Began his military service Jan 13, 1943; served in Europe 18 months; discharged Feb 26, 1946; went in active Reserves, Sarasota, FL as staff sergeant from June 1953-1960; returned to active duty and assigned to Ft Hood, TX in Co A, 142nd Sig Bn as motor sergeant.

July 1960 sent to school at APG; November 1960 to Korea with 516th Ord Co; January 1962 assigned to Camp Roberts, CA, 573rd Ord Co. Went to Verdun, France October 1964, served in the Army Depot with 97th Engr Bn, then moved to K Town, Germany.

November 1967 returned to Ft Riley, KS in the 265th Maint Bn; went to Vietnam April 1969 and joined the 243rd Field Svc Co at Plaeku. Appointed WO CW1 Sept 7, 1969, assigned to the 1st Inf Div; April 1970 returned to Darmstadt, Germany with the 93rd Sig Bn as a Mt Officer; June 1973 went to Ft Benning, GA, 444th Trans Co. Left Ft. Benning October 1974 back to APG, MD; February 1975 back to Stuttgart, Germany, 2nd Bn, 4th Inf. Left Germany March 1978 to Homestead, FL to 3rd Bn, 68th ADA BN.

Awards/Medals: WWII Victory, Army Occupation, Nat Def w/OLC, Good Conduct, Vietnam Svc, Vietnam Campaign, ETO, American Campaign, Bronze Star w/OLC, 20 year Army Reserve. Retired Oct 1, 1979, as CW3.

Married Florence Head Aug 18, 1947, has two children and four grandchildren.

JOHN B. ALLNATT, CW4, born Richmond, England. Attended St Paul's School and HM S Worcester. Joined first ship as a 4th officer February 1945. Sailed on Persian Gulf-India-USA run. Immigrated to USA May 1947 (naturalized USA citizen May 1949) and spent many years in travel industry.

Enlisted in NJNG July 1951; commissioned 2LT, MPC, October 1953, Co A, 161st MP BN. Became ill with tuberculosis until May 1961. Appointed W01 December 1961 as vessel master, 362nd Trans Co, USAR. Unit deactivated and transferred to 306th MP DET USAR as criminal investigator. Transferred to the 12th Spec Forces Gp (abn) USAR as property book officer; attended Supply Mangagement School, Ft Lee, VA, 1968.

Approved for active duty December 1968, served as supply inspector, USA Garrison, Ft MacArthur, CA until August 1970. Went to Vietnam as PBO, 1/11th Inf Bn, 1st Bde, 5th Inf Div (mechanic), Quang Tri Cbt Base. Transferred to Germany September 1971. PBO 2/13th Inf Bn, 8th Inf Div. Extended tour in June 1974 as PBO, Army Mat Mgmt Agency Eur and retired August 1977.

President Zweibruecken Ch USAWOA, 1975-76; president European Region USAWOA, 1976-77. Originally joined Mannheim Ch, European WOA in 1972.

Awards/Medals: Bronze Star, Meritorious Svc, Army Commendation and various US and British Campaign awards.

After retirement attended post graduate courses in management studies in England; graduated June 1980. Wrote and directed courses in basic supervisory techniques for Jamaican Government employees in Kingston. December 1980 accepted post with the Industrial Society in London, England as course director. Opened first overseas office for them in Nassau, Bahamas as Caribbean Regional Director September 1983.

Retired from active business April 1993. Continues part-time as adjunct professor, School of Business and Industry, Miami-Dade Community College. He is life member of USAWOA, ROA; member of The Institute of Management (London) and The Institute of Directors (London).

RICKIE J. AMERICA, CW2, USA (ACT RES), born Dec 6, 1950, to Clarence and Mildred America of Muirkirk, MD and raised in Beltsville, MD. Drafted and began Army career on March 21, 1970.

Received basic training at Ft Dix, NJ and assigned to 6/1 Armd Cav, Ft Hood, TX. Joined active Reserve July 1973. Assigned to 2122nd US Army Garrison, Baltimore, MD as unit supply sergeant. September 1980 assigned to the 220th MP BDE, Gaithersburg, MD as chief supply sergeant. February 1985 assigned to 450th CA Co, Riverdale, MD as Co 1SG. He achieved the ranks of SSG, SFC, MSG and 1SG.

Enlisted schools completed were: QM Supply Crs, Senior NCO Crs, 1SG Crs, 95B MP Crs and the enlisted CA Crs. Applied and met the qualification to be WOC for QM Supply under the new program, Total WO System. Completed WO Tech Tactical Certification Crs June 15, 1990, and commissioned property accounting technician, 920A.

Called to active duty December 1990 for Operation Desert Shield/Storm. Served with 82nd Abn Div in Saudi Arabia. Assigned to 2070th USAR School, Ft Belvoir, VA as certified instructor for Logistics. Presently assigned to 400th MP BN, Ft Gen Meade, MD as battalion property accounting tech.

Awards/Medals: Kuwait Lib Med, AR Comp Overseas Trng Rib, Overseas Svc Rib, Army Svc Rib, NCOPDR w/4, Armed Forces Res Med w/HG, Humanitarian Svc Med, SWA Svc Med, Nat Defe Svc Med w/Bronze Star, AR Comp Achiev Med, Good Conduct Med, Army Achiev Med w/2 OLCs, Army Comm Med w/2 OLCs and Army Lapel Button.

Employed as postmaster, Upper Marlboro, MD, with over 25 years with the USPS. Received a BS degree in business management from the Univ of Maryland, University College. Married Patricia Stroud and has two wonderful children, Wendy and Rickie Jr. Hobbies are basketball, gospel singing and playing both lead and bass guitars.

CARL S. ANDERSON, CW3, USA (RET),born March 24, 1933, Detroit, MI. Graduated from Univ of Florida with BBA. Drafted October 1954, served with HQ 376th Abn, FA BN, and 82nd Admin Co, 82nd Abn Div upon completion of basic training, artillery AIT and parachutist training. Separated from the service October 1956.

Re-enlisted May 1960. Served enlisted assignments as personnel or administrative NCO; 82nd Admin Co, 82nd Abn Div, 1960-1961; AG Div, HQ USAREUR, 1961-1963; HQ SACOM, Munich, Germany, 1963-1964; HQ CO, US Army Garrison, Ft Carson, CO, 1964; Co C, 6th Spec Forces Gp, 1965; HQ MACV, Saigon, 1965-1966; HQ CC, USA JFK Ctr for Special Warfare, Ft Bragg, 1966-67; HQ 18th Abn Corps, Ft Bragg, 1967-69.

Appointed W-1 February 1969 as unit personnel tech and attended Unit Personnel Officer Crs at Ft Benjamin Harrison during same year. Served as general staff administrative tech with following units subsequent to appointment: HQ, 18th Abn Corps, Ft Bragg, 1969; HQ II Field Force, Vietnam, 1970; Office of Chief of Staff, SHAPE, Belgium, 1971-74; Ballistic Missile Defense Program Office, OCSA, Pentagon, 1975-76; HQ, 1st USA, Ft Meade, 1976-78. Retired from service November 1978.

Awards/Medals: Bronze Star, Meritorious Svc, Joint Svc Comm, Army Comm w/3 OLCs, Nat Def Svc, Meritorious Unit Comm, Prcht Badge, Vietnam Svc Med, Vietnam Campaign w/60 device, Vietnam Civil Actions Honor Med First Class, Vietnam Gallantry Cross w/palm (2nd Awd) and a Good Conduct Med w/Bronze Clasp.

Married Joyce Ann Screws of Friendship, TN. Active in USAWOA since the formation of ACE Ch at SHAPE, Belgium in 1972. Served as national treasurer 1976-78 and 1984-85. Currently working for state of Pennsylvania and residing in New Cumberland, PA.

RICK F. ANDREWS, CW5, born Sept 13, 1946, Wilmington, DE. Entered active Army December 1966 with basic training at Ft Polk, LA; Flight School, Ft Wolter's, TX and Ft Rucker, AL. Graduated Dec 14, 1967; went to Vietnam until January 1969. Assigned as aircraft commander, maintenance officer with 191st AHC (Boomerangs) in III Corps, located at Bear Cat and Dong Tam, RVN. Assigned to 6th Cav, Air Cav Trp, Ft Meade, MD. Completed active duty Sept 13, 1970.

Joined DEARNG February 1972, served as rotary wing instructor pilot and fixed wing aviator until conditional release to NJARNG in January 1981. With NJNG as technician flight instructor and instrument flight examiner until the Title 10 tour with the NG Bureau. July 1992 assigned to the ARNG Avn and Safety Directorate as a special project officer and as aviation standardization and training officer.

Awards/Medals: Soldiers Med, Meritorious Svc and Air Med w/V.

Special memory as WO was to be the national program manager for ARNG Aviation Standardization, and to do so as a CW5 is an unsurpassed experience.

Married Dorothy Andrews of Ridley Township, PA and has one daughter, Kristin.

BILL L. ARMOUR, CW4, RA (RET), born June 22, 1931, Hooker County, NE, the youngest of five boys. Enlisted in USAF Oct 11, 1950, with 1st Computations Sq (later became 1370th Photo Mapping Gp) completed the first known Geodetic tie of Africa, Europe and North America. Retrained in crypto/communications maintenance, security service in Tokyo; IBM computer system analyst in Air Defense.

Became readiness officer of first COSTAR unit in Army, taking it to Vietnam. Commander of 56-man unit attached with 11th Armd Cav Swan Loc; commander of 34-man unit attached with 9th Div and Thai Div; commander of 72-man unit attached with 1st Inf at Lai Khe. Bootstrap to UofNE for BGS degree. Soc Trang Vietnam with 13th Avn Bn. Germany 11th Sig (three years); MS (mgt) UofArk; 134th Sig (four years) Stuttgart. Commander of DOD main satellite terminal in Maryland (Presidential hot line to Moscow). Retired in 1980 with 30 years of service.

Awards/Medals: Bronze Star w/2 OLCs, Meritorious Svc, Air Med, Purple Heart, Army Comm, Good Conduct w/4 kts, several service and campaign medals w/8 Battle Stars, Pres Unit Cit, Valorous Unit Awd, Meritorious Unit Cit w/OLC, Vietnamese Pres. Unit Cit, Vietnamese Cross of Gallantry w/palm, Viet Civil Action Hon Med first class, Air Force Outstanding Unit Awd w/2 OLCs.

Started a WOA at Ft Hood in 1966. One of the original members who met in Mannheim in October 1971 to form the EuRegWOA. President of the Stuttgart Chapter for two years, founder of Bad Canstatt Chapter. Lifetime member of USAWOA #22.

Started a turkey breeding business in North Carolina, sold out and retired second time in 1986. Retired third time in January 1994. A 32° Mason, Shriner, pilot and commander of SE Reg of Scottish American Military Society.

Married Maureen Mahoney of St Petersburg, FL, and has four sons (one is a Vietnam veteran) and six grandchildren (five boys and one girl).

MARVIN R. ATKINS, CW4, USA (RET), born Aug 21, 1941, Greenup County, KY. Entered Army Feb 4, 1960, Hagerstown, MD. Basic training at Ft Jackson, SC. Served as tracked vehicle mechanic during the early 1960s with the 4th Inf Div and the 11th Armd Cav Regt. Served from August 1965-1968 as aircraft crewman, mechanic, and inspector with the 10th Avn Bn and the 1st Cav Div in Vietnam.

He was Service School instructor at Trans School during the late 1960s and the Army Ord Ctr and School during the 1980s. In addition to Vietnam, spent tours in Germany, Korea and Okinawa.

Appointed W01 in 1976 as automotive maintenance tech assigned to the 3rd Armd Div in Friedberg, Germany. Retired in 1991 after 31 and a half years at APG, MD.

Awards/Medals: Legion of Merit, Bronze Star, Meritorious Svc w/5 OLCs and various other medals.

Holds Master degree in business and Maryland State Vocational Teacher's Certificate. Married Kay Avington of Weston, WV and has two children. Currently employed as the maintenance manager of FMC's Bradley Fighting Vehicle Project in Saudi Arabia. Hobby is woodworking. Future plans are to complete doctorate degree at Temple University.

SHERRY JOYCE MORREY-AUGSBURGER, MAJ, born Nov 25, 1949, Austin, TX. Enlisted USAF 1968; served as inventory management specialist, 1968-1972. Attended Rutgers University, New Brunswick, NJ, obtained BA degree in psychology, 1975.

Attended Physician Assistant (PA) Program, Univ of Texas Medical Branch. Graduated August 1978 with BS degree in health care sciences and certificate as a primary care PA. Served as member of TXARNG as medic during two years of PA training.

Joined Army as WO1 PA October 1978. Served in HHB 1/41 FA (Pershing Missiles), Schwaebisch Gmuend, Germany as battalion surgeon 1978-81. Secretary, then president, of the Schwaebisch Gmuend Ch. Second tour as PA in Troop Medical Clinic at Eisenhower Army Med Ctr. Returned to Germany October 1983, assigned to 547th Gen Disp, Grafenwohr.

Returned to States January 1987. Attended Army Med Dept Officer Advance Crs, Ft Sam Houston, followed with tour as instructor of PA Training Program. Performed special mission at the Officer Procurement Div, Health Professionals Support Agency, Office of the Army Surgeon Gen, the Pentagon, 1990.

Completed MA degree in health systems management at Webster University, December 1990. Promoted to major Feb 4, 1992.

Served as Army Med Dept Regimental Adj, Ft Sam Houston, TX and promoted sense of family among medical personnel and educated Army and public on proud traditions of Army medicine.

Returned to PA Training Program August 1994. Future challenges include the assimilation of the AF and USN PA training programs into a single tri-service program hosted by the Army at Ft Sam Houston.

Awards/Medals: Meritorious Svc Med w/OLC, ARCOM w/2 OLCs, Army Achiev Med, Nat Def Svc Med w/star, AF Good Conduct, AF Outstanding Unit Awd, (2) Overseas Ribbons, Army Svc Rib, Expert Field Medical Badge and Order of Military Medical Merit.

Her military memberships include USAWOA, Society of Army Physician Assistants and the Association of Military Surgeons of the US.

Married to Maj Russell Augsburger of the Med Svc Corps. Retired from the Army and currently an attorney in San Antonio, TX.

WILLIAM B. AUMAN, CW3, USA (RET), born July 25, 1931, Bellefonte, PA. Entered USN March 1949; Army in April 1951; the USAF in April 1954. Returned to Army in April 1958. Served as seaman, infantryman, microwave tech, air traffic controller, GCA instructor, flight tech, personnel and administrative tech.

Assignments at Camp Cook, CA; Camp Wood, Ft Monmouth, NJ; Bolling AFB, DC; Dover AFB, DE; Olmstead AFB, PA; Ft Jackson, SC; Ft Eustis, VA; and multi-overseas tours to Korea, Germany, Japan and Vietnam.

Awards/Medals: Bronze Star, Meritorious Svc, Army Comm w/OLC, Army and AF Good Conduct Medals and numerous badges, service and campaign medals with Battle Stars. Retired January 1972 as assignment management officer of Army Trans Ctr, Ft Eustis, VA. Retired from Army Civil Service October 1991.

Resides on Gulf Coast of Dixie County, FL with wife, Barbara Burnham, of Jasper, FL. They have three sons and three grandchildren.

HARLEY B. BACK, CWO3, born in Menetee County, KY. Enlisted in the service Nov 8, 1936, and served with the 1st Armd Div, 1st Ranger Bn during WWII and 101st Abn Div, from 1951-53 for Korean War. Stationed at Ft Knox, KY; Ireland; Scotland; North Africa; Sicily; Italy; Germany and France. He participated in battles in North Africa; Tunisia; Sicily; Italy; ETO, Germany and France.

Memorable experiences: the period at El Guettar, Tunisia with the 1st Ranger Bn; while a POW and being rescued by British engineers March 11, 1943.

Retired from HQ 101st Abn Div, Ft Campbell, KY on May 1, 1965, with the rank of CWO-3. Awards include Bronze Star w/OLC, Purple Heart w/OLC, Army Comm, POW Med, Good Conduct, Pres Unit Emblem, Am Def Svc Med, Am Camp Med, EAME Camp Med, WWII Victory Med, Korean Svc Med, Combat Inf Badge, French Fourragere, UN Svc Med and Honorable Svc Lapel Button WWII.

Married Irene and has one son Steven. He is retired from civil service.

DARYL G. BAKER, CW3(R), born March 24, 1951, Redding, CA. Enlisted in Army May 5, 1968, as mechanical maintenance tech. Stationed at Camp Grieves, Korea; 3 AD Butzbach Frg; 1st AD Nuremberg; maintenance officer at Ft Ord, CA; the Netherlands and Vietnam (three campaigns).

Memorable experiences were working with and training all of the fine soldiers he served with.

Awards/Medals: (2) Meritorious Svc Med, (3) Army Comm Med, (3) Army Achiev Med, (3) Army Good Conduct, (2) Vietnam Svc Med, Army Svc Rib, Overseas Svc Rib, NOOR and the Vietnam Cross of Gallantry. Discharged March 1, 1990, with rank CW3.

Has wife Dola, three children and two grandchildren. In building repair and small engine repair business.

FRANKLIN L. BAKER, CW4, USA (RET), born May 27, 1933, Arapahoe, CO. Entered Army August 1952. Basic and AIT (radar operator), Ft Bliss, TX. Served latter part of Korean War as radar operator with AAA Gun Bn.

Returned to States, assigned to AAA Gun Bn, Washington, DC area. Attended Radar Maintenance Crs, Ft Bliss, TX. Appointed WO W1, Aug 1, 1957.

Next 22 years served tours in the States, Taiwan, Europe and Vietnam at all levels in air defense from battery to Army Air Defense Cmd, including North America Air Defense Cmd and as instructor at Army Air Defense School. June 1979 was assigned to MILPERSCOM, WO Div, as career manager for Air Defense WOs. From 1982 until retirement January 1989, with over 36 years of active service, of which 31 of those years were served as WO, he served as the technical services branch chief in WO Div.

Awards/Medals: Legion of Merit, Bronze Star, Meritorious Svc, Joint Svc Comm and the Army Comm Medals.

A military personnel management specialist with the Adjutant General Directorate, Total Army Personnel Cmd in Alexandria, VA where he resides.

HELENE A. SCHIMEK BAKER, CW4(L), IRR, IMA, USAR, born April 30, 1945, Chicago, IL. Entered USWAC July 1963, taking basic training at Ft McClellan, AL and personnel administration schooling, Ft Knox, KY. Completed training the sad day President Kennedy died. Traveling the next day to her assigned duty in Washington, DC, Maryland area, found all transportation lines disrupted and unscheduled. Final transportation by bus was determined by asking each bus driver which direction Edgewood Arsenal, MD was in.

Arriving at a roadside diner near midnight at Edgewood Road, uncertainties still existed until assisted by a courteous diner patron. Served in AG sections and 1st-2nd Army CID Office at Edgewood Arsenal, MD until discharged July 1966. Advanced to SP5, re-enlisted for tour in Germany with critical occupational skills September 1966. Arrived Bad Canstatt in time to add one qualifying team member to play and receive 2nd place in the USWAC championship basketball.

Misassigned with critical occupational skills, was transferred to HQ, 2nd Gen Hosp-Landstuhl serving in deployment and headquarters duties. Received ACM for chief clerk, adjutant and XO duties performed by vacated personnel rotating to Vietnam. Transferring Stateside, completed re-enlisted period at Fitzsimmons Gen Hosp, Aurora, CO where she administered medical discharges and veterans affairs until Sept 1969. A new era began by watching man televised "walking on the moon" while on NCOIC duty.

Re-entered USAR October 1974, served HQ, 801st Gen Hosp and 30th Hosp Ctr, Ft Sheridan, IL. Transferred to 18th PSYOP Co Chicago, IL upon obtaining the Army supply technician civil service position. Using active duty skills assisted her in obtaining the unit an OIG outstanding rating. Received direct appointment to WO1 Jan 11, 1979, as supply officer with 18th PSYOP CO.

Transferred 1980 to Individual Ready Reserves, Individual Mobilization Augmentee, Directorate of Contracting, HQ, USAG, Ft Sam Houston, TX. Indirectly supporting Desert Shield while on annual training. While waiting for IMA to call-up, found out funding was being used to send desperately needed water technicians to Saudi Arabia. Completed various military logistics and financial schooling to include depot operations, contracting, resource management, comptrollership courses and graduate studies. Addressed to Congress and the President of the US a study on implementing a reimbursable welfare package plan.

Member of USAWOA-Pentagon, ROA and Marauder Squadron Composite, CAP, Porter, TX. Obtained BA degree from Northeastern Illinois University, CFE. Awards/Medals: Army Comm, Army Res Achiev, Good Conduct w/2nd awd, Nat Def, Armed Forces Res, Army Svc Rib, Overseas Rib, City of Chicago Citation-Election Board, US Dept of the Army Outstanding Performance Awd and Dept of Interior, Minerals Management Svc, Spec Achiev Awds.

Married George Baker of Hanover Park, IL. They reside in Humble, TX. Has three sisters, two nephews, two nieces, four step-sons and a step-grandson residing in Chicago, IL. Employed as lead auditor, DOI, MMS, Houston, TX. Hobbies include continuous education classes and traveling. Highlighting activity was attending Veterans Celebration during the 1993 Presidential Convention at the Astrodome, Houston, TX and obtaining autographs of Sen John McCain, Pat Robertson and Arnold Schwarzenegger.

ALBERT W. BAMSCH JR., CW4, USA, born June 28, 1952, Barstow, CA. Entered Army Sept 3, 1970. Stationed at Ft Lewis, WA for basic; AIT, Ft Ord, CA; March

1971-June 1971, 93rd Evac Hosp, Ft Leonard Wood, MO; June 1971-March 1972, A/62nd Engr Bn, RVN; April 1972-August 1975, C Co/D Co, 52nd Engr Bn, Ft Carson, CO; September 1975-August 1978, D Co, 249th Engr Bn, Karlsruhe, Germany; September 1978-March 1979, 7th MI CO, Ft Ord, CA; April 1979-September 1984, D Co, 249th Engr Bn.

Appointed WO1 Feb 2, 1980, transferred to HQ Co, 78th Engr Bn, Karlsruhe, Germany B Co; February 1982, 79th Engr Bn; September 1984-March 1985, WO Advance Crs; April 1984-November 1986, A Co, 864th Engr Bn, Ft Lewis, WA; December 1986-October 1992, 16th Engr Bn, Germany-SWA; November 1992, assigned to 317th Maint Co, Nuremberg, Germany.

Awards/Medals: Bronze Star, Army Comm w/3 OLCs, Army Achiev w/2 OLCs, Good Conduct (4th awd), Nat Def w/star, Vietnam Campaign Rib w/2 stars, SW Asia w/3 stars, NCOPDR, Army Svc Rib, Overseas Rib, Vietnam Svc Rib, Kuwit Lib Med. Citations include: Vietnam Cross of Gallantry w/palm and Unit Valor Awd.

Married Jan Benton of Widefield, CO. Life member of USAWOA and VFW Post 03885.

DARRELL L. BARBER SR., CW4, USA (RET), born June 14, 1931, Idaho Falls, ID. Entered Army Dec 6, 1949, taking basic training at Ft Ord, CA. Graduated from Jump/Glider School, Ft Benning, GA June 16, 1950. Assigned to 82nd Abn Div, Prcht Maint Co. Served as aerial resupply tech during Korean Conflict with QM Abn Air Sup and Pkg Co, 8081st Army Unit, Ashiya AB, Japan.

After tour with 505th QM Co, 55th QM Depot Korea, reassigned to Japan in 549th QM Co (Air Supply). Deployed 1958 with 549th to Tai Chung AB, Taiwan, where instructed ROC soldiers' rigging procedures for dropping door bundles from C-46 and C-47 aircraft to off-shore islands of Matsu and Quemoy during Red Chinese bombardment. Returned to States 1961 and assigned to Army Depot, Memphis, TN (Sup and Maint Cmd) Abn Equip Det, moved with them to Army Depot, Atlanta, GA.

Appointed WO February 1966 as Prcht Rigger Warrant and assigned to 82nd QM Co, 82nd Abn Div, Ft Bragg, NC. Tours included Co C, 173rd Spt Bn, 173rd Abn Bde (SEP), RVN, 1967-68; 11th QM Co (AES) 8th Inf Div, Germany, 1968-69; AES Co, 15th S&S Bn, 1st Cav Div (airmobile) RVN, 1969-70. While assigned to 1st SFG Okinawa, ordered to Clark AB, Republic of the Philippines, as part of Army Homecoming Team, Operation Homecoming, POW release, January-April 1973.

Returned to States 1974 and assigned to USAG Presidio of San Francisco Parachute Shop for support of 6th Army Area. Inducted Nov 18, 1977, and placed on Honor Roll of Prcht Rigger WO Hall of Fame, Ft Lee, VA. Retired at Ft Hood, TX, Dec 31, 1979, with 30 years of service, of which 29 and a half were on jump status.

Awards/Medals: Bronze Star, Meritorious Svc w/OLC, Nat Def Svc, Air Med, Army Comm w/2 OLCs, Korean Svc w/4 Bronze Stars, Good Conduct w/clasp, Bronze 3 loops, Army Occupation (Japan), Armed Forces Exped w/Bronze Svc Star, Vietnam Svc w/1 Silver and (2) Bronze Svc Stars, Meritorious Unit Comm, Vietnam Cross of Gallantry w/ Palm, RVN Campaign Med, UN Svc Med, Master Parachutist Wings, Glider Wings and Prcht Rigger Badge.

Employed by Vinnell Corp, working in Kingdom of Saudi Arabia instructing Logistics to Saudi Arabian NG. Medically evacuated 1985, with non-Hodgkin's Lymphoma cancer, back to States. Retired again and resides in Harker Heights, TX, with his wife, Fumiyo Fujise of Kyushu, Japan. They have three children. Lifetime member of DAV, TROA,

Spec Ops Assoc, 82nd Abn Div Hist Soc, 82nd Abn Div Assoc, International Assoc of Abn Vets, Century Club, and the 1st SFG. Hobbies are fishing, traveling and jumping (last jumped in 1989).

HOYT F. BARBOUR, CW4, AUS (RET), born Aug 20, 1914, Chillicothe, OH. Enlisted in Reg Army November 1936 with Co B, 10th Inf and Finance Office, 5th Corps area. Discharged January 1939 to accept civil svc position in the finance office, 5th Corps area. Appointed WOJG May 15, 1942, Ft Hayes, Columbus, OH. Assigned to 29th Finance Disbursing Sect September 1942.

Served in North Africa and Italy during WWII. Returned to States in November 1945. Assigned to 37th Inf Div, OHARNG October 1947 as administrative assistant to chief of staff. Recalled to active duty with 37th Inf Div, 1951-1953. Returned to NG status until retirement, August 1974, with over 36 years of service. Retired from the civil service in December 1968. Employed by state of Ohio as fiscal officer until December 1980.

Member of ROA, TROA, NGA of the US, NGA of Ohio, USAWOA, Assoc of the US Army and the NRA.

Married to Marian Von Driska of Hilliard, OH, has eight children and 11 grandchildren.

JAMES MCCLURE BARKER, CW2, AUS (RET), born Aug 18, 1934, Pueblo, CO and currently lives in Leavenworth, KS. MI Order of Battle Tech. Enlisted in Army October 1952. Initially trained as FA survey specialist. Received warrant in 1969.

Education includes: Army FA Survey Crs, 43rd Inf Div FA Fire Direction Crs, 7th Army NCO Academy, Army FA Ops and Intel Crs, Army Intel Analysts Crs, 7th Army CBR Crs, Army Unit Supply Crs, Def Dept Computer Security Crs and Programming and various USAF and Def Dept Programming Crs.

During early 1970s was instrumental in formation of WO organizations at Ft Bragg, NC and Heidelberg, Germany. Was first secretary and second president of Heidelberg Ch of USAWOA. Late 1970s was active with Sooner Plains Ch, Ft Sill, OK with terms as secretary and president. Was recording secretary 1978 for USAWOA National Convention held at San Antonio, TX.

Awards/Medals: Legion of Merit, (5) Army Comm, Good Conduct (5 awds), Nat Def Svc w/OLC, Army Occupation Med (Germany), Vietnam Svc Med, (2) Overseas Bars, RVN Campaign Med, RVN Gallantry Cross Unit Cit w/Palm.

Completed college at Cameron University. Obtained degree in business administration with data processing and secondary education track. Did his graduate work at Oklahoma Christian University and worked for several years as an operations analyst, systems engineer, project group leader, software product testing, configuration, and quality assurance branch managers and support division manager. Had his own business providing consultant, turn key computer and software service and support, as well as related services. Currently under contract as quality assurance manager for NATIONS, Inc at Ft Leavenworth, KS.

Became active in partisan politics, including a run at elective office. Was Comanche County, OK Republican Chm for two terms and Republican Chm for 4th Congressional Dist of Oklahoma for one term. Served as Long Range Planning Committee Chm for Republican Party for state of Oklahoma four years. Has been active within the Methodist Church for several years and is a certified lay speaker. Retired after nearly 25 years of service as a CW2(P), to Lawton, OK. Resides in Leavenworth, KS.

Married to the late Edith Marie Blakey for 27 years. She passed away in 1984. They had two children, James Michael and Brigitte Ann. Married to Deborah Lynn Wilson and has one child, Sarah Elizabeth.

GEORGE E. BARTON JR., CW4, USA (RET), born May 25, 1927, Charleston, SC. Enlisted in USN July 31, 1944. Completed boot camp at Camp Perry, VA. Served aboard USS *West Point* troop transport from 1944 until it was decommissioned at the end of WWII. Remained in USNR until 1955, then transferred to USAR as MSG-E7. Ap-

pointed WOW1 in 1957; resigned as CW2 to accept 1SG-E8 in 1965; 1969 promoted to SGM-E9 at HQ, 120th ARCOM; reappointed CW2 in 1971; promoted to CW4 in 1978.

Called to active duty in AGR Program in 1983 at HQ 157th Sept Inf Bde and served until 1985, transferred to HQ 120th ARCOM. Retired from AGR in 1987; from USAR in 1988; served more than 44 years in Active and Reserve duty.

Awards/Medals: Legion of Merit, Meritorious Svc Med w/3 OLCs, Army Comm Med w/OLC, Army Achiev Med, EAME Campaign Med and the Asiatic-Pacific Campaign Med.

Married the former Jennie Ackerman of Cottageville, SC. They have three sons and seven grandchildren.

PETER WILLIAM BASKER, CW3, born July 29 1945, Honolulu, HI. Entered the Army Feb 13, 1974. Received basic training at Ft Leonard Wood, MO and AIT at Ft Lee, VA. Served as cook, first cook and shift leader at Yuma Proving Ground, AZ, and Karlsruhe, Germany with the 78th Engr Bn and DIVARTY, 7th Inf Div, Ft Ord, CA (1974-83). Served as dining facility manager with 3rd Ar Div at Kirchgoens, Germany (1983-84).

Appointed WO CW2 Oct 26, 1984, following training at Ft Rucker, AL and Ft Lee, VA. Served as installation food advisor at Ft McClellan, AL (March 1985-April 1990); and command food advisor with 32nd Army Air Def Cmd at Darmstadt, Germany (April 1990-December 1992). Currently serving as installation food advisor at Ft Gordon, GA.

Awards/Medals: Meritorious Svc Med w/OLC, Army Comm Med w/4 OLCs, Army Achiev Med, Good Conduct Med, Nat Def Svc Med w/star, NCOPDR, Army Svc Rib and Overseas Rib.

Member of the USAWOA, AOQM and the ACF.

Married Charlene Hardy and has three children, one step-son and one grandchild. Hobbies include gourmet cooking, culinary arts, running and stamp collecting.

WILLARD W. BATIEN (BILLY), CWO4, USA, born Sept 2, 1947, San Francisco, CA, grew up in Appomattox, VA. Joined the Army June 6, 1966, with 915E Ord Corps. Appointed to WO May 23, 1979.

Awards/Medals: (2) Meritorious Svc, (2) Nat Def, (5) Army Comm, (1) Joint Svc Comm, (2) Army Achiev, (5) Army Good Conduct, (2) SWA Bronze Star, (1) AFEM, (1) Army Svc Rib, (2) Overseas Rib and Driver/Mechanic Badge.

Married Mindy Sulman. Has four children from previous marriage: Nicole, Jessica, Shawn and Stephanie. Still on active duty assigned to HQ CMD, Armed Forces in South Naples, Italy. Next assignment will be to Army Material Cmd, Alexandria, VA.

RAYMOND A. BELL, entered military service December 1963 with the 38th Inf Div, INNG. Ordered to active duty by Presidential direction in 1968, deployed to Ft Carson, CO as supply sergeant of the 890th Trans Co, USAR, Ft Wayne, IN. Promoted to staff sergeant with this unit, converted to the

RA in 1969 when the unit returned to Reserve status.

While a NCO, he served in various supply positions with combat and combat support units in Vietnam and Germany. In December 1974 he was appointed WO1. As WO he held two specialties, organizational supply tech and supply systems tech. Served in 299th Engr Bn; 394th Trans Bn (AVIM); 800th Mat Mgmt Ctr; 2nd Spt Ctr; 528th Arty Gp; Information Systems Cmd, Pentagon; 22nd Sig Bde; and Office of the dep chief of staff for personnel, HQDA. Bell was designated as MWO as member of the last MWO Class in September 1993.

Awards/Medals: Bronze Star, Meritorious Svc Med w/ 3 OLCs, Army Achiev Med w/4 OLCs and various service and campaign ribbons.

Bell and wife, Frances (LTC, USA), reside in Fairfax, VA.

CLARENCE E. BENNETT, CW4, USAR (RET), born April 9, 1927, Cleveland, OH. Began military career in USN. Enlisted May 12, 1944. Became engineer in landing craft on USS *Hocking* APA-121. Participated in landings at Iwo Jima and Okinawa. Received an honorable discharge May 24, 1946.

Enlisted Jan 9, 1947, in USMC. After boot camp at Parris Island, transferred to Camp Lejeune, NC, became criminal investigator in Prov Marshal's office. Received honorable discharge Jan 8, 1950.

Enlisted June 26, 1950, in Army as criminal investigator and sent to Camp Fuji, Japan as infantryman with A Co, 17th Inf Regt, 7th US Inf Div. From August 1950-November 1951, he served in Korea as infantry assistant platoon and platoon sergeant.

Returned to Conus, November 1951-January 1953. Served as criminal investigator in Prov Marshal's office, Camp Breckinridge, KY. Requested transfer to Germany and served from January-June 1953, assigned to 109th Cbt Engrs, Kaferta, Germany. Received honorable discharge June 4, 1953.

August 1953, he enlisted in USAR and assigned to 406th MP CID, Cleveland, OH. Became 1st sergeant and applied for WO in 1957. Became WO1, March 2, 1959. Unit was deactivated. Assigned to the 83rd Inf Div, Prov Marshal's office, as criminal investigator. Unit deactivated March 1963 and assigned to 342nd MI Co, Cleveland, OH as counter-intelligence agent until July 1969.

Transferred to the 259th MI GP, Sharonville, OH until 1974. At that time unit was redesignated 259th MI Co. Reassigned to 342nd MI Co, Cleveland where he stayed until his retirement in April 1987 with almost 42 years of Active and Reserve duty.

Active duty stations were for a month at a time while in the USAR at the 109th MI GP, Ft Mead, MD which later became designated the 902nd MI GP. The 470th MI GP Panama Canal Zone, the 101st Air Assault, Ft Campbell, KY. The Pentagon Counter-Intellence Forces; USN Counter Insurgency School, Coronado, CA; 107th ACR NG Unit, Ohio; Joint Chief of Staff Office, Pentagon, Washington DC; Camp Ripley, MNNG Unit. Duties during assignments were as agent or counter part training or instructor, Intell Subjects, Sec Mgr - Sect Chief.

Awards/Medals: Cbt Inf Badge, Legion of Merit, Bronze Star w/V Device, Army Comm, Army Achievment, USMC Good Conduct, Army Good Conduct, Armed Forces Res Med w/3X, American Theater, Asiatic-Pacific Med w/ 2 Battle Stars, China Svc Med, Occupation Med, WWII Victory Med, Nat Def, Korean Svc Med w/6 Battle Stars, UN Med, Army Res Achievment Med, AR Res Overseas Med, Army Res Svc Rib and Korean Pres Rib.

Married Eleanore Feb 6, 1954.

DALE M. BERG, CW5, born March 29, 1947. Enlisted at San Rafael, CA, August 1965. Received basic training at Ft Ord; AIT at Ft Rucker; Flight School CL 66-13; Vietnam 174th Avn Co, 1966-67; Ft Wolters IP Flt B-11 1968-69.

Reserves, 90th Div Trng, Presidio SF 1970; AMOC then Vietnam C Trp Maint 3/17 Air Cav, 1971; Germany Inst IP/Maint two SUPCOM Flt Det 1972-75; Adv Crs then Ft Ord GS Co 7th Avn Bn Maint, 1976-79; Korea B Trp Maint 4/7 Air Cav, 1979-80; Ft Ord E Co Maint 7th Avn Bn, 1980-83; Ft Gillem 2nd Army CART Team, 1983-87; HQ DA TWOS Team Staff, 1987-88; MWOT & MAM Crs then Ft Eustis USAALS Staff, 1989-92; Germany 70 Trans Bn DCO staff.

Promotions: WO1, 1966; CW2, 1968; CW3, 1972; CW4, 1978; MW4, 1988; and CW5, 1992.

Awards/Medals (6) Meritorious Svc Med, (28) Air Medals, ARCOM, (2) Army Achiev Med and Master Army Aviator.

Married Mary Casciano, of Phoebus, VA, and has two sons, Douglas and Russell.

JAMES R. BERG, CW3, USA (RET), born June 1, 1944, Joplin, MO, raised in Antioch, IL. Graduated from Campion High School, Prairie du Chien, WI, 1962. Married Elizabeth Ann McBride from Duluth, MN in May 1967. Entered the Army in Waukeegan, IL July 1967. Attended basic training at Ft Leonard Wood, MO and AIT (utility helicopter mechanic and LOH mechanic) at Ft Eustis, VA.

Held various capacities in helicopter maintenance until accepted into the Nuclear Power Plant Operator Course at Ft Belvoir, VA in October 1976, where he was 1st Honor Graduate in October 1977. Final assignment in aviation was as member of the Army Avn Precision Helicopter Demonstration Team (Silver Eagles) where he served as crew chief. Was Honor Graduate from both the 3rd Army NCO Academy in February 1970 and the Avn Maint Sr NCO Crs at Ft Eustis, VA in February 1976.

Accepted appointment as WO in August 1978. Served as utility operations and maintenance tech. Assignments included the 10th CSH/MASH, Ft Meade, MD; HQ, Allied Land Forces Southeastern Europe, Izmir, Turkey; and Ft Hood, TX where he served in the 21st Evac Hosp, the Directorate of Engineering and Housing and HQ, TEXCOM. Retired from active duty Jan 31, 1990.

Awarded BA degree, Magna Cum Laude, in management studies from the Univ of Maryland June 1, 1986, and MS with a concentration in computer information systems management from the Univ of Central Texas August 1988.

Awards/Medals: Bronze Star, Meritorious Def Svc Med, Army Meritorious Svc Med, Army Comm w/2 OLCs, Joint Svcs Achiev Med, Army Good Conduct 3rd awd, Nat Def Svc Med, Vietnam Svc Med w/6 campaigns, Vietnamese Campaign Med, Senior Acft Crewmember Badge, Excellence in Competition Badge (pistol) and the Nuclear Reactor Operator Badge (basic).

He is a widower living in Austin, TX. Was recognized as a certified plant engineer in December 1993 by the American Institute of Plant Engineers. Joined the WOA in the Spring of 1979 and holds Charter Life Member Card #192.

MICHAEL J. BERKERY, CW4, born July 9, 1923, Brooklyn, NY. Enlisted in Army Sept 6, 1940. Participated in the Aluetian Island and Europe invasions.

Memorable experiences were taking back the Aluetian Island and Europe under combat conditions. Awarded the ETO, Asiatic Theater, American Theater, Meritorious Svc Awd. Discharged Aug 9, 1945 with rank CW4.

Berkery re-enlisted in Reserves in 1948 and completed 20 years of service. Very active in the VFW and American Legion activities.

PAUL BERRY, CW3, born July 15, 1917, Plumer, PA. Enlisted Oct 30, 1935, with Co K, 35th Inf, Schofield Bks, HI. Discharged June 3, 1938, as corporal. Graduated Army Admin School. Re-enlisted March 15, 1939, Ft Niagara, NY, with 28th Inf. December 1940 the regiment moved to Ft Jackson, SC.

Overseas to North Africa with 2nd Gp Regulating Stations, TC March 1943. Discharged Sept 24, 1943, to accept WO and assigned to HQ, 3rd Port TC. Served as assistant adjutant, adjutant, personnel officer, director of personnel and assistant adjutant general: 3rd Port as air courier delivering classified documents for accomplishment of emergency war missions until December 1944 (Served as Air Courier delivering Classified Documents for accomplishment of emergency war missions); Lyon Depot, France (operating and training French Forces to operate depot) until return to States July 1945 on second Green Project flight from Europe.

Participated in Rhineland Campaign; Adj Gen Pool, NOPE until Sept 29, 1945; HQ 4th Svc Cmd, Atlanta, GA, March 25, 1946; Ft Jackson, SC, April 10, 1946; Camp Kilmer, NJ, Dec 31, 1946; Ft Hamilton, NY, July 5, 1948; NYPOE, Oct 21, 1948; 7117 QM School Center, Darmstadt, Germany, March 8, 1949; HQ 223 QM Reclamaton Depot, Marburg, Germany, Feb 7, 1952; served as asst adj, Wetzlar Military Post; HQ 7th Armd Div, Camp Roberts, CA, Nov 25, 1952; HQ III Corps, Ft MacArthur, CA, Feb 12, 1953; admitted in Fitzimmons Army Hospital, Denver, CO, untill Nov 11, 1954, and G-1 Office, 4th Inf Div and HQ, Ft Lewis, WA until his retirement as CWO3 Jan 31, 1957.

Memorable experiences include serving as air courier delivering classified documents for accomplishment of emergency war missions.

Awards/Medals: Good Conduct w/clasp, Meritorious Unit, American and EAME Occupation, American Defense, WWII Victory Medal, Nat Def and Armed Forces Res.

Sold real estate for three and one-half years; US Customs Service stationed at Oroville, Danville, McChord AFB, WA; VanCouver International Airport, British Columbia, Canada. Attained title of Supervisory Customs Inspector and Port Director. Retired Sept 15, 1975. Life member of ROA, American Legion and DAV.

Married Mary and has three sons: Leland, Paul Jr, and Robert; 11 grandchildren and nine great-grandchildren. Fully retired and enjoys traveling in his RV around the country.

JOHN O. BIRCHMAN, CW4, USA (RET), born June 11, 1923, Detroit, MI. Attended Univ of Detroit, 1941-42. Drafted in Army 1943. Overseas duties included North Africa and invasion of Italy. Discharged Dec 1, 1945.

Moved to Seattle, WA, 1947 and enlisted in the USAR March 1950. In 1958 appointed WO1 and served with the 104th Div for 25 years as a food advisor. Assigned 1979 to the 174th Gen Support Gp and the unit received the runner-up "Connley Award" for field feeding. Retired June 11, 1983 (his 60th birthday), with 36 years of service. He was awarded the Legion of Merit.

Married Domenica Rossetti of Seattle in 1953; has six sons (four served in the USAF and two in Desert Storm).

RANDY J. BLACKBURN, CW2, born June 22, 1955, Sioux Falls, SD and raised in Brandon, SD. Enlisted as military personnel tech, 420A, Aug 7, 1974. Stationed with the 1st Inf Div, Ft Riley; 5th Sig Cmd, Germany; Dugway Proving Ground, UT; Div Arty, 1st Armd Div, Germany; USAAVNC, Ft Rucker; 32nd AADCOM, Germany; and PERSCOM.

Memorable experience was having the opportunity to serve with the WO DIV PERSCOM.

Awards/Medals: Meritorious Svc w/2 OLCs, ARCOM w/4 OLCs, (4) Army Good Conduct Med, (2) Nat Def Svc Med, (3) NCOPDR, Army Svc Rib and (3) Overseas Svc Rib.

Blackburn married Debbie and has four children. A personnel actions officer, PERSCOM, Alexandria, VA, PCSing to Ft Sam Houston, TX to be chief, Personnel Services Branch Aug 15, 1994.

ROBERT W. BLANCHARD, CW4, USA (RET), born April 18, 1935, Lansing, MI. Enlisted in MIARNG May 7, 1952. Employed by Combined Fld Maint Shop, 1953-65. Entered active duty and assigned to Ft Leonard Wood. Received Warrant Jan 17, 1969, at APG. Other assignments include Vietnam, Germany (two tours), Ft Riley, Ft Bliss, Korea and APG (two tours). Retired Feb 1, 1986, after 27 years of service.

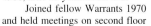

Joined fellow Warrants 1970 and held meetings on second floor Officer's Club, then given a room in basement which they decorated to resemble a cave, and finally began work on the Eagle Room in the basement of HQ and Co A, 85th Maint Bn

Automotive Shop, Hanau, Germany. As a delegate he attended the 3rd Annual Convention 1975 in Berchtesgaden.

Awards/Medals: Legion of Merit, Army Comm w/ OLC, Army Achiev, Meritorious Unit, Good Conduct, Armed Forces Res Med, NCOPDR and numerous service and campaign medals. Member of AUSA, VFW and American Legion.

Married to the former Beatrice Wise of Meadville, PA.

EDMUND B. BLANCHETTE, CW4, USA (RET), born March 9, 1926, St Kitts, West Indies. Immigrated to New York February 1944 and drafted in the Army September 1944.

His 35 year career included service in Louisiana, California, New Jersey, Kansas, New York, Texas and Alaska; overseas at Germany, Korea and Crete. Specialty field was Nike Missiles. Retired in November 1979.

Awards/Medals: Legion of Merit, Meritorious Svc Med, Army Comm w/3 OLCs, Good Conduct, American Campaign, Armed Forces Exped Med, WWII Victory Med, Armed Forces Res Med w/X year device, Army Occupation Med and a Nat Def Svc Med w/1 OLC.

Served in inactive Reserves from 1947-50 and the active Reserves from 1950-52. Received BA in law and justice; served 10 years as paralegal in King County, WA; retired July 1993; and a member of the TROA, Nat Assoc of Uniformed Svcs, VFW, American Legion and FOE.

Married Patricia and has six children, two step-grandchildren and numerous grandchildren.

CESAR A. BLANCO, CW2, USAR, born May 3, 1947, Havana, Cuba. Arrived in States 1960 and lived in Chicago, IL area since 1962. Graduated HS. Received BA degree in criminal social justice from Lewis University, Romeoville, IL and MPA from Illinois Institute of Technology in Chicago.

Entered service April 1979; attended basic training at Ft Knox, KY; AIT as medical aidman at Ft Sam Houston, TX; 1982 cross-trained as infantryman; 1987 as counterintelligence spec agent. As an enlisted completed various courses of instruction: ANCOC, Abn, SEC MGR, Spec Sec Officer, DAME, Anti-Terrorist and Battlefield Deception Crs's and served with 33rd Inf Bde (Sep)(ILANG), 5034th USARFS, 86th USARCOM (DCSOPS), C/1/7 SFG (ABN), JTF-B (J2), JCIOE and TF-164 in Honduras, CA, the 138th MI BN (CEWI) and the 902nd MI GP, MI BN (CI)(SEC).

Promoted MSG; accepted in WOC Program and attended WO School (RC), Ft McCoy, WI, graduating August 1993. Attended WOBC, Ft Huachuca for technical certification as CI tech.

Assigned to Co B, 138th MI BN (HVYDIV) as chief, CI Section; serves as BN security manager. Continues to serve as adjunct instructor to 4th Res Forces School-Intelligence, Ft McCoy, WI in the fields of CI, SEC MGMT and Languages.

Awards/Medals: Meritorious Svc Med, Army Comm Med, Army Achiev Med, Nat Def Svc Med, Armed Forces Res Med and received the Expert Fld Med Badge and the Honduran Prcht Badge.

A deputy chief paramedic and commanding officer of Chicago Fire Department's Support and Log Div. Life member of WOA and member of ROA.

THOMAS C. BLAUL, CW3, AUS (RET), born March 5, 1941, Chicago, IL. Enlisted in 1/131 Inf ILARNG 1963 with initial training at Ft Leonard Wood, MO. Served with HHC 3rd Bde, 33rd Inf Div and HHC 33rd Inf Bde as intelligence sergeant and MP platoon sergeant. Activated

five times for Chicago civil disorders including a Presidential Order in 1968. Transferred as SFC, Commo Chief, to USAR, 1972, with 314th Army Security Agency Bn.

Appointed WO, Crypto tech, 1974; assigned communications officer, CE repair tech, and supply tech. Developed "cheap-fix," an inexpensive electronic warfare training device. Unit redesignated 138th MI BN (CEWI). Retired Reserve, 1984. Received Air Crewman's Badge, Meritorious Svc, Army Achiev and other service medals.

A journeyman tool and die maker; and since 1967, a Chicago police officer assigned to Chicago O'Hare International Airport. Married Marianne Pick in 1964 and has two daughters.

DONALD W. BLAZEK, CW4 (RET), born April 7, 1928, Montana and raised in Forsyth, MT. Entered Army March 14, 1947, and had basic training at Ft Lewis, WA.

Assigned as driver for Post Commander, Ft Lawton, WA. Left for Germany September 1947 and assigned to IG Farben Building, Frankfurt USARA HQ. March 1948 went to Bamberg, Germany to 1st Inf Div, 26th Inf Regt. Returned to States December 1951 and assigned to Ft Sill, OK April 1952. Re-assigned to Germany October 1952 and assigned to 4th Inf Div, 40th TKBN, Friedberg, Germany until May 1956.

Returned to States to 1st Armd Div, 1st TKBN, Ft Polk, LA, 1956-59. Unit moved to Ft Hood May 1959-62. Assigned to Korea with 17th Trans, 7th Div ITT to Germany December 1963 with 2/34 24th Div. Promoted to WO1 June 1964 and assigned to Berlin 4/18 Inf October 1966. Reassigned to Vietnam, 9th Inf Div Returned to States December 1967 to Ft Carson, CO. Returned to Vietnam August 1969-70; ITT to Germany 1/68 Armor, Baunholder, Germany. Returned to Ft Carson, CO July 1975, 2/34 Armor then 704th Ord 1977-78.

Awards/Medals: Legion of Merit, Meritorious Svc Med, Bronze Star w/OLC, Army Comm w/2 OLCs (3) Good Conduct, Army Occupation (Germany), Vietnam Svc w/6 stars, Nat Def w/3 OLCs, (4) Overseas Bars and Vietnam Campaign w/60 device. Retired May 1978 after 31 years of service.

Married since January 1956, has three children: David, Gerald and Linda. He is a part-time automotive instructor.

ARNOLD A. BOCKSEL, born Oct 10, 1913, New York. Enlisted in Army February 1941 in Mine Planter Service. Stationed in Boston; Ft Monroe, VA; Corregidor, Philippines. Participated in campaigns at Bataan and Corregidor, Philippines.

Memorable experience was being a Japanese POW for three and one-half years. Retired in 1949 with a physical disability as a CWO4 chief engineer.

Awards/Medals: Bronze Star, POW Med, (3) Pres Citations, (4) Battle Stars, Nat Def, American Def w/Bronze Star, Asiatic-Pacific w/2 Bronze Stars, Philippine Def w/ Bronze Star, Philippine Pres Unit Cit, WWII Victory Med, American Campaign, NY State Conspicious Svc Cross.

Wife passed away; has four children and nine grandchildren. Author of book, *Rice, Men and Barbed Wire*. He is retired.

ANTON BOKOR, CWO3, USAR, AGR, born Dec 7, 1944, Budaors, Hungary, now naturalized US Citizen. Enlisted in Army 1966. Duty assignments, 1966-92: basic training, AIT, cartographic draftsman, cartographic sergeant, intelligence sergeant, photomapping tech, team chief (CDR); and present assignment as property accounting tech with 303rd Ord Gp (AMMO) with rank CWO3.

From 1967-92 completed numerous courses at various military schools: Cartographic Drafting, Charting and Reproduction, NBC Basic, NCP Crs, Battalion Trng Mgmt, Institute For Packaging, Spec Security Trng, WO Prof Development, Topographic Work Station Crs, Sup and Svc Mgmt Crs, Intel Trng, Hazardous Mat Crs, and others.

Civilian education includes: high school; three years commercial art (diploma) and College of Lake County, 92 credit hours, continuing.

Awards/Medals: Meritorious Svc w/2 OLCs, Army Comm w/3 OLCs, Army Achiev w/4 OLCs, Res Component Achiev Med w/3 OLCs, Humanitarian Svc Med, Nat Def Svc Med w/Bronze Svc Star, Armed Forces Res Med w/ HGD, Vietnam Svc Med w/7 Campaign Stars, Vietnam Campaign Med, SWA Svc Med w/3 Campaign Stars, Kingdom of Saudi Arabia Lib of Kuwait Med, Army Svc Rib, (6) Army Res Overseas Deployment Trng Rib, Overseas Rib, (4) Overseas Bars, Sharpshooter Badge.

GARY DAVID BOSWORTH, CWO4, SIG, ARNGUS, born Dec 3, 1941, Pinehurst, Moore County, NC. Completed HS, Pinehurst, NC; Mercer County Community College, Trenton, NJ; Servicemans Degree Program (62 credit hours); AAS gen business.

Enlisted in Army Aug 1, 1959. Attended military schools: ATT; Projectionist; Armor Radio Maint; Radiological Monitoring; Fld Radio Repair; Elec Maint Off Crs; CE WOAC; WOSC; Comm Sec Custodian Crs; Def Hazardous Materials Waste and Handling Crs, USA Log Mgmt Col; Battle Focus Crs, Wayne Comm Col, Goldsboro, NC; HAZ-MAT Trans Crs, Pryor, OK LSC-3; Environmental Coordinators Crs, Ft Bragg, NC; Leadership/Management Development Crs; Vinson Installation Crs, FT Huachuca, AZ; and M1 Abrams Electrical Crs, Warren, MI.

Awards/Medals: (2) Army Comm, (2) Army Achiev, Army Res Comp Achiev, (2) Nat Def, Armed Forces Res, (4) Overseas Trng Rib, Army Svc Rib, Expert Rifle, OSD Unit Citation, 30th Inf Div Citations and NG Recruiter Badge.

Memberships: NG Assoc. US, life member of NCNGA, USWOA (president of Ft Bragg Silver Ch), American Legion Post 303 (vice commander) and USPA GW 1670 D3963 and FAA Senior Prcht Rigger.

Presently assigned as C-E equip repair tech with 256AO DET-1 Co B, 230th Spt Bn 30th Inf Bde (M)(S), NCNG, Benson, NC.

CARLO BRACCI, CW3, USA (RET), born March 6, 1938, New York City. Began his career Jan 13, 1956, Ft Dix, NJ. Attended Crypto Operator School, Ft Gordon, GA. Served in various Commcenter/Comsec assignments at Arlington, VA; Italy; Ft Ritchi, MD; Ft Jay, NY; Thailand; Ft Carson, CO; and Germany. He was also a truckmaster SFC E7 in Germany and appointed WO in November 1967.

Served as WO crypto custodian, instructor, operations officer and automated software tech at Ft Monmouth, NJ, Vietnam, Italy, Germany and chief AUTODIN Training Facility, Ft Gordon, GA until he retired as CW3 in December 1978 with 23 years of service.

Awards/Medals: Meritorious Svc Med, Bronze Star, Army Comm Med and various service and campaign medals.

Special memory as operations officer AUTODIN Switching Center Leghorn, Italy and the start up and shutdown of Gablingen AUTODIN Switching Center in Augsburg, Germany (also as operations officer).

Lives in Martinez (Auga), GA and 4th degree member of K of C, Martinez Masonic Lodge; WOA; life member DAV; American Association for Artificial Intelligence.

Married to Carmela Campanella of Naples, Italy, over 35 years. They have three children and two grandsons.

GARY D. BRAMAN, CW3, USA (AD), born Oct 25, 1954, in Lansing and raised in Grand Ledge, MI. Graduated HS, 1972; entered Army May 1973. Basic training, Ft Knox, KY; AIT (FA Surveyor), Ft Sill, OK; promoted to PFC. Assigned to C Btry, 2/25th FA, Wertheim, Germany in October 1973, promoted to SP4, SGT and S/SGT.

Assigned July 1979 to HHB DIVARTY, 101st Abn Div; began WOC flight trng August 1980; appointed WO1 June 1981. Assigned to 4/12th Cav, Ft Polk, LA as UH-1 pilot; attended Avn Safety Off Crs, and promoted to CW2 June 1983. Attended Degree Completion ERAU, Ft Rucker, AL January 1985; assigned to 4/11 ACR, Fulda, Germany.

Attended Fixed Wing Qualification Crs, February 1988, received National Safety Officers Awd from AAAA April 1988. Assigned to 56th Avn Co, Mannheim, Germany May 1988; promoted to CW3 October 1988, reassigned to Ft Rucker, AL July 1992.

Awards/Medals: Meritorious Svc, ARCOMS and Army Achiev Med.

Married Louise Schmied December 1976 and has three sons and one daughter.

TODD JOSEPH BRANDA, CW2, USAR, born July 19, 1968, Bay City, MI. Entered Army July 11, 1986; basic training, Ft Dix, NJ; AIT, Ft Eustis, VA; served as CH-47 mechanic with 210th Cbt Avn Bde, USA South, Ft Kobbe, Panama.

Accepted to USA Avn School, Ft Rucker, AL January 1989; graduated Flt School March 28, 1990; attended AH-64 Apache Qualification Crs; assigned to 2/227 AHB 3rd Armd Div Hanau, Germany Aug 23, 1990. Deployed to SWA Dec 29, 1990, served as a co-pilot/gunner during Operation Desert Shield/Desert Storm and Provide Comfort.

Awards/Medals: Air Med (2nd awd), Army Commendation w/OLC, Army Achiev w/2 OLCs, Good Conduct, Nat Def, SWA Med w/3 stars, NCOPDR, Army Svc Med, Overseas Svc Rib w/2nd awd, Kuwaiti Lib Med.

Married Carolyn Reno, of Standish, MI; has two sons, Corey and Kyle. Currently assigned to 1/227 AHB 1st Cav Div, Ft Hood, TX and member of WOA and VFW Post 3724. Hobbies include building models of WWII fighters and he has an avid interest in aviation history.

THOMAS F. BRANDT, CW5, OHARNG, one of twins born Aug 30, 1941, Columbus, OH. Began his military career in OHARNG, Columbus area October 1963. Assigned to HHC 37th Inf Div, Prov Marshal's Sect. Served continuously in numerous assignments and units of OHARNG. Last enlisted assignment was 1SG of HHC 73rd Inf Bde (Sep); appointed CW2 April 5, 1979, with 16th Engr Bde as brigade food advisor.

Transferred to HQ STARC (Det 1-5) in 1985; assigned as auditor in Internal Review and Audit Compliance Div (IRA) of U.S. Property and Fiscal Office. Assigned 1989 as chief auditor of the M-Day personnel of IRA Div. Promoted to CW4 Nov 3, 1990.

Awards/Medals: Meritorious Svc, Army Commendation w/2 OLCs, Army Achiev Med, Army Res Comp Achiev Med w/SLC, Nat Def Med, Humanitarian Svc Med, Armed Forces Res Med w/2 HGs, NCOPDR w/3, Army Svc Rib, Army Res Comp Overseas Trng Rib w/2, Ohio Comm Med, Ohio Faithful Svc Med w/4 OLCs, Ohio Spec Svc Rib, Ohio Awd of Merit Rib w/4, and Ohio Basic Trng Rib.

Retired as police officer from Columbus, OH Div of Police in 1987. During his 24 1/2 year police career, he received awards for bravery (was shot in the line of duty); and special commendations.

Appointed Marshal of The Supreme Court of state of Ohio in 1987, where currently employed. Member of USWOA, NGA, Assoc of QM, USAA, Enlisted Assoc of the NG of US, FOP, Police and Fire Retirees of Ohio, Columbus Maennerchor. In 1993 elected as member of the board of directors for the Columbus Municipal Employees Federal Credit Union.

Married Evalyn Mack in 1966; they have twin daughters, Lynn Ann and Lori Kay.

HOWARD M. BREEDING, CWO, W3, AUS (RET), born Dec 15, 1925, Arcola, MO. Entered Army April 18, 1944; basic training with 214th Ord HM Co (FA) at various bases in States. Served as heavy artillery repairman with the 214th in Germany during WWII. Instructor at Ord School, APG, MD. Appointed WOJG Nov 26, 1951.

Served as ordnance supply officer in Korea with 30th Ord HM Co, 1951-52; Japan at Tokyo Ord Depot, 1952-December 1954. Retrained 1961 as nuclear weapons assembly supervisor; served in Germany and Seneca Army Depot, NY. Supervisor of Tech Trng Branch at SOD until voluntary retirement as CWO, W-3, AUS, with over 20 years of service, Oct 31, 1965.

Awards/Medals: Army Comm Med (2nd Awd), Good Conduct Med (2nd Awd), Army Comm Med, EAME Campaign, WWII Victory, Army of Occupation (Germany), Nat Def, Korean Svc, Armed Forces Res Med, UN Svc Med, Meritorious Unit Emblem (2nd Awd) and Rep of Korea Pres Unit Cit.

Second career as safety engineer with a major national insurance company in Albuquerque, NM, retiring after 25 years of service on Jan 1, 1991. Member of TROA, Professional Member Emeritous of American Society of Safety Engrs, past president of New Mexico Chapter of ASSE, member of NRA, Amateur Radio Operator (HAM) N5QBD and American Radio Relay League, Inc.

Married Catherine Rose Green (Katie) of Nevada, MO; has four children and six grandchildren. Has a motor home and travels a lot, spending winters in Yuma, AZ.

IVAN L. BROOKBANK, CW5, USARNG, born Nov 20, 1935, Mitchell, SD. Began his military career in SDARNG, 100th Ord Co, Mitchell, SD March 19, 1954. Through the years he attended several MOS related courses. Graduated June 1958 from South Dakota OCS and commissioned 2LT September 1958. Served as assistant platoon leader in Ord Co for three years.

In 1961 accepted a full-time position with unit, but would not allow him to be an officer, so March 6, 1960, resigned commission and reverted to SP5 E5. Held various positions throughout Automotive Sect Chief with rank SFC E7. On June 18, 1968, appointed to rank WO1 as automotive tech in 665th Heavy Maint Co (GS), SDARNG where he continued to serve as staff support maintenance tech. Promoted to CW5 Sept 9, 1992. Attended Advance and WOSCs at APG, MD and WOSC and MWOC at Ft Rucker, AL.

Awards/Medals: Army Comm Med w/OLC, Army Achiev Med w/OLC, Armed Forces Res Med w/2 HGs, Army Component Achiev Med w/Silver OLC, South Dakota Soldier of the Year 1961, and South Dakota Tech of the Year 1989.

Retired March 7, 1991, after 32 years as a tech completing his career as automotive shop foreman of the Combined Sup Maint Shop #1; continues to serve SDARNG. Oct 1, 1993, he concluded a 15 month tour of active duty that included six months in Panama with Fuertes Caminos 93. Resides Mitchell, SD with wife, Delores Cunningham; has two children and one grandchild.

RUSSELL D. BROOKOVER, CW4, AUS (RET), born July 15, 1920, Greenfield, OH. Enlisted in RA June 26, 1940, at Ft Hayes, Columbus, OH and assigned to the 67th Coast Arty, AA BN stationed at Ft Bragg, NC. Upon completion of "Schooling of a Soldier," he performed all artilleryman duties including AAA fire control. He was in charge of maintaining and operating one of the first Model 268, Mobile AAA radar units delivered to the Army. Shortly after Pearl Harbor, he hit the cadre circuit and later was permanently assigned to the 627th FABN as sergeant major (E-7).

He departed for Europe with the battalion and participated in WWII battles of Central Europe, Northern France and Rhineland. He was unit administrator with HQ Btry, 77th FABN, 1st Cav Div in Korea, 1951, and in Korea again as personnel officer with the 99th FABN, 1st Cav Div, 1953. He participated in Korean battles of UN Summer-Fall Offensive, 2nd Korean Winter Offensive; 3rd Korean Winter Offensive and Korean Summer-Fall Offensive 1952.

After returning from Korea and Japan, he served as chief, Officers Branch, HQ 5th Army, Chicago; administrative assistant to the adjutant general, US Army Pacific, Hawaii; XO to the Director Military Operation, Pentagon; Personnel Officer USA Element JUSMMAT, Ankara, Turkey; Personnel Officer, US Army Element Allied Forces SE Europe, Izmir, Turkey; and last assignment as XO to Comptroller of the Army, Pentagon. He accompanied the US Army flag officers to Vietnam during the 1960s.

Held every enlisted rank from private to sergeant major (E-7 was tops in those days). Appointed WOJG (half bars) April 1, 1951; promoted CWO (split bar) April 8, 1953. Under the new grade system, he was promoted to CWO, W-3, in August 1958, and to CW4 on Feb. 7, 1964. Primary WO MOSs during his career were 2600 admin asst, 2200/711A personnel offier, and 712A general staff administrative tech.

Awards/Medals: Legion of Merit, Meritorious Svc, Army Comm w/2 OLCs, Good Conduct, American Defense, American Campaign, EAME Campaign w/3 stars, WWII Victory, Army Occupation (Germany and Japan), UN Svc Med, Nat Def Svc Med, Korean Svc Med w/4 stars and Armed Forces Res Med w/HG.

Retired at Pentagon as CW4 Sept 1, 1970, with over 30 years of service. Second career was director of administration for large corporation in Dallas, TX. Retired from industry June 1, 1979, because of health problems. Primary avocation for many years has been Amateur Radio (HAM). Holds an Amateur Extra Class FCC license with Call Sign of NB5Z. Life member of TROA, The Greater Dallas ROA, USAWOA, VFW, and American Radio Relay League.

Married 51 years to the former Marion Hocking of Highwood, IL; has two daughters, four grandchildren and two great-grandsons. They reside in Duncanville, TX.

BRUCE R. BROOKS, CW3, born Sept 14, 1945, Spartenburg, SC. Began military career enlisting in TNNG with 5th Bn, 109th Armor Div, Knoxville, TN, July 1965. Attended basic training at Ft Campbell, KY and IAT at Ft McClellan, AL. Relocated to Michigan in January 1970 and transferred to 156th Sig Bn in Monroe, MI for remainder of service obligation in June 1971.

Re-entered MIARNG March 1973 with 1/182nd FA, Detroit, MI. Transferred to 70th Div (training), USAR in Livonia, MI, July 1982 as chief administrative NCO for Division Inspector General Section.

Appointed CW2 April 14, 1985, as assistant to inspector general at Div HQ. July 1987 assumed position of battalion adjutant with 3/330th 1st Bde (infantry); transferred to brigade HQ as military personnel tech. January 1991 activated for Desert Shield/Desert Storm, Ft Benning, GA for three months. Promoted CW3 April 14, 1991. October 1992 transferred back to 70th Div HQ, Livonia, MI to G-1 Div as CIP team chief of G-1 Section.

Awards/Medals: Armed Forces Res Med w/OLC, Army Res Comp Achiev Med w/3 OLCs, state of Michigan Legion of Merit, NCOPDR "4", ARCOM w/2 OLCs, Army Achiev Med w/OLC, and Meritorious Svc Med.

Married Margaret Brooks and has two sons. Employed by Ford Motor Co since April 1970, works in Parts Redistribution Ctr, Brownstown TWP, MI. Hobbies include staying active in USAR Program and managing younger sons hockey team.

CLIFFORD L. BROWN, CW5, entered active duty April 1, 1968. Completed basic training, went directly to Flight School. Completed Flight  School Class 69-3, March 23, 1969; served first tour as WO1 HU1 pilot in Korea.

Assignments: 1970-80, instructor pilot (IP) and ops officer, Army Primary Helicopter School, Ft Wolters; avn maint officer/test pilot for 62nd Avn Co (Corps), RVN; standardization IP and instrument flight examiner at Army Avn School, Ft Rucker; IP and ops officer for 295th Avn Co (CH-47), Mannheim, Germany;

1980-91, completed resident WOSC; ops officer for 295th Avn Co (CH-47), Mannheim, Germany; HHC and ops platoon leader for D Co (CH-47), 34th Spt Bn, Ft Hood; personnel proponent systems manager for avn branch of Ft Rucker; completed MWOTC.

1990-91, battalion standardization officer, safety officer and S-3 for 2-105th Avn Bn (CH-47) in Korea. 1991-present, chief, avn WO personnel proponency, avn branch, Ft Rucker. Subject matter expert on AWO structure coding, utilization and training and responsible for implementing WOMA and WOLDAP for avn branch and writing AWO personnel plan and career guide. Received BS degree in aviation science; master army aviator with 6,000 flying hours. Awards/Medals: Bronze Star, Air Medal, Meritorious Svc w/4 OLCs.

Married Dorothy; has two sons. One is WO1 aviator at Ft Campbell and the other a major in JROTC, National Honor Society and Black Belt in karate.

EDDIE C. BROWN, CW3, USA (ACTIVE), born May 14, 1951, Orangeburg County, SC. Entered Army Oct 26, 1970, taking basic training at Ft Jackson, SC and AIT (technical) at APG, MD. Served in automotive repair with 295th Spt Co, Ft Lewis, WA from June-October 1971.

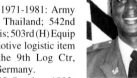

November 1971-1981: Army Maint Activity, Thailand; 542nd Maint Co, Ft Lewis; 503rd (H) Equip Maint Co; automotive logistic item manager with the 9th Log Ctr, Kaiserslautern, Germany.

March 1982-October 1992: maintenance repair and production control supervisor with C Co, 27th Maint Bn, 1st Cav Div Ft Hood; battalion automotive maint tech with HHC, 3rd Bn, 69th Armor, 4th Bn, 66th Armor, Aschaffenburg, Germany; HHC, 2nd Bn, 34th Inf and 3rd Bn, 7th Inf Regt, Ft Stewart; maint sup tech with HHD and Co B, 224th Maint Spt Bn, Ft Stewart; battalion maint tech with the 5th Bn, 20th Inf Regt, Camp Casey, Korea; 3rd Bn, 73rd Armor, 82nd Abn Div, Ft Bragg from October 1992-present.

Awards/Medals: Meritorious Svc Med, Army Comm w/OLC and numerous service and campaign medals. Desert Shield/Desert Storm veteran and member of USAWOA and past president of Ft Stewart Chap of WOA.

Married Marva Scott of Columbia, SC, has two children and one grandchild.

RICKEY P. BRUMFIELD, CW2, born Dec 21, 1949, Tell City, IN. Enlisted in Army Sig Corps Oct 20, 1980; basic trainee and AIT trainee for tactical field wireman, Ft Gordon, GA; 1981-85, wire systems section chief, OJT for telephone repair/switchboard operator and sattelite systems maint and operations in Alaska followed by service school for same at Ft. Gordon, GA.

1985-90, WOC, rotary wing student, Aviator (Cobra helicopter pilot), tech supply officer, worked in MATO Section of DISCOM as material manager and from 91 to present with HHC, 6th Sig Bn, 6th Inf. Div(L), Ft Richardson, AK as signal systems maint tech in the Direct Support Maint. Shop. Currently fielding MSE.

Worked in maint and log section of 1/123rd Avn Regt, Ft Ord, CA during Panama Conflict; provided log sup for Desert Storm while assigned to HHC, 707th Maint DISCOM (DMMC), 7th Inf Div(L) as material manager in MATO Section DISCOM.

Memorable experience was the team work towards a common goal to complete mission successfully.

Awards/Medals: ARCOM (2), Army Achiev (2), Army Good Conduct, Nat Def, Army Svc Rib, Overseas Rib (2), ARAVBAD and ECB-R.

Married Grace Emma Schneider Aug 26, 1972, in Tell City, IN. Has three children: Jamie Nicole, Yancey Sinclair and Dakota Ryane.

DANIEL BRYAN, CW4, USA (RET), born July 30, 1942, Attleboro, MA. Enlisted in Army Dec 14, 1960. Assigned to 2nd Armor Div, Ft Hood, TX for basic training. Stationed at Ft Hood, TX; Ft Benning and Ft Gordon, GA; Ft Polk, LA; APG, MD; Korea; Okinawa; Thailand; Vietnam; Germany; and Egypt.

1965, senior small arms, artillery and turret repairman, 1st Cav Div (airmobile), Vietnam; 1973, senior armament shop foreman and inspector, platoon and 1st sergeant 66th Maint Co(H) in Kitzingen, Germany; 1982, armament maint tech and senior instructor for XO of 1st Ord WOCC, APG, MD; 1984, armament maint chief/senior instructor and armor TAFT leader, Cairo, Egypt; 1987, regimental armament tech/asst mat off/automotive and armament platoon leader, 2nd Armd Cav Regt, Nuremberg, Germany.

Education included commanders NBC, Adv NCO Academy, Sup Maint Supervisor Academy, WOSC, associate degree in general studies.

Awards/Medals: Legion of Merit, Meritorious Svc Med w/OLC, Army Comm Med w/6 OLCs, Army Achiev Med w/OLC, Nat Def and Army Svc ribbons. Good Conduct w/4 knots, NCOPDR w/#3, Overseas Svc Rib w/#7 and numerous other service and campaign medals.

Married Mamie R. Howell of New Bern, NC and has two children, Daniel Eugene and Anita Jean. Lives in Palm Bay, FL. Retired 1991 with over 30 years of continuous service in the Ord Corps.

FREDERICK J. BRYANT, CW4, USA (RET), born July 18, 1948, Wabash, IN. Entered active duty with Army March 1972; completed basic training at Ft Jackson, SC and AIT and basic NCO training at Redstone Arsenal, AL. Served as nuclear weapons electronic specialist in Germany, February 1973-May 1976 and Seneca Army Depot, Romulus, NY, June 1976-November 1976. Appointed WO November 1976; served tours in Germany, Korea and States as nuclear weapon maint tech.

Stateside tours included Ft Devens, MA, APG, MD, and Picatinny Arsenal, NJ. Served as instructor at Ord Ctr and School. Last tour with Army Project Manager's Office for Nuclear Weapons. Retired from active duty July 1992 with 20 years of service.

Service Schools: WOSC; Svc Sch Instr Crs; Nuclear Weapons WOAC; Hazardous Mat Tech Escort Crs; and Nuclear Weapons Tech Crs.

Awards/Medals: Legion of Merit, Meritorious Svc Med, Army Comm Med w/4 OLCs, Army Achiev Med, NCOPDR (2), Good Conduct, Nat Def Svc Med (2), Army Svc Rib and Overseas Rib.

Married Barbara (Judy) Sergent of Sanford, FL and has one daughter, Catherine.

JOHN FRANKLIN BUCHANAN, born May 13, 1926, Gallipolis, OH. Enlisted in USAR and Army, serving in different branches. Stationed at Ft Bliss, TX for basic training; Cp Howze, TX for AIT; and ETO. Returned to States 1946 and discharged as staff sergeant.

Joined USAR; recalled to active duty 1951. Stationed at Army Chem Ctr, Edgewood, MD; 190th Med Det USAREUR, Idar-Oberstein, Germany; and 937th Engr Gp (Cbt), Ft Campbell, KY. Re-enlistment duty for three years at Post HQ; Korea; Ft Knox, KY; Offenbach and Mannheim, Germany; Vietnam; Indian Head, MD. Retired Nov 30, 1970.

Memorable experiences: Gardelegan, Germany in 1945 where prisoners of German army burned to death in barn; flying with great WO helicopter pilots in Vietnam who saved his life a couple of times.

Awards/Medals: Bronze Star, Air Med, Good Conduct w/Loop, Nat Def Med, EAME Rib w/star, WWII Victory Med, Army of Occupation (Germany), Nat Def Med w/star, Armed Forces Exped Rib, Vietnam Svc Rib w/2 stars, Res Svc Rib, Vietnam Med, Vietnam Cross of Gallantry w/Palm and Army Comm Med. Discharged Nov 30, 1970, with rank CWO (W-3) (CW) (W-4) USAR.

A retired antique dealer and free lance writer. Author of *Antiques and Collectible Humor*, and several masonic essays. Currently writing a clean book about the Army. Memberships include USAWOA, American Legion, VFW, DAV, AMVETS, ROA, and most Masonic Bodies including the Shrine.

Married Adaline Jane Ruble Oct. 4, 1954, and has three children: Jeremy, Robert Clegg (MSG E08, soon to retire) and Adelyn Christina Thomasset; one grandson, Mark; three granddaughters: Jennifer, Samantha and Brittany.

ROBERT E. BUFFUM, CW4, AUS (RET), born Oct 24, 1921, Milford, CT. Enlisted with Btry B, 197th CA (AA) Regt NHNG Oct 25, 1939. Regiment ordered to AD Sept 16, 1940, Camp Hulen, TX. Departed from States Feb 17, 1942; arrived Brisbane (Queensland) Australia March 9, 1942; served in New Guinea, Morotai, Philippines and given honorable discharge as sergeant at Ft Devens, MA Sept 4, 1945.

Re-enlisted as sergeant with 978th CA (DH) Btry NHNG June 30, 1947; WOJG November 1950; CW2 in February 1954; CW3 in February 1960; CW4 in February 1966; ordered to AD with Svc Btry 3rd Bn, 197th FA on April 23, 1968 at Ft Bragg, NC. Left the States on Oct 8, 1968, and arrived in the RVN on Oct 10, 1968.

Awards/Medals: Bronze Star, Meritorious Svc Med, Army Comm Med w/OLC, Good Conduct, ADSM, APCM w/AH and 3/BSs, WWII VM, NDSM, AFRM w/2 HG Devices; VCM w/4 BSs, PLM, PIR, PPUC, VSM w/60 device, VCOV w/Palm, and 8/OSB. Returned to States Sept 4, 1969, and released from active duty Sept 16, 1969; reverted to NHNG Sept 17, 1969.

Employed as NG tech, Adj Gen's Dept from April 1949-December 1978. Retired from civil service Dec 31, 1978, as purchasing and contracting officer, USPFO for New Hampshire; retired as personnel officer 3rd Bn, 197th FA on Oct 24, 1981.

DONALD W. BULLEN, CW4, (RET), born July 7, 1936, Medfod, OR. Entered Army April 1955; basic training at Ft Ord; ATT at APG, MD; served with 8th Ord Co, 6th Armd Cav Regt, Straubing, Germany, 1955-1958, as fuel/electrical system repairman and tank mechanic. Transferred 1959 to 802nd Avn Const Engr Bn, Pyongtaek, Korea; returned to CONUS, Post Ord, Ft Belvoir, VA; May 1962 Detach B, Korean MAG, Chunchon until 1963.

1963-70 stationed in Ludwigsburg, Munich, Nurnberg, Zirndorf, Kaiserslautern and Baumholder, Germany; Ft. Lewis, WA; Long Than, Dau Tieng and Long Binh, Vietnam. Returned to CONUS, completed Degree Completion Program, Macomb College, 1973. Served as maint staff officer and chief, USARSUPTHAI CMD Maint Mgmt Insp Team; completed WOSC, reassigned to MILPERCEN, Alexandria, VA until retirement in 1980.

Awards/Medals: Legion of Merit, Bronze Star w/2 OLCs, Purple Heart, Meritorious Svc Med w/OLC, Army Comm Med w/OLC, Vietnam Svc Med, Vietnam Campaign, RVNGCUCWP, VCOFGWP, Pres Unit Cit, Meritorious Unit Cit, Good Conduct Med and various service and campaign ribbons.

Currently employed by IBM Federal Systems as senior engineer and scientist.

Married a dependent school teacher, Patti Posey, wife and lifelong companion.

CHARLES R. BURACK, CW3, AUS (RET), born April 23, 1932, Royal, PA. Enlisted RA May 3, 1949; basic with 9th Inf Div, Ft Dix, NJ. Served the greater portion of his military career as a special agent, US Army Counterintelligence.

Units of assignments: 502nd MI BN, 8th Army and 191st MI DET, 1st Cav Div, Korea; Nurnberg, Stuttgard and Germersheim, Germany; Angouleme and Braconne Depot, France; Dong-Ha Cbt Base (attached to 3rd March Div), 517th MI DET, 1st Bde, 5th Inf Div (mech), Quang-Tri Cbt Base (Camp Red Devil), Vietnam.

Stateside assignments: Ft Dix, NJ; Ft Jackson, SC; APG, MD; Valley Forge, PA; Ft Sam Houston, TX; Ft Sill, OK; Ft Carson, CO; Ft Hood, TX; and several field office assignments.

At the time of appointment to WO August 1967, he was 1SG of HHC, 66th MI GP, Stuttgart, Germany. Awards/Medals: Vietnam Svc w/SS, Vietnam Camp, Bronze Star, Purple Heart, VN Cross of Gallantry w/Palm, Army Comm and Army Occupation Med (Germany).

Married former Dwanda Simmons of Masontown, WV. Has two children and one grandchild. Self-employed for past 10 years, wife is a nurse and they both plan to retire soon.

LAWRENCE R. BURBANK, CW4, born Sept 26, 1936, Topeka, KS. Enlisted in KSARNG, Btry B, 127th FA BN Nov 16, 1953, while still attending HS. Transfered 1957 to 137th Trans Co, Kansas City, served as AST and supply sergeant. Completed Flight School, Ft Rucker, AL, October 1961 and Aircraft Maint Off Crs, Ft Rustic, VA, February 1962. Returned to Kansas and assigned to 137th Trans Co as aircraft maint off/tech of newly formed AAFA, Fairfax Airport, Kansas City.

Transferred to 169th Avn Co, 69th Inf Bde May 1965 as aircraft maint tech until May 1968. Ordered into federal service 24 months, assigned to Ft Carson, CO. January 1969 ordered to RVN with CH-47 Pilot Qualification Crs en route; served as aviator/material readiness officer/motor officer for the 242nd Avn Co until release from active duty December 1969.

Returned to Kansas and reassigned to 69th Inf Bde as aircraft maint tech/off, AAFA, Kansas City. Feb 1, 1972, appointed to IP and aviation safety officer; Dec 1, 1986, transferred to 1st Bn, 108th Avn, KSARNG Topeka, KS as flight safety tech. Accepted transfer as aircraft maint officer in ARNG Avn Spt Fac, Salina, KS. June 1989 accepted AGR tour with ARNG Avn Div, APG, MD where still serving.

Awards/Medals Army Aviator Badge (AAB), Armed Forces Res Med, Nat Def, Army Comm w/OLC, Bronze Star, Distinguished Flying Cross, Vietnam Svc Med, RVN Campaign Med w/60 device, Sr AAB, Master AAB, and KSNG Svc Med (18 awards).

He and wife Susan have six children and nine grandchildren.

ROBERT A. BURKHARDT, CW3, USA, born June 11, 1950, Cleveland, OH. Entered Army April 4, 1970; basic training at Ft Campbell, KY; served with 5th Spec Forces and P/75 Ranger Co, Vietnam; 173rd Abn Bde and 101st Abn

Div, Ft Campbell, KY; advisor to German Labor Service, West Germany; 1SG HQ Rapid Deployment JTF, McDill AFB, FL; IG with 1st Armd Div; West Germany; NCOIC Weapons Pool, JFK Ctr, Ft Bragg, NC.

Appointed WO1 in 1987 as armament tech, 82nd Abn Div. Participated in Ops Just Cause, Desert Shield/Desert Storm. Currently resident trainer in 218th, a roundout brigade in South Carolina for 1st Inf Div.

Awards/Medals: Combat Infantry Badge, Master Parachutist Badge, Special Forces Tab, Purple Heart w/2 OLCs, Meritorious Def Svc Med, Meritorious Svc Med, Army Comm w/2 OLCs, Good Conduct w/5th Clasp, Nat Def Svc w/star, Vietnam Svc w/2 stars, SWA Svc w/2 stars and numerous service and campaign medals.

Married Paula Watts of Akron, OH, has four children.

ROBERT W. BUSBY, CW3, USA (RET), born June 22, 1950, Waco, TX. Entered Army June 16, 1970. Basic training, Ft Lewis, WA; MP training, Ft Gordon, GA; served as SP4 MP attached to Army Security Agency, 509th Radio Research in Saigon, Nah Trang and Can Tho, Vietnam; 256th MP Co as patrolman; correctional guard at Ft Hood, TX. Served with TXNG as MP sergeant convoy router in Waco, TX prior to re-entering active duty at Ft Gordon, GA.

Performed duties as SGT and SSG MP customs investigator and SP6 Army CI, Stuttgart, Germany. Assignments with Army CID as SP6 and SFC were: Ft Ord Dist CID and Hanau Resident Agency CID; appointed WO at Hanau Resident Agency. Duties as Army CID WO at Hanau, Germany; Ft Hood, TX; Wuerzburg, Germany; Wertheim, Germany; and Ft Gordon, GA.

Awards/Medals: Army Svc Rib, Army Good Conduct (4th award), Meritorious Unit Comm, Vietnam Svc, Overseas Rib (3), Vietnam Camp, NCOPDR (4), Nat Def Svc Med, Army Comm Med w/3 OLCs and Meritorious Svc Med. Retired from Army July 1991 at Ft Gordon, GA as a Res Army CW3.

His parents, Jack and Bea Busby, along with his favorite uncle and aunt, Edward and Linda Busby, inspired him to join and make the Army a career. Married Ann Gibbs; Christy Goosman; and currently married to Ann McNabb. Has one daughter from his marriage to Ann Gibbs, Julie Busby Neal, and a granddaughter, Britney Neal. Hobbies are computers and trains.

EDWARD J. CALHOON SR., CW3, USAR (RET), born June 28, 1942, Los Angeles, CA. Active enlisted service, 1960-66; basic and band training at Ft Ord, CA; was a tuba player with the 1st Army Band, Ft Jay, NY and Army Field Band, Ft Meade, MD. Nike Hercules Internal Guidance Sp/Sup, Ft Wainwright, AK; ordnance calibration sp/instr, APG, MD.

Res enl/off svc, 1966-69; supply instr/trng off, 2071st USAR School and supply plt leader, 611th Rep Parts Co, Baltimore, MD. Active officer svc, 1969-72; EOD Off, 549th Ord Det, Ft Meade, MD and Kwajalein Missile Range, Marshall Island maint officer, CO cdr and ammo officer, 92nd CS Bn and HHC 5th Trans Cmd, Da Nang, Vietnam. Res officer svc, 1972-81; Sup Comm Chief, 78th Div Trng, Edison, NJ; missile maint/supply/ ammo off, 510th Fld Depot, Baltimore, MD; log systems analyst, IMA to ODCSLOG, DA, Pentagon; Res WO service, 1981-91; data processing tech, IMA to Log Systems Agency, Ft Lee, VA; and SIDPERS Branch USAG, ODCSIM 1st Army and ADP Sec Det, 902nd MI BN, Ft Meade, MD.

Awarded Meritorious Svc Med, Army Comm Med, Good Conduct Med (2 awds), Vietnam and Res Svc Medals and Ribbons, Sr EOD Badge. Retired with over 30 years total active and Res service.

Played tuba with 1st Army Band, his first unit, at his retirement ceremony. Honor graduate of six service schools;

BS degree in sociology, 1972; Towson State University, Baltimore, MD; graduate study, 1972, 1974 and 1975, Princeton Theological Seminary, Princeton, NJ; graduate study, 1973-75, Rider College School of Ed, Trenton, NJ; BS degree, business, 1987, Regents College, USNY, Albany, NY; certified data processor, 1987; certified NARTE telecomm tech, 1990; and certified FCC volunteer examiner, Laural and ARRL VECs.

Federal Civil Service, 1978-present. Employed by Dept of Commerce as computer programmer analyst with Nat Telecommunications and Information Admin, Annapolis, MD, since 1985. Life member of ROA since 1967. Married Katherine Myers in 1974 and has three children.

MAURICE E. CAMMACK, CW4, USA (RET), born Feb 25, 1938, in Terry, MS. Began military service with 114th MP Co, MSNG in 1955; entered active duty May 1956.

Served in various Infantry, Artillery, Sig Corps, ASA and MI assignments. Appointed WO Oct 1, 1963; performed duties as cryptographic tech, automated software tech, ADP tech and telecomm tech.

Retired as CW4, RA, September 1982. Awards include Legion of Merit w/OLC, Bronze Star w/2 OLCs, Meritorious Svc Med, Army Comm Med w/OLC and many service and campaign medals.

Cammack is Distinguished Graduate of WO Sr Crs, Class 75-1. Graduated from civilian universities with BGS degree, MBA degree and completed numerous post graduate courses in computer science.

Worked in management positions with Lockheed Corp and Northrop Corp. Presently an instructor of computer science at Copiah-Lincoln Community College, Wesson, MS. Member of 1st Cav Div Assoc, Hon Order of Kentucky Colonels, American Legion and VFW.

Married to Katie Hall of Crystal Springs, MS and has two children and two grandchildren.

MATTHEW P. CAPUTO, CWO4, born Brooklyn, NY in 1936. Enlisted in Army in 1955 as automotive mechanic. Discharged as SFC, April 1967, and appointed WO1 at APG. Served in numerous assignments, including Vietnam, Germany and CONUS.

Major contributions include assisting in establishment of AMDF; improving supply and maintenance support for low-density engineer equipment; improving the lighting on standard, emergency and oversized vehicle fleets; and recoding of over 400,000 items from Class II to Class IX which saved the Army millions of dollars.

While assigned in Europe, he initiated several USAREUR wide programs that reduced maintenance down time and accidents. Material Readiness Programs included rotating 20,000 low mileage tactical wheeled vehicles with vehicles from inactive Army units; a three million dollar upgrade of the M151 jeep; and a repair program that rebuilt 60 amp alternators; and the submission of over 300 recommended changes to publications, 97% of which were approved.

Retired November 1988 as CWO4 and continues to serve the nation and the Ord Corps in his position as equip spec with the Army, Europe and 7th Army, ODCSLOG. Has held this position since 1988. His tireless and selfless dedication to the Ord Corps and the Army has earned him the richly deserved reputation as an expert in all aspects of supply, readiness, safety, maintenance, cataloging and operation of automotive equipment.

CARL R. CARNES JR., CW3, born April 7, 1951, Muskegon, MI. Entered the US Army June 25, 1970; basic training at Ft Knox, KY. Assigned as helicopter crew chief in Ninh Hoa, Vietnam, 1971 and 1972. Reassigned to III Corps AG, Ft Hood, TX; changed MOS to personnel management. Next two assignments were to 2nd Corps Sup Cmd, Nellingen, Germany and Admin Ctr, Ft Harrison, IN. Served as Army recruiter in Lansing, East Lansing and Jackson, MI.

Returned in 1983 to III Corps AG, Ft Hood, TX where he was selected WO. Upon completion of Entry Crs and Pers Officer Crs, he was appointed as pers tech on Feb 15, 1985. Initial assignment was Pers Records in Baumholder, Germany and later assigned to the G1, Personnel Actions, 8th Inf Div in Bad Kreuznach, Germany. The Readiness Group and the 1st Inf Div at Ft Riley, KS were his next two assignments.

Deployed to Saudi Arabia, Kuwait and Iraq with the Big Red One. Next assignment was to the WO Recruiting Team at Ft Sheridan, IL and later moved with the Recruiting Cmd to Ft Knox, KY. Currently Chief, Soldier Actions, 25th Inf Div, Schofield Bks, HI.

Awards include Bronze Star, (4) Meritorious Svc Med, Air Medal for valor, (5) Army Comm Med, (2) Army Achiev Med, numerous service and campaign medals, Aircraft Crewman Badge and the Gold Recruiter Badge w/2 Sapphire Stars.

Married Anna Moore of Fruitport, MI, and has three children: Kelly, Cheryl and Jason.

JIMMY E. CARPENTER, CW4, USA (RET), born Oct 9, 1948, Ft Worth, TX. Entered US Army Sept 8, 1968, Ft Polk, LA in the WO Flt Trng Program. graduated from Flt School at Ft Rucker, AL, November 1969; attended Attack Helicopter Qualification Crs en route to RVN. An 18 month combat tour was followed by assignments to Germany (twice), Ft Bragg, Ft Rucker and Ft Hood. While his primary duty was instructor pilot, he also served in staff positions at Division, Corps, Army and Army School during his 20 year career.

One of his more pleasurable tasks in the military was to coordinate the retirement ceremony for CW4 George Eby at Grafenwoehr, Germany. Due to inclement weather, the ceremony was held in the tiny gymnasium, but was very moving all the same.

Carpenter retired from the Army at Ft Hood, TX Dec 31, 1988. Awarded the Legion of Merit, Bronze Star, 50 Air Medals, Meritorious Svc Med w/OLC, Army Comm Med, Army Achiev Med and numerous service and campaign medals.

He is currently employed by Cartwright Electronics, Inc as field service manager on contract to the US Army for support of attack helicopter weapons training world-wide. Member of the USAWOA, VHPA, AAA, VFW, American Legion and TROA. Lives in Killeen, TX with wife, Donna, and son, Chris. His daughter, Kim, lives in Austin, TX.

KEITH E. CARTER, military service began Feb 25, 1944. Enlisted in the USAAC for aviation cadet trng. Program was terminated when Germany surrendered. Enlisted in USN July 1945 and served in the Pacific Islands until June 1946. In 1951 he joined the USAR FA. Appointed WO on full-time status as admin and sup tech from 1954-1964.

Recalled to active duty, Jan 31, 1964, assigned to 703rd Maint Bn, 3rd Inf Div, Kitizen, Germany. Returned to CONUS and assigned as platoon leader of equip for the 100th Engr Co (float bridge) Ft Belvoir, VA and for deployment to Vietnam.

September 1967 assigned to Safeguard Anti-Ballastic Missile Central Trng, Ft Bliss, TX. Appointed OIC of Power Barge Weber in Panama CZ for one year. Returned to Ft Bliss, TX, 1969 to Safeguard Anti-Ballistic Missile Program until February 1971; served second tour in Vietnam as contracting officer rep for utilities; later assigned to support the Four Power Peace Commission to oversee a cease fire that ended the war. February 1972 transferred to CONUS, Engr Branch OPD as WO assignment and professional development officer.

Next tour was Safeguard Complex, Nekoma, ND, until its deactivation in July 1976. Reassigned to Facility Engr Spt Agency, Ft Belvoir, VA. Retired from active duty March 31, 1983. Awarded Legion of Merit (2) Bronze Stars, Joint Svc Comm Med, (3) Army Comm Med and (3) Meritorious Unit Cit.

MARY F. CARTER, CW3, USAR, born Dec 6, 1946, Union, SC. Entered WAC in November 1965 and served as admin specialist with HQ, USCONARC, Ft Monroe, VA until her discharge in 1967. Established residence in California and began employment with county of Los Angeles in 1968; entered the USAR in 1973.

Appointed WO in 1984 with the 349th Gen Hosp; transferred to 6222nd USARF School and served as instructor, personnel records specialist for the 6th Army MOSTC during annual training for three years; transferred to 6218th Army Reception Bn where she utilized her skills of primary and secondary MOSs. She is the Unit Equal Opportunity representative and Alcohol Drug Abuse Prevention Program Coordinator.

Earned master degree of public administration in 1986, completed Systems Automation Crs and the WO Sr Crs in 1988. Awarded the Army Achiev Med w/OLC, Army Comm Med w/OLC, Armed Forces Res Med w/HG, Nat Def Svc Med w/BSS and other service medals and ribbons. Memorable experience was first assignment as WO at Ft Drum, NJ.

Lifetime member of WOA and interim president of Southern California Chap, member ROA, NAofBMO and several civilian organizations. Sr Dept Employee Relations Rep with public health programs and services. Formerly married to Carl Carter Sr and has one son.

NICKLAS R. CAUDILL, CW2, USA, born Aug 2, 1965, Great Falls, MT, and raised in South Whitley, IN. He earned the rank of Eagle Scout in 1982. Graduated from Whitko HS and entered the AFANG, Ft Wayne, IN; attained rank of sergeant in the position of ground/airborne radio operator with the 235th Air Traffic Control Flt in 1988.

He graduated from Ball State Univ, Muncie, IN with BS in business in 1988. Transferred to US Army to begin basic training at Ft Jackson, SC in 1989. After appointment to WO1 in 1990 as OH-58 A/C pilot, he joined the 2nd Inf Div in South Korea. Subsequently assigned to the 101st Abn Div (air assault), Ft Campbell, KY.

Awarded the Meritorious Svc Med, Humanitarian Svc Med, AF Outstanding Unit Awd, Army Achiev Med, Good Conduct, Nat Def Svc Med, Army Svc Rib, Overseas Rib, AF Trng Rib, Army Aviator Badge and Air Assault Badge.

Resides in Clarksville, TN, h is assigned to the 1/101st Avn Regt qualified in the UH1, OH-58A/C and the AH64A. Currently enrolled in Embry-Riddle Aeronautical University working towards masters degree in aeronautical science and retains membership with the Army Avn Assoc of America and the WOA.

MICHAEL A. CHALMERS, CW3, USAR, born Feb 22, 1952, Lima, Peru (father was in USAF). Entered Army April 14, 1972; attended basic training at Ft Dix, NJ and AIT at Ft Huachuca, AZ. Served on active duty with 5th Spec Forces Gp, Ft Bragg; HQ-USAINTA, Ft Meade; 209th MID (CI), Korea; Pentagon CI Force. USAR assignments include 226th MID (CI); Co B, 338th MI BN; and currently serving with 214th MI Co (CI).

His memorable experience was when walking along with a fellow WO (CW2) on USAR drill weekend. An E-1 approached them (they could see the confusion on his face as to whether or not they were a 'salutable' breed) and walked by without saluting. Chalmer's friend stopped the private and half-heartedly chewed him out. The young soldier was standing there, braced, when Chalmer's friend finished "educating" him. He asked the private if there were any questions, to which the soldier replied, "Sir, what do the black dots on your silver bar stand for?" Chalmers' friend said, "Young man, these so-called black dots are awarded each time we give punishment to disrespectful soldiers. As you can see we have given out five between us." The young soldier's face was aghast-believing that he was about to become another "dot". With that they turned and walked away and the young soldier hurried off to tell his comrades of his near escape with two "old Chiefs."

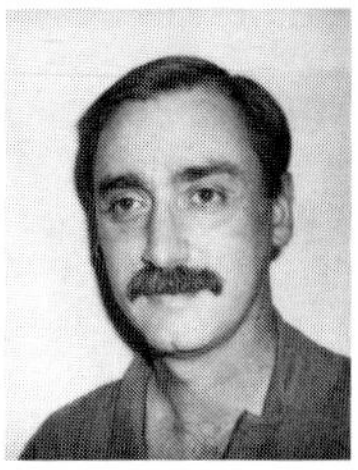

He was appointed WO1 in August 1980, and received WO commission in November 1987. Attended Intel Analyst and CI Agent Crs at Ft Huachuca, SF Qualification Crs at Ft Bragg, and basic airborne training at Ft Benning.

Awarded the Meritorious Svc Med, ARCOM w/4 OLCs, Army Achiev Med w/3 OLCs, AFRAM, Army Res Comp Achiev Med (3 awds), Overseas Rib, RCODTR. Member of Army CI Corps Veterans, WOA, ROA and the OPSEC Professional Society. Currently employed with the Federal Government.

CHARLES H. CHARLTON JR., CW2, born July 31, 1934, in Harrisonburg, VA. Entered the US Army in April 1957; basic training with the 43rd TSB, Ft Benning, GA; Clerk Typist School, Ft Knox, KY; 63rd Ord Co APO 166 (Germany) Cook School, June 1961, Ft Lee, VA; September 1961, 2nd QM Bn, later to be the 502nd S&T, Ft Hood, TX; November 1963, Mess Steward Crs, Ft lee, VA; March 1964, 1st Bn 68th Armd Div APO 09034 (Germany); June 1966, 1st Bn OCS Regt, Ft Lee, VA; August 1967, 9th Avn Bn, 9th Inf Div (Vietnam); August 1968, 2nd Inst Co, Ft Lee, VA; September 1968, Instructor Trng Crs.

Food service supervisor Crs, June 1969, while assigned to the 2nd Inst Co at Ft Lee, VA; March 1971, HQ Cmd, Ft Ord, CA; May 28, 1971, appointed WO; attended QMC USARV Trans Det, Ft Lee, VA, Food Advisor and Tech Crs; October 1971, 32nd Med Dep USAPAC RVN to HQ MACV, USARPAC RVN; departed RVN on March 29, 1973; May 1973, 2nd BCTB, Ft Leonard Wood, MO; October 1975 Co B 2nd Bn USAECBDE, Ft Belvoir, VA; August 1977, 2nd Bn 37th Armor 1st Armd Div (Germany).

Retired Oct 1, 1980, Ft Myers, VA. Awards include the Bronze Star, Joint Svc Comm, Army Comm, Good Conduct, Nat Def Svc Med, VN Svc Med, Valorious Unit Awd, Meritorious Unit Emblem, RVN Cross of Gallantry w/palm, VN Civic Actions Med, five Overseas Svc Bars, RVN Camp Rib w/D and one BS and SS.

Married and has eight daughters and two step-daughters. After retiring he returned to the trade of brick mason. He enjoys hunting, fishing, cooking and bowling.

JAMES F. CHATT, CW4, AUS (RET), born Nov 19, 1923, Chicago, IL. Enlisted on Sept 25, 1942 in the US Army. Received basic training at Cp McQuaide, CA as Coast Artillery man. After basic he was assigned to B Btry, 18th CAC at Ft Stevens, OR; assigned to the 283rd CA BN, Ft Cronkhite, CA; then overseas to the Pacific Theater. Served in Fiji, Wallis, Guadalcanal, New Guinea and Luzon. When his unit arrived on Luzon, it was redesignated the 4614th QM Truck Co, in which he served until being reassigned to the States. Discharged on Dec 25, 1945.

Joined the ORC in January 1946 and was inactive until his recall in September 1950. Assigned to A Btry, 61st FA, a unit of the 1st Cav Div. Served in Korea and was released on Aug 28, 1951. In 1952 he became a member of the 374th AAA Bn, which evolved to the 4th/75th Arty Bn where he was promoted to WOW1 in June 1958. Upon relocation of the 4th/75th Arty, he became the supply specialist and PBO for HQ, 472nd Cml Bn (SG). When the toe slot was eliminated, he became a member of the 5034th USAR where he served as instructor, S-4 and PBO.

Retired Dec 1, 1983, with over 40 years of service. Awards include the Meritorious Svc Med w/OLC, Army Achiev Med, Good Conduct Med, Nat Def Med, Asiatic-Pacific w/2 stars, Korean Svc w/3 stars, Armed Forces Res Med, Army Res Achiev, WWII Victory Medal, Philipppine Lib Med and the UN Svc Med.

A retired postal service employee with 34 years of service, he is a member of ROA, TROA, USAWOA, NRA, VFW, AL and BSA. Hobbies include scouting and fire buffing. He is now living in Florida.

LYLE E. CHEADLE (CHAD), CW3, (P) (RET), born Aug 7, 1939, Billings, MT. Entered the US Army Jan 8, 1955; attended basic training at Ft Carson, CO; AIT and Jump School at Ft Campbell, KY; and Ranger School at Ft Benning, GA. Served as infantryman from PVT to SFC, 1955-66. Served with the 101st and 82nd Abn Divs, 5th and 7th Sped Forces, 4th Armd Div, 1st Cav Div, 2nd Inf Div, 9th Inf Div and 23rd Inf Div (Americal). Served three tours in Vietnam, 1961-62, 1965-66 and 1971-72. Appointed WO1 November 1969.

Retired in 1981 as CW3 promotable. Awards include the Silver Star, Legion of Merit, Bronze Star w/V and 2/ OLCs, Meritorious Svc Med w/3 OLCs, Army Comm Med w/3 OLCs, Purple Heart w/2 OLCs, Air Medal w/3 device, Ranger Tab, Master Parachutist Badge, Combat Inf. Badge, Expert Infantryman Badge, Vietnam Svc w/7 Campaign Stars, Armed Forces Exped w/OLC, Nat Def Svc Med w/ OLC, etc. Greatest experience was being able to serve in the world's finest Army for 26 plus years.

Degrees include BS, business admin; MBA; MS (psychology) and Ph.D. in business admin.

He is working for the US Govt as chief, Resource and Systems Mgmt Div, HQ, US Forces Korea and 8th Army, ACofS, J4/G4. He is the father of five children: Jacqueline, David, Larry, Robert and Janet.

WILBUR A. CHRISTOPHER, CW5, inducted into the US Army on April 7, 1958, at Detroit, MI; in-processed at Ft Knox, KY; basic training with C Co, 66th Armor, Ft Hood, TX; AIT as personnel specialist with 502nd Admin Co, 2nd Armd Div.

Served as personnel specialist with 122nd Ord Bn, 3rd Armd Div, Hanau, Germany. Released from active duty at Ft Sheridan, IL, returned to Detroit and joined 3rd Bn, 329th Regt, 70th Div (trng). Served as 1st sgt and regt per sgt. Appointed WO1 Sept 1, 1965, and served as personnel officer with the 329th Regt and 70th Div HQ. Transferred to 5064th US Army Garrison, Detroit, MI in 1974 and remained until 1990.

July 15, 1990, transferred into AGR Program, assigned to 4th Bde, 84th Div (trng), Milwaukee, WI as the unit per tech. He was promoted to CW5 in January 1993 and assigned to ARPERCEN as chief, WO Branch, his present assignment. Awards include Meritorious Svc Med, ARCOM w/3 OLCs, Good Conduct Med, Army Achiev Med, Nat Def Svc Med, Army Svc Rib, Overseas Svc Rib, Armed Forces Res Med w/2 devices and Army Res Comp Achiev Med w/4 OLCs.

Resides in St Peters, MO with wife, Kathryn; they have five children, and three grandchildren.

WILLIAM A. CHURCH, CW4, USA, born June 8, 1948, Flint, MI. Raised in Holly, MI, graduated high school

and entered US Army in June 1965. Basic training and AIT (clerk school) at Ft Knox, KY. Advanced to SP5E5 (AGC), serving as company clerk, personnel specialist, and administration specialist at Sinop, Turkey, Tokyo, Japan and Ft Benning, GA. Entered IRR in 1968, discharged in 1971 and entered MIARNG as MP in 1975. Served with 46th MP Co, Lansing MI as SGTE5 squad leader and SWAT team member for three years.

Returned to active duty in February 1978, attended WOCMDC/Flight School, and was appointed WO1, USAR in January 1979.

Served with 3rd AB(C), Geibelstadt, FRG as Aeroscout Pilot and Border Unit Trainer. In 1982 became an instructor pilot and taught the Aeroscout IERW Crs at Ft Rucker, AL until 1985. He graduated from Embry-Riddle Aeronautical University with AS and BS degrees in December 1986, followed by tours to Ft Campbell, KY and Chunchon, ROK to form and deploy the 309th AHB.

Assigned to the 1-24th AHB, Savannah, GA in 1988; helped form, train, and deploy the 5-501st Avn Regt to Wonju, ROK in 1989; served with the 5-501st and 4-501st Avn Regt from July 1989-February 1994; acted as EUSA Flight Standards designated OH58 SIP, 1990-1991. Currently assigned as Standards Officer/OH58 SIP at 4-501st Avn Regt at Chunchon, ROK. Flight experiences: 5,600 (1,000 NVG) accident free hours. Will help train up a new Apache Bn at Ft Hood, TX and deploy it to the ROK in late 1994.

Awards include Meritorious Svc Med, ARCM (2), Army Achiev Med, Good Conduct Med, Nat Def Svc Med (2), Overseas Svc Rib w/#8, Army Svc Rib; badges include SS (M-14), EXP (M-16), EXP M-16, EXP .38 cal and 9mm pistols and Master Army Aviator.

Divorced, father of three children: Shannon, Dayton, OH Robert and James, Flint, MO. Member of USAWOA and AAAA since 1979.

WALTER W. CLARK, CW3, USA (RET), born Feb 10, 1928, Ryegate, MT. Graduated high school and entered US Army 1946; basic training at Ft Lewis, WA; assigned to 1st Guided Missile Bn, White Sands, NM. Helped fire first seven German V-2 rockets. He served in Korea with the 8th FA, 25th Div. While there he flew with the 8th AF as aerial observer and directed fighter strikes and artillery fire.

Reassigned to 4054th Board #4 at Ft Bliss, TX. Graduated SAM Fire Control Crs; appointed WO1 in October 1955. Assigned to AARADCOM in Pittsburgh and Philadelphia; 52nd Bde HQ, Atlantic Highlands, NJ; assigned 32nd Bde, Baumholder, Germany in 1964.

Received the Nat Def Svc Med w/OLC, Good Conduct Med, WWII Victory Med, Korean Svc Med, UN Svc Med w/O/S Bar, Air Medal, Armed Forces Res Med and the Army Comm Med.

Married Ruth Sovil in 1949 and they raised three daughters. Married Sharon Robbins in 1967 and raised one daughter. He retired in October 1968.

PAUL H. CLARKE, CW3, RA, born July 8, 1947, Park Ridge, IL, and raised in Winnetka, IL. Graduated from New Trier HS in 1965 and attended Luther College in Decorah, IA. Entered the service in 1975 to attend the Initial Entry Rotary Wing Aviator Crs. Basic training was at Ft Polk, LA.

Served with the D/158 Avn Bn, 101st Abn Div, 1976-1979, UH-1H pilot; Air Trp, 2 ACR, 1979-1982, AH-1S pilot; B/D Trp, 2-17 Cav, 101st Abn Div, 1982-87, AH-1F instructor pilot; B Co, 2-3 Avn Regt, 3ID, 1987-1990, instrument flight examiner, standardization officer; 3-17 Cav, 10th Mtn Div (LI), 1990-, instrument flight standard-

ization officer, ARFOR/TF 3-17 Standardization Off, Operation Restore Hope, Somalia.

Awards include Army Comm Med w/2 OLCs, Army Achiev Med w/3 OLCs, Good Conduct, Nat Def Svc Med, Armed Forces Exped Med, Army Svc Rib, Overseas Rib (2nd awd), Joint Unit Meritorious Awd and the Master Army Aviator Badge.

Married Elaine Marie (Duby) of Wheatland, PA.

B. COHEN, CW2, served during WWII and awarded the Legion of Merit for technical ingenuity for fabricating a vehicle frame straightener and axle straightener. Without his innovation many vehicles that were returned to combat would not have been available.

During the Korean War, he won the Bronze Star w/V device for heroic action near Chupari, South Korea on Sept 11, 1951; awarded a second Bronze Star w/OLC for technical contributions in the fabrication of a device that prevented track laying vehicles from sliding on hazardous, icy, Korean mountain trails. He also fabricated parts that allowed deadlined equipment to be repaired and returned to service. His initiative saved a great deal of immobilized equipment from falling into enemy hand.

From 1956-76 served the Ord Corps as civilian employee at Army Ord Ctr and School. His three major accomplishments included: designing the Metal Body Repair Crs, developing instructional materials and serving as primary instruction for the first two years of the course; updating the Welding Crs to include introduction of metal inert gas welding; supervising all welding and metal body repair during training, 1970-76.

While in uniform and again as a civilian, he successfully supervised welding and metal body repair training at the USAOC&S during the Korean and Vietnam conflicts. During both periods, he displayed great initiative and saved the US Government a great deal of money.

DONNA D. ZAMPI-COLON, CW4, USA, born Aug 27, 1956, Harmon AFB, Stephenville, Newfoundland, Canada, and raised in Vestal, NY. Entered the US Army in December 1974; attended basic training at Ft Jackson, SC; AIT at Lowry AFB, CO, MOS 35H, test, measurement and diagnostic equip spec (TMDE). Served as electronic tech with MICOM/95th Maint Co, Redstone Arsenal, AL; 257th Sig Co, Camp Humphreys, Korea; 521st Maint Co, Hanau/ Schwanheim, Germany. As E6 she received direct appointment to WO1 March 1981, TMDE tech, MOS 252A/918A.

Assignments included VII Corps TMDE Coordinator, 2nd SUPCOM, Stuttgart, Germany; commander of TMDE detachments at Ft Ord, CA and Ft Stewart, GA; and 5th Sig Cmd's TMDE Program manager, Worms, Germany. Today, she is a combat development staff officer, USAOMMCS, Redstone Arsenal, AL.

Awarded the Meritorious Svc Med w/OLC, Army Comm Med w/OLC, Army Achiev Med, Humanitarian Svc Med, Good Conduct (2nd Awd), Nat Def Svc Med w/2 stars, Army Svc Rib, AOR (3), and NCOPDR (2).

Graduated from Univ of Maryland in 1989 with BS degreee in business management; and MS in systems management from Univ of South Carolina in 1991, Phi Kappa Phi. She has one son, Anthony Mitchell, born on March 5, 1992.

ROBERT NEILL COOPER (BOB), CW4, USA (RET), born Dec 14, 1941, in Church Hill, TN. Entered Army in September 1957; attended basic training at Ft Benning, GA as member of 3rd Inf Div "New Marne Men," then gyroed to Germany in March 1958 with 10th Engr Bn.

Returned to States in 1961. Further assignments with 4th Engr Bn at Ft Lewis, WA; 23rd Engr Bn, Hanau, Germany; 5th LOG Cmd and 12th Spt Bde at Ft Bragg, NC; 171st Inf Bde, Fairbanks, AK; attained the rank of E-7 prior to beginning Army Flt School at Ft Wolters, TX, February 1969.

Appointed WO1, November 1969. Assignments as

WO were with 240th Avn Co, Bearcat, RVN, liaison officer to Vietnamese AF Cadets and 214th Avn Bn, Hunter AAF, GA; 52nd Avn Bn, Yongsan, Korea; US Army Avn Safety Ctr and Dir of Eval and Std at Ft Rucker, AL; and US Mil Trng Mission to Saudi Arabia.

Retired from Army October 1987 as CW4 with over 30 years of active service. Employed by flight training contractor at Ft Rucker, AL as Asst Dir of Safety. Currently member of ROA, AAAA, VHPA, charter member of Seoul Korea Ch of WOA and life member of VFW.

Married Ditte of Copenhagen, Denmark. They have two children and two grandsons. Sons, David Cooper followed fathers' footsteps and became Army aviator in March 1993 and Robert is paratrooper in GAARNG.

DONALD V. COPELAND, CW3, USA (RET), born May 24, 1937, Ft Madison, IA. Entered Army Nov 14, 1958, taking basic training at Ft Carson, CO. Attended Auto Mechanics Helper Crs at Ft Leonard Wood, MO and served as unit mechanic with the 362nd Sig Co, Ft Gordon, GA; senior auto repairman with the 3rd Inf Div, H97th US Army; and several separate maintenance units in Europe. Instructor at Ft Leonard Wood, MO and Army Ord Ctr and Ord OCSs, APG, MD.

Appointed WO1 Sept 12, 1967, and served with the 101st Abn Inf Div, RVN, During TET 1968 at Bien Hoa, Phan Rang and Camp Eagle (Phu Bai) RVN with 2/502nd Abn Inf, 501st Sup Det, 101st Truck Co (Prov) and 426th S&SBN. Served in several FORSCOM maint units at Ft Sill, OK, Ft Meade, MD, Ft Polk, LA and maint units assigned to the 7th Army Corps in Europe.

Attached to Cam Rahn Bay Army Depot from the 69th Maint Bn and served as chief, Inspection-Identification Section with retrograde responsibilities and OIC Project Keystone, Jan 11, 1971-Jan 31, 1972.

Awarded Bronze Star w/OLC, Meritorious Svc Med, Army Comm Med w/OLC, Air Med, Good Conduct Med (3rd Awd), Nat Def Svc Med, RVN Cross of Gallantry (personal awd) RVN Svc Med w/8 Battle Stars, RVN Campaign Med, Pres Unit Cit, Meritorious Unit Cit (2 Awds), RVN Cross of Gallantry w/Palm Unit Citation, RVN Civil Actions Unit Citation and (4) Overseas Bars.

Retired Dec 31, 1978, and currently employed by Good Year Tire and Rubber Co in Shipping Dept at Lawton Plant in Oklahoma where he has 14 years of service.

ALFRED E. COX, CW3, AUS (RET), born July 24, 1938, Claiborne County, TN. Entered Army May 15, 1958; basic training, Ft Chaffee, AR; AIT at Ft Monmouth, NJ. Served in 57th Sig Co Seoul Korea, 1959-60; 69th Sig Bn, Ft Meade, MD, 1960-61. May 1961 joined USAF as airborne radio/radar operator/repairman. Duty involved aerial photographing of Cuban Missile removal activities, 1962, special duty with Peruvian Embassy, 1963, and removal of troops and equipment from France, 1966.

Appointed WO in Army Sig Corps; September 1968-February 1971 served with Army Avn Units for two tours of

duty in RVN and in between tour at Butts AAF, Ft Carson, CO. Reassigned to the Sig Corps February 1971 for tour of duty in Hanau, Germany. Selected June 1974 for assignment with White House Communications Agency.

Retired from active duty Dec 31, 1978. Entered FCS June 1979, Ft Ritchie, MD; served as Cmd Ops Sec Off for 7th Sig Cmd; assigned to Spec Ops Div in support of JSOC. Promoted to Chief, Ops Div, Deputy Chief of Staff Ops and Plans, HQ, 7th Sig Cmd. August 1988 promoted to current position as Chief, Army Infor Systems Cmd, Technology Applications Office, Ft Ritchie, MD.

Received the Legion of Merit, Bronze Star w/2 OLCs, Meritorious Svc Med, Air Medal w/OLCs, Army Comm Med w/2 OLCs, AFCM w/OLC, Good Conduct Med w/OLC, Nat Def Svc Med, RVN Svc Med, Vietnam Cross of Gallantry, Pres Svc Badge.

Joined EWOA 1971; USAWOA, 1972; president of Hanau Silver Ch, 1972; president European Region, 1973-74; national president USAWOA. 1974-75. Lifetime trustee of USA WOA, 1975-present; member of ROA, VFW, AL, AUSA, AFCEA and NRA.

Married former Doris Stiner, a federal employee since 1974. They have three children: Melissa, Teresa and Douglas, and three grandchildren, all living in Waynesboro, PA.

JESSE C. COZART, CW3, USA (RET), born May 14, 1924, Heath, AK. Entered Army in February 1943 and attended basic and airplane mechanics training at Ft Sill, OK. Served as an airplane mechanic with the 5th Armd Div in Europe during WWII and 7th Inf Div in Korea and Japan during Occupation and the Korean Conflict. Other assignments during this period included Ft Sill, OK and the Army War College.

Called to active duty as WO in May 1955. Served as aircraft maint officer and tech at Ft Hood, TX, Europe, Vietnam and Ft Eustis, VA until he retired as CW3 in November 1965 with over 22 years of service.

He was awarded the Air Medal, Meritorious Svc Med w/OLC, Army Comm Med w/OLC, Decoration of Meritorious Civilian Service and numerous service and campaign medals.

After active duty retirement he was employed by the Army as an aircraft maint instructor, training administrator and as chief of the New Systems Trng Div at the Trans School and later the same duty with the Avn Log School as aviation became a separate branch. Retired from civil service in March 1988 after 23 years of service. During his 45 years with Army Avn, he was involved with the maint, trng and log for Army aircraft ranging from the L-4 Cub to the AH-64 Apache.

He is member of TROA, USAWOA, Assoc of the US Army, Army Avn Assoc, National Assoc of Civilian Conservation Corp alumni and Rutitan National.

Married Nina Speight of Brownsville, TN; they have one daughter, Lynda.

WENDELL R. CRAIG, CW4, (RET), born Oct 9, 1941, Lynchburg, VA. Entered Army March 31, 1960, taking basic training at Ft Jackson, SC and Wheeled And Tracked Vehicle Mech School at Ft Sill, OK. He served as mechanic and parts clerk in Germany until discharge. He was employed by a mechanic in a new car dealership for two years before enlisting in the USAF on March 25, 1965. Served as mechanic and maintenance supervisor in Myrtle Beach AFB, SC and Hickam AFB, HI.

Appointed WO1 in February 1968 and served as automotive maint tech in various overseas locations including Korea, Vietnam, Hawaii and Saudi Arabia. CONUS assignments included Ft Bragg, NC (2); Ft Rucker, AL; St Louis, MO; and APG, MD. He retired as CW4 in January 1984 with over 23 years of service.

Awards include the Bronze Star, Meritorious Svc Med w/OLC, Army Comm Med w/OLC, AF Comm Med, Army and AF Good Conduct and numerous service and campaign medals.

Life member (99) of the USAWOA and member of American Legion and American Defence Preparedness Assoc. Since retirement he has been employed as log analyst, senior log analyst and program manager for JAYCOR in

Vienna, VA. Currently ILS program manager at JAYCOR for a government acquisition program.

Married Alice Geraldine Winston of Altavista, VA and has two children, Malia and David.

ROBERT J. CRAWFORD, CWO4, USA (RET), born July 11, 1912, Chicago, IL. Began his military career with Med Det 265th Coast Arty, FLNG, in October 1940. The unit was inducted into the Army in January 1941 taking basic training at Ft Crockett, Galveston, TX. Stationed at William Beaumont Gen Hosp, El Paso, TX; Ft Taylor, Key West, FL; Ft Jackson, SC; Ft Hancock, NJ; Camp Barkley, TX; CAMA (California/Arizona Maneuvers Area) Yuma, AZ; Camp Chaffee, Ft Smith, AR; 1944-45, European Theater (England and France), 123rd and 77th Station Hospitals, 11th, 2nd and 10th Repl Depots, Med Det of 41st and 533rd QM Bn; returned to the States on *Queen Mary* with the 393rd Med Coll Co in November 1945.

Discharged at Ft Levenworth, KS as staff sergeant Feb 1, 1946. He is active ORC M/SGT, 82nd Abn Div, 485th GIR, 3rd Army, Jacksonville, FL. Appointed WOJG, 1951 and in 1972 retired as CWO-4, Food Svc Tech, 345th Evac Hosp, 3rd Army.

Awards include the Campaign and Svc American Def, 1941, Campaign and Svc Nat Def, WWII Victory Med, Good Conduct Med, Armed Forces Res and Armed Forces Res for Achiev.

Before entering military service he was employed as veterinary pathologist with Jacksonville Humane Small Animal Hosp, 1935-40. He is licensed as a single engine pilot. After WWII he was employed by Seaboard Railway as lab tech; 1951-70 with Florida Mil Dist, Dir Audio Visual Spt Ctr, US Army; 1970-75 with the Florida Dept of Health as manager, Audio Visual Library.

Married Lillie Rollins Stacy of Jasper, AL and had two children and two grandchildren. He passed away on February 24, 1992.

EDWARD D. CREWS, CW4, USA (RET), born Dec 16, 1924, in Sanderson, FL. Entered Army Aug 25, 1943, at Camp Blanding, FL, attended basic training and AIT with the 42nd Rainbow Div at Camp Gruber, OK. Released from active duty April 15, 1946, and joined the active Reserve on April 16, 1946.

Appointed WO in May 1957 and served as Pers Officer with 3017th Station Hosp. Finance and Maint Officer with the 345th Cbt Spt Hosp.

Retired Dec 15, 1984, with over 40 years of continuous service with all Reserve units of Jacksonville, FL. Awards include the Army Comm Med, Army Achiev Med, Good Conduct Med, Nat Def Svc and Armed Forces Res Med w/2 HGs.

Married Joyce Shaw and has three children and five grandchildren. Retired from Ford Motor Co in 1988 with over 42 years of service. He is a life member of the ROA and American Legion.

MACK H. CRIDDELL, CW4, USA (RET), born June 25, 1936, Dallas, TX. Entered Army Aug 2, 1959, and took basic infantryman training at Belvoir, VA. Served as draftsman and illustrator at Staff and Faculty Btry, Ft Sill, OK; Electronic Warfare Countermeasures School, Ft Monmouth, NJ; and EW repairman at military installations in the US Army, Asia and Europe.

Appointed WO in January 1967 while on duty in Berlin, Germany. Served as EW tech, comm off, crypto tech, Depot Elec Maint Sup Off and Avionics Off until he retired as CW4 in September 1981.

Awarded the Bronze Star, Meritorious Svc Med, Army Comm Med w/OLC and numerous service and campaign medals.

Married Verniece McCoy of Palestine, TX; there are no children. Currently employed by Enviro/Max, Inc as project manager and principal of consulting firm in Dallas, TX. He is a charter and lifetime member of the USAWOA.

HENRY ALVIN CROWDER, CW3, USA (RA), born Aug 30, 1953, Panama City, FL. Graduated from HS in Beckley, WV; Univ of Maryland with associates degree. Enlisted in Army April 4, 1974, Jacksonville, FL; basic training at Ft Jackson, SC; AIT training at Ft Huachuca, AZ.

Assigned to 502nd ASA Gp, Field Station Augsburg, West Germany; 1st Tac 856th ASA Co, Frankfurt, Germany; Spec Analyst, US Army FA School (USAFAS), Ft Sill, OK, 1977; re-enlisted 1978 at Ft Sill, OK.

December 1979 reported to 2nd MI Det/G2 2nd Inf Div, Camp Casey, Korea; served as NCOIC of SCIF analysts. Prepared WO packet and boarded at Camp Casey. Reported to 504th MI Gp, III Corps, Ft Hood, TX; deployed with elements of III Corps to Germany for WINTEX exercise. Appointed WO April 17, 1981, Ft Hood, TX; attended third class of WO Off Orientation Class, Ft Rucker, AL, June 1981.

WO, OB and ASI assignments, 1981-91: OB Tech, 109th MI Bn and G2 9th Inf Div; Ft Lewis, WA; MI WOAC, Ft Huachuca, AZ; OB tech, 501st MI Bn and G2 1st Armd Div, Ansbach, West Germany; completed WOSC correspondence crs from Ft Rucker, AL; OB tech, 174th MI Co (174th EACIC) Ft Monmouth, NJ; ASI tech, ARCENT EACIC, Riyadh, Saudi Arabia (Ops Desert Shield/Storm); senior ASI tech, 297th MI Bn EACIC, Ft Monmouth, NJ; senior ASI tech, 513th AMISE (Dett), HQ 3rd US Army/ARCENT, Ft McPherson, GA.

Awards include Bronze Star, Meritorious Svce Med, Army Comm Med, Army Achiev, Joint Meritorious Unit Awd, Unit Meritorious Comm, Saudi Arabia-Kuwait Lib Med, SWA Svc Med, Nat Def Svc Med, Army Svc Rib, Overseas Svc Rib, Good Conduct and several civilian awards.

Married Beth Marie Burlingame and they have two children, Heather Elizabeth and Jeremy Allen.

HARVEY L. CURRY, CW4, USA (RET), born June 5, 1939, Alva, OK. Graduated from Carmen HS, Carmen, OK in 1957. Enlisted in Army Feb 13, 1958. Basic training at Ft Carson, CO and AIT at Ft Monmouth, NJ. Served with the White House Comm Agency from May 1959-April 1967.

On April 5, 1967, received a direct appointment to WO1 and served two tours in Vietnam, one with the 4th Inf Div and one with the 509th Radio Research Gp. Other assignments include two tours in Germany, The Lexington Bluegrass Army Depot and the 25th Inf Div.

Awards include the Legion of Merit, Bronze Star w/2 OLCs, Meritorious Svc Med, Army Comm Med, Good Conduct Med and the Pres Svc Badge. He is 20 year member of the USAWOA.

Graduated from the Northwestern State College, Alva, OK in 1974 with BS degree and from Morehead State University, Morehead, KY in 1977 with an MBA.

Married Leslie Rogers of Wayside, NJ and has three sons and a daughter. Since retiring from Army, he has worked in the natural gas pipeline industry.

GEORGE W. DAHLQUIST, CWO, USA (RET), born May 14, 1896, Sweden. Began music career as bandsman in Swedish Army. Arrived in States 1917 and learned the English language. Joined the Army June 5, 1919, Ft McDowell, CA. Assigned to band at Presidio of San Francisco. February 1921 attended Army School of Music until

June 1923; promoted to staff sergeant with Army Band in Washington, DC. Assignments took him to Langley Field, VA; Ft Hoyle, MD; 2nd Cav Band, Ft Riley, KS as band leader; promoted to tech sergeant.

Appointment to WO May 15, 1928. Transferred to Schofield Barracks, HI; 1931 to Ft Monroe, VA; October 1934 back to Hawaii and in July 1938 to 14th Coast Arty Band, Ft Worden, WA. December 1942 promoted to CWO.

A symphony conductor and composer of over 20 military marches including *The 34th Infantry March*, and *Semper Peratus;* pageant music director for the Yorktown Sesquicentennial in 1931 for which he composed the march, *Yorktown Sesquicentennial*.

September 1944 received medical retirement from Army and settled on small farm at Lake Stevens, WA. He passed away in 1959.

JAMES R. DAMRON, CW5, USA, born July 1, 1940, Shelbyville, TN. Enlisted in Army June 15, 1958; basic training at Ft Ord, CA. Enlisted assignments at Ft Huachuca, KMAG in Korea; Camp McCoy, WI; Ft Leonard Wood and 25th Div in Hawaii. Deployed with 25th Div to Vietnam and appointed to WO during 1966-67 tour. Completed first Vietnam assignment at HQ, 1st Log Cmd. Assigned to 6th ACR at Ft Meade, MD where participated in civil disturbance actions involving the "March on the Pentagon," October 1967, and riot control duties in Washington DC, following the assassination of Martin Luther King.

Another Vietnam tour with 1st Bn, 27 Inf (Wolfhounds); Korea, Ft Wainwright, the 1st Cav Div at Ft Hood, and again with the 25th in Hawaii. In 1980 assigned to HAWK Project Office, Redstone Arsenal, AL with duties involving Foreign Military Sales to Mid-East countries.

Served four year tour at US Military Academy, West Point; tour with 6th Inf Div (L) in Alaska. Attended Master WO Crs January 1989. December 1991 assigned to Master WO Crs at Ft Rucker as instructor. Served as charter member of the Leader Development Decision Network that developed the WO Leader Development Action Plan. The Total Army WO Career Ctr was established at Ft Rucker; he was appointed as first commandant. Promoted CW5 Nov. 1, 1992.

Awards/Medals: Purple Heart, (5 awds) Bronze Star, Air Med, multiple awards of Army Comm Med, Meritorious Svc Med and Army Achievement Med.

Married Lee Damron in 1962 and has two children, Jimmy and Sandy.

JACK L. DANIELS, CW2, born April 28, 1927, Detroit, MI. Drafted in service Aug. 7, 1945, Kalamazoo, MI. Served in Sig ASA Trans Ord Inf 25th Div in 1968. Basic training at Camp Fannin, TX. Overseas to Austria, Japan, Germany, Italy and two tours in Vietnam.

Participated in seven battles with the 25th Inf Div in Vietnam. Retired July 31, 1972, at Ft Polk, LA. Highest award is Bronze Star.

Divorced, has three children and six grandchildren. Writes letters to editors, several newspapers and *Army Times.*

GERALD A. DAVIES, CW3, born July 9, 1938, Syracuse, NY and raised in Cazenovia, NY. Graduated Cazenovia HS; entered the Army and attended basic training at Ft Dix, NJ in August 1956. Attended school at Ft Belvoir, VA, December-March 1957; assigned to the 141st Sig Bn, Ft

Polk, LA with 1st Armd Div; transferred to 205th Sig, Ft Polk. September 1958 transferred to Kaiserslautern, Germany, Kleber Kaserne with 69th Sig Co (Photo). Left active service November 1959.

Re-enlisted January 1964 and after basic went to Ft Greely, AK to US Army Artic Test Ctr, April 1964-October 1965. Assigned to 196th Light Inf Bde at Ft Devens, MA; B Co, 8th Spt Bn, June 1966 en route to Tay Ninh, Vietnam; unit moved up north.

Left service January 1967 and re-entered USAR September 1974 with 1209th USAG, Mattydale, NY with unit as SGT E5 until promoted to CW2 Aug. 28, 1985. Went with 1209th Ft Drum Det with DEH; April 1990 assigned to 359th Sig Bde as supply technician.

Later as Property Book Officer at North Syracuse, NY. Attended Sr WO Crs April 1992. Still in USAR and enjoys being member of USAWOA the last eight years. His memorable experience was kissing the ground in Oakland, CA, Jan. 17, 1967, first day back in real world. Received Army Achievement Med, Good Conduct (2nd Awd) and Meritorious Svc Med.

Married Geneveive Corbett of Watertown, NY and has two sons, Michael and Mark. After 20 years with US Postal System, he retired as letter carrier. Enjoys building homes for Habitat for Humanity.

HAROLD L. DEAL, CW4, USA (RET), born Jan. 27, 1925, Newville, AL. Entered Army June 17, 1943, Ft McCellan, AL. Attended Inf basic training at Camp Fanning, TX. Sent overseas (SW Pacific) as infantry replacement. Due to civilian training in aircraft engine mechanics, he was reclassified and assigned to 13th AF. Discharged AAC as corporal Jan. 5, 1946.

Recalled to active duty with B Co, 200th Inf, 31st Inf Div ALNG, Jan. 16, 1951, as WOJG, unit administrator. Completed Aircraft Maint Officer Crs, Class #4, Ft Eustis, VA, Feb. 3, 1955. Upon completion of AMOC assigned to 93rd Trans Co (HCPTR), Ft Riley, KS; served with 6th Trans Co (HCPTR), Japan; 7th Avn Gp, Germany; and tour in Vung Tau, Vietnam with 138th Trans Det.

Retired as CW4 at Ft Rucker, AL on June 30, 1968. Worked with aircraft maintenance contractor at Ft Rucker, AL for nine years after retirement.

Awards/Medals: Bronze Star, Army Res Comm Med w/2 stars, Air Med, Good Conduct Med, WWII Victory Med, Asiatic-Pacific Campaign Med, Philippine Lib Rib, Army Comm Med (Japan), Nat Def Med w/OLC, five Overseas Bars, Armed Forces Res Med w/10 year device, Philippine Pres Unit Cit, SR Acft CRM Badge, Vietnam Svc Med, Air Med and Vietnam Unit Awd.

Married Betty Ann Evans from Dothan, AL. Has three children, eight grandchildren and two great-grandchildren.

PHILIP A. DeHENNIS, CWO4, USA (RET), born Nov. 27, 1927, DeLancey, PA. Entered Army Feb. 25, 1946; basic training at Ft Knox, KY; served with Gen MacArthur's HQ as occupation forces in Tokyo, Japan. Assigned as escort for WWII dead and stationed at Philadelphia, PA, returning bodies to seven different states from 1948-49.

Transferred from active Reserve status to PANG July 5, 1949. Called to active duty Sept. 11, 1950, with 235th FA Observation Bn during Korean Conflict. Sent to Camp McCoy, WI and Korea, serving with 2nd Inf Div in and around Iron Triangle.

Returned to Pennsylvania state control Sept. 11, 1952, served with NG units: 416th AAA AW Bn; 709th AAA Gun and Msl Bn; 3rd Msl Bn, 166th Arty; 2nd Msl Bn, 166th Arty; 166th Sup and Svc Bn; 1066th Engr Bn; 28th Sup and Trans Bn; C Co, 103rd Engr Bn; and Det 1, 723rd MP Co.

Honorably discharged from Det 1, 723rd MP Co Jan. 1, 1983, and assigned to USAR Control GP (Reinforcement) with final discharge Jan. 7, 1987. Placed on retired list Nov. 27, 1987, with retired grade of CWO-4, having completed 41 years, nine months and two days of military service. Campaigns were 2nd Korean Winter and Korean Summer-Fall Offensive.

Currently employed as security guard at retirement home. Active member of Artillery Corps, Washington Grays (a unit which dates back to June 19, 1777), Veteran Corps 1st Regt. Inf PANG and American Legion.

Married Elizabeth Keely and has four children and five grandchildren.

PATRICK R. DERBY, CW2, USA, born Dec. 22, 1955. Enlisted in Army Feb. 16, 1976, with MI, 350L. Stationed in US Defense Attaché Office at Windhoek and USDAO in Rome.

Memorable experience was first US Military Attaché accredited to Government of Namibia.

Received the Defense Superior Svc Med, Meritorious Svc Med w/OLC, Army Res Com Med w/3 OLCs and Army Achievement Med. Currently a CW2.

Married Lynn Martin of King of Prussia, PA. Currently an attaché technician, USDAO in Rome, Italy.

JOHN B. DERDEN, CW4, USA (RET), born June 27, 1919, Ellijay, GA. Began military career by enlisting in 66th Inf light tanks at Ft Benning, GA. Served as private to tech sergeant in E and B Co, 66th Armd Regt.

Appointed WOJG April 1943 and assigned assistant maint officer HQ, 1st Bn, 66th AR and served as such for the remainder of war. Member of 2nd Armd Div, July 15, 1940-Aug. 26, 1945. Participated in all battles and campaigns the division was involved, Africa, Sicily and across Europe.

Awards/Medals: Bronze Star Med, (2) Invasion Arrowheads, (7) Campaign Stars, Army Comm Med w/OLC and the Belgian Forragere.

On the instructional staff of the Army Inf School for six and a half years and the US Army Armor School for two years. Served as maint officer in Calvary, Armor and heavy artillery units including the 280mm atomic cannon.

Has commercial pilot rating and flown many search missions with Hawaiian, Kentucky and Georgia CAP Sqdns. Served more than 26 years in Army and retired September 1965.

Joined teaching staff of Dekald Tech Institute and retired from there in 1979 at Clarkston, GA. He and wife, Virginia, have visited all 50 States. Hobbies include flying, camping, fishing and making the Appalachian Dulcimer.

WALTER DESMOND, CWO4 (RET), born Feb. 3, 1916, Chicago, IL. Entered Army May 1, 1942; attended basic training at Ft Knox, KY. Attached to 12th Armor Div at Ft Campbell, KY when activated. Appointed WO in January 1943 as a medical supply officer in 82nd Med Bn.

In September 1944 the Division sailed to England; then sent to Rouen, France as part of the 7th Army. In March 1954 attached to XX Corps, 3rd Army. Progressed through southern Germany with final destination being Kurstein, Austria. Received Bronze Star in recognition of moving medical supplies closest to the battlefield.

Remained in service until Aug. 2, 1962, having served

at Ft Sam Houston, TX; Ft Bragg, NC; Ft Custer, MI; Ft Sheridan, IL; Bad Constadt, Germany; Korea; Ft Leonard Wood, MO; and the 5th Army HQ, Chicago.

Married Eileen McNerney and had six children and seven grandchildren. He passed away May 18, 1977, and is laid to rest at Ft Sheridan Cemetery, IL.

ALLAN O. DETTMANN, CW4 (RET), born Aug. 17, 1919, Sparta, WI. Enlisted in US Army Feb. 27, 1941, at old Camp McCoy, WI. Appointed WOJG March 20, 1943, and assigned to HQ, 15th Port per par 32, Special Orders #79, War Dept. Departed for overseas with 15th as excess on Dec. 6, 1943. Transferred to HQ, Western Base Sect, February 1944, and after D-day to HQ, United Kingdom base as assistant AG (2110).

Returned from overseas Nov. 30, 1945, and relieved from active duty Feb. 15, 1946. Assigned to Reserves; transferred to AG Section, 32nd Inf Div, WING January 1947. Promoted to CW4 Oct. 15, 1959, recalled to active duty with 32nd (BC) Oct. 15, 1961-Aug. 10, 1962. On deactivation of 32nd, he was assigned to 105th Light Maint Co (301A). Employed by USPFO WING as logistics officer, Dec. 9, 1946-July 1976.

Awards include Bronze Star, WWII Victory Med, EAME Theater, Am Theater, Am Def Med and Good Conduct Med. Retired from NG and Civil Service Aug. 4, 1976. Now living in New Mexico.

JOSEPH DIAZ, CW3, March 19, 1943, New York City, NY. Enlisted NJARNG Feb. 24, 1960. Basic training at Ft Benning, GA; school training at Ft Benjamin Harrison, IN; QM in Giessen, Germany; 1st Army, Ft Jay, Governors Island, NY; and 7th Army, Zweibrucken, Germany.

Military education included computer operations (MOS 74) and recruiting and retention at Ft Benjamin Harrison, IN; corresponding courses in Personnel Management and Automated Data Processing (basic/advance/senior). Given honorable discharge after six years and 15 days of service; inactive service from March 1966-July 1971.

Army Security Agency, Ft Hancock, NJ, July 1971-July 1972; NJARNG, July 1972-May 1978, with the 50th AG Co NJ; NJARNG, commissioned as WO to the 50 PSC Co, June 1978 to present.

Awards/Medals: Army Comm Med (2nd), Good Conduct Med, Nat Def Med, Armed Forces Res Med, New Jersey Med of Honor, New Jersey Merit Awd, Unit Strength Awd and New Jersey Desert Storm Svc Rib.

Memorable experiences include learning a career, starting his family, traveling and continuing his education, which all helped his profession, personal growth and a wonderful family.

Received associate degree in computer science and is working on BA in business. Currently employed with Continental Ins Corp as system analyst (hardware, software, communication installation and troubleshooting) for the past 15 years.

Married in 1963 and has two daughters, Melissa and Sharon. Currently living in Jackson, NJ.

RAY M. DILDINE, CW4, USA (RET), born Dec. 6, 1928, Wynona, OK. Entered US Army Jan. 30, 1951; attended basic training at Ft Leonard Wood, MO. Assigned to 4th Army Co A, 701st Armed Inf Bn on May 30, 1951, in Korea. Transferred to Ready Reserve Oct. 31, 1952; discharged Oct. 31, 1956. Re-enlisted Jan. 2, 1958, and appointed by the USNG and state of Oklahoma as SFC E6, Jan. 7, 1958, with HQ Btry, 145 AAA Bn (AW)(SP) general mechanic, Pawhuska, OK.

Received appointment as WO WO1 April 15, 1962; transferred March 27, 1963 to HHD 145th Sig Bn, auto maint tech in Edmond, OK. Transferred Jan 1, 1969, with HHC 120th Engr Bn, Okmulgee, OK as organization maintenance shop chief and served there until retirement Dec. 6, 1988.

Awards/Medals: Korean Svc Med w/2 Bronze Stars, Combat Inf Badge, UN Svc Med, numerous Oklahoma Guardsman Exceptional Svc Meds, Superior Performance Awds, certificates of accomplishment and commendations.

Married Frances Forrest of Barnsdall, OK. Has three children: Charles Ray, Cheryl Ann and Chris Alan. He passed away Dec. 19, 1989.

LLOYD S. DILLARD, CW5, born Aug. 12, 1936, Boxwood, VA, but considers Reidsville, NC, home. Enlisted in Regular Army Jan. 6, 1959, as Pers Tech 420A. Stationed at Ft Jackson, SC; Germany (Giessen and K-Town); Vietnam; Ft Bragg, NC; Indianapolis, IN; Milwaukee, WI; Iran, Taiwan; Ft Rucker, AL; Huntsville, AL; Birmingham, AL; Pentagon; and Ft Monroe, VA. Participated at LAMSON 70.

Memorable experiences include obtaining BS, MS and M.Div degrees in the service; being ordained a Minister in Baptist Church; co-developer and member of the 1st Master WO Class; and being on first CW5 selection list.

Awarded the Legion of Merit, Bronze Star, Meritorious Svc Med (2), Army Res Comp Med (6), Good Conduct Med (3), Army Achiev Med, Nat Def Med Svc Med (2), Vietnam Svc Med and Meritorious Unit Cit (2).

Married Barbara Pegues and has two children, Lloyd S. II (air traffic controller) and Leslie (computer analyst and 1LT, Chem Corps, USAR). Currently assigned to WOCC at Ft Rucker, AL as instructor.

CLARENCE ARTIE DILLMAN (ART), CW2, INARNG (RET), born Aug. 1, 1939, English, IN. Attended U of Kentucky and Murray State U. Enlisted in USNR January 1957; transferred to USAF September 1957. Attended basic training at Lackland AFB, TX and Computer Maintenance School, Keesler AFB, MS.

Served on active duty until April 1966 at Hanna City AFS, IL; Sault Ste Marie AFS, MI; Snow Mt AFS, KY; Fire Island AFS, AK; and McClellan AFB, CA.

Re-enlisted in USNR in 1967, served at different stations while working for NASA. In 1972 returned to Indiana and transferred from USNR to INARNG serving as Artillery Fire Direction Chief and later Chief of Firing Battery in 155mm Btry. Appointed as WO1, Sig Maint Officer for 138th Sig Bn, 38th Inf Div in April 1982. Served in that position until retirement in May 1987.

Awards/Medals: Army and Air Force Good Conduct Med, Indiana Comm Med, Army Achiev Med, Armed Forces Res Med and Nat Def Med Svc Med.

Resides in Spencer, IN and is currently a field sales specialist for Perkin Elmer selling scientific instrumentation for chemical and medical use. Retained his membership with WOA and the 38th Inf Div Assoc. Married Agnes Irene Toby in December 1959 and has four children and four grandchildren.

THOMAS J. DITTMAN, CW3, June 1977-July 1979 entered Army as PVT E-1, Prch Rigger for 10th Spec Forces Gp (Abn), Ft Devens, MA. Earned Abn and Prcht Rigger Wings. July 1979-July 1980 cadet candidate at West Point Prep School, Ft Monmouth, NJ. Member of skydiving, track and field teams. Honor graduate, second of 215. July 1980-January 1981 cadet at the USMA, West Point, NY.

Completed "Beast Barracks" and one semester as plebe with above average grades and resigned after Christmas break. As member of skydiving team he represented USMA at Collegiate National Skydiving Championships and placed second in accuracy and fourth overall in category.

January 1981-June 1982, classified a civilian. June 1982-June 1983 WO Candidate in Flight School at Ft Rucker, AL. Graduated Aeroscout tracks as OH-58 pilot in May 1983; OH-58 pilot, 2nd Inf Div, Camp Casey, Korea, June 1983. Attended Korean Ranger School and earned ROK Ranger Badge. UH-60 transition at Ft Rucker, AL, July 1984; medevac/instructor pilot, 421st Med Bn, Darmstadt, Germany. Attended UH-60 Instructor Pilot Crs and Advanced Crs (honor graduate), while TDY at Ft Rucker. Earned AA Wings. December 1988-July 1989 "boot strap" full time civilian schooling at Embry-Riddle Aeronautical U, completed associate degree in aviation business administration. August 1989-August 1990 instructor pilot, 377th Med Co, Seoul AB, Korea; completed BS degree in aeronautics. October 1990-May 1991 completed U-21 and OV/RV-1D fixed wing qualifications at Ft Rucker, AL and Ft Huachuca, AZ.

June 1991-present assigned to 1st MI Bn (Aerial Exploitation), Wiesbaden AB, Germany as surveillance pilot (Imagery Intelligence) flying the OV/RV-1D Mohawk. Currently undergoing transition training into RC-12K airplane (Sig Intel) employing Guard Rail Common Sensor. Recently selected to attend Naval Test Pilot School, Patuxent River, MD. He will then be assigned as Army engineering test pilot at Edwards AFB, CA.

DANIEL E. DODGE, CW3, entered active Army Oct. 28, 1975. Attended basic training at Ft Leonard Wood, went in for 34G, but broke his foot in basic training and had to switch to MOS 74F. Graduated AIT, 74F COBOL Programmer School at Ft Ben Harrison June 1976 as distinguished graduate. Sent to West Point, support of Corps of Cadets at post computer center. October 1978 ETS as Spec-5.

Joined Active Reserves October 1979 with 425 PSC, Inkster, MI, which is part of the 300th MP Cmd as 74F programmer. Promoted to SSG. After OIC transferred and applied for direct promotion to WO, receiving in December 1982 as 741A data processing tech.

Transferred to 409th PSC, Tonowanda, NY, attached to 1209th US Army Garrison, Syracuse, NY March 1983. Both are part of 98th Div (trng). Duty was to support garrison data processing requirements while part of Ft Drum Det. Transferred to 2365th Sig Det October 1987 as communications section officer in charge of nine 72G soldiers. Mission was to support Camp Edwards, MA and Ft Drum ISC. Promoted CW3 January 1992. Sept. 15, 1993, the 2365th was deactivated and he transferred to 98th Div (trng) HQ as communications tech in charge of COMSEC for the division, commo training and operation of division WMMCCS terminal.

Last school, COMSEC Custodian Crs, Ft. Gordon. Recently graduated from WO Tactical and Technical Certification Crs at Ft Gordon, awarded 250A MOS. Current goal is to be promoted to CW4 before retiring.

Civilian job as sr. data base administrator with Martin Marietta Ocean and Radar Systems, Syracuse, NY.

Married and has three boys, ages 16, 13 and nine.

ROBERT D. DODSON, CW4, USA (RET), born July 4, 1932, Best, NE. Enlisted July 8, 1948, taking basic training at Ft Ord, CA. Entire military career was in Sig Corps (completing a total of eight service schools). After one year of duty in Japan he was among the first troops deployed to Korea (arriving on July 2, 1950), and served in seven campaigns there. Served four years with HQ, Allied Land Forces Central Europe and second Korean tour with 8th US Army Sig Long Lines BN. Appointed WO Sept. 15, 1961.

Duty assignments encompassed all levels of sig maint (direct, general and depot) including general support (avionics) of all Army aircraft in Vietnam and two assignments at Sacramento Army Depot, serving successively as repair and return-Southeast Asia project officer; assistant chief, Mech and Spec Spt Branch; assistant chief (and acting chief), Elect Branch. Non-maintenance assignments were with the Frequency Control Branch, J-6, HQ, MACV and 3rd Army CMMI Team.

Awards/Medals: Bronze Star Med w/OLC, Meritorious Svc Med, Joint Svc Comm Med, Army Comm Med w/ 2 OLCs, Parachutists Badge and numerous service and campaign medals. Retired in 1977 with 29 years of service.

Graduated from California State U at Sacramento. Active in Masonic bodies and past master and past patron; past charter president of USAWOA. (Heilbronn, Germany Chapter); charter and life member of Veterans of Underage Military Service.

Married Catharina Mulder of Rotterdam, Holland and has two children and four grandchildren.

CHARLES R. DOWD, CW4, USAR, born June 16, 1948, Oswego, NY and raised in Baldwinsville, NY. Entered USAF in Baldwinsville, 1966-1970. Served tours as Security Policeman in Greenland and Panama Canal Zone. USNR, March-July 1973, candidate for naval flight officer but withdrew. USAR active duty 1974-1977 as criminal investigator WO with duty at Ft Ord, CA. USAR Troop Program Unit April 1977-present as a military intelligence WO.

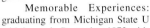

Memorable Experiences: graduating from Michigan State U with honor in December 1972 with BS in criminal justice; Criminal Investigator Basic Crs; USAF NATO Equipment Interpretation Crs; first USAR WO to graduate from the Intelligence Officer Basic Aerial Surveillance Crs; class leader of first RC MI WO Adv Crs; WO Sr Crs; Tactical Exploitation of National Space Capabilities Crs.

Awarded (4) Army Comm Med, (2) Army Achiev Med, AF Good Conduct Med and Nat Def Svc Med with service star.

Married Jennie and has two sons, Matthew and Eric. At the present he is a counter-intelligence WO with the 307th Mil Intel Co at Ft Lewis, WA and instructs imagery analysis at the 6th Res Forces Intel School at Ft Huachuca, AZ.

ARTHUR J. DOYLE, CW4, USA, A/D, born Feb. 22, 1948, New York, NY. Entered active duty Dec. 9, 1968, taking basic training at Ft Polk, LA. Attended Rotary Wing Aviator Crs at Ft Wolters, TX and Ft Rucker, AL, receiving WO appointment Nov. 17, 1969, and Aviator Wings Nov. 19, 1969. Served in Vietnam until December 1970 in first F Trp, 8th Cav, 123rd CAB, Americal and later in HHC, 123rd CAB. Returned to Ft Rucker, AL as assistant S-3, ATB.

Left active duty April 1971 and served in both IRR and Active Reserve until recalled in October 1979. Returned to active duty and served as Medevac pilot and aviation maint tech with first 3/498th Med Co, Ft Stewart, GA, then with 15th Med Det, Grafenwoehr, Germany.

Returned to the States and served as QC Safety Officer Div MTFE in the 536th TAMC, Ft Ord, CA. Medically grounded in July 1986 and reclassified into the Army's marine field as marine engineer (881A).

Served at Ft Eustis, VA as chief engineer of LCU and as the 7th Trans Gp mar maint officer. Converted to Ord Corps as support and staff maint tech in July 1989 and subsequently served as chief of maint for the newly created Cbt Mnvr Trng Ctr (CMTC) Hofenfels, Germany. Arrived at Ft Rucker, AL in February 1992 where currently serving as senior instructor, WO Career Ctr.

Assisted in USAWOA by reactivating Hampton Roads Chapter, Ft Eustis, VA in 1988; founding the Bayern-Juna Chapter in 1991; and reactivating the Aviation Center Chapter, Ft Rucker in 1992.

Received Bronze Star, Meritorious Svc Med w/2 OLCs, Air Med, ARCOM w/2 OLCs, Army Achiev Med w/OLC, Nat Def Svc Med (2), Master Army Aviator, Vietnam Svc Med, AF Res Med, Army Svc Rib, Overseas Rib (2), RVNGCUC, Broken Wing and Vietnam Comm Med.

He and wife, Norma Grace Ray, have one daughter, Julia.

LOYD S. DRENNAN, CW4 ARNGUS (RET), born Jan. 13, 1928, Morris, OK. Entered USN June 25, 1945, and discharged Feb. 7, 1950. Entered CANG March 2, 1950, and retired Jan. 13, 1988.

Served with Co C, 149th Med Tk Bn (Tank Commander) 49th Inf Div, Btry D and HHB 1st Bn 1/144th Arty (1SGT) 40th Inf Div and various other units of CAARNG. Served full time with USPFO for California, July 1951-June 1978, as state publications officer, admin services officer and chief, internal review officer. Transferred July 1978 to Camp Roberts, CA as installation supply officer. Retired from technician status April 1984 but continued on full time active duty from April 1984-January 1988 as facilities engineer supply officer.

Attended Mil Per and Internal Review Courses at Ft Benjamin Harrison, IN. Served three separate tours with NG Bureau. In 1977 and 1978 participated in program to establish the Internal Review Program in the ARNG and helped to establish Internal Review Crs at Camp Robinson, AR.

Awards include (3) NGB Minuteman Awds, Meritorious Svc Med, Army and Navy Pres Unit Cit, Asiatic-Pacific Campaign Med, Am Def Svc Med, WWII Victory Med, Armed Forces Res Med w/3 10 year devices, Army Comm Med and numerous other awards.

Married Doris Lannon of Paso Robles, CA who became the first female SGM (E9) in CANG. They have one son, Kerry, a SFC AGR Recruiter for ARNG and daughter-in-law, Karen, SSG with ARNG, a technician at Camp Robinson, AR.

Member of USAWOA; life member NGAUS, NGAC and TROA.

MICHAEL P. DUGGAN, CW3, USAR, born Oct. 15, 1935, Lackawanna, NY. Entered NYARNG Feb. 22, 1954, and US Army June 7, 1954. Attended basic training at Ft Knox, KY and AIT at Camp Chaffee, AR. Afterward served with the 510th FA in Austria, Germany and Italy.

In May 1957 transferred to the Stand-by Reserve until 1974; enlisted in the 365th Evac Hosp (USAR). Served as hospital supply sergeant and obtained rank of SFC.

April 20, 1984, appointed CWO and assigned as motor officer to 338th Gen Hosp (USAR) Niagara Falls, NY. March 8, 1988-May 10, 1992, served with the 152nd Engr Bn as construction officer and HQ&HQ company cmdr. Served with the 221st Engr Gp as track vehicle maint tech, NYARNG.

August 1991-March 1992, activated for Desert Storm and assigned to APG as a wheeled vehicle tech. At Aberdeen he operated a repair shop for returning vehicles. Presently assigned to 365th Evac Hosp (USAR) as maint tech.

Awards/Medals: Meritorious Svc Med, Army Comm Med, Army Achiev Med and several other decorations.

Retired from Buffalo Fire Depart and presently proprietor of Michael P. Duggan Co, a building contractor in Buffalo, NY.

Married Grace McGowan of Buffalo, NY and has five children and three grandchildren.

CHARLES EDWARD DUNN, CW4, USA (RET), born May 6, 1933, Graysville, TN. Entered US Army Oct. 20, 1954, taking basic and intermediate speed radio operators training at Ft Jackson, SC. Served with 4th and 9th Inf Divs in Germany. Discharged in October 1956.

Employed in construction work until recalled to active duty in 1962. Appointed WO1 and served with the 809th Engr Bn as engineer equipment repair officer until 1964. Served as service school instructor at Ft Belvoir, VA until sent to Vietnam in July 1965. Returned to Ft Belvoir, 1966-1968, and again sent to Vietnam in 1969 as South Vietnam Army Advisor.

Attended U of Nebraska from 1970-71 for Degree Completion School. Assigned to Engineer Research and Development Ctr as equipment manager and served in Germany with 81st Pershing Msl Unit from 1976-79. Last assignment was with DOD Mobile Electric Power Project.

Received the Meritorious Med w/OLC, Army Comm Med w/OLC and numerous service and campaign awards. Retired from active duty April 1, 1980.

Currently employed by Global Associates as quality control manager in Reston, VA. Member of National Assoc of Quality Participants, Total Quality Management Assoc, 20+ years as member of the USAWOA, having held office as chapter president, Region 1 VP, nat sec, nat treas, pres of Region VI, dir of Region VI, nat dir and member of EXCOM.

Married Peggy Heath of Kinston, NC and has three sons and six grandchildren.

MICHAEL J. DURANT, CW3, USA, born July 23, 1961, Berlin, NH. Entered US Army August 1979; attended basic training at Ft Leonard Wood, MO and AIT (Spanish voice intercept operator) at the Defense Language Institute, Presidio of Monterey, CA and Goodfellow AFB, San Angelo, TX.

After assignment to the 470th Mil Intele Gp, Ft Clayton, Panama, he was accepted and attended the WO Basic Crs followed by Primary Flight Training at Ft Rucker, AL. Appointment to WO1 November 1983; completed UH60 Blackhawk Qual Crs and assigned to the 377th Med Co, Seoul, Korea.

Next assignment was the 101st Avn Bn, Ft Campbell, KY. Performed duties as instructor pilot. Joined the 160th Spec Ops Gp Aug. 1, 1988, and participated in real-world operations Prime Chance, Just Cause, Desert Storm and Restore Hope.

Oct. 3, 1993, while piloting an MH60 Blackhawk in Mogadischu, Somalia, he was shot down and held captive by supporters of clan leader Mohamed Farrah Aidid. Released 11 days later and returned to his current home in Clarksville, TN. Plans to enter the degree completion program and return to the 160th.

Received the Distinguished Flying Cross, Purple Heart, (2) Air Med and Army Comm Med w/2 OLCs.

Married Lorrie Todd of Clarksville, TN in April 1988. Currently enrolled in BS degree program with Embry-Riddle Aeronautical U.

LOUIS L. DUVERNAY, CW2, USAR (RET), born Aug. 10, 1936, New Orleans, LA. Enlisted in US Army Aug. 18, 1955, and attended basic training at Ft Chaffee, AR and Radar Repair School, Ft Monmouth, NJ.

Stationed at Toby Hanna Sig Depot, Toby Hanna, PA; Ft Bliss, TX; 94th Arty Gp, Kaiserslautern, Germany; Niagara Air Defense, Lock Port NY; 6th Arty Gp, Ft Bliss, TX; 61st Sig Det, Inchon, Korea; Calibration School, APG, MD; Flight School, Ft Wolters, TX; Ft Stewart, GA; Ft Rucker, AL; flight instructor at Ft Stewart, GA.

Participated in Vietnam Summer and Fall Campaigns in 1969 and Vietnam Winter and Fall Campaigns from 1969-1970. Served as a fixed wing aviator, Sig Corps.

Memorable experience: direct hit with a 3.75 inch rocket on the enemy ammo stockpile. Retired in August 1975 at Ft Stewart, GA, as CW2. Received the Nat Def Med Svc Med, Good Conduct Med (4th Awd), Aviation Badge, Vietnam Svc Med, Army Res Comm Med, Bronze Star and RVN Comm Med w/V device.

Married Rosemary French of Wilkes-Barre, PA, has one son and two daughters. Works as real estate agent and is a member of the WOA and TROA.

FRANK H. DYER, MW4, USA, born July 20, 1933, Valley View, TX. Started military career with NG in October 1952. Drafted in Active Army October 1953 and has been on active duty since that date.

While in enlisted status he served as cook, AAA gunner, commo chief, radar computer operator and fire control maintenance tech. Appointed WO March 1957 at Ft Bliss, TX where he was radar instructor in Fire Control.

First WO assignment was in Germany as fire control tech for radar controlled 90mm AAA guns. Due to the introduction of missiles and nuclear weapons into Army inventory, he retrained as a nuclear weapons tech and has continued in that specialty since April 1958. He performed duties at company, battalion, group, brigade, division, MACOM and at DA level and currently assigned to US Army Nuclear and Chemical Agency, Springfield, VA.

Attended first ever Master Warrant Crs where he was class leader and the first to be pinned with that grade. For several years he was the senior warrant on active duty; however, having been retired and recalled at 30 years of active duty he was unable to compete for CW5 due to restrictions in the WO Management Act. When he retires he will have more than 40 years of active duty of which 36 was served as a WO.

Received the Legion of Merit w/OLC, Meritorious Svc Med w/6 OLCs, Army Comm Med w/OLC and numerous service medals and awards.

Married the former Jean Mitchell of Gainesville, TX and has two children, Frank Jr. of Frankfurt, Germany and Lorrin of Dallas, TX.

GEORGE W. EBY, CW4, USAR (RET), born Sept 4, 1928, and graduated from Wisconsin HS in 1946. Joined the USNR February 1947 and joined the Army Jan 3, 1951. Served with 2nd and 4th Armd Div from 1951-61. Enlisted rank was SFC E-7 when appointed WO1 at Ft Benning, GA March 12, 1962.

Served with the 562nd Nike Herc Bn LA; assigned to the 121st Evac Hosp in Korea, 1964-1965; 6/60th Hawk Msl Bn, Germany, 1965-68; USARV 1G Office, Vietnam, 1968-69; USAREUR Schools, Murnau, Germany, 1969-71; moved school to Vilseck, Vietnam, Cam Ranh Bay, 1971-72; Heidelberg, Germany 503rd TC, June 1972-October 1972; transferred to 7th Army Trng Ctr as chief of maintenance.

In 1972 joined Nord Bayern Chapter of EWOA and elected VP 1973-74; 1975 started Oberpfalf Franken Chapter of USAWOA; 1978-1979, elected president of Region One of the association. Still active with the chapter and life member six of the association. Retired in 1981.

THEODORE M. ECKMANN, CW2, USAR, born May 14, 1941, Brooklyn, NY. Graduated from Long Island U and entered USAR in December 1961; attended basic training at Ft Dix, NJ. Served as infantryman, 305th Inf, 77th Inf Div and was honorably discharged in 1967.

Re-enlisted in USAR April 1977 in the 24th MI BN as image analyst. Served in various positions including Det 1SGT before becoming a WO in October 1989. Also served as faculty advisor and instructor for Image Analyst Crs, 6th

Res Forces Intel School, Ft Huachuca, AZ. Served in Operation Desert Storm as Tactical Recon Officer, ARCENT G2.

Awarded the Army Comm Med w/OLC, Army Achiev Army Res Comp Achiev Med w/3 OLCs, Nat Def Svc Med SWA Svc Med, Armed Forces Res Med, NCOPDRw/#3 and the Lib of Kuwait Med.

Member of the Statue of Liberty Chapter WOA.

ANTONIO B. ECLAVEA, CW5, USA, born Sept 19, 1939, Agana, Guam. Member of military for over 33 years first 10 years were with the USAF. Achieving rank of maste sergeant as personnel tech, he decided to become WO and switched to the US Army in 1969. Attended Army Adj Ge Corps Mil Per Officer Crs, Ft Benjamin Harrison, IN; 198 graduate of Master WO Crs; holds a BS degree in economic and business administration from Marymount College, Salina KS. Currently serving as senior doctrine writer and instruc tor for Training and Doctrine Division, US Army Soldier Sp Ctr, Ft Benjamin Harrison, IN, and holds the distinction a first active Army WO to be promoted to CW5 in the Adj Ge Corps.

Military service includes tours of duty, in peace an war, in Vietnam, Taiwan, Germany (Personnel Officer fo the 570th Arty Gp, Munster) and the ROK (two tours wit 2nd Inf Div as Per Mgmt Office, a tour with the Combine Field Army, Uijongbu, as gen staff tech to the commandin general, CFA, and tour with the Combined Forces Cmc Seoul, Korea, as admin asst to the Commander-in-Chie CFC) as well as in numerous stateside locations.

Awarded the Legion of Merit, Meritorious Svc Med w 6 OLCs, Joint Svc Comm Med, Army Comm Med w/ OLCs, Army Achiev Med w/OLC, Army and AF Goo Conduct Med.

Married for over 30 years to the former Yong Ngo Anh (Rose Marie) from Vietnam and has four sons: Johnn (1LT), Anthony (med student), Michael (at home) and Mar (ROTC student).

DON G. ELLIOTT, CW4, ARNG (RET), born Oct 3 1935, Pax, WV. Graduated from Warren County HS Jun 1953. Enlisted November 1955 in ARNG HHC Bn 211th In Reg 51st Inf Div, Miami, FL. Basic training at Ft McClellan AL; MOS as communications specialist; attended NCC Academy at Ft Jackson, SC.

Re-organized as Bn Cmdr, Chief HQ 2nd AW Bn (SP 265th Arty as E5. Rose in ranks with duties as Intel NCO an later as Operations NCO. Promoted to MSG E8 as 1SGT HQ 2nd AW Bn (SP) 265th Arty; reorganized in 1968 as 1SGT HHC 124th Inf and served as SGM 1st Bn 124th Inf Commissioned CW2 May 1970, as battalion auto main tech six years HHC 1/124th Inf. Completed jungle operation training at JOTC, Ft Sherman, CZ, with first NG troops (1s Bn, 124 Inf) to receive training there.

May 1976 promoted to CW3 and reassigned as logis tics tech HHC 1st Bn 124 Inf for three years. In 1979 reassigned as ballistics med tech HHB 2/116 FA, Lakeland FL. May 1982, promoted to CW4 and served as meteorolo gist until retirement in August 1986 with over 30 years o service.

Received the Good Conduct Med, Armed Forces Re Med w/silver OLC, Armed Res Comp Achiev Med w/2 OLCs, Army Svc Rib, Florida Comm Med w/silver OLC FLAARNG Drill Attend Rib w/3 OLCs, FLAARNG Activ State Svc Rib w/silver OLC, Jungle Expert Badge and Pres Unit Cit.

Previously married to Elizabeth Rouse, Miami, FL three children and two grandchildren. Married to Iva Rex Slater of Sheridan, WY and has three stepchildren. Enjoys hunting, camping and building restoration. In business as air conditioning and heating contractor since 1966.

LAURENCE E. ELLIS, CW4, USA (RET), born April 1929, Letcher, NY. Entered service April 1952; basic training at Ft Chaffee, AR; served three tours in Germany; two tours in Vietnam. Positions included company commander logistics officer at battalion level, logistics officer at Yuma Proving Ground; and WO in 1967.

Awards/Medals: Army Svc Rib, Overseas Svc Rib, Bronze Star, Army Comm Med w/3 OLCs, Good Conduct Med, Army Achiev Med, Meritorious Unit Comm, Army Occupation Med, Nat Def Svc Med, Vietnam Svc Med, UN Campaign Med, UN Campaign, Vietnamese Gallantry Cross w/palm, Meritorious Svc Med and Legion of Merit. Retired February 1988 as CW4.

Organized one of the first WOA Chapters in Europe in 1972 (Nord Bayern) and served as president three years; fraternal organizations include the USAWOA, VFW and DAV. Retired in February 1988 with 36 years of service.

ORVILLE N. ELMORE, CW3, USA (RET), born Jan 6, 1916, Fancy Prairie, IL. Enlisted in US Army Feb 3, 1934, and assigned to Co C, Ft Sheridan, IL. Served in following organizations: HQ C, 35th Inf, Schofield Barracks, HI TH, May 1937-December 1940; Co L, 32nd Inf, Ft Ord, CA, July 1940-October 1941; transferred to 102nd Sig Radio Intel Co, October 1941.

They were on a troop ship headed for Philippine Islands Dec 7, 1941, when suddenly ship's captain announced that Pearl Harbor had been bombed by Japanese. Returned to San Francisco, CA and assigned to 838th Sig Svc Bn, operating through NWT, Canada. Was in charge of weather and radio station at Ft Wriggley, NWT, Canada until 1943; assigned to Ft Logan, CO as provost sergeant 1943-1945; assigned as provost sergeant Denver MP 1945-1946; appointed CID agent, June 1946, Denver MP; assigned to 13th CID, Munich, Germany, October 1949-October 1952; assigned to 75th CID, Ft Carson, CO, October 1952-1955; assigned to 19th CID Uijonbu, Korea, January 1955-May 1957; assigned to the 1st CID Ft Gordon, GA, May 1957-June 1950. Retired July 1, 1959.

Attended Criminal Investigation School, Carlisle Bks, PA; Denver Police Academy, U of Austria, Vienna, Homicide and Arson, Lie Detector School, Ft Gordon, GA.

Received Army Comm Med for service in Sig Corps, NWT, Canada. He had no combat service.

Wife deceased, he is the proud grandfather of six and great-grandfather of six wee ones.

ERNEST A. EMIG, CW3, USAR, born Nov 7, 1951, Canton, IL. Joined USAR June 1970; entered basic training Oct 3, 1970; graduated AIT on March 13, 1971, at Ft Carson, CO. Enlisted in service with 724th Trans Co and 733rd Maint Co (DS), Canton, IL until 1983. Appointed WO1 July 8, 1983, as auto maint tech and accepted into the Active Guard and Reserve Program on June 17, 1985, with first tour in Bardstown, KY in 396th Engr Co (Panel Bridge). Transferred to 961st Engr Bn (CBT) (HV), Milwaukee, WI, June 1989, serving as battalion maint tech and twice as an interim property book officer. Transferred to present assignment as maint tech with 3/75th FA BN, Ft Leonard Wood, MO April 5, 1992.

Awarded Meritorious Svc Med, Army Comm Med w/

3 OLCs, Army Achiev w/OLC, Overseas Rib, Nat Def Svc Med and Res Comp Achiev Med. Member and chapter president of SHO-ME Chapter, USAWOA, February 1993-February 1994.

Held special assignments as Logistics OIC from June-July 1990, operating on island of Western Samoa. Projects completed by three 40 man rotations of reservists include a 120' cable foot bridge, three concrete fiords and the renovation of a college dining facility.

Married Sheila Jordan in 1971 and has two children, Cindy and Daniel.

DAVID A. EMMITH, CW2, USA, born Sept 18, 1956, Beverly, MA, raised in Newburyport, MA, and graduated from Newburyport HS in June 1975. Entered US Army June 24, 1975, taking basic training at Ft Knox, KY. Served as finance specialist from 1975-1983 at the 105th Fin Sect in Augsburg, Germany and at the Finance and Accounting Office, Ft Devens, MA. In 1983 obtained the 98J MI MOS through the Bonus Extension and Retraining (BEAR) Program. Served in Chun Chon, Korea; Ft Bragg, NC and Sinop, Turkey before becoming a WO in 1988.

Served with 103rd MI Bn, Wurzburg, Germany from 1988-1992. In July 1992 he was assigned to the 319th MI Bn, Ft Bragg, NC.

He plans to retire in spring of 1995 and pursue a career as an information systems manager. He possesses an associate of arts degree in business administration from the Methodist College, Fayetteville, NC; BS degree in information systems management from U of Maryland and expects to complete MA degree in computer resources and information management from Webster U on Pope AFB, NC in December 1994.

Married Katherine Weber of Dittmer, MO in May 1977 and has one child, Nicole, born in 1981.

FLOURNOY T. ENGLISH, (Jack) CW4, USA (RET), born Aug 2, 1930 in Linnville, TN. Enlisted US Air Force November 1947. Following basic and speciality training at Lackland Air Force Base, TX served as Ground Equipment Maintenance Technician, Gnd Equip Cold Weather Test Branch, 3200th Climatic Test Sqdn, Eglin Air Force Base, FL from April 1948 until levied for overseas assignment July 1950. Served as Maint Supervisor 13th Equipment Support Gp, Japan from August 1950 until reassigned to the 6410th Far East Air Materiel Command Depot, Japan from March 1951 until July 1951. Following completion senior automotive repair course July 1951, served as Motor Sergeant, 6401st Fld Maint Sqdn Korea until discharge Jan 23, 1952.

Post discharge (Jan 23, 1952) employment: E. I. duPont de Nemours & Company, Aiken, SC from February 1952 until August 1952; US Army Corps of Engineers, Tullahoma, TN from August 1952 until April 1956.

Enlisted in the US Army April 16, 1956. Following infantry leadership training Fort Jackson, SC, served as Automotive/Engineer Equipment Maintenance Supervisor in combat and construction engineer organizations in CONUS, Germany and France from July 1956 until March 1962.

Appointed Warrant Officer, WO1 March 9, 1962 as Automotive Maint Tech (631A). Following appointment to WO1, served as Bn Maint/Motor Officer Headquarters, 143 Sig Bn Gp Maint/Motor Officer HQ, 7th Special Forces Gp (Airborne), Fort Bragg, NC from July 1965 until reassigned 80th OD GP, Fort Bragg, July 1966. Helped activate (July 1966 until December 1966) and deployed with 632nd HEMCO (GS) to Vietnam, arriving at Cholon (Rice Mill) Feb 21, 1967. Reassigned HQ 79 Maint Bn (GS), 506th Fld

Depot Materiel Office with special duty assignment US Army Procurement Agency, Saigon Support Command. Following this assignment, served as Maint Officer, HQ 506th Fld Depot, Cam Davies, Saigon and Assistant Materiel Officer, HQ 79th Main Bn (GS), Long Binh until completion of tour Jan 28, 1968. Via intra-theater transfer to Germany, served as Shop Officer, 903rd HEMCO (GS), 87th Maint Bn (GS), Nellingen, Germany from January 1968 until levied for second Vietnam tour October 1969; arrived in Vietnam November 1969, served as Plt Leader and Tech Supply Officer 632nd HEMCO (GS), 79th Maint Bn Long Binh from November 1969 until July 1970. Reassigned July 1970 as Shop Officer, 548th LEMCO (GS), 79th Maint Bn (GS) until completion of tour November 1970.

Via intra-theater transfer to Germany, served as Assistant Maint Officer, G-4 HQ VII Corps, Kelly Barracks, Germany from December 1970 until April 1973. Returning to CONUS April 1973, retired July 19, 1973 at Fort Eustis, VA with more than 22 years active military service.

Post military retirement has been with the Federal Civil Service Commission. Awards include: US Air Force Good Conduct Medal, Korean Presidential Unit Citation, Occupation Ribbon (Japan), US Air Force Commendation Medal, Korean Service Medal w/2 stars, US Army Meritorious Service Medal, US Army Bronze Star; US Army Commendation Medal w/3 OLC, Army Officer Reserve Medal, Meritorious Unit Commendation w/1 OLC, Army Officer Reserve Medal, Meritorious Unit Commendation w/1 OLC, Armed Forces Expedition Medal (DOM REP), Republic of S. Vietnam Campaign Medal with 60 device, Vietnam Service Medal w/5 stars, National Defense Service Medal w/2 stars, Parachutist Badge, US Army Achievement Medal.

His hobbies include gardening, hunting, and fishing. He is married to the former Ute Schnitz of Berkheim, Germany. They have three children and four grandchildren. He is a member of the American Legion, Retired Officers Association and the Disabled Veterans Association.

RICHARD F. ESTERON, CW3, USA, born Aug 10, 1954, Honolulu, HI. Began military career when he enlisted in US Army Feb 4, 1972. Entered active duty June 26, 1972, at Ft Ord, CA for basic training and AIT at Ft Monmouth, NJ. Served as strategic microwave systems maintainer with 69th Sig Bn, Augsburg, Germany and USA Electric Proving Ground, Ft Huachuca, AZ. Managed GS electronics maintenance with 71st Maint Bn, Nuremberg, Germany and direct support with the 24th Sig Bn, Ft Stewart, GA.

Appointed CWO2, sig sys maint tech in 1987 upon completion of entry training, Ft Sill, OK and technical certification, Ft Gordon, GA. Assignments include 724th Maint Bn, Ft Stewart, GA and 11th Sig Bn, Kaiserslautern, Germany. Graduated from the WO Advanced Crs, Class 03-93, Ft Gordon, GA; advanced to present grade Aug 1, 1993, and presently assigned to 208th Sig Co, 18th Abn Corps, Ft Polk, LA. Married former Marjorie Ann Hill and has two children, David Timothy and Aaron Cheyne.

FRANK W. ETHERIDGE, CW3, USAR (RET), born June 29, 1916, Thomaston, CT. 1934 graduated high school; 1939 Automotive Sales and Svc Crs, General Motors Institute; 1948 Master Gunners Crs, Artillery School, Ft Bliss, TX; 1954 Armor Officers A/Adv Crs, Armor School, Ft Knox, KY; 1956 Nike Ajax Fire Control Crs, Artillery School, Ft Bliss, TX; 1961 Nike Hercules Fire Control Crs, Artillery School, Ft Bliss, TX; 1948-1958 completed Army Estension Courses Series 10-16, Ground General School, Armor School and Cmd and Gen Staff College; 1965 BS degree in business administration, U of Palm Beach, West Palm Beach, FL.

Enlisted in US Army Aug 8, 1935. Served as utilities clerk, Hawaiian QM Depot (PFC Sp 4cl) and discharged Oct 27, 1937; March 1942-October 1945, served as tank commander and battalion operations sergeant, 68th Tk Bn, 6th Armd Div (T/SGT).

Participated in action in Normandy, Northern France, Rhineland and Ardennes. April 1948-March 1952, served as operations sergeant, 16th AAA Gp (M/SGT), Ft Bliss, TX and Ft Hancock, NJ (Air Defense of New York City); March 5, 1952, appointed WOJG and assigned as instructor, Armor to Armored School, Ft Knox, KY. May 1954, assigned as ops officer, General Subjects Dept., Armor School.

Released from active duty March 31, 1955. Ordered back to active duty Oct 12, 1955. Served as fire control officer (CW2) in 1st Msl Bn, 60th Arty in Chicago Air Defense. Transferred to Retired Reserve (CW3) February 1963. Returned to school and earned BS degree in business administration in 1965.

Employed by Florida Regional Office, VA as adjudicator, rating specialist and chairman of a Rating Board from May 1967 to April 1983 when retired from civil service. Life member of TROA, VFW and DAV and member of American Legion, 6th Armd Div Assoc and Moose Lodge. Current hobbies include visiting old Army Posts west of the Mississippi and Military History.

MARION D. EVERHART, CW3, USA (RET), born May 17, 1922, Hymera, IN. Entered US Army July 17, 1963, as CW2 aviation and commissioned USMCR Naval Aviator, June 20, 1944-May 20, 1952, 1LT. Entered USAF Dec 7, 1953, KC-135 boom operator. Also instructor pilot with commercial multi-engine and instrument licenses with SAC Aero Club, Offutt AFB, Omaha, NE. Logged 22,000 hours. As M/SGT transferred to US Army July 16, 1963, as CW2. Assigned to Ft Wolters, TX, Primary helicopter training September 1963, then to Ft Carson, CO with 5th Div.

Served in Vietnam September 1964-May 1965 flying UH1B Huey gunships. Next assigned to 45th Arty Bde, Army Air Defense, Arlington Heights, IL flying OH23, UH19, U6A and OIC of Air Det. Promoted to CW3 April 24, 1967; CH47 Chinook Transition, September 1967; Senior Army Aviator, Nov 27, 1967. Vietnam Jan 3, 1968-Dec 18, 1968 with 1st Cav Div flying Chinooks and OIC Engine Shop. Assigned to ARADCOM Colorado Springs, CO; command pilot on U21, U8F and C47.

Retired June 30, 1970, with 36,775 hours flying time and 350 combat assault missions. Awards include Navy-Marine Med, Bronze Star w/V, Purple Heart, Meritorious Svc Med, Air Med w/V 14 OLCs, Army Comm Med, WWII Victory Med, Nat Def w/OLC, Expert Marksman, Vietnam Svc w/7 stars, Vietnam Campaign, ASM, AOSM, Combat Readiness, Combat Action and numerous service and campaign medals.

Married Betty Bakke July 6, 1944, and has three children, six grandchildren and one great-grandchild. Graduated from Nebraska U at Omaha Aug. 22, 1955, and Naval Air Trng Ctr, Pensacola, FL June 20, 1944. Currently self-employed in ranching Brookston, TX.

SUZAN R. FARRELL, CW3, USA, born Dec 4, 1953, Fredericksburg, IA. Entered military service June 1, 1976, Ft McClellan, AL in Women's Army Corps. AIT at Ft Sam Houston, TX, as food inspection specialist (91R). Enlisted assignments included Ft Riley, KS, 106th Med Det (VS) Korea and Ft Stewart, GA with duty at Jacksonville NAS, FL.

Direct appointment to WO1 June 1, 1983, and first WO assignment with the 72nd Met Det (VS), Nuremberg, Germany. Subsequent assignments included Ft McClellan, AL, Walter Reed Army Med Ctr, and Ft Leonard Wood, MO, with duty at Great Lakes NTC, Great Lakes, IL.

Most memorable event as warrant was her first re-enlistment as commissioned Warrant was her husbands last re-enlistment.

Received Meritorious Svc Med, Army Comm Med w/ 3 OLCs, Army Achiev Med, Army Superior Unit Awd, NCO PDR, Army Good Conduct, Nat Def Svc Med, Army Svc Rib and Overseas Svc Rib.

Married Thomas Farrell and has two sons, David and Matthew.

BARRY D. FARRIS, CW4, USA (RET), born May 11, 1937, Grinnell, IA. Joined USMC July 8, 1955; boot camp at MCRD, San Diego, CA; AIT at Camp Pendleton, CA. Served on Okinawa, January 1956-March 1957, with 1st Bn, 9th Mar (Rein), 3rd Mar Div (Reinf) FMF. Completed enlistment at MCSC, Barstow, CA as rifle instructor, April 1957-July 7, 1959. Awarded the USMC Good Conduct and Expert Rifle Badge.

Enlisted in US Army with 101st Abn Div and Jump School May 31, 1960. Served in 502nd Abn BG as infantryman. Appointed WO1 USAR AGC Oct 19, 1966, from rank of SFC E7 while assigned to 503rd Admin Co, 3rd Armd Div in Frankfurt, Germany; appointed CW2 RA (DOR Oct 19, 1969) in 1971. Served as personnel and administration tech at division, battalion, brigade and MACOM levels.

Attended Mil Pers Officer Crs in 1971 and Pers Mgmt Crs in 1976 at Ft Ben Harrison, IN. Attended WO Sr Crs at Ft Rucker, AL in 1977. Retired as Ch, Asmt Mgmt Br, HQ USACIDC effective Jan 31, 1980.

Awarded the Parachutist Badge, Army Good Conduct Med (2nd Awd), Nat Def Svc Med, Vietnam Svc Med, RVN Comm Med, ARCOM (2nd OLC), Meritorious Svc. Med, Bronze Star (2nd OLC), VCOFGWP, AFOUS and Legion of Merit. Life member #39 USAWOA. Served as pres Pikes Peak Chap, 1974-75. Region 3 dir in 1981. Also member of TROA, Am Legion and life member 11th ACVVC.

Overseas tours include Germany, November 1964-November 1967; Vietnam with the 69th Sig Bn, July 1968-July 1969; Alaska with the 171st Inf Bde, August 1970-September 1971; and Vietnam with the 2nd Sqdn, 11th ACR and DRAC USMACV, November 1971-November 1972.

Most memorable experiences include: 65 mile, three day hikes on Okinawa; Jump School when he broke his foot on the last day of ground training and still ran the 5-mile run the following day; Charley's mortar attacks and getting shot at while in command helicopter; trying to balance morning reports during Vietnam draw down; USMC boot camp and first jump; winter in Fairbanks, AK; and getting his WO appointment.

Married LeEtte Peterson July 12, 1957, and has one daughter and three grandchildren. Retired in Colorado Springs, CO and currently working as a private investigator.

KEITH A FENRICH, CW4, USA, entered US Army Feb 6, 1968. Basic training at Ft Polk, AIT at Ft Gordon. Attended Army's first Skill Development Base Crs in preparation for tour in Vietnam starting April 1969.

Subsequent assignments include: 67th Sig Bn, Ft Riley; two tours with 122nd Maint Bn, Hanau, Germany; 25th Sig Bn, Ft Bragg, NC; US Army Sig School, Ft Gordon; Technical Advisory Field Team, Iran; 440th Sig Bn, Darmstadt, Germany; 504th MI Gp, Ft Hood; 1st Maint Bn, Boelingen, Germany; 706th Maint Bn, Ft Richardson, AK; 13th Sig Bn, and DMMC 1st Cav Div, Ft Hood. Served as communication and elect maint tech, service school instructor, shop officer, Bbattalion and DISCOM staff officer and foreign military advisor.

One of the most challenging events of his career was FTX BRIMFROST 89 during assignment to 6th Inf Div (Light) in Alaska. BRIMFROST 89 took place during a record breaking cold snap in Alaska. It was the coldest winter in over 100 years with temperatures dipping -70 degrees below zero and wind chills exceeding -100 degrees. Despite the extreme difficulty caused by low temperatures and persistent ice fog, his platoon's teamwork operated like a Swiss watch in setting up their section of the defensive perimeter, maintenance support area and living area. The extreme cold and isolation of the field site quickly turned FTX into an extended survival training exercise. The cold made the simplest tasks difficult. Teamwork ensured that supplies dropped from C-130s were recovered and distributed. The ultimate test of teamwork came with the unfortunate crash of a Canadian C-130. They were the first to respond. It was a massive team effort to find, provide first aid, and evacuate the victims during the dark Arctic night with temperatures at -61 degrees. Several lives were saved because of their efforts.

On February 2, returning in convoy to Ft. Richardson, the ice fog began to lift for the first time since their deployment. They all felt good, not only because the sky was blue and the sun was finally shining, but because of their sense of accomplishment and confidence that they could depend on one another when they really needed to.

Awards/Medals: Meritorious Svc Med w/3 OLCs, Army Comm Med w/OLC, Army Achiev Med w/3 OLCs, numerous service and campaign ribbons and West Germany's Cross of Honor.

Earned AA and BA degrees while on active duty. Married Maj Debra Fenrich, Ord Corps. Life member of USAWOA and belongs to the ROA and Amateur Radio Relay League.

DANIEL C. FENTZKE, CW2, USAR, born June 27, 1949, in Buffalo, NY. Entered US Army May 9, 1969, and attended BCT and AIT at Ft Dix, NJ. Served as wheel vehicle mechanic, PLL clerk and unit motor sergeant with Battery C, 2nd TAB, 25th FA at Peden Barracks, Wertheim, Germany from 1970-1973. Reassigned to Ft Jackson, SC to be instructor at the Wheel Vehicle Mechanics Crs. Discharged from active duty in November 1974.

Employed as locomotive machinist by Southern Railway Norfolk Southern Corp from 1975-1986; entered USAR in October 1987 as a requisite to employment as an Army Reserve tech. Served as senior mechanic with 273rd MI Co, Dobbins AFB, Marietta, GA and as maintenance section sergeant with Co A, 337th MI Bn (TE), East Point, GA. Attended WOCS-RC, Ft McCoy, WI and WOTTCC at APG, MD; returned to Co A in February 1990 to serve as foreign equipment analyst.

Currently serving as battalion maintenance officer for the 357th Supply and Service Bn, Athens, GA. Employed by 81st ARCOM as heavy mobile equipment repairer, ECS 43G, Ft Gillem, GA from September 1987-February 1993. Currently employed by Forces Command, Ft McPherson, GA as unit movement data manager.

Married Marilyn Owen of East Aurora, NY. Has three children and four grandchildren. Their son and son-in-law both served in Operation Desert Storm with the US Army.

COREY J. FERGUSON, CW4, USAR, born Sept 18, 1953, Erie, PA, and moved to Los Angeles, CA in 1959. Entered US Army Feb 28, 1972, taking basic infantry training at Ft Polk, LA. Appointed WO candidate at age 18 and transferred to Ft Wolters, TX for basic helicopter training; completed advanced helicopter training, appointed WO and designated an Army Aviator at Ft Rucker, AL April 3, 1973.

Served four years active duty as a UH-1 and OH-58 Aviator with B Co 227th Avn Co, 1st Cav Div, Ft Hood, TX. Employed as pilot for United Airlines while being assigned to the USARs 336th Avn Co, Los Alamitos, CA and served as UH-1 and U-21 instrument flight examiner and standardization instructor pilot. Transferred to ORARNG in 1987 and assigned as OV-1 instrument flight examiner until 1992.

Currently employed by United Airlines as Boeing 727 captain based in San Francisco. Life member of USAWOA, Army Avn Assoc of America, ROA and TROA.

Married Barbara Westerbeck of Los Angeles, CA, and has three children: Paul, Stephen and Kathyrn.

WILLIAM F. FERGUSON, CWO, enlisted 1936, Chicago, IL in NG, 202nd CA AAA, Regt, Inducted Sept 16, 1940, as sergeant at Ft Bliss, TX. Served as comm sgt, mess sgt and range sgt. Attended Fire Control Data Transmission School, Ft Monroe, VA; assigned to 210th CA AAA Bremerton Ship Yards, Seattle, WA. May 1942 shipped out to Dutch Harbor, AK to set up antiaircraft and antimech positions and supervised construction of 22nd AAA gun emplacements and underground ammunition shelters.

December 1942 appointed WOJG and assigned to Kodiak, AK; served as assistant S-3; appointed CWO in June 1942 with the 599th Sep Bn (AAA). Unit returned to Ft Bliss following 31 months in Alaska and reclassified CWO AUS Recon Officer, 599th Sep Bn. Departed from States for Europe, Salisbury Plains, England, 1944. Attended Passive Air Defense School and assigned to 3rd Army, France, last strong stand of Germans at Opeenheim, Germany, crossing of Rhine River and ended at Czech Border at meet up with Russian and Mongolian Troops and horse wagons.

In Paris, France for V-E Day attending Troop Information and Education Officer Courses. Attended Durham University, Durham, England. Discharged in Etampes, France in October 1945 and appointed assistant field director of American Red Cross, GI War Bride Program. Received Reserve commission and remained overseas for 35 years with Coca-Cola Export Corp, Europe, Latin America, China Region and vice president; board representative director for Coca-Cola Company to Coca-Cola Company Japan LTD.

Retired with 28 years credited service as CAPT USAR RET. Sole proprietor of Wm. F. Ferguson and Associates, Marketing Consultants, Coral Gables, FL for the past eight years.

Joined the Service Corps of Retired Executives, serving as chapter president, district representative and assistant regional director of eight southeastern states with 60 chapters.

BILLY K. FLANAGAN, CW4, USA (RET), born Feb 4, 1927, Van Wert, OH. Drafted June 11, 1945, attended basic training at Camp Blanding, FL. First assignments included B Co, 803rd MP Bn, Naples, Italy and B Co, 503rd MP Bn Livorno and Pisa, Italy. Discharged in 1947 and enlisted in Reserves.

In 1949 re-enlisted and completed Auto Elec Crs at APG as honor student. Further assignments included MP, Marburg, Germany, 62nd MP, Heidelberg, 574th Ord MAM Co, Heidelberg. Participated in the first reforger. Discharged in 1952 and enlisted in L Co 148th Inf OHNG and promoted to MSGT. Transferred to 913th Ord Gas Co and was appointed WO1 in 1966.

Requested active duty and first WO assignment was with Svc Btry 6th Bn 12th Arty, Korea. Further assignments as WO include 507th HEM Co, Hanau, Germany, Svc Btry, 5th Bn, 27th Arty, Vietnam; 507th HEM Co, 296th CCS Co, Hanau, Germany; Svc Btry, 1st Bn, 82nd Arty, Ft Bragg; 189th Mt Bn, Ft Bragg; HQ CEBW CEGE, Landstuhl, Germany as QA Team Chief; participated in first winter REFORGER, First Night Issue of Equipment; appointed Regular Army, May 1978; HHD 189th Mt Bn, Ft Bragg; 84th Ord Bn, Muenchweiler, Germany; HHC 59th Ord, Pirmasens, Germany. Last duty assignment with HHD 189th Mt Bn.

Retired as CW4 at Ft Bragg, May 1, 1989, after 43 years of service. Charter life member #48 USAWOA. Awards/Medals: Legion of Merit, Bronze Star, Meritorious Svc Med w/OLC, Army Comm Med w/3 OLCs, Good Conduct Med, WWII Victory Med, Army Occupation Med, Nat Def Svc Med, Armed Forces Exped Med, Vietnam Svc Med, Humanitariam Svc Med, Armed Forces Res Med, NCO PDR, Army Svc Rib, Overseas Svc Rib and Vietnam Campaign Rib. Married in 1951 to Cpl Gloria Acker, C Co, 7774th Sig Bn.

WILLIAM T. FLEMING, CW4, USAR, born April 12, 1939, Somerville, MA. Began military career May 1956 with MAARNG, Tank Co, 101st Inf Regt, 26th Inf Div; basic

training at Ft Dix, NJ and armor training at Ft Knox, Ky. Worked as full-time NG tech 1957-1960. Entered active military service July 1960, as enlisted Reservist and assigned to HQ Co, USAG, Ft Dix, NJ as Personnel NCO.

September 1960 transferred to US Army Reception Station, Ft Hood, TX as NCOIC of Testing Division. Discharged and re-enlisted in Regular Army September 1960. Remained with US Army Reception Station during relocation to Ft Chaffee, AK, 1961, and Ft Polk, LA in 1962. Served in Korea from September 1962-October 1963 with HQ Co, 2nd Battle Gp 4th Cav. 1st Cav Div. Reassigned to the US Army Advisor Gp, Augusta, ME, where he served as group personnel sergeant as well as enlisted advisor to HQ MEARNG. In 1965 attended counterintelligence agent and investigative photography training at US Army Intelligence School, Ft Holabird, MD. January 1966 reassigned to Germany with HQ, 66th MI Gp, Stuttgart, Germany.

November 1966 appointed WO1 as a counterintelligence technician; 1969, reassigned as field office commander, New Cumberland Field Office, Region II, 109th MI Gp, New Cumberland, PA. In August 1970, transferred to the USAR. Assigned to the 2090th USARF School, Harrisburg, PA where he held positions as MOS instructor, asst MOS director, Unit S-4 and Sr WO Crs instructor. In September 1986, selected to assist in the activation of a new organization, the 1079th USAR Garrison, FT. Indiantown Gap, Annville, PA. Served as senior team leader in the directorate of Logistics of the 1079th USAR Garrison until August 1989, when he transferred to the 1073rd Spt Gp, a reinforcement training unit located at Defense Distribution Region East, New Cumberland, PA doing research for the Armed Forces Med Intel Ctr, Ft Detrick MD. In addition to being assigned to the 1073rd Spt Gp, he holds an IMA assignment with the Federal Emergency Management Agency as an operations officer.

Awards/Medals: Meritorious Svc Med, Army Comm Med w/3 OLCs, Good Conduct Med w/2 loops, Nat Def Svc Med w/star, Armed Forces Res Med w/2 HG, ARCAM w/5 OLCs, Army Svc Rib, Overseas Svc Rib w/#2.

Member of Assoc of the US Army, 1st Cav Div Assoc, ROA, USAWOA, TROA, American Legion and VFW. Serves as member of Advisory Council of Officers Club, US Army War College, Carlisle Barracks, PA. Employed as investigator with the Commonwealth of Pennsylvania.

Married Susan Swires and has four children and five grandchildren.

DAVID FOLEY, CW3 (RET), born Sept 24, 1916, Moosic, PA. Military career began in 1934 stationed in Panama, at Panama Pacific General Depot. Appointed WOJG in June 1950, and assigned to the Pennsylvania Military College. After promotion to WOSG in 1951 he was assigned to the 2nd Logistics Cmd Provost Marshal Section. Other assignments included Adjunct of Military Missions to Bolivia and Kokira, Japan.

Awards/Medals: Army Comm Med w/OLC, Am Def, Asiatic and Pacific Def w/2 Battle Stars, Good Conduct Med, Am Theater Rib and Am Victory Med.

Retired in 1958 and began a career with Chase Federal Savings and Loan in Florida. After retirement in 1971, he relocated to Dothan, AL with his wife Edith.

Their three children and grandson have continued the Army tradition: MAJ David L. Foley served 24 years (RET); CW3 Donald E. Foley is on active duty; and daughter Diana L. Kalahan married CW3 Jim Kalahan on active duty; grandson, Michael Foley, is on active duty with the US Army in Hawaii.

DAVID LEROY FOLEY, MAJ, born Oct 22, 1942, Baltimore, MD. Enlisted in US Army Aug 21, 1961. Overseas assignments included: Vietnam, Special Forces Operational Det A, 1963, 1965-1966 and armed helicopter pilot, 1968-1969. Republic of Panama, Bn Cmdr, School of the Americas TDY assignments: Korea, Japan, Alaska, Germany, Honduras, El Salvador, Peru and Paraguay.

Assignments: Spec Forces Operational Det A; primary flight instructor, helicopter; aerial gunnery instructor; aerial gunnery subjects academic instructor; commanding officer pathfinder, airborne company; Dept of Tactics Staff Officer, Avn Ctr; VIP flight platoon commander; assistant S-3, inf bn; company commander, Co B, 3rd Bn, 187th Prcht Inf; intel officer S-2, inf bn; aviation safety officer, Cbt Avn Gp; co commander, Co B, 2nd Spec Forces Bn, 7th Spec Forces Gp; log S-4 officer, Spec Forces Gp; instructor, Command and General Staff Dept, School of the Americas; battalion commander, School Battalion, School of the Americas.

Promoted through the grades from private (E-1), Aug 22, 1961 to major on Feb 1, 1979. Retired Feb 28, 1985, as major. Awards include Master Parachutist Badge (USA, Vietnam, Korea and Paraguay), Parachutist Badge (Panama and Honduras) Combat Infantry Badge and Sr Aviator Badge.

Married Joan Masterman and has two children, Michael on active duty in Hawaii; daughter, Kathy; and two grandchildren.

DONALD E. FOLEY, CW3, born Oct 14, 1949, Wilkes-Barre, PA. Military career began Nov 4, 1968; attended basic training at Ft Gordon, GA and AIT at Ft Jackson, SC. Other assignments included Pleiku, Vietnam; Ft Sam Houston, TX; Okinawa; Ft Leavenworth, KS; Heidelberg, Germany; and Vint Hill Farms Station, VA.

Appointed WO in 1980; transferred to Ft Monmouth, NJ; Ft Richardson, AK; Ft Polk, LA; Northwestern State University (where he received his BA in Computer Information Systems) and Ft Gordon, GA.

Awards/Medals: Meritorious Svc Med, Army Comm Med, Vietnam Svc Med, Vietnamese Civic Action Med, Good Conduct Med w/5 awards and Nat Def Rib.

Married to Lonnie and has four children, three boys and one girl.

LESTER O. FOLTZ JR., CW3 (RET), enlisted in US Army November 1948. Attended basic training at Ft Ord with 4th Inf. Served in 2nd Armd Div; 161st Ord; 311th MP Bn (USAR); 5th Inf Div; USATA, Ft Knox; 7th Inf Div; 124th Sig Bn; 22nd Arty; 4th Msl Bn; 349th Trans; 808th Engr; and the 3/187th Inf, 101st Abn Div and 23rd Inf.

Permanent RA SFC E-7 appointed to WO1 December 1966; CW2, December 1967 and CW3, July 1973. All assignments were exciting but first assignment under LTC Mike Fleck (then capt) as new WO1 wearing all those "new hats" was his most memorable, i.e., PBO, mess officer, asst adj, etc.

Awards/Medals: Good Conduct Med (3rd Awd), Nat Def Med w/OLC, Vietnam Svc Med, Vietnam Comm Med w/6 stars, Meritorious Unit Cit, Comm Med w/OLC, Res Med, Vietnamese Gallantry Cross, Vietnamese Civil Actions w/OLC, Valorous Unit Med and Jungle Expert Patch.

Resides in Redmond, WA with wife Joan. They have three children and four grandchildren. Involved in church, art, writing and a new profession as "Clown" to children, elderly and handicapped. Memberships include 101st Abn Div Assoc, TROA, WOA and American Legion. Retired Feb 1, 1974, at Ft Richardson, AK.

DAVID H. FORD, Master WO, born March 24, 1944, Cartersville, GA. Upon completion of basic and AIT, was assigned to Germany as supply clerk. Awarded a degree in business admin from Floyd College.

Attended Troy State U and U of Maryland, European Division. Military education includes the completion of Supply Mgmt Officers Crs, Standard Property Book System Crs, Standard Army Retail Supply System Crs, Division Automated Supply and Support Crs (DS4), WO Training Crs.

He has held a wide variety of important logistics and staff positions culminating in current assignment as systems integrator and logistics staff officer, assistant chief of staff, G4, XVIII Abn Corps. Other key assignments include: property book officer, 82nd Abn Div, accountable officer, combat equip group, Europe, assistant community life officer, US Army Inf Ctr, Mat Off, 67th Maint Bn, log staff officer and property book officer, HQ USAREUR/7A, supply and service officer, assistant chief of staff, G4 and property book officer, 3rd Inf Div, chief, Support Branch, director of logistics, Inf Ctr, assistant S4 and property book officer, Infantry Training Group, Infantry School, S4, 1st Bn, 65th Air Def Arty and S4, 39th Sig Bn (Vietnam).

Awards/Medals: Legion of Merit, Bronze Star, Meritorious Svc Med w/3 OLCs, Army Comm Med w/2 OLCs, Army Achiev Med w/OLC, Good Conduct w/OLC, Nat Def, Vietnam Svc Med w/5 Service Stars, Army Svc Rib, Overseas Svc Rib and the RVN Campaign Med.

Married the former Barbara Gibbons and has one daughter, Amanda; daughter-in-law, Maria; four sons: David Jr, Jeffery, Joey, Terry; and granddaughter, Ashley.

RONALD E. FORRER, CW3, USA (AGR), born Aug 26, 1937, Columbus, OH. Began military career in OHANG, 121st Sup Sqdn, Lockbourne AFB, OH, Oct 23, 1955. Entered basic training at Lackland AFB, TX Jan 6, 1956, as supply specialist.

Enlisted in USMC Oct 22, 1956, and served actively through Sept 21, 1959. Attended basic training at USMC Recruit Depot, San Diego, CA with additional infantry training at Camp Pendleton, CA. Assigned as data processing specialist with duty assignments in post and intramural sports areas. Received early release from active duty to attend Ohio State U and received BS degree in business administration from Franklin U, Columbus, OH, 1971, and MA in management from Webster University, St. Louis, MO, 1983.

After nearly a 13 year hiatus from military service, he entered US Army for three years on May 28, 1974. Remained in active Reserve program rising to rank of SFC. Appointed CWO2 June 27, 1985, and began active guard Reserve tour Sept 29, 1986, and second tour April 8, 1994. Returned to civilian occupation as inventory management specialist with Dept of Air Force at Wright-Patterson AFB, OH.

Awards/Medals: Army Comm Med, Army Achiev Med, Nat Def Svc Med, Armed Forces Res Med, Army Svc Med, Army Overseas Rib, and Army NCOPDR#3. Member of ROA and WOA.

Married Alfreda Ann Goslee of Columbus, OH.

LARRY E. FORRESTER, CW4, USAR, born May 8, 1946, West Chester, PA. Military career began with basic training at Ft Jackson, SC in June 1964; AIT, Ft Belvoir, VA; assigned to 78th Engr Co, Dachau, Germany, February 1965; assigned to 504th Sig Bn, Boblingen, Germany; HQ

71st Maint Bn, Zirndorf (Nuremberg) Germany until September 1966; Ft Belvoir, VA Engr School as instructor, Precise Power Generation.

Discharged from active duty June 1968 and immediately enlisted with 157th Spt Bn, 157th Inf Bde, 79th ARCOM USAR as SSG. Promoted to SFC and accepted appointment as WO1 on Aug 1, 1976; promoted to CW2 Aug 1, 1979; assigned as sig systems maint tech; transferred to 449th Maint Co, 77th ARCOM USAR, 1984, as signal systems maintenance tech; promoted to CW3 Aug 1, 1985; completed AWOC and SWOC and promoted to CW4 Aug 1, 1991. Presently with 449th Maint Co, 695th Maint Bn, 77th ARCOM USAR.

Memorable experiences include first day in basic training and now 30 years later.

Employed by Unisys Corp for the past 25 years working in research and development engineering as staff engineer developing the next generation of computer equipment and being able to use that experience in serving as WO of the US Army.

Has three wonderful children: Ryan, Adina and Amy, whom he loves very much.

DON E. FORSHEE, CW4, USA (RET), born March 26, 1929, Peru, IN. Entered US Army June 18, 1947, Ft Knox, KY. Assigned to Ft Ord, CA for basic training and Ft Lee, VA for QM Crs. Served with 514th QM Bn at Inchon, Korea until January 1949. Assigned to HQ I Corps, Japan, serving with the Kobe and Osaka QM Depot until January 1952.

Joined exercise Longhorn at Ft Sam Houston, TX as battalion supply sergeant; assigned to HQ Btry, 1st Div Arty, Ft Hood, TX in May. Transferred to USARAL in September 1954; HQ Yukon Cmd in Fairbanks, AK, November 1954-September 1957; reported to Ft Leonard Wood, MO, September 1957 as battalion supply sergeant until January 1961; assigned to 12th Cav, Korea; 85th Evac Hosp, Ft Hood, TX, which transferred to Ft Chaffee, AR.

Appointed WO Nov 15, 1964. Assigned back to Ft Wainwright, AK as unit supply tech and served another tour in Korea in 1967; two tours in Vietnam, 1968-69 and 1970-71; assigned to 25th Inf Div in Hawaii; last assignment was Homestead AFB, FL.

Retired with 30 year's service on Feb 28, 1977. Awards/Medals: Legion of Merit, Army Comm Med w/OLC, Bronze Star w/OLC, Air Med, UN Svc Med, Army Occupation Med, RVN Campaign Med, Armed Forces Res Med, Vietnam Svc Med, Korean Svc Med, Good Conduct (4th awd), etc.

Presently working for Raytheon Co with the last 17 years working in Kuwait and Egypt. Life member of the WOA.

CHARLES T. FOUTS, CW4 (RET), born April 13, 1937, Douglas County, GA. Enlisted in US Army September 1960, taking basic training at Ft Jackson, SC. Served with USAFS VHFS Warrenton, VA; 3rd RRU VN; USASATC&S, Ft Devens, MA; 14th USASAFS, Hakata, Japan.

Appointed WO February 1967 upon graduation from Flight School. Served as pilot, IP or SIP at the 56th Avn Det in France, Germany and England; 200th Aslt Spt Hel Co VN, A & C Co of 159th ASHB, 101st Abn Div Vn, Co D, 227th Avn Bn and 34th Spt Bn 6th ACCB at Ft Hood, TX; 205th Avn Co, 4th Trans Bde, Germany.

Retired February 1982 as CW4 with over 21 years of service. Awards/Medals: Distinguished Flying Cross, Bronze Star, Air Med w/#13 and numerous service and campaign medals.

Employed by the NTSB as air safety investigator from February 1983-November 1988. Currently employed as MANPRINT manager for the Boeing Sikorsky, RAH-66 Comanche Team.

Married Jennifer Spencer of Newton-Le-Willows, England and has one son.

KENNETH R. FRANKLIN, CW2(P) ARNG, born Feb 25, 1957, Tunica, MS. Raised in Chicago, IL; entered military Jan 27, 1981, as AF engineering assistant based at Homestead AFB, FL. Transferred to US Army Jan 19, 1993 to attend Army's Rotary Wing Flight School.

Appointed WO and aviator Feb 2, 1984, at Ft Rucker AL. Graduated as OH-58 A/C aeroscout pilot and transferred to Ft Polk, LA. Served as scout pilot and unit supply officer in the 4/12th Cav Sqdn, February 1984-February 1988. Left calvary and active duty to join ARNG in 1988. NG units were Co A 1/185th Avn, Jackson, MS and Co A 1/114th Avn North Little Rock, AR. While in these units, he served as OH-6 and AHIS pilot respectively. He was the first black AHIS pilot in the ARNG.

Awards/Medals: Army Svc Rib, Sr Army Aviator Wings, Good Conduct, AF Trng Rib, Small Arms Expert and Army Comm Med.

A resident of Memphis, TN, he is employed by Northwest Airlines. Married Judy Steinberg of Memphis, TN. Member of Kappa Alpha PSI Fraternity, Quad A and WOA.

WILLIAM W. FRANKLIN, CW4, born July 23, 1920. Enlisted with the US Army and was commissioned WO on May 16, 1952. Served as a master mechanic; shop foreman, electronic chief; senior auto repairman; OMS chief; shop inspector; admin specialist to SMO; supervisory distribution facilities specialist; and warehouse foreman; PBO for CSMS. Qualified in the following MOS's: 631A; 632A; 711A; 761A; 0606; 4440; 4806; 762A; 762AO; 630AO; 915AOO1

Attended the Univ of Utah, 1937-38, Aircraft and Engine Mechanic FAA, 1941-42; completed 24 correspondence courses; and attended numerous Army and Air Force Schools from 1952-78 in Fallon, NV; Ft Bliss, TX; Carson City, NV; Ft Lewis, WA; Ft Carson, CO; Reno, NV.

Retired on July 23, 1980, as CW4. Awards include the Meritorious Svc Med; Medal of Merit, NVARNG, Army reserve Components w/2 OLCs; NVNG Service Medal (6 awds); NVNG Meritorious Svc Rib; NVNG Meritorious Svc Med, WWII Victory Med and Am Campaign and Svc Med.

He is a member of Carson Lodge #1, F&AM, and he enjoys hunting, fishing and trailering.

KEVIN L. FRENCH, CW2, USA, born July 19, 1964, Burlington, KS and raised in LeRoy, KS. Graduated Allen County Community College in 1985. Entered US Army basic training at Ft Knox, KY, January 1987. Attended AIT at Ft Eustis, VA, where he graduated as distinguished graduate, Medium Helicopter Repair Crs in July 1987. Assigned to B Co 2/159th Avn Regt 18th Abn Corps, Hunter AAF, Savannah, GA, as CH-47D flight engineer. Transferred October 1988 to C Co, 228th Avn (6th ID), Ft Wainwright, AK, where he served as member of High Altitude Rescue Team, 1989-1990.

On Jan 28, 1992, appointed WO1 as utility helicopter pilot; transferred to B Co, 4/123D Avn (6th ID), Ft Richardson, AK, where he served as quality control officer for "Artic Knights." Currently on orders for CH-47D transition en

route to Ft Campbell, KY. Awards/Medals: Army Comm Med, Army Achiev Med, Good Conduct, Nat Def Svc Med, NCO PDR, Army Svc Riv, Overseas Svc Rib, Expert Badge Pistol and Army Aviator Badge.

Married Laurie French (Graham) of Chanute, KS June 1, 1985, and has two children, Clayton Derrick and Adrienne Niccole.

LYNN A. FREUND, WO1, entered active duty Sept 23, 1973, Milwaukee, WI. Appointed WO1 Dec 9, 1977, Arlington Hall Station.

President, Ft Bragg Silver, 1978-1980; secretary, European Region, 1980-1981; director, European Region, 1981-1983; president, European Region, 1983-1985; vice president, National, 1985-1987; and secretary, Frankfurt Silver, 1992-1993.

Retired Oct 1, 1993 at Ft Jackson, SC. On May 8, 1994, settled in Huntersville (Charlotte), NC.

MICHAEL D. FRIEDBERG, CW2, USAR, AGR, born Dec 8, 1952, Cleveland, OH. Entered USN July 1971, and served six years that included three tours of Western Pacific, a tour in Vietnam and in the Philippines. Entered USAR in 1980 with the 350th Psychological Ops Co in Parma, OH as a 31V and later as intelligence analyst with the loudspeaker platoons and the Propaganda Development Section.

Took an AGR assignment with 350th in 1987 and served as operations sergeant and HB section sergeant before being appointed WO1 in August 1991 as an all source intelligence technician, (350B). Assigned to 403rd MI Det (strategic), with duty at the 81st ARCOM in East Point, GA.

Married his beautiful wife Elizabeth of Manila, Philippines in 1976. Elected president of the Greater Atlanta Chapter of the WOA in 1993 and is also a member of the Harley Owners Group (HOG), and lifetime member of DAV.

RONALD G. GALLOWAY, CW2, USA (RA), born Feb 23, 1959, Martin, SD. Began military career in US Army Aug 1, 1978; entered basic training and AIT for administrative specialist (PMOS 7IL) at Ft Jackson, SC. Held various positions up through personnel administrative sergeant with the rank of SSG.

Assignments include 1/60th Inf Bn in Alaska, MI School and 11th Sig Bde at Ft Huachuca, AZ, 1/503rd Inf Bn in Korea, Total Army Personnel Command in Des Moines, IA. On Nov 2, 1989, he was appointed WO1 as a military personnel tech (420A). Assigned to 7th Personnel Svc Co at Ft Ord, CA and later transferred to the 575th Personnel Svc Co in Darmstadt, Germany.

Awards/Medals: Meritorious Svc Med, Army Comm Med w/3 OLCs, Good Conduct w/2 OLCs, Air Achiev Med w/2 OLCs and Nat Def Svc Med.

Married former Paula Goodwin of Merriman, NE and has two children, Travis and Rhonda.

ROBERT L. GAMBERT, CWO-4, USA, born on Nov 11, 1943, in San Francisco, CA. Enlisted in the US Army Sept 29, 1961, at the Presidio, San Francisco, CA, with the USA WO Corps, as an ADP tech. His assignments were the RVN, 1966-67 and 1971-72; Germany, 1969-71 and 1978-91; and many stateside assignments.

Appointed WO1, ADP tech on Jan 13, 1975, from enlisted grade SP7. First WO assignment was chief, SIDPERS (programming), 101st Abn Div, Ft Campbell, KY, 1975-77. Subsequently assigned to the 800th Material Mgmt Ctr, 2nd COSCOM, 1978-79; 198th Pers Svcs Co, 38th Pers and Admin Bn, 1979-84; 16th Data Processing Unit, 2nd Spt Cmd, 1984-89. All assignments were on Nellingen Barracks, Stuttgart, Germany.

Final active duty assignment and subsequent retirement was with the G-6, 93rd Sig Bde, VII Corps, Kelley Barracks, 1989-91. Combat tours include the 11th Armd Cav Regt, 1966-67; RVN, having served as a door gunner for part of the tour and the 539th Pers Svcs Co, 1971-72; RVN as a SP-6 programmer; SWA Campaign, 1990-91. Attended Orange Coast College through the Enlisted Undergraduate Training Program from June 1972-June 1974, is a graduate of the Sig Sr WO Crs, and has a BS degree from the Univ of Maryland.

His memorable experience was his appointment to CWO4 on Jan 13, 1975; attending Orange Coast Junior College, 1972-1974; achieving first place on the two man patrol, while competing in a 100 km race held in Biel, Switzerland in the time of 11 hours, 20 minutes in 1982.

Retired as a CWO-4, with 27 years of active duty (30 years total service). Awards include the Legion of Merit, Air Medal, Meritorious Svc Med, Army Comm Med w/4 OLCs, Army Achiev Med w/OLC, Good Conduct Med w/3 loops, Aircraft Crew Member Badge and the Air Assault Badge.

He is a life member #98, USAWOA and holds additional life memberships in the VFW and Assoc of the US Army as well. He is a past-president of the Stuttgart Silver Chapter, USAWOA, and now serves as vice-president, Retired Affairs, European Region. Currently a member of the USAREUR Retirees Council.

He actively lobbies for the retention of retiree entitlements and benefits and encourages others to petition their congressmen as well. For health reasons, he became an avid runner and has run 135 marathons in 32 countries. Best marathon time is 2:44 for a total of 19 sub-3 hour marathons. He has competed and placed in USAREUR marathons, 10 km running races, triathlons and cross country skiing championships. During his last year of service, he won the masters age category in the USAREUR sponsored marathon and 10 km cross country championship. An injury while participating in the SWA Campaign limited his running, however, he continues to volksmarch and has completed over 700 marches.

Currently employed as Patch American High School, Stuttgart, Germany, as the school information management specialist. With his Mercedes Benz Mobile Home "Odyssee," he travels extensively throughout Europe in the company of his special lady friend. He continues to follow a good health regimen, and is active in several community organizations to include the Stuttgart Silver Chapter, VFW Post #10810, Stuttgart Chapter, AUSA and the Stuttgart Germany-American Wandering Club. He is single.

ROBERT J. GAMBINO, CW3, NJARNG, born Oct 25, 1950, Woodbury, NJ. Entered the NG October 1970; attended basic training at Ft Dix, NJ; AIT at APG, MD, May 1971. Graduated from Gloucester County Community College in June 1971 and from Camden Police Academy in June 1974 as a Patrolman for Washington Twp Police Dept. Received lifesaving award with Valor in 1975.

In 1982 he switched to 63H as SSG and promoted to SFC. Attended ANOC, Sea Girt, NJ military Academy the same year. Served as section chief, automotive for three years in 117th HEMCO; received direct appointment to CW2 (915E), April 1985; completed SWOT, APG, MD, June 1991; promoted to CW3, August 1991; and currently

support staff maint tech (915E) with the 117th HEMCO (23 years of service).

Awards/Medals: NJ Desert Storm Rib, Army Achiev Med, ARCM, NCO PDR, Army RC Overseas Trng Rib.

Cvilian occupation as police computer administrator, Washington Twp PD with 20 years of service. He has a daughter, age 12; son, age 10; and recently married Arleen. They are residing in Turnersville, NJ.

JON W. GANUES, CW2, was born on June 30, 1960, in New Rochelle, NY. Entered the US Army on June 30, 1978, as supply systems technician. Served at Camp Casey, Korea; Ft Carson, CO; Grafenwoehr, Germany; Ft Devens, MA; Argyroupolis, Greece; and Ft Bragg, NC.

Most memorable experience was his first jump out of airborne aircraft at Airborne School at Ft Benning, GA.

Received the Army Comm Med w/3 OLCs, Army Achiev Med w/2 OLCs, Good Conduct w/3 Clasps, Nat Def Svc Med, NCOPDRw/#2, Army Svc Rib and Overseas Svc Rib w/#3.

Married Carolyn Etheridge of Virginia Beach, VA. They have two sons, Jon Jr and RaShawn. He is a supply systems technician for Main Warehouse, 782nd Main Support Bn, 82nd Abn Div, Ft Bragg, NC. He is a member of the USAWOA.

JAY E. GARBUS, CW2, USAR, born on Oct 6, 1950, Suffern, NY. Enlisted in service on April 28, 1970. Attended basic training at Ft Campbell, KY, 1970; Military Police School, WOTTCC, CID Agent (311A), 1989; and US Military Police School, Advance Fraud Investigation, 1993.

Military assignments include Gunner, Btry B, 156th Arty, Newburg, NY MP, 42nd MP Co, 42nd Inf Div, Mt Vernon; NY drill sergeant, 78th Trng Div, Lodi, NJ; OPNS sergeant, 1163rd USARF School USAR, NYNY; CID Agent, Desert Shield and Desert Storm, Ft Benning, GA; CID Agent (IMA), Ft Jackson, SC.

Awards/Medals: Army Comm Med w/OLC, Army Achiev Med w/2 OLCs, Army Res Comp Achiev Med w/2 OLCs, Nat Def Svc Med w/Star, Armed Forces Res Med, NCOPDRw/3, Army Res Comp Overseas Trng Rib and Drill Sergeant Badge.

Married Robin Garbus and has two children, Wendy and Aaron. Member of the AUSA and WOA and is employed as a Compliance Safety Officer with the state of North Carolina.

GERALD GARCIA, CW4, born May 23, 1934, Richmond, CA. Joined the USAF, CAARNG and the US Army (AGR). Stationed at Parks AFB, CA in 1952; Hunter Ligget, CA; Etain AFB, France, 1954-1956; Operation Desert Storm; Ft Bragg, NC; Watts Riot, Los Angeles, CA for 17 days in 1965.

His most memorable experience was with the 347th Gen Hospital Cdr Col asking him to accept maintenance officer WO1 in the US Army.

Awards/Medals: Army Legion of Merit in 1944, and the EIB in 1966. Discharged on May 23, 1994, at Ft Lewis, WA with 43 years and 4 months of total service.

Married Marlys and has four children: Steve, Scott, David and Maura Lia. He is attending college to establish new WO Retention Programs past age of 60.

MICHAEL D. GAY, WO1, born Aug 24, 1963, in Barre, VT. Enlisted in VTARNG July 1981; attended basic training and AIT at Ft Jackson, SC as 63B. Entered active duty May 1985 with US Army at Ft Hood, TX. Duty stations with 628th Trans Co, Ft Hood, TX; 6/10th FA Bn, Bamberg, FRG; 514th Med Co, Ft Devens, MA; 51st Sig Bn, Ludwigsburg, FRG; 440th Sig Bn, Darmstadt, FRG. He participated in Desert Storm.

Awards/Medals: Good Conduct (2nd Awd), Army Achiev Med w/4 OLCs, ARCOM w/4 OLCs, Kuwait Lib Med w/3 Bronze Stars, 22nd Sig Bde NCO of year 1992; Sergeant Morales Club Inductee January 1993, Distinguished honor Graduate WOCS, Class 9-94, Ft Rucker, AL.

Married Kimberly Clark and has three children: Amanda, Christina and Justin.

WILLIAM STINSON GEORGE III, CWO, USA (RET), born Sept 7, 1944, West Point Military Academy, NY. Joined the US Army March 1966 in enlisted ranks. Appointed WO August 1977 and retired from the Army Criminal Investigations Cmd (CID) in April 1986 at Frankfurt, Germany. In Mainz, Germany following retirement, he became the first civilian deputy provost marshal in USAREUR. Currently resides in Warner Robins, GA.

Served at Ft Polk, LA; Redstone Arsenal, AL; Ft Dix, NJ; various locations in the Orient including Korea, Vietnam and Cambodia; Ft Meade, MD; Ft Shafter, HI; Ft Knox, KY; and Wiesbaden, Germany.

Awards/Medals: Meritorious Svc Med, two Vietnamese Crosses of Gallantry, Vietnamese Civil Actions, Armed Forces Exped Med, Korean Pres Cit, Good Conduct w/3 Clasps, Infantry Badge, and numerous service, campaign and unit commendation medals.

Campaigns include Vietnamese Phase VI Counteroffensive, Tet Counteroffensive, Vietnamese Summer-Fall Offensive, Vietnamese Winter-Spring Offensive, Sanctuary Counteroffensive, Vietnamese Phase VII Counteroffensive and Cambodian Parrot's Beak Offensive.

Married Cynthia Morrow of Warner Robins, GA and has one daughter, Katrina Nicole Alohaleilani. He is a member of the Former CID Agents' Association and the VFW.

JOSEPH F. GERVAIS, CW3, born Jan 15, 1931, Madawaska, ME. Attended the U of Maryland and Pima Community College, Tucson, AZ with associate degree. Attended the WO Advance Crs, Ft Monmouth, NJ while in the service.

Entered the USAF in March 1951 as enlisted serviceman. Assigned in the communications field at Sampson AFB, NY; F E Warren AFB, WY; Scott AFB, IL; HQ SAC, Offutt AFB, NE; Selfridge AFB, MI; Point Barrow AFS, AK; Fuchu AS, Japan; Darmstadt, West Germany.

Appointed WO in US Army June 1966 and served as cryptographic tech with assignments to the 35th Sig Gp, Ft Bragg, NC; 1st Cav, An Khe, South Vietnam; USASETAF, Vicenza Italy; 12th Sig Gp, Da Nang, South Vietnam; Signal School, Ft Monmouth, NJ; USACSLA, Ft Huachuca, AZ; and US South Command/J6, Ft Clayton, Panama.

Retired from the military service after 26 years of service in June 1977. Awards/Medals: Legion of Merit, Bronze Star, Meritorious Svc Med, Army Comm Med, USAF Comm Med, Vietnam Honor Med, Vietnam Signal Badge and nine other service awards.

Entered civil service February 1985 as communications mgmt specialist, GS-391-12, at HQ, 7th Sig Cmd, Ft Ritchie, MD with staff supervision of 220 communications centers in US, Alaska, Puerto Rico and Panama. Promoted to GS-13 with assignment to Ft Monmouth, NJ as project manager for communications center terminals. Represented the US Government to the contractor, Astronautics Corp of America, for total of 640 Standard Remote Terminals (SRT) as procured by the US Army, USAF, and USN. Assigned to USARJ, Camp Zama, April 1988, in the Plans, Programs and Systems Division. Transferred to USFJ/J61 in April 1989. Completed 32 years of federal service in February 1991.

Married the former Juanita MacLean of Edmundston, New Brunswick, Canada. They have four sons, Ken, Steve, William, Carl; and two grandchildren.

THOMAS B. GIBSON, CW2, born July 12, 1947, Ft Payne, AL. Enlisted in USN August 1965 and served on board the air craft carrier USS *Intrepid* for three consecutive tours to Vietnam. He was honorably discharged in July 1969. Served two years in ALNG from 1974-1977 and attended Air Crewman Crs at Ft Rucker, AL in 1977.

Enlisted in US Army November 1977, in supply field as 76Y. Served as supply sergeant in basic and AIT training C-1-1 in Ft Benning, GA, January 1978-April 1979; CIF NCOIC in 802nd Eng Bn, Camp Humphreys, Korea, April 1979-June 1980; supply sergeant in basic training, Ft Dix, NJ, June 1980-May 1982; supply sergeant in C Troop 4/7 Air Cav, May 1982-June 1984; supply sergeant, CIP NCOIC, master sergeant, instructor, property custodian in ROTC at August College, Augusta, GA, July 1984-September 1986.

Appointed to CW2 920A in September 1986 and served as Property Book Team Chief 1st AD Nuremberg,

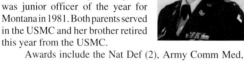

Germany, November 1986-January 1992. Deployed to SWA, December 1990-April 1991, with 1st AD. January 1992 was assigned to the 28th Trans Bn.

Awards/Medals: Bronze Star, Meritorious Svc Med, ARCOM (4), Army Achiev Med (4), Overseas Rib (3), NCOPDR(3), VNS w/4 stars, VNC w/device, Nat Def, Army Svc, SWA, SWAC, Army Good Conduct, Navy Unit Comm and Air Crew Badge.

Married Han Chin Su on March 16, 1981. He is property book officer, 28th Trans Bn.

RUTH LEE (ANTONSEN) GIEBEL, CW3(P), born March 22, 1945, Bozeman, MT. Enlisted in USMC on March 27, 1964, and the USAR on Aug 26, 1974. Stations included Parris Island, SC; Electronics School, MCRD, San Diego, CA; 420th MP Co, Bozeman, MT, 1974, 889th S&S Co, 1974-1977 and 125th Ord Bn, 1977-present.

Her whole career has been great. Her children have all served, two still on active duty in Army. She was junior officer of the year for Montana in 1981. Both parents served in the USMC and her brother retired this year from the USMC.

Awards include the Nat Def (2), Army Comm Med, Army Achiev (2), ARCAM (4), AROTR and Armed Forces Res Med.

Married Edmund Giebel on July 1, 1989. He was a former Army Reservist. They have two sons, Michael Tebbedeaux, SPC Mark; daughter, SPC Marjorie Bellow; son-in-law, Tom Bellow; and four grandchildren.

She is a GS-9 Army Reserve Tech during the week and just completed the WO Advanced Crs at Redstone Arsenal. They raise paint horses, hunt, fish and enjoy life. She was past commander of the American Legion Post, life member of ROA, Woman Marines Assoc, Vietnam Veterans of America, Beta Sigma Phi Sorority, Marine Corps League and best of all USAWOA.

ROBERT P. GIFFIN, MW4, born Oct 13, 1941, Carmel, CA. Entered the USAF CAANG in November 1958 and was discharged in 1964. Entered the Army in February 1969 taking basic training at Ft Polk, LA.

Went to primary helicopter training at Ft Wolters, TX, finishing his training at Ft Hunter-Stewart in January 1970.

Served with the 240th Aslt Hel Co in RVN. Also served with units in Alaska, Ft Campbell, Ft Irwin, ROK and Ft Rucker, AL as aviation safety tech and instructor pilot. Served as senior TAC officer for the WO Candidate School.

Awarded the Distinguished Flying Cross, Bronze Star w/OLC, Meritorious Svc Med w/2 OLCs, Air Med w/15 OLCs, ARCOM w/4 OLCs and numerous service and campaign medals.

Currently still on active duty serving as battalion safety officer for 1/14th Avn Regt at Ft Rucker, AL. He is a member of Queen City Lodge #761, Clarksville, TN and Scottish Rite of Nashville, TN. Member of AAAA, past president of the Kenn-Tenn, Ft Irwin-Barstow and Aviation Center Chapters of the USAWOA.

Married Martha Tyson of Hacienda Heights, CA. They have four children and two grandchildren.

VINCENT A. GIOVANIELLO, CW3, USA (RET), born Oct 4, 1940, New York City, NY. Enlisted Aug 11, 1958. September-November 1953, basic training, 2nd Inf Div, Ft Benning, GA; December 1958-March 1959, Track Vehicle Mech Crs, USAARMS, Ft Knox, KY; April-July 1959, instructor, USAARMS, Ft Knox, KY; August-July 1961, Track Vehicle Mech, 519th Arty Bn, Ft Clayton, Canal Zone. Received honorable discharge July 16, 1961.

Re-enlisted Oct 17, 1961, and served as instructor, USAARMS, Ft Knox, KY, 1961-1962; Instructor, CAS, 7th

Army Trng Ctr, Vilseck, Germany, 1966; service evacuation section chief, 7th Spt Bn, 199th Lt Inf, Long Binh, Vietnam, 1966-1967. Appointed WO1, 632A, 1967. WO Orientation Crs, USAARMS, Ft Sill, OK, 1968. Auto maint tech, 293rd Engr Bn, Baumholder, Germany, 1968-1970; Vehicle Park Maint Officer, US Army Depot, Long Binh, Vietnam, 1970-1971; auto maint tech, 380th Trans Co, Ft Meade, MD, 1971-1973; auto repair tech, 66th Maint Co, Kitzingen, Germany, 1973-1976; Mech Maint WO Adv Crs, APG, MD, 1976-1976; auto repair tech, 707th Maint Bn, 7th Inf Div, Ft Ord, CA, 1977-1979.

Assigned as instructor on track vehicle maintenance and procedures at Combined Arms School, Vilseck, Germany. He not only taught enlisted personnel and officers up through rank of generals, but also had the opportunity of presenting classes to the officers of the British War College. A time he will never forget.

Awards/Medals: Bronze Star, Army Comm Med w/2 OLCs, Good Conduct, Nat Def Svc Med, Vietnam Svc Med, RVCM, RVGC w/P, RVCAVC, Meritorious Unit Cit and Meritorious Svc Med. Retired Nov. 30, 1979. Graduated as honor student and distinguished graduate from the WO Officers Advance Crs, APG, MD. Life member of USWOA since 1976.

He presently works as an operational manager for Sunrise Rock and Redi-Mix, in Modesto, CA.

WILLIAM R. GLEICHAUF, CW4, USA (RET), born Jan 25, 1918, Foxboro, MA. Entered the US Army on April 30, 1942, and attended basic training in Ft Harrison, IN. He served with the Finance Office, 90th Inf Div in Europe and was discharged on Oct 28, 1945.

Recalled to active duty with the 1013th Reception Center, Ft Devens, MA on Sept 4, 1950. Appointed WO on March 27, 1951, and served in Korea with the Finance Office, 2nd Inf Div and I Corps. Served with the following Finance Offices: 3rd Inf Div, Ft Benning, GA; Florida Military District, Jacksonville, FL; Ft McPherson, GA; 59th FDS, Bremerhaven, Germany; Ft Campbell, KY; 3rd US Army Support Group, Homestead, FL.

Participated in battles in Normandy, North France, Rhineland, Ardennes, Central Europe, 3rd Korean Winter, Korean Summer-Fall. He retired on April 30, 1967.

Awards/Medals: Bronze Star, Good Conduct, EAME Campaign Med, WWII Victory Med, Army Comm Med, Army Ocupation Med (Germany), Armed Forces Res Med, UN Svc Med, Korean Svc Med, Bronze Star (2nd awd), Nat Def Svc Med w/OLC, 10 year service Armed Forces Res Med.

Divorced, he has three children and seven grandchildren. Presently retired, he served with the Treasury Dept, IRS from May 1967-January 1980 and retired as GS-12. Currently attends courses in computers at community college. He is a member of the American Legion, DAV and ROA.

BOBBY K. GOFORTH, CW3, USA (RET), born June 21, 1938, in Murfreesboro, TN. Enlisted in TNNG in 1954 and in the US Army Sept 14, 1956, taking basic training at Ft Chaffee, AR. Assignments included the 782nd Maint Bn, 82nd Abn Div (1956-64); 6th SFG, Ft Bragg (1964-65); 173rd Abn Bde, Vietnam (1966-67) where promoted to WO; 7th SFG, Ft Bragg (1967-68); 5th SFG Vietnam (1969-70); 7th SFG Ft Bragg (1971-72); 46th SF Co, Thailand (1973); 82nd Sig Bn, Ft Bragg (1974-76). Attended Automotive Repair School, Food Service School and Radar Repair School.

Retired in 1976 with rank CW3. Awards/Medals: USA,

Thailand, Vietnam Master Parachutist, Centurion Wings, Good Conduct, ARCOM w/OLC, Bronze Star w/OLC, Air Med w/OLC, Vietnam Cross of Gallantry, Vietnam Svc Med and Nat Def Svc Med.

Married Norma Parks of Bristol, TN, and has three children and four grandchildren. Currently employed by Holston Defense Corp, Kingsport, TN as information analyst and programmer.

JACK GOLDMAN, CW4, USA (RET), born July 20, 1926, New York City, NY. Began his Army Service on Oct 25, 1944, and was honorably discharged Nov 9, 1946. Served with the active Reserve until recalled to active duty Sept 11, 1950. Served overseas in Austria, Korea, Bolovia, two tours in Vietnam and Germany (Augsburg, Karlsruhe and Stuttgart).

Enlisted in the service with the 4th Cav Sqdn (scout car commander), 325th Tk Bn (platoon sergeant) and 522nd MP Co (1st sergeant). Appointed WOJG June 23, 1951, and promoted to CW4 on Sept 23, 1965. Received a BS degree in Military Science from the U of Maryland in 1960. His WO service included tours with the 3rd Armd Div, 43rd, 5th and 24th Inf Div, 82nd and 101st Abn Div, 17th Sig Bn, 50th Sig Bn (ABNC), Stratcom-South (Panama), 472nd Sig Co, HQ-USARV, and HQ-VII Corps (C-E).

Awards/Medals: Legion of Merit, Bronze Star w/2 OLCs, Army Comm Med w/OLC, Meritorious Unit Cit, RVN Cross of Gallantry w/Palm, RVN Civic Action Med, Good Conduct w/3 Loops, Army of Occupation, Nat Def Svc Med wOLC, WWII Victory Med, Am Campaign Med, Armed Forces Res Med, Vietnam Svc Med, RVN Campaign Med and Parachute Badge.

Married the former Doris Renate Bundschuh of Karlsruhe, Germany and has one son Glen Harry who is currently serving on active duty as a major, FA. Since retirement on Nov 1, 1978, he has served as senior Army instructor, AJROTC, Patch American High School, Stuttgart, Germany.

BENJAMIN F. GOTTFRIED, CWO, born April 13, 1939, Philadelphia, PA. Joined the US Army, Corps of Engineers, on March 24, 1959, and the Ordnance Corps. Stationed in Europe, Vietnam and Thailand.

Memorable experiences include holding the position of Officer in Charge of the Motorcade for President Carter's Inauguration Parade; being ambushed in Vietnam in 1970; and receiving his commission as a WO from the grade of SFC.

Retired on March 31, 1979, with 20 years of active service. Received the Bronze Star, Army Comm Med, Purple Heart Med, Meritorious Svc Med, Vietnam Campaign Med w/2 Bronze Palms, Vietnam Svc Med, Good Conduct (4th Awd), Vietnam Cross of Gallantry, Who's Who in the East, 1993-94, Who's Who in Industry, 1993-94, Who's Who in the World, 1994-95.

He is the son of Harry Gottfried (deceased) and Sylvia Gottfried, and brother of Mrs Diane Krupnick. Married

Nancy in June 1994 and has one son, Hal. He is senior director of service for Iveco Trucks of North America.

DAVID T. GOUGH, CW2, born Nov 26, 1942, Kansas City, MO. Enlisted in the MOARNG May 10, 1960, and the US Army Corps of Engineers Dec 18, 1961. Stationed in Korea, 1962; Greenland, 1963; RVN, 1965-66 and 1969; Germany, 1974-76; and Antarctica in 1972. Served with the Seabees at PM-3A Nuclear Power Plant and Ross Station, Antarctica.

Discharged June 30, 1983, with the rank CW2. Received the Meritorious Svc Med, (2) Army Comm Meds, (5) Good Conduct, Nat Def Svc Med, Vietnam Svc Med, Antarctica Svc Med, Army Svc Rib, Overseas Svc, RVN Civil Actions Hon Med, Vietnam Cross of Gallantry w/palm, RVN Campaign Med w/7 stars, NCO PDR, Nuclear Reactor Operator 1/c, and Safe Driver Badge.

Married Billie Rose April 26, 1993; he has a son, David, from a previous marriage. Presently in administration and management of commercial properties.

JOHN T. GRANTHAM, CW3, AUS (RET), born Dec 28, 1934, Day, FL; graduated from Melbourne HS, Melbourne, FL June 2, 1952; U of Nebraska in Omaha (bootstrap program) on May 30, 1970; Kansas State U (MA), Dec 15, 1972; U of Cambridge (England, Ph.D.), Nov 12, 1977. Entered US Army July 1952; basic training, Ft Jackson, SC and photo interpreter training, Ft Riley KS.

Served in 4th API Co, Korea; and intelligence assignments in Ft Sam Houston, TX; Allied Forces, Southern Europe (Naples, Italy); and Ft Meade, MD. Appointed WO1 in 1963 and served at Ft Hood, TX; 73rd Avn Co, Vietnam; Ft Bragg, NC; back to Vietnam with the 9th MI Det and subsequently the 73rd Avn Co for second time. Following bootstrap he served on the staff of the US Army Intel School, Ft Holabird, MD; transitioned to counterintelligence and served in Manhattan, KS Field Office. Retired July 1972.

He was subject matter expert on research projects ran by the US Army Pers Research Office, Washington, DC, including the development and evaluation of the tactical Imagery Interpretation Facility. Served as infra red imagery evaluator during arctic test of UAS-4 infra red surveillance system in 1962-63 and qualified as an aerial observer.

Awards/Medals: Bronze Star w/OLC, Meritorious Svc Med, Air Med w/#3, Army Comm Med w/3 OLCs and Vietnamese Cross of Gallantry w/Palm.

Taught international relations and comparative politics for the Open University and U of Cambridge Board of Extra Mural Studies in England.

Married Barbara Joan Hentall and lives in Cambridge, England, where he presently works for a firm of lawyers and is active in the retiree community in Britain.

GEORGE C. GRATCHEN, CW4, USA (RET), born Sept 29, 1929, Joffre, (Washington County) PA. Entered the US Army April 12, 1950, from Pittsburgh, PA. Took 16 weeks of armored and infantry basic training at Ft Knox, KY, then assigned to the 503rd Engr Light Equip Co in Mannheim, Germany as a wheeled vehicle mechanic. Served in enlisted status for 11 years culminating his enlisted service as engineer operations sergeant at HQ, 7th Army, Stuttgart and Vaihingen, Germany. Appointed WO in June 1961 and completed more than 17 years of warrant service in a variety of assignments in Europe, the US, Pacific area and Vietnam as tank and automotive repair tech and as commanding officer of Equipment Spt Ctr, Mannheim, Germany.

He was instrumental in forming the European WO Assoc in the early 1970s that later merged with USAWOA.

Member of Triangle Masonic Lodge #834, AF&AM, Mannheim, Germany and a life member in the USAWOA.

Retired in October 1978 with over 28 years of service. Awards/Medals: Bronze Star, Meritorious Svc Med, Army Comm Med and numerous service and campaign medals. Inducted into the US Army Ordnance Corps Hall of Fame at APG, MD, May 12, 1989.

Married the former Margot Antoni of Ludwigshafen/Rhein, Germany. They have a son, two daughters and four grandchildren. Presently enjoying total retirement in Virginia Beach, VA and working on his stamp and coin collections and the arrangement of his photograph and slide collection that was accumulated over the years.

LEAMON L. GREEN, CW4 (RA), born March 14, 1933, in Merrelton (Calhoun County), AL. Entered the US Army June 8, 1953; attended basic training and organizational level Automotive Maint Crs at Ft Jackson, SC. As an enlisted soldier E-1-E-6, he served in Japan; Ft Lee, VA; Korea; Ft Myer, VA; Germany, Washington, DC and Germany.

Appointed WO1 Aug 28, 1966, as maint officer of Munich Equipment Maint Center, Dachan, Germany, 149th Lt Maint Co, Vietnam, 48th Trans Gp, Vietnam, 508th Heavy Equip Maint Co, Ft Meade, MD, HQ Med Cmd Vietnam, 95th Evac Hosp, Vietnam, 85th Med Gp, Ft Meade, MD, 902nd MI Gp, Washington, DC, HQMDW, Ft McNair, DC.

Retired July 31, 1975. Recalled to active duty Aug 1, 1984, and assigned to 66th Maint Co redesignated 66th Light Equip Maint Co. HQ US Army Cbt Systems Test Activity, APG, MD, 296th Fwd Spt Bn, Korea and returned to CSTA.

Awards/Medals: Bronze Star w/OLC, Good Conduct, Meritorious Svc Med w/3 OLCs, Army Comm Med w/OLC, Nat Def Svc Med W/2 stars and other service and campaign medals.

Married Therese Langer Haese and has six children and three grandchildren.

J.T. GREENHAW, W4, born Oct 29, 1926, Kemp, TX. Enlisted in US Army March 15, 1945. Stationed at Ft Sam Houston, TX; Ft Hood, TX; Ft Sill, OK; Germany; and Vietnam.

Most memorable experience was with the 5th US Army Arty Gp in Germany. Retired Oct 1, 1977. Awards/Medals: EIB and Parachute Badge.

Married Millie and is in ranch management in Kemp, TX.

ERNIE L. GREENING, CW4, USA (RET), born June 8, 1937, in Stoutsville, MO. Entered US Army on Sept 5, 1955, taking basic training at Camp Chaffee, AR and Operations and Intelligence Training at Ft Bliss, TX. First posting was to Camp Lucas, MI; served as MP in Korea, 1957-58. Short tour at Ft Ben Harrison in 1958; then to Germany. Entered Aviation from Ft Carson in 1962 and served as Aviator until 1976.

Recalled to active duty during the Falklands uprising and served at Ft Campbell from 1981-85. Presently an Adult Probation Officer in Harrison, AR. Received the Silver Star, (3) Distinguished Flying Crosses and numerous service and campaign medals.

Married Kris, who runs a Corporate Day-Care in Harrison, and has five children and five grandchildren.

WILLIAM A. GRIMES, CW3, USA, born May 17, 1951, St. Augustine, FL. Entered the US Army June 9, 1975, taking basic training at Ft Jackson, SC. Assignments included the 24th Spt Bn and D 724th Spt Bn at Ft Stewart GA; 182nd Maint Co at Nuremberg, FRG; HHC Committee Gp, Ft Knox, KY; 539th Maint Co at Ft Polk, LA; the 45th Spt Bn in Gelnhausen, FRG.

Completed WO Candidate Crs and the Advanced Crs at APG, MD. Appointed WO June 28, 1984, and served with the 3rd Armd Div during Desert Shield/Desert Storm in SWA. Currently serving with the 24th Spt Bn at Ft Stewart, GA with 19 years of active service.

Awards/Medals: Bronze Star, ARCOM w/OLC, Army Achiev Med w/OLC, Good Conduct, Nat Def Svc Rib, HSM, NCO PDR, Army Svc Rib, Overseas Rib and service and campaign medals.

Member of WOA and has been married to Linda Morris of Brunswick, GA for 23 years. They have two children, Angela and Thomas.

LANCE S. GROMME, CW4, USA (RET), born June 8, 1946, San Francisco, CA. Began his military career as draftee in February 1966 and progressed to the rank of specialist 6 while serving as radar, microwave, and satellite communications repairman.

Appointed to WO1 in June 1970, and served as a communications and electronics repair technician in a variety of assignments including the 1st Cav and 1st Inf Div; 24th Sig Bn; 394th Avn Maint Bn; 597th and 903rd Maint Co's; 800th Corps Mat Mgmt Ctr and overseas in Germany, Korea, Thailand and Vietnam.

Graduate of Elect Maint Officer Crs, Comm and Elect WO Adv Crs and the WO Senior Crs, he holds an associate in arts degree for social sciences. Most memorable experiences include serving aboard the USS *Hornet* aircraft carrier during the Apollo 12 Recovery Mission; with the Armed Forces Korea Network, broadcasting the 1972 Bob Hope Christmas Show; and with the Advanced Attack Helicopter Program Managers Office fielding the Apache AH-64A Helicopter.

Retired in August 1988. He received the Bronze Star, Army Meritorious Svc Med w/2 OLCs and Army Comm Med w/4 OLCs. Member of the American Legion, La Societe des 40 Hommes et 8 Chevaux, Optimist Club, ROA and USAWOA.

Married Katherine Holmes of Walnut Creek, CA and has six children and a granddaughter.

JOHN H. GROTE, CW4, AUS (RET), born July 3, 1931, Neola, IA. Enlisted in IAARNG on July 9, 1951, and drafted AUS Jan 28, 1952. Basic training at Ft Leonard Wood, MO; assigned to airborne battalion, 1st Stu Regt, Ft Benning, GA, July 1952. Reassigned HHC, 1st Stu Regt, Sept 23, 1952, relieved from active duty Jan 27, 1954, and transferred to the USAR.

Served various positions and promoted to 1SG June 6, 1960. Rejoined the NG in August 1963 and began full time employment with IANG as staff administrative specialist May 25, 1964. Appointed WO Jan 14, 1965, as supply section leader. Reassigned as automotive maintenance technician Jan 1, 1968, due to reorganization of IAARNG; activated by presidential order May 13, 1968, and served tour of duty in Vietnam with the 54th Trans Bn; and released to NG on Dec 12, 1969. Completed 30 years tech service as battalion admin spec, battalin property book officer, Supv Sup Spec (OUSPFO IA) and Organ Maint Shop Chief.

Retired July 1991 with 40 years of military service. Awards/Medals: Meritorious Svc Med, Army Comm Med, Good Conduct, Army Res Achiev Med w/4 OLCs, Nat Def Svc Med w/2 stars, RVN Campaign Med w/3 stars, Armed Forces Res Med w/2 devices, Pres Meritorious Cit, Vietnam Gallantry Cross w/Palm and several service ribbons.

Married Mary Lee Jorgensen and has six children (two sons serving with IAARNG) and 14 grandchildren.

JAY G. GRUWELL, CWO-4 (RET), born April 20, 1931, in Muncie, IN. Entered the US Army and attended basic training with Co A, 83rd Mech Sqdn, Ft Knox, KY. He graduated from Central High School, Muncie, IN in 1949; has a vocational-industrial education teaching certificate, Univ of Maryland; 64 hours of general education credit, Univ of Maryland; NCO Academy, US Army Europe; several specialty and technical schools, US Army; and Officers Automotive Maint and Repair Crs, APG, MD.

February 1950-June 1961 he served as MP, Ft Sill, OK and Camp Polk, LA; wheel vehicle mechanic and wheeled vehicle repairman inspector with 4th Inf Div in Germany; ordnance supply clerk, 1st Inf Div, Ft Riley, KS; motor sergeant, Arlington Heights, IL; ordnance vehicle inspector, 881st Ord Co, 8th Ord Bn, Hanau, Germany; maint tech, 39th Trans Co, HQ, VII Corps, Germany.

October 1961-76: brigade maint tech, HHC, 2nd Inf, Ft Devins, MA; ordnance supply advisor to the Republic of China Army, HQ USAMAAG, Taiwan; battalion maint officer, HQ, 4th Inf Div, Ft Lewis, WA; shop officer, 538th Engr Bn Const, Thailand; shop officer, C/51st Maint Bn, Mannheim, Germany; battalion maint officer, HQ, 25th Inf Div, RVN; inspection and identification section leader, Kaiserslautern, Germany; brigade automotive repair tech advisor, HQ, 1st Spt Bde, Mannheim, Germany; chief of inventory, HQ Miesau Army Depot, Germany; battalion maint officer, 1st AIT Bde Trng Cmd, Ft Knox, KY.

Retired in June 1976 as CWO4. Awards include the Legion of Merit, Bronze Star w/2 OLCs, Meritorious Svc Med, Purple Heart, Army Comm Med w/V Device and 2nd OLC and Good Conduct Med.

Worked as a quality control engineering supervisor, M60 Tank, Defense Div. and as management information and project control analyst, M1 tank, Defense Div, Chrysler Corp. From March 1982 to present with General Dynamics Land Systems Div as manufacturing program specialist, Program Office, Lima Army Tank Plant.

JAMES JOSEPH GUYRE, CWO-3, USA (RET), born July 3, 1947, Teaneck, NJ, the fourth oldest of 14 children. Entered the US Army in May 1966, completed Aircraft Instrument Repairman Crs, and assigned to B Co, 708th Maint, 8th Inf Div in Mainz, Germany.

Went to Vietnam as electrician with 92nd AHC, 10th Bn, 1st Avn Bde; returned to Germany to 122nd (later 73rd MI) OV-1 Mohawk Avn Co. Served four years as aviation maintenance instructor at Ft Eustis, VA, where, as a staff sergeant, he was selected for appointment as WO.

Following completion of AMOC he was assigned to the 1st AD Avn Co, 501st Avn Bn in Ausback, Germany; then 4th ID, Ft Carson, CO; back to the 1st AD, 10th Avn Bn at Illesheim, Germany where he retired as CWO3 after completion of more than 20 years of service.

Awards/Medals: Meritorious Svc Med, ARCOM, Master Instructor Awd, and numerous service and campaign medals and ribbons. Graduate of St Leo College with AA in business, Embry-Riddle Aeronautical U with BS in professional aeronautics, and holds a current FAA airframe and power plant license with inspection authorization.

Holds the position of director for an international multi-faceted investment corp with headquarters in Munich, Germany and aviation holdings in Asia, Africa, US, France, Germany and other countries.

Married the former Christel Mayer of Burgbernheim, Germany and lives in Bavaria.

RONALD L. HACKETT, CW3, USA (RET), born Aug 5, 1950, Portland, ME. Entered the US Army Aug 12, 1968, taking basic training at Ft Dix, NJ. Served as radar tech at Homestead AFB, FL until he transferred to Germany with the 7th Army. Continued as radar tech and service school instructor until appointed WO1 in Ft Bliss, TX, June 1979.

Transferred to 3rd Bn, 7th Air Def Arty, 32nd Army Air Def Cmd Hawk Msl Maint Officer; promoted to CW2 in June 1981 and remained until June 1982. Transferred to I Corps, 35th Air Def Arty Bde, 1st Bn, 4th ADA, Ft Lewis, WA until reassigned in 1985 to the 32nd Army ADC, 606th Ord Co as missal maint officer. Promoted to CW3 in 1986 in support of Hawk Msl Bn in Bitburg, Germany, and affiliated with the US Army Ord Corps. Served as logistician at Ft Lee, VA from July 1989-August 1990 and retired with over 22 years of military service.

Awards include the Army Achiev Med, Good Conduct Med, Army Svc Rib, NCO PDR, Army Comm Med w/2 OLCs, Meritorious Svc Med w/OLC and the Legion of Merit.

Served as past-president of the Eifel Chap, WOA in Bitburg, Germany and is currently a member of the Americal Legion, TROA and Masonic Lodge.

Married Christina Stanglmeir of Munich, Germany and has two step-children and three grandchildren. Currently employed as production manager in a manufacturing firm.

JAMES D. HAGER II, WO1, USAR, born July 29, 1959, Portsmouth, VA. Entered the US Army Sept 2, 1977, taking basic and MP training at Ft McClellan, AL. Served as MP with the 258th MP Co, Ft Polk, LA and C Btry, 2/56th ADA until discharged in August 1980.

Returned to active duty in October 1981, receiving training as basic laboratory specialist. Employed as a medical photographic tech at the USAMRIID, Ft Detrick, MD until March 1984 when selected for training as CI agent. Served as CI agent with the 1st Armd Div until March 1987 when selected as military instructor (CI and intelligence photography) assigned to the US Army Intel Ctr and School, Ft Huachuca, AZ. He was selected as WOC in April 1988.

Discharged from US Army and concurrently entered the USAR as WOC in August 1988. Completed WOEC/WOCS in August 1989, WOTTC in July 1990 and appointed WO1 in the USAR on July 16, 1990. Promoted to CW2, effective July 16, 1992 (promotion orders dated March 9, 1993). Received the ARCOM w/2 OLCs, Army Achiev Med, Army Good Conduct Med (3), Overseas Svc Rib (2) and Army Svc Rib.

Currently employed by Salvation Army, Columbia, SC as executive assistant to the commanding officer. Graduated Magna Cum Laude with a BS in human resources mgmt from Central Wesleyan College in December 1992, and presently pursuing an MA in Christian Ministries. Lifetime member of Alpha Chi National Scholastic Honor Society, Beta National Honors Society, Assoc of Former Intel Officers, SC Emergency Preparedness Assoc, USAWOA, The Salvation Army, and ECS committee member of the American Red Cross, Midlands Chap, Columbia, SC.

He is the father of one son, James D. Hager III.

FANNY J. HAINE, CW3, born May 1947 in Zaire. Graduated from high school in Paris, France; moved to Florida in 1972; became a resident and joined the Army in January 1973 as personnel specialist. Naturalized in 1974 while stationed at Ft Ord, CA. Enlisted assignments were Ft Belvoir, Pentagon, 1st PERSCOM, GE.

Appointed WO1 in August 1981 as a personnel tech. Assignments were Ft Campbell, KY as chief, Pers Records; Rheinberg, GE as MILPO chief; Heidelberg, GE, USAREUR IG as pers inspector; Heidelberg, CENTAG as G-1; currently at Grafenwoehr, GE as assistant AG.

Holds a master's degree in human resources and services from Boston University. Single, no children. Hobbies are biking, hiking, skiing and more.

JULIETTE ANITA HALLMAN, CW3, USAR, born June 22, 1946, in Prichard, Mobile, AL. She served a total of 24 years, which includes 15 years of enlisted service.

Attended Admin Spec School; USAR Tech Basic School; Personnel Mgmt School; USAR Tech Refresher School; NCO Basic Engineer; USAR Tech School, Training/Operation Crs and mobilization Crs; QM School, Food Svc Sr Crs and Sanitation Crs; USA Inst of Prof Dev, QM, Food Svc Mgmt Crs; Ft Levenworth School, Observer/Controller Crs; Army Trng Spt Ctr, Test Standards Off Crs; and Bay Business College.

Duty stations include basic and AIT training, Ft McClellan, AL; Ft Dix, NJ; USA Vietnam; Ft Lesley J. McNair, Mil Dist, Washington, DC; S&S Bn, 85th Div, Chicago, IL; HHC, 1/337th Regt, 85, Arlington Heights, IL; admin NCO, E7, HHC, 2/337, 85, Chicago, IL; A/863rd Engr Bn, Harvey, IL; 434th FA Bde, Chicago, IL; 85th MEC, Ft Sheridan, IL.

Awards include the Nat Def Svc Med (2 awds), VN Svc, Army Comm (5 awds), Good Conduct, Army Res Comp Achiev (5th awd), Humanitarian Svc Awd, Armed Forces Res Med (2 awds), Army Achiev Med (2 awds), St Barbara Medal (FA Ceremonial Awd), Adjutant, II District, Cook County, AMVETS, Queen, OWS Chap.

Present assignment is food service tech, Mobilization Sect, 1st Bde, BCP/SIM, 85th Div, Ft Sheridan, IL, with the rank of CW3. Her civilian occupation is federal employee, USAR full time tech, supervisory staff admin (SSA), HQ, 138th MI Bn, Rosemont, IL.

Married Jack Hallman, retired active duty soldier; they have four adult children: Lendra, Gerard, Leander Coleman, Michael; one teenage daughter Ophelia Coleman; seven grandchildren. She enjoys cooking and sewing and is a member of the AMVET and Order of Eastern Star. .

ROBERT L. HAMILTON, CW4, USA (RET), born May 21, 1936, Hanford, CA. Enlisted October 1954 at Ft Ord, CA; attended Helicopter Maint School, Camp Rucker and assigned to 2nd Armd Div, 1955-57. Graduated from WO Flt Trng in 1958; assigned to Ft Benning, 1958-61; participated in aerial recon and surveillance troop tests at Ft Stewart.

After tour in Germany, 1961-64, and Ft Rucker, 1964-66 (ARCOM), he was assigned to the 1st Air Cav Div from 1966-67; Dept of Army Staff, 1967-70 (ARCOM 1st OLC); attended second WO Advance Crs, Ft Rucker; attended Aerospace Mgmt and Safety, U of Southern California, 1971; HQ US Army, Vietnam, 1971; USARV Safety Office; assigned to HQ 1st Avn Bde, 1971-72.

Helped establish the USAWOA in 1972 and is life member #3. Assigned to the director of Army Aviation Office in the Pentagon, 1972-75 (MSTARAVB/LOM). Was responsible for survival equipment and flight simulation.

Retired in 1975. Awards include the Dist Flying Cross, Bronze Svc Star, Meritorious Unit Cit, VUA, VN Gal Cross w/Palm Unit Cit, Air Med w/23 OLCs, ARCOM w/OLC, MSTARAVB and Legion of Merit.

Inducted into the US Army Aviation Hall of Fame in 1986. Elected member of Santa Clara County Republican Central Committee, 1989-90, and elected town council member, town of Los Gatos, 1986-90.

JOHN WILLIAM HAMPTON, CW3, USAR, born April 23, 1947, in Cleveland, OH. Duty assignments include Navy boot camp, Great Lakes, IL; Mobile Const Bn Eight, Vietnam; Naval Reserve, St Louis, MO; 70th Div Trng, Ft Wayne, IN; 199th Sup Co (GS), Grisson AFB, IN; 300th Sup & Svc Bn, Lafayette, IN; ARPERCEN, St Louis, MO; 805th MP Co, Raleigh, NC; Control Gp (reinforcement), St Louis; 5033rd USAR School, Lansing, MI; Control Gp (reinforcement), St Louis; 2nd Bde, 70th Trng Div, Flint, MI; HQ, 70th Trng Div, Livonia, MI.

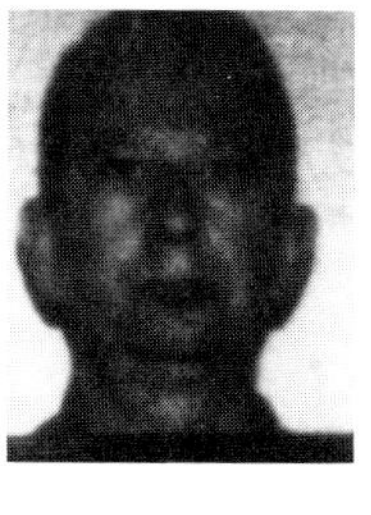

Attended Naval Weapons School and Personnel and Administration School. From 1967-93 he completed 48 courses. Civilian education at Lakewood HS, Lakewood, OH; Akron Univ, Akron, OH; Central Vocational College, Ft. Wayne, IN; International Jr. College, Ft. Wayne; Upper Iowa Univ, Lansing Computer Institute, Lansing, MI; State of MI Assessor's Crs, Holloway's Real Estate Institute.

Awards include the Army Comm w/2 OLCs, Army Achiev Med w/OLC, Combat Action Rib, Navy Unit Comm Med (2), Navy Meritorious Unit Comm Med, Army Good Cond Med, Army Res Comp Achiev Med w/3 OLCs, Nat Def Svc Med w/SS, Vietnam Svc Med w/Fleet Marine Force Combat Operation Insignia w/9 Campaign Service Stars and two Bronze Arrowheads, Army Svc Rib, NCOPDR w/#3, Army Svc Rib, Navy Expert Marksmanship Rifle Rib, RVN Camp Med w/D, RVN Meritorious Unit Cit - Navy Gallantry Cross Medal with Palm (2nd awd), RVN Meritorious Unit Cit - Navy Civil Actions Medal Color with Palm (2nd and 3rd awd), FORSCOM Bronze Excellence in Competition Pistol Badge, Army Pistol Expert Badge, Army Rifle M-16 (SS) Badge, Army Drivers Badge with Bar (Wheel Vehicle) and Overseas Service Bars (5). He is assigned to HQ, 70th Trng Div, Livonia, MI and works as a school administrator, 123rd ARCOM, Lansing, MI.

RANDALL S. HANSEN, CW5, born June 29, 1951, in LaPeer, MI. Enlisted in the US Army Jan 21, 1972. Basic training at Ft Polk, LA; basic flight training, Ft Wolters, TX; advanced flight training, Ft Rucker, AL. Assigned to D Trp 3rd Sqdn (air), 5th Cav, Ft Lewis, WA, where he completed the demanding Artic Military Mountaineering (summer) Crs at Ft Greely, AK.

Completed UH-1 Instructor Pilot Crs; arrived in Korea and assigned to HHC 52nd Avn Bn (CBT); returned to Ft Lewis and 3rd Sqdn, 5th Cav/214th Attack Heli Bn in 1978; departed Ft Lewis in 1981; attended Instrument Flt Examiner Crs en route to A Co 3rd Avn Bn (CBT)/225th Gen Spt Avn Co, Giebelstadt, Germany; completed both WOAC and WOSC by correspondence while performing duties for 3rd Inf Div. Returned to CONUS in 1985 for assignment with the 5th Trans Bn (AM) 222nd Avn Bn 8-101st Avn Regt (AASLT), Ft Campbell, KY. Promoted to CW4, April 16, 1987.

Spent three years at Ft Campbell then PCS'd to Korea; assigned to the 17th Avn Bde; selected to attend the Fixed Wing Multi Engine Qualification Crs; departed Korea in 1990 for Ft Rucker. Assigned to the 7th Army Trng Cmd (7ATC) at Grafenwoehr, Germany. Completed Army Avn Safety Off Crs and U-21 Instructor Pilot Qualification Crs. Departed Germany for present assignment in Atlanta, GA; promoted to CW5 in 1993 and attended the first WO Sr Staff Crs in January 1994.

Awards include the Meritorious Svc Med w/2 OLCs, Army Comm Med w/2 OLCs and numerous service medals.

Received his AA degree in business administration from Fullerton Jr College, Fullerton, CA and a BA degree in professional aeronautics from Embry-Riddle Aeronautical Univ, Daytona Beach, FL. Life member of WOA and the Army Aviation Assoc of America and past vice-president of Wuerzburg and Grafenwoehr WOA chapters.

Married the former Deborah Danen (BSN).

ROGER L. HARDMAN, CW4, USA, born Sept 4, 1951, Crawford, WV. Entered the US Army in June 1971; attended basic training at Ft Dix, NJ and AIT at Aberdeen Proving Ground, MD, September 1971. Held various positions as enlisted and obtained rank of SSG(P). On Jan 13, 1981, he was appointed WO1 as automotive repair tech. Served five overseas assignments: three long tours in West Germany; one short tour in Korea; and one short combat tour in Kuwait. Retired as CW4.

Awards include the Meritorious Svc Med w/OLC, Joint Svc Comm Med, Army Comm Med w/5 OLCs, Army Achiev Med, Army Good Conduct Med w/3 Bronze Loops, Nat Def Svc Med w/BS, SWA Svc Med w/BS, NCOPDR, Army Svc Rib and Overseas Svc Rib w/#4, Expert Badge (pistol and grenade). He is a member of the WOA.

Married Hannelore Scheiermann of Esslingen A/M Neckar, West Germany.

FRANK R. HARGIS, CW4, USA (RET), born April 7, 1917, Danville, KY. Drafted in the Army June 17, 1942; attended basic training at Ft Leonard Wood, MO. Served with the 411th Engr Bn, 2nd Amph Bde in the South Pacific until his discharge in September 1945.

Re-enlisted in the Army in 1947 and spent 14 months in Adak, AK with the 210th Ord Co. Returned to March AFB and assigned to the 817th Engr Bn, SCAWAF, then to England for five years. Appointed WOJG in March 1955.

After duty at Camp Wolters and Ft Sill with the 1902nd Engr Co as maint officer, he joined the 8th Engr Bn, 1st Cav Div in Korea in 1959 as maint officer. Year later was assigned to the 46th Engr Bn at Ft Hood, TX as maint officer and CO of the Maint Co.

Assigned duty with MUS10 in Rabat, Morocco for a three year tour as advisor to the Moroccan Engr Bn; transferred to 102nd Engr Co, Vietnam. After one year assigned to 63rd Engr Bn at Ft Hood, TX as battalion maint officer for two years; returned for second tour in Vietnam in 1969 with the 45th Engr Gp as S-4 maint chief; returned to Ft Hood as billeting officer in charge of BOQs, BEQs and Guest House.

Retired May 1973 with 29 plus years. Makes his home in Austin, TX. Awards include the Meritorious Svc Med, Bronze Star w/OLC, Army Comm Med w/2 OLCs, Good Conduct Med, Nat Def Svc Med w/2 stars, Armed Forces Res Med w/3 OLCs, and service ribbons and medals from Asiatic-Pacific, Philippine Liberation and Vietnam.

Married to Marcella Mink for 52 years and has six children, 12 grandchildrean and eight great-grandchildren. Life member of ROA, DAV, American Legion and VFW. Stays active by golfing and fishing.

BETTY JANE HARPER, CW4, born April 8, 1933, in Emeigh, PA. Entered the WAC on March 3, 1953; went to Ft Lee, VA for basic training; transferred to Ft Knox, KY at the 2048th Reception Ctr. One year later transferred to the Far East and served there until her discharge July 30, 1957.

Returned to the States, became a civil service employee at the Atlanta Army Depot and retired as a USAR Tech with over 40 years of service on Sept 1, 1993. During her government service she never used any her sick leave, so one-half years was added to her 40 years of service.

In 1968 she joined the USAR and stayed in the same unit working her way up through the ranks to MSG, then was the 5th female appointed to CW2 in 1977 and the 6th female appointed CW4 in 1989). Having served 29 1/2 years of military service, she retired April 8, 1993 from the USAR.

Received the Legion of Merit, Meritorious Svc Med, Army Comm Med w/3 OLCs, Army Achiev Med w/2 OLCs, UN Svc Med, Nat Def Svc Med, Korean Svc Med, Good Conduct Med, Army Svc Rib, Armed Forces Res Med w/X device, Army Res Component Achiev Med w/5 OLCs and Meritorious Unit Cit.

Married Laurice Harper and lives in Conley, GA. Currently does volunteer work for the 81st ARCOM, Family Support and Reserve Retirement. Recalled for active duty during the month of March 1994 for Exercise Certain Sage. Retains membership in TROA, VFW and WOA.

ROBERT C. HARRISON, CW3, born Sept 25, 1916, Walton County, GA. Enlisted in US Army May 12, 1943, with the Medical Svc Corps; appointed WO in February 1951. Stationed at Camp Grant, IL; Ft Lewis, WA; Korea; Luzon, 1944; Philippine Islands, 1944-45; France, 1957-60; Japan, 1959-61; Ft Dix, NJ and Aberdeen Proving Ground, MD, 1960-63.

Most memorable experience is having served 20 plus years and survived. Retired Aug 1, 1963, with rank of CW3.

Awards include the Bronze Star, Army Comm Med and numerious service medals.

Married and has three children and two grandchildren. Retired and enjoys doing volunteer work in Central Florida.

MARTIN FRANCIS HAYDEN, CW4, USA (RET), born Aug 21, 1929, Clarksburg, WV, the son of the late Martin F and Margaret Kraus (RN) Hayden of Alum Bridge, Lewis County, WV. Childhood was spent working on family farm on Crooked Run and attending school.

Enlisted service: Feb 11, 1948-Oct 16, 1950 as SGT E-5; Dec 17, 1960-Aug 25, 1962 as SSG E-6. Enlisted Feb 11, 1948, in WVARNG, Clarksburg, WV as PVT-1, Co D, 197th Tk Bn. Ordered to active duty during Berlin crisis with Clarksburg Guard Unit, Trp F, 2nd Sqdn, 150th Armd Cav WVARNG. Sent to Ft Meade, MD, Oct 15, 1961-Aug 15, 1962. On Aug 16, 1962, returned with HQ 150th Armd Cav to Charleston, WV as regt pers officer. Total enlisted service was four years, four months and 15 days.

Appointed WOJG-1, Oct 17, 1950; as unit administrator; promoted to CWO-2, Nov 2, 1953; CWO-3, Nov 19, 1959-Dec 16, 1960; reappointed CWO-3 as a unit personnel tech, Aug 26, 1962; promoted to CW4 July 28, 1967, and remained in that grade for over 24 years. Retired Aug 31, 1991, with total of 39 yrs, 2 mo and 6 days of WO service, and a total of 43 yrs, 6 mo and 21 days of military service at age 62 on Aug 31, 1991. This is the longest period of continuous active NG service in the WVNG to date.

Assignments include unit admin with Co C, 197th Tk Bn, 29th Inf Div, Clarksburg, WV, Oct 17, 1950-Feb 28, 1959; Trp F, 2nd Sqdn, 150th Armd Cav, March 1, 1959-Dec 16, 1960; plt sgt, Dec 17, 1960-Oct 14, 1961; active duty supply sgt, Oct 15, 1961-May 31, 1962; regt pers sgt, June 1, 1962-Aug 25, 1962; regt pers officer with HQ 150th Armd Cav, Charleston, WV, Aug 26, 1962-Nov 11, 1965.

Assigned to HQ&HQ Det WVARNG, Mil Spt Sect, Nov 12, 1965-Dec 31, 1973; pers officer, State Selective Svc Sect, Jan 1, 1974-Oct 31, 1976. Returned to State HQ&HQ Det WVARNG as gen staff admin tech, Nov 1, 1976-Nov 30, 1987; appointed general staff secretary and served until his retirement, Aug 31, 1991. Additional assignments included secretary to commandant for the WVARNG USAR Sch Cmd and General Staff College Program from 1964-89 and on the Staff of the WV Military Academy (OCS) as a pers officer from 1962-87.

Awards include the Legion of Merit, Meritorious Svc Med, Army Comm Med w/OLC, Army Res Component Achiev Med w/4 OLCs, Meritorious Svc Awd-Selective Svc, Nat Def Svc Med w/Svc Star, Humanitarian Svc Med w/ Svc Star, Armed Forces Res Med w/3 10 yr Devices, Army Svc Rib, WV Legion of Merit, WV Achiev Rib, WV Emergency Svc Med w/2 Gold Mountain Laurel Blossoms, WV State Serv Rib w/4 Bronze Stars, WV Svc Med w/Silver Eagle and XV (over 40 yrs service) and the WV Dist Unit Awd.

Employed as full-time tech for the WVARNG, Oct 20, 1948-Nov 30, 1990, when he retired with 42 yrs, one month, 10 days of actual service plus credit for 3,379 hours of accrued sick leave which gave him a grand total of 43 yrs, 8 months, and 23 days of tech service. This is a record of service for a tech in the state. Positions included admin sup tech, staff admin spec, ops and trng in military spt to civilian authority, senior cmd admin spec, enlisted military pers manager, officer pers readiness manager and cmd program spt spec to chief of staff.

Attended Army General's School, 10 series, Civil Def Staff Col Planning and Ops Courses I, II, III, Mil Pers Offs Crs, Selective Svc System Mil Crs and WOSC. Graduated from St. Patrick's HS in Weston, WV, June 1947; WV Business and Career College in Clarksburg, WV in October 1948 with honors; BS degree in accounting and mgmt, WV State Col, Institute, WV in May 1977.

Memberships: K of Cs, Benevolent and Protective Order of Elks, TROA, life member of the USNGA, WVNGA and the USAWOA. Served under the command of eight adjutant generals in the WVARNG: BG Charles Fox, BG William Blake, BG Gene Williams, MG Jack Blair, MG Robert Childers, MG John Wilson III, BG (WV) Harlan Wilson JR, and MG Joseph Skaff, from Feb 11, 1948-Aug 31, 1991.

Married Betty Linger of Weston, WV, Nov 12, 1960. They have three sons: Cpt Martin F III; Sgt Stephen, both on active duty with the WVARNG and John R.

Hayden is currently employed by the state of West Virginia as admin assistant to the adjutant general and to the Secretary, Dept of Mil Affairs and Public Safety in Charleston, WV.

CHARLES E. HENDRICKS (CHUCK), CW4, USA (RET), born May 8, 1930, Tacoma, WA. Entered US Army April 21, 1947, and was discharged in June 1950 as T5 radio repairman. In the ARNG he progressed through both civilian and military ranks. As a full-time employee he progressed from radio repairman to IFC System Tech. As a soldier he was appointed a WOJG in 1955, commanding an SRMU.

Commanded SRMU and Nike Ord Det as a CW2. Returned to the Army in August 1963, commanding various Sig Det in CONUS, Korea, Europe and Vietnam. Class leader and distinguished graduate of 1st Sig Maint WO Crs at Ft Monmouth. Graduated Magna Cum Laude from Troy State Univ. in 1976 with BS degree in electronics, after completing the WOAC at Ft Rucker.

Retired October 1981 from the logistic staff of USAISC, Ft Huachuca. Awards include the Legion of Merit, Bronze Star, Meritorious Svc Med, Army Comm Med and other service and campaign medals.

Retired as project leader at PRC Inc (McLean, VA) in May 1993. Provided support for operational testing of Army Weapons Systems; previously at Litton Industries, he was manager of the Saudi Arabian Air Def System Integration Laboratory.

He is past-president of AZ Chapter USAWOA and Rhine-Neckar Chapter of the European WOA.

Married Florence (Polly) Robinson of Seattle and has six children and seven grandchildren.

THOMAS J. HENNEN, CW4, USA, born Aug 17, 1952, in Albany, GA and joined the US Army Aug 28, 1972. Military education: distinguished graduate of the III Corps and Ft. Hood Leadership Crs; honor graduate of the 5th US Army NCO Academy; distinguished graduate of the Defense Sensor Interpretation and Applications Training Program; Distinguished Graduate of the USAF Eur Advanced Imagery Interpretation Crs and completed numberous courses in related field. .

Served over 21 years in the Imagery Intel Fld. Has extensive technical training and experience as an operational imagery analyst at both the national and tactical levels; experience as an instructor; training, force, and combat developer; extensive material development and acquisition management experience making him one of the most qualified imagery intel techs within the Dept of Def.

Stationed at Ft Hood, TX; Ft Huachuca, AZ; Washington, DC; NASA Johnson Space Center, Houston, TX; Wiesbaden, Germany.

Currently assigned to the USAF Space and Missile Systems Ctr, NASA, and responsible for development, integration, and operations of designated DOD space shuttle payloads.

Most memorable experience was being the first WO in space, flying aboard the Space Shuttle Atlantis which launched from Kennedy Space Cneter Nov. 24, 1991 and orbited the earth 109 times, 2.9 million miles before landing at Edwards AFB, CA Dec. 1, 1991.

Awards include the Def Superior Svc Med, Legion of Merit, three Meritorious Svc Med w/2 OLCs, Army Comm Med and Army Achiev Med w/OLC.

Single, he has three children, ages 16, 12 and eight. He is a member of the USAWOA, The Assn of Space Explorers, TROA, The Planetary Society and the American Legion.

ANDREW A. HENRY, CWO (RET), born in November 1919 Lewiston, ID. Enlisted in the USN in 1939; served in the USS *Canopus* at the beginning of the war as QM. On April 9, 1942, he was a member of the scuttling crew that scuttled the *Canopus;* on May 6, 1942, he was captured on Corregidor and taken to Camp #3; and transferred to Japan in October 1942.

Worked at Yodogawa Steel Mill and later in the coal mines. Retired from the Navy in 1959 as a CWO. He had a real estate office in Chula Vista for over 20 years; was president of the Board of Realtors in 1972; and was state vice-president in 1974. Now lives in Thousand Palms, CA and is commander of the Inland Empire Chapter American Ex-POWs, 1989, and junior vice-commander for the state of California for 1989 and 1990.

Married Virginia and has eight grandchildren.

CARL. L. HESS, CW4, born Nov 12, 1936, Donna, TX. He began his military career in the 49th Armd Div, TXNG and was called to active duty Oct 15, 1961, during the Berlin Crisis. Appointed WO upon completion of Flt School in 1963; served in the 11th Air Aslt Div (Test). During two tours in Vietnam, he served with the 114th Avn Co and the 1st Cav Div. Other assignments were Ft Rucker, AL; Ft Hood, TX; Panama and Ft Sill, OK.

Retired as CW4 in February 1982. Awards include the Expert Inf Badge, Armed Forces Exped Med, Air Med w/54 OLCs, Nat Def Svc Med, RVN Camp Med, Armed Forces Res Med, Bronze Star, Army Comm Med, Dist Flying Cross w/3 OLCs, VN Cross of Gallantry w/Silver Star, four Overseas Svc Bar, VN Svc Med w/5 Svc Stars and the Meritorious Unit Cit, Pres Unit Cit (Army), Valorous Unit Awd, Master Army Aviator Badge, RVN Gallantry Cross Unit Cit w/ Palm, Humanitarian Svc Med, NCOPDR-1, Army Svc Rib, Overseas Svc Rib, Expert (pistol .38), Meritorious Svc Med and Pres Svc Med. He is member of the USAWOA (life) and the Army Avn Assoc.

Married the former Virginia Smith and has two children and one grandchild. Presently he is employed with UNC and works as a helicopter instrument flight instructor at Ft Rucker, AL.

RAYMOND J. HILGART, CW4, USA (RET), born Nov 10, 1931, Park Falls, WI. Entered the US Army in October 1950 and completed basic and AIT with the 85th Inf at Ft Riley. He served with the 45th Inf Div (Korea) in 1952-53 and the XVI Corps, Japan, in 1953-54, until discharged in 1954.

Re-entered the US Army in 1955 with the most significant enlisted assignment in post Korean War era being that of plt sgt, 50th Sig Bn, with plt mission of supporting tactical command communications for XVIII Abn Corps. He was appointed WO in December 1961 and joined the 82nd Abn Div from 1962-63. His service in the RVN included a MAAG assignment with the 21st Inf Div (RVN) in 1964, and with units of the 5th Spec Forces Gp located throughout III and IV Corps regions in 1966 and 1967.

Other WO assignments included that of command elect maint officer for the US Army JFK Ctr for Special War at Ft Bragg and the Spec Action Force, Asia (Okinawa). This was followed by a three year assignment as Communications Project Officer with the US. Def Liaison Gp (Indonesia) advising Indonesian armed forces officials in the planning, procurement, installation, maintenance and training activities associated with Project INDOCOM. Retired from the service in August 1978.

His education includes a BS (management) from the Univ of Nebraska and a BS (electronic engineering) from

North Carolina State Univ. Awards and decorations include the Legion of Merit, Bronze Star w/2 OLCs, Air Med, Meritorious Svc Med, Joint Svc Comm Med, Army Comm Med, Comb Inf Badge, Master Parachutist Badge, Pres Unit Cit (Korea and US), and the RVN Cross of Gallantry.

Employed by PAN-AM in Saudi Arabia as radio engineer, 1978-80 and joined Science Applications Inernational Corp (SAIC) of McLean, VA in 1984 where he is employed today as a communications systems engr. Both he and his wife, Hisako, reside in Warrenton, VA. Their son Kenneth is pursuing a law degree in New York.

KENNETH B.N. HILL, CW2, USA, born Feb 9, 1956, Pomona, CA. Entered the US Army on April 10, 1974, taking basic training at Ft Polk, LA and served as mechanic with D/782nd Maint Bn, 82nd Abn Div from October 1974-May 1978. Served as shop office NCOIC with D/122nd Maint Bn, 3rd Armd Div, June 1978-January 1981; DAC in Giessen, March-September 1981.

Re-entered USAR at Philadelphia, PA on April 14, 1982, with duty at HHC, 330th Engr Bn; motor sergeant with C Co, 330th Engr from September 1983-September 1986; appointed WO in February 1987 at APG, MD and transferred to Germany. Served as battery and battalion tech, February 1987-June 1990; battalion maint tech with 82nd Sig Bn, 82nd Abn Div, July 1990-present; deployed to SWA with 82nd Sig Bn in November 1990; redeployed USA in April 1991. Current duty assignment is battalion maint tech, 82nd Sig Bn.

Awards include the Bronze Star, Army Comm Med w/ OLC, Army Achiev Med w/3 OLCs, Para Badge, Good Conduct Med w/3 knots, Nat Def Svc Med w/2 Bronze Stars, NCOPDR w/#3, Army Svc Rib, Overseas Svc Rib w/#2, Kuwait Lib Med and Mechanic/Driver Badge.

Member of the USAWOA; secretary and president, Eifel Chapter, vice-president, Ft Bragg Chapter and life member of the 82nd Abn Assoc.

Married Barbara Shively and has four children. His hobbies include fishing and golfing.

JOSEPH A. HINES, CW4, USA (RET), born Dec 17, 1948, and raised as a military dependent in Germany; Hawaii; Phillipines; Washington, DC and San Antonio, TX; where he joined the Army in 1967 at the age of 18. Basic training was at Ft Polk, LA and WO flight training at Ft Wolters, TX and Ft Rucker, AL.

Served two tours in Vietnam, 1968-69 and 1972-73 with the 117th Aslt Heli Co, the 48th Aslt Heli Co and D Trp, 4/7 Cav. Two tours at Ft Hood, TX, 1973-77 and 1978-80 with the 7/17th Attack Heli Sqdn, interrupted by a tour in Korea with D Trp, 4/7 Air Cav in 1978. In 1980, after attending the WOSC, he was assigned to 210th Avn Bn in Panama with duties as battalion safety officer and assistant S-3. Subsequently assigned to WO Div, Dept of the Army in 1983 as assistant branch chief of Professional Development.

In 1984 he was given the job of Assoc Branch chief, Avn Branch, as well as the position of career manager for over 2,000 WO aviators in the utility and observation category.

Departed DA in 1986 for assignment to the Ft Sam Houston Flight Det in San Antonio, TX where he retired in 1988. From 1970-80 he completed a bachelor's degree in psychology and a master's degree in counseling. Awards include the Dist Flying Cross, Meritorious Svc Med (2), Air Med (50), Army Comm Med (2), Army Achiev Med, and numerous other awards. Additionally, he holds qualification as a master Army aviator.

He resides in San Antonio, TX and currently flies as a pilot for American Airlines.

JOHN HOBER, CW3, USA, (RET), born Sept 19, 1920, Brooklyn, NY. Began his military career in the NYNG, HQ 1st Bn, 212th Coast Arty, 12th Inf Div on Nov 18, 1940. Federalized into active duty Feb 10, 1941 and held NCO grades of corporal, sergeant, tech sergeant (pers. sergeant

major), master serteant (battalion sergeant major).

Was part of a cadre, forming the 462nd AAA (AW) Bn, Camp Haan, CA on Sept 1, 1942; ETO, 1943; Scotland; Wales; England; Normandy (Liberation of Paris); Belgium (Battle of the Bulge); Luxembourg, Germany; and until the war's end at Pilsen, Czechoslovakia in 1945. Served under Patten's 3rd Army and also the 1st Army. Appointed WO at Meng Kofen, Germany in 1945 as battalion personnel officer of the 462nd AAA (AW) Bn (personally proud of the best field personnel section in the ETO).

Awarded five campaign stars (Normandy, Northern France, Rhineland, Ardennes and Central Europe), Am Def Svc Med, Army Comm Med, Good Conduct Med, EAME, Normandy Med, Army of Occupation w/Germany Clasp, Army Meritorious Unit Cit from 2nd Inf Div, Med of Liberated France w/2 clasps, France and Germany; French Croix de Guerre Awd (Cord), Croix du Combattant Voluntaire Medal, Medaille Commemorative Francaise Medal, Belgium Fourraguere Awd (Cord), Victory Med, Armed Forces Res Med w/HG Device, WWI Certificate of Merit, 15-year Res Svc Med, 102nd Med Bn Svc Med, Army Res Components Achiev Med, and the NY State Conspicious Svc Cross.

Arrived back in England on July 16, 1945. While in the ETO he was assigned additional duties as postal officer, naturalization officer, legal assistant officer and finance officer. Returned to Southampton, England on Sept 17, 1945. Boarded the *Costa Rica* victory ship on Sept 27, 1945. Honorably discharged on Oct 26, 1945, and transferred to Officers' Reserve on Oct 29, 1961. His Army life was quite an experience.

Married Catherine Williams of Inverness, Scotland, a war bride whom he met on Nov 23, 1943, and married at a mil wedding on Sept 11, 1945, at Cheltenham, (Ashchurch) England. They have three children and two grandchildren. His hobbies are surf fishing, metal detecting and dancing. Retired from business on Dec 1, 1982.

JAMES MICHAEL HOLDER, CW2, USA, born Sept 20, 1963, Gulfport, MS. Joined the GAANG April 24, 1982 and served as a medical service tech until accepted into the USAWO Flight Trng Program in 1988. Attended basic training at Ft Jackson, SC before proceeding to Ft Rucker, AL for WOC School and Initial Entry Rotary Wing Crs. Upon graduation and qualification in the AH-1 Cobra attack helicopter, he was assigned to the 2/17 Cav Regt, 101st Abn Div at Ft Campbell, KY in January 1990.

Deployed with the unit to SWA in September 1990, participating in Operation Desert Shield/Desert Storm before returning to the States in April 1991. He attended the AH-64 Apache Qual Crs en route to his current duty station in Hanau, Germany, assigned to the 3/227 Avn Regt, 1st Armd Div.

Awards include Air Medal (3), Army Comm Med, SWA Svc Med w/3 Bronze Stars, Kuwait Lib Med and various service medals.

Married the former Alicia Weiss of Clarksville, TN and is looking forward to a house full of children.

MARY L. HOOTMAN, CW4, USA (RET) born Dec 15, 1934, near Newcomerstown, OH. Enlisting in the WAC on April 30, 1953, she attended basic training at Ft Lee, VA and AIT at Ft Benjamin Harrison, IN. She served as summary court clerk, Ft Bragg, NC and as personnel clerk, HQ Camp Yokohama, Japan.

Discharged in 1956 she joined a USAR Hosp unit in Columbus, OH; was promoted through the ranks to WOJG and continues affiliation with this unit as a member of the 2291st Club. Serving as a USAR AST, she volunteered for recall to active duty in 1966. From 1976 until her retirement in April 1983, she was the only female CW4 serving on active duty. Primary career assignments were as personnel officer and as an instructor and advisor to USAR and ARNGUS units and overseas assignments were in Japan, Germany, Vietnam and Italy.

Selected for civilian schooling she bootstrapped at the Univ. of Nebraska at Omaha; was selected as the first woman to attend the Avn WOAC; and subsequently earned an MS degree from Western Kentucky Univ.

Awards include the Bronze Star, Legion of Merit, Meritorious Svc Med w/2 OLCs, ARCOM w/2 OLCs, and numerous service ribbons and campaign medals.

She is active in veteran's organizations and has served as second vice-commander, American Legion; commander, DAV; commander, Coshocton County Veterans Council; and judge advocate and chaplain, AMVETS.

During Operation Desert Storm she worked as assistant office manager and sales representative for the Colonial Flag Co. She resides in Coshocton, OH, spending retirement building things; assisting senior citizens and disabled veterans; taking vacations, visiting friends and attending reunions.

DONALD M. HOSKINS, CWO3, USA (RET), born Jan 5, 1937, Jacksonville, FL. Enlisted in the Army April 17, 1957, with the 250 Alv 3B and 3C. Attended basic training at Ft Jackson, SC and AIT Sig School at Ft Monmouth, NJ. Enlisted service included ASA BN, Ft Bragg, NC; HQ ASA, Frankfurt, Germany; USASACUPI, PI; Vint Hill Farms Station, VA; Sinop, Turkey.

WO service includes the 32nd Sig Bn, Frankfurt, Germany; 414th Sig Co, Ft Meade, MD; 97th Sig Bn, Mannheim, Germany; HQ USCENTCOM, McDill AFB, Tampa, FL; USATCLSC-E, Worms, Germany; HQ USATRADOC, Ft Monroe, VA. Served as cryptographic maint tech, supervisor and maint NCOIC in ASA BN and CRITICOMM relay stations, TEMPEST Red and Black insp while enlisted; COMSEC custodian, communications platoon leader; COMSEC COMCEN staff officer, OIC COMSEC Storage and Distribution Depot and staff manager for fielding of new tactical COMSEC equip.

Deloyed overseas in C-124 and assisted in installation of CRITICOMM Relay Station, upgraded stations; participated in Bright Star exercise; assisted in deployments of new COMSEC equip for new tactical control system.

Assigned to the Army Theater Comm Sec Log Spt Ctr in Europe, he was OIC of the Inventory Control Div.; upgraded and coordinated the plans for the purchase, receipt, installation, training and use of a new on-line ACCLAIMS Level IV system. Also for the purchase and installation of 25 stand alone PCs for the HQ element of TCLSC-E and its two COMSEC Log Spt units. He was the OIC of the Material Mgmt Div and instituted a program that reduced the time required for units to receive ordered parts by 30 days.

Discharged Dec 31, 1988, with rank CWO3. Awards include the Meritorious Svc Med w/3 OLCs, Army Comm Med w/2 OLCs, Army Achiev Med, Good Conduct Med w/5th awd, Nat Def Svc Med, NCOACG, CRSCOM, and OTC.

Married Linda Harbaugh from Fairfield, PA (no children). He is retired and participates in community activities and is secretary, Flagler County ROA.

JOHN A. HRUBIK, CW5, USA, born July 15, 1943, Cleveland, OH. Enlisted in the US Army 250A Sig Corps in January 1964. Was the first Sig Corps Warrant to be selected for CW5, Senior Sig Corps WO. Assignments 1969-78: 191st Aslt Heli Co, Dong Tam, RVN; US Army Avn Sch, Ft Rucker, AL; HQ Svc Co USASAFS, Sinop, Turkey; USAREC Flt Det, Glenview NAS; 1978-81, USA COMM-E E/I AGY, Ft Huachuca, AZ; 270th Sig Co, Pirmasens, FRG; USAISC Det Kunia, Kunia, HI; and May 1990-present, USAISEC, Ft Huachuca, AZ.

In August 1972 he entered on the Army Roll of Economy Champions a suggestion for the improvement in the method of tracing unauthorized telephone calls charged to the government. From 1981-86 he was OIC of the Pirmasens Autodin Switching Ctr, one of the largest communications facilities in the world.

Awarded the Legion of Merit, Nat Def Svc Med, Bronze Star w/ OLC, VN Svc Med, Meritorious Svc Med w/OLC, Army Svc Rib, Air Med w/21 OLCs, Overseas Svc Rib, Army Comm Med w/4 OLCs, VN Campaign Med, Army Achiev Med and Senior Aviator Badge.

Married Nancy Elizabeth Kay of Cheyenne, WY and has two daughters, Jennifer and Amanda3.

JERRY L. HUCKELBERY, CW4, RA (RET), born Sept 22, 1936, Seymour, IN. Began his military service Oct 1, 1953, in the INNG; entered active service June 7, 1954; received basic and clerical training at Camp Chaffee, AR. Enlisted service included company clerk, S1 clerk, personnel specialist, personnel sergeant, and service school instructor. Appointed WO1, military personnel tech May 13, 1966, at USAAGS, Ft Benjamin Harrison, IN. Served four tours in Germany and two tours in Vietnam.

Retired Oct 1, 1981, at DLIFLC, Presidio of Monterey, CA, with 28 years of service. Awards include the Legion of Merit, Bronze Star w/OLC, Meritorious Svc Med, Army Comm Med w/3 OLC, Good Conduct Med (4th awd), Nat Def Svc Med w/OLC, VN Svc Med, VN Comm Med, VN Cross of Gallantry w/Palm, VN Staff Svc Med (2nd class), Meritorious Unit Cit, German Marksman Awd in Bronze, Dist Instr Awd (USAAGS). Presently lives in Fresno, CA with his wife, Deane.

ROBERT M. HULL, CW4, USAR (RET), born April 22, 1924, Milwaukee, WI, and raised in Milton, WI. Attended four years at the Univ of Washington, Whitewater, business education, 1951-55. Enlisted in the NG, 32nd Div, Co B, 107th QM Co, in October 1940 and was discharged in February 1942. Enlisted in the USMC in December 1942 and assigned to the 1st Marine Avn Bn, 1st Marine Div, Guadalcanal, New Zealand, Tinian, Okinawa and China.

Discharged January 1946 as sergeant. Enlisted in the USAR in March 1954 with the HHC Inf Regt, Madison, WI, and discharged November 1956 as master sergeant to accept WOJG appointment (2200) personnel officer.

Subsequently qualified for 411A, 632A and 941A with the 395th Ord Co, Appleton, WI; 633rd Spt Gp, Madison, WI; 314th Army security agency, Chicago, IL; HQ Maint Depot, Ft Huachuca, AZ as MOBDES. Retired from Ft Huachuca, AZ on April 22, 1984.

Married Vergene Flood from Evansville, WI in October 1947; they have a daughter Pam and a son Cory. Retired from the USDL, Wage and Hour Div as compliance officer in April 1986. He has lived at Appleton, WI since 1965 and raises and trains Arabian horses as a hobby.

HOWARD B. HUNT JR., CW4, USAR, born Nov 24, 1946, Louisville, KY. Enlisted in US Army Security Agency Sept 15, 1966, as general cryptographic repairman. Served in the 14th USASA Field Station, Hakata, Japan and the 175th Radio Research Co, Bien-Hoa, Vietnam with TDY to Okinawa and Taiwan.

Transferred to 168th Spt Gp, Louisville, KY, USAR in 1972; advanced to staff sergeant and appointed WO1 telecommunications tech in 1973; transferred to 259th MI Co, Sharonville, OH in 1974 and became counterintelligence special agent; instructed Counterintelligence and Security Manager Courses at the 5th US Army Area Intel School during the school years 1976-79. Upon unit inactivation in September 1990, he became the Corps CI OPS section leader, B Co, 314th MI BN, Detroit, MI. Presently an S-1, HHD 1404th Log Cmd (B) (RTU) Cincinnati, OH.

Life member of USAWOA, WO Protective Assoc, ROA, VFW, American Legion, American Veterans of WWII, Korea and Vietnam and the National Rifle Assoc.

JOSEPH BOYD HUNT, CW4, born May 21, 1911, San Francisco, CA. Enlisted in the Army at Ft Sam Houston June 14, 1932; served 10 years as EM in Inf and Cav (horse) at Ft Sam Houston and Ft Brown, TX and warrant as 1st sergeant HQ Trp, Ft Brown, TX in July 1941. Appointed WOJG Sept 1, 1942, and assigned to Camp Livingston, LA in November 1942 as camp assistant adjutant and publications officer.

Reassigned to the 326th Glider Inf, 1st Bn, 13th AB Div at Camp McCall, NC as Bn S-1 in October 1944 and awarded the Glider Inf Badge. The unit transferred to the ETO in November 1944 and detached duty with the 17th Abn Div HQ; participated in airborne ops in March 1945 at Rhine Crossing where he was wounded. Reassigned to HQ Co 504th PIR as assistant S-1; served with unit of occupation of Berlin from July-November 1945.

Returned Stateside in December 1945; participated in victory parade in New York City in January 1946; served with regiment as assistant adjutant from February-October 1946; was reassigned to civil affairs, Vienna, Austria in November 1946; served in American Occupied Zone, Austria, as team leader of 10 civilians on implementation of Marshal Plan.

Returned Stateside in November 1949 and assigned special service supply officer, Ft. Bliss, TX on Jan 1, 1950; reassigned to 10th AAA BN and transferred with unit to Fairchild AFB, WA, as battalion supply officer in November 1952.

Reassigned to KMAG, Tague, Korea, as advisor to ROK Army G-4, in December 1953; returned to CONUS in July 1955 and was assigned to the 5th Inf Regt, Ft Lewis, WA as assistant adjutant and assistant intelligence officer; reassigned to HQ 22nd Inf Battle Gp, January 1956, as asst adj and later adj and served until September 1958 (received Certificate of Achiev from MG William Quinn, 4th Div Cmd).

Promoted CW3, January 1956; reassigned to EVCOM, September 1958, for duty as personnel officer with HM Ord Bn; promoted to CW4, January 1959; returned to the States on early out (surplus MOS) June 30, 1959, and retired at Ft Hamilton, NY.

Awards include the Bronze Star, Purple Heart, Am Theater, ETO Rib w/OLC, Good Conduct Med, Army Comm Med, WWI Vic Med, Army Occupation Med (Germany), UN Med (Korea), Combat Inf Badge, Glider Badge and Pcht Badge w/star.

He is retired and keeps house for his sick wife.

JAMES DANIEL IVEY, CW3, USA, (RET), born March 28, 1948, Atlanta, GA. Entered the US Army in June 1967, taking basic training at Ft Leonard Wood, MO and AIT at Ft Gordon, GA. Began his career with the Army Security Agency in Japan and Radio Research Communication Unit-Vietnam. Served with USDAO, American Embassy, Tehran, Iran.

Appointed as WO in April 1978 at Ft Huachuca, AZ in the Sig Corps; as telecommunications tech, he served as COMSEC custodian for the US Army Sig Sch, Ft Gordon, GA; and the US Army Readiness Gp, Puerto Rico as COMSEC advisor to the USAR and NG in the Caribbean.

Retired in December 1987 with over 20 years of service. His awards include the Legion of Merit, Meritorious Svc Med (2), Army Comm Med, Army Good Conduct Med (4), Nat Def Svc Med, NCOPDM, Overseas Svc Rib (3), VN Svc Rib, VN Campaign Med (four campaigns), VN Cross of Gallantry w/palm, Overseas Svc Bars (2) and Army Svc Rib.

Married Sussan Ivey and has one daughter Jennifer and one grandson Sterling. He is employed as a security specialist senior on the Advanced Tactical Fighter Program.

WILLIAM IWANICKI, CW4, RA (RET), born Dec 24, 1917, DePue, IL. Volunteered for combat engineer in February 1942, taking basic training at Ft Leonard Wood, MO. Served with the 5th Engr Spec Bde (Amph) and the 1st Inf Div, 16th Regt on D-day, June 6, 1944. As intelligence section chief he carried $4,000 in French Frs and gold certificates (money belt) to use as rwards for information furnished by the local inhabitants.

The Cbt Engr Unit shipped to Korea in July 1950; arrived in Pusan, Korea in July 1950 as support unit for the 25th Inf Div from Pusan Perimeter to Kuna Ri about 25 miles from Manchuria; they were forced back to Central Korea then renewed attacks north to 38th Parallel 1X Corps; unit transferred to Vietnam in June 1965 and arrived north of Saigon responsible for stock piling ammunition and explosives on the Vietnam/Cambodian border in preparation for future 1st Div combat sweeps in that area (Black Virgin Mountains area).

School assignments included Engr Sch, Ft Belvoir, VA; mountain and cliff climbing, Seneca Rock Cliff Climbing Sch, 10th Mtn Div, WV; Amphibious Landing and Assault Sch, Ft Pierce, FL; Intel Trng Sch, Shrivingham, England; and Tank Sch, Ft Sill, OK.

Unit assignments included the 5th Engr Spec Bde (Amph), ETO; 1st Inf Div, 16th Regt, ETO; 29th Topographical (survey), Phillippines; 3rd Armd Div, Ft Knox, KY; 74th Cbt Engr, Ft Campbell, KY; IX Corps (combat engr), Korea; 6th Inf Div, Ft Ord, CA; 1st Inf Div Arty, Ft Riley, KS; 44th Inf Div, 135th Cbt Engr, Ft Lewis, WA; 11th Armd Regt, Ft Meade, MD; 35th Arty Bde (AD), Ft Meade, MD; and I Corp, Vietnam.

Overseas assignments included: ETO, September 1943-July 1945; PTO, August 1946-August 1948; Europe, June 1954-December 1954 and May 1959-May 1964; Korea, July 1950-December 1951; and Vietnam, June 1965-June 1966.

Received the French Croix de Guerre w/Palm Leaf for assault on Omaha Beach, Dist Unit Cit, ETO Camp Med w/ 2 stars and Bronze Arrowhead, Am Camp Med, Army Comm Med w/3 OLCs, WWII Victory Med, Am Def Med, Korean Camp Med w/7 stars, Korean Pres Cit, UN Svc Med, Nat Def Med w/OLC, VN Camp Med w/60 D; VN Pres Unit Cit, VN Svc Med and VN Cross of Gallantry w/Palm.

Married Jeannine Molley and they have one child and two grandchildren. He is a member of TROA (RA).

FORREST A. JACKSON, CW3, AUS (RET), born Aug 28, 1922, Spain, SD. Enlisted in the US Army in 1942. Served in enlisted status until March 1952, attained rank of master sergeant and appointed to WO status in March 1952 as personnel officer and served in WO status until retirement Feb 1, 1966, at Ft Bliss, TX.

Served in WWII with the 1st Inf Div, 88th Inf Div, 10th Mtn Div, 5th Army, in North Africa, Sicily, Italy and ermany. Served two tours in the Korean War with the 1st nf Div and 1st Cav Div. His military stations were Ft Riley, .S; Ft Gordon, GA; Ft Sheridan, IL; Cp Roberts, CA; residio of San Francisco HQ, 6th Army; Ft Barry/Baker, 'A; Ft Bliss, TX and served overseas in Germany and Korea.

Awards include numerous service and campaign med- ls, Purple Heart w/OLC, Army Comm Med w/2 OLCs, rmed Forces Res Med w/10 yr device, Bronze Star, Dist nit Badge and Combat Inf Badge.

After retirement from military service he was em- loyed as director of personnel of Electronics Corp, then as ersonnel director of county (local) government in the state f North Carolina. He retired on April 1, 1985. He is a nember of the Masonic Fraternal Organizations and Shrine.

Married Kirsten Schmidt and has two daughters, Su- an, graduate of American Univ., and Mette, graduate of lorth Carolina State Univ.

IARVEY J. JACKSON, CW3, RA (AD), born Jan 9, '956, Hartsville, SC. Entered the US Army June 11, 1974, nd attended basic training and AIT at Ft Jackson, SC. erved as light wheel vehicle mechanic with the 839th Trans 'o (deactivated), Abn, Ft Bragg, NC, from 1974-79; G Co, 02nd Maint Bn 2nd Inf Div, from November 1979-Novem- er 1980; was instructor at Ft Jackson Wheel Vehicle Me- hanic Sch and attended Warrant Sch in April 1985.

En route to Germany served with B Co, 54th Spt Bn, 3rd rmd Div, Friedburg; was a material maint tech for Div Spt md, 3AD (DISCOM), Frankfurt, Germany from 1987-90; eparted Germany in July 1990 en route to the 82nd Abn Div.

Served in Desert Storm with 3/319th Abn FA Regt 82nd bn; attended WOAC, January 1992; was assigned as direct upport maint tech for A Co, 782nd Maint Bn; and is currently vorking as (DS) maint tech for the 307th Med Fwd Spt.

Received the Bronze Star, Meritorious Svc Med w/2 LCs, Army Comm Med w/3 OLCs, Army Achiev Med, Nat ef Svc Med, SWA Army Svc Rib and Saudi Kuwait Lib led. Married Nancy Lynn Harris of Andrews, SC.

IOSEPH S. JAWORSKI, CW2, USA (RET), born in 932 on the south side of Chicago, IL, in the shadows of the teel mills. He began his military career as enlisted man from 949-52 in the ILANG, then enlisted in the USAF from 952-56. Discharged in 1956 and worked as journeyman nechanic at International Harvester Motor Trucks.

From 1956-58 was enlisted with the 85th Inf Div, and rior to re-enlisting in the USAF, he transferred from the 5th to the USAFR unit. Re-enlisted in the USAF, served rom 1958-67 and was appointed warrant in 1967, 631AO uto maint tech. Overseas assignments included Alaska, ingland, Germany, Korea and Vietnam.

Memorable experience occurred when he was informed y two chief warrants, CW4 Chavis and CW4 Furr, USAAC, hen changed to USAF, that they both felt that Jaworski had he ability to become a WO in the US Army.

Retired in 1974 with the rank of CW2. Awards include he VN Svc Med, VN Campaign Med, Civil Actions Medal v/1st Cl, Bronze Star, Nat Def Svc Med w/OLC; (4) Over- eas Bars, Armed Forces Exped Med (Korea), Small Arms ixpert Rifleman, AF Outstanding Unit Awd, AF Good Conduct w/2 Bronze Loops and Army Comm Med.

Married the former Audrey Jean Churchyard from pswich, Suffolk, England. Presently working as a material andling mechanic with three years remaining until social ecurity.

DENNIS M. JINKS, MW4 (RET), born May 30, 1933, Neillsville, WI. Entered the US Army on Sept 15, 1953;

served as automotive mechanic, senior truck mechanic, motor sergeant, maintenance instructor and NCO Academy instructor. He was appointed WO1, 630A8, auto repair tech on Dec 11, 1962, at Ft Riley, KS. He served three tours in Germany with the 2nd Armd Div, 3rd Armd Div, 7th ATC and short tours in Korea, Vietnam, Thailand and Saudi Arabia.

He was the senior WO on the TWOS group and directed the study of improved professional development training for WO Corps; served as chief of Professional Development Branch, WO Div, MILPERCEN (now PERSCOM); directed the establishment and operation of the MWOTC from inception in 1988 until retirement on Oct 1, 1991.

His military decorations include the Legion of Merit, Bronze Star (2), Meritorious Svc Med (3), Army Comm Med (6) and the Humanitarian Svc Med. He served the WOA as the national president, 1986-88; past-national president, 1988-92; president, European Region, 1984; chapter secre- tary, 1983; chapter president, 1984; Oberpflaz-Franken; and chapter president, Aviation Ctr Chapter, 1990.

Jinks married the former Florence Hope Edmonson Ford of Dothan, AL. They have three children: Dennis Jr, Julie and Elizabeth (Betsy); three grandsons; one grand- daughter (and still counting). He is an active member of the First United Methodist Church, Gideons International, Kiwanis and a life member of the USAWOA. He presently owns and operates DMJ's Fine Wood Products, a business specializing in the manufacture and sale of custom-made furniture and cabinets in Ozark, AL.

BRYAN LEE JOHNSON, CW2, USAR/IMA, born on Aug 23, 1961, in Fairfield, IA. He graduated from Fairfield HS, 1979, and Central Texas College in 1984. Joined the US Army in December 1979 and assignments included MP basic and AIT at Ft McClellan, AL, 1980; 463rd MP Co, Ft Leonard Wood, MO (patrolman); HQ USMCAD, Darmstadt, Frg, 1982 (MP desk sergeant); HQ Co, MP Activity, Ft Leonard Wood, MO, 1983 (MP investigator and SRT squad leader). Completed US Army Criminal Investigations Basic Crs, Ft McClellan, AL, 1984; reassigned as special agent, Ft Knox District, USACIDC.

Appointed WO1 in 1987 and promoted CW2 in 1989. Assignments included team chief, Property Crimes and Drug Suppression teams, Ft Knox District; special agent-in- charge, Honduras Branch Office; operations officer, Det D, 10th MP Det (CI), Port Area Spt Element, Dhahran, Saudi Arabia; senior agent, 3rd ACR (Operation Desert Storm); Asst SAC, Ft Knox Resident Agency.

ETS'd in July 1991 and joined the USAR/IMA. Served with the Protective Svc Unit, USACIDC for Secretary of Defense and chairman, JCOS, Washington, DC, in the au- tumn of 1991, then assigned to 3rd MP Gp, USACIDC, Ft Gillem, GA.

Received the Bronze Star (Operation Desert Storm), Joint Svc Achiev (Honduras, SA), Army Achiev w/OLC, Good Conduct (2nd awd), Nat Def Svc Med, SWA Svc Med w/2 BS, Kuwaiti Lib Med, NCOPDR (3rd awd), Overseas Svc Rib, and Army Svc Rib.

Currently employed as special agent, National Insur- ance Crime Bureau, residing in Raleigh, NC.

RALPH JOHNSON, CW5, USA, born Jan 6, 1949, Cincinnati, OH. Began his military career Feb 26, 1969, with basic training at Ft Polk, LA. Entered Flt School in May 1969. Combat tours included helicopter pilot/aircraft maint tech in the 173rd Aslt Heli Co in Vietnam. In 1991 he served in Kuwait with the 1th ACR as maint tech.

Other tours included B Co, 124th Maint Bn; the HHT 3/4 Cav (AIR); and HQ, 45th Gen Spt Gp as aircraft maint tech; HHC, 84th Engr Bn (CBT), 50th Sig Bn, HHC 130th Engr Bde, XVIII Abn Corps G-4; HHT, CS/11th ACR as automotive maint tech. He was instructor/writer at Avn Ctr and School, Ft Rucker, AL.

Awards include the Dist Fly- ing Cross, Bronze Star w/OLC, Meritorious Svc Med w/4 OLCs, Army Comm Med w/3 OLCs, Air Med, Army Achiev Med w/OLC, Good Conduct Med, Nat Def Rib w/star and the VN Cross of Gallantry, VN Svc Med, and VN Campaign Rib and SWA Svc Med.

Married Bessie Watford of Ahoskie, NC and they have one daughter Carolyn Teresa.

RICHARD E. JOHNSON, CW4, AUS (RET), born June 14, 1930, Chicago, IL. Began his military career in the ILNG, A Btry, 122nd FA. Enlisted in the RA Sept 22, 1948, taking basic at Ft Sill, OK with the 37th Inf Regt. Served in Germany, January 1949-May 1952, with H Co, 18th Inf Regt, 1st Div.

Rejoined NG in 1952 and served in A Btry, 122nd FA where he became 1st sergeant in 1966. Reorganized as the 106th Cav, became tank commander and platoon sergeant. Activated in 1968 by Presidential order and again released to the NG.

Transferred to AR and served as 1st sergeant, 305th PSYOP BN, 1968, promoted to SGM, then assigned as CSM, 363rd CA GP. Appointed WO CW2, 1977, as maint officer, 305th PSYOP (SOF); transferred to the 85th Div as tank automotive officer and served three years; returned to 305th PSYOP (SOF) as maint officer.

Retired in October 1990 as CW4 and recalled again in February 1991 for Desert Storm. Served as maint operation officer at Ft Sheridan, IL under DOL. He was in charge of overseeing maintenance faculties, handling and movement of vehicles, weapons, and radio equipment to SWA, as well as the return of the equipment to become serviceable before returning it to units.

Retired again in July 1991 with over 40 years of service. Awards include the Legion of Merit, Meritorious Svc Med w/OLC, Army Comm Med w/OLC, Army Achiev Med w/OLC, Army of Occupation, Good Conduct Med, Nat Def Svc Med w/2 stars, Army Res Achiev Med w/4 OLCs, Armed Forces Res Med w/2 HG, NCOPDR, Army Svc Rib, Overseas Svc Rib. Also received the state of Illinois Longev- ity Medal w/2 OLCs, State Svc Ribbon w/5 OLCs.

Formerly married to Betty Scholtz and has seven children and five grandchildren. A retired postal employee, member of ROA, USAWOA, American Legion, VFW, NRA, Boy Scouts and ARA. Hobbies are hunting, canoeing, camping and a collector of scouts on stamps.

URBAN R. JOHNSON, CW4, USAR, born June 3, 1934, Douglas, AL. Drafted into the US Army in October 1955; attended basic training and AIT (morse code radio operator) at Ft Jackson, SC. Completed training in March 1956 and shipped overseas to Japan. Assigned to the 8th Cav Regt, 1st Cav Div.; advanced to the rank of specialist 3rd class.

Returned to CONUS in August 1957 and was assigned to the USAR. Served with the 348th Engr Gp until October 1978, advancing to rank of master sergeant. Served with the 3392nd and 3385th USAR schools as senior instructor until

August 1985. In August 1981 he was appointed to WO CW2 and assigned to HQ 121st USAR Cmd in August 1985, where he currently serves.

Promoted to rank of CW4 in August 1993 and served in the active Reserves until his retirement in June 1994. Awards include the Army Comm Med, Army Achiev Med, Good Conduct Med, Army Res Components Achiev Med w/ 3 OLCs, Armed Forces Res Med w/X Device, Army Svc Rib and Overseas Svc Rib.

Life member in the ROA and active annual member of WOA.

Married Margaret Jean and currently resides in Birmingham, AL.

WILLIAM R. JOHNSON, CW4, AUS (RET), born Nov 29, 1938, in Oskaloosa, IA. Enlisted in regular Marine Corps Jan 4, 1956; received basic training at Parris Island, SC and AIT at Cp Pendelton, CA, where he served as rifleman with the 2nd Div.

Discharged April 13, 1958, and enlisted in the regular AF on April 14, 1958. After receiving a month's training in customs and traditions of the AF, he was sent to Keesler AFB, MS, then to Gunther AFB, AL and awarded dual MOS of morse intercept operator and medical records specialist.

Served entire career in SAC. Duty stations were McConnell AFB, KS; Ernest Harmon AFB, Newfoundland; and Grand Forks AFB, ND. Discharged June 1, 1962; enlisted in the USMCR on Feb 28, 1963, and served as rifleman with the 102nd Rifle Co, 4th Div, Des Moines, IA. Discharged Feb 27, 1966.

Received direct appointment as WO1 after being told he was too old for 1st lieutenant commission. Initial tour was with the 830th Station Hosp as med maint facilities officer. A year later transferred to 394th Ord Bn, 103rd COSCOM (commanded by Gen Evan Hultman) as a conventional ammunition officer, where he spent 15 years.

Additional duties were as NBC officer, and he took additional courses on his own to be proficient as a biological warfare officer. Duty stations were mostly at McClellan Army Depot, Anniston, AL; Redstone Arsenal, Huntsville, AL; Lexington Army Depot at both Lexington and Richmond, KY; and Savannah Army Depot, IL. Last six years were spent as MOBDES officer with HQ, Ft Riley, KS.

Retired April 21, 1991, with 36 years of service. Awards include the Meritorious Svc Med, Marine Corps Good Conduct, AF Good Conduct, AF Longevity Svc Med, Nat Def Svc Med, Organized Marine Corps Res Med, Army Svc Med w/4 OLCs, Armed Forces Res Med w/3 HGs.

Served five years as deputy sheriff and 25 years as federal officer with the General Services Admin. Retired as federal officer Jan 29, 1989. Final job with military and ammunition, 1991-1992, at KKMC (Northern Def Sector for Kingdom of Saudia Arabia) teaching non-English speaking 3rd country nationals (Indians, Bangledesh and Sri Lankins) how to preserve and prepare ammunition for shipment back to the United States. Member of the ROA, USAWOA, Polk County Peace Officers Assoc, Masonic and Scottish Rite.

DAVID C. JONES, CW4(P), born June 25, 1935, Troy, MO. Enlisted in the USMC and after basic and AIT (radio/telegraph operator), was assigned to HHC, 9th Marines, 3rd Div, Okinawa. Completed enlistment as a corporal in 1st AAA AW BN, 29 Palms, CA. In 1965 he enlisted in the USAR as a SP4 (MP) and was assigned to the XI USAC, Control Gp (Reinf), St Louis, MO.

Upon the creation of the 399th MP Det (Crim Inv), St Louis, MO on Jan 31, 1968, he joined as a charter member. He became an accredited special agent in 1971 and was

appointed WO1 in 1973. In 1992 he was appointed unit operations officer and selected for CW5 in June 1993.

Military schools include CID Crs, WOSC, CILMOC, Advanced Inv Mgmt, DEA, Hostage Negotiation, Protective Services and The Instructor Training Crs. Awards include Meritorious Svc Med w/OLC, ARCOM w3 OLCs, Army Achiev Med w/OLC, Nat Def Svc Med w/star, ARCAM w/ 2 OLCs, AFRM w/HG, Gold Dist Pistol Shot Med, Bronze Rifle Shot Med, and the "President's 100" Tab.

His interest in marksmanship resulted in the following additional duty appointments: 1965-present, 5th USAR Pistol Team (OIC since 1981); 1969-1974, All-USAR Pistol Team; 1973-1985, marksmanship coordinator, 300th MP PW Cmd (Michigan); 1985-present, marksmanship coordinator, 102nd ARCOM (Missouri); 1986-present, All-USAR Marksmanship Training Team.

Joined the St Louis Police Dept in 1959 and served in virtually all areas of law enforcement before retiring as a sergeant in 1990. He entered college in 1971 and graduated from Webster Univ, St Louis, MO, 1978, with a master's degree in criminal justice and business administration.

Married Loyce East from Winfield, MO, in 1959. They have three daughters and one son David, who is a St Louis Police Officer, a member of the 399th MP Det (CI), and a member of the All-USAR Pistol Team. Jones is a member of the USAWOA, ROA, Missouri Peace Officers Assoc, American Legion and a host of other police and military associations.

FRANKLIN D. JONES, CW2, AUS (RET), born on Sept 4, 1939, in Ft Payne, AL. Entered the US Army on Dec 29, 1958, and completed basic training at Ft Jackson, SC and US Army Finance School at Ft Benjamin Harrison, IN. Served with HQ Co, Spec Troops, Ft Rucker, AL, June 1959-March 1961; was assigned to Armish/MAAG, Iran, March 1961-September 1964; transferred to the Def Attaché Office, American Embassy, Managua, Nicaragua, October 1964-October 1965, when he returned to the Log Spt Branch, Def Intel Agency, Washington, DC.

Discharged in September 1968 and returned to active duty in September 1970. Served with the 38th Finance Disbursing Section, Heilbron, Germany, October 1970-June 1972; returned to the Def Attaché System and served in the Def Attaché Officer, American Embassy, Moscow, USSR, July 1972-July 1974; transferred to the Foreign Liaison Office, asst chief of staff Intelligence, Army, August 1974-December 1975.

Jones was appointed WO1 in December 1975, as Army Attaché Tech Asst, MOS 961A. He served as operations coordinator, defense attaché office, American Embassy, Rangoon, Burma, May 1976-June 1978.

Returned to the Log Spt Branch, HQ Def Intel Agency in July 1978 where he served until his retirement on Dec 31, 1980. Awards include the Def Meritorious Svc Med, Joint Svc Comm Med, Good Conduct Med and Nat Def Svc Med.

He is currently employed by the US Dept of State as foreign service officer and is a member of the TROA.

HUMPHREY B. JONES, CW2, USA (RET), born Dec 15, 1911, in San Antonio, TX. Entered the US Army on March 20, 1941, and attended basic training at Cp Wolters, TX. Served with the 393rd QMC Port Bn, New Orleans, LA; assigned to the 398th Port Bn, platoon sergeant, Charleston, SC, February 1941; served as 1st sergeant with Bn in ETO and Mediterranean Theater of Operation from January 1942-December 1944.

Returned to the States in December 1944 and assigned to the 1207th SCU as 1st sergeant. Re-enlisted in RA on

December 4 as personnel and admin sergeant and attended Advance Admin School at Cp Lee, VA. He was assigned to HHC 9th Inf Div in March 1945; AG Div, 1951; Ft Slocum, NY, personnel sergeant; appointed WO on Feb 14, 1952; and assigned personnel officer.

Transferred to the 40th Inf Div, Korea, June 7, 1952; personnel officer HHC AG Div; reassigned personnel officer 140th FA BN; returned to the States on Oct 25, 1953; assigned administrative officer Provost Marshal Office; promoted to CW2; assigned administrative officer, G-3 Section, Cp Drum, NY, April 7, 1955; assigned HQ Ft Slocum, Oct 5, 1955, as asst adj. Assigned HQ 4th Log Cmd, IG Div, April 23, 1957; performed duties inspecting non-appropriated funds and procurement activities; attended US Army QM/ Sig School, Europe; and returned to the States on April 22, 1961.

Jones retired on April 30, 1961. His awards include the Comm Rib w/OLC, Good Conduct Rib w/2 pendants and other service and campaign medals.

Married Melvina of Atlanta, GA. Retired in August 1979 from the service as a USAR tech after 17 years of service. He is a member of the National Assoc of Uniformed Services, West Point Retiree Council, Kingston New York YMCA Advisory Board.

JOHN DELBERT JONES, CW4, USA (RET), born Sept 28, 1938, at Marrietta, OK. Entered the USN on March 20, 1956, and attended basic training at San Diego, CA. Trained to jet engine mechanic and served on the aircraft carrier USS *Ranger* on initial training cruise from Oakland Bay, CA. Also served on aircraft Carrier USS *Shangri La* during the Far East cruise as crew chief on F11F jets. He was discharged on Feb 28, 1959.

Enlisted in the US Army during August 1960. Attended basic training at Ft Ord, CA and trained initially as ammunition records clerk, later promoted to SP5 in technical supply of nuclear weapons unit. He was selected and reassigned to training as helicopter pilot at Ft Wolters, TX and Ft Rucker, AL, graduating class of 65-3RW on May 11, 1965.

He later cross trained as a fixed wing pilot and as an instructor pilot, instrument instructor pilot and instrument flight examiner in both helicopters and airplanes. Also trained as aviation safety officer at the Univ. of Southern California. His assignments included three combat tours in the RVN.

Awards include (3) Dist Flying Crosses, (4) Bronze Stars, Meritorious Svc Med, (35) Air Medals (one with V Device), Army Comm Med w/V Device, Army Good Conduct Med, Navy Good Conduct Med, Nat Def Svc Med, (5) VN Campaign Awds, VN Svc Awd, Unit Pres Med, Unit Dist Svc Awd, Unit VN Svc Awd and numerous Letters of Commendation, one Letter of Congratulations from the US Army Chief of Staff, Senior Aviator Wings and Expert Marksman.

Married Sue Ellen Nitchsky on Feb 14, 1961, Albuquerque, NM. They have two children, John David and Julie Diane. Both were born during his tours in Germany. He retired on May 31, 1979, and they reside in Oklahoma City, OK.

RICHARD R. JONES, CW3, USA (RET), born Oct 31, 1938, in Shade, OH. Entered the US Army on Oct 15, 1957, taking basic training at Ft Knox, KY and serving in Ethopia with the USA Security Agency. He was 1st sergeant at Mat Spt Cmd, VHFS, VA in 1967 and again in 1971. Served in Vietnam in 1968 during the TET Offensive and served with the White House Communications Agency. Appointed WO1 in 1976 and assigned to the 2nd Armd Div (Fwd) and the 7th Light Inf Div, CA.

He was discharged on Jan 16, 1989, and received the Army Meritorious Svc Med, Army Achiev Med w/OLC, Meritorious Unit Cit w/OLC, Pres Svc Badge, VN Svc Med w/4 Bronze Svc Stars and numerous service awards.

Married Geri Wordan of Whittemore, MI and they have two children, Richard (a captain in the US Army) and a daughter Pamela (of Columbus, OH), and one granddaughter, Jessica.

Currently employed as an instructor at Indian River Community College, Ft Pierce, FL.

JACK D. JORY, CW4, AUS (R), born on March 30, 1933, Salem, OR. Moved to Silverton, OR in 1941; enlisted in the USAF in October 1951; transferred to Okinawa in 1952 (during the Korean War, 1952-54). Duty at Andrews AFB; Japan; TDY in Vietnam (1964) during the installation of the radar site on Monkey Mountain, Da Nang.

Received BA degree (1967) from the Univ of Maryland. Subsequent assignments at Altus AFB and Malatya, Turkey. Appointed WO March 26, 1968, at Incerlic AB, Adana, Turkey. Assignments in the Army included duty with the 14th, 125th and 293rd Avn Co's and the 146th Sig Co in Germany, Vietnam and Ft. Hood, TX and USASTRATCOM Sig Gp in Okinawa, 1972-76.

Received MBA degree from the Univ of Hawaii; taught in Maryland and Okinawa; transferred to Germany then to Ft Lewis as OIC in 1976 until his retirement in February 1983.

Entered civil service in December 1983; transferred CECOM in 1986; served in Germany and currently serving in Korea as a CECOM LAR at Taegu with the LAD, 19th TAACOM.

Awards include the Legion of Merit, Bronze Star, Meritorious Svc Med w/OLC, Army Comm Med, UN Svc Med, Korean Svc Med, Armed Forces Res Med, Army Svc Rib, AF Outstanding Unit Awd, VN Campaign Med, VN Cross of Gallantry w/Palm, RVN Gallantry Cross Unit Citation w/Palm, Small Arms Expert Marksmanship Rib, two civilian Sustained Superior Performance Awds and an Army Civilian Achiev Awd.

Joined the WOA in 1973; past-president Northwest Chap, USAWOA; past member, Okinawa, Rhein Neckar and Frankfurt Chapters, USAWOA; member, MOWW; and life member, Univ of Maryland Alumni Assoc.

Married the former Bonnie Stryker and has one son Robert, who is a desk officer for the III Corps and SOUTHCOM at ATCOM HQ in St Louis.

ALVIN JULKES SR., CW2, USAR, born on Dec 12, 1954, in east Chicago, IN. Entered the US Army in August 1975, taking basic training at Ft Dix, NJ. Served in many positions as medic, clarinet player and med sup tech. Duty assignments: 1976-87 at Bad Kissingen, Germany (medic); Wurzburg, Germany (band); Ft Sill, OK (band); 97th Gen Hosp, Frankfurt, Germany, NCOIC of the medical warehouse; 93rd Evac Hosp, Ft Leonard Wood, MO; MCOIC of Prop Mgmt at Vicenza, Italy; WO candidate, Ft Sill, OK; WO basic course, Ft Lee, VA; and appointed to WO1 September 1987

1987-91, HHC/MMC DISCOM 2nd Armd Div, Ft Hood, TX; 1991-93, property book officer of HHD 565th Engr Bn, Karlsruhe, Germany. The 502nd Engr Co, 565th Bn won the Dept of the Army Sup Excellence Awd under his direction. On orders to Ft Stewart, GA in December 1993.

Awards include the Meritorious Svc Med w/3 OLCs, (3) Army Achiev Med, (3) Good Conduct Med, NCOPDR, Army Svc Rib (4) OSRs. Member and elected official of the WOA in Karlsruhe, Germany.

Married Dortheia (Hall) Julkes in June 1975. They have three children: Kimberly, Tabitha and Alvin Jr.

JAMES R. KALE, CW5, born March 27, 1945, in Dover, OK. Entered active duty Oct 14, 1968, and basic training at Ft Polk, LA.

Assignments included Vietnam, 1969-70, B Co, 228th Avn Bn, 1st Cav Div and 1972-73, 237th Med Det; Ft Rucker, AL, 1970-72, instructor pilot; Ft Sill, OK, 1973-75, 178th Avn Co; Ft Meade, MD, 1976-79, 661st Avn (GS) Trans Co, 247th Med Det; Korea, 1979-80, 19th Avn Bn; Ft Sill, OK, 1980-85, 14th Avn Bn; Germany, 1985-89, 205th Avn Co, B 6-158 Avn Regt; Philadelphia, PA, 1990-93, ARPRO and DPRO Boeing; and Ft Rucker, AL, 1993-94, Avn Proponency.

Kale attended Southwestern State Univ of Oklahoma and received BS degree. Awards include the BS and 23 Air Meds. Has 7,000 hours flight time.

JEFFREY A. KAUFMAN, CW4, USA, born Jan 26, 1954. Began his mil career in the NJNG, assigned to 50th Armd Div MP Co, and received basic training at Ft Jackson, SC and AIT at Ft Gordon, GA. On July 15, 1973, enlisted in RA and proceeded to the 241st MP Co, Ft Monmouth, NJ, serving as MP and MP investigator. In July 1975 reassigned to SHAPE, Belgium as international MP, NCOIC, International MP Investigations Sect, and CID special agent and returned to Ft Dix as a CID special agent.

Appointed WO1 Nov 16, 1979, served as team chief special agent in Baumholder, Germany, and special agent in the Protective Svc Div, HQ, USACIDC until 1986. Returned to Germany and served as special agent in charge of the Grafenwoehr and Baumholder Resident Agencies, USACIDC with a short trip to Cp Blackhorse, Doha, Kuwait. In June 1993 was sent back to Ft Dix Dist, USACIDC, as the operations officer for the nine northeastern states.

Medals: Meritorious Svc w/3 OLCs, Joint Svc Comm, Army Comm w/2 OLCs, Army Achiev, Good Conduct 2nd Awd, Nat Def Svc w/star, SWA Svc w/star; and NCOPDR, Army Svc and Overseas Svc Ribbons.

Kaufman is a member of the International Assoc of Chiefs of Police, American Society for Industrial Security, Criminal Investigation Div Agent's Assoc, Federal Investigator's Assoc, USAWOA, Assoc of the US Army, MP Regimental Assoc, 8th Inf Div (mechanized) Pathfinder Assoc, 1st Armd Div Assoc and the Univ of Maryland Alumni Assoc.

Married Paula DeMarco and has two children, Jenny, who is attending college in Boston, and Jeffrey II, who is attending high school at Mt Laurel.

WALTER L. KEESECKER, CW4, USA (RET), born Feb 4, 1935, Martinsburg, WV. Began military career Aug 6, 1953, with 16 weeks of advanced inf basic trng with the 3rd Armd Div at Ft Knox, KY. Rank of master sergeant (E-8) was obtained through assignments with inf and armd units in Italy, Austria, Germany, Iceland, Ft Ord, CA, Ft Knox, KY, Ft Meade, MD and Ft Myer, VA.

Assignments as heavy weapons platoon leader, certified master pistol shooter for the All Army Marksmanship Team, as task force leader for a combat team to the congo crisis and as NCOIC for the Old Guard S4 at Ft Myer, VA. Attended numerous leadership and special military crs. Obtained the grade of WO1 on April 26, 1966, and deployed to Vietnam via troop ship.

Received assignments with the artillery, communications, and MI organizations during three tours to Germany, a second tour to Vietnam and three tours to Washington, DC. Obtained a college degree under the "Bootstrap Program" in 1974, completed the WOSC in 1976 and promoted to CW4.

Retired in 1987 after being nominated, selected and serving two years with the AID as the US Disaster Log Off. Returned as a civilian employee to the Office of US Foreign Disaster Assistance and continued to perform as its logistics officer.

Received the Legion of Merit, Bronze Star w/OLC, Meritorious Svc Med w/OLC, ARCOM w/4 OLCs, Meritorious Unit Cit w/3 OLCs, Army Achiev Med w/OLC, VN Cross of Gallantry and 18 other service connected awards and decorations.

Served as USAWOA chap president for the Augsburg Silver Chapter, European Region parliamentarian for three years, charter member of the USAWOA and remained highly active until retirement to the hills of West Virginia with his wife Irmy. They have one daughter Cynthia and a grandson Michael.

CLAY E. KELLEY, CW4, born on Sept 22, 1949, Orlando, FL. Entered the Army in 1966, attended basic training at Ft Benning, GA and QM AIT at Ft Lee, VA. First permanent assignment was in Korea, 1967. Sgt. Kelley attended Drill Sergeant Sch and served as drill sergeant at Ft Bliss, Ft Knox and Ft Jackson. Assigned in 1971 to Vietnam with the 23rd (Americal) Inf Div, 277th QM Bn and also served as a linguist/logistics advisor with the South Korean (ROK) Army operating in Vietnam.

Selected in 1976 to become one of the first school trained enlisted IGs in the Army and served as IG supply inspector at Ft Leonard Wood, MO until his promotion to WO in 1978. Because of his background, he was the first WO to serve as the Director of the Army's Sup Sch at Ft Jackson, SC. Involvement with the school and development of the school curriculum paved the way for other WOs to serve as directors.

From 1981-86, he was at Cp Zama, Japan. Was the first WO to serve on the IX Corps G-4 staff as a major contributor to the development of the logistics system in the Japanese Army. In 1985 he wrote the original standards and established the criteria for the Army's Supply Excellence Program. Was responsible for the implementation of automated property accountability programs in non-tactical organizations. Overseas assignments spanned five years in Korea, one year in Vietnam, five years in Japan and three years in Germany.

Current assignment is at the Pentagon working in the office of the Secretary of the Army on a special project with property accountability and logistics advisor to the Secretariat Staff. He completed his master's degree in education administration from Michigan State Univ. Undergraduate degrees were in Asian studies, Korean language, social science and business. He is the current national vice president of the USAWOA and the past-president of the Heidelberg Chap. An active member on the board of directors of the National Assoc of Uniformed Services; a former president of the Czech-American Friendship Assoc in Europe; and avid boater and holds a USN Skippers license. His sailing experiences have covered almost half of the world's oceans.

Awards include the Bronze Star, Meritorious Svc Med w/3 OLCs, Army Comm Med w/3 OLCs, Army Achiev Med, VN Cross of Gallantry w/Palm, Vietnam Campaign Rib w/3 Campaign Stars, Vietnam Svc Rib and Drill Sgt Identification Badge.

Married Karla Reichert of Dayton, OH and has a daughter Kimberly Ann from a previous marriage.

RUTH N. KELLY, CW2, USA (AGR), born Oct 7, 1942, Las Marias, Puerto Rico, graduated Graceland College with BA in 1972 and Drake Univ with MA in 1977. Entered the US Army in April 1974 and attended basic training at Ft McClellan, AL and Treasure Island, CA.

In 1978 received a direct appointment to 1st lieutenant; May 14, 1982, entered AGR status and held various positions up to the grade of major in New Mexico, Indiana, Puerto Rico and the Army Pers Ctr in St Louis, MO. On Aug 31, 1992, she was appointed WO2 as a military personnel technician.

Awards include the Meritorious Svc Med, Army Comm Med, Nat Def Svc Med, Armed Forces Res Med, Army Svc Rib and the Overseas Svc Rib. She is a life member in the ROA, WOA, NCOA and American Legion.

Kelly is married to an Iowa native and mother of two. She is currently working toward her doctorate's degree.

DAVID R. KENNEDY, CW3, AUS (RET), born July 6, 1924, Philadelphia, PA and attended schools in Philadelphia. Entered the US Army in October 1942; attended basic training at Ft McClellan, AL; transferred to the 572nd Ord Co, Ft Sill, OK; attended school at BPG, MD and trained in foreign ammunition. Served in England, France, participated in D-day landings, Southern, Northern, St Malo campaigns. He was discharged in January 1946.

Re-enlisted in ORC in 1947 and held various positions up through 1st sergeant. Later assigned to the 175th Heavy Boat Co; appointed as enlisted det commander of the 304th TC DET; appointed to CW2 on June 7, 1973, and served as instructor of the 2072nd USAR School.

Awards include the Bronze Star, Army Comm Med, Army Achiev Med, Good Conduct Med, Am Camp Med, EAME Campaign, WWII Victory, Nat Def Svc Med, Humanitarian Svc, Armed Forces Res w/3 HG Devices, Army Res Comp Achiev Med, Expert Badge (rifle and pistol), Mech Badge w/Driver-T&W and Mechanic. Life member of ROA and a member of the WOA.

Married Eloise and has five children: Patricia, Jacquelyn, David, Dennis and Gina. He the Pennsylvania State Constable.

GORDON R. KENNEDY, CW4, AUS (RET), born Feb 3, 1932, Niagara Falls, NY. Enlisted in RA on July 28, 1949, taking basic training at Ft Dix, NJ, followed by assignment to H/H Co, 2nd Armd, Cp Hood, TX. In August 1950 assigned to GHQ, FEC, Tokyo; assigned to a special planning staff (later known as HQ X Corps) and saw service in Korea from Sept 15, 1950 (Inchon landing and Chosin Reservoir Engagement) until December 1951.

Returned to CONUS as sergeant and assigned to Georgia Mil Advisory Gp, training reservists until 1956; then as a G-1 sergeant major with the JUSMAG, Tawian; 1959, returned to Georgia to serve with the Reserve Gp; 1960-1966, assigned to OACSI/DA, Washington DC, later know as DIA serving in the US Embassies in Poland and Hong Kong as an Intel NCO.

Appointed WO1 in 1966 and assigned to US Embassies in Syria, Finland, Vietnam and Jamaica as Ops coordinator for the Def Mil Attaché. Also had assignments with the Def Investigative Svc in Rochester, NY and Bryan, TX.

While serving in Vietnam, January 1974-January 1975, he was one of 50 officers allowed to serve in country under the peace accords; departed just prior to the evacuation of the Embassy.

Retired as CW4 in Texas with 22 years overseas service and 31 years active duty. Awards include the DMSM, Joint Svc Comm Med w/OLC, Meritorious Svc Med, Army Comm Med, Nat Def Svc Med w/OLC, Good Conduct Med w/5 Loops, KSM w/Silver and Bronze Star, UN Svc Med, Meritorious Unit Cit, and ROK Pres Unit Cit.

Married the former Lucille VanBrunt and has one son (retired from the US Army), a daughter and four grandchildren. He is a retired postal employee; member of the VFW, Military Order of Cooties, American Legion, 40/8, TROA, The Chosin Few, and BPOE.

ARTHUR F. KILPATRICK, CW4, born Sept 8, 1932, Mason, MI. Enlisted in the US Army on Aug 19, 1952, with the MI Gp. Served in Vietnam and the Cambodia Cross Border Operation in 1970. He was appointed WO on Oct 25, 1965.

His memorable experiences include two excellent tours in Germany, teaching at Ft Devens, MA, Korean experiences (five tours) Vietnam, and the National Intel Ctr, Ft Meade, MD.

Kilpatrick retired on Sept 30, 1985, with 33 years of active service and 20 years as a Warrant. His rank at retire-

ment was CW4. Awards include the Legion of Merit, Bronze Star w/OLC, Meritorious Svc Med w/OLC, Army Comm Med w/OLC and numerous service and campaign medals.

Married the former Ruth Bray from Fitchburg, MA and has three children and three grandchildren, all living in Maryland. Employed by the Dept of Def at Ft Meade, MD and is active in local church and leads work teams to foreign countries to build buildings for mission stations, churches and schools, usually one per year. Each team consists of 20-30 people.

ROSA L. KING, CW2, USA, born April 8, 1959, in Wilcox County, GA. Entered the US Army on May 29, 1979; attended basic training at Ft Dix, NJ; AIT at Ft Lee, VA and served with the 853rd ASA and the 124th MI BN, 24th Inf Div HAAF at Ft Stewart, GA, 1979-

82, as a supply clerk and P11 clerk. Assigned with the 142nd Sig Bn, Ft Hood, TX as a P11 clerk, 1982-83; from 1983-86 served as a supply sergeant, NBC NCO and orderly room clerk at Herzo Base and Monteith Barracks in Nuremburg, Germany and as supply sergeant and PBO Team NCOIC for the 1st Inf Div, Ft Riley, KS from 1986-89.

Attended WOEC/WO orientation at Ft Rucker, AL and Ft Lee, VA in 1989 and appointed WO on June 15, 1989. Assigned as PBO Team Chief HHC Discon, 24th Inf Div (to include SWA, Desert Shield and Desert Shield), served with the 24th Inf Div from 1989-91; served as PBO, 2nd Inf Div, Cp Casey, Korea from 1991-93; assigned as chief of Cmd Sup Discipline Program Monitor at Ft Gordon, GA and as PBO 63rd Sig Bn, Ft Gordon, GA in January 1994.

Served as vice president and secretary for USAWOA at Cp Casey, Korea and Ft Gordon, GA. Hobbies are traveling shopping and reading.

Awards include (6) ARCOM, (2) Army Achiev Med, (2) NCOPDR, (3) Army Good Conduct Med, Nat Def Svc Med, (2) SWABS, Army Svc Rib, (2) DSR, SAKULIBM and DRV/MECH.

THOMAS I. KNEDLER, CW3, USA (AGR), born Jan 17, 1951, in Portland, ME. Entered US Army Jan 22, 1971, completed basic training at Ft Leonard Wood, MO and AIT at Ft Monmouth, NJ, November 1971. Served in Germany at the 532nd Sig Co from December 1971-June 1976; PCS to USAEPG, Ft Huachuca, AZ as a SP5 in July 1976; worked as an electronic technician for the US Army until ETS May 29, 1977.

Transferred into the USAR at C Co, 3/16th Inf at Auburn, ME; served as the bn commo chief E-7 and bn motor sergeant at HHC, 3/16th Inf Bn, Scarborough, ME. Worked for US Customs from 1977-85 in Portland, ME; received appointment as WO on May 11, 1983 in MOS 630AO automotive maint tech. Completed WO orientation crs at Ft Rucker, Al in 1984; promoted to CW2 on Nov 1, 1984; received additional MOS of 256A communications electronics equipment repair tech on Nov 29, 1984; and began AGR tour on June 10, 1985 at HHC, 368th Eng Bn (CBT) as a staff support maint tech.

Completed WO professional development crs on March 13, 1987, at Ft McCoy, WI and WO senior crs at Ft Rucker, AL in May 1988. PCS to 5A on July 11, 1988, at Co L 158th Avn Regt (AVIM). Worked as avionics maint tech; received promotion to CW3 on Nov 1, 1990; PCS to 1A on Aug 24, 1992; and currently assigned to the 378th Sup and Svc Bn as a 915A wheeled vehicle maint tech.

Awards include the Army Comm Med w/OCL, Army Achiev Med w/OLC, Good Conduct Med, Army Res Achiev Med, Armed Forces Res Med, NCOPDR, Army Svc Rib, Overseas Svc Rib.

Founder and past president of the USAWOA, North Texas Chapter; founder and president of the USAWOA, Keystone Chapter, PA. Completed BS degree in May 1990 at Northwood Univ and completed AS degree at the Univ of Southern Maine in May 1982.

Married Marlene Kloft of Bad Marienburg, Germany and has one son, Thomas I. Knedler Jr.

WILLIAM E. KNIGHT, CW3, USA, born on July 2 1952, in Sunbury, NC. Graduated with AAS from the Co lege of The Albermarle and BS from the Univ of New Yor Attended basic training in July 1973 at Ft Jackson, SC followed by AIT (71H) at Ft Ord, CA.

Assignments with the QM Sch Bde, Ft Lee, VA, 1973 74; 19th Avn Bn, 1975; HQ, USA Electronic Proving Groun Ft Huachuca, AZ, 1976-78; 17th Avn Gp, Korea, 1979; 25t Sig Bn, Ft Bragg, NC, 1979-80; Def Comm Spt Uni Thurmont, MD, 1982-84; USA Tk Automotive Cmd, War ren, MI, 1984-87; 2nd Armd Div, Garlstedt, Germany, 1987 89; 4th Trng Bde, Ft Jackson, SC, 1989-92; and 258th PSC Wuerzburg, Germany, 1992-present.

Awards include Legion of Merit, Meritorious Sv Med, Joint Svc Comm Med, ARCOM w/4 OLCs, Arm Achiev Med w/3 OLCs and the Pres Svc Badge.

Served as external vice-president of the Cp Humphrey Chap of the US Jaycees, secretary and acting secretary for th Norddeutchland and Wuerzburg Chapters of the USAWOA 1989 and 1994 respectively. Hobbies include writing an antique auto restoration and his motto is "Helping other achieve their best."

Married to the former Rosalind Johnson and has tw sons, Anthony and Marcus.

EDWARD B. KOLOSVARY, CW3, born Oct 6, 1942 in McKeesport, PA. Enlisted in the US Army Oct 24, 1961 basic training at Ft Dix, NJ; AIT at Ft Devens, MA, ASA M Morse Code Intercept Direction Finding and Radio Finge Printing. Military stations (1962-83): 3rd RRU, Saigon Ru ARDF; HSASATC&S instructor, DF, TA, RFP, Ft Devens 8th SF, Panama, 8th SFGA; USASATC&S instructor ARDF 101st Abn Camp Eagle RVN, Left Bank, 1st Cav 1-9 407tl Bien Hoa RVN, Left Bank, 175th RR NCOIC Direction Finding; 409th MI platoon leader OPNS Co Rear; USASA Fld Station Augsburg Germany, 502nd MI OPNS Rear Pl Ldr DF, 538th MI Bn, 5th Corp, Frankfurt, Germany, TA OIC; Chief SIT Branch USASATC&S, Ft Devens, MA CMA Kunia, HI; and XVIII Abn Corps TCAC black boo officer, operations officer, 1st Trojan Mount. Appointed WO1 in Bein Hoa RVN, while with the 175th Radio Re search 1-9 1st Cav Div.

Awards inlcude the RVNCOG w/Palm, VCM, NDSM MUC, VSM, AM w/2 OLCs, ACM, BSM, MSM, GCM Senior Jump Wings, ACB, and six OSBs. Discharged on Dec 31, 1983, at Ft Shafter, HI, with the rank of CW3.

Married Peggy Jean Haneline of Slaydon, TN. He is a vocational rehabilitation specialist and private investigator holds a M.Ed, counseling from Boston Univ; master's degree in labor relations, Western New England College; and a BA/BS degrees in business and management, Univ o Maryland. Active in BSA, Member of Shriner Mosia Temple Dallas, TX; York Rite, Munich, Germany; Scottish Rite Heidelburg, Germany; Masonic Lodge 831, Augsburg, Germany and Cherrydale, Arlington, VA; and Knight of Columbus, Leominster, MA. Life member of the American Legion Paris France Post 1; VFW, Holiday, FL; WOA #96; and NRA. He is certified protection professional; American Society for Industrial Security; PI licensed and registered in the state of Virginia.

IGNATIUS J. KONING, CW4, USA (RET), born Feb 22, 1922, in Poughkeepsie, NY. After five weeks of basic training at Ft Lee in 1946, a student at the USA CI Corps Sch, Ft Holabird, MD. Shipped overseas in 1947 as a CI investigator to the 430th CIC Det, Hrs USFA (United States Forces Austria) in Vienna.

Appointed WO (WOJG) in 1948 and worked as a

counterintelligence officer at the same unit. In 1950 assigned to the 108th CIC Det with duty in New York City, Poughkeepsie and Albany, NY. During 1951 transferred to the 450th CIC Det at SHAPE, Paris, France and served as a counterintelligence officer and DASE (Defence Against Sound Equipment) specialist. Also employed as interpreter-translator and liaison officer to French intelligence organizations; speaks four foreign languages.

In 1955 assigned to the field office of the 450th CIC at AFSOUTH (Allied Forces Southern Europe) in Naples, Italy. Security type investigations were conducted plus DASE operations in Italy, Malta, Turkey and Greece. Returned to CONUS in 1957 and assigned to the 902nd CIC Det Washington DC, performed routine duties as an intel tech and also OIC of the technical section.

Transferred in 1960 to B Co (CI), 532nd MI BN HQ 7th Army, Stuttgatt, Germany. In 1963 his unit merged with the 66th MI Gp and during the last two years of military service, he performed the routine duties of a junior grade company officer, supply property book, communications, crypto, motor and maint officer.

Member of the ROA and lives in Key West, FL.

WILLIAM ROGER KRUMMREI, CW4, USA (RET), born Dec 16, 1940, in Merrill, WI. Joined the US Army in November 1958 and attained sergeant first class selection just prior to accepting appointment to WO in June 1973.

Served four tours with varied assignments in infantry and artillery motor pools and direct support maint companies and battalions in Germany: Karlsruhe, 1959-63; Mainz, 1967-70; Bamberg, 1972; Bremerhaven, 1972-73; Mainz, 1973-75; Weisbaden, 1978-85; six months TDY in Geissen in 1984; one tour in Vietnam, 1965-66; one tour in Korea, 1989. CONUS assignments included Ft Wood, Ft Riley, Ft McCoy, Ft Eustis, Ft Carson, Cp Ripley, APG MD and Ft Sill, OK.

Best assignments were with the 1st, 2nd, 4th and 8th Inf Div Units and the best unit was the 509th Abn Inf Bn (Mech), Lee Bks, Mainz, Germany.

Memorable experience was chasing a tactical Army ambulance on the Germany Autobahn from Karsruhe to Heidleberg Army Hosp for the birth of his first daughter, Deonne, who was born in the ambulance on the Autobahn.

Retired Jan 1, 1990. Awards include Legion of Merit, Meritorious Svc Med, Army Comm Med, VN Svc Med and campaign medals.

Married Roswitha Peter from Karsruhe, Germany and has four children: Patrick, Deonne, Belinda and James; and two grandchildren, Hilary and Hunter. Member of the Sooner Plains Chapter of the WOA at Ft Sill, OK and belongs to the Alumni, Cameron Univ, Lawton, OK.

EDWARD B. LANCE, CW2, USA, born Aug 12, 1950, in Georgetown, SC. Entered the US Army May 26, 1970, taking basic training at Ft Jackson and AIT in aircraft armament maint at APG, MD. Served 15 years as an enlisted aircraft armament maint repairer in the US, Korea and Germany.

Commissioned as aircraft maint tech WO on April 27, 1987, after completing WOEC at Ft Rucker, AL and the Aircraft Maint Officers Crs at Ft Eustis, VA. Served as aircraft maint tech at Katterbach, Germany and in Desert Storm with 1-1 Cav 1st Armd Div. Awards include the Bronze Star, Air Med, Army Comm Med w/OLC, Army Achiev Med and numerous service and campaign medals.

Serving with 23 years en route to Hunter AAF, Savannah, GA. Member of Thomas A. Simms Mil Lodge of Free Masons and a third degree mason. Member and past-president of the Ansbach Chap of the USAWOA. Married Carolyn Moor of Savannah, GA, have three children and one grandson.

THOMAS L. LANNING, CW4 (RET), born Feb 23, 1931, in Webster City, IA. Enlisted in MTARNG Dec 3, 1948-April 12, 1956; WO, April 13, 1956-Sept 8, 1960; enlisted Sept 9, 1960-Aug 9, 62; WO, Aug 10, 1962-Feb 23, 1991. Held various positions as aviation, wheel, track, artillery and staff support maint tech. Was an instructor at the Montana Mil Academy for 15 years as additional duty and employed as a civilian tech by the MTARNG from 1953-86, M1 General Abrams Tk Fielding Off, Active Duty AGR from 1988-89.

Military education included track vehicle mechanic, Ft Knox, KY, 1951; M41 tank transition, Ft Knox, KY, 1953; Operation Taper, Ft Lewis, WA, 1962; armament maint and repair officer, APG, MD, 1963; automotive maint and repair officer, APG, MD, 1965; material readiness, Ft Lewis, WA, 1966; supply management, Ft Lewis, WA, 1968; engineer tech repair officer, Ft Belvoir, VA, 1969; Chemical, Biological and Radiological Crs, Ft Lewis, WA, 1970; Mechanical Maint WO Advanced Crs, APG, MD, 1977; WOSC, Reno, NV, 1980.

Civilian education includes Helena HS, Helena, MT, 1949; Helena VO-Tech Ctr, 1950; Basic Labor Relations, OPM, 1983; Basic Labor Contract Negotiations, OPM, 1983; and Motor Fleet Mgmt, Wright State Univ, 1985.

Member of the USAWOA for 16 years and NG Bureau Maint Advisory Committee from 1980-1981.

Awarded (3) Armed Forces Res Med, Legion of Merit, (5) Army Component Achiev Med, Army Achiev Med, Meritorious Svc Med, Army Svc Rib, MTNG Dist Svc Med, MTNG Svc Rib w/3 OLCs, M16 Rifle Sharpshooter.

Civilian awards: Meritorious Action from the Boy Scouts of America for life saving, Dept of Army Meritorious Civilian Svc, Federal Employee of the Year, Helena Chamber of Commerce, 1981, Montana Fish, Wildlife, and Parks for 15 years of service to Hunter Safety Education Program and the MTNG Unit Trng Equipment Site Building was dedicated to him in 1984.

He and wife Nora have six children and enjoy their retirement life, children, grandchildren and great-grandchildren. Hhobbies include snowmobiling, golfing, hunting and fishing.

BILLY J. LAUBACH, CW3, USA (RET), born Dec 27, 1940, in Rock Springs, WY. Entered the Army in September 1961; basic training at Ft Carson, CO and first assignment at 141st Sig Bn 1st AD, Ft Hood, January 1962-July 1963. Served as Comm Ctr Specialist at USATRS Tehran, Iran from August 1963-September 1964. After a break in service returned to duty in November 1965 and served as a Sig Operation instruction clerk, HQ 5th Sig Bn, Ft Carson until July 1966.

Assigned to the 23rd USA Msl Det in The Netherlands from August 1966-March 1968. Served in Vietnam from April 1968-March 1969 as Comm Ctr Specialist, HHC, 18th Engr Bde USARPAC; April 1969-December 1970 as cryptographer clerk and comm specialist, USASTRATCOM NY, Phila Sig Co HAADS, Highlands, NJ.

From April-June 1970, attended school at Ft Benjamin Harrison, IN for computer programming; student with HQ USA Student Det 6th Army Presidio of San Francisco, CA with duty station Orange Coast College, Costa Mesa, Ca; received AA degree with a certificate in business information systems; assigned to DPD, MILPERCENEUR in Heidelberg, Germany, February 1973-August 1977; received BS degree in business management from Univ of Maryland; computer programmer at Div of Biometrics, Walter Reed Army Institute of Research.

Appointed WO in 1979; assigned to MILPERCEN WO Div in 1980, was the first automated data processing tech to serve at the WO Div; then assigned to Mil Traffic Mgmt Cmd in Rotterdam, The Netherlands from 1984-1989 as chief, 778th Trans Det.

Retired in January 1989 on medical disability. Awards include the Army Comm Med, Joint Svc Achiev Med, Good Conduct Med, RVN Cross of Gallantry w/Palm, RVN Campaign Med, VN Svc Med, Nat Def Svc Med, Army Svc Rib, Overseas Svc Rib and Marksman Qualification Badge.

Currently living in Littleton, CO with his wife Jennie and two sons.

MARY H.T. LAWSON, CW2 (P), QM, USAR, born June 26, 1949, at Ft Benning, GA. Graduated HS, Columbus, GA, 1967; Univ of North Florida, Jacksonville, FL, graduated 1974 with a BA degree in sociology and social welfare.

Military education: Unit Sup Tech Crs (nonresident), 1986; WO Prof Dev Crs (resident), 1986; Sup Mgmt Off Crs (nonresident), 1987; Org Sup Man Sys Facility Crs (resident), 1987; Std Pro Book Sys Crs (resident), 1987; Sup Staff Off (G4/S4) Crs (nonresident), 1987; Gen Sup Tech Crs (nonresident), 1989; Food Serviceman Crs (nonresident), 1989; Def Small Purchase Crs (nonresident), 1991; RC WOTTCC Rep Tech Crs (nonresident), 1992; and Qm Sup Spt Activity Crs.

Duty assignments: USAR, 301st Fld Hosp, 1975-76 and from 1978-82; Control GP (Reinforcement), 1976-78; supply sergeant, 3rd US Army, 1982-85; property book tech, 449th Sup Gp (TASG), 1985-88; property book tech, 361st CA Bde, 1988-92; provide humanitarian assistance for Hurricane Andrew, 1992; property book tech, 361st CA Bde, 1992-present.

Appointments were WO1, 1985; CW2, 1988; and CW2(P), 1993.

Awards include the Army Comm Med w/2 OLCs, Army Achiev Med w/1st OLC, Meritorious Svc Med w/OLC, Armed Forces Res Med w/10 year and Good Conduct Med.

JEFFERSON W. LEE, CW2, USA, born Oct 22, 1940, in Seoul, South Korea. Immigrated to the States in 1974 and entered the Army on July 31, 1975. Attended basic training and AIT (Engr Equip Rep Crs) at Ft Leonard Wood, MO, followed by three assignments at Ft Meade, MD, three tours in Korea and one at Ft Belvoir, VA.

After three years as a sergeant first class, working as maint NCOIC, he entered the WO Candidate Crs in October 1987, leading to his appointment as a WO1 as engineer equipment repair tech in April 1988. First assignment as WO1 was with the 2nd Engr Bn at Korea, followed by an assignment with the Ord School at APG, MD and currently assigned to the 61st Maint Co, Korea. In addition to a BS in engineering from Seoul National Univ, he has an AA and an AS from Central Texas College.

Awards include the Meritorious Svc Med, Army Comm Med, Army Achiev Med w/OLC, Army Good Conduct Med (4th), Nat Def Svc Med w/star, NCOPDR (4th), Army Svc Rib, Overseas Svc Rib (4th).

He and his wife, Maryann, have three children; his oldest son received his commission through ROTC and is an active duty Armor Officer; his other son is a computer engineer; and his daughter is a senior in high school. He is an active deacon with his church and is a member of the USAWOA.

JAMES W.B. LEGGITT, CW3, USA (RET), born July 24, 1935, in St Louis, MO. Entered the USAF in August 1952. Following basic training, attended Radio School at Keesler AFB, MS and sent to Korea in 1953. Completed Crypto School, Scott AFB, IL and reassigned within USAF Security Svc, Clark AB, PI.

Assigned to AFSSO Key West during Cuban crisis; promoted to tech sergeant and later assigned to AFSSO 2nd Air Div, RVN; reassigned to AFSSO Strike, MacDill AFB, FL where he applied for Army WO appointment.

Appointed WO in June 1967 and attended Comm Cen Off Crs at Ft Monmouth, NJ. Assigned to STRATCOM, Munich, Germany for 15 months and later to the 121st Sig Bn, 1st Inf Div RVN as COMSEC custodian. Won two Bronze Stars, Army Comm Med and Air Medals.

Following 18 month tour with USASA at Ft Hood, TX, attended ADMSC Crs at Ft Monmouth, NJ and on to STRATCOM in Okinawa where he was promoted to CW3; attended Advanced Crs for senior WO at Ft Gordon, GA and subsequently retired as CW3 in June 1975.

Married Myrna McCord of Port Arthur, TX and has three children and 10 grandchildren. Currently employed in warehousing.

CARYNN B. LEMIEUX, CW3, born Dec 31, 1951, in Townsend, MT. Enlisted June 2, 1973, and attained rank of master sergeant, MOSs 73C and 75Z. Worked as civilian tech at the US Property and Fiscal Off in Mil/Tech Pay from 1974-81; SIDPERS senior personnel sergeant, 1981-86; SIB chief, 1986-92; and currently officer records manager for the state at HQ STARC, MTARNG.

From 1973-87 was stationed at BCT, Ft McClellan, AL; AIT 71L, Ft Jackson, SC; AIT 73C, Ft Benjamin Harrison, IN; WOCS, Ft Sill, OK; MOS 420AO WOTTC and WOAC, Ft Benjamin Harrison, IN.

Awards include the Army Comm Med w/2 OLCs, Army Achiev Med, Nat Def Svc Med, Army Res Component Achiev Med w/4 OLCs, Armed Forces Res Med, NCOPDR w/3 Dev, Good Conduct Med w/2 Knots and Army Svc Rib.

Married MSG Phillip LeMieux on Sept 12, 1979, and has two step-daughters and two granddaughters. Currently Active Guard Reserve with the MTARNG, chief of officers records section. They reside in Helena, MT and her hobbies include snowmobiling, camping and fishing. Member of the WOA, Arlington Hall Branch, National Guard Assoc and lifetime member of the Enlisted Assoc NG of the US.

FRANCIS A. LEONE SR., CW4, USA (RET), born May 18, 1921, in Utica, NY. Enlisted Oct 1, 1940, with Co M 106th Inf, 27th Div in the NYARNG. The unit was activated into Federal Services Oct 15, 1940. Stationed at Ft McClellan, AL; attended basic and AIT and rose to the rank of sergeant. In 1942 his unit moved to the Asiatic-Pacific Theater of Operation and he saw combat at Eniwetok, Saipan and Okinawa. Honorably discharged on Nov 15, 1945, as staff sergeant.

In May 1946, he re-enlisted in the NYANG with the 132nd Ord as a small arms repair chief and promoted to 1st sergeant. Appointed WOJG as small arms and ord supply officer, Jan 9, 1950; unit was activated into federal svc for the Korean War, Sept 10, 1950; stationed at Ft Pickett, VA and in November 1950 he was transferred to Ft Pickett Staff HQs 2114 ASU and served as post ord and supply officer.

Transferred May 11, 1952, to Germany and served with the 93rd(L) Gun Maint Co as gun supply officer; May 13, 1952, separated from federal svc and released to NYANG Control and assigned Svc Co 101st Armd Cav as maint officer. Unit was redesignated 102nd MP BN, March 7, 1959, and served as maint officer; promoted to CW4 Sept 9, 1966.

Assigned to 205th Lt Equip Maint Co as engr pep tech, 1970-71; reassigned to 102nd MP BN as maint officer, 1971-76; and transferred to the 127th Maint Co as service and supply officer, March 10, 1976, until dischaged on May 18, 1981.

Memorable experiences include the Empire State Military Academy from 1968-80 with Weapons and Tactics Committee; Operation Empire Glazier, 1978; Operation "ReForager," 1979 (Mannheim, Germany); and Operation Gold Plum, 1979.

Awards include Army Comm Med, Bronze Star, Combat Inf, Good Conduct, Am Def, Am Theater, A/P Campaign w/Arrowhead and 3 Battle Stars, WWII Victory, Army of Occupation w/Japan and Germany Clasp, Nat Def Med, Armed Forces Res Med w/30 yr clasp, Army Res Components Achiev, NY State Conspicuous Svc Cross, NY Mil Comm, NY Aid to Civil Authorities Med, NY Conspicuous Svc Med w/1979 clasp, NY Exercise Spt Rib "Europe Mannheim" and NY Long and Faithful Svc Ribbon w/35 yr clasp.

Married Mary Fusillo and has two sons, Francis Jr (has six years in the USAR) and Dennis, (has four years in the USAF and 15 years in the NYANG). He is a member of the WOA.

ROBERT J. LETENDRE, CW4, USA, born Jan 25, 1947, in Fall River, MA. Joined the Army in October 1966 and served with the 1st Inf Div in Vietnam from 1967-68. Other enlisted assignments included the 86th Ord Det in Japan; the Engr Reactors Gp at Ft Belvoir; and the Floating Nuclear Power Plant STURGIS in the Panama Canal Zone.

After appointment to WO1 as a power systems tech in 1975, he served with the 41st Cbt Spt Hosp at Ft Sam Houston, the Facilities Engineering Support Agency at Ft Belvoir and commanded the Army's floating poser barges Weber and Impedance in the Dominican Republic. Currently assigned to the WO Div, TAPC in Virginia.

Awards include the Meritorious Svc Med w/OLC, ARCOM, Reactor Operator Badge and other service and campaign medals.

His wife Lucy is from Fall River, MA and they have two children.

BUDDY L. LIGGENSTOFFER, CW4, USA (RET), born Jan 14, 1946, in Hardtner, KS. Enlisted in the Army Oct 4, 1965; basic training at Ft Benning, GA; followed by Engr Sch on heavy equip at Ft Leonard Wood, MO; and Fixed Wing Aircraft Maint Sch at Ft Rucker, AL. Went to Vietnam as crew chief on the CV-2 (C-7A) Caribou.

Returned to Ft Rucker in 1967 and assigned to the Army Avn Test Board as a member of Project U-21 and assisted in taking delivery of the Army's first U-21 aircraft. Left the Army in 1968, and re-entered in 1970 for the WO Fixed Wing Flight Training Program.

Warrant assignments: 1971-1972, Vietnam, flying the YO-3A surveillance (Night Rider 16) and U-21 aircraft; 1972-77, 101st Abn Div flying airplanes and helicopters; 1977-79, Germany with the 173rd AHC; 1979-82, 101st as an instructor pilot in UH-1Hs and UH-60s. He was a key instructor in the beginning of the NVG Program and taught the first UH-60 Qualification Crs outside Ft Rucker. 1983-87, Ft Rucker as fixed wing evaluation sect leader, fixed and rotor wing instructor and flight examiner.

1987-88, Korea with the 201st AHC (Red Barons) as UH-60 instructor/examiner (Red Baron 10); 1988-90, Ft Rucker as a fixed wing evaluation plt leader, standardization instructor/examiner responsible for quality control of all fixed wing courses at Ft Rucker.

Provided instructor support for the Grisly Hunter surveillance system test/evaluation and was a DES fixed wing designee; 1990-91, Korea 3rd MI BN as RC-12H standardization instructor/examiner (Rail 01); 1991-93, Ft Rucker as flight commander and standardization instructor/examiner responsible for initial planning, implementation and execution of the first Army taught C-12/RC-12 Aviator Qual Crs.

Retired in June 1993 as CW4 with over 26 years of service. Awards include the Meritorious Svc Med, Air Med, Army Comm Med, Army Achiev Med, Good Conduct Med, Nat Def Svc Med w/Bronze Star, VN Svc Med w/5 Svc Stars, Army Svc Rib, (4) Overseas Svc Rib, RVN Cross of Gallantry w/Palm, RVN Campaign Med and Master Army Aviator Badge.

Married Carolyn Curry of Kiowa, KS and has two children. Member of the USAWOA, AAAA, TROA, VFW, The American Bonanza Society and the Christian Coalition.

CHARLES J. LILLIS, WO4, born Feb 7, 1915, in Winchester, VA. Enlisted with Co I, 3rd Bn, 116th Inf in the VANG March 27, 1934. Graduated Inf OCS in October 1942 as plt ldr 14th Ar Dic at Ft Chaffee, AR. Served in Europe with XXII Corp HQ as mess officer in England, France, Germany, Czechoslavakia. Was special service officer HQ Assembly Area Cmd, Reims, France.

Re-entered the VANG in 1947, resigned commission and appointed WO as full-time personnel officer. First contact with the WOs was while in the XXII Corps, so when the opportunity came up in the Guard he resigned his commission to except position of WO.

Retired February 1976, after 42 years of service, with the rank of WO4.

Lives in Winchester, VA with his wife Hilma and has five daughters, 16 grandchildren and two great-grandchildren. He was the Virginia weightlifting champion and participated in the 29h Inf Div show (Snap It Up Again as a weightlifter).

GERALD H. LIMBACH (JERRY), CW2, USA, (RET), born Nov 8, 1926, in Canton, OH. Began his military career in Army Reserve in May 1944. Attended Ohio Univ, Athens, OH and called to active duty on Jan 17, 1945. Basic at Ft Sill, OK; served in the USAAC at Sheppard Field and Randolph Field; January 1946 transferred to Saudi Base until discharged in August 1946.

Attended college and worked until March 1950; served in Guam, Army and Navy Hosp, Naval Hosp at Great Lakes, IL, 121st Evac Hosp, Walter Reed Army Institute of Research and the Enlisted Branch Army Surgeon General Office, Washington, DC and was a sergeant first class.

Appointed WO1 in 1962 as personnel officer with the 32nd Tk Bn, 3rd Armd Div in Europe. Transferred to 3rd Armd Div AG Sect as chief, Machine Records Div and later chief, Personnel Records. In 1965 transferred to a Nike Msl Bn at Edgewood Arsenal; 1966 transferred to the US Army Elm JUSMMAT Turkey; January 1968 transferred to Ft McNair, Washington, DC as pers tech and retired in July 1968.

Employed by the College of Wooster, Wooster, OH as manager of Scot Lanes and retired from the college in 1988. Was co-owner of the Dairy Queen Store in Wooster for 15 years and now retired. His hobby is bowling.

JOHN L. LIPNICKY, CW3, USA (RET), born June 17, 1945, in Indiana, PA and raised near Pittsburgh. Entered the US Army in August 1965, attended basic training at Ft Dix, NJ and AIT (morse code intercept) at Ft Devens, MA.

Served in Thailand, Udorn, 1966-1967, 7th RRFS and Korat, 1969, USARSUPTHAI; Japan, Chitose, 1968, 12th USASAFS; Vietnam, Bienhoa, 1968, 145th Cbt Avn Bn; Phu Bai, 1968, 101st Abn Div; Binh Tuy, 1971, MACV Advisory Team 48; Germany, Boeblingen, 1970-71, 198th PSC; Ft Wolters, TX, 1972-74; Nigeria, 1974-77.

In 1977 appointed as WO1, MOS 961A (attaché tech); assigned to US Def Attaché Offices in Ghana, Ivory Coast, Zimbabwe and Tanzania. Retired as Chief Army Attaché Mgmt Div, Ft Meade, MD in 1989. Awards include the Legion of Merit, Def Superior Svc Med w/2 OLCs, Bronze Star w/Valor, Def Comm Med w/2 OLCs and Army Comm Med w/OLC.

Married Ubon Saripant from Thailand in 1989; they reside in Vienna, VA. He owns his own flag and banner business.

PAUL A. LOACH, CW4, AUS (RET), born March 30, 1930, in Cleveland, OH. Enlisted June 23, 1948, with Btry A,

730th AAA Gun Bn, 251st Arty Gp CALARNG. Served with the Armor Ord 915D4 Armor Cav Systems Maint Tech HHC, 2nd Bn, 185th Armor, 40th Inf Div (mech).

Enlisted with Btry A, El Cajon, CA; transferred to HHC 2nd Bn, National City, CA April 1, 1964; served 42 years with the CANG in the same unit. The 730th AAA Gun Bn redesignated 6th Bn 185th Armor on June 1, 1962; redesignated 2nd Bn, 185th Armor Jan 29, 1968. Although some units of the 40th were called to serve in Korea, the 2nd Bn, 185th Armor was not called. The 40th also participated in Vietnam, and again the 2/185th was not called.

Received active duty training at Ft Bliss, TX AAAGM Sch FCSM33 (one year). Designated as class leader of 44 students and completed as second in the class. Progressed from private E-1 cannoneer to master sergeant E-7 range plt sergeant prior to attending FCSM33 at Ft Bliss. Appointed WOW1 July 17, 1960; CWO W-2, June 16, 1963; CWO W-3, Sept 23, 1969; CW4, Nov 29, 1976. WO service consisted almost entirely as auto maint tech 631A.

Discharged March 30, 1990, as CW4. Awards include (4) Army Comm, (4) Armed Forces Res, (6) California Continuous Svc Med, Army Svc Rib and California Comm Med.

Married Chesalie Self June 16, 1957, they have son Charles Arthur (b 1959) and daughter Catherine Ann (b 1964). He is continuing automotive pursuits by restoring vehicles and upholstering; semi-retired.

GEORGE HOWARD LOYD, CW4, USA (RET), born May 31, 1933, in Plant City, FL. Joined FLNG, B Btry, 149th FA BN, Lakeland, FL in 1947. Volunteered for active duty in 1954, completing basic at Ft Jackson, SC; served as field 1st sergeant, basic training unit, Ft Chaffee, AR; served in Germany from December 1954-December 1955 as chief of operations, C Btry, 44th FA BN, 4th Inf Div.

Enlisted in USAF, April 1956; served as instructor, bombing nav system, Lowry AFB, Denver, CO; rejoined FLNG in 1966; promoted to WO1, radar tech, HQ&HQ Btry 2/116 FA BN, Lakeland, FL. Enlisted in KYNG, Lexington, KY, 1967; rejoined FLNG in 1970, HQ&HQ Btry, 227th FA Brig; promoted to 1st Sergeant HQ&HQ Btry 227th FA Brig, 1972; promoted to CW2, radar tech, Sept 1977; HQ&HQ Btry 2/116 FA BN, Lakeland, FL.

Called on state active duty after Hurricane Andrew, August-October 1992 in Miami, FL.

Retired in June 1993 after 43 years of service in the Army, Air Force and FLNG. Awards include the Army Comm Med, Army Achiev Med, Army Occupation Med, Overseas Svc Rib, Army and AF Good Conduct and numerous service and state mil awds.

Life member of FLNGOA, ROA, NG Officers Assoc of the US. Retired form the International Business Machines in June 1991 after 30 years as a computer tech and field manager.

Married Shirley R. Keene of Plant City, FL. They have three children and seven grandchildren.

JOHN M. LUKE, CW4, USA (RET), born Feb 1, 1948, in Philadelphia, MS. Entered the US Army on June 24, 1970, taking basic training at Ft Ord, CA. Received intelligence training at Ft Holabird, MD; assigned to the 502nd MI BN, 8th US Army, Korea as an image interpreter in 1971; served with the US Electronic Proving Grounds, Ft Huachuca, AZ; the 652nd Engr Bn (TOPO), HI; the 548th RTG, Hickam AFB, HI.

Appointed WO1 Aug 27, 1976, as an imagery interpretation tech; assigned to the 7th MI CO and the 107th CEWI Bn, 7th Inf Div and served as the div tactical surveillance

officer; reassigned to the 452nd MI Det, 172nd Inf Bde, Ft Richardson, AK; 581st MI CO, 502nd ASA MI BN, Zweibrucken AFB, Germany; transferred to the Def Intel Agency, Washington, DC. 1985; served as senior intel analyst with the National Photographic Interpretation Ctr, Central Intel Agency.

Retired as CW4 in August 1992 with 22 years of service. Awards include the Def Meritorious Svc Med, Meritorious Svc Med, AF Comm Med, Army Achiev Med, Good Conduct Med (2nd Awd), Nat Def Svc Med w/BS, Army Svc Rib, (3) Overseas Rib, Armed Forces Exped Med, two unit awards and two Central Intel Agency Outstanding Performance Awds.

Married Maj Barbara J. Luke, USAFR; they have two children, Matthew Mark and Emily Mary-Louise. Currently employed as a national security analyst with the Pacific-Sierra Research Corp, Arlington, VA.

JAMES T. LUTTRELL, CW4, USA (RET), born May 2, 1929, at Warrenton, VA. Entered the DCNG May 1948; ordered to active duty May 15, 1951; served in Korea during 1952 and joined the RA Dec 31, 1952. After four year tour in Worms, Germany, he returned to CONUS and entered the Army Nuclear Power Plant Operators Crs from which he graduated in 1961.

Appointed WO1 in the Reserves June 1967 and ordered to active duty to start his WO career. Served two tours in Vietnam, March 1968-December 1971.

During his tour with the 19th Mat Mgmt Ctr V Corps, he was officially assigned by DA to fill a captains slot, but due to a shortage of qualified majors available in the CE Mat Mgmt field, he was slotted as chief, Elect/Avn Div. Service in this position earned him several commendations during three AIGs. During next assignment at the Lakehurst Satellite Installation, he actually commanded for a period of nine days.

Retired at VHFS on June 1, 1981, having completed 30 years, 60 days active and 33 years total service. Awards include Bronze Star, Meritorious Svc Med (3 awds), Army Comm Med, Good Conduct (5 awds), Nat Svc Def (2 awds), Army Occupation Med, KSM, VN Svc Med, UN Med, RVSM and the RVN Cross of Gallantry.

Received his Ph.D. in 1986 and is now fully retired and resides in Sterling, VA. He married the former Hedi Martha Seifert from Worms, Germany.

JOHN F. LYNCH (JACK), born on June 15, 1935, in Newark, NJ. Enlisted in the NJARNG Aug 11, 1953. Assignments included company clerk, pers sgt, sup sergeant, 1st sergeant and command sergeant major. Appointed CW2 April 20, 1972, as a mil pers tech, 44th Area HQ (LS) NJARNG. Assigned to records branch chief, 50th AG Co, NJARNG in April 1976.

Promoted to CW3 April 20, 1978; entered AGR status February 1981 at the NG Bureau and assigned as PAC action officer and chief SIDPERS-ARNG QA Fld Spt Teams; separated from AGR status in February 1985; assigned to STARC NJARNG as MPT; promoted to CW4 on April 20, 1984; entered AGR status in March in March 1988; assigned as PSB action officer; assigned as ARNG WO programs manager, September 1990; promoted to CW4 April 1, 1992.

Awards include the Meritorious Svc Med, ARCOM, Army Achiev Med, Armed Forces Res Med w/3 Devices,

Army Svc Rib, Army Staff Identification Badge. Education includes MPO, WO senior, Manpower Staffing Standards, and MWOT Crs and BA degree.

His civilian experience included ARNG full time support 1955-1981; AMC Manpower Staffing Standards Systems Analyst, 1985-86; and NGB Supervisory Mil Pers Mgmt Specialist, 1986-88.

JOHN P. MADRID, CWO2, born Aug 22, 1949, in Basilan City, Philippines. Enlisted in the US Army on June 18, 1969; attended basic training at Ft Ord, CA, 1969; Calibration Tech School, APG, MD, 1969-70; WOAC, Ft. Gordon, GA, 1984; Student, degree completion at Washburn Univ., Topeka, KS, 1985-86.

Stationed at Cp Carroll, Korea, 1970-71; APG, MD, 1971-72; Sagami Depot, Japan, 1972-75; Ft Riley, KS, 1976-77; Cp Humphreys, Korea, 1977-78; Redstone Arsenal, AL QA inspector, 1978-80; Mannheim, West Germany Det NCOIC, 1980-81; Schweinfurt, West Germany Det OIC, 1981-83; Ft Riley, KS, 1984-85; Pirmasens, West Germany, 1986-88; Ft Ord, CA, Det Cmdr, 1988-89. Appointed to WO1 on May 29, 1981.

Awards include the Meritorious Svc Med, Army Comm Med (2nd), Good Conduct Med (3rd), Nat Def Svc Med, Armed Forces Exped Med, NCOPDR, Army Svc Rib, Overseas Svc Rib and Meritorious Unit Cit. Achieved the rank of CWO2 at the time of his retirement, Sept 30, 1989.

Has one son John Madrid II. After retirement, returned to college and attained BS degree in electronics engineering technology from South Dakota State University. Presently employed with Raytheon Spt Svcs Co as a precision electronics measurement tech at Offutt AFB, Omaha, NE.

EDDIE E. MALLARD, CW4, USA, born April 7, 1948, in Ludowici, GA. Enlisted in the US Army June 18, 1965, taking basic and AIT at Ft Jackson, SC. Served in Korea as a telephone wireman with the 6/12 Arty. Was honorably discharged in June 1968, and re-entered the Army in December 1969.

Served in Germany from January 1970 to December 1974 as radioteletype repairman with the 2/13th Inf; a CI agent with the 902nd MI Gp until appointed WO1 in May 1979. Served as counterintelligence tech with the Defense Investigative Service, Santa Clara, CA; 102nd MI Det OIC, 2nd Inf Div; supply officer/property book tech, 902nd MI BN (CI)(CE); 501st MI Bde case control officer and service school instructor, Ft Huachuca, AZ, 1979-90. Currently assigned to the DCSOPS-HU/CI, HQ USAINSCOM, Ft Belvoir, VA as the counterintelligence plans, programs and policy officer.

Awards include the Meritorious Svc Med w/2 OLCs, Joint Svc Comm Med, Army Comm Med w/2 OLCs, Army Achiev Med w/4 OLCs, Good Conduct Med (4th Award), Nat Def Svc Med w/BS, Armed Forces Exped Med, NCOPDR (3rd), Overseas Svc Med (3rd) and two Superior Unit Awds.

President of the Lord Fairfax Silver Chap of the USAWOA, member of the United Supreme Council 33 Degree and a certified literacy instructor.

Married Betty Wagner of Ft Knox, KY and has four children and four grandchildren.

CHRISTOPER M. MANDIC, CW4, USA, born Jan 6, 1954, in Sellersville, PA. Graduated from Pennridge Senior HS, 1972; entered the Army in July 1972; basic training at Ft Polk, LA; AIT (field radio mechanic) at Ft Benning, GA; field radio repairman at Ft Gordon, GA.

Assignments included 358th ASA Co, Ft Bragg, NC; USASAFS-K, Khang Wha Do, Korea; 504th ASA Gp,

Hunter AAF, GA; 415th ASA Co, Idar-Oberstein, Germany; Svc Co, 10th SFG, Ft Devens, MA; 16th Sig Bn, Ft Hood, TX; 699th Maint Co, Hanau, Germany; 801st Maint Bn, Ft Campbell, KY; 129th SOA Co (later redesignated 3/160th SOAR), Hunter AAF, GA; 3/160th SOAR, Saudi Arabia; 3/160th SOAR, Hunter AAF, GA. As a staff sergeant, he was appointed to WO on June 27, 1980.

Awards include the Bronze Star, Meritorious Service, Army Comm, Army Achiev, Good Conduct, Nat Def, Armed Forces Exped Med, SWA Svc Med, NCOPDR, Army Svc Rib, Overseas Svc Rib, Saudi Arabian Def and Kuwait Lib Med, Air Crewmember Badge, Army Prcht Badge, Air Assault Badge, Joint Meritorious Unit Awd and Valorous Unit Awd. Received his AA and BA degrees from St Leo's College.

Married Sheila Mahan of Ludlow, KY and has three children: Andrea, Melonie and Danny.

VICTOR JOHN MARASCHIELLO, CW4, born
June 15, 1921, in Buffalo, NY. Enlisted in the US Army Sig Corps, Ft Monmouth, NJ on Sept 4, 1940, and attended Open Pole Construction Crs for telephone line foreman. During WWII served in North Africa, France, Alsace-Lorraine and Germany. Attended Spiral-Four Cable School in Oran, Africa, 1943.

Honorably discharged July 10, 1945; enlisted in the 174th Inf NYARNG, 1947; accepted WOJG-1, Dec 10, 1950. Graduated Canisius College with BS in social studies, 1952; attended Univ Admin Crs, Ft Ben Harrison, IN, 1954. Transferred to 174th AIB NYARNG, 1955; attended Motor Officer Crs, Ft Knox, KY, 1957. Attended Inf Motor Off Crs, Ft Benning, 1965; CW4 DOR Dec 10, 1965. Honorably discharged NYARNG, Jan 31, 1971.

Assigned to 1151st USAR Sch, 77th Army Res Components Med USAR on Feb 1, 1971. Transferred to 409th Pers Svc Co, 98th Div USAR on Dec 1, 1973, due to unit reorganization. Attended ADP Tech Crs at Ft Ben Harrison, IN, 1975; attended Senior WO Crs, Ft Rucker, AL; class leader, 1979 and 1980.

For 10 years he was map reading instructor at ESMA Officer's School at Cp Smith, NY. While serving with the 409th Svc Co, USAR, he held 24 different MOSs, simultaneously. Retired from Army June 15, 1981. Commissioned major, New York Guard, May 9, 1984, G-3 4th Bde. DOR colonel March 13, 1989, placed on NYS retired Reserve list at age 68. His service motto: "Keep the old man out of trouble."

His memorable experiences include 46 years combined military service, RA, NYARNG, USAR and NYG, including three years overseas duty during WWII; creating an efficient driver's dispatch and maint board made of tiddly-winks, bathroom tiles, empty Alka-Seltzer bottles and plywood; re-establishing annual training preventive maint checkpoints for track and wheel vehicles as early as 1955; created OPLAN "Tell it to Sweeny," the servicemen's welfare emergency effort for the state of New York; assisting guardsmen and their families in the event of an emergency or crisis in or out of the continental limits of the US during annual field training periods. Was awarded the NYS Meritorious Svc Med; and was class leader of the SWOC 1979-80 at Ft Rucker, AL.

He married Delores Breil on Nov 5, 1955, and has six children and five grandchildren. Erie County Probation Officer and retired after 33 years of service.

FRANCIS E. MARTIN, CW4, USA (RET), born Dec 7,
1928, in Saranae Lake, NY. Enlisted in the NYARNG Nov 11, 1947, with the 3rd Bn, 105th Inf, 27th Div. Changed over to 186th FA in 1954 and attended Track Maint School, Ft Sill, OK, 1957. Became WO1, September 1957; CW2, 1960; CW3, 1966; CW4, 1972; maint tech, 127th Mt Co, HEM

Overseas tour December 1978 in Germany and in 1988 in Italy. He retired in December 1988 with 41 years of service.

Activated from control group in March 1991 for Desert Shield/Storm. Served at Ft Drum, NY with the Family Assistance Ctr until October 1991 with seven months additional service.

Memorable experiences are places traveled and the fine people he met and served with; his many, many tours; Ft Ritchie, MD and tour of Site "R," the tour in Mannheim, Germany; and LAD at Tyrennia, Italy.

Awards include the Army Svc Rib, Armed Forces Res Med, Army Res Component Achiev Med, Nat Def Svc Med, Army Lapel Button and state of New York Aid to Civil Authorities.

Married Helen Callaghan in Gabriels, NY on Aug 25, 1951, and they settled in Saranae Lake, NY. There are four children and four grandchildren. Retired Saranae Lake Central School employee. Member of the USAWOA, American Legion, ROA and National Assoc of Uniformed Services.

EDWARD NATHANIEL MARTIN, CW3, born May
22, 1948, in Baltimore, MD, and raised in Virginia. Entered the US Army on May 20, 1968, and served in Germany, Panama, Korea, Okinawa, Redstone Arsenal, AL and Ft Sill, OK. Military education includes the USAWOAC; Platoon Leader Trng work shop; USA MLRS Cadre Crs; USA System Approach to Trng; USA Instruction Trng Crs; USA Methods Of Instruction Crs; USA Electronic Mechanical PII Crs; USA Pershing Electronic Repairman Crs PII; and USA Pershing Msl System Tech Crs.

Martin's civilian education includes a BS degree, business, Athens State College; AA degree, general education, University of Maryland; AS degree, missile munitions and technology, John C. Calhoun.

Discharged on Sept 30, 1989, with the rank of CW3. Awards include the Meritorious Svc, (3) Army Comm, Army Achiev Med, (4) Good Conduct, Nat Def Svc, Armed Forces Expeditionary, (2) NCOPDR, Army Svc Rib and (4) Overseas Svc Ribs.

Single and has two daughters. He is member of fraternal organizations and presently an education tech GS-4 in Babenhausen, Germany.

EMANUEL MASSARELLA, CW4 (RET), born June
30, 1920, in New York City, NY. Enlisted in the US Army Nov 6, 1941; attended basic training at Ft Belvoir, VA; served as launcher maint off, cryptographic custodian, div arty motor maint off, asst supply off and labor off (KSC).

Stations included: basic engr trng, Ft. Belvoir, VA; Co F, 20th Engr Cbt Bn, Ft Blanding, FL; Svc and Sup, HQ Engr Sect, ETO; 773rd AAA Gun Bn, NYARNG, NY. Recalled for Korean Conflict, 773rd AAA Gun Bn, Ft Stewart, GA; Co B, 116th Engr Cbt Bn, 8th Army, Korea (Punchbowl); 773rd AAA Gun Bn, NYARNG; 212th and 244th Msle Bn, NYARNG; and 42nd Inf Div Arty, NYARNG.

Participated in the EAMETO (WWII) and the Korean Conflict. Memorable experiences in Antwerp, Belgium (WWII) when Germany V-1 and V-2 bombs were falling. A V-2 hit the Rex Theater where hundreds of people were trapped, and he assisted in clearing debris and trying to locate survivors. Also memorable was serving as sergeant major in HQ, Western Base Section, England, during WWII and being fortunate to meet and talk to Gen George Patton.

Final discharge from Army Oct 25, 1953, WO2 and on Oct 7, 1980, from NYARNG as WO4. Awards include the Bronze Star, Army Comm, Belgium Fourragere, Army of Occupation (Germany and Japan), Good Conduct, Nat Def w/5 Stars, Armed Services, EAMETO, A-P/TO, Korean Svc, Korean Pres Unit Cit, Armed Forces Res, Am Campaign, Am Def w/clasp, Army Res, NYS Conspicuous Svc Cross, Mil Comm Med for service to the State of New York (NYARNG).

Married Veronica Kleinman of NYC, on June 7, 1941; they have three daughters and six grandchildren. Retired superintendent of the worlds largest armory, Kingsbridge Armory, NYARNG; member of the WO Corps, Bronx, NY;

past commander of American Legion Post; past commander of VFW Post; K of C; and actively engaged in the Benevolent and Protective Order of Elks as a lodge secretary for 10 years.

RAYMOND J. MATUS, born Dec 27, 1939, Tarentum,
PA. Enlisted in the USAR December 1956 and the US Army in June 1958. Attended basic training at Ft Benning, GA; Sig Sch, microwave repairman, Ft Monmouth, NJ, 1958-59. Assignments 1959-64 to Ft MacPherson, GA; Paris; various sites in France; Belgium; Ft Ritchie, MD (SP5). Assigned to DLI in 1964.

MI assignments 1965-88 to Ft Holabird for initial MI POW interrogation trng; 11th ACR, Ft Meade and Xuan-Loc Vietnam with major operations in Attleboro, Cedar Falls and Junction City; Intel Analyst 5th Psyop Bn, USAREUR (SP-7); MACV Combined Mil Intel Ctr, NCOIC PW Intg Team (SP7 to WO1); XO 203d MI Det, III Corps, Ft Hood, TX (WO1); intg tech, 25th ID, HI, (CW2); liaison officer, 18th MI Bn, Office, Zierndorf, Germany, (CW3); intg ops off, 511th MI Bn, VII Corps, Ludwigsburg, Germany, (CW4).

Education: associate's degree, 1974; bachelor's, 1976; MA, 1977; Ed.D, 1991; sig trng, 1959; SerboCroat (DLI), 1965; Basic POW Intg, 1965; Intel Analyst, 1968; NCOA, 1968; Vietnamese (DLI), 1971; C-141 Loader Crs, Hickham AFB, 1977; MI WOAC, Ft Huachuca, AZ, 1978; German (DLI), 1979; WOSC, Ft Rucker, 1984; various routine periodic short courses.

Married Claudine Lamotte of Willerzie, Belgium; they presently reside in Dusseldorf, Germany. Retired in 1988 and presently employed as DAC, GS-12, 18th MI Bn, with duty at APO AE 09234.

ROY J. MAULT, CW3, USA (RET), born March 11,
1941, in Portsmouth, VA. Entered the USAF on Oct 6, 1959, and served in weapons repair for eight years and four months. Appointed as WO on Feb 16, 1968, and served in Ordnance as an armament tech until retirement on Nov 1, 1979.

Assignments include Goldsboro, NC; Madrid, Spain; Victorville, CA; Thailand; Tucson, AZ; Ft Lewis, WA; Pleiku, Vietnam; Crailsheim, Germany; Quinhon, Vietnam; Nurenburg, Germany, 101st Abn Div, Ft Campbell, KY. Campaigns include Vietnam Defense; Vietnam Air; Vietnam Air Counteroffensive; Vietnam Air Counteroffensive Phases IV, V and VI; TET 1969 Counteroffensive; and Consolidation I.

Memorable experiences include the participation in the 2nd Annual USAWOA Convention, European Region, May 1974, in Berchtesgaden, Germany.

Awards included the Bronze Star, Meritorious Svc Med, Army Comm Med w/2 OLCs, AF Comm Med, Army and AF Good Conduct, Nat Def Svc Med, Armed Forces Res Med, RVN Comm Med and the AF Outstanding Unit Award w/10 OLCs.

Divorced, and has son and daughter. Employed as a management analyst (GS-0343-11) with the Naval Avn Depot, Norfolk, VA. Received BS degree from the Univ of New York in 1984.

HERCULES MAXWELL, CW4, born in Lake City,
FL. Joined the Army on Oct 1, 1956; stationed at Germany; Italy; Ft Rucker, AL; Ft Meade, MO; Ft Jackson, SC; Ft Sill, OK; Ft Bliss, TX; Redstone Arsenal, AL; served as support role only for long range missile systems.

Memorable experiences include the WO Senior Crs educational experiences.

Discharged Sept 30, 1986, with rank of CW4. Awards include the Army Meritorious Svc Med, Army Achiev Med, ASM, Army Comm Med w/3 OLCs, and the Legion of Merit.

Married Annie Maxwell and they have four children: Ryan, Keith (staff sergeant, USA), Craig (sergeant, USAF) and Meggan. He is director of corrections with the Columbia County Sheriffs Office.

RUSSELL V. McCONNELL, CW4, USA (RET), born Aug 7, 1932, in Oak Park, IL. Graduated from the music program at Lane Technical HS in Chicago, 1950. Drafted in the Army on July 24, 1953; served as acting platoon sergeant at Ft Leonard Wood, MO and company clerk in the 1st Log Cmd, Ft Bragg, NC. Released from active duty June 10, 1955.

Enlisted as a French horn player in the 5th USA Band, Ft Sheridan Feb 17, 1959; promoted to WO1, Aug 25, 1960. Assigned as CO and bandmaster of 328th Army Band, Brooklyn Army Terminal, 1960-65. Assignments 1965-80: 214th Army Band, Ft Richardson; 113th Army Bank, Ft Knox; 2nd Inf Div Band, Korea; 2nd Armd Div Band, Ft Hood; was the first bandmaster to graduate from the WO Sr Class, Ft Rucker (1974); 1st Armd Div Band, Ansbach, FRG; USA Band, Europe (33rd), Heidelberg, FRG; 74th Army Band, Ft Benjamin Harrison; and served as staff bands officer in the Chief, Army Bands Off until retirement June 1, 1987.

Awards include the Legion of Merit, Meritorious Svc Med w/3 OLCs, Army Comm Med w/2 OLCs.

Presently resides with his wife Mary in Martin, TN, where he plays French horn in the Paducah Symphony, the University of Tennessee at Martin French Horn Sextet and serves as the director of the Martin Cumberland Presbyterian Church Choir.

HARRY C. McCURDY, CW3, NJARNG, born May 29, 1940, in Camden, NJ. Enlisted in the USMC on Aug 15, 1958, taking basic training at Parris Island, SC. Duty as field radio operator with various 2nd Mar Div Inf Regts, including duty in the Caribbean during the Cuban revolution and a Mediterranean tour of duty.

Received an honorable discharge in 1961; entered the NJARNG, 50th Armd Div in 1978 as SSG, intelligence analyst; promoted in 1979 to SFC and assigned as the S-2 NCOIC and supervisor of the 2nd Bde Battlefield Intel Coordination Ctr.

Appointed WO1 in 1982 with the 119th Maint Bn; commissioned CW2 in 1984, and served ODT tour in the Netherlands for Reforger 87; transferred to the 117th HEMCO in 1988 as Stf/Spt Tech; and ODT tour at EMC-E, Kaiserslautern, Germany in 1991.

Awards include the Army Comm Med, Army Achiev Med, USMC Good Cond Med, Nat Def Med w/star, Army Res Comp Achiev Med, Army Svc Rib, Overseas Svc Rib, Res Overseas Trng Rib (2nd award), NJ Good Cond Med, Meritorious Svc Med and Desert Storm Ribbons.

Married Alfreda "Cookie" Ciechanowicz of Riverside, NJ; they have three children. Retired as lieutenant from the NJ State Police and is currently employed as a deputy attorney general with the NJ Attorney General's office.

JOHN COLLINS MCDUFFEY, CW3, AUS (RET), born Jan 14, 1921, in Wichita Falls, TX. Enlisted in RA on July 21, 1942; completed basic training at Ft Sam Houston, TX; ordered overseas in May 1944 and served in CBI until

end of WWII. Honorably discharged as tech sergeant in March 1946.

Enlisted ERC and called to active duty as master sergeant in August 1950; appointed WOJG in September 1951 and served with the 8th Army until June 1953, then Japan until September 1954. Returned to CONUS for training at Ft Bliss in Guided Msl Fire Control System, SSM. Graduated number one in class and served as instructor at The Artillery School, antiaircraft and guided missile branch, Ft Bliss until January 1957; transferred to Ft Sill, duty station Redstone Arsenal for cadre training in Redstone FA Msl System until September 1958.

Promoted to CWO2, moved with arty cadre to Ft Sill and was instructor at Arty and Msl School until August 1961. Promoted to CWO3 and served in corporal missal units in 7th Army and later in Southern European TF.

Returned to CONUS, April 1964; attended Pershing Specialist Crs, Ft Sill, OK; last STRAC Unit assignment was with B Btry, 2nd Msl Bn, 44th Arty. Later assigned as instructor, Pershing Msl Maint Crs. Participated 1955-66 in live Corporal, Redstone and Pershing missile firings at Ora Grande Range, Ft Bliss at the British Msl Range in Outer Hebrides Islands, Scotland and at Green River, UT.

Retired in January 1967 at Ft Sill with the rank of CWO3. Awards include the Army Comm Med w/OLC, Korean Svc Med w/3 campaign stars, Armed Forces Res Med w/HG and UN Svc Med.

Received BS and MS from Southern Illinois Univ and served as associate professor in engineering technology at Lewis and Clark Community College in Illinois and Texas State Technical College.

Married Virginia Metcalf in Houston, TX. Member of the USAWOA, Assoc of USA, TROA and ROA.

PHILIP ANDREW McGIBNEY, CW4, USA (RET), born Aug 25, 1942, in Lubec, ME and raised in Brookton, ME. Entered the US Army in October 1960, basic training at Ft Dix, NJ and AIT (SIGSEC Specialist 05G) at Ft Devens, MA. Assignments in Germany, RVN and CONUS include the 318th USASA Bn, Det A; 11th/337th RRU, 1st ID; 352nd USASA Co; 407th RRU, 5th ID; 201st USASA Co (achieved Army high 05G MOS score in 1971) where he was appointed a WO1, MOS 721A, in 1973; 261st Sig Co; 333rd Sig Co; 472nd C-51st Sig Bn; Chief, SIGSEC Branch, USAISD, Ft Devens, MA thus completing cycle from 05G trainee to Branch OIC which he eventually closed out for transfer of the mission to Ft Huachuca, AZ; USAITIC-PAC, Ft Shafter, HI as the USAINSCOM Cryptofacility Inspector responsible for the Pacific Theater.

While at USAITICPAC he developed and wrote a basic COMSEC Custodian Crs which was taught theater wide. This course later served as the basis for the US Army Standardized COMSEC Custodian Crs which was taught as a mandatory requirement to all US Army COMSEC Custodians. For this effort he was chosen as the 1983 recipient of the "Commanders Plaque for Operational Achievement" presented each year by the USAINCSOM commanding general.

During his career he attended 4th AD NCO Academy; 5th USA RECONDO Crs; USA Sig School approved courses for MOSs 05B, 05C, 72B; CE WOAC (honor graduate); WOSC, USAF TEMPEST for Mint and Installation Supervisors Crs; DODCI, USA and USAF COMPUSEC Courses; NSA CY-300 National Cryptologic Crs; and various instructor training, course development and job aids courses while at USAISD.

Retired at Ft Devens, MA in February 1989. Awards include the Bronze Star, Meritorious Svc Med w/3 OLCs,

ARCOM w/3 OLCs, ACM w/OLC and numerous service, campaign medals and ribbons.

Earned an AA degree in management from Univ of Maryland, a BGS in computer science from Roosevelt Univ and a MBA from Western New England College.

Married Joan Hope of Edinburgh, Scotland in 1967 and currently resides in Shirley, MA. Works for Massachusetts Institute of Technology, Lincoln Laboratory since 1989, currently as a program administrator.

ROBERT W. McGILLICUDDY, CW2, AUS (RET), born Sept 12, 1918, Williamsburg, IA. Enlisted in the USN on his 17th birthday. During WWII he participated in convoy operation to Murmansk, an Arctic seaport in the Soviet Union. He was present in Tokyo Bay when Gen Douglas MacArthur accepted surrender of the Japanese forces in August 1945. Left the USN at the end of WWII.

In September 1948, he enlisted in the Army where he rose to the rank of CW2, criminal investigator. Assignments included Carlisle Barracks, PA; Ft Gordon, GA; Korea (in charge of the Masan sub-det), Tokyo; Washington DC, where he served as special assistant to the Provost Marshal General; and Puerto Rico.

Retired in September 1959 in Arlington, VA, after 23 years of service. Awards include the Am Def Svc Med, Army Comm Med, EAME Camp Med, WWII Victory Med, Korean Svc Med and the UN Svc Med.

He passed away Feb 2, 1965, and is buried in Arlington National Cemetery. He is survived by his wife Helen, four sons and one daughter.

THOMAS P. McLAUGHLIN, CW4, USAR, born Feb 17, 1944, in Washington, DC. Entered the Army in 1967, receiving basic training at Ft Dix, NJ. Joined the US Army Security Agency (USASA) in 1968 as a cryptanalyst and traffic analyst. From 1977-79, he was senior instructor in traffic analysis at Army Intel Sch.

Appointed RA WO in October 1979; served with USASA and its successor organization, the US Army Intel and Security Cmd as a traffic analyst, intel analyst and area intel officer in CONUS, Thailand, Japan, Korea and Hawaii until 1987.

Joined the USAR as an individual mobilization augmentee in the Office of the Deputy Chief of Staff for Intelligence (DCSI/G2), HQ, USA Japan/IX Corps. Recalled to active duty during Desert Shield/Desert Storm.

Awards include the Meritorious Svc Med w/OLC, Army Comm Med w/OLC, Good Conduct Med w/3 Knots, Nat Def Svc Med w/star, Armed Forces Exped Med, Vietnam Svc Med w/3 stars, NCOPDR w/#4, Army Svc Rib, Overseas Svc Rib W/#4, Army Res Comp Overseas Trng Rib w/#6 and VN Camp Med.

Graduate of Lake Forest College, IL and holds a master's degree in systems management and public administration. Charter life member of USAWOA; member of AUSA and ROA; former information officer for the mayor's office, city and county of Honolulu, and currently works as a civilian with the C3I Systems Directorate, CIC, US Pacific Forces in Hawaii.

SHERMAN RANDOLPH McNEELY (RANDY), CW4, USA (RET), born April 23, 1942, in Homeville, PA. After graduating from Waynesburg HS, Waynesburg, PA, in June 1961, he was sworn into the US Army July 5, 1961, at Fairmont, WV. First assignment basic combat training at Ft Knox; transferred to the Ord School, APG, MD. In November 1961 he graduated from the Ord Sup Crs and received overseas assignment to the ROK. This was the beginning of what was to become a 30 year plus career in Army Air Def Arty. While serving a tour at C Btry, 4th Bn (Nike Hercules), 44th Arty (also know as Camp Safari) as a parts clerk, his aspiration of becoming a USAWO was realized.

On July 11, 1969, he took the oath of office as a WO1 in the active duty Reserves with the MOS of Nike Hercules fire control tech. In 1972 he received a RA appointment as a

CW2; in 1987 he was commissioned by the President and administered the oath as a commissioned RA CW4.

His education includes certificate of promotion to high school, Greene County, PA (1957); Waynesburg High School, diploma, Waynesburg, PA (1961); AAS degree, with distinction, industrial technology, The University of Akron, Akron, OH (1974); BS degree (cum laude), technical education, The University of Akron, Akron, OH (1993); diploma (1961) Ord Sup Crs, US Army Ord School, APG, MD; diploma (1966) Improved Nike Hercules Fire Control System Maint Crs, US Army Air Def School, Ft Bliss, TX; certificate (1968) honor graduate, Instructor Trng Crs, Air Defense School, Ft Bliss; certificate (1969) WO Orientation Crs, US FA School, Ft Sill, OK; diploma (1970) honor graduate, Air Def Electronic Airfare Crs, US Army Air Def School, Ft. Bliss; diploma (1971) Improved Nike Hercules High Power Acquisition Radar Maint Crs, US Army Air Def School, Ft Bliss; diploma (1978) Surface-to-Air Missile Systems Maint WO Adv and Sr Courses, US Army Air Def School, Ft Bliss; diploma (1981) Allied Central Europe Officer's Nuclear Weapon Release Procedures Crs, Supreme HQ Allied Powers Europe, The NATO School, Oberammergau, Germany; certificate (1983) Patriot Air Def System Maint Tech Crs, Raytheon Co, Missile Systems Div, El Paso, TX.

As a young soldier and junior WO, he served over 18 months in various Nike Hercules guided missile system assignments with the 38th Air Def Arty Bde, Korea; Army Air Def Cmd and (ARADCOM), Pittsburgh, PA Def; ARADCOM, Seattle, WA Def; and 32nd Air Def Cmd, Germany.

As a senior WO, he served over 12 years in various Nike Hercules and PATRIOT missile system major command staff positions with HQ, 94th Air Def Arty Gp, Kaiserslautern, Germany; HQ, US Army Air Def Arty School, Ft Bliss, TX; HQ, 10th Air Def Arty Bde, Darmstadt, Germany; HQ, 32nd Army Air Def Cmd, Darmstadt, Germany; and HQ, Allied Air Force Central Europe, Ramstein, Germany.

As a commissioned CWO4, he was the first warrant officer to command a PATRIOT battery at Ft Bliss, TX.

His memorable experiences include: (1961) Riding the bus from in front of Bailey's Drugstore in Waynesburg, PA to the Recruiting Ctr at Fairmont, WV; scared, sad and homesick, he receiving basic combat training at the same time the Berlin Wall was going up; life suddenly became very precious when faced with the prospect of war. (1962) Working around the clock at a Nike Hercules Missile Battery in Korea during the 13 days of the October 1962 Cuban Missile Crisis. Bone-weary and feeling like a very old man at the age of 20. (1963) Hearing Walter Cronkite announce the assassination of President Kennedy while watching television in the launcher platoon dayroom at the Nike Hercules Missile Battery at Herminie, PA. Grief stricken, like everyone else in that dayroom, and trying to buck up and stay dry-eyed. (1964) Deciding to re-enlist and make the Army a career with mixed emotions. The military establishment wasn't held in very high esteem in those days. (1965) Getting married for the first time; happy and proud, the way it should be; choosing Nike Hercules Missile System training over Counterintelligence Corps training as his re-enlistment option. Disappointed that his young bride did not want him to be a CIC agent. More than likely she saved his life as the life expectancy for intelligence types in Vietnam wasn't very long. (1966) Graduating from a very long (55 weeks) and difficult Nike Hercules Crs. (1967) Hearing his name announced as a selectee for temporary duty in Vietnam during formation while serving a second tour in Korea. Mixed emotions, enjoying the limelight and well-wishes of fellow soldiers and being scared of what was to come. (1969) Seeing his newborn daughter at William Beaumont Army Medical Ctr. Joyful and very unsure—learning to be a good parent is difficult even for the highly motivated. (1969) Taking the oath as a brand new "Wobbly One," such a proud day.

(1970) Watching Soviet bombers being tracked by the Nike Hercules System at the Seattle, WA Defense. Felt the entire world was on his shoulders; profound relief when they turned north and went home. (1972) Being speechless when his career manager called to tell him he had been selected for the Army's full-time, two-year degree completion program. Nearly chickened out, but sure glad he didn't. (1974) Graduating from college; for the son of a poor dirt farmer from Pennsylvania who had been told "You will never amount to anything," his day had come. (1975) Living through a divorce while serving in a nuclear duty position. A double whammy, coping with one's world coming apart while not showing any unsuitability under the ever watchful eye of the human reliability program. (1978) Graduating from the Advanced and Sr Crs, and proud about reaching another important milestone. (1978) Finding, falling in love with and marrying his best friend, his dream come true, Gabrielle-Octavia Boehme McNeely.

(1981) Attending NATO School at Oberammergau, Germany. Quite an ego trip being part of a team of officers training in nuclear weapons release procedures that involved the White House. (1981) Leaving the Nike Hercules System for the PATRIOT System. Mixed emotions, transition is never easy. (1985) Fielding the first PATRIOT Systems in NATO. Hard work rewarded. WOs were vital to that success. (1987) Taking the oath as a commissioned CWO. Truly feeling a part of the officer corps. (1989) Assuming command of A Btry, 3rd Bn (PATRIOT) 6th ADA, Ft Bliss, TX. (1990) Receiving notification of below-the-zone selection for MWO training and eventual promotion to CW5, proud and sad. Proud to be among the best of the best and sad because the opportunity came after committing to retirement; watching the invasion of Kuwait while on vacation with his family; being locked in at the Air Def School while everyone else went off to war (frustrating); being inducted into the Ancient Order of St Barbara (very honored indeed); conducting emergency training for the Israeli Air Force in PATRIOT, a true feeling of contribution to the war effort. (1991) Watching PATRIOT intercept SCUDs over Saudi Arabia and Israel with mixed emotions, feeling both pride and left out; preparing for and briefing the vice president on PATRIOT during his visit to Ft Bliss, TX; standing retirement, truly a mixed bag of emotions, a joyful occasion tempered with the air of a funeral.

Total number of decorations awarded is 19. They include the Legion of Merit, Meritorious Svc Med w/OLC, Army Comm Med w/2nd OLC, Good Conduct (2nd awd), Nat Def Svc Med w/Bronze Svc Star, Armed Forces Exped Med, Overseas Svc Rib (4), Expert Missileman Badge and Expert M-16 Rifle Badge.

He is affiliated with Kappa Delti Pi, Air Defense Arty Assoc, Ancient Order of St Barbara, Univ of Akron Alumni Assoc, El Paso Junior Chamber of Commerce, American Assoc of Retired Persons, United We Stand America and USAWOA.

His career came to a close on Aug 1, 1991. After 30+ great years, it was time to move on to something else. Currently in the process of pursuing his third college degree, this time from the Univ of Massachusetts at Amherst. Future plans include a second career with some firm in El Paso, TX. In the meantime, he will continue to enjoy retirement and help his wife, Gaby, as she moves into her 24th year as a high school teacher. Life is good!

WALTER R. McNUTT, CWO, born Feb 24, 1912, in Salt Lake City, UT. Enlisted in the service on Aug 24, 1938, at Ft Hayes, Columbus, OH with the Coast Arty, Sig Corps. Stationed at Ft Scott, San Francisco, CA; Ft Crockett, Galveston, TX; Base X, Manila; GHQ, Tokyo, where he had seven years of detached service.

His memorable experiences include serving 16 years overseas in Japan, France, Vietnam and the Philippines.

Discharged on March 31, 1959, with the rank of CWO. Awards include the Army Comm Med and service ribbons.

Married and has one daughter. He retired after 11 years as chief of document reproduction and preservation at The National Archives of the US.

JOHN E. McPOLAND, CW5, USA (AGR), born April 1, 1937, in Dubuque, IA. Entered the Army on Feb 7, 1956, taking basic training at Camp Chaffee, AR and AIT at Ft Hood, TX. Served with the 21st Inf Regt, 24th Inf Div in Korea from July 1956-November 1957 as supply clerk.

Joined the USAR in 1958, serving with the 410th Inf, 389th Engr Bn, becoming battalion supply sergeant (SFC) until appointment as WO1 in September 1966. Served as supply and personnel tech and employed as a federal civil service in several positions at unit and battalion level from 1960-83.

Entered AGR status in April 1983 as supply tech, CW4, serving with the 389th Engr Bn, 245th Engr Bn and presently with the 89th USAR Cmd.

Memorable experience was in August 1985 when the 389th Engr Bn HQ was located in Dubuque, IA and tasked with providing logistical support in preparation for "Blazing Trails," a humanitarian mission in Honduras, Central America.

Awards include the Meritorious Svc Med w/OLC, Army Comm Med w/OLC, Army Achiev Med, Good Conduct Med, Nat Def Svc Med, Humanitarian Svc Med and other awards. Life time member in the ROA; member of the WOA, Assoc of the USA, American Legion and Knights of Columbus.

Married Betty Schmerbach of Sherrill, IA.

JAMES A. McQUAIG, CWO3, called to active duty with the 31st Inf, 124th Inf in November 1940; completed basic training at Camp Blanding, FL; transferred to 156th Inf at the beginning of WWII and served with that unit primarily as a security unit.

Discharged as E5 in September 1945 and re-enlisted in September 1948 in the 325th Inf, 82nd Abn as light avn mech. Transferred to 15th Inf, 3rd Div and served 13 months in Korea; transferred to JMAG until September 1954 when appointed W1 USAR with a concurrent call to active duty. Assigned to the 11th Abn Engr Bn; went to WO School, Ft Belvoir, VA and upon completion was post engr at Ft Belvoir; then to 49th Engr Depot Co; 1st Engr Arctic TF; 806th Engr Bn (HC); 587th Engr Field Maint Co; 577th Engr Bn (const). Retired Sept 1, 1963.

Employed at a CAT dealership in northeast Florida. In June 1963 employed by a contractor for the Corp of Engr southeast Asia; transferred in 1971 to Thailand as facilities maint sup; departed Thailand and employed as a general foreman Marshal Islands; inter-company transfer sent him to Saudi Arabia where he remained until May 1981.

Since returning, he has worked various jobs as a store manager, a counselor aide and for the last five years as nursery tech.

JERRY A. MCREE (MAC), CW4, USA (RET), born Aug 19, 1938, in Puryear, TN. Began his military career in September 1955 in the ARNG. Enlisted in the USAF Nov 20, 1956, and served as accountant and as special agent, office of special investigations (OSI) until direct appointment as WO, USA, November 1967.

Served as criminal investigator, operations officer, executive officer, acting commanding officer, polygraph examiner and special agent in charge in CID organizations until he retired in July 1982 as a CW4.

Awards include the Legion of Merit, Bronze Star Med, Meritorious Svc Med w/OLC and several service and campaign medals. He remembers serving as CID ops off, managing and conducting police investigations of major crimes within combat areas under very "primitive conditions" during the Vietnam War.

Married Beverly Gee of Gibson City, IL; they have two

children and six grandchildren. Received BS degree from the Univ of Nebraska, June 1971. He is a charter member of the USAWOA and of the International Assoc of Chiefs of Police and CID Agents Assoc.

DAVID E. MEADE, CW3, USA (RET), born Jan 4, 1947, in Camden, NJ, and raised in Easton, PA; graduated Kutztown State College, 1968. Entered the Army in 1969, attended basic training at Ft Dix, NJ and AIT (military stenographer) at Ft Ben Harrison, IN. After assignment to the 902nd MI Gp, Baileys Crossroads, VA, he met and married a Fairfax, VA woman, Riva Roland.

Re-enlisted for Counterintelligence (CI) Agent Crs at Ft Huachuca, AZ and served with the 14th (later 519th MI Bn, Ft Bragg, NC and Defense Investigative Service in Orlando, FL. Attended Technical Surveillance Countermeasures (TSCM) Crs in 1975 with subsequent assignment to 650th MI Gp, supporting NATO Allied Forces Central Europe in Brunssum, The Netherlands.

Appointed WO1 in 1978 and returned to Pentagon CI Force, 902nd MI Gp, as team leader of an Ops Security team, and later chief, TSCM Sect.

Transferred to the CI Det, 902nd MI Gp, HQ Defense Nuclear Agency, Washington, DC, as assistant ops off and TSCM chief. While with the 902nd, he took the TEMPEST Coordination Off Crs, several computer security courses, and several specialized technical courses.

Was selected to head the TSCM Det, 519th MI Bn, 66th MI Bde, Munich, Germany, and established the office there as brigade TSCM assets were centralized. He returned in 1988 for a one-year terminal assignment to the Washington Resident Office, MI Bn (CI) Technical, 902nd MI Bn where he assisted in the relocation of the office from Arlington Hall Station to Ft Belvoir, VA.

Awards include the Meritorious Svc Med, Def Meritorious Svc Med, Joint Svc Comm Med and Army Comm Med.

Studied at the graduate level with Pepperdine Univ and has attended weapons and VIP protection courses sponsored by the FBI and secret service. Residing in Virginia, he is currently a security consultant with USATREX International, INC, McLean, VA, is a member of the American Society for Industrial Security and the WOA.

ALBERT R. MEDEIROS, CW4, AUS (RET), born Dec 25, 1930, in New Bedford, MA. Entered the USA in April 1951 with basic and AIT at Ft Lee, VA. Served in Korea from September 1951 to April 1953. Discharged and recalled to active duty in May 1957. Served as a dental supply specialist at Ft Polk, LA and Ft Sill, OK until December 1962; S2 NCO, OCS, Ft Sill, OK, December 1962-December 1963.

Transferred to MI; graduated from Ft Holabird, MD, April 1964; served as CI agent 1964-67 with the 66th MI Gp, Heidelberg, Germany and from May 1967-May 1968 with 109th MI Gp, Madisonville, KY. Appointed WO1 1967 as a CI officer. June 1968 attended WO Orientation Crs, Ft Sill, OK.

Served as CI officer in Vietnam with 1st Cav Div (Air Med), July 1968-July 1969. Served as senior CI officer at 66th MI Gp (Munich and Garmisch); 519th MI Bn, Ft Bragg, NC; 4th PSYOPS Gp, Ft Bragg; and senior adjudicative tech, USA "CCF," Ft Meade, MD.

Retired in April 1987 with the rank of CW4 with over 32 years of service. Awards include the Legion of Merit, Meritorious Svc Med w/OLC, Armed Forces Res Med, Army Comm Med w/OLC, Nat Def Svc Med, Bronze Star Med w/OLC, Vietnam Svc Med, Air Med, UN Svc Med and Korean Svc Med. Member of USAWOA, TROA, Phoenix Soc, AAFMAA and past Scout Master BSA.

Currently employed by DOD as a senior Security Specialist, Ft Meade, MD. He married Virginia Lanier of DeRidder, LA and they have one son and two grandchildren. He is a

FRANKLIN D. MEEKS, CW4, USA (AGR), born Jan 23, 1947, in Washington, NC. Began his military career in the USAR, 398th Engr Co, Greenville, NC Aug 23, 1965. Entered basic training on Nov 1, 1965, at Ft Jackson, SC and AIT at Ft Belvoir, VA Jan 14, 1966. Held various positions up through motor sergeant with the rank of staff sergeant.

On July 30, 1974, appointed WO1 as engineer equip repairman, 398th Supply Co. Transferred to HQ, 362nd QM BN in April 1983; entered AGR status June 3, 1985, as unit supply tech for HQ, 362nd QM BN; transferred to Army Res Readiness Trng Ctr at Ft McCoy, WI Sept 17, 1990, as the assistant branch chief in the Logistics Branch.

Received the Meritorious Svc Med, Army Comm Med w/2 OLCs, Army Achiev Med w/4 OLCs, Nat Def Svc Med and Armed Forces Res Med w/HG, Army Svc Rib, Army Res Overseas Trng Rib w/#6, Expert Rifle Badge, Mechanic Badge, Operator Badge w/S and Driver Badge w/T and W.

Married to Wanda Gail Butts of Greenville, NC. He is a life member in the ROA and WOA.

MANFRED FREDRICK MEINE, CW5, USA, born Jan 7, 1944, and grew up in Salem, OH. Enlisted in the US Army June 1, 1962, attended basic training at Ft Gordon, GA and armor training at Ft Knox, KY. Assigned to the 24th Inf Div, Augsburg, Germany and accepted for OJT transition to MP.

CID School at Ft Gordon then served as investigator in Seoul, Korea and Ft Bragg, NC. Appointed Feb 11, 1969 to WO1. After tour in Vietnam from 1969-1970, returned to Augsburg, Germany and became the special agent in charge of the CID resident agency. In 1975, selected for bootstrap attendance at Univ of Nebraska, earning his bachelor's in 1976. Served two years with Secretary of Defense, Washington, DC. Selected in 1978 to attend the FBI National Academy and in 1979 was special agent in charge of the CID resident agency at the USMA at West Point, NY. In 1982 selected as career manager for CID WOs at DA PERSCOM.

Returned to Germany in 1984 as a CID District Ops Off. Moved in 1986 to the 6th CID Region HQ in San Francisco. Selected as one of the Armies first MWOs in 1988, graduated from the first MWO Trng Crs and completed his doctoral degree in public administration. Selected in 1991 to be WO Leader Development Staff Officer/Branch Chief HQ, US Army Trng and Doctrine Cmd. Promoted to CW5 on Feb 1, 1993.

Awards include the Bronze Star, Meritorious Svc Med w/4 OLCs, Army Comm Med w/3 OLCs, Good Conduct, Nat Def Svc w/2 devices, Army Exped Med, NCOPDR, Overseas Svc Rib, VN Campaign w/4 devices, VN Svc Med and RVN Cross of Gallantry (unit). Member of the USAWOA, CID Agents Assoc, FBI National Academy Assoc, TROA, American Legion and several academic honor societies.

Married the former Rita Stegmueller of Augsburg, Germany. They have the distinction of an all military family. Their twin son and daughter were the first ever to be accepted in the USMA and graduated in 1985; their youngest daughter graduated from AF ROTC at the Univ of California; their sons-in-law are an USAF captain and an US Army captain.

THEODORE R. MELINE, CW4, USA (AGR), born Dec 20, 1935, in Eagle Grove, IA. Entered military service March 10, 1952, Co E, 133rd Inf Regt, 34th Div. Completed basic training at Camp McCoy, WI; held various positions in infantry, engineer and QM units attaining enlisted rank of master sergeant E-8. Appointed CWO2 Jan 21, 1978, as property book tech, USAR, HQ, 423rd Sup and Svc Bn, Albuquerque, NM.

Transferred to HQ 244th Engr Bn, Denver, CO; HQ 259th QM Bn, Pleasant Grove, UT; HQ 162nd Spt Gp, Ft Douglas, UT; HQ 96th Army Res Compo-

nents Med, Ft Douglas, UT. Entered AGR status 1985-88, HQ 259th QM Bn, Pleasant Grove, UT; AGR status 1990, 2291st USA Hosp, Columbus, OH; Desert Shield/Desert Storm, 1990-91, Kenner USA Hosp, Ft Lee, VA; 1991 Walter Reed AMC, Washington, DC; 1991-93, 2291st USA Hosp, Columbus, OH; 1993-present, HQ 91st Div, Ft Baker, CA.

Significant assignments: div prop book officer, 91st Div; Med Ctr Bde S-4, Walter Reed AMC; prop book officer, 2291st USA Hosp and 259th QM Bn; and task force assignments (7) to Republic of South Korea, 1982-88.

Awards include the Meritorious Svc Med w/2 OLCs, Army Comm Med w/3 OLCs, Army Achiev Med w/OLC, Res Component Achiev Med w/6 OLCs, Nat Def Svc Med, Armed Forces Res Med w/3 HGs, Army Svc Rib, USAR Components Overseas Trng Rib w/#7, Expert Badge w/ Rifle, Carbine, Pistol.

Married Carolyn McCune of Lusk, WY in July 1961. They have one daughter Krista and son Shawn (USA, Ft Lewis, WA). Completed 42 years of continuous military service (active and reserve) on March 9, 1994, and is still on active duty. Civilian service includes logistics management specialist (CLRT), 6th USA; administrative officer, Utah and Nevada, Dept of Ag; supervisor staff administrator, 96th ARCOM; staff training assistant; 96th ARCOM; and admin sup tech, 96th ARCOM.

THOMAS I. MENDENHALL, CWO, born Aug 21, 1908, at Beatrice, NE. Joined the 110th Med Regt Svc Co NENG in 1927; transferred to Band 110th Med Regt for five years. AUS March 1940-October 1942; attended Army Music School, September-October 1942, and graduated in top 10 of the class.

Appointed WOJG in November 1942; assigned to the 94th Div Art Band, Camp Phillips, KS and made CWO on May 10, 1943. September 1943 Art Band combined with the 302nd Regt Inf Band to form the 94th Inf Div Band; was appointed CO of combined band. Trained at Camp McCain, MS until August 1944.

Overseas September 1944 for stand-by duty in western France. January-April 1944, duty on the Ardennes front where the band did perimeter guard duty, no music. June-November 1944, did occupation duty in Czechoslovakia, their Bokoo music making (the natives loved it). Returned Stateside in December 1944 and final discharge in March 1945.

Joined the ILNG in 1946, made CWO and assigned CO of 33rd Div Band. Reserves in 1949. Retired from the US Postal Service in 1977.

JAMES H. MERO, CW3, AUS (RET), born Aug 14, 1918, in Escanaba, MI. Inducted in the US Army on March 7, 1941, taking basic training at Field Arty Replacement Trng Ctr (FARTC), Ft Sill, OK. Assigned to cadre, FARTC as clerk for Btry D, 27th Bn; transferred to HQ, Army Ground Forces, Washington, DC, 1942, serving as administrative NCO. Discharged as master sergeant on Dec 9, 1945.

Employed by federal service with the Army, Washington, DC and Ft Monroe, VA. Enlisted in the USAR in 1948 as master sergeant with assignments to Co E, 318th Prcht Inf, 421st Trans Port Co and Hampton Roads POE, 9248th ARTSU.

Appointed WO1 in 1952 as adjutant, Hampton Roads POE, 9248th ARTSU. Other assignments: mobilization designee to Office Chief of Staff, Office Chief Army Field Forces and 7613th USAR Trans Unit Trng Ctr; served as administrative officer, military personnel officer, adjutant, inspector general and civilian personnel officer.

Retired with over 20 years of active duty and active Reserve service on Aug 14, 1978, as CW3. Awards include the Meritorious Svc Unit Insignia, Good Conduct Med, Am Def Svc, Am Theater Svc, WWII Victory Med and Armed Forces Res Med.

Retired from the federal civil service as personnel and equip analyst, Cbt Developments Div, Trng and Doctrine Cmd, Ft Monroe, VA in December 1974. He is member of St Tammany Lodge #5, AF&AM, ROA, TROA, Tidewater Genealogical Society (charter member), American Air Museum, Duxford, England, and elder of the First Presbyterian Church, Hampton, VA.

Married Leona Harris of Adair, OK on Jan 29, 1943; they have one daughter.

JOHN C. MEYERS, CW2, USA, born March 5, 1963, in Racine, WI. Began his military service in the US Army in B 268 AHB, Ft Lewis, WA (1983-1984) as a Cobra crew chief (67Y10) after completion of basic training at Ft Jackson, NC and AIT at Ft Eustis, VA.

Reassigned to B-205 Trans (AVIM), Fleigerhorst, Germany and promoted to the rank of staff sergeant; selected for Flight School in 1987 and was appointed to WO1 on Nov 16, 1989. Assigned to C Trp 2-7 US Cav, Ft Carson, CO as an Aeroscout (152B). Attended the Aeroscout Instructor Pilot Crs in 1992 and served in D Trp 2-7 Cav until August 1993. Reassigned to Ft Hood, TX after Warrior Qualification (152DO) for collective training with CATB in order to deploy to the ROK assigned to D Trp 5-17 US Cav.

His awards include the Army Comm Med w/OLC, Army Achievement Med w/3 OLCs and Aviator Badge.

Meyers married Kathy A Herriott of Texas in February 1985 and they have a daughter, Brigitte Marie, born on Jan 14, 1991.

RICKEY L. MILLER, CW2, born June 28, 1959, in Macomb, IL. Entered the Army Oct 25, 1976, and served in various positions for 14 years prior to appointment as an engr equip repair tech, 919A, Sept 21, 1990. Assigned to Charlie Co, 708th Spt Bn, 8th Inf Div, Baumholder, Germany, October 1990-November 1992. Attached to the 12th Engr Bn (combat), 8th Inf Div, as the bn maint officer, 33rd Engr Bn (provisional), 3rd Bde, 3rd Armd Div, during Operation Desert Storm.

Awards include the Bronze Star, Army Comm Med, Army Achiev Med, Army Good Conduct Med, Humanitarian Svc Med, SWA Svc Med, Kuwait Svc Med, Prcht Badge and Mechanics Badge.

Currently assigned to the Foreign Mat Intel Bn, APG, MD as the foreign engr equip and systems analyst.

Married the former Rosemarie McCoy of Macomb, IL and together with their children: Jennifer, Meleiah, Rikki and Jacob, reside in Edgewood, MD.

S.W. KENT MILLER III, CW4, USAR, born March 10, 1938, in Martinsburg, WV. Holds AAS in business admin, Vincennes Univ, IN; 30 additional SH from Ball State Univ and Marian College, IN; various other prof dvlmt courses. Mil ed includes WOSC; Mil Complr Crs; Fin Off Adv Crs; MP Sch Crim Inves Crs; various DA and NGB fin rel prof dvlmt courses; and C&GSC Opn Sgt/Sgt Maj Crs.

Enlisted in DCARNG 1955; assigned to various positions including CO MP Ops supervisor, Bn Pers NCO, DCNG Sate HQ Ops and trng dir SGM and asst commd't of State NCO Academy and inf bn CSM. Assigned to 1-380th Inf; ord to AD with NGB Fin Svc Br, 1974-82. Transferred to INARNG; Ord to AD as NGB fin svc br off January-July 1987 and November 1987-March 1989; transferred to DC ARNG in March 1989; ord to AD with NGB Fin Svc Div, January-July 1991. Transferred to MDARNG 1991-93; ord to AD with NGB Fin Svc Div 1992-93. Transferred to USAR IRR in Jul 1993. Currently assigned to the USAR IRR attached to the 157th IMA Det (Joint), Washington, DC.

Awards include the Meritorious Svc Med w/OLC, ARCOM, Army Achiev, NCOPDR w/#4 D, Nat Def Svc Med (2nd awd), AFRM w/2 HG devices (30 years of service), and ARCAM w/5 BSs for subsequent awards, and numerous civilian, state and honorary state awards.

Married and has two children.

WILLIAM W. MILLER, CW3, USA (RET), born March 28, 1951, in Owensboro, KY, and raised in California and Kentucky. Enlisted in the USMC in 1970, completed basic training at MCRD Parris Island, SC; AIT at Camp Geiger, NC; AIT in the telecommunications and maint field at San Diego, CA; 29 Palms, CA; Albany, GA; Lowry Technical Trng Cmd, Lowry AFB, Denver, CO.

Served WestPac; tours with the 3rd Mar Div and Force Troops FMF Pac; tours with the 2nd Mar Div and 2nd Mar Air Wing. Discharged as E-6 and enlisted in the USAR in 1978; promoted to SFC and applied for WO direct appointment. Selected and appointed as WO1 in 1981 with a 630A MOS; completed basic and advanced courses in both 630A and the 252A fields.

Completed the USMC Officer Basic, Amphib Warfare and Command and General Staff College Courses; served as maint evaluator-controller for the 100th Div MTC, 1981-93; served during Desert Storm-Desert Shield as the readiness officer for the 100th MTC and work at Ft Knox, KY in assisting Readiness Gp Knox in processing mobilized units on their way to the desert.

Retired Nov 1, 1993. Awards include the Meritorious Svc Med w/2 OLCs, Army Comm Med, Army Achiev Med, USMC Good Conduct (2nd awd) and numerous campaign, service medals and unit decorations.

Married the former Sumiko Sueyoshi of Okinawa, Japan; they have three children: Tresa (served in the Army for four years as 71L and discharged as SP4), Katherine (currently serving as E-3 with the KYANG as an information management specialist), Christian (high school senior and currently going through the paper work and tests prior to joining some branch of the Armed Forces). Graduated from the Univ of the state of New York with AS and BA degrees with dual major in history and geography.

DONALD R. MILLS, CW3, AUS (RET), born Dec 16, 1928, in Seattle, WA. Entered the US Army May 27, 1954; took basic training and Clerk Typist School at Ft Ord, CA; assigned as 2nd Bn clerk, Medical Trng Ctr, Ft Sam Houston, TX. Re-enlisted in RA 1957 and assigned to Air Def Msl Fire Control School, Ft Bliss, TX; upon graduation became an instructor in the Niki Hercules Radar Branch.

Retrained in aviation electronics, 1959, Ft Gordon, GA; transferred to the 124th Sig Bn, 4th Inf Div, Ft Lewis, WA; appointed WO, May 1962 at Ft Lewis, WA. Assignments as WO included div sig maint officer, 7th Inf Div, Camp Casey, Korea, 1962-63; Sig officer, 4th Terminal Cmd and Sig maint officer, 69th Sig Bn (Army), Ft Eustis, VA, 1963-64; Sig Det commander and maint officer, 5th Maint Bn, USAREUR Augmentation Readiness Group, Pirmasens, Germany, 1964-67; Sig Maint Advisor to the RVN, 4th Corps, Vinh Long, VN, 1968-69; Sig Maint and Log Officer, S-4, Sig Gp 22, Manheim, Germany, 1969-71; Satellite Comm Terminal Commander and Maint Off, Tun Son Nhut AFB, VN, 1971-72.

Retired on disability at Ft Lewis, WA in April 1972. Awards include the Bronze Star, Army Comm w/OLC, Army Good Conduct, RVN Honor Med, Sig Corps Badge and numerous service and campaign medals.

Married 40 years to the late Hilda Hughes of Elba, AL and Seattle, WA. He is a retired postal employee, member of the ROA, VFW Post 3057, Westport, WA.

JOHN S. MILUCKY, CW2, USA (RET), born May 3, 1916, in Chicago, IL. Inducted into the US Army on April 10, 1941; basic training at Camp Forrest, TN, with the 33rd Inf Div. Appointed WOJG Oct 7, 1942, at HQ Army Ground Forces, Army War College, Washington, DC.

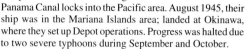

He participated in Arkansas-Louisiana Red River maneuvers; April 1944 joined the 58th QM Base Depot at Camp Lee, VA; June 1944, arrived in Liverpool, England; landed on Utah Beach; September 1944, moved to Ablis, France; December 1944, at Bressoux, Belgium. After V-E Day, all of the 58th QMBD personnel staged near Marseilles, France.

July 1945, personnel boarded the troop ship AT-125 *Admiral Mayo*, destined for the CBI Theater of Operations and sailed through the Panama Canal locks into the Pacific area. August 1945, their ship was in the Mariana Islands area; landed at Okinawa, where they set up Depot operations. Progress was halted due to two severe typhoons during September and October.

Returned to the States in December 1945 and after 60 days of R&R was assigned to the Army Medical Center in Washington, DC as asst adjutant. Joined the Valley Forge Army Hospital, Phoenixville, PA as asst registrar in July and acquired additional duty as asst det commander.

During his service as a WO he was privileged to see and meet some of the great military commanders during WWII. At HQ, Army Ground Forces, he worked with the liaison officer for Armored Forces and together they worked for Brig Gen William Dean.

The exceptional qualities of those commanders was very inspiring. He felt compelled to put forth his very best effort and accomplish each and every assignment to the best of his ability.

JOHN JOSEPH MITCHELL, CW3, USA, born June 21, 1953, in Washington, DC. Entered the US Army July 31, 1973, taking basic training at Ft Jackson, SC and AIT at Ft Devens, MA. Served with the 1st Ops Bn, USAFS, Augsburg, 1974-76. Assigned to the 408th ASA Co and 470th MI Gp, Ft Amador, Panama Canal Zone.

Present during the 1977 treaty exchange between President Carter and Gen Omar Torrijos; assigned to USAFS Augsburg from 1981-84; appointed as WO (CW2) Aug 15, 1984, and assigned to the 313th MI Bn (CEWI)(ABN), 82nd Abn Div, Ft Bragg, NC. Held position as secretary for the Ft Bragg Chap USAWOA.

Assigned to USAFS Berlin from 1988-92; served as SIGINT/EW systems analyst and OIC, Analysis and Reporting Sect. Present during the fall of the Berlin Wall and the Oct 3, 1990, unification of East and West Germany. Assigned to his current position as chief, Target Development Div with the 743rd MI Bn, 704th MI Bde.

Awards include the Meritorious Svc Med w/OLC, Army Comm Med w/3 OLCs, Army Achiev Med, Army Good Conduct Med w/3 knots, Army of Occupation Med, Overseas Svc Awd (3), Nat Def Svc Awd w/star, NCOPDR (3). Awarded the Army Parachutist Badge, USAF Space Badge and German Parachutist Wings (Bronze).

Married Teresa Lee Gonzles of Memphis, TN; they have two children. Life member of NRA and USAWOA; past president (two terms) of the Berlin Chap USAWOA. Active in Boy Scouts; hobbies include golf, camping, fishing and hunting.

NASH DENNIS MONTGOMERY, CW2, born July 26, 1954, in West Point, MS. Enlisted Aug 20, 1973; served in the US Army as military personnel officer, 420AO. Stationed at Ft Campbell, KY; Turkey; Germany; Los Angeles, CA; and Ft Meade, MD.

Memorable experiences include the USA recruiting in Los Angeles, CA and his appointment to WO.

Awards include the Meritorious Svc Med, Army Comm Med w/OLC and Army Achiev Med. Currently on active duty.

Married Frankie Lucas; they have two children, Tammy and Nash II. He is chief, Personnel Services Branch, Ft George G. Meade, MD.

ARCHIE C. MOORE, CW3, USA (RET), born May 28, 1952, in Brooklyn, NY. Entered US Army Sept 28, 1972, taking basic training at Ft Dix, NJ and AIT at Ft Ord, CA and

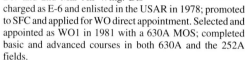

Ft Harrison, IN. Served as administrative specialist at Ft Dix, NJ with the 42 AG Reception Bn until his discharge Sept 28, 1976.

Immediately enlisted in the USAR serving with the 78th MTC, Ft Dix, NJ as an administrative NCO. Received direct appointment June 15, 1985, to CW2 as personnel tech and began serving with HHC, 78th Div, Edison, NJ as assistant inspector general. Reassigned to present unit, 1018th USARECBN, 76th Div, Ft Dix, NJ Nov 16, 1990; unit was activated during the Persian Gulf War and he served from January 1991-May 1991.

Awards include the Meritorious Svc Med, Army Comm Med w/2 OLCs, Army Achiev Med, Army Res Comp Achiev Med w/3 OLCs, Armed Forces Res Med and the Nat Def Svc Med w/star.

Member of the USAWOA, AG Corps Regimental Assoc and the Army Reserve Assoc. Resides in New Jersey and is currently a supervisor, Commodity Distribution with the New Jersey Dept of Ag.

ERNEST A. MOORE, CW2 (RET), born Sept 6, 1952, in Houston, TX. Entered the US Army on June 5, 1972; basic training at Ft Polk, LA, B Co, 3rd Bn, 1st Trng Bde. Completed AIT as tracked and wheeled mechanic with 1st Bn 67th Armor, 2nd AD, Ft Hood, TX; assigned with same unit during the Vietnam era until October 1974. Reassigned to the 42nd MT Co, Furth, West Germany as recovery specialist from 1974-77.

Transferred to B Btry, 1st Bn, 77th FA, III Corps, Ft Sill, OK as battery motor sergeant through November 1979. Completed tour and reassigned to HHQ Co, 2nd Bn, 36th Inf (Rangers), 3rd AD, Kirch-Goens, West Germany as company motor sergeant until departure in November 1982. End of tour reassigned as motor sergeant 2nd Bn, 36th Inf, 3rd AD, Ft Hood, TX, serving until selected to attend Class 2-83 WOCC, 2nd Bn School Bde, APG, MD. Graduated WOCC and promoted to WO1, December 1983; reported to Svc Btry, 1st Bn, 77th FA, 1st Cav Div, Ft Hood, TX; promoted to CW2 1985 and served with unit until July 1986.

Due to a service connected disability he retired from the Army in April 1989. Awards include the Army Comm, Good Conduct (3rd awd), Nat Def Svc Med, Drivers Badge, Parachutist Badge, Drivers-Mechanic Badge, Air Assault Badge, Army Svc Rib, Overseas Svc Rib (2), NCOPDR, Expert Qualification (.45 cal and M16 rifle) and German Marksmanship Badge (Gold).

Life member of the WOA, DAV; member of NRA, American Legion, Boy Scouts of American and the Order of the Arrow, Texas Parks and Wildlife as a hunter safety instructor. Education includes two associates degrees, one with honors from Central Texas College, Killeen, TX.

Married Mary Joyce Bryan of Amarillo, TX; they have three sons.

JOHN O. MORGAN, CWO4, born July 17, 1930, in Talladaga, AL. Enlisted in the US Army in 1949. Demonstrated leadership ability as an NCO during the Korean War by taking charge in combat when his platoon leader was killed. He assisted in the inspection and repair of small arms in ROK Army support units and helped establish war reserve cannon and tank tube requirements for Army in Korea.

Appointed WO (1965) and became armament platoon leader, 4th Inf Div, where he reduced weapons backlog to near zero; provided customer relations and maint standards. In Vietnam his forward support area contact teams provided direct support maint for units from Fire Base JJ Carrol to the coast. While shop officer at the 705th Maint Bn, he reduced the 2nd Bde's backlog and improved operational readiness to 80 percent.

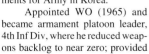

In 1971 he became chief of the heavy equip div in Korea and completed a special program, the rebuilding of M16A1 rifles, two months ahead of schedule. Extended his tour to organize and set up shop to rebuild 150 M60A1s and 25 M102s, light 105mm howitzers two months ahead of schedule. During 1974-75, was responsible for the recovery of $7 million of equipment; planned, supervised, coordinated, and executed the worldwide, total package unit material fielding of more than 1,500 backup computer systems; negotiated and expedited the return of M102 howitzers from Europe for rapid depot modification and also contributed to the Army wide readiness of the 8-inch M11A2 self propelled howitzer.

Though mandatorily retired in 1983, he returned to active service the next day as arranged by LTG Register to continue his service to the Army. He subsequently retired a second time in July 1988.

ROBERT MORRIS, CW3, AUS (RET), born April 20, 1923, in Cambridge, MA. Enlisted in RA July 23, 1942, in Boston, MA. Stationed at Cold Bay, Aleutian Area, 1942-44; England Gen Hosp, NJ, 1945; 97th Gen Hosp, Germany, 1946-48; SGM Valley Forge Gen Hosp, 1949; SGM Fitzsimons Gen Hosp, Denver, CO, 1950.

Appointed WOJG April 10, 1951; registrar, 8076th MASH; 544th Gen Disp, Korea, 1952-53; adjutant Osaka Gen Hosp, Japan, 1954; Med Admin Off, Ft Leonard Wood, MO, 1955; HQ VII Corps, Germany, 1956-59.

His memorable experiences include the waning days of the Korean War when he obtained the necessary material, supplies and equip with which he redesigned, rebuilt and refurbished the 544th Gen Disp in the town of Chunchon, Central Korea. .

Retired in July 1962 at Ft Bragg, NC. Received BA and MA degrees from the Univ of Pennsylvania in 1964 and CPCU in 1966. Life member of the Ambassadors Club and TROA and currently the secretary of the Manchester Masonic Lodge, Manchester, MA.

Married Sigrid Margarete Henker of Frankfurt, Germany; they have three children and six grandchildren.

GEORGE B. MORTON, CW3, entered the US Army in January 1970, at Ft Polk, LA as 55B, ammo records, operations specialist. Assigned to MMC V COSCOM in Frankfurt, Germany from 1970-1972. Reclassified to 72B, Telecommunications Ctr Specialist and assigned to STRATCOM-EUR in Worms, Germany. Assigned to the 232nd Sig Co in Germany; USAISC Det, Ft McPherson, GA; USAG USALANDSOUTHEAST, Ismir, Turkey; USAISC, Ft Gordon, GA; 169th Sig Co, Taegu, Korea; USAISC, Ft Benning, GA.

Attended WOEC October 1986 and completed the WOTC May 1987 as 250A. Assigned to the 522nd MI Bn, 2nd Armd Div at Ft Hood, TX as the COMSEC officer and Bn Sig officer, 1987-89; reassigned to the 141st Sig Bn, 1st Armd Div as MSE project officer and Div COMSEC officer, 1989-91. Unit deployed to Operation Desert Shield-Desert Storm, 1990-91; and current assignment is 102nd Sig Bn as OIC of Telecommunications Branch which is responsible for all Telecommunication Centers in the Frankfurt, Darmstadt and Hanau area.

Awards include the Bronze Star, Meritorious Svc Med, Joint Svc Comm Med, Army Comm Med (2), Army Achiev Med (2), Good Conduct Med, Nat Def Svc Med (2), SWAM (3), NCOPDR (3), Army Svc Rib, Overseas Svc Rib (4) and Kuwait Lib Med.

Married the 15 years to the former Pamela Hobbs and has two sons, Michael and David. Currently working on his bachelors degree in education.

GEORGE E. MORTON, CW3, born Feb 24, 1941, in Greensboro, NC. Enlisted in the RA on Jan 26, 1962; attended basic training at Ft Knox, KY; served with the 43rd Msl Bn, Omaha, NE, 1962-65. Ordered to Korea and served with the 76th Engr Bn, January 1966 and served three tours in Vietnam units, 1099th Med Boat Co, 19th Engr Combat Bn and the 363rd Trans Co.

Served with A Co, 63rd Armor Bn as maint sergeant; final assignment as enlisted A Co 1st of 5th Cav, 1st Cav Div, Ft Hood, TX, until Nov 25, 1975. Appointed WO1 Nov 26, 1975, as maint officer, 43rd Engr Bn, Ft Benning, GA; transferred to the 17th Bn FA, Camp Phelam, Korea; reassigned to 1st Bn 7th Cav 1st Div, Ft Hood, TX; reassigned to Germany, 1981-83 with the 66th Maint Bn general support at Kissinger, Germany; final assignment was with the 551st Trans Co, Ft Eustis, VA.

Discharged on Aug 1, 1984, with the rank of CW3. Awards include the Bronze Star, Meritorious Svc Med w/ OLC, Army Comm Med w/4 OLCs, Army Achiev Med and numerous service and campaign medals.

Married a wonderful woman and has five children and four grandchildren. Currently employed with the Kuwait AF as maint tech and advisor.

TRICE W. MOTT (WES), CW4, USA (RET), born Feb 20, 1939, in West Carrol, Parish, LA, and raised in Bastrop, LA. Joined the USAF in October 1956; trained as communications and cryptographic specialist; assigned to the 2nd Mbl Comm Gp (France) and served with UN forces in the Republic of the Congo, Leopoldville and Stanleyville.

Participated in the arms airlift to India to counter an invasion from China; assigned to listening stations in Africa in the early manned space flights; participated in operations hard surface in Saudi Arabia. Appointed in the USAR as WO October 1966 while assigned to the NORAD Hardsite and to the RA in October 1969.

Completed the USA Inf School Basic Abn Crs, 82nd Abn Div Jumpmaster Crs and the Ft Bragg Chem School's Radiological Def Off Trng in 1969. Completed the Communications and Electronics WOAC at Ft Gordon in 1973 and the WOSC at Ft Rucker in 1976. Graduated from Campbell College in 1972 under the Degree Completion Program, with a BBA in accounting and economics. Graduated from Univ of Northern Colorado in 1975 with MA in business mgmt. Served with HQ ARADCOM (Colorado Springs), 7th Inf Div (Korea), HQ I Corps (Group) (Korea), 82nd Abn Div (Ft Bragg), Military Assistance Cmd (Vietnam), 1st Sig Bde (Vietnam), 11th Sig Gp (Ft Huachuca), and the Mil Pers Ctr (Alexandria, VA).

Primary MOS was COMSEC Off; served as platoon leader; small arms CBR and Ops Off and performed as jumpmaster. Initially an assignment officer and later served as professional development officer.

Memorable experience while in the service was over Fryer Field, Ft Benning, GA during his first jump from a C-119. The individual he most respected while on active duty was Emmit Paige Jr, colonel, commander of the 11th Sig Gp.

Retired from active duty in February 1978. Medals include the Bronze Star, Exped Forces, VN Svc Med, RVN w/Palm, AF and Army Comm and others.

A financial operations manager, he joined Parsons Brinckerhoff Quade and Douglas (international engineering firm) in 1985 and was assigned to the Office of Finance in NYC

Resides with his wife Joyce Autry Mott in Anaheim Hills, CA.

WILLIAM C. MULLINS, MW4, USA, born Aug 12, 1934, in Allen, OK. Entered the US Army in November 1955; served over 13 years as an enlisted soldier. Appointed WO1 in September 1969; served as supply officer at virtually every level of Army Logistics, career manager for QM WOs at MILPERCEN, chief of DA WO Recruiting Team; analyst on DA Total WO Stud (TWOS) Gp, Personnel Proponent Officer for USALOGC and CASCOM, CWO of the QM Corps, USAQMS, chief, WO Div, USAQMS and chief evaluator for CSA Supply Excellence Award Program.

Graduate of the first MWO Trng Crs. CONUS service includes Fts Chaffee, Jackson, Hood, Sill, Lee and Alexandria, VA; OCONUS service includes Germany, Hawaii, Vietnam and Korea. Holds an AS degree from Troy State Univ. Member of TROA, USAWOA, Loyal Order of the Moose, American Legion and several Masonic organizations.

Awards include the Legion of Merit, Bronze Star w/ OLC, Meritorious Svc Med w/7 OLCs, Army Comm Med w/

4 OLCs, Humanitarian Svc Med, EIB, Army Good Conduct Med, Air Med and several campaign and service medals.

Married Gertraud Guhl of Eger, Sudatenland; they have three children and three grandchildren.

WILLIAM C. MURPHY, CW4, USA (RET), born Jan 1, 1915, in Chicago, IL. Entered the USA on July 31, 1941; took basic training and Sig School at Ft Monmouth, NJ; served as 1st sergeant, 3254th Sig Svc Co in WWII, including Battle of the Bulge; 1948-49, military attaché office, Dominican Republic; appointed WO on Sept 1, 1951 at SHAPE HQ, Paris, France.

Served 1957-1958 in Korea as asst AG (prov MAAG-K); in Vietnam as asst AG, 937th Engr Gp; June 1969 until his retirement as personnel officer of the 2nd Psyop Gp, Ft Bragg, NC.

Retired as CW4 with 30 years of service on Jan 1, 1972, and took a position with the North Carolina Employment Security Commission. In 1980 moved to Port Orange, FL where he passed away on July 16, 1983. He is survived by his widow Helen and a son Michael (Raleigh, NC).

GRAHAM MURRAY JR., CW3, AUS (RET), born Nov 21, 1927, in Pender County, NC. Enlisted with several classmates, all with ROTC training, in June 1946. Basic training at Ft McClellan, AL; assigned to Intel School, Ft Riley, KS; graduated Aerial Photo Interpretation Crs and assigned to the 3rd Bn, 20th Inf, 6th Div near Kwang Ju, Korea. Discharged to active Reserve in December 1947 (347th Engr Ponton Bridge Co).

Attended Wilmington, NC Junior College and obtained aircraft mechanics license; requested and recall to active duty at the beginning of the Korean War in November 1950 with duty at Recruiting Main Station Induction Ctr, Fayettville, NC. Assigned to Mil Pers Proc Div, OCS Sect HQ 3rd Army, Ft McPherson, GA.

Departed for Germany, September 1952, and MOS changed to aircraft mechanic. Assigned to 36th FA Gp, but excess in 36th Gp so reassigned to 2nd Bn, 2nd Armed Cav, Bamberg Germany. Remained with them throughout Operation Gyroscope; moved to Nurnberg, then departed in April 1962. Assigned to Ft Stewart, GA; G-3 NCOIC Liberty AAF; requested and reassigned to Imagery interpretation School, Ft Holabird, MD; graduated and assigned to IMDO.

Involved in Army tests and helped develop the vehicle mounted imagery interpretation facility, AN/TXQ-43; appointed WO1 Dec 10, 1965, with orders to RVN; assigned CICV, then to 1st MI BN ARS with duty at Tan-Son-Nhut AB; assigned to Det C, 2nd MI Bn with duty station RAF Alconbury, England; spent 364 days in England, then back to RVN where assigned to 219th MI Det II FFV.

Completed tour and assigned to HQ 2nd MI BN, ARS Kaiserslautern, Germany; liaison officer working with USAF, Canadian Air Force and German Air Force. Member of NATO panel of experts on aerial photography, with meetings including French speaking nations due to official languages of NATO-English and French writing reports. When his tour in the USAEUR completed he was assigned to the US Army Image Interpretation Ctr with duty station, Washington, DC.

Retired on April 30, 1975. Awards include the Nat Def Svc Med w/OLC, VN Camp Med w/60 Device, VN Gallantry Cross Unit Cit w/Palm 2nd awd, Aircraft Crewman Badge, Good Conduct Med w/Bronze Clasp and 5 loops, Army of Occupation Med (Germany), WWII Victory Med, Army Comm Med w/OLC, Bronze Star w/OLC, Meritorious Unit Cit 2nd awd, Army of Occupation Med (Korea) w/4 Overseas Bars and Meritorious Svc Med.

Married over 38 years to the former Lucille Weiss.

JERIEL LEE MUSIC, WO1, USA, born Feb 16, 1962, in Wabash, IN. Education includes distinguished graduate of the US Army Basic Non-Commissioned Officer Crs; USA Precommission Crs; Unit Level Log System Mid-Level Mgrs, Crs; Dist Graduate of the USA WO Candidate School; Honor Graduate of the USA WO Basic Crs; USA Instr Trng Crs; and the USA Bn Mtr Off Crs.

Enlisted in the USMC from Sept 28, 1980-Sept 28, 1984, then enlisted in the US Army from Jan 14, 1986, to present. Military stations include Marine Bks with duty in Philippines; 2nd Bn 2nd Mar Div, Camp Lejeune, NC; 3rd Bn, 35th Armor, Bamberg, Germany; B Co, 1st Bn, 81st Armor, Ft Knox, KY; and 3rd Bn, 7th Inf Div, Ft Stewart, GA.

Most memorable experience is being accepted as a WO. Awards include (2) Army Comm, (3) Army Achiev, Army and USMC Good Conduct, Nat Def Svc Med, Meritorious Unit Cit (Navy).

Married the former Vickie Lynn Shankle; they have two children, Meghann and Ethann. Presently assigned to the 3rd Bn 7th Inf Div, Ft Stewart, GA as the bn maint tech.

LASZLO NEMETH, CW4, USA (RET), born Feb 21, 1942, in Szekelykeresztur, Hungary and lived with his family behind the Iron Curtain until his escape from the soviet controlled communist regime, Nov 21, 1956, to Austria. As a 14 year old, he witnessed the short-lived Hungarian Revolution of 13 days, Oct 23-Nov 4, 1956; after two and one-half years in Austria, he emigrated to the States and lived in St Louis, MO until his enlistment in the Army on Jan 17, 1962.

Training took him to Ft Leonard Wood, and Ft Lee. First duty assignment was B Co, 23rd Engr Bn, 3rd Armd Div, in Hanau, Germany. Promoted to WO1 at Ft McNair, Washington DC; first WO assignment took him to Ft Carson, CO, 4th Inf Div Arty.

Served over 15 years in West Germany and Berlin Bde, two tours in the Far East, seven years in Ft Bragg, NC (five years were with DISCOM, 82nd Abn Div) and one year as the XVIII Abn Corps and Ft Bragg installation food advisor. Final assignment with G-4, USA Spec Forces Cmd, Ft Bragg, NC from where he retired on Jan 31, 1992.

Memorable experiences are the privilege of serving his country for 30 years and having been part of the winning team, NATO, which toppled the cold war adversaries without firing a shot.

He and wife Sigrid selected Fayetteville, NC as their retirement home town.

GENE A. NEWTON, CW2, USA, born March 21, 1940, in Millhaven, GA. He entered the USA AG Corps on Sept 7, 1961; attended basic training at Ft Gordon, GA and AIT at Ft Leonard Wood, MO. Other stations include Ft Gordon, GA; Ft McClellan, AL; Ft Campbell, KY; Ft Rucker, AL; Korea; two tours in Vietnam, 1966-67 and 1969-70; Panama City 1972-75.

Retired Oct 15, 1985, with the rank of CW4. Awards include the Legion of Merit w/2 OLCs, Bronze Star, Joint Svc Comm Med, Meritorious Svc Med, Army Comm Med w/2 SCL, Army Achiev Med, Good Conduct Med w/2OLCs and numerous service and campaign medals.

Newton married Tina and they have three children: Tammy, Alani and Michael. He is district manager in Augusta, GA for EMRO Marketing Speedway stores. Member of the TROA, NOA, Ft Gordon Retired Council, USAWOA, established and is president of a chapter at Ft Gordon, Panama CZ, Ft McClellan and currently director of region 5 of USAWOA.

ED NICHOLLS (NICK), CW2, USA, born on July 31, 1937, in Pasadena, CA. Enlisted in the USMCR Oct 14, 1954. After four years in the USMC, he served with the Los Angeles Police Dept (LAPD), 1959-1964. Graduated from LAPD Trng Acad Feb 5, 1960; did two short tours and one long tour of duty in RVN, 1965-70.

Participated in 14 major infantry ops, 350+ combat patrols, ambushes and medcaps. Wounded in a 122mm VC rocket attack at Chu Lai Cbt Base, RVN in May 1970 and was injured by friendly fire twice. Served during seven RVN campaigns; (1970-74) in the CI Div IIIMAF, Da Nang and USMC Air Station, El Toro, CA; transferred (1974) to the Army as a CI and spec agent USACIDC (WO Corps).

Assigned to USACIDC, 7th Reg in charge of the Western Corridor of Korea; served at Ft Sam Houston USACIDC Field Office in the Gen Crimes, Drug, Burglary and Larceny Teams as spec agent and CI coordinator.

Retired as CWO2 in 1981. Awards include the Meritorious Svc, Purple Heart w/star, Navy Comm w/V, Army Comm, MC Cbt Act Rib, MC Good Conduct w/2 stars, Navy Unit Comm w/3 stars, Pres Unit Cit w/star, Nat Def Svc w/star, RVN Svc w/silver and Bronze Star, RVN Cross of Gallantry w/palm frame, RVN Unit Cross of Gallantry, RVN Civic Action Rib, San Diego County Civic Apprec Awd and Certificates of Apprec from numerous law enforcement agencies in various states and Korea.

Resides with his wife Ellen from Toronto, Canada; they have two children, Ian and Dawn Lynne. Worked as a US Post Office city letter carrier in SATX from 1983 to retirement in 1992. He is seasonal worker at the Fiesta Texas as park services tech; researches USMC combat ops from the RVN War; is member of the SAR; 3rd Mar Div Assoc and MOPH.

GREGORY B. NICHOLS, CW2, USA, born Aug 6, 1950, in Salt Lake City, UT. Began his military career on April 7, 1969, taking USN boot camp at the NTC, San Diego, CA. Following initial training he attended Radioman A and C School, graduating in October 1969. On Christmas Eve 1969 he reported for duty aboard the USS *Hancock* (CVA-19) and for the next three years, participated in three combat Western Pacific tour cruises, which encompassed 22 1/2 months off the coast of Vietnam in the gulf of Tonkin.

On Jan 23, 1973, the day the Paris Peace Talks began, he was mustered from active service. Following eight years as a civilian, during which he received his bachelor's degree in information and communications studies from California State University, Chico, CA and nearly four years work as a newspaper photojournalist and reporter, he re-entered active military service on April 7, 1981.

Following a second basic training session, and subsequent initial counterintelligence training at Ft Huachuca, AZ, he was assigned to the 588th MI Det, 2nd Armd Div (FWD), Garlstedt, GE. In May 1983 he returned to Ft Huachuca for additional CI training and in July 1983, was assigned to the 902nd MI Gp, CI Det, Defense Nuclear Agency, Alexandria, VA.

In June 1984, he re-enlisted for European duty with the 527th MI Bn, Mainz, Germany. In May 1987, he reported to the WOEC, APG, MD for initial WO training. Following initial training and subsequent training at Ft Huachuca, AZ, and appointment as a USAWOA, he was assigned to the 201st MI Bde (communications, electronics warfare intelligence), Ft Lewis, WA. In January 1991, he was reassigned to the 527th MI Bn, Kaiserslautern, GE. With the reorganization of the Bn, his next assignment was to the 18th MI Bn (communications and electronics), Kaiserslautern, GE. In January 1994, he reported for duty to the Ft Monmouth Resident Office, 902nd MI Gp, Ft Monmouth, NJ.

Awards include the Joint Svc Comm Med, Army Comm Med w/2 OLCs, Army Achiev Med w/OLC, Good Conduct Med (3rd awd), Nat Def Rib (2nd awd), RVN Comm Med (3rd awd), Armed Forces Exped Med, NCOPDM, Army Svc Rib, Overseas Rib and VN Svc Med.

EDWARD E. NOSBAUM, CW2, USA (RET), born Nov 4, 1928, in Chicago, IL. Entered the US Army Jan 15, 1947; following basic training at Ft Knox, KY, he served with the MP Det at Oliver Gen Hosp in Augusta, GA.

Other assignments included the 709th MP Bn and the 62nd MP Hwy Patrol Co in Germany; the 505th MP Bn,

Presidio of San Francisco, CA; personnel NCO with V USA Corps, Frankfurt A/M, Germany; CCA, 1st Armd Div, Ft Hood TX; advisor to several USAR units in Northern California; administrative NCO at XV USAC and HQ, 6th Army, Presidio of San Francisco, CA; PSNCO with the 85th Evac Hosp, Vietnam, and PSNCO, 144th Sig Bn, 4th Armd Div, Germany.

Accepted appointment as WO in Dec 1968 and assigned to Cp Carrol Depot, Korea as depot personnel officer and adjutant; then assigned to the 212th FA Gp, Ft Lewis, WA as a unit personnel tech.

On July 1, 1971, he retired from the Army after having served on active duty for over 24 years. Returned to civilian life and accepted employment with the Dept of the Army, serving in various responsible positions with elements of the 91st Div (training), Ft Baker, Sausalito, CA until his retirement from active Federal Civil Service on March 31, 1993, with over 22 years of civil service.

Civilian awards include the Meritorious Civilian Svc Awd and the Superopr Civilian Svc Awd. Military awards include the Meritorious Svc Med w/OLC, Army Comm Med w/OLC and numerous service and campaign medals.

Married the former Edith Menges of Frankfurt A/M, Germany; they have two daughters and two grandsons. Lifetime member of TROA and a member of the USAWOA.

WILLIAM GEORGE O'BRIEN (OBIE), CW4, USA (Ret), born Oct 7, 1925, in Rochester, NY. Enlisted in the USN in October 1942, and was assigned Destroyer Escort 47 for USS *Decker*. Underwater Demolitions Naval Gun School, SEAL qualified and a qualified master diver; participated in the Normandy invasion on June 6, 1944, as a LST pilot landing troops. Participated in landings at Iwo Jima, Okinawa and Occupation of Japan. Discharged in April 1946.

Re-enlisted in the USAR in October 1952. Active duty, Korea, corporal 2nd ID, earned Combat Inf Badge. May 1, 1953, appoint WOJG, Trans Corps Marine Div. Mentored by "old warrants" of Mine Planter Service; was first officer and master on Army water craft. Diving officer, 50th Engr Co (Port Const), Korea. First diving officer, USS *Belgrove*, Arctic resupply.

Graduate of Army Flight School, Class 56-5, April 21, 1956, and assigned to Ft Sill, OK. Nuclear exposure test flights Desert Rock, AZ; Discharged in October 1959. Served as pilot for PHI; Sunshine Helicopter, Jacksonville, FL; Keystone Helicopter, South America; Kenting Helicopter and Autari Helicopter, Canada, Greenland.

Founder and vice president of Delta Marine Divers. Active duty in May 1964, 11th Air Assault, Ft Benning; 1964-65, Vietnam, med-evac to Tripler. Assigned to Ft Wolters, TX, qualified CH-54. Second tour to Vietnam; assigned to Ft Rucker; instructor, History of the WO at WO Career Ctr; awarded Master Aviator Wings; 1975-1976, Korea; chief, WO assignments. Returned Ft Rucker, AG Officer.

Retired Feb 1, 1986, with 32 years of active duty. He was one of only two WWII combat veterans still on active duty. Awards include the Combat Inf Badge, Master Aviator, Master Diver, (4) Bronze Star, Purple Heart, Air Med, 30 campaign and service ribbons.

O'Brien passed away on March 16, 1994, at his home in Ozark, AL. Interment in the Arlington National Cemetery. He is survived by his wife Elizabeth Ann and three daughters: Leilane, Sharon and Susan.

ROBERT C. O'DAY, CW4, born July 26, 1935, in Butler, PA. Enlisted in the US Army on Sept 8, 1953, as a food advisor tech. Stationed in Germany, France, Korea, Vietnam, Ft Knox and Ft Sam Houston.

Participated in the Vietnam campaigns from 1965-1970. Retired April 1, 1981, with the rank of CW4. Awards include the Bronze Star w/3 OLCs, Meritorious Svc Med w/4 OLCs, and the Army Comm Med w/3 OLCs.

Married and has four children. He is a Reserve Component Food Advisor, ACES at Ft Lee, VA.

KENNETH D. OLSON, CW4, USA (RET), born Dec 25, 1931, in Eagle Bend, MN. Entered the US Army June 20, 1949, with basic and clerical training at Ft Riley, KS. Served at Ft Jackson, SC and 1st Cav Div in Korea and Japan until discharged in October 1952. Re-enlisted October 1954 with retraining at Ft Leonard Wood, MO.

Served with the Nebr Mil Dist, 8th Inf Div, Ft Carson, CO; joined the 10th Inf Div (Gyroscope) at Ft Riley, KS; transferred to Germany. Served with the 2nd Inf Div at Ft Benning as Repl Sect pers sergeant and as NCOIC of Pers Mgmt Sect, Div Adj Gen Sect.

Appointed to WO in 1961; served with 35th Armor Bn and 8th Inf Div in Germany as Unit Pers Tech and special consultant to the div adj gen; returned to the US to attend MILPERS Off Crs and assigned to Scott AFB, IL. Reassigned to 223rd Avn Bn in Vietnam. Assigned as adj and unit pers tech for the 43rd Arty Bn (Msl) at Ft Richardson, AK; reassigned to the 4th Inf Div, Vietnam as security control officer for the G-1 Sect in 1970-73 and served as pers mgmt off, WO Assignments, Adj Gen Branch, Washington DC.

Awards include the Bronze Star w/3 OLCs, Meritorious Svc Med, Army Res Comp Med w/2 OLCs and numerous service and campaign medals.

Member of the USAWOA and a lifetime member of the VFW. Currently retired and residing in Minnesota. Married Diana Niemann of Breckenridge, MN; they have four sons and 11 grandchildren.

WILLIAM K. OLSON, ARNG, born June 20, 1945, in Newburgh, NY and raised in Charleston, WV and Westfield, NJ. Graduated Parsons College, Fairfield, IA with a BA in 1967; Seton Hall Univ with MA in 1973. Enlisted RA in 1968, attended basic training and AIT at Ft Dix, NJ; Track Vehicle Mechanic School, Ft Knox.

After serving as NCOIC of the Flagged Records Sect in the Armor School Pers Off, he was assigned to the 2nd Log Cmd on Okinawa as pers staff NCO for the Trans Bn (Prov). Released from active duty in 1971.

Enlisted in 1973 in the 2nd Bn, 102nd Armor, NJARNG as pers staff NCO. He was appointed WO1 in 1978 and assigned to the 5th Bn, 102nd Armor as unit pers tech. Upon reorganization of the 5th Bn in 1991, he was reassigned to HQ, State Area Cmd in the Office of MILPERSMGMT in 1992 as a military pers tech.

Awards include the Army Achiev Med, and Army Comm Med w/OLC.

Married Pamela Richter of Warren, NJ.

JACK W. PACE, CW4, USA (RET), born Jan 9, 1943, in Bellingham, WA and raised in Pacific Northwest. Entered the US Army from California in 1961 and served three years with the 82nd Abn Div, discharged and returned to school. Re-enlisted in January 1965 for the CI Agent Crs at Ft Holabird, MD with subsequent assignments as chief, Counterespionage Section, Seoul Field Office, Korea.

Received appointment to WO1 in 1968 with initial assignment as Staff CI Chief, G2, V Corps, Frankfurt, Germany. Was a charter member of Defense Investigative Svc with assignments as senior agent in charge of Camp Lejeune field office and Raleigh field office in North Carolina.

Overseas locations included specialty assignments in countering hostile intelligence espionage, sabotage and terrorist efforts with assignment locations in Korea, Germany and Vietnam. Subsequently selected for assignment to Staff, Proponency Office for MI at Ft Huachuca, AZ, where he served until he retired in 1985.

Education included two years at Coastal Carolina Community College, Jacksonville, NC and a host of military schools, including CI Agent, Criminal Investigator Crs, Area intel Off (RVN), abn training and technical courses relating physical security, sound and electronic emanations, as well as language training in Laotion and French. Was also a graduate of the WOSC at Ft Rucker, AL.

Awards include the Legion of Merit, Bronze Star, Meritorious Svc Med, Def Comm Med, Army Comm Med and Honor Medal from Vietnam.

Resides in Bellingham, WA and is past Exalted Ruler and active supporter of Bellingham Elks Lodge and the general manager of a major cordage manufacture in support of the Pacific Northwest Fishing Industry.

WALLACE BRUCE PAGE, CW2, USAR, born May 7, 1933, in Bronx, New York City, NY. Enlisted service from May 7, 1949-Feb 23, 1978, in the NYARNG, USN, US Army and USAR. Commissioned service, Feb 4, 1978-present.

Military Schools: WO College, Security Manager, Area Intelligence, Technical Intelligence and Staff Officer, Electronic Warfare, Interrogator, Physical Security, Nuclear, Biological and Chemical, Airborne, Ranger, Supply, and Jump Master. Also completed numerous correspondences in MP duties and CID.

Participated in the Korean War with the USN from 1950-54 and with the Army in Vietnam from 1968-70. Retired in November 1987 with the rank of CW2. Awarded the Army Comm Med, Army and Navy Good Conduct Med, NY State Meritorious Svc Medal, Sr Prcht Badge, Armed Forces Res Med and (2) Army Res Comm Med.

His civilian education included John Jay College BS degree in police science, 1975 and MPA in 1977. A licensed polygraph examiner in the state of Florida and worked as a NYC police officer, September 1959-February 1980.

GEORGE R. PATT, CW4, born Aug 13, 1930, in East Bridgewater, MA. Entered the US Army Sept 2, 1948, completed basic training at Ft Dix, NJ and Logistics School at Ft Lee, VA.

Served three years in Japan in direct support of the Korean War (two separate tours in Korea) one with Hawk BN and another with 280mm Arty; three years in Ethiopia (ASA); two tours in Vietnam, one with the 25th Div and one with Heli Maint Support plus a tour of duty in Europe. Also performed logistic duties at Ft Hood, TX; Ft Riley, KS; Pittsburgh Air Defense; Ft Benning, GA; Ft Bliss, TX and other locations.

Patt retired from the USA as a CW4 on Nov 30, 1978. His awards include the Bronze Star w/OLC, Army Comm Med w/3 OLCs, Good Conduct Med (4th awd), Nat Def Svc Med w/OLC, Korean Svc Med, UN Svc Med, VN Svc Med w/6 stars, RVN Camp Med w/60 device, Armed Forces Res Med, RVN Civil Action Med (2nd awd), RVN Cross of Gallantry w/Palm (unit) and Pres Unit Cit.

Married Helen Burris in 1951; they have two sons, Jerry and David, and two daughters, Sarah and Marsha.

DENNIS E. PATTERSON, CW3, USA (RET), born May 23, 1947, in Roswell, NM. Entered military service Nov 14, 1966; basic training at Ft Bliss, TX; AIT at Ft Holabird, MD where he trained as imagery analyst. Served two tours in Vietnam with the 519th MI BN, 525th MI GP with the Combined Intel Ctr Vietnam until his discharge July 1969.

Re-enlisted July 1971, proceeded to Ft Hood, TX and assigned to the 163rd MI BN until April 1972. In May 1972 transferred to Heidelberg, Germany as imagery analyst with the Imagery Intel Prod Div, HQ USAREUR and 7th Army. Returned to Ft Hood, TX and was assigned to the 15th MI BN, 504th MI GP.

Appointed to WO May 1979 and moved to Washington DC. From 1979-85 was assigned to the Intel Threat Analysis Center as imagery analyst in the science and technology arena; 1985-87, assigned to the 581st MI DET, 502nd MI BN in Zweibruecken, Germany; 1987-88, assigned to the 513th MI Bde, Ft Monmouth, NJ.

Retired Aug 1, 1988, as a CW3 with 20 years of service. Awards include the Legion of Merit, Meritorious Svc Med w/OLC, Army Comm Med, Army Good Conduct Med (2 awds), Nat Def Svc Med, VN Svc Med, RVN Cross of Gallantry w/Palm, VN Camp Med, Army Svc Rib and Overseas Svc Rib.

Married Viola Tankersley of Roswell, NM. Currently works for the Army with the Intel Threat Analysis Ctr in

Washington DC and is a free lance artist by avocation and a member of the Woodbridge Art Guild.

THOMAS L. PATTERSON, CW3, (RET) born Sept 4, 1917. Entered the US Army in November 1938 and assigned to MG Troop 12th Cav. Served as MG in 1st Cav, 91st Inf Div, 70th Inf Div during WWII, France and Germany. Met all requirements for aviation cadet training in October 1941, but could not meet call in January 1942.

Called in August 1946 for helicopter training but refused. Assigned to Ft Benning, GA from August 1946-February 1948 and attended Communications Chief Crs, instructor training; assigned to Communications Sector to teach international Morse Code; February 1948, assigned to Armed Forces Special Weapon Project and Atomic Energy Commission and assigned to two different stock pile sites.

August 1950, appointed WO, nuclear weapon assembly tech; August 1955, transferred to Japan; July 1958-March 1961, assigned to Ord Ammo Cmd. As a new equipment overseas training instructor, he taught firing and fusing of various nuclear weapons and made trips to the Far East, Germany, Alaska and Thule, Greenland.

Retired March 31, 1961. Awards include the Bronze Star, Good Conduct Med, Am Def, Nat Def, Am Camp, EAME and Pres Unit Cit. Worked at Red River Army Depot as nuclear weapon assembly, general foreman and integrated electrical system foreman, chaparral.

Married Myrtle Phillips and they have one daughter, one grandson and one great-granddaughter. Hobbies include traveling, fishing and amateur radio, W5UKY.

JOSEPH B. PAUL JR., WO1, born in 1919 in Pennsylvania. Enlisted in the Corps of Engineers in February 1941. Stationed in Melbourne, Sicily, New Guinea and the Philippines.

Memorable experiences included riding shotgun on a supply train from Manila and his 30 month stay in Melbourne.

Discharged with the rank WO1. He received all the usual awards and medals.

He is a resident at Fairview Nursing Home in Pennsylvania.

STANLEY W. PAYNE, CW4, RA (RET), born Dec 6, 1931, in Gallia County, OH. Began his military career in the Ohio State Guard and the OHNG. Enlisted in the RA in 1949 and served in Japan in GHQ from 1949-52. After discharge in 1952 he rejoined the OHNG until transferred to active duty in 1958, serving continuous active duty until his retirement as CW4 in 1974.

Active duty assignments included FECOM-Japan, USARPAC MAAG (Laos), USAREUR-Germany, ASARPAC (Okinawa), and USA Element Defense Mapping Agency, Washington, DC. Career highlights were working in conjunction with USIS, USOM, and the US Embassy in establishing a printing plant in Laos; serving as the operations officer of the 1st PSY OPS BTN, Okinawa while managing the printing plant in support of the psychological ops effort in Vietnam; serving as the assistant S-3 ops officer of the 656th Engr Bn (TOPO) while managing the Center Reproduction Plant (CRP); serving as the officer in charge of the reproduction portion of the Topographic Engr Officers Crs at the Defense Mapping School.

His occupations specialties were 831A map reproductions officer, 831AO map reproduction instructor, 832A psychological operations tech and 833A reproduction tech. Military schools included Jungle Warfare School, Topographic Engr Officer Crs and WO Intermediate Crs. Appointed WO W-1 in 1962, CW2 in 1964, Cw3 in 1968 and to CW4 in 1973.

Honored by being the first WO reproduction tech to be assigned to a psychological operations unit when he was ordered to report to the 7th Psychological Ops Gp in 1968.

Awards include the Army Comm Med w/OLC, Nat Def Svc Med w/OLC, Army of Occupation Med-Japan, UN Svc Med, Korean Svc Med, Good Conduct Med, Armed Forces Res Med, AF Exped Med, Joint Svc Comm Med, VN Svc Med, VN Camp Med and the Alabama Comm Med.

Married the former Rita Lyon of Marion, OH; they have two children and one grandchild. Lifetime member of the DAV; member of the VFW and American Legion.

VAUGHN R. PEERMAN, CWO3, born July 26, 1938, in Evansville, IN. Enlisted in the USAR Oct 6, 1960, received his direct appointment on March 19, 1983, and commissioned CWO on July 4, 1987.

Spent six months in training at Ft Knox, KY beginning on April 14, 1961. Duty assignments: enlisted service USAR 1960-83; USAR AGR (active duty), MPO, 78th Trng Div, Ft Dix, NJ, 1983-89; MPO, 123rd ARCOM, Ft Harrison, IN, 1989-91; MPO, 77th ARCOM, Ft Totten, NY, 1991-Present.

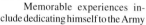

Memorable experiences include dedicating himself to the Army family and being awarded the Humanitarian Svc Med for his work in the 1982 flood relief effort at Ft Wayne, IN; sharing and caring attitude that insured that all soldiers and their families were properly cared for during the mobilization of Reserve Forces for the Persian Gulf War and his ability to inspire others to win in a time of need was outstanding, a truly professional soldier.

Awards include the Meritorious Svc Med w/2nd OLC, Army Comm Med w/2nd OLC, Army Achiev Med w/3rd OLC, Nat Def Svc Med w/BS, Humanitarian Svc Awd, Army Res Comp Overseas Trng Rib and Army Excellence in Competition Badge, Bronze, Pistol.

Still on active duty; current assignment MPO for the 77th Army Reserve Cmd headquartered at Ft Totten, NYC, for his over 32 years of outstanding military service and devotion to duty.

Married Patricia Vaupel of Evansville, IN.

JOHN M. PELOSE, CW2 (P), USAR, born Sept 28, 1946, in Nashville, TN. Began his military career in January 1967; basic training at Ft Benning, GA and AIT at Ft Gordon, GA. Served in Vietnam, 1967-68; Picatinny Arsenal, 1968-70 with the US Army Spec Sec Gp, ACSI, DA. After release from active duty in 1970, he completed requirements for an AB degree from the Boston College and a MS degree from Simmons College.

Re-entered the USAR in September 1975 with the 505th ASA CO, Ft Devens, MA and served in various leadership positions up to and including field 1st sergeant. Appointed WO in 1985 with assignment as communications security tech for the 187th Inf Bde (SEP), Ft Devens, MA.

Awards include the Army Comm Med w/2 OLCs, Army Achiev Med, Good Conduct Med, Nat Def Svc Med, Vietnam Svc Med, Armed Forces Res Med, Army Res Comp Achiev Med, Army Svc Med, Army Res Overseas Trng Rib w/#8, RVN Camp Med.

Married the former Gloria Joy Crawley and they have two children, Jennifer Beth and Michael Philip. They reside in Braintree, MA. Employed at the Boston Public Library as a librarian-manager responsible for automated cataloging and telecommunications.

HERBERT R. PENNINGTON JR., CW3, USA (RET), born April 11, 1931, in Fairfield, IL. Enlisted in the US Army April 19, 1949, attended basic training at Ft Chaffee, AR and served with the 2nd Inf Div in CONUS and Korea; then the 101st Abn Div, where he became sergeant major of the 3rd Bn, 53rd Abn Inf Regt, at 20 years of age.

After school tours he served at Ft Myer, VA; 2nd Army HQ, Ft Meade, MD as administrative assistant to deputy CG, 2nd Army; post sergeant major, Cp, Breckinridge, KY at the age of 26. Appointed WO, AGC, April 28, 1961, and served

in Germany, Ft Leonard Wood, MO and Vietnam. Returned to Ft Wood for a final tour as chief, officer assignment branch.

Retired May 31, 1969. Awards include the Meritorious Svc Med, Army Comm Med w/OLC, Good Conduct Med, Nat Def Svc Med, Korean Svc Med, VN Svc Med, Armed Forces Res Med, UN Svc Med (Korea), RVN Cross of Gallantry, RVN Camp Med and numerous unit and individual citations.

Married Anna Paul of Newburgh, IN; they have four children and nine grandchildren.

EUGENE L. PERRINO SR., CW3, born July 17, 1959. Entered the US Army July 10, 1978; assignments include Ft Jackson, SC; Ft Gordon, GA; Ft Campbell, KY; Ft Bragg, NC; Germany; APG, MD; two tours to Korea; and two tours to Ft Stewart, GA.

He was the bn maint officer for the 24th Inf Div, Ft Stewart, GA during Operation Desert Storm and Desert Shield. Presently assigned to the 124th MI BN, Ft Stewart, GA; MOS includes 63B, 76C, 630A, and 915A.

Received the Bronze Star, Meritorious Svc Med, Army Comm Med w/4 OLCs, Army Achiev Med w/3 OLCs, Meritorious Unit Comm, Army Good Conduct Med-3, SWA Svc Med w/2 BSs, NCOPDR and SAKULIBM.

He married Kathy and they have two sons, Eugene Jr and Michael.

HENNING PETERSEN, MW4, USA (RET), born Dec 23, 1938, in Asserballeskov, Denmark. Drafted into the US Army July 28, 1961; basic training at Ft Ord, CA and AIT at Ft Eustis, VA; Jan 15, 1962, assigned to the 75th Trans Co (heavy boat), Inchon, Korea.

Returned in late 1964 to the States and assigned to the 344th Trans Co (LARC), Ft Story, VA. 1967-68 performed two tours of duty in Qui Nhon, Vinh Long, Mekong Delta in RVN and in Pusan, Korea; returned to Ft Eustis, VA to attend Harbor Craft Deck Off and Marine Radar Observer's Courses.

Appointed WO1 in 1969; assigned to the 612th Trans Co (HB); returned to RVN for tour of duty at Cat Lai; assigned to the 384th Trans Det, Naha, Okinawa, Japan; attended the WOAC; selected to command the 469th Trans Det, USAV LTC *John U.D. Page.*

Returned in 1977 to Korea, Port Terminal, Pusan; 73rd Trans Co (HB), Ft Eustis, VA; Coast Guard Marine Inspection and Safety School en route to Military Traffic Mgmt Cmd (MTMC), Azores, Portugal; 1984 assigned to the 5th Trans Co (HB), Ford Island, HI for duty in the USAV LTC *John UD Page*; attended the Def Basic Traffic Mgmt Crs and the Gen Trans of Haz Mat Crs and assigned to the 45th Gen Spt Gp, Ft Shafter, HI; assigned to the 10th Trans Bn (TML); attended MWO Trng Crs; 1992-93, tour of duty in Mogadishu, Somalia with the 710th Trans Co (HB).

Retired Aug 31, 1994. Awards: Bronze Star, Purple Heart Med, Meritorious Svc Med w/OLC, Joint Svc Comm Med, Army Comm Med w/3 OLCs, Army Achiev Med, Army Good Conduct Med, service awards and foreign awards.

DAVID MICHAEL PETERSON, CW2, born Dec 30, 1958, in Berwick, PA. Enlisted in the US Army on Dec 30, 1975, taking basic training at Ft Dix, NJ. Assignments included C Co, 1st Bn, 5th Inf Regt, 25th Inf Div, Schofield Bks, Hawaii, 1976-1980; 227th GS CO, Eagle Spt Bde, 101st Abn Div, Ft Campbell, KY, 1980-1984; Wilkes-Barre Recruiting Station, Scranton Rctg Co, Harrisburg Rctg Bn, 1984-1987; HSC 6th S&T Bn, 6th Inf Div (L), Ft Wainwright, AK, 1987-90; promoted to sergeant first class; appointed WO1 on March 12, 1991, at Ft Lee, VA; B Co, 324th Spt Bn, 3rd Bde, 24th In Div (M), Ft Benning, GA, 1991-93; current assignment is with the 598th Maint Co, 13th CSB, 36th Engr Gp, Ft Benning, GA.

Attended Inf AIT, 1976; Mat Storage and Handling Specialist Crs, 1980; BNCOC, honor graduate, 1987; ANCOC, distinguished honor graduate, 1990; WOEC, 1990; WO Technical and Tactical Certification Crs, honor graduate, 1991.

Awards include the Army Res Comp Med w/3 OLCs, Army Achiev Med w/2 OLCs, NCOPDR w/3, Overseas Svc Rib w/2, Gold Recruiter Badge (5th awd), Army Svc Rib and Good Conduct Med (5th awd).

Married the former Jimmel Lee Gordon of Berwick, PA and has one daughter Elizabeth Ann. He is member of the WOA Nat and Forever Forward WOA, Ft Benning, GA.

RONALD G. PETERSON (PETE), CW3, USA (RET), born Aug 25, 1939, in New Britain, CT. Entered the USAF on Aug 5, 1957. While serving in a recon unit at Barkdale AFB (Shreveport, LA) he applied for his warrant in MI and was accepted in November 1967 while stationed at Clark AFB Philippines. Discharged from the AF and sworn in the Army on the same day in Manila.

After WO Orientation Crs at Ft Sill, his first Vietnam tour started in Long Binh in April 1968. Most of the year was spent in the back seat of an 0-1 Cessna participating in the hand held camera program. After two 'years at Ft Carson, CO it was back to CICV (Combined Intel Ctr Vietnam). From 1972-76 he was assigned to the National Photographic Interpretation Center in Washington DC and gave numerous briefings in the Pentagon and DC area before retiring at Ft Hood, TX in August 1977.

Awards include the Bronze Star, Joint Svc Comm Med, Air Med and non-crew member wings.

Married Linda and has four children and 10 grandchildren. A banker in Victoria, TX, he stays busy with his children, grandchildren, woodworking, travel and golf.

DONALD G. PFEIFFER, CW3, USAR, born Nov 21, 1947, in Annapolis, MD. Entered the US Army May 19, 1968; basic training at Ft Jackson, SC; AIT at Ft Monmouth, NJ. As fixed microwave radio repair he was stationed in Teague, Korea for 23 months, Cp Walker Communications Center. Discharged on Dec 11, 1970, from Ft Lewis, WA.

Rejoined the USAR 399th Cbt Spt Hosp in December 1976; attended FAMC 35G and 35T Bio Med Eng Repr School, Denver, CO, 1977-78; graduated and returned to 399th CSH. Applied for and received appointment to WO position at the 804th Hosp Ctr AFB, MA, October 1979. Selected in May 1993 for promotion to CW4 and presently assigned to the 804th Med Bde. Member of USAWOA and president of Ch 17 of ROA.

Married Maj Audrey MacLeod, USAR, ANC; they have two children, Alastair and Marjorie.

DONALD DALLAS PIERCE, CW4, USA, born in February 1953 and raised in Hampton, VA. Awarded a ROTC scholarship to Texas A&M. Won the draft lotto and entered basic training in March 1973, Ft Polk, LA. Member of the Omega Flight, last class at Ft Wolters, TX.

Scout pilot for several cal units, Ft Hood and Korea; attended Instructor Pilot and Maint Officer Courses; unit maint off, Korea, Germany and Ft Sill, OK. Instructor; Maint Test Pilot Crs, Ft Eustis, VA; Bde maint off for 82nd Abn, Ft Bragg, NC; 1st Inf Div, Ft Riley, KS. Awarded degree in Avn Maint Mgmt from Embry Riddle Univ; graduated WO Advanced and Senior Courses.

Awards include Sr Aviator Badge, Meritorious Svc Med, Army Comm Med, Army Achievement Med, Army Good Conduct Med, Nat Def Svc Med, Army Svc Rib and Overseas Svc Rib.

Married Lynn Simpson of Madison, SD; they have two sons, Don Jr and Joshua, and a daughter Victoria.

JAMES L. PIERCE, CWO2 (RET), born April 20, 1924, in Pine Bluff, AR. Enlisted in the US Army May 26, 1961. Stations from 1943-53: Panama, college, Korea and Ft Hood, TX. From 1953-66 at Ft Sam Houston; Ft Ord Language School (Spanish); Lima, Peru; Panama; Ft Eustis, VA Ft Benning, GA; Ft Bliss, TX; Ft Bragg, NC; Venice and Verona, Italy; Edgmont, PA.

Retired July 31, 1966, with the rank of CW2; transferred to the USAR; last duty assignment was with the HQ Btry, 3rd Bn (HERC), 43rd Arty, HQ ARADCOM. Awards include the UN Svc Med, Army of Occupation Med, Pres Unit Cit (ROK), Armed Forces Res Med, Nat Def Svc Med w/2nd OLC and Korean Svc Med w/SS and BSS.

Married Janis Scogin on June 15, 1952.

RENZIE M. POE JR., CW4 (RET), born Nov 10, 1929, in Kennedy, AL. Drafted into the US Army Aug 9, 1951; basic training at Ft Jackson, SC. Served as heavy weapons squad leader with the 40th Inf Div in Korea, 1952 as CPL; reassigned to the 47th Ord Bn at Ft Rucker, AL January 1953; promoted to SSG (E-5) in March 1953.

Discharged and re-enlisted in May 1953; promoted to SFC (E-6) in November 1953. From 1954-67 served with 703rd Maint Bn, 3rd Inf Div, Ft Benning; assigned to 725th Maint Bn, 25th Inf Div, Hawaii; US Army Garrison, Ft Douglas; 30th Ord Co, Korea; Co D, 705th Maint Bn, Ft Devens; promoted to SFC (E-7) and assigned to the 196th (L) Inf Bde, Ft Devens and in Vietnam.

Assigned 1967-83 at Tooele Army Depot, UT; appointed to WO1, armament tech; reassigned to 543rd HEM Co, Hanau, Germany; HQ Co, 707th Maint Bn, 7th Inf Div, Cp Casey, Korea; reassigned to the 503rd HEM Co, Ft Bragg; reassigned to D Co, 708th Maint Bn, Mainz, Germany; reassigned to the 556th Maint Co and the 701st Maint Bn, 1st Inf Div, Ft Riley.

Retired 1983 at Ft Riley with over 31 1/2 years of active military service. Awards include the Good Conduct Med (5th awd), Army Comm Med w/OLC, AF Exped Med, UN Svc Med, Combat Inf Badge, Korean Svc Med, VN Svc Med w/2 BS, Overseas Svc Rib w/#6, VN Camp Med, Bronze Star w/OLC, VN Cross of Gallantry w/Palm, Meritorious Svc Med w/OLC, and NCOPDR #1.

Married 37 years to Lula Marie Madison of Newbern, AL; they have four children and six grandchildren. Presently employed by the US Government Contractor (CSI) at Post

Locksmith and armament tech at Ft Riley, KS. Vice president of the ROA, member of the WOA, American Legion, VFW, NRA and NASA.

JAMES C. PRESTON, MW4 (RET), born Jan 22, 1943, in Bessemer, AL. Joined the US Army June 15, 1960, and appointed WO on June 30, 1967, after completion of Heli Flt School. Assigned to the 7th Sqdn, 1st Cav at Ft Knox, KY and deployed with them to RVN in January 1968.

In June 1968 assigned to the 121st Avn Btry where he flew *Viking Surprise*. Second tour from November 1970-November 1971 where he served with the Cobra Nett Team, which was later renamed the 5th Avn Det.

Awards include the Legion of Merit, Meritorious Svc Med w/OLC and numerous others.

Married Donna Jan 25, 1964, in Bessemer, AL; they have two sons. Retired and living in Anniston, AL, he is a member of the ROA, National Officers Assoc, the Amateur Softball Assoc (ASA) and the International Softball Assoc.

DENNIS D. PRICE, CW4, born May 19, 1952. Joined the US Army and served with the 321st MI Co, Paducah, KY and the 325th MI Co, Louisville, KY.

Married Deborah and has two sons, Patrick and Andrew. Presently serving with the CI, 325th MI Co in Louisville, KY.

JOHN D. PRIMAVERA, CW3, USA (RET), born Aug 7, 1922, in Philadelphia, PA. Entered the US Army in December 1943. After basic training and engineering training at Ft Belvoir, VA, he served with the 138th Engr Cbt Bn, Co C.

Participated in the Central Europe and Rhineland campaigns. Appointed WO in 1959 and served as maint tech and MTO for various Arty units; staff and faculty (instructor) service school; developed four complete maint mgmt training courses for inclusion in schools curriculum.

His memorable experiences include a reunion with a neighbor at the American Red Cross in Munich, Germany, prior to boarding the famous 40 & 8 box cars for travel to Bremerhaven, NG destined for Stateside demobilization.

Retired in May 1946 as CW3 with over 25 years of service. Awards include the Good Conduct Med, Am Camp, EAME w/2 campaign stars, WWII Victory Med, Army of Occupation Med w/Germany Clasp, Armed Forces Res Med w/2 devices, Army Res Comp Achiev and a diploma from the USA Ord Center and School.

Married Antoinette D'Alessandro of Philadelphia, PA. Member of the USAWOA, MOWW, Rhin Et Danue and 138th ECB Assoc and is a 4th degree K of C. Currently involved in local and county senior adult programs and plays banjo in a string band.

LUIS E. RAIGOSA, CW2, USA, born Jan 3, 1955, in Columbia, South America. Entered the US Army June 10, 1980; basic training at Ft Jackson; AIT at the Academy of Health Sciences, (MOS 91R). Assigned as procurement inspector in Germany from 1987-89; worked as operation NCO for the Veterinary Det Europe.

Received direct appointment in January 1990 to WO1 as veterinary services tech (640A) and subsequently reassigned to Ft Riley, KS. This position closed after his departure in 1991; reported to Subic Bay, a few days after the eruption of Mt Pinatubo.

In November 1991 he received his promotion to CW2 and after his departure in September 10 1992, this assignment closed along with the closure of all military bases in the Philippines. As of September 1993, he is serving as the OIC of the Food Inspection Branch in San Diego.

Awards include the Meritorious Svc Med w/OLC, Army Comm Med w/2 OLCs, (4) Army Achiev Med, (3) Overseas Svc Ribs, Army Good Conduct Med (4th awd) and the NCOPDR.

HOWARD G. RAPPOLD, CWO4, USA (RET), born March 26, 1927, in Baltimore, MD. A college graduate from the upper Iowa Univ. in 1975 in public administration (Magna Cum Laude). Joined the US Army and served as an infantry soldier and med tech, March 1945-December 1946.

Attended Basic Special Agent Crs at Ft Holabird, MD, July-Oct 1948; special agent, 66th CIC Det Germany, January 1949-May 1952; CI Agent, 513th INTC Gp Berlin, Germany, December 1961-November 1964; SAIC 113th INTC Gp Denver, CO, March 1965-November 1966.

Special agent and asst S-2 3rd Bde, 25th Inf Div, Vietnam, November 1966-November 1967; SAIC 115th MI Gp Seattle, WA, December 1967-May 1969; operations officer, Defense Attaché Office State Dept, Kuala Lumpur Malaysia, August 1969-August 1971.

Instructor in CI Courses in MI School, Ft Huachuca, AZ, September 1971-July 1973; case supervisor, Defense Investigative Service HQ, Washington DC, August 1973-January 1976; appointed WOJG, April 1954, in MI, Baltimore, MD.

Retired as CWO4 in January 1976 at Ft Meyers, VA. Received the Combat Inf Badge, (2) Purple Hearts and Bronze Star.

In civilian life was a county police officer for six years, investigator for Dept of Defense overseas for three years, polygraph examiner for private security firm for seven years and Deputy US Marshal for seven years.

Rappold married Geraldine Adamson over 42 years ago. Retired and lives in Florida. Charter member of the USAWOA in 1972.

CURTIS W. RANDOLPH, CW2, USA, born Oct 12, 1955, in London, England. From 1981-92 he attended basic combat training, Ft Knox, KY; Walter Reed Army Medical Center, Washington DC; NCOIC, US Army MEDDAC, Ft Polk, LA; NCOIC Anesthesia Sect, US Army Med Mat Ctr, Europe, APO NY; Medical Maint Branch, Brook AMC, Ft Sam Houston, TX; 312th Evac Hosp, Damman, Saudi Arabia.

New Brooke Project Office, Ft Sam Houston, TX; Med Equip and Optical School, Aurora, CO; Primary Leadership Development Crs, USA 5th Inf Div, Ft Polk, LA; Basic Noncommissioned Officer's Crs, Ft Sam Houston, TX; WO Orientation, Ft Rucker, AL; Health Serv Maint Tech Crs, Ft Sam Houston, TX; Supervisor Development Program, Ft Sam Houston, TX; and presently stationed at New Brooke Project Office, SGFP-PM-35, Brooke Army Med Center, Medic Equip Specialist, Ft Sam Houston, TX.

Received his BS degree in business administration in 1993 from Wayland Baptist Univ, TX and AS degree in biomedical engineering in 1987 from Regis College, Denver, CO.

Awards include the Meritorious Svc Med, Army Comm Med w/3 OLCs, Army Achievement Med w/OLC, Nat Def Svc Med, SWA Svc Med w/2, NCOPDR w/2, Army Svc Rib, Overseas Svc Rib and Kuwait Lib Med.

Married the former Paulette Simmons in July 1980; they have two children, Curtis Samuel and Nessira Paulette. President of South Texas Biomedical Instrumentation Society, member of the Assoc for the Advancement of Medical Instrumentation, National Fire Protection Assoc and Beacon Light Lodge F&AM.

JOSEPH B. RAY, CW4, USA, born in Karlsruhe, Germany as part of a military family. After many CONUS and OCONUS assignments, home is not atop the western Bull Run Mountains in Haymarket, VA.

Received BA (Magna Cum Laude) from St Leo College and graduated on the dean's list with MBA from Troy State Univ. Completed the WOSC, Off DP Crs, as well as a myriad of other IBM, Honeywell and Cabletron software, hardware and communications courses.

Completed one tour in Vietnam, four tours in Germany, and one tour at the Pentagon. As a family member in 1960, he saw the Berlin Wall being built and in 1991, as a soldier, saw the wall being dismantled. His job was to reduce the number of computer facilities from 14 to two; personnel from 576 to 204; eliminating all military personnel from the facilities. The mission was accomplished in November 1993.

Awards include the Def Meritorious Svc Med, (3) Army Meritorious Svc Med, Joint Svc Comm Med, (2) ARCMs, Army Achiev Med, Nat Def Svc Med, VN Svc Med and VN Camp Med.

His wife Donna, also an Army brat, has served in support of soldiers and families at the installation level as a staff and director of the Army Community Svc Program; as a division chief at USAREUR and HQDA and now insures that the Army receives an adequate proportion of the Defense budget to support soldiers and families. She does all this while parenting two daughters, Melissa (an Army wife) and Jennifer (active duty soldier).

BENJAMIN A. REED, enlisted in the USA and served most of his enlisted status as a 1st sergeant in armored units. Appointment for WO was made, accepted and he was pinned WOJG Dec 28, 1951. Served as unit administrator in his company until February 1952, then assigned to M Co, 160th Inf, 40th Inf Div in Korea, serving as UA and plt leader, then assigned to the 522nd Inf Bn, Ft Sill, OK.

Applied for the Aircraft Maint Officer Crs at Spartan Aero School, Tulsa, OK, graduating in August 1954. Assigned to 3rd Cbt Avn Co, 3rd Inf Div as maint officer; spent three years on the AFTA tests and expanded avn activities in the Army. In 1957 he was assigned to the 245th Acft Maint Co in Germany and the 41st Bn as a maint officer. Assignment was curtailed for attendance at A&E School at Embry Riddle Aero School, Miami, FL, then to Ft Eustis, VA to serve as an instructor in the Avn Maint Dept.

In 1962 was sent to Korea for assignments as a contracting officer's representative with the Korean AF on an Army aircraft overhaul contract to oversee quality control and production scheduling. Next assignment was with the Army Material Cmd Field Office, Ft Benning, GA as aircraft maint and supply coordinator, developing the 11th Air Assault Div and finally the 1st Cav Airmobile Div.

Shipped out to Vietnam and assigned to the 610th TC Acft Maint Co as maint and quality control officer. The unit was shipped to RVN to perform 4th Echelon support for the 1st Cav and 101st Abn. From RVN he was assigned to the Trans School Avn Dept where he served until his retirement on March 1, 1969.

Participated in Rhineland and Central Europe during WWII; 2nd Korean Winter, Korean Summer and Fall 1952, 3rd Korean Winter, Korean Summer and Fall 1953 during Korean War; VN Counteroffensive 1965-66, VN Counteroffensive Phase II, and VN Counteroffensive Phase III during Vietnam War.

Retired from active duty on March 1, 1969, with the rank of CW4. Awards included the Combat Inf Badge, Bronze Star, Air Med, Army Comm Med w/3 OLCs, Good Conduct Med, Am Theater Med, ETO Med w/2 BS, Victory Med, Occupation Med w/Germany Clasp, Nat Def Svc Med w/OLC, Res Med w/HG, Korean Svc Med w/4 BS, UN Svc Med, VN Svc Med w/3 BS, RVN Camp Med w/60 D, RVN Cross of Gallantry w/Palm, Pres Cit Badge, Korean Pres Unit Cit Badge w/OLC, RVN Unit Cit Badge w/palm and Sr Acft Crewman Badge.

Married Irma Goyette Oct 14, 1949. Retired real estate broker and lives in Florida; he is active in the VFW and community activities.

EDDIE R. REED, CWO3 (RET), born Feb 3, 1947, in Richmond, IN. Enlisted in the US Army Oct 2, 1964, as a general supply tech. Attended basic training and AIT at Ft Knox, KY; assigned to Btry C, 4th Msl Bn, 57h ADA, Furth Germany; 506th Fld Depot, Vietnam; Co A USASAFS, Herzogenaurach, Germany and US Army Recruiting Cmd, Freeport, IL.

Assigned to HHB III Corps Arty, Ft Sill, OK; 409th ASA Co, 502nd ASA Gp, Augsburg, Germany; HHC 504th ASA Gp, Hunter AAF, GA; 24th Inf Div MMC, Hunter AAF, GA; Tuslog Det 4, Sinop, Turkey; Co D, 1st Bn, Ltng Bde, Ft Knox, KY; HHT 1st Sqdn, 2nd ACR, Bindlach, Germany; Readiness Gp Sheridan, Ft Sheridan, IL; 1st QM WOAC in 1982.

Retired March 1, 1987, with the rank of CW3. Awards include the Meritorious Svc Med w/3 OLCs, Army Comm Med w/2 OLCs, Army Good Conduct Med (3 awds), Nat Def Svc Med, VN Svc Med, VN Camp Med w/60 D, VN Cross of Gallantry w/Palm, Army Svc Rib, Overseas Svc Rib (3) and Armed Forces Res Med.

Married Susan Horigan and has two daughters, Sherry and Kimberly. He has worked for NCR Corp in Dayton, OH since retirement.

WILLIAM S. REID, CW4, USA (RET), born March 29, 1950, in Royal Oak, MI, and raised in Valparaiso, IN. Entered the Army in October 1969; basic training at Ft Campbell, KY and AIT (stock control, accounting and mechanized stock control) Ft Lee, VA. Duty assignments from 1970-76 included Korea, HQ&HQ, A Co, 55th Maint Bn; 620th Sup Co, Ft Carson, CO; Korea, 1st Sig Bde (AMSF); Fitzsimons Army Med Ctr, Denver, CO. Held various positions up through supply NCOIC with the rank of staff sergeant. Appointed WO1 July 8, 1976, as general support tech and transferred to the 1st Inf Div, Ft Riley, KS.

Stations 1976-93, Korea, 1st Bn, 2nd ADA; 9th Inf Div (mech), Ft Lewis, WA,; Germany, 142nd S&S Bn; Germany, 29th S&S Co; 9th Inf Div (motorized), Ft Lewis, WA; Yemen, LOGTAFT; 274th SSD, 7th ID (L), Ft Ord, CA.

Participated in Desert Shield and Republic of Yemen. Attended the Intermediate Level Supply System Mgmt Crs, Directorate of Industrial Ops Crs, QM WOAMC; Sup Mgmt Crs and Electronic Warfare Off Crs, Ft Riley, KS.

Retired on June 30, 1993. Awards include the Meritorious Svc Med w/OLC, Army Comm Med w/OLC, (2) Army Good Conduct Med, (2) Nat Def Svc Med, SWA Svc Med w/star, Armed Forces Exped Med, Army Achiev Med, (4) Overseas Svc Rib and Army Svc Rib.

Married Toddy Lynn Woods of Valparaiso, IN, and has two sons, Jason and Travis. Life member of the WOA; member of TROA, AUSA and NMRA. Received his AA degree in 1982 from Pierce College, Tacoma, WA.

ROBERT RENN, CWO3, USA, born Aug 31, 1932, in New Bedford, MA. Entered the USMCR, 12th Amphib Tractor Bn; September 1949 enlisted in the US Army with basic training at Ft Ord, CA; transferred overseas with the 85th Engr Boat Co assigned to the 39th Topo Bn, at Cavite, P.I.

Unit transferred to Cp McGill, Japan with eventual duties at Inchon, Korea. Re-enlisted in 1952 in MP Corps and assigned to Presidio of San Francisco, 505th MP Bn. Completed Adv MP School, Cp Gordon; 18 months patrol duty. Transferred to the Armed Forces Police Det, Honolulu, HI.

Returned to CONUS and assigned to the Armed Forces Police Det, Treasure Island, CA until July 1959; served with the 55th MP Co in Korea until August 1960. Returned to CONUS and assigned to the 163rd MP Co, PSFC as an MPIS investigator with the local CID office. Attended Criminal Investigative School, Cp Gordon, GA and assigned to Det B, 6th MP (CID) Gp, PSFC. In September 1963 reassigned to the Army Log Ctr, TOKOROZAWA, Japan.

Transferred to Cp Zama; TDY in Bangkok; returned to Japan; assigned duties in Vietnam in December 1969. First five months of duty was an exciting undercover assignment in Saigon which cumulated in the seizure and arrest of large amounts of currency, contraband and black marketer's.

Balance of tour consisted of commanding CID Det E at Qui-Nhon, Vietnam, until his return to CONUS in December 1970. Awarded the Bronze Star, Army Comm Med w/OLC and others.

Retired at Presidio of San Francisco, CA. Began work Nov 1, 1971, as senior and chief criminal investigator at the Marin County District Attorney's Office where on Nov 8, 1982, he retired. After working as a private investigator for several years, he retired to his home in Lake Tahoe. Divorced and has two children.

GEORGE T. RENO (TED), CW5, USA, born Aug 18, 1937, in Long Beach, CA. Began his WO career on Nov 12, 1962, as maint officer for the 1st Bn, 63rd Armor, Ft Riley, KS. For the next 16 years he served with various combat arms and support units. From 1979-82 he was the ordnance assignment officer, WO Div, USA MILPERCEN.

Moved to the Office Chief of Ordnance, APG, where he participated in the total WO study and development of the first formal WO training system. In 1987 he became maint officer for the 7th Army Trng Cmd, Grafenwoehr, Germany, where he developed the maint support plan for the newly activated Cbt Mnvr Trng Ctr in Hohenfels.

Returned to the Office Chief of Ordnance in January 1992 and on Oct 1, 1992, became the first RA WO to be promoted to CW5. Overseas tours included Korea, Germany, Vietnam, Thailand and Hawaii.

Awards include the Legion of Merit, Bronze Star w/ OLC, Meritorious Svc Med w/2 OLCs, Army Comm Med w/ 4 OLCs and the Army Achiev Med w/OLC. Education includes BS degree from Troy State Univ, WOSC and MWOTC.

Married the former Gerry Elzenga; they have four children: George Jr, John, Rochelle, Michael, and six grand-children.

PAUL B. RICHARD, CW4, USA (RET), born Feb 22, 1940, in Baltimore, MD. Entered the US Army Dec 18, 1961; basic training at Ft Jackson, SC; completed AIT at Ft Holabird, MD as an image interpreter. Served at HQ USARPAC, Ft Shafter, HI from 1962-65; served at the 497th Recce tech in Wiesbaden, Germany as member of Det A, 2nd MIBARS from 1965-68.

Appointed WO in 1968 as an image interpretation tech 962A; served in the 73rd Surveillance Airplane Co at Vung Tau, RVN, 1968-69; in the 203rd MI CO, III Corps, Ft Hood, TX, 1970-71; and in the 131st Airplane Co (SA) in Hue-Phu Bai, RVN, 1971-72.

In 1971 he attended the Defense Sensor Interpretation and Applications Training Program (DSIATP) at Offutt AFB, NE and was the first WO honor graduate. In Washington DC served in the Spec Activities Div, USAINTC, 1972-78; attended the WOSC, Ft Rucker, AL in 1978; returned to Washington and served in the Image Intel Prod Div of USAITAC.

Retired as CW4 July 31, 1983. Awards include the Legion of Merit, Bronze Star w/OLC, Air Med, Meritorious Svc Med, Army Comm Med, Good Conduct Med, Nat Def Svc Med, Overseas Svc Rib, VN Svc Med w/5 Campaign Stars and Air Crewman Badge while serving as observer and sensor operator during combat missions in the OV-1 Mohawk surveillance airplane.

Married Harriet Heil of Catonsville, MD and has three children. Employed by Autometric, Inc, Alexandria, VA as a senior imagery analyst coordinating support to military operations. He is a member of the Nat Mil Intel Assoc and the USAWOA.

JAMES C. RICHARDS, CW3, USA (RET), born June 6, 1946, in Oceanside, NY. Began his USN career Sept 19, 1965, in Attack Sqd 72 (VA-72) NAS Oceana, VA; Patrol Sqd 18 (VP-18) NAS Roosevelt Roads, P.R.; Heavy Attack Sqd 21 (VAH-21); USS *Franklin D Roosevelt*; USS *John F Kennedy*. Discharged in 1969.

Recalled to active duty in 1975; served in the following units: Patrol Sqd 64 (VP-64) Nas Willow Grove, PA; Patrol Sqd 94 (VP-94) NAS New Orleans, LA; Patrol Sqd 69 (VP-69). Interservice transfer to USAWO and Flight Program; graduated Flt Sch (1983) and assigned to C Trp 4/6, 6th Cav Bde and C Co, 227th Avn Bn, 1st Cav Div, Ft Hood, TX. Went to Honduras as UH-1 pilot flying missions in Honduras and El Salvador and made many trips to SOCOM Panama.

Returned to States in 1987; transferred to Ft Eustis for Avn Maint and Test Pilot Crs and Ord and Wpns Crs. Departed Ft Eustis for Ft Lewis, WA and the 228th ATK Bn. Returned twice to Central America in support of the units missions in Honduras, El Salvador and a new mission in Panama (was present for the downfall of dictatorship in 1989).

Returned to the States in 1989 and attached to several units; finally to C Co 214th from where he retired in 1991. Awards: Meritorious Svc Med, USN Air Med (5th awd w/v), Army Comm Med, Army Achiev, Good Conduct Med (2nd awd USN), Nat Def Svc Med w/BS, VN Svc Med w/3 stars (USN), Humanitarian Svc Med (USN), RVN Civil Actions Med (USN), RVN Cross of Gallantry w/Palm (USN), RVN Spec Svc Med (USN), Armed Forces Exped Med (USN) and numerous ribbons, unit citations and badges.

Married Kathi White and has two children, Kyla and Adam. Currently employed by Washington State Patrol. Memberships in 1st Cav Div Assoc, TROA, Vietnam Veterans of American Assoc, USS *FDR* CV-42 Assoc, USS *JFK* CV-67 Assoc, WOA.

ALLAN E. RICKARD, CW4, USA (RET), born Dec 23, 1938, in Wood Stock, VA. Commissioned 2nd lieutenant QMC from ROTC July 28, 1961 and entered active duty at Ft Lee, VA Nov 29, 1961, serving in a commissioned status in the following positions: maint and util officer, AC/S G4, Ft Lee, VA, 1962-64; club officer and asst S4, US Army School of the Americas, Panama, 1964-67; S4, 7th RRFS, Udorn, Thailand, 1968-69.

Chief, Sup Div, DCSLOG, US Army Intel Cmd, Ft Holabird, MD, 1969-70; subsistence staff officer, G4, HQUASARV, Long Binh, RVN, 1970-71; Chief, Spt Svcs, Walter Reed Army Med Ctr, 1971-74; Logistics Staff Officer, DCSLOG, 8th US Army, Seoul, Korea, 1974-76; Chief, Concepts and Doctrine Div, US Army Tp Spt Agency, Ft Lee, VA, 1976-78. Discharged as a major Nov 30, 1978.

Appointed WO1 Dec 1, 1978; served as Chief, Customer Branch, DIO, Ft Bragg, NC, 1979; supply tech, 125 ATC Bn, Seoul, Korea, 1980-81; supply systems analyst, USLOGC, Ft Lee, VA, 1981-83; supply tech, 4th Trans Cmd, Oberursel, Germany, 1983-86; administrator and senior evaluator, chief of staff, Army, Sup Excel Award, USA QM School, 1987-91.

He was the first CW4 to be promoted (March 1, 1990), by commissioned MWOs, MW4 John Zimmerman and MW4 Bill Mullins. Retired Feb 1, 1992, with over 30 years of active service. A graduate of VA Polytechnic Institute with a BS in agronomy; US Army QM School; USA Log Mgmt College; Army Cmd and Gen Staff College; Industrial College of the AF; and WOSC, Ft Rucker, where he was the distinguished graduate of his class.

Awards include the Legion of Merit, Bronze Star Med, Meritorious Svc Med w/2 OLCs, Army Comm Med w/3

OLCs, Army Achiev Med, Nat Def Svc Med w/BS, VN Camp w/2 stars, Armed Forces Res Med w/HG, Army Svc Rib w/#5, Korean Order of Military Merit, VN Svc Med, Meritorious Unit Comm and RVN Cross of Gallantry w/ palm.

Married the former Pamela Thompson of Christchurch, New Zealand; they reside in Petersburg, VA, and he is employed as a travel consultant in Chesterfield, VA. He has two children from a former marriage. Member of the USAWOA, TROA, American Legion, Abou Saad Shrine Temple and other civic organizations.

HARRY D. RIDER JR., CW4, USA (RET), born July 13, 1934, in E. Stroudsburg, PA. Enlisted in the US Army Nov 10, 1953, with assignments to the 71st Inf Div; 1st BG, 1st Inf; 7th Inf Div; and active advisor to KYARNG. Completed abn and spec forces trng.

Appointed from master sergeant to WO1 June 3, 1966. Duty assignments in both finance and personnel were with the 101st Abn Div; 3rd Bn(A) 508th Inf; 173rd Abn Bde; 6th SFGA; 7th SFGA; SF Det(A) Europe; 10th SFGA and USAJFKSWCS.

Retained in service beyond 30 years, reclassified as spec ops tech and assigned duty as WO manager, Proponency Off, USAJFKSWCS. Actively sought WO enhancement as member of TWOS. Overseas service was in Alaska, Panama, Korea, Vietnam and Germany.

Retired May 1, 1986, with 32 1/2 years of active duty. Awards include the Legion of Merit w/OLC, Bronze Star w/ V and 3 OLCs, Meritorious Svc Med w/OLC, Air Med, Army Res Comp Med w/Silver OLC, Army Achiev Med, Good Conduct Med w/4 Bronze Loops, Master Parachutist Badge and Spec Forces Tab.

Retirement honors include the Distinguished WO of Spec Ops, past Honorary WO of AG Corps Regt Assoc and current Honorary WO of 1st SF Regt Assoc.

Now a sales manager for a building products firm. He and his wife Shirley reside in Tobyhanna, PA.

LYNN D. RIDLEY, CW5, USA, born Jan 29, 1949, in Estherville, IA. Entered the US Army in September 1970 as a watercraft operator and appointed WO1, Marine deck officer in September 1973; served

on virtually every class of the Army watercraft in the capacity of mate, XO and master.

Commanded both the 469th and 790th Trans Det, two of the largest ships in the Army Fleet. Twice served as harbormaster of a major Army Port. Served as regt CWO of the Trans Corps Regt; as team chief, WO recruiting, HQ Recruiting Cmd responsible for developing and implementing the first formal WO recruiting effort in the Army.

Twice served as personnel proponency officer on General Officer staff and currently serving as senior personnel proponency officer, HQ, Combines Arms Support Cmd, where his duties include serving as a member of the Chief of Staff Army, directed leader development decision network to draft and then implement the WO Leader Development Action Plan.

Career included CONUS service at Ft Eustis, VA, Ft Sheridan, IL and Ft Lee, VA. Overseas service includes Vietnam, Thailand, Hawaii and Saudi Arabia. He holds a master's degree in business administration.

Member of the USAWOA and a life member and past-post adjutant in the VFW. Married Kristie Lee Klemme of Brunsville, IA. They have two daughters, Melissa and Patricia.

LEO RIVERA, CW3, USA (RET), born April 26, 1928, in Puerto Rico. Entered the US Army Aug 13, 1948, in New York; basic training at Ft Bragg, NC, followed by four years at Munich QM Depot and three years at Florida Military District, Jacksonville, FL. Attended Nuclear Weapons Maint School, Sandia Base, NM.

Stationed at Killeen Base, TX; received additional nuclear weapons training at Sandia Base; reassigned to nuclear weapons unit on Okinawa. Appointed WO June 1,

1959, reassigned to Turner AFB, GA; assigned to Korea; Vietnam, 1964-1965; Army Geodesic Svc, Panama, 1966 and returned to Vietnam with the 4th Inf Div, Pleiku.

Retired as CW3 in August 1969. Completed his bachelor's and master's degrees and 20 years service with Brevard County, FL schools as counselor and guidance director at Rockledge and Satellite High Schools. Retired in June 1990 and is now serving as family counselor at Crosswinds YCS, Merritt Island, FL.

Married Kay Christian in 1955 and has four children.

JAMES D. ROBBINS, CW4, USAR, born Dec 29, 1938, in Big Spring, TX and grew in Corpus Christi, TX. Entered the USMCR in January 1957; transferred to the US Army in 1960. Army Arty in Germany, 1961-62; transferred to aviation as air traffic controller; served as ATCS at Ft Benning, Seoul, Korea and Ft Hood.

Entered Flight School in January 1967; joined 1st Cav in December 1967; flew 2nd Bdg Avn and later became 1st Cav ATC officer. Returned to Ft Hood as air traffic facilities officer and left the Army in May 1970 to work for the FAA.

Except for a two-year tour with the FAA in St Croix, USVI, he remained in the USAR and TXNG. Last active duty tour was with the Army Safety Center during Desert Shield and Desert Storm; performed as accident investigator in El Salvador and Saudi. He is currently a member of the 467th S&S Bn, Corpus Christi, TX.

He is the bn safety officer and mob officer and retired from the civil service in 1994. He plans to spend as much time in the USAR as allowed.

Awards include the Vietnam Svc Med-4, RVN Comm Med, Bronze Star Med, Air Med-12, AMV, Army Svc Rib, Armed Forces Res Med, Nat Def Svc Med-02, Good Conduct Med-2, ARCAM and SRARAVBDG.

He has seven grandchildren and is retired from the civil service.

ROBERT L. ROBBINS, CW4, USA (RET), born July 20, 1922, in Red Oak, OK. Enlisted in the US Army in June 1940; assigned to the 18th FA Regt, Ft Sill, OK. Cadred to the 80th Inf Div, Cp Forrest, TN in June 1942. Appointed WOJG in the 80th Div, Dec 24, 1942; promoted to CWO in July 1943; crossed the Atlantic on the *Queen Mary* and served with the 80th Inf Div, 3rd Army during WWII.

Returned to CONUS in 1945, reassigned to Germany in 1946 and served three years; returned to CONUS in 1949. Reassigned to Japan as a member of the 279th Gen Hosp in 1951 and returned to the States in 1953.

Reassigned to Europe, 1945-58; reassigned to CONUS and to the USATC-E, Ft Leonard Wood, MO; promoted to CWO4 in January 1959. Retired from active service in September 1960.

Employed as a civilian employee at Ft Leonard Wood, MO, upon retirement and served as Chief, Trainee/Student Personnel, Adjutant General's Division until retirement on July 20, 1985. Completed over 45 years of service with the US Army.

Awards include the Bronze Star and numerous service and campaign medals. Additionally awarded two civilian awards, Meritorious Civilian Service Award and the Commanders Award for Civilian Service.

Married Gloria Head from Borger, TX in 1941; they currently reside in Crocker, MO.

JAMES J. ROBERT, CW4, USAR, born March 19, 1940, in New York City, NY. Joined the NYNG May 4, 1956; RA June 1, 1958; USAR on Nov 11, 1961. Appointed WO1 Dec 22, 1972; served with C Co, 826th MIB, 339th MIC, 211th MIC.

Enlisted service with 259th AAA Bn E-4, 82nd Abn Div Trp A 17th Cav E-4, 3rd Sqd 10th Cav E-5, 77th MP Co E-6. Memorable experience was participating in Desert Shield.

Graduated with BS degree from Iona College, Criminal Justice Prof Cert Risk Management. Currently serving as a CW4 in the USAR.

Married Anne and has two children, Louis and Dawn Marie. He is employed by the New York City Police Dept as a lieutenant.

DONALD W. ROBERTS, MAJ, USA (RET), born Sept 24, 1948, in Itawamba County, MS. Graduated from Itawamba Agricultural High School in Fulton, MS in 1966. Entered the US Army in February 1967; basic training at Ft Benning, GA; AIT (automotive mechanic) at Ft Jackson, SC. After his assignment to the 352nd Trans Co in Ft Carson, CO, he went with them to Vietnam in January 1968.

In January 1969 he was assigned to the 52nd Arty Bde, Highlands, NJ; reassigned to Ft Benning, GA as motor sergeant, 609th Trans Co. Assigned to Army Recruiting Cmd, Jackson, MS, 1971; appointed WO1, automotive maint tech, February 1975; assigned to the 2nd Armd Div, 1st Bn, 41st Inf as bn maint tech; promoted to CW2, February 1977.

Assigned to the 42nd Maint Co, Fuerth, Germany and Det 3, 614th Maint Co, Amberg, Germany. Received BA degree in 1979 and MA degree in Communications from California State Univ, 1980; received direct commission to captain, May 1980; ordered to active duty as captain of Ord, May 1981. Given command of 4th Cbt Equip Co, Germersheim, Germany until June 1983.

Returned to McDonnell Douglas Space Co, Huntington Beach, CA as a training with industry student; assigned to the Armament, Munitions and Chemical Cmd, Rock Island, IL as chief, training devices, 1984. Returned to Germany as commander, Geinsheim staging activity, Geinsheim, Germany, 1986. Promoted to major, April 1988; reassigned to Gen Spt Ctr, Germersheim, Germany, as material officer until his retirement in 1990.

Awards include the Purple Heart w/2 OLCs, Bronze Star Med, Legion of Merit, Meritorious Svc Med w/2 OLCs, Army Comm Med w/3 OLCs, Army Achiev Med, Good Conduct Med, Nat Def Svc Med, Combat Inf Badge and Parachutist Badge.

Married Phyllis Newell of Fairview, MS. He is a life member of USAWOA, served as chapter president, Nord Bayern 1978-79 and Ober-Pflaz Franke, 1979-80. Currently a personnel officer at the Mississippi Dept of Trans, Tupelo, MS and resides in Fulton, MS.

HERBAL ERNEST ROBINETTE, born Jan 22, 1904, in Blackwater, VA. Entered the US Army on May 19, 1919, taking basic training at Ft Knox, KY. Stationed at Duffield, VA; 81st FA, Ft Knox, KY; FA School, Ft McDowell, CA; 8th FA and 11th FA Bde, Schofield Bks, HI; Southern Pacific Ry, San Francisco, CA; Repl Ctr, Ft Hamiliton, NY; 5th FA, Ft Bragg, NC; Sig School, Ft. Monmouth, NJ; 3rd FA Bde, Ft Lewis, WA; 9th FA Ft Ord, CA; HQ 9th Corps Area, Presidio of San Francisco, CA; Washington, DC; OMA, Am Embassy, London, England; WD, AGO, A&I Br, Washington, DC; Office, Chief of Staff, War Dept; WD, AGO, Casualty Br; HQ US Constabulary, NY; Munich Mili Post, Munich, Germany; Ft Sam Houston, TX and Dallas, TX.

Served as clerk; battery clerk; supply clerk, radio operator, clerk-typist, radio chief, communications chief, instructor, detail clerk, assistant to OIC, assistant chief clerk,

OIC, assistant XO, OIC of Sub-Section, Chief of Section, assistant AG, Deputy AG, S-1 and adjutant.

Promoted through the ranks and retired from the service on Oct 31, 1951, with the rank of lieutenant colonel. Awards include the EAME Theater, Good Conduct, Am Camp Rib and WWII Victory Rib.

Married Ruth Robinette and has one daughter Jacqueline Robinette Davis. He passed away on March 8, 1974.

HARRISON EVANS ROBINSON, CWO, born in 1927 in Atlantic City, NJ; entered the US Army as an inductee in 1946. He rose to the rank of master sergeant in seven years and served as bn maint sergeant in several units and as NCO in charge of heavy equip and wheel vehicles for the 282nd Maint Bn of the 82nd Abn Div.

In 1951 he was appointed a WO and for 10 years served as maint officer with a number of units in the States, Europe, Korea and Vietnam, including the 82nd and 101st Abn Div, then promoted to the grade of CWO.

Upon his retirement in 1978, he was described by one of his former supervisors "as the most outstanding WO with whom he had served during a 30 year career." Had he been commissioned officer," this former supervisor continued, "he would have achieved general officer rank."

Robinson passed away in 1978.

JACK W. ROBSON, CW4 (RET), born on May 29, 1920, in Billings, MT. Enlisted in the MTNG Nov 27, 1936, in Great Falls, MT with the 41st Div, Co D, 116th Med Regt. Inducted into federal service on Sept 16, 1940, as a corporal and transferred to Cp Murray, WA with the 41st Div. On May 1, 1941, transferred to Ft Lewis, WA and promoted to the rank of sergeant. From 1941-44 he was the swimming instructor at Ft Lewis, WA; 1944-45, he served in the South Pacific Theater with the 37th Div, 129th Inf Regt, Med Det.

As a section leader he saw action on Bougainville, New Guinea, Lingayen Gulf, Bagio, Apailae, the Island of Luzon and Manila where Sgt Robson was the 9th American soldier to enter Manila when it was liberated. During these actions he administered to the wounded on the battlefield and transported them back to first aid stations. Sent back to the States and discharged on Oct 9, 1945, at Ft Lewis, WA.

When the NG was reactivated in Washington State he re-enlisted on Feb 2, 1947, in Olympia, WA where he served with HQ Btry, 115th AAA Bde as the first sergeant. Discharged on June 6, 1951, when he moved to California. After arriving in California, he re-enlisted on Nov 14, 1952, with the CANG as a WOJG and served with Co B, 40th Div, 40th Armd Ord Bn at Ontario, CA.

On March 2, 1956, he was promoted to CWO W-2; Nov 23, 1959, transferred from the CANG to the AR serving with the 63d Inf Div HQ and Co B, 763rd Ord Bn, Bell, CA; March 1, 1962, promoted to CWO3; March 1, 1968, promoted to CWO4.

Robson ended his military career with over 34 years of dedicated service on Sept 18, 1975. Awards include the Combat Inf Badge, Bronze Star, Combat Med Badge, Philippine Lib Med w/BS, AP Camp Med w/2 BSs, Am Def Svc Med, Pres Unit Cit, Honorable Svc Lapel Button, WWII Victory Med, Expert Badge w/rifle bar, Good Conduct Med, Armed Forces Res Med w/HG.

Employed on March 31, 1956, with the Dept of Defense Logistics Agency as a quality assurance representative

GS-12. On Dec 19, 1968, he was the recipient of the commemorative Apollo 8 Medallion for his work on the Saturn Program. He retired from federal service on June 6, 1980, with over 24 years of service.

He was a member of the ROA, American Legion, Grand Master Independent Order of Odd Fellows Post #345, Ontario, CA; vice-president International Little League, Ontario, CA chapter, honorary citizen of Boys Town.

Married to Fae Vincent for 52 years, he passed away on Feb 5, 1993; he is loved and missed by all who knew him. Survived by two sons, one daughter, four grandchildren, and five great-grandchildren. Hobbies included flying single engine aircraft and sea planes, wood working and fishing.

JOSEPH R. RODRIGUES, CW4, USA (RET), born Feb 5, 1932, in Puunene, Maui, HI. Entered the US Army May 6, 1949; received basic training at Schofield Barracks, HI; served in various units in Hawaii, Korea, Japan, Oklahoma, USAREUR and Ft Bliss, TX. Appointed WO1, MOS 761A, unit supply tech Oct 1, 1964. Served as special service property officer at Ft Bliss, TX with orders to the 8th Inf Div.

Arrived March 1965 and was assigned as property book officer 2nd Bn, 87th Inf; April 1966, promoted to CW2; April 1966, 2/87 Inf redesignated 5th Bn, 68th Armor. Served as S-4 Officer/PBO/Support platoon leader until October 1967; reassigned to Vietnam in January 1968; assigned to 4th Inf Div, 1st Bn, 22nd Inf as PBO. Consolidated all company supply functions into one supply support group for faster response to needs of forward combat elements.

Reassigned to the US Army FA School (USAFAS) as S4/PBO Arty combat leader bn; promoted to CW3, October 1969. Reassigned to Vietnam and the 25th Inf Div, 3rd Sqdn, 4th Cav in July 1970; received order to stand down in 1971; processed all equip for turn in to depot located at Long Bien then reassigned to D Trp, 3/4 Cav (air) and later chosen to clear HQ Co, 2nd Bde, 25th Inf Div, property records. Reassigned in 1971 to USAFAS Ft Sill, OK as division supply chief, Target Acquisition Dept; reassigned October 1972 to the 25th Inf Div to the 25th S&T Bn and was placed in charge of Property Book Team #1 which supported all inf bns.

Promoted to CW4 in May 1975 and later reassigned as Chief Document Control Officer Div Log Spt System (DLOGS). He later developed a readiness DLOGS report which was used to control all assets within the division. He was reassigned in June 1976 to Readiness Region 9 at Presidio, CA and was responsible to train over 200 NG and USAR located in Nevada and California.

Retired on July 31, 1978. Awards include the Legion of Merit, Bronze Star w/3 OLCs, Meritorious Svc Med, Purple Heart, Good Conduct Med (4th awd), Nat Def Svc Med w/ OLC, Army of Occupation (Germany), Korean Svc Med w/ Silver Star, VN Svc Med w/Silver Star, VN Cross of Gallantry w/Palm, UN Svc Med, VN Camp Med w/60 D, Pres Unit Cit (Korea), Combat Inf Badge and Army Comm Med w/5 OLCs.

Married and has six children. He enjoys fishing, camping and volunteer work.

FERNANDO CASTRO-RODRIGUEZ, CW4, USA (RET), born Sept 19, 1932, in Rio Grande, Puerto Rico. Drafted Sept 9, 1953, taking basic training in Ft Dix, NJ. Served in Korea from April 1954-August 1955 with B Btry, 15th FA BN, 2ID, 1st Field Observation Bn, 8A and finally with I Corps Arty. Honorably discharged as sergeant E-4 and remained in active USAR until recalled to active duty during the Cuba-Berlin crisis. Served as admin supervisor SFC E-7 in the Directorate of Civil Affairs, 301st Log Cmd C at Ft Bragg, NC from October 1961-September 1962.

Discharged and returned to USAR as personnel sergeant, HHC 11th Spec Forces Gp (Abn) first sergeant; appointed WO1 in January 1965; recalled to active duty during the mail strike in March 1970 as CW2 and discharged after a three-day call up. Served in various USAR assignments in Special Forces, Military Intelligence, Civil Affairs and finally as food service tech, CW3 with HQ 77th ARCOM in Ft Totten, NY until June 1979; returned to active duty in the newly created AGR Program as budget analyst in the Office Deputy Chief of Staff, Resource Management and promoted to CW4 in January 1980.

Served as team manager in the Bde PBO, 157th Separate Inf Bde (mech) in Horsham, PA and PBO with Svc Co, 11th Special Forces Gp (Abn) first sergeant in Ft Meade, MD and 7th Bn, 9th FA in Ft Lauderdale, FL. Retired on Sept 30, 1992, at Ft Benning, GA after 39 years and 22 days of service and selected for promotion to CW5.

Awards include the Meritorious Svc Med w/OLC, Army Comm Med w/2 OLCs, Army Achiev Med w/OLC, Korean Svc Med, UN Svc Med, Army Good Conduct Med, Nat Def Svc Med w/Silver Star, Army Res Comp Med w/2 #2, Army Svc Rib, Master Parachutist Badge, Pathfinder Badge, Prcht Rigger Badge, Panamanian Prcht and the Spec Forces Tab.

Married Angelina Louise Fiore Castro of New York City and has one daughter and two granddaughters. Life member of the ROA, DAV, TROA, 77th USARCOM, Officers Assoc, USAWOA and the AUSA.

JAMES F. ROUHAN, CW4, USAR, born July 7, 1944, in Detroit, MI. Began military career in the USAF in the mid-1960s. Served in various positions through sergeant. Positions included mechanized personal, finance and instructor for both Army and AF personnel in computer programming. After four years active duty he entered the USAFR and later discharged on Aug 2, 1973.

Entered the USAR Aug 6, 1976, and served in many administrative positions. On May 6, 1978, he was appointed WO1 as data processing tech, 424th PSC and helped develop the SIDPERS training materials and later the *SIDPERS Reserve Component Manual.* Also served as a member of several Reserve units and taught regression analysis in the Officer Advanced Course for Personnel.

Awards include the Nat Def Svc Med-1, Pres Unit Cit, AFOEA, AFOUA, AF Good Conduct Med, AFRMSR, AFCOM, Army Res Components Med, Army Svc Rib, Army Achievement Med, NCOPDR, AFRM-1 (860805), ARCAM-1 (800805), ARCAM-2 (840805), ARCAM-3 (880805), ARCOTR-1, Nat Def Svc Med-2, ARCAM-4 (920805) and Expert Badge w/Rifle.

Resides in Livonia, MI with wife Janet and daughters, Karen and Lori. Currently a consultant with Management Technologies and holds membership in the American Statistical Assoc, American Society for Quality Control, Project Management Institute, WOA and the ROA.

THOMAS T. SANDERS, CW4, USA (RET), born March 6, 1933, in Loraine, TX. Graduated from Portales High School, Portales, NM, in 1950; attended Eastern New Mexico Univ and graduated with BS degree from the Univ of Maryland. Entered the US Army on Nov 26, 1954; basic training at Ft Bliss, TX and AIT at Ft Chaffee, AR. He served as an infantryman with the 350th Inf Regt in Austria and Germany. He served with the 3rd Armd Cav Regt in Germany; Ft Meade, MD and with various arty units in Germany, CONUS and Korea. Appointed WO1 on Dec 1, 1966;

served as personnel tech with the 3rd Armd Div and the 14th Armd Cav Regt in Germany and with the 108th Arty Gp in Vietnam. Return in 1969 and served with the 187th Pers Svc Co in Mannheim, Germany.

As a CW4 he retired in May 1984 with over 29 years of service. Awards include the Meritorious Svc Med, (13) Bronze Star Med w/OLC, and numerous service and campaign medals.

Currently employed as chief of the Status and Recon Sect of the area Maint and Sup Facility-Europe, Mannheim, Germany. Life member of TROA, Nat Assoc of Uniformed Services, USAWOA, VFW and a member of USAREUR Retiree Council.

Married to Doris Auerbach of Mannheim, Germany; they have two children and two grandchildren.

S. WILSON SANDRIDGE, CW3, USAR (RET), born Sept 5, 1931, in McGaheysville, VA. Enlisted in the US Army Sec Agency at Alexandria, VA Oct 29, 1951; basic training with the 3rd Armd Div, Ft Knox, KY and served in Germany from September 1952-August 1954 with HQ&HQ Co 502nd Comm/Recon Gp and the 331st Comm/Recon Co as radio operator and radio traffic control analyst. Discharged with the rank of sergeant in August 1954. Served with the H/H Btry, 787th FA Bn (Res) Elkton, VA, December 1954-October 1956, while attending college. Re-enlisted in November 1956 and assigned to Stu Bn, USAIS, Ft Holabird, MD. Graduated as special agent and served as MI specialist with the 3rd Ops Gp USAPC, Camp Drake, Japan from May 1957-June 1958. Assigned from June 1958-March 1961 to USAAG, Washington, DC as a MI specialist and promoted to rank of SSG E-6.

In June 1962 assigned to the 902nd INTC Gp, Washington, DC; on Jan 24, 1963 appointed to the rank of WO. Completed the Area Intel Off Crs, Ft Holabird, MD, August 1963; assigned to the 500th INTC Gp, USARPAC, Japan as asst OIC, technical laboratory. In 1966 assigned to the 116th MI Gp, Washington, DC and conducted intelligence command operations and investigations within Military District of Washington. Completed Polygraph Examiner Trng Crs at Ft Gordon, GA in March 1967. Served from June-September 1968, as polygraph examiner, 1st Bn (Prov), 135th MI Gp, Vietnam, then with Tech Spt Bn, 525th MI Gp as polygraph examiner until July 1969. Assigned to HQ, USAINTC, Ft Holabird, MD and evaluated MI polygraph examinations conducted world wide. In July 1970 assigned to HQ 902nd MI Gp, Falls Church, VA to provide direct polygraph support to The White House Communication Agency, all CONUS MI Gps and other highly sensitive CONUS commands as directed by USAINTC. In 1971 became Chief, Polygraph Branch, CI Svcs, 902nd MI Gp. In July 1972 assigned as team chief Region V, 650th MI Gp, USA Element, SHAPE, Belgium with direct supervision of all enlisted special agents providing counterespionage, countersubversion and counterintellignece support for SHAPE.

Retired in 1975. Awards include the Legion of Merit, RVN Cross of Gallantry w/Palm, Armed Forces Res Med, (2) Overseas Svc Bars, Meritorious Unit Cit, Army Comm Med w/OLC, RVN Comm Med, VN Svc Med, Nat Def Svc Med w/OLC, Good Conduct Med (1st and 2nd awd).

Retired in 1975 and currently working as substitute teacher in middle and high schools. He is member of the Shrine of North America, Civitan International and American Polygraph Assoc. Married Frances Mahan Sandridge and has two sons and two grandchildren.

RICHARD A. SAUER, CW4, RA (RET), born July 8, 1934, in West Brighton, NY. Entered the US Army Jan 11, 1957; basic training at Ft Dix, NJ; served in chemical, signal, MP, armored and infantry units before appointment to WO status in November 1967. Served five years as administrative assistant to Gen Westmoreland in Vietnam and Washington.

During a later HQ DA tour he was appointed the first WO member of Compassionate Review Board; first WO on DCSPER staff and first WO Chief of Professional Development, WO Div, before retiring in October 1981.

Memorable experience: the helicopter guided tour of Washington in April 1968 with tour guide by then President

Lyndon B Johnson. Gen Westmoreland and Sauer were in Washington at President Johnson's direction and he put them both up in the White House (Sauer slept in the same bed as Abraham Lincoln had used). The tour was an extra the President gave us as he escorted us to Andrews AFB for the flight back to Vietnam.

Awards include the Legion of Merit w/2 OLCs, Bronze Star, Meritorious Svc Med, Army Comm Med w/OLC and several service and campaign medals.

Subsequently graduated from the seminary, licensed to ministry and presently serves with Pioneers, a Christian missionary organization in Orlando, FL. Married Adele Crosby and has three children and two grandchildren.

RICHARD M. SCALZO, CW5, USAR, born May 16, 1940, in Utica, NY. Enlisted in the USAR July 20, 1962; attended basic and AIT training at Ft Dix, NJ; returned to USAR status in February 1963 to the 969th Ord Co, (DAS) as a wheeled vehicle mechanic. Appointed as WO1 on Jan 22, 1968, as automotive repair tech.

Served with 816th Station Hosp; 2nd Bn, 389th Regt, 98th Div (Trng), Utica, NY; HQ 98th Spt Bn, Rochester, NY; HQ, 98th Spt Bn, Rochester, NY; HQ, 1st Bde, 98th Div (Trng); 1209th USA Garrison, Mattydale, NY; HHC, 464th Engr Bn, Schenectady, NY; Log Gp, 98th Div (Trtng), Rochester, NY; Co B, 464th Engr Bn, Horseheads, NY; 969th Maint Co., Horseheads, NY; 98th Div (Trng), Rochester, NY; Mat Div, ACofS, G-4, 98th Div (Trng), Rochester, NY.

Memorable experience was being among the first 10 USAR WOs promoted to CW5.

Discharged Jan 21, 1968, to accept Wo1 appointment. Awards include the Army Res Comp Med w/3 OLCs, ARCAM w/S OLC, AFRM w/2 HD, and the Nat Def Svc Med.

Married Phyllis and has three children: Gina, Kim and Richard. Retired from Federal Civil Service June 30, 1993, with 29 years of service. Last duty assignment was the supervisory log mgmt specialist (SLMS, GS-12), 98th Div (Trng). Was full time representative of the ACofS G-4 and supervised the full-time work force.

DOROTHY J. SCHLEGEL, CW3, USAR, born May 2, 1943, in New York City. Graduated with BBA from City Univ of NY, 1967; MS from Hofstra Univ, NY 1974; entered the USAR in April 1976 in the Civilian Acquired Skills Program and completed basic at Ft McClellan, AL in the WAC. Promoted to SP5 and ordered to attend Instructor Trng School at FTIG, PA.

Assigned as 76Y instructor 1154th USARF School and taught classes in the 76 series at Ft Totten, Ft Lee, VA and Tobyhanna Army Depot; 1981 assigned to the 99th Sig Bn, NY and received direct appointment to WO1 as PBO. Reassigned to 1154th USARF School; 1983-1987 completed the five phases of the Assoc Level Exec Devel Crs at the Army Log Mgmt College, Ft Lee.

As assist inspector gen, she was the first female WO to

serve in the 77th USARCOM; June 1993 transferred to the 695th Maint Bn as property book tech.

Awards include the Meritorious Svc Med w/1 OLC, Army Comm Med w/2 OLCs, Army Achiev Med, Nat Def Svc Med, Army Res Comp Achiev Med w/2 OLCs, Armed Forces Res Med w/HG.

She organized the Statue of Liberty Chap of the UWAWOA, Metropolitan New York area and has held the office of president since October 1992. Other affiliations include the ROA, ASTD and FBLA.

Divorced, she has one daughter who graduated from Hofstra Univ in 1991. Worked for the NYC Board of Ed for 15 years and currently working on a 2nd master's degree with the goal of earning a Ph.D. in organizational sociology.

DALE F. SCHNABEL, WO1, born Sept 21, 1951, in Minot, ND. Entered the RA Aug 14, 1970, and discharged May 15, 1973. Entered the USAR at Minot, ND May 16, 1973, and discharged May 15, 1975. Entered the SDARNG Aug 8, 1981, and began working for them as AGR May 1, 1984, until present.

Began his full-time tour with the ARNG as the administrative clerk with Svc Btry, 1st Bn, 147th FA. On June 1, 1985, became the unit supply sergeant and was promoted to staff sergeant. On Dec 10, 1989, he transferred to Sioux Falls as the Det 1 Readiness NCO until his appointment April 1, 1991, as PBO for the 1st Bn, 147th FA. Upon completing WOC Crs at Ft Rucker and WOTTCC at Ft Lee, he was appointed WO1 June 12, 1992.

Awards include the Joint Svc Comm Med, Army Comm, Army Achiev (2nd awd), Nat Def Svc Rib (2nd awd), Army Good Conduct (3rd awd), Army Res Comp Achiev Med, NCOPDR w/3 Device, Army Svc Rib, SD Dist Svc Rib (2nd awd), SD Recruiting Rib, SD Svc Rib, SD Desert Storm Rib.

He and Dianne have been married for over 19 years and have one son Andrew (Andy). His wife works for the VA and they currently make their home in Sioux Falls, SD.

WILLIAM H. SCHNAKENBERG, CWO, USA (RET), born Oct 22, 1915, in Staten Island, NY. Entered the USA in 1943 at Camp Upton, NY; basic training MP and Investigators Crs, Ft Custer, MI; 1944-46, New Guinea and Philippine campaigns as MP and Provost Marshal Investigator. Joined 402nd CID in NYC, 1947; Bolan Academy of Investigation 1948; Criminal Investigation Crs, Ft Gordon, 1949; fingerprinting recruits, Ft Jay, 1949.

Recalled to active duty during Korean War; assigned to the 331st CID, Ft Dix, NJ, 1950; assigned to the 7th and 12th CID, Austria, Italy, 1952; CIC, University of Vienna, 1952; returned to the 43rd CID and 1st Armd Div, Ft Hood, TX, 1954; Def Language Institute, Monterey, CA, 1955 (Spanish).

Sent to CID, Puerto Rico, 1956-59; returned to Sacramento Sig Depot, 26th CID; graduated Sacramento Police Academy, 1959; left for 534th MP CID, Panama. Promoted from SP-7 to WO, 1963. Returned to USA, resident agent, Ft Jay, NY; Federal Bureau of Narcotics Crs, Washington, DC, 1965; Vietnam service with the 40th CID, 1965-66; returned to 10th CID, Ft Hamilton, NY; retired as CWO2, 1969; attended SI Community College, NY and NYC Civil Service with NYC Hospital Police, 1969; later Pinkerton Detective Agency, US Public Health Security; relocated to Harleysville, PA in 1987.

Retired in 1987; awards include the Asiatic-Pacific, Philippine Liberation, WWII Victory Med, Am Def and Svc, Good Conduct, VN Campaign and Svc, Army Comm Med and NY State Conspicuous Service Cross.

Married the former Barbara Hortenhuber of Linz, Austria. He is a member of the CID Assoc, VFW, DAV, Vietnam Vets, ROA, TROA and WOA.

OTTO F. SCHOLZ JR., was born on May 9, 1914, in Chicago, IL. Drafted into the US Army in November 1942 and discharged for medical reasons in June 1943. Volunteered for draft recall and entered the USMC in January 1944, serving until June 1946 in the Pacific area. Enlisted in the Army in January 1949 and attended CIC School at Ft Holabird, Baltimore, MD.

Served with the 430th CIC Det in Salzburg, Zell am See and Innsbruck, Austria until September 1952. Employed by National Security Agency from October 1952-March 1954, serving also in the USAR, 268th CIC Det, Ft Myer, VA.

Attended Army Language School, Monterey, CA as E-7 studying Hungarian and graduated in April 1957. Assigned to the 513th MI Gp, 1957-63, as interrogator and intel ops specialist; appointed WO1, August 1963 and CWO2 in September 1964. Due to a heart attack in October 1964, he retired with a physical disability in December 1967 at WRAMC. Employed as DA civilian from May 1968-January 1982, serving with the US Army Field Activities Cmd in Washington, DC, five years with DCSI, USAREUR, Heidelberg, Germany and five years with HUMINT Div, ACSI, DA.

Resided near Gettysburg, PA for two years then in Virginia until present time. Worked part-time with KETRON, Inc, Carlisle, PA, 1982-93, as a security officer, editor and proofreader. Permanently retired and resides with his wife Hermine Treml in Annandale, VA. They were married in 1953 and have two daughters, Johanna Farrell-Sutton and Charisse Phillips with the Dept of State. He is a member of the TROA, AFIO, ACICV, AUSA and now with the WOA.

KURT A. SCHULTZ, WO1, born Feb 9, 1963, in Mechanicburg, PA. Enlisted in the USA on April 16, 1982, as a 915A unit maint tech. Served with the 3rd ACR, 2/11 ACR, 1/52 Inf (M) OPFOR, 18th CEC, DCD Armor Ctr. Held various positions up through motor sergeant with the rank of SSG (P).

Memorable experiences include 33 rotations at NTC, Ft Irwin, CA. Awards include (6) Army Achiev Med, (3) Army Res Comp Med, (3) Good Conduct Med and (2) Overseas Svc Ribs.

Married Sherri Keenan July 17, 1982, and then have two children, Kurt Jr and Jennifer. Presently assigned to the BMT 302nd MI Bn.

TERRY W. SCHUMACKER, WO1, USAR, born May 5, 1959, in Sparta, WI. Began his military career in the USAR June 30, 1977, and held various positions up to motor sergeant and grade of staff sergeant. Appointed WO1 as unit maint tech (L) in the 85th Div, 2nd Bde LSU at Ft McCoy, WI Sept 15, 1992.

Awards include the Army Achiev Med, Army Res Comp Achiev Med w/3 OLCs, Nat Def Svc Med, Armed Forces Res Med, NCOPDR w/3 Army Svc Ribs, Army Res Comp Overseas Trng Rib w/2 Mech Badges, Driver (W), Mechanic (W), Expert Qualif Badge and Ord Regt Crest.

Resides in Sparta with his wife Ginger and their two sons, Nathaniel and Nicholas. He is treasurer of the USAWOA, Ft McCoy Chap. Civilian occupation is tactical vehicle automotive inspector ECS 67, Ft McCoy, WI.

KENNETH L. SCHUMANN, CW3, born Oct 6, 1935, in Meeker County, MN. Began his military career as a senior in high school. Enlisted with Co B, 682nd Engr Bn (47th Inf Div) Dec 9, 1953, at Hutchinson, MN.

Held various positions through motor and supply staff sergeant. Was the company supply sergeant for 17 years and received a merit promotion to sergeant 1/c in 1973. He was with his home town unit for 28 years. Transferred in June 1982 to CAC HQ MNARNG, then attached to troop command as chief supply sergeant.

On March 15, 1984, was appointed WO1; Dec 20, 1984, appointed CW2; April 7, 1993, appointed CW3 as the PBO for troop command MNARNG.

Awards include the Army Achiev Med w/Bronze OLC, Army Res Comp Achiev Med w/Silver OLC, Nat Def Svc Med, Armed Forces Res Med w/4 HGs, MN Comm Rib w/Pendant and Bronze OLC, MN Good Cond Rib w/2 Silver Stars, MN Active Duty Rib w/Silver Star and MN Svc Rib (40 years).

Married the former Carolyn Ann Selland has five children and 11 grandchildren. Worked for the MN Dept of Nat Resources for 36 years and retired in September 1991. He works for the NG when ever needed and plans to retire in October 1995 with 40 years in the Guard and 36 years with DNR.

JOHN A. SCHWARTZ III, CW2, USAR, born Sept 7, 1954, in Philadelphia, PA. Joined the USAR, HHC 330th Engr Bn (c)(c) Philadelphia, PA May 5, 1973. The unit moved to Worcester, PA in February 1975; entered basic training Aug 30, 1973, at Ft Wood, MO; completed AIT (electricians course) at Ft Wood Dec 14, 1973; held various positions in the 51 career management field up to construction supervisor with the rank of SFC; March 20, 1990, appointed WO1 as utilities operation and maint tech after attending WOS-RC at Ft McCoy, WI and WOTCC at Ft Wood, MO; July 1990, participated in the renovation of an Adult Vocational School in Grenada; returned in September 1991, to provide guidance in the construction of barracks for the Grenadian Special Service Unit; went to Ft Sherman, Panama, July 1992, to supervise the renovation of the NCO School Barracks; transferred to the 404th Civil Affairs Bn (FID/UW) in Trenton, NJ, Sept 1, 1993, as the property accounting tech, due to the deactivation of the 330th Engr Bn in February 1994.

Awards include the Army Comm Med, Army Achiev Med w/OLC, Armed Forces Res Med w/10 year Device, Army Res Comp Achiev Med w/4 OLCs, NCOPDR w/#3, Army Res Overseas Trng Rib w/#2, Nat Def Svc Med and Army Svc Rib.

Married Christine Marita Blinebury on Sept 8, 1984. Currently employed at Boeing Heli Co, member of the WOA, Engr Regt Assoc and the ROA. Attended Spring Garden College and Penn State Univ.

BRADLEY J. SCOTT (SCOTTY), CW3, ARNGUS, born Jan 12, 1952, in Pontiac, MI. Graduated from Oxford Area community HS in 1970 and Northern Virginia Community College in 1990. Entered the MIARNG in December 1970; basic training at Ft Campbell, KY and AIT at Ft Lee, VA. Initial assignment with HHC, 1/125th Inf Div, Flint, MI, as armorer; reassigned to Spt Co as the full-time administrative and supply tech then went to Personnel Mgt School, Ft Ben Harrison, IN.

Assigned on a six month active duty short tour with the NG Bureau continuously from 1974-94 (240 months); worked at Accession Mgt Br, PERSCOM from 1974-79 (SFC); NG Bureau Enl Pers Br, Pentagon from 1970-83 (MSG); ARNG Recruiting School, Ft Ben Harrison, IN (1983); in service

recruiter, Ft Ord, CA (1983-85); appointed as CW2 on Sept 16, 1985; returned to Mil Pers Tech Certification School, Ft Ben Harrison, IN (1985); reassigned back to NGB Enl Pers Br, Pentagon, 1985-87; Chief, Recruit Quota System (RE-QUEST) Ops Ctr, ARNG Recruiting Br, Skyline Six, Falls Church, VA and ultimately today at the brand new ARNG Readiness Ctr, Arlington Hall Station, VA, since its dedication in March 1993.

Awards include the Meritorious Svc Med w/OLC, Army Res Comp Med w/2 OLCs, Army Achiev Med, Good Conduct Med (3rd awd), ARCAM w/2 OLCs, Nat Def Svc Med w/star, Armed Forces Res Med (2nd awd), NCOPD (3), Army Svc Med, DA Staff ID Badge, Master ARNG Recruiter Badge and CNGB's Eagle Plaque.

Married the former Phyllis Ann Green and has two children, Jenna May and Jonathan Bradley. Remarried to Susan Kay Harris and they live in Virginia. He is currently planning on retirement to Florida as a travel consultant. He has been the USAWOA national secretary since March 1989.

ROBERT D. SCOTT, CW4, USA (RET), born Nov 14, 1935, in Marlboro, MA. Entered the US Army Nov 19, 1952, taking basic training and leadership training at Ft Dix, NJ. Served as infantryman with the 45th and 24th Inf Div in Korea and the 606th AAA Bn in Grand Island, NY until his discharge in November 1955.

Employed as a radar tech by the NYNG and the Federal Civil Service until recalled to active duty as a WO in November 1962. Served as a radar tech, personnel officer, crypt tech, communications officer, Service School instructor and automated software tech until he retired as CW4 in January 1978 with over 24 years of service.

Awarded the Bronze Star, Meritorious Svc Med w/OLC, Army Comm Med w/OLC and numerous service and campaign medals.

Currently employed by the Army as the director, business operations and management diretorate, USA Personnel Information Systems Command, Alexandria, VA. Member of the K of C and the 4th Degree K of C, TROA, Nat Assoc of Uniformed Svcs, lifetime member and past national president of the USAWOA.

Married Rose Cirrito of Niagara Falls, NY and has four children and nine grandchildren.

THOMAS J. SCUTTI, CW4 (RET), born Nov 5, 1928, in Philadelphia, PA. Graduated from South Philadelphia HS; entered the US Army in 1951; attended basic training at Camp Carson, CO; Engr Sup Spec Crs at Ft Belvoir, VA; 7th Army NCO Academy, Munich, Germany, graduating in 1957.

In 1960 assigned to the USA Trng Ctr, Ft Knox, KY; 1961 appointed WO1 and initial assignment as the Chief Supply Branch G4, Ft Knox, KY; 1963 transferred to the 7th Inf Div, Korea as the accountable property officer. In 1966 returned to Germany and service with the 4th Armd Div; 1968 brought an assignment to the Americal Div, Chu Lai, Vietnam.

After one year at Ft Bragg, he returned to Vietnam and served with the Da Nang Spt Cmd. Returned to Ft Bragg in 1972; 1973 brought an assignment to the Southern European Task Force in Vicenza, Italy; 1977 returned to Ft Indiantown Gap and retired in 1978.

Awards include the Bronze Star w/OLC, Meritorious Svc Med w/2 OLCs, Army Comm Med w/4 OLCs, Good Conduct Med (2nd awd), Nat Def Svc Med w/OLC, Armed Forces Res Med, VN Svc Med, RVN Camp Med and RVN Cross of Gallantry w/Palm.

Married and has three children, whom all have degrees and doing well; his wife works for a stock broker. Retired, and has an auto hobby.

JAMES C. SEACOTT, CW2, USAR, born Sept 15, 1942, in Johnson City, TN and has lived most of his life in New York City. Entered the USAR as a postal clerk with the 312th BPO, attending basic training in January 1962. In 1965 he transferred to the 363rd Chem Co as a smoke generator operator and served as mechanic and motor sergeant.

Left the Reserves in 1969 and re-enlisted as an intel analyst in the 24th MI Bn in 1982; 1989, attended WOCS; 1990, appointed WO after completing technical certification; 1991 mobilized for Desert Storm and served at the 3rd Army ARCENT Intell Ctr, Riyadh, Saudi Arabia as a liaison for the US Army, logging and requesting reconnaissance or BDA missions to be flown by the USAF and RAF.

At the present he is still serving at the 24th MI Bn as an imagery intelligence tech. Awards include the Army Comm Med, Army Res Comp Achiev Med w/OLC, Nat Def Svc Med, SWA Svc Med, NCOPDM, Army Svc Rib, Army Res Comp Overseas Trng Rib w/#2, Kuwait Lib Med.

Married Jo-Anne D'Errico in 1965.

DONALD L. SHAW, CW3, USA (RET), born May 17, 1931, in Shoals, IN. Entered the USAF in May 1948 and promoted to master sergeant in May 1954 as an administrative supervisor. Changed career fields in June 1955 to become an OSI special agent. January 1968, accepted WO appointment in MI, as a counterintelligence tech. Overseas assignments included Japan, Korea (1951-52), Germany and Taiwan, Vietnam (1968-69) during Army service with the 5th SFG (Abn). Stateside bases with the USAF were Lackland AFB, TX; Warren AFB, WY; Camp Stoneman, CA; Chanute AFB, IL; Bakalar (formerly Atterbury) AFB, IN; Wright Patterson AFB, OH; Bolling AFB, DC; OSI Det 504 Louisville, KY; and Sawyer AFB, MI. His Army service stateside was at Ft Sill, OK; Ft Meade, MD; and Ft Knox, KY.

Retired in July 1978 after more than 30 years of service. Awards include the Legion of Merit, Bronze Star, Meritorious Svc Med, Joint Svc Comm Med, AF Comm Med, two awards of the Army Comm Med, Korean Svc Med w/2 Battle Stars and the VN Svc Med w/4 Battle Stars.

After military retirement, he worked in civil service as a personnel security specialist with the directorate of security, Ft Knox, KY, from spring 1979-81 when he began work as special agent with the Def Investigative Svc, in which capacity he continues to serve.

Married the former Linda Fahr. He has been active with the Masonic Fraternity since 1955, was elected to receive the 33rd degree at the Supreme Council Sessions, AASR, NMJ, Boston, MA in August 1993. Currently serves as a national vice-president of National Sojourners, Inc. and is scheduled to become the National President for the period of June 1995-June 1996.

JAMES A. SHAW (JIM), CW4 (RET), born in December 1937 in Ludowici, GA. Began his military career with the

GANG and entered active duty in October 1956 with the Army Security Agency. Appointed WO in February 1964, Ft Stewart, GA.

Overseas tours were Lubeck, Kirchgons, Heidelberg, Bamburg and Frankfurt, Germany; Thailand; Vietnam. While in Frankfurt, July 1971-July 1975, he activated the Frankfurt Silver Chap of the Eur WOA and served as its first president, and vice-president and editor for the EWOA Newlsetter.

Retired at Hunter AAF, Savannah, GA after 23 years of service. Presently a communication and electronics specialist (computer) with Defense Information Service Organization located at Ft Ritchie, MD.

Awards include the Bronze Star Medal and many other awards and decorations from active duty and civil service.

He and Heinke live in Chambersburg, PA.

DANIEL K. SHISHIDO, CW3, USA (RET), born Dec 20, 1947, in Puunene, HI. Entered the US Army in February 1967; basic training at Ft Ord, CA; AIT at Ft Devens, MA; assigned to the Pacific (Okinawa, Vietnam, Korea, Thailand) and upon appointment to WO1 in 1975, he returned to Ft Meade, MD. Subsequent assignments included the 372nd ASA Co, 25th Inf Div; USAICS, Ft Huachuca, AZ; 302nd ASA Bn, V Corps; and the 125th MI BN, 25th Inf Div (L).

Retired from active duty in March 1987. Awards include the Bronze Star, Meritorious Svc Med w/2 OLCs, Joint Svc Comm Med, Army Comm Med w/3 OLCs and the Army Achiev Med.

Resides in Honolulu and is currently an intelligence operations specialist with USARPAC in Ft Shafter, HI. He is a life member of the WOA.

ROGER LEE SIFFORD, CW3, USAR, born in Bluefield, WV Jan 23, 1944. Initially joined the US Army in March 1961, at Roanoke, VA; attended basic and AIT training at Ft Benning, GA (2nd Inf Div) as a radio repairman. Served six months (TDY) Germany; six months (TDY) Vietnam; and "Operation Big Lift" (Airlift of 2nd Armd Div from Ft Hood to Germany). He was discharged from active duty in March 1964.

Entered USAR in January 1981 at Ft Worth, TX; USAR assignments include 223rd Mn Bn, Ft Worth, TX; 279th Mn Bn, Dallas, TX; 158th Avn Reg, Grand Prairie, TX. Best assignment as WO was 279th Mn Bn (Operation Desert Shield/Storm, 17 months active duty). Heroes are his oldest brother, SFC Nathan D. Sifford (Korea 1950-1953, Purple Heart) and Gen Dwight D. Eisenhower.

Awards include the Army Comm Med w/OLC, Army Achiev Med, Good Conduct Med, Army Res Comp Achiev Med, Nat Def Svc Med w/BSS, SWA Svc Med w/2 BSS, VN Svc Med, NCOPDR, Army Svc Rib, RVN Camp Med, Lib of Kuwait Camp Med, SE Asia Svc Med.

Has BS in economics from the Univ of Texas, Dallas and is a career employee of Texas Instruments, Inc. He has two children, Anna and Julie, and is active in home life, community affairs with daughters, and the military. He is member of the USAWOA and ROA. He would like to be

remembered as a good father and a professional soldier. His hobbies include running and health.

EARNEST L. SMILEY, CW2, USA, born Sept 23, 1961, in Alexander City, AL. Entered the US Army Sig Corps Sept 18, 1979, at Ft Gordon, GA as a communications specialist. Completed basic training and AIT in January 1980; served with 7th Corps, 34th Sig Bn, Ludwigsburg, Germany, January 1980-September 1982. Assigned to 7th Inf Div, 127th Sig Bn, Monterey, CA, from October 1982-October 1983; assigned as a communications security NCOIC and platoon sergeant in 5th Sig Cmd, 44th Sig Bn, Darmstadt, Germany, November 1983-November 1989. Served as an instructor at US Army Sig School from November 1989-May 1990; completed WO Candidate School, Signal Systems Tech Crs and Abn School, March 1991. Assigned as a communications-electronics tech in 4th Inf Div, 124th Sig Bn, Colorado Springs, CO, from April 1991-May 1993.

Awards include the Meritorious Svc Med, Army Comm Med, (2) Army Achiev Med, (2) Overseas Svc Ribs, (3) Army Good Conduct Meds and NCOPDR.

Married Jewel Johnson of Philadelphia, PA; she is an Army nurse currently assigned to Walter Reed Army Med Ctr. Graduated with BS degree in computers and management from Univ of Maryland, 1988; MS in management from Troy State Univ, 1989; master of business admin in information systems and finance from Regis Univ, 1993. He is a member of the USAWOA and AFCEA. Currently assigned to Pers Infor Systems Cmd as a networks tech in Alexandria, VA.

DARRELL E. SMITH, CW2, USA (RET), born March 10, 1933, in Latrobe, PA. Enlisted in the USAF Nov 4, 1953, taking basic training at Sampson AFB, NY. Completed formal training as aircraft jet engine tech at Chanute AFB, IL. Subsequently served with the 366th Ftr BG (TAC) equipped with F-84, F-86 and F-100 jet aircraft at England AFB, LA; 354th Tac FW, Myrtle Beach AFB, SC; Aviano AB, Italy (NATO); Osan AB, Korea; and 4042nd Strategic FBW (SAC) equipped with KC-135 refueling tankers and B-52H bomber aircraft having achieved the rank of tech sergeant.

Further served as special agent, 21st Dist, Off of Spec Investigation (OSI), Langley AFB, VA until November 1967. Transferred into US Army on Nov 21, 1967; appointed WO with subsequent duty as criminal investigator Det D, criminal investigation Div (CID), Ft Leonard Wood, MO; and Det A, CID, Ft George G. Meade, MD until 1971.

His overseas assignments included 8th MP Gp (CID) with duty at Cam Rahn Bay, RVN and as OIC of Vung Tau Resident Agency (CID), RVN; served at Ft Dix Field office, First Region, USACIDC, Ft Dix, NJ.

Memorable experience as a WO, USA, was having the opportunity to serve as a criminal investigator with the elite and very professional team of CID investigators conducting in depth criminal investigative activities into alleged war crimes involving US Combat Forces and South Vietnamese civilian nationals during combat operations on March 16, 1968, at My Lai IV Province, RVN, upon which he was awarded the Bronze Star for meritorious service.

Retired in February 1974 with 20 years of service. Awards include the AF Comm Med w/OLC, Meritorious Svc Med w/OLC, Army Comm Med w/OLC, AF Good Conduct Med w/2 Bronze Loops, Army Good Conduct Med, Nat Def Svc Med, AF Outstanding Unit Awd w/Bronze OLC, AF Longevity Awd w/2 Bronze OLC, Army Svc Rib, VN Svc Med, RVN Comm Med and numerous letters of commendation and appreciation.

Married Barbara Jean Gibson of Greensburg, PA; they have five children and six grandchildren. He is a member of the USAWOA and TROA; active with hobbies in wood working crafts, photography, collecting and restoring antique cars, trucks and farm tractors.

DONALD LEE SMITH, CW3, AUS (RET), born Nov 13, 1933, in Murphysboro, IL. Enlisted in the US Army in January 1952; attended basic training at Ft Leonard Wood, MO and AIT (offset press platemaker) at Ft Belvoir, VA. Assigned to the 332nd Engr Co (topographic), Frankfurt, Germany from July 1952-December 1954; assigned to Field Printing Plant, Ft Leonard Wood, MO, June 1955-June 1956; served with US Army Tech Services Pacific, Ft Clayton, Canal Zone from July 1956-February 1959 as map editor.

Graduated from Plastic Proofing Crs and Basic Photogrammetry Crs given by Inter American Deodetic Survey; February 1959, assigned to Ft Belvoir, VA and became instructor after graduating from Map Compiling Crs. Graduated from Topographic Surveying Crs in April 1960 and promoted to SFC E7 in September 1961. Assigned operations sergeant, 34th Engr Co (base photomapping, 29th Engr Bn, base topographic) January 1964 in Japan.

He was appointed to WO1 in December 1964, as operations officer, 34th Engr Co (base photomapping) until February 1966; assigned to Ft Belvoir, VA as photomapping tech instructor, Topographic Engr Off Crs and Corographic Drafting Crs until June 1969; July 1969, served as operations officer, 34th Engr Co Base Topographic, 29th Engr Bn, base topographic, located on Ford Island, HI; promoted to CW3 in August 1969; March 1971, selected chief, Bn Quality Assurance Branch with direct responsibility for quality of all topographic maps issued to US Forces in Pacific Theater.

Additionally, he managed the USARPAC Program of Foreign Mapping Agreement Agency Acceptance Review and was responsible for assuring that all foreign maps accepted into the USARPAC Map Stockage System met USA Topographic Cmd, and Def Intel Agency standards.

Smith retired in July 1972 as a CW3 with over 20 years of service.

Awards include the Army Comm Med, Army of Occupation, Good Conduct Med w/2 clasps, and Nat Def Svc Med w/2 stars. Married to Irene Brasel of Jasper, AR until her death in May 1966. They had three children. He married in 1968 to Betty Woodward Holt from Bainbridge, GA; she was a widow with five children. He is a member of the USAWOA, VFW, and life member of TROA.

CRAIG L. SODERBERG, CW4, USA (RA), born June 22, 1953, at Oakland Naval Base, CA. Entered the US Army in July 1972; basic training and infantry AIT at Ft Ord, CA; assigned to the 25th Inf Div, December 1972; subsequently assigned to Ft Lee, VA, and promoted to the rank of staff sergeant. Appointed WO1 July 25, 1980, as property accounting tech and transferred to 1/2 ACR, Bindlach, Germany.

Assigned in September 1982 with the 222nd Avn Bn, Ft Wainwright, AK; completed QM WOA Crs as an honor graduate, September 1985. Further assignments include the technical escort unit, APG, MD, October 1985; Berlin Bde, Germany, September 1988, directly experiencing the fall of the Berlin Wall; and 1/12 (MLRS) FA, Ft Sill, OK, November 1991, where his contributions were recognized through presentation of the Artillery's Honorable Order of St Barbara Medallion.

Awards include the Meritorious Svc Med w/3 OLCs, Army Comm w/3 OLCs, Army Achiev w/2 OLCs, Nat Def

Svc w/BSS, Army of Occupation, Army Superior Unit Awd and the Expert Inf Badge.

Married Patti Dodds from Atlanta, GA. Stationed at Cameron Univ, Lawton, OK, August 1993, to complete a baccalaureate degree in business management under the Army's fully funded degree completion program for WOs. Graduated in July 1994 and attends the new WO Staff Crs at Ft Rucker, AL.

FRANK D. SPANNRAFT, CW4, USA (RET), born Sept 8, 1913, in Wienerneustadt, Austria and retired from active duty on May 31, 1961. During his career he had many assignments that he was proud of, the most memorable of which are: Admin O(AG), HQ OMGUS, Berlin, Germany; Admin O, 11th MPCID Det; Asst Adj, HQ 5th US Army, Ft Sheridan; and Admin O, HQ Co Spec Trps, 7th US Army.

Awards include the Good Conduct Med, Army Comm Med, Am Def Med, Army Comm Rib w/Medal Pendant, EAME Campaign Med, Army Occupation Med (Germany), WWII Victory Med, Korean Svc Med, UN Svc Med, Nat Def Svc Med, Armed Forces Res Med and Bronze Star.

Married Marie-Louise of Paris, France and has two sons and three grandsons. He is past active member of the Ft Sheridan Retirees Council and past member of the American Legion. *Submitted by his son Daniel Spannraft, April 1994.*

DAVID MYRON SPURGEON, CW5, born Jan 13, 1942, in Gadsden, AL. Enlisted in the US Army in June 1960. His assignments from 1967-90 include 117th Avn Co, Dng Ba Tien, RVN; 15th Med Bn, 1st Cav Div, An Khe, RVN; MOI training branch USAPHS, Ft Wolters, TX; 116th Avn Co, Cu Chi, RVN; 117th Avn Co, Camp Stanley, Korea; 295th Trans Co, Finthen, FRG; 478th Trans Co, Ft Benning, GA; WOSC, Ft Rucker, AL; 180th Avn Co and HHC, 11th Avn Gp, Schwab Hall, FRG; B Co 159th Avn Bn, and HHC, 101st Avn Gp, Ft Campbell, KY; DLI Presidio of Monterey, Monterey, CA; 205th Avn Co, B Co 6/158th Avn Regt, Finthen, FRG; and USA Safety Center, Ft Rucker, AL.

Education includes WOMC, 1990; MS, Law Enforcement Admin; BS in criminology; BA in history; AA in Germany studies and AA in professional aeronautics.

Awards include the Dist Flying Cross, Bronze Star, Merit Svc Med-2, Air Med-24, Army Comm-2, Army Achiev, Nat Def Svc, VN Svc, Armed Forces Exped, Army Svc Rib, Overseas Svc Rib, VN Camp Med, VN Cross of Gallantry, SWA Svc Med, Master Army Aviator Badge, Combat Medic Badge and Air Assault Badge. Promotions from WO1 in 1965 to CW5 in February 1992.

Married and has one son and one daughter.

FRANK STAMEY, was born July 21, 1936, in Athens, GA. Entered the US Army in October 1955; basic training at Ft Jackson, SC; then the Engr Drafting Crs at Ft Belvoir, VA. Transferred to AG Corps and served in progressive administrative and personnel support assignments at Ft Leonard Wood, MO, Ft Richardson, AK; Ft Gordon, GA; and in Washington, DC attaining the rank of SFC in January 1965.

Appointed WO1 in May 1966 and reassigned to Ft Sill, OK; deployed to RVN in September 1966 as personnel officer of 1st Bn, 40th FA. Reassigned to Ft Bragg, NC in September 1967 as OIC of Officer and Senior Enlisted Personnel Team, 573rd Pers Svcs Co. Reassigned to Washington, DC in March 1969 as assistant executive and military assistant to the assistant Secretary of the Army (research and development). Reassigned in December 1977 as Chief, Pers Svcs for the office of the Chief of Staff, Army. Reassigned in January 1981 as adjutant and chief, Pers and Admin Svcs Div, White House Communications Agency.

Professional organizations include charter and life member of the USAWOA. Served seven years as member of Board of Directors and Executive Committee, with two years as national secretary, one year as national vice-president, and two years as national president; currently serves on Past-Presidents Council and Lifetime Trustees Council. He is a life member of the VFW and member of TROA.

Retired Dec 31, 1989, with more than 34 years of active duty. Awards include the Def Sup Svc Med, Legion of Merit w/OLC, Army Meritorious Svc, Army Comm w/OLC, Army Comm Med w/3 Bronze Knots, Nat Def Svc Med, Army Svc Med, Overseas Svc Rib, VN Svc Med w/2 campaign stars, Navy Pres Unit Cit, Joint Meritorious Unit Awd, VN Camp Med, RVN Cross of Gallantry w/Palm, Pres Svc Badge and the Army General Staff Badge. He is listed in the 37th Edition of *Who's Who in America.*

Married the former Mary Janes of Athens, GA with residence in Stafford, VA. They have two grown children and two grandsons. Currently employed with DynCorp of Reston, VA as manager, Family Housing Management Department, Ft Belvoir Div.

PHILIP MICHAEL STAMM, CW4, USA (RET), born June 19, 1941, in Muncie, IN. Entered the US Army on April 13, 1960, with basic training at Ft Knox, KY and advanced Finance School training at Ft Harrison, IN. First duty assignment was Ft Irwin, CA; first overseas assignment was in Poitiers, France in 1962 where he was branch transferred to the Chemical Corps and promoted to staff sergeant E-6 with three and one half years of service.

Returned to CONUS to Ft McClellan, AL, in 1965 and appointed QM Corps WO in 1966 with six and a half years of service. Attended QM School with following assignment to Camp St Barbara, Korea as PBO for the 2/76th FA Bn, ITT;'d to Ft Clayton, Panama in 1968 and served as PBO for the 4/20th Mech Inf Bn; volunteered for duty in Vietnam that same year with assignment as the PBO for the 9th Sig Bn, 9th Inf Div in Dong Tam. Returned to CONUS in 1969 via Schofield Barracks, HI to Ft Knox, KY for duty as PBO for the 2nd AIT Bde; again volunteered for Vietnam in 1972 and assigned to the G-4 Staff for the 1st Avn Bde first at Long Binh and alter at Ton Son Nhut AB.

Departed Vietnam in 1972 for civilian college at the Univ of Nebraska at Omaha where he was awarded a bachelor's of general studies degree. After graduation assigned to Ft Campbell, KY as the PBO for the 20th Cbt Engr Bn; departed in 1976 for Camp Coiner, Korea to serve as the PBO for the 501st MI Bde. In 1977 was selected for promotion to CW4 with 17 years of service; returned to Ft Campbell in 1978 as the accountable officer for the DMMC's Class II, IV, VII Sect, 101st Abn Div. Attended the Univ of Southern California's Ft Campbell campus and awarded a MS in systems management degree just prior to retirement in May 1980.

Awards include the Bronze Star w/2 OLCs, Meritorious Svc Med w/2 OLCs, Army Comm Med w/2 OLCs and numerous service and campaign medals.

After retirement went to work for Vinnell Corp in Saudi Arabia training the NG. In 1982 he started his current career with Civil Service as a GS-11 accountable officer and chief of the VII Corps DIO Field Office, Augsburg Regional Supply Support Activity in Augsburg, Germany.

Promoted to GS-12 in the same position and in 1985 accepted a GM-13 position as the Chief, Supply Branch, Logistics Div, Dept of Defense Dependents Schools - Germany Region located in Wiesbaden, Germany. In 1988 was promoted to GM-14 as the Chief of the Logistics Div for DoDDS - Germany Region. In March 1993 returned to CONUS to the Defense General Supply Center in Richmond, VA still working for DoDDS as the liaison officer between DoDDS and DGSC.

In August 1993 accepted a promotion to GM-15 working for the Defense Logistics Agency as the director for the Directorate of Logistics Information Distribution for Defense Logistics Services Ctr in Battle Creek, MI. He is a 20 year member of the WOA. Married to Linda Barria-Herrea, a native of Panama, who is now a proud US citizen.

WILLIE E. STARNES, CW4, born Dec 17, 1949, in Murfreesboro, TN. Graduated from Eagleville High in 1968 and attended MTSU Univ as Upward Bound Student. Entered the US Army July 22, 1969; basic training at Ft Campbell, KY; AIT at Ft Knox, KY and Ft Leonard Wood, MO.

Served with 3/35th Armor, 4th AD (Bamberg) 1970-73; assigned to Ft Knox, KY in 1974; returned to Bamberg in 1974 to 1/75th FA; appointed WO1 in February 1977 and moved to 6/10th FA. PCSed to Ft Carson, CO in 1979 to serve with 1/22th Inf.

Returned to Bamberg in 1980 to 2/78th FA. Attended SWOC, 1985-86; assigned as project officer, Directorate Of Training and Doctrine, APG, MD, 1987; June 1987 assigned to Regimental Spt Sqdn 2ACR with duty in Bamberg supporting the 2nd Sqdn; Desert Shield/Desert Storm from December 1990-May 1991 as 2nd Sqdn DS Maint Tech, then 2ACR's MMC Chief; in January 1992 assumed duties as the 7ATCs (Grafenwoehr) Consolidated Maint Center's chief.

Awarded the Meritorious Svc Med w/OLC, Army Res Comp Med w/Silver OLC, Army Achiev Med w/OLC, SWA awd w/3 stars and numerous other awards including the Thayer Award (2ACR's Best WO).

Served as vice president of Bamberg WOA Chap and currently president of the WOA Oberpfalz-Franken Chap (Grafenwoehr and Vilseck). Holds AA degree from the Central Texas College and currently chief of 7ATC;s Consolidated Maint Center.

Married the former Gertrude Hopf of Bamberg, Germany and they have two lovely daughters, Cynthia and Susanne.

WILLIAM C. STATON, CW3, born Nov 28, 1939, in Danville, KY. Enlisted in the US Army on Jan 4, 1957, in Anderson, IN as an engineer. Military stations include Ft Leonard Wood, MO, 1957-77; Ft Hood, TX, 1961-62; Vietnam, 1965-66 and 1969-70; Okinawa, 1971-73; Germany, 1958-61, 1968-69 and 1973-76; Ft Wolters, 1962-64; Thailand, 1964-65; and Ft Stewart, GA, 1967.

His memorable experience includes being military advisor with the 5th ARVN Div Run in 1970.

Discharged Jan 1, 1978, as a CW3. Awards include the Good Conduct Med, Nat Def Svc Med, VN Svc Med, RVN Comm Med, Bronze Star, Meritorious Svc Med, Army Res Comp Med, Meritorious Unit Cit, UNCAHM, AFEM, and RVN Gallantry Cross Unit Citation w/Palm.

Married Sue and has two sons, Brian and Richard. He is a maint supervisor for FFE Transportation Services, Inc.

FRANK A. STEELE, CW3 (RA), born Aug 7, 1946, in Montgomery, AL. Entered the US Army on March 21, 1968, taking basic training at Ft Benning, GA and flight crew training at Ft Eustis, VA. Served with A Co, 228th Avn Bn, 1st Cav Div, RVN, 1969-70.

Appointed WO in 1982, serving in positions as maint officer, Bn motor officer and executive officer with assignments in Germany, Korea, Ft Polk, LA and Ft Benning, GA. Graduated from WOSC in 1988 and currently assigned as contractor logistics support officer for the Bradley Fighting Vehicle Training and Fielding Team, Taif, Saudi Arabia.

Awards include the Bronze Star, Meritorious Svc Med w/OLC, Army Comm Med w/OLC, Air Med w/31 OLCs, Good Conduct Med (5th awd) and numerous service and campaign medals.

Married the former Diana Patterson of Louisiana. He is a member of the USAWOA, VFW, AUSA and lifetime member of NCOA.

JOSEPH B. STEIN, CW4, USA (RET), born Feb 14, 1934, in New York, NY. Entered the military service in May 1950, with the 1st Bn, 156th FA BN, 27th Inf, Div NYANG. Assigned to Ft Sill, OK ATVMC-12, 1959; enlisted in RA in October 1963 and attended basic training at Ft Dix, NJ.

Assignments included the 413th Sig Co, Ft Meade, MD; 3rd RECON SQDN 11th ACR, 1964; deployed to RVN, 1966; 499th Trans Co, Ft Devens, MA, 1967; HQ 46th Gen Spt Gp, 1968; HQ 2/1 Arm Cav Regt RVN, 1969; 76th Trans Co, USAEUR, 1970; 581st Maint Co (DS), Ft Meade, MD, 1973; 223rd AV BN USAEUR, 1975; WO Advanced Crs, APG, MD, 1978; HQ 10th Spec Forces Gp, Ft Devens, MD, 1978; WO Senior Crs, Ft Rucker, AL, 1982; 15th Maint Co (DS) 19th Maint Bn USAEUR, 1982; HQ 513th MI Bde, Ft Monmouth, NJ, 1985; 10th DISCOM, 10th Mtn Div, Ft Drum, NY, 1987. Appointed to WO on April 18, 1969 and to CWO4 in November 1982.

Most pleasant experience and assignment was as the shop officer for the 15th Maint Co (DS) when they issued the M-1 Abrams Tank to the 11th Armd Cav Regt. He had the pleasure of working with the most ideal combination of professional WOs ever assembled for one mission.

Retired in March 1990. Awards include the Bronze Star w/clusters, Meritorious Svc Med w/clusters, Army Comm Med w/clusters and several service and campaign medals and qualification medals and badges.

Married and has two sons, J. Eric and Gregory. He is a member of the VFW Post 5218, American Legion Post 1627, USAWOA, Assoc of USA and NRA.

CHARLES E. STEPHENSON, CW3, AUS (RET), born Sept 15, 1933, in Wells, TX. Enlisted in the US Army Feb 3, 1953, taking basic training at Ft Bliss, TX. Enlisted service in HHB and B Btry, 92nd AAA Bn, 32nd Bde (Brize Norton, England) 1953-56; HHB, 41st FA Bn and HHB, 3rd Inf Div Arty (Ft Benning, GA and Kitzingen, Germany) 1956-61; HHB, 1/73rd FA Bn, CCA and HHB, 1st Armd Div Arty (Ft Hood, TX) 1961-63.

Discharged as SFC (E-7) with immediate recall to active duty as WO1 Ballistic Meteorology Tech May 24, 1963. Served in TAD, USAAMC (Ft Sill, OK) 1963-65; HHB, 4th Armd Div Arty (Zirndorf, Germany) 1965-67; HHB, IFFV Arty and HHB, 8th TAB, 26th Arty (Vietnam) 1967-68; TAD, USAAMC (Ft Sill, OK) 1968-70; and HHB, XXIV Corps Arty and HHB, 2/94 FA Bn (Vietnam) 1970-71.

Retired after his final assignment with TAD, USAFAS (Ft Sill, OK) on March 1, 1973. Awarded the Bronze Star, Meritorious Svc Med w/OLC, Army Comm Med w/3 OLCs and numerous service and campaign medals.

Married Sheila Traynier of Cromer, Norfolk, England. They have two daughters, Debbie and Sharon; sons-in-law, Mark Mossavat and Brock Lawson; three granddaughters:

Jocelyn and Brooke Mossavat and Nicholette Lawson. Retired from the Univ of Texas at Austin on Aug 31, 1993.

GLENN W. STEVENS, CW5, USA, born Nov 5, 1938, in Tamaqua, PA. Enlisted in the RA on Nov 7, 1961, (two days prior to being drafted). Completed basic training at Ft Jackson, SC and AIT at Ft Leonard Wood, MO. While enlisted, he served as a heavy equipment operator, eng supply sergeant, stock control supervisor and senior supply sergeant.

Appointed to WO in 1973, as a unit supply tech; served as PBO, supply support tech and property accounting tech. Stateside assignments include Ft Bliss, Ft Leonard Wood, Ft Indiantown Gap and Key West, FL. Overseas tours include Korea, Thailand, Vietnam and five tours totaling more than 19 years in Germany.

Awarded the Bronze Star, Def Meritorious Svc Med, Meritorious Svc Med w/OLC, Army Comm Med w/OLCs and Army Achiev Med and numerous service ribbons, unit citations and campaigns medals.

Married the former Margitta Rhein of Hanau-Steinheim, Germany. Currently serving with HHC, DISCOM, 1st Armd Div, Bad Kreuznach, Germany. He is also a member of the TROA, USAWOA, FVW and AF&AM Masons of Texas.

JOHN McGREGOR STEVENSON, CW4, USA (RET), born Aug 7, 1935, and raised in Chatham, Cape Cod, MA. Entered the US Army in October 1956; basic training with 2nd Bn, 15th Inf, Ft Benning, GA; AIT, Finance School, Ft Harrison, IN. In March 1957 served as a statistician for USAFFE, 8th Army (rear) Assignment Team, Ft Lewis, WA; May 1958, assigned to G2, USAREUR, Heidelburg, FRG; pers sec investigations analyst and adjudicator.

Discharged in December 1959; re-enlisted in March 1960; assigned to USARMS, Boston Army Base, MA; Intel School, Ft Holabird, MD, June-September 1962; assigned as special agent and NOCIC CE Branch, 513th MI Gp, Oberursel, FRG, October 1962; appointed WO, November 1963; source control officer, 513th MI Gp; reassigned May 1966; special cases officer G2, US Army, Vietnam with duty en route as S1, 14th MI Bn (FA), Ft Bragg, NC, arriving RVN October 1966.

Chief, Liaison Branch, 902nd MI Gp, Washington, DC, December 1967; close liaison and operational support functions with other executive branch intelligence and investigative agencies and departments; operational security activities, support of intelligence operatives worldwide. As a special agent, he participated in sensitive CI operations and investigations at National level. He was nominated for assignment in May 1969 to (and later became Chief of) WO Plans Branch, Deputy for Career Planning, Officer Personnel Directorate, HQDA. Single point of contact for policy matters related to professional development and utilization of Army WOs; prepared second (unsuccessful) study and proposal for WO grades CW5 and CW6. Assisted in preparation and publication of first definitive career progression plan for Army WOs (DA Pam 600-11). Awarded Legion of Merit for duties performed in this position.

Appointed in RA. Under Officer Undergraduate Degree Completion Program, he attended Mt St Mary's college, Emmitsburg, MD, January 1973-December 1974; graduated magna cum laude; member of Joint OACSI/OTJAG Special Litigation Team and technical advisor to US Attorney, January 1975-July 1976 for matters related to alleged conduct of CI activity involving US citizens abroad. Until his retirement in October 1978, he was operations officer and special agent, 902nd MI Gp Field Office, Ft Ritchie, MD responsible for liaison with other governmental agencies,

OPSEC surveys, unique CI investigations.

Awards include the Legion of Merit, Bronze Star, Meritorious Svc Med w/OLC, Army Comm Med w/OLC, Good Conduct Med (4), Nat Def Svc Med, VN Svc Med w/ 2 Campaign Stars, VN Campaign Med w/60 D, and numerous certificates and commendations.

Married Mary Robertson on Sept 17, 1961, in Chatham, MA. She owns and operates The Recovery Place, a drug and alcohol outpatient counseling center in Gettysburg. They have three daughters: Deborah (1962), Cynthia (1963) and Jennifer (1967); three grandchildren as of 1993: Joshua, Alyssa and "Jamie."

They reside in Gettysburg, PA where he is territory supervisor and marketing representative (So Central PA, DE, MD northern half of VA) for Millers Mutual Insurance Co. Active in Episcopal Church, licensed Lay Eucharistic Minister, past Sr Warden, past member of Diocesan Council and Finance Comm, member of Vestry. He attended 3-year Diocesan School of Christian Studies and is a life member of TROA, member of USAWOA, American Legion, Sparks Club, Delta Epsilon Sigma (National Scholastic Honor Society), Monsignor Tierney Honor Society (Mt St Mary's), US Golf Assoc, Gettysburg Country Club, and charter member of PGA Tour Partners.

JAMES I. STONE, CW3, USA (RET), born July 23, 1946, in Detroit, MI, and raised in Gaylord, MI; graduated from Central Michigan Univ with BS in education in January 1969. Enlisted in the US Army in February 1969, commissioned in the FA in March 1970; served in a variety of arty and logistical assignments from 1970-82 to include 1-22FA, 4th Armd Div, Germany; 1/42FA, 4th Msl Cmd, Korea; HQ DIVARTY, and 2-19FA, 1st Cav Div, Ft Hood; Special troops, I Corps (ROK/US), Korea; and two tours with the USA FA Board, Ft Sill.

Appointed CW2 (MOS 762A, supply support tech) in February 1982, and assigned to the 226th Maint Co, Ft Sill. Conducted the initial automation of the supply support activity and expansion of the customer base from three units to over 30. Reassigned in July 1984 to the 22nd Maint Co, 1st Maint Bn, 2nd SupCom, Heilbronn, Germany. Participated in two REFORGER exercises, organized and planned physical upgrade of warehouse storage operations as well as conversion of automation software. Assigned as the div repair parts tech, Div Mat Mgmt Ctr, 1st Inf Div, Ft Riley, March 1988, assignment included deployment to, participation in, and recovery from Operation Desert Shield/Desert Storm.

Awards include the Legion of Merit, Meritorious Svc Med w/OLC, Army Comm Med w/3 OLCs, Nat Def Svc Med w/star, AFEM, SWASM w/2 stars, Armed Forces Res Med, Army Svc Rib, Overseas Svc Rib w/3 Device, and the Lib of Kuwait Med. Also honor graduate in Supply and Service Management Course (1984) and distinguished graduate, QM WO Advanced Crs (1988).

Married Chong Nam (Kim) Stone and they reside in Manhattan, KS. He retired Sept 30, 1991.

WILLIE D. STONE, CW4, USA (RET) born Oct 3, 1940, in Jacksonville, FL. Enlisted in the US Army Oct 28, 1958. Attended basic training and AIT at Ft Jackson, SC. Appointed WO1 July 22, 1966; promoted to CW4 Oct 1, 1977. His first WO assignment was with the 25th Inf Div, Cuchi, RVN; last assignment was with USA Readiness Gp, Los Angeles.

His tours of duty included Germany (4); Vietnam (2); Republic of Panama, Ft Sill (2); Ft Benning, Ft Stewart; and Seneca Army Depot, NY. All assignments were finance or personnel.

Most memorable experience was flying throughout RVN to pay hospitalized soldiers of the 25th Inf Div.

Retired on Aug 1, 1981. Awards and decorations include the Legion of Merit, Meritorious Svc Med, Bronze Star w/3 OLCs, Army Res Comp Med w/2 OLCs, Good Conduct Med, Nat Def Svc Med, VN Svc Med, Meritorious Unit Cit, VN Cross of Gallantry w/Palm, and VN Campaign Med.

Married Charlene and has three children: Erwin, Ava Maria and Tanya. Currently serving as a social services specialist with the Richmond County (GA) Depart of Family and Children Services.

DANIEL M. SULLIVAN, CW4, AUS (RET), born Sept 13, 1929, in Craigsville, VA. Entered the US Army in 1946 and received basic training at Ft Bragg, NC. Served in Japan, 1946-49; Ft Sill, OK, 1949-50; Korea, 1950-51; Ft Bliss, TX, 1951-52; Panama, 1952-54; Japan, 1954-57; Army Air Def Cmd, 1957-66; Vietnam, 1966-67; Army Air Def Cmd, 1967-69; Vietnam, 1969-70; USA Europe, 1970-72.

Promoted to first sergeant in 1954 and appointed WO in 1961. Retired in 1972 after 26 years of active duty. Awards include the Bronze Star, Air Med, Army Comm Med, Good Conduct Med, WWII Victory Med, Army of Occupation Med, Nat Def Svc Med, Korean Svc Med, VN Svc Med and Armed Forces Res Med.

Received BA degree in business and administration from St Leo College in 1980 and employed as officer manager for 16 years. He is a member of the DAV and ROA.

JEFFREY A. SUMNERS, CW2, USA, born May 1, 1961, in Athens, TN. Enlisted in the US Army in January 1983, attended basic training at AIT for Chaparal Crewman at Ft Bliss, TX. Enlisted assignments were: May 1983, D Btry, 1/67th ADA, Ft Lewis, WA; April 1985, C Btry 6/56th ADA, Haha AFB, Germany; May 1987, C Btry, 3/6th ADA, Ft Bliss, TX. He held all crewmemeber positions from assistant gunner to squad leader, attaining the rank of sergeant.

In May 1988 he attended Flight School at Ft Rucker, AL; May 1989, appointed to WO1, as a UH-1 pilot; June 1989, posted Ft Campbell, KY, B Co 6-101 AV; piloted lead aircraft for B 6-101 AV Regts Air Assault with the 101st Abn Div into Iraq on Feb 24, 1991. The historic air assault by the 101st to the Euphrates River cut off supplies and retreat for Iraq's Army in Kuwait. October 1992, stationed AV Co, 1SB/MFO Sinai, Egypt; December 1993, student with Embry-Riddle Aeronautical Univ, Ft Campbell, KY.

Awards include the Air Med (2), JSCOM (1), Army Res Components Med (2), Army Achiev Med (8), Army Good Conduct Med (2), Nat Def Svc Med, SWABS (3), Humanitarian Svc Med, NCOPDR, Army Svc Rib, Overseas Svc Rib (3), MFOSM (2) and SAKULIBM.

HARRY W. SWEEZEY, MWO, USA (RET), born Sept 27, 1939, in Malden, MA. Served 10 years in naval aviation on anti-submarine patrol aircraft, search and rescue helicopters and as a survival, escape and evasion instructor. Transferred to US Army for flight training in 1968 and earned his bachelor's degree from Troy State Univ.

Served in Asia, Europe and the States with Air Cav. Performed as safety officer, maint officer and standardization instructor pilot. Special assignments included Liaison officer 8th Army HQ, HQDA RETO Study, TRADOC Avn Branch Study, HQDA Enlisted Aviator Study, Personnel Proponent Systems manager and special assistant to commanding general.

Awards include the Legion of Merit, Meritorious Svc Med, Army Comm Med, NCM, Army Achiev Med, Army Good Conduct Med, Navy Good Conduct Med, Nat Def Svc Med, Armed Forces Exped Med, Army Svc Rib, Overseas Svc Rib, Parachutist Badge, Air Assault Badge and Master Army Aviator Badge.

He resides in Panama City Beach, FL.

HAL A. TABERNER, CW3, USA (RET), born June 27, 1941, in Worcestor, MA. Entered the US Army Sept 30, 1961, taking basic and AIT at Ft Ord CA; served in Saarbrucken and Mannheim, Germany in the 594th Trans Gp until his discharge in 1963.

Re-enlisted in 1965 attended US Army Guided Missile School, Redstone Arsenal, AL and retrained as Nike radar and computer repairman, graduating in 1967. Sent to Ft Richardson, AK with the 524th Ord Co; assigned to Ft Bliss, TX then back to Redstone Arsenal for WO training, graduating from WO Land Combat Missile/Short Range Repair Tech Crs in 1970.

Assigned to 92nd Det, Ramstein AB, Germany; reassigned to the 71st Ord Co (Hanau, Germany); served in F Co, 709th Maint Bn, Ft Lewis, WA until 1977; went back to Worm, Germany to HHC, 3rd Ord Bn in 1977, supporting 563rd and 41st Ord Companies where he was assigned to Lance Missile Tech School at UK School of Ammunition in Kineton, England, graduating in 1980; returned to Co E, 707th Main Bn, Ft Ord, CA.

Supported Israelis during Arab/Israeli in October 1973 and won unit citation for V Corps; also supported Russian Bear Bombing runs of Alaskan air defenses between 1967-68.

Retired March 31, 1983. His awards include the Army Svc Rib, Overseas Svc Rib, Vietnam Svc Rib, Army Comm Med w/2nd OLC, Good Conduct (2nd awd) and Nat Def Med.

He is a member of TROA, VFW, USAWOA. Graduated from Univ of Maryland with BS degree; City College of Chicago with AS degree; Univ of the State of New York with AA degree.

Presently employed with Lockhead Missile and Space Co, Inc, Sunnyvale, CA as a system test and design production engineer senior. He has two children and lives in El Sobrante, CA.

ROBERT G. TADLOCK, CWO3, born April 5, 1929, on a southern Illinois farm, where they maintained a stable of stud horses, raised grain, cattle and hogs. He always wanted to fly and soloed at age 17. Flying has been his life time love. He enlisted in the USAF December 1950, where he trained as an aircraft mechanic and became an aircraft maint tech instructor.

In November 1951, he joined the 3499th Mobile Training Wing; spent five years with F86 D Mobile Trng Detachments. Re-enlisted September 1955 as technical instructor with the B52 special school to train SAC bomber maint personnel at Chanute AFB, IL.

Selected as technical instructor with the new Field Training Det (415C). Taught B58 maint for six years at Carswell AFB, TX. Completed civilian flight training and volunteered off-duty hours as flight and ground instructor with the Aero Club.

During the Vietnam War, he made an in-service transfer to the US Army as an 062B MOS and trained at Ft Wolters, TX and Ft Rucker, AL. Due to 15 previous years in aircraft maint training, he returned to Maint School and attended Aircraft Maint Officers School, then became OIC of Aircraft Hydraulic Committee at Ft Eustis, VA.

In 1966 he was ordered to the 1st Cav Div RVN and served with D Co, 15th TC BN at Camp Radcliff, RVN as the QC OIC and supported the 1/9th Cav Regt. He was next assigned to RVN with the REAL CAV Hg Hg Trp 1/9th Cav as asst maint officer, with lots of flying to the LZs along the coastal plain. In 1968 he returned to Ft Eustis, VA, as training officer and night OIC of HI and E Branch. In 1970 returned to RVN as OIC of Retrograde Unit at Saigon Helport #3. Participated in Vietnamization (turning the war over to the Vietnamese).

Returned to Ft Rucker, AL for Advanced Aviation Wo Career Crs. Retired from the Army as RA CWO3 June 30, 1972, after serving 22 years.

Awards/Medals: Bronze Star, Air Medals, Army Comm Med, numerous service and campaign medals and Master Aircraft Crewman Badge.

Second career with the Newport News Shipbuilding (NNS) as nuclear power plant inspector for 21 years. Completed college and volunteered as a pilot and teacher for CAP, Coast Guard Auxiliary and the Virginia Defense Force. Upon his retirement Nov 30, 1993, he became active with PTA, Meals on Wheels, Emery Riddle College Recruiting and teaching aviation ground school volunteer programs.

He and wife, Mary Lou, celebrated their 44th wedding anniversary in August 1993. They raised two children and are helping to raise two grandchildren.

BRUCE T. TAIJI, CW3, born June 25, 1946, Minneapolis, MN. Entered the Army Sept 12, 1967, taking basic training and AIT at Ft Ord, CA. Served in Vietnam with the 1st Bn, 83rd Arty; reassigned to HQ XXIV Corps, Vietnam. Discharged from active duty.

In September 1974 returned to the USAR and assigned to 916th Field Depot, Bell, CA until it was deactivated in September 1981. Transferred to 304th MMC for two years. In 1983 volunteered for assignment with the 335th Data Processing Unit which was just activated. Promoted in 1983 to WO1 and continued to serve the unit for the next 10 years. In 1993 the 335th Data Processing Unit was deactivated and as CW3 ADP maint tech, he was transferred to 489th (L) Equip Maint Co, San Bernadino, CA.

Awards/Medals: Meritorious Svc Med, Army Comm Med w/OLC, Army Achievement Med w/OLC, Nat Def Svc Rib w/2 stars, Army Res Component Med, Army Res Overseas Trng Rib and numerous other service and campaign medals.

Member of VFW, TROA and the USAWOA. Previously involved with the US Jr Chamber of Commerce (Jaycee's) and Boy Scouts. Currently employed with the county of Orange (Santa Ana, CA) as systems/programmer analyst. Married to Gayle Uyeno of Cypress, CA (23 years) and has one son, Darryl.

DONALD G. TALBOT, CW4, born March 1, 1940, Norfolk, NE, but considers Midland, TX his hometown. Entered Army in El Paso, TX Aug 29, 1958. Education includes associate of science degree, liberal arts and electronics, 90+ semester hours; Carrier Equip Rep Crs, 7th Army NCO Academy at Bad Toelz; MW Rad Rep Crs; Computer Data Equip Rep Crs; Avionics Maint Officer's Crs; Navigation and Stabilization Crs; Comm Elect WO Adv Crs; Abn Crs, Spec Forces Qual Crs; SF Jumpmaster's Crs; CBR Officer's Crs; Instructor Crs.

Awards/Medals: Master Prcht Badge, Combat Inf Badge, (3) Bronze Stars, Purple Heart, Meritorious Svc Med, (4) Army Comm Med and 3rd awd of Army Good Conduct Med, Vietnam Svc Med w/8 Battle Stars, ARVN Tech Med and Sig Qual Badge. Two of his units were awarded Meritorious Unit Citations. Qualified for Bronze, Silver and Gold Germany Army Shooting Proficiency Badges and awarded the Bronze and Silver German Officers Qualification Badges for sports and shooting proficiency. Qualified for Bronze and Silver German civilian sports proficiency medals. An avid skier and sports parachutist, he holds USPA license numbers of B-2402 and C-3404 The North Vietnamese Army invaded South Vietnam in 1972, and his unit was overrun on three separate occasions.

Worked with Cincinnati Electronics Corp, TRW Electronics Products, Inc, and retired Sept 1, 1984. Now a full time real estate sales consultant in Fayetteville, NC. He is a 32nd Degree Scottish Rite Mason and Shiner.

Single with two wonderful daughters.

KENJI TANAKA, CW4, born Nov 5, 1939, Kona, HI. Entered the Army on Jan 30, 1958, taking basic training at Ft Ord, CA. Attended Diesel Eng Rep Crs at Ft Belvoir, VA. Served with 83rd Ord Co and Co B, 4th Tk Bn, 37th Armor, Ft Knox, KY; Co B, Long Line Sig Bn and 600th Engr Co, Korea; H&H Co, 588th Engr Bn, Ft Lee, VA 185th Engr Co and 555th Maint Co, Okinawa, in the mechanical equipment repair field.

Received direct appointment to WO May 9, 1968, as engineer equip repair tech and attended WO orientation at Ft Sill, OK. Served two combat tours in Vietnam (seven campaigns) as engr equip repair tech (maint officer) and platoon leader with 497th Engr Co (port construction) in Cam Rahn Bay and Saigon and the 59th Engr Co (land clearing) in Chu Lai and Da Nang. Served with 44th Engr Bn, Korea; Army Depot, Okinawa, 84th Engr Bn, 25th Med Bn, 65th Engr Bn, 25th Inf Div in Hawaii. Attended various military schools including Senior WO, Engr Equip Repair Tech and Army instructor's training.

Awards/Medals: Legion of Merit, Bronze Star w/2 OLCs, Meritorious Svc Med, Army Comm Med w/OLC, Army Achievement Med, Good Conduct Med (3rd Awd), Nat Def Svc Med, Humanitarian Svc Med, Armed Forces Exped Med, Vietnam Svc Med w/7 D, AFRM, Army Svc Rib, Overseas Svc Rib w/7 D, RVN Campaign Med, Meritorious Unit Citation w/3 OLCs, RVNCOF w/Palm and RVN Civil Action Unit Citation.

Retired as CW4, July 31, 1984, with 26 1/2 years of service; currently employed as service manager in Honolulu.

MICHAEL WILLIAM TANNENBAUM, CW3, born Chateauroux, France July 18, 1957. Joined the Army Sept 27, 1976, Ft Knox, KY and appointed WO April 24, 1984. Has two associate degrees and BA from Regents College of New York. Completed basic training and AIT for diesel mechanics in 1977.

Assignments: Kirch Goes, Germany, Delta 122nd Maint Co, track and wheel vehicle mechanic, 1977-79; Ft Dix, NJ, 63B Wheel and Power Generation School, wheel vehicle instructor, 1979-82; Ft Bragg, NC, 7th Spec Forces Gp, motor sergeant, 1982-83; Aberdeen, MD, WO Candidate School Class 1-84, candidate, 1983-84; Wiesbaden, Germany 11th Avn Bn (CBT) maint tech, 1984-86; Ft Bragg, NC, 6th Psychological Bn, maint tech, 1987-90; Ft Bragg, NC, Spec Forces Cmd, G4, maint officer, 1990-91; Frankfurt, Germany, 205th MI Bde, S4, staff support maint officer, 1991-92; Frankfurt, Germany, V Corps HQ, G4, maint officer, 1992-93; Columbus, OH, Army training with industry program at UPS, 1993-94; and Ft Lee, VA, US Army Comb Arms Spt Cmd, training development and evaluation, 1994-present.

Awards/Medals: Army Svc Rib, NCO Rib, Overseas Svc Rib (3), Good Conduct Med (2nd awdd), Army Achievement Med (4), Army Comm Med (2), Meritorious Svc Med (2), Air Assault Badge, Master Prcht Badge and the German Jump Wings.

Married Faith and has daughter, Christina, and a son, Caleb.

RICHARD L. TARBOX SR., CW4, born May 28, 1936, Olin, IA. Completed USAWO Sr Crs, Basic and Advanced Adj Gen Off Crs, Army Recruiting Off Crs. Enlisted in USN June 5, 1955, attended basic and AIT at Great Lakes, IL; graduated Aug 15, 1955. Assigned to FASRON 12 US Miramar, CA; transferred to Guided Missile Group One, San Diego, CA.

Relocated to Oahu, HI; transferred to VA-155 San Jose, CA. Released from active duty June 1959 to USNR, Cedar Rapids, IA. Back on active reserve June 1964.

Offered in 1967 a civilian position as unit administrator GS-06, with USAR 301st Field Hosp, Cedar Rapids, IA. Selected staff administrative specialist GS-07 with 457th Trans Bn, Ft Snelling, MN, May 1970. In 1974 selected USAR recruiting off GS-09; 1976 selected mil pers off, GS-11 (civ) and dual CW2 drilling Army Reserve with HQ 425th Trans Bde, Forest Park, IL.

In 1976 transferred with brigade to Ft Sheridan, IL; 1985 applied for AGR position with 477th Pers Svc Co as SIDPERS Chief, Ft Sheridan, IL, serving five years; transferred June 1990 to HQ 89th USARCOM, Wichita, KS.

Released from active duty Sept 17, 1993, immediately assigned to admin tech Res position with DCSIM, HQ 89th USARCOM.

Awards/Medals: Army Svc Rib, Nat Def Svc Med w/ Bronze Star, ALB, Navy Good Conduct, Army Comm Med w/OLC, Army Achiev Med w/OLC, Armed Forces Res Med w/OLC, Army Res Components Achiev Med w/OLC, Overseas Svc Rib, Army Res Components Overseas Trng Rib and Marksman Rifle M-16. Spent almost 17 years on active duty, 22 years of reserve duty and over 25 years of civil service. Highest civilian grade to date is GS-11; highest military grade is CW4.

Currently working as civilian unit admin GS-06 with HHD 331st Med Gp, Wichita, KS and attending Res drills with the HQ 89th USARCOM, Wichita as CW4 admin tech.

Lives in Rose Hill, KS with wife and two sons. Oldest daughter and family lives in Columbus, GA; second daughter and family in Waukegan, IL; oldest son and family in Wichita, KS. Member at large with WOA.

DALE C. TAYLOR, CWO, born Aug 18, 1956, Peoria, IL. Joined the USA in March 1976; attended basic combat training and AIT at Ft Leonard Wood, MO. Served as motor sergeant in Germany, at Ft Sill and Ft Bragg before being selected for drill sergeant duty in 1983. He was assigned as a drill sergeant in the same unit that he had taken basic training with several years earlier. After a successful tour of duty as a drill sergeant, he was assigned as the motor sergeant for the 463rd MP Co at Ft Leonard Wood until he was selected to attend WO School at APG, MD in April 1986.

After his appointment to WO in October 1986, he has served as maint officer in Alaska and New Jersey and is currently stationed in Hawaii. Participated in Operation Desert Storm in Saudi Arabia and Operation Restore Hope in Somalia, both times as member of the 513th MI Bde. Besides these two events his most memorable experience was serving as the protocol officer for TF 1-17 in Sinai for eight months as part of the Multinational Peacekeeping Force.

Awards/Medals: Meritorious Svc Med, (5) Army Comm Med, (2) Army Achievement Med, (2) Good Conduct Med, Nat Def Svc Med, Armed Forces Exped Med, Multinational Force Observers Med, Kuwait Lib Med, SWA Svc Med, Meritorious Unit Citation, Expert Mechanics Badge and Drill Sergeant Identification Badge.

Married to former Vickie Lady and has one child, Amanda Gail.

THOMAS E. TAYLOR, CW4, born Jan 29, 1938, Chestnut, LA. Entered the Army in January 1955; basic training at Ft Jackson, SC with AIT at APG, MD as ordnance supply specialist. Served at Nancy General Depot, Nancy, France from 1955-59 attaining grade of E-5; in the 539th Heavy Equip Maint Co, Ft Benning, GA from 1959-60; in 3rd Army Combined Guided Missile Field Maint Activity, Albany, GA from 1960-61; in the 47th Ord Gp, Stuttgart, Germany, from 1961-63 attaining grade of E-6. Also an honor graduate of the 7th Army NCO Academy during this period.

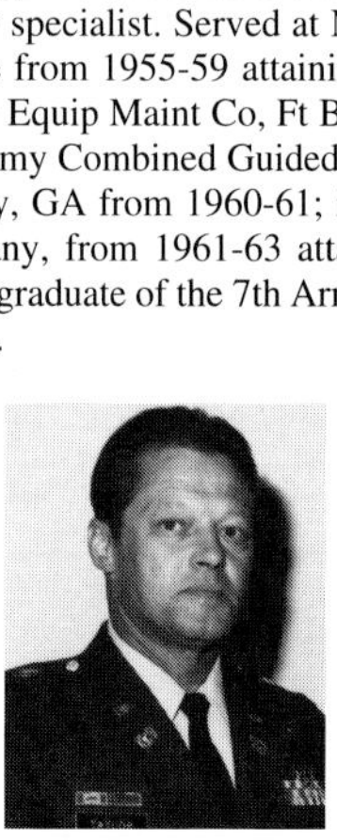

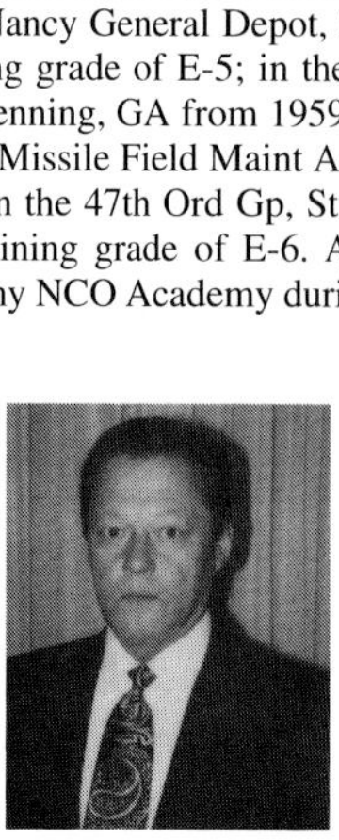

Served with the 87th Maint Bn, Nellingen, Germany from 1963-66, attaining grade of E-7. Appointed to WO at Texarkana Army Depot in May 1966; served as property book officer 15th Engr Bn, 9th Inf Div from 1966-67, Ft Riley, KS and in Vietnam; as PBO 79th Engr Bn, Neu Ulm, Germany from 1967-69; as PBO 3rd Bn 7th Inf, 199th Inf Bde, Vietnam from 1969-70; as S-4 supply tech 68th Trans Bn, Ft Carson, CO, 1970-72; S-4/Sup Tech 101st Ordnance Bn, Heilbronn, Germany from 1972-77; S-4 701st Maint Bn from 1977-79; as chief, USAREUR Equip Survey Team, Heidelberg Germany from 1979-89.

Awards/Medals: Legion of Merit w/OLC, BS w/3 OLCs, Meritorious Svc Med w/OLC, Army Comm Med w/ OLC and various service medals.

Retired on March 31, 1985, with concurrent recall to active duty and returned to retired rolls on March 31, 1989, with over 34 years of active duty.

Married Helga Binder of Stuttgart, Germany, and they have three sons. They currently reside in Germany and he is employed as chief, equipment survey team, HQ USAREUR and 7A, Heidelberg, Germany. He has also retained his membership with the WOA.

LEVI A. TERBIO, CW2, born March 2, 1954, Republic of the Philippines. Entered Army October 1976, taking basic training at Ft Dix, NJ and AIT at Ft Lee, VA. First assignment was HHC, 94th Engr Bn Cbt (Hvy), Darmstadt, Germany from April 1977-August 1981.

Subsequent assignments were with CSC and HHC, 2/19th Inf Bn (M), Ft Stewart, GA, September 1981-June 1983, as TAMMS clerk and supply sergeant, C Trp, 1/11th Armd Cav Regt, Germany, August 1983-August 1990, where he initially served as senior supply sergeant and later served as property book officer (PBO) and chief, Central Issue Branch.

Attained rank of SFC in his 10 years of enlisted service.

Appointed WO in QM Corps December 1990; honor graduate of his class at WO Entry Crs, Ft Rucker, AL; and distinguished graduate of his class at the WO Technical/Tactical Certification Crs, Ft Lee, VA. Initial PBO duty as WO was brief and memorable. Last PBO for the 2nd Bn, 20th FA Regt, Germany prior to its deactivation in June 1992. Current assignment is PBO for 2nd Bn, 14th FA (MLRS) 3ID, Germany (June 1992-January 1996).

Awards/Medals: Meritorious Svc Med, Army Comm Med w/4 OLCs, Army Achievement Med w/6 OLCs, Nat Def Rib and various service ribbons.

Married Maureen Cruz of Metro-Manila, Philippines. They have two sons, Dennis and John Christopher.

WILLIAM E. TERRELL, PFC, born Blanchard, OK, on Oct 31, 1918. He enlisted in OKNG July 1, 1937, and discharged as PFC June 30, 1940. Drafted during WWII June 29, 1944; attended basic training Ft Hood, TX. Qualified for Parachute School, Ft Benning on Sept 16, 1944. Advanced training with 541st Prcht Regt, Camp Mackall, NC. Joined 187th Parachute Regt in Batangas Province in Philippines and served in occupation of Japan until 1946. Discharged April 4, 1946.

Joined 45th Sig Co, ONG 1949, and called to active duty as M/SGT for Korea Sept 1, 1950. Trained at Camp Polk, LA, then shipped to Hokkaido, Japan. Made AUS Warrant, W-1 in Hokkaido May 15, 1951. Served with division in Korea until 1952 when his family joined him in Japan. Attended nine months of Army Security Agency School, Ft Devens in 1953, and promoted to W-2. Served with agency in Alaska, then transferred to Ft Huachuca where he made W-3. Served four years in Italy where he acquired BS degree from U of Maryland.

Returned to Ft Hood where he was involved with Desert Strike and Big Lift, then returned to Korea. Promoted to W-4 and selected for RA in 1965. Stationed with USAICA in Virginia, then sent to Army Crypto Depot in Worms, Germany. Retired at Ft MacArthur Nov 30, 1970.

Married Lavelle Johnson in Oklahoma in 1938.

WILLIAM H. THOMAS, CW2, born Nov 8, 1918, Seattle, WA. Enlisted in USNR March 23, 1936, as apprentice seaman, rose to chief carpenters mate January 1944. Served aboard battleship, two cruisers, a destroyer, mine sweeper, net tender.

Ended WWII on a refrigeration ship in South Pacific. Promoted warrant carpenter in October 1944 and retained rank until his discharge in Mary 1949.

In May 1949 accepted Army commission and served

with 18th Inf, 1st Inf Div in Germany. Transferred branch to MPC and remained in MPC until December 1963 totaling 28 years service. During Army service attained rank of captain, was relieved from active duty October 1957 and reverted to RA E-6 until appointed to CW2 June 1, 1961.

As accredited criminal investigator instructed at Provost Marshal General School, Ft Gordon, GA. Later transferred to PM Section, HQ, 7th Army in Germany until retirement in December 1963. Attained BA degree from U of Washington, initiated and taught criminal justice education at Shoreline Community College, Seattle for 16 years. Retired as professor emeritus June 1981.

Awards/Medals: Army Comm Med and numerous service campaign medals. Member of TROA, VFW, DAV and CIDAA.

Married Shirley Jennings of Seattle; they have five sons and 11 grandchildren.

WILLIAM K. THOMAS, CW5, born June 7, 1942, Connersville, IN. Enlisted Nov 9, 1960, 231st Trans Co (FC), USAR, St Pete, FL. February 1961 BCT, Co A-4-1, Ft Jackson, SC; April 1961 AIT, Ft Eustis, VA, as Marine engineman; July 1961 RFRAD to 231st TC.

Reclass to Harbor craft crewman and activated with 231st for Berlin Crisis from Oct 1, 1961-Aug 13, 1962, Ft Eustis, VA. Appointed WO1 on Dec. 21, 1965, as marine deck officer. Jan 22, 1968-Jan 22, 1969, served as mate, USAV *Rendezvous* (freight ship [FS] 476), 70th Trans Plt (FC). Dec 21, 1968, promoted CW2; Jan 22, 1969-June 4, 1976, served as master, small tug 2129; mate, USAV *Resource* (FS), 72nd Trans Plt (FC); Dec 21, 1975, promoted CW3.

Entered AD June 6, 1976; Marine Deck Officer Advance Crs MOS 500A, August 1976-December 1976; December 1976-May 1978, commanded USAVs LCU 1507 and LCU 1671 (test vessel of new class of landing craft utility (LCU)), 97th Trans Co (heavy boat), 10th Trans Bn, 7th Trans Gp. May 1978, Cdr USAV large tug (LT) 2088, 73rd Trans Co (FC), 11th Trans Bn, 7th Trans Gp. July-November 1979, Harbormaster, 3rd Port, Ft Eustis, VA; November 1979-December 1980, chief mate and XO of motor vessel, USAV *Gen Wm. J. Sutton* (469th Trans Det).

January-July 1981, attended WO Senior Crs, Ft Rucker, AL; July 1981-March 1984, chief instructor of Marine navigation, Army Trans School, Ft Eustis, VA. March 1, 1982, promoted to CW4; March 1984-July 1986, harbormaster, MTMC Trans Terminal Unit, Azores, Portugal. July 1986-April 1991, training developer Marine WO Courses (MOS 880A/881A), USA Trans School, Ft Eustis, VA. April 1991 commanded and delivered USAV Five Forks (LCU-2018), a new class of Army ship to 1097th Trans Co, Rep of Panama.

April 1992-present, chief, Marine Qualification Div, Office of the Chief of Transportation, Ft Eustis, VA. March 1, 1993, the first CW5 promoted in Trans Corps. August-September 1993, Master WO Crs, 93-4. Best assignment was command of any Army ship and training Army soldier/ mariners.

Awards/Medals: Meritorious Svc Med w/OLC, ARCOM w/OLC, AResCAM, Nat Def Svc Med w/star, AFR and two Overseas Svc Rib.

Married Sue Deas of Lake Alfred, FL, and has one daughter, Erin. Hobbies include golf, computers and mechanics. Member of USAWOA, USN Institute and US Army Trans Corps Regt Assn.

REGINALD L. THORNHILL, CW2, born Sept 13, 1931, in Winnsboro, LA. He enlisted in the US Army on Nov 17, 1950, and Feb 20, 1959. Basic training at Ft Chaffee, AR

with the 347th Cbt Engr Bn, Korea; Ft McCoy, WI; Co B, 9th Armd Inf Bn, Ft Leonard Wood, MO; Rec Co USATC (I) GAR, Ft Ord, CA; 1st ETC USAOS, APG, MD; Co A 708th Ord Bn; HQ Co, USAG&LSOE, Camp Roberts, CA; Co 707th Ord Bn; HQ & Co A, 124th Maint Bn, 2nd Armd Div, Ft Hood, TX.

With 1st CS Bn Maint USAREUR; HQ & Co A, 1st Maint Bn USAREUR; HHC VII Corps USAREUR; USAOC&S, APG, MD; HHC 1st Bn USAOC&S, APG, MD; US Mil Asst Cmd, VN; WTD HQ & Co USAOC&S Sch Bde, APB, MD; B Co, 124th Maint Bn, Ft Hood, TX; D Co, 702nd Maint Bn, 2nd Inf Div, Korea; and Co D, 27th Maint Bn, 1st Cav Div Ft Hood, TX.

Retired Feb 29, 1976, with the rank of CW2. Awards include the Nat Def Svc Med w/OLC, UN Svc Med, Good Conduct Med w/clasp (bronze, 3 loops), Korean Svc Med w/ 3 BSs, VN Svc Med w/SSS, RVN Camp Med, Vietnamese Ord Badge, Bronze Star, Vietnamese Cross of Gallantry w/ palm (two awds), Vietnamese Armed Forces Honor Med 2/ c..

Married Marie Jackson in 1965 and has two children. Retired in 1993 from maint tech in Community Hospitals in Central California. He enjoys fishing, deep sea and fresh water.

ROBERT THURMAN, CW4, born May 30, 1935, Ruston, LA, but considers Wichita Falls, TX his hometown. Military education includes USA NCO Academy, Army Logistics Service Schools and USAWO Crs.

Served as property book officer for HQ 980th Engr Bn, September 1981-July 1986 in Wichita Falls, TX; property book officer for HHC 353rd Engr Gp, July 1986-March 1991, Oklahoma City, OK; property book officer for USAR Ctr, Dallas, TX, March 1991-present.

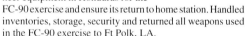

Selected by his command over numerous other WOs to fulfill property control requirements for engineer equipment in Honduras for the FC-90 exercise and ensure its return to home station. Handled inventories, storage, security and returned all weapons used in the FC-90 exercise to Ft Polk, LA.

Awarded a plaque for the best staff technician during the year of 1984, Meritorious Svc Med, (2) Army Comm Med, (2) Army Achievement Med, (3) Army Good Conducts.

Currently assigned as property account tech, HQ 493rd Engr Gp, Dallas, TX. Additional duties include environmental compliance officer and property book officer USAR Ctr.

Married and has two children at home, ages 15 and 17.

JOHN A. TIMM, CW3, born Aug 6, 1952, Inglewood, CA. Enlisted in US Army as supply tech and served at Ft Campbell; Ft Dix; Ft Drum; Ft Hood; Ft Sill; Presidio SF; Stuttgart and Mannheim, Germany.

Memorable experience was being a drill sergeant from 1980-82, and WO hut renovation at Mannheim, Germany.

Awards/Medal: Meritorious Svc Med w/5 OLCs, Army Comm Med w/OLC and Army Achievement Med w/OLC. Still in the service with rank CW3 as property book officer. He is a seven year member of the USAWOA.

WILLIAM M. TREAT, CW4, born Dec 5, 1920, Staten Island, NY. Enlisted September 1939 for Panama. He was a private with the 11th Engr Bn; PFC, MPs (was honor guard for FDR's visit in 1940); AC photographer, corporal staff

sergeant; photo sergeant assigned to original 501st Prcht Inf Bn in Panama, 1940-41; photo NCOIC at Ft Kobbe-Howard Field, Dec 7, 1941.

After OCS acceptance, but long delay for return to CONUS, took exams for WO. After Pearl Harbor sent with group of RA first three graders to man gun crews on civilian ships taking dependents from Panama and Hawaii back to States.

Returned to Panama where WOJG "red border" letter appointment from War Dept came later in 1942, as aerial photo officer, MOS 8502. First duty as adjutant and also assigned the dreaded yearly Post PX inventory officer.

Following secret clearance and secret courier duty, eventual duty as aerial observer/aerial photo officer and liaison officer for secret mapping project "Casey Jones" in Europe. Duty covered South Central American, Pacific, Africa, Middle East, India, England, Europe with Army and B-17 units with 306th BG and 19th Photo Recon; MOS 9302 added (CIC agent).

Returned from Europe in 1946 and released from active duty. Went into active Reserve with 70th CIC Det, then 65th and 346th CIC Dets. Made CW4 in 1965 and retired in 1978.

Spent 40 years in civilian job as special agent with Burlington and Denver, Rio Grande Western Railroads, retired in 1985. Collector of military insignia, etc., and advisor to antique dealers on military and other specialties.

Married Betty over 50 years ago and has five children (three boys with Army/Navy service), 12 grandchildren and one great-grandson. Member of American Legion, TROA, ASMIC, life member of Colorado Law Enforcement Officers Assoc.

EDRYCE N. TUCKER, CW3, born July 22, 1955, Montclair, NJ. Graduated from East Orange High School, East Orange, NJ, 1973. Entered the WAC in September 1974. Upon completion of basic training at Ft Jackson, SC, she completed an On-The-Job Training Program as 76Y at Ft Leonard Wood, MO.

First duty assignment was as supply clerk A-4-4 Engr Trng Co. In 1976 promoted to sergeant and assumed duties as supply sergeant with same unit. In 1979 reassigned to HHC Wildflecken Training Area, Wildflecken, FRG as supply sergeant. Promoted to staff sergeant in 1981 and assigned to 179th MID, 197th Inf Bde, Ft Benning, GA, as supply sergeant; was selected to be automated property book NCO (DLOGS) with 197th Spt Bn and fielded SPBS.

Completed ANOC at Ft Lee, VA in September 1984 as distinguished graduate. Promoted to SFC November 1985. Attended WOEC in April 1986, completed WOTCC at Ft Lee, VA as honor graduate Sept 30, 1986, and appointed to CW2.

First assignment as property book officer was with 72nd Sig Bn, Karlshrahe, FRG, where she converted five manual property books to SPBS-R. In 1989 she was assigned to the 44th Med Bde, 18th Abn Corps as property book officer, brigade budget officer and brigade logistical advisor.

Deployed to SWA for Operation Desert Shield/Desert Storm from October 1990-April 1991. Reassigned to present duty station, 50th Sig Bn, 35th Sig Bde, 18th ABN Corp as property book officer in August 1991. Promoted to CW3 in March 1993.

Awards/Medals: Bronze Star, ARCOM, Army Achievement Med, (3) Army Good Conduct, Nat Def Svc Rib, SWA w/2 Bronze Stars, (3) NCO Professional Development, (2) Overseas Svc Rib and KLM.

Married SFC Ricky Tucker of Virginia and has two sons, Ramone and Larry. Member of USAWOA, QM Assoc. and AUSA.

CARRIE E. TUNING, CW2, born Roanoke Rapids, NC July 29, 1958. Attended Halifax Community College, Weldon, NC. Entered US Army in June 1977. Basic training at Ft Jackson, SC and AIT at Ft Benjamin Harrison, IN. Received BS degree in business management from U of Maryland, 1984.

Assigned to Staff Judge Advocate Office, Ft Dix, NJ; attended WO Entry Crs, Ft Sill, OK, graduating with honors. Completed certification training and received recognition as first black female to be appointed WO in the Judge Advocate General Corps.

Received MS degree in administration from Central Michigan University, 1987. Spearheaded establishment of first electronic income tax filing program for Staff Judge Advocate Office, Ft Belvoir, VA. After three years transferred to HQ, US Army, 7th Army Europe, Office of the Judge Advocate, Heidelberg, Germany. Spearheaded establishment of first electronic income tax filing program for the entire Army throughout Europe.

Authored and published a quarterly automation newsletter for the Judge Advocate General Corps with distribution throughout Europe and the States. Completed tour in Europe and assigned as the Chief, Information Management Officer for US Army Litigation Ctr, Arlington, VA. Currently pursuing doctoral studies at George Mason Univ.

Awards include (4) Meritorious Svc Med, (4) ACMs, (2) AAMs and recognition as 1987 Outstanding Woman in *The World Who's Who of Women.* Member of WOA.

Married Lucas Tuning and they hs two children, Careka and Lucas II.

RALPH L. TURNER, born Sept 6, 1933, Gastonia, NC. Began military career in August 1949 with SCARNG 713 AAA Gun Bn, York, SC. Called to active duty Aug 15, 1950, and attended basic and AIT training at Camp Stewart, GA.

Appointed WO1 Sept 22, 1961, and served overseas with 50th AAA AW BN, Korea, 32nd AD Cmd. Germany, 110th Maint Co, Vietnam and the 284th Avn Unit, Korea.

Stateside assignments included Ft Jackson, SC; Monmouth, NJ; Ft McNair, Washington, DC; Ft Bliss, TX; Ft Meade, MD; Camp McCoy, WI; and Ft Benning, GA.

Presently a contractor for wide body aircraft maintenance with Federal Express Corp in Korea.

CHARLES BERNARD TYLER SR., born Sept 30, 1884, in Hayes, KS. Joined the US Army in 1905 after graduating from the Institute of Musical Art, NY. Was one of the first 10 people appointed WO upon that rank's creation and one of the first three people promoted to CWO upon creation.

Served with Black Jack Pershing, both in the interior of Mexico and at the border, in the Philippine Islands. With the 28th Inf Band, was part of the first American band to land in Europe during WWI. With the 1st Inf Div, spearheaded the attack throughout France, Luxembourg, Belgium and were the first to cross the Rhine. Last 19 years of active duty were at Ft Sill, OK.

Awards: Legion of Merit, French Croix de Guerre, French Fourragere, Interior of Mexico, Mexican Border, Philippine Campaign, WWI Victory w/5 Battle Stars, German Occupation (WWI), Nat Def Svc Med, Good Conduct Med w/3 clasps, American and WWII Victory. Composed, recomposed, and arranged numerous military marches, including one dedicated to the 18th FA. A long time Mason and member of the American Legion. He has two sons, Charles Jr and John, who graduated from West Point and retired after distinguished careers as commissioned officers. Daughter, Louise, served during WWII as commission Army nurse; and grandson, William George, retired as a CWO.

Tyler retired at Ft Sill, OK in 1946. He passed away Jan 26, 1951, at Lawton, OK.

MAYNARD M. UHLIG, CW4, born Feb 22, 1949, Sheboygan, WI. Entered US Army Sept 18, 1969, taking basic training at Ft Campbell and AIT at Ft Knox. Received airborne training at Ft Benning and assigned to the 82nd Abn Div, Ft Bragg, as field radio mechanic, RATT operator and tactical comm chief, 1970-77.

Served the 72nd Armor Bn, Korea, July 1977-August 1978 as tactical comm chief; September 1978 assigned to communication electronic test board, Ft Gordon, as RAM/LOG evaluator; transferred to Arlington Hall Station, VA as OIC, Communications-Electronic Installation Det supporting INSCOM and Engineering Applications Branch Chief, USACC-INSCOM.

Served as Bn CE Maint Chief, 26th Sig Bn, Heilbronn, and 44th Sig Bn, Mannheim, Germany, August 1983-October 1986 and July 1989-1992, respectively; served with 112th Sig Bn, Ft Bragg as CE maint officer, November 1986-July 1989; deployed to Operation Desert Shield/Storm in January 1991. Currently serving in system engineering directorate, USAISEC, Ft Huachuca, as satellite systems engineer.

Awards include Meritorious Svc Med, Army Comm Med, Army Achievement Med, Meritorious Unit Cit, Army Good Conduct, Nat Def Svc Med, NCO PDR, Army Svc Rib, Overseas Svc Rib, SWA Kuwaiti Lib Med and Master Parachutist Badge.

Member of Electronics Technicians Assoc; lifetime member of VFW and USAWOA; served as PAO in the Ft Bragg and Mannheim USAWOA chapters and as vice president at Mannheim.

Married Carolyn Chesshire of Elgin, OK and has a daughter, step-daughter and grandson. Hobbies are hunting, gardening, woodworking and reading.

DONALD E. UMLAUF, CW3, born Feb 13, 1935, Lackawanna, NY. Began military career Aug 7, 1951, in NYNG, HQ 134th Med Bn, 27th Inf Div. Served with HQ Btry 102nd AAA, 817th Evc Hosp, 402nd CA, HQ, 1st Bn, 391st Regt 4th Bde, 98th Div. In 1961 called to active duty with 134th Ord, Ft Dix, NJ.

Appointed WO CW2 June 4, 1985, as 920B; as IMA served as DAAS-3 officer, HQ 10th Mtn Div, Ft Drum, NY; supply system tech, Army Material Cmd, Alexandria, VA. Supply system tech, SARD-MS, Pentagon June 1991; called to active duty with 164th Maint DS Co.

Retired from CECOM, Ft Monmouth, NJ in March 1988 as general supply spec.

Member of USAWOA, American Legion, VFW, DAV, Mason, National Sojourners, ROA and NARFE. Hobbies are model railroads, civil war, collect unit chest and patches and collect coffee mugs.

Wife Barbara Ann is deceased; he has two children and six grandchildren.

ROY A VALIANT, CW4, born Oct 22, 1949, in Elmhurst, IL. Began his military career in basic training at Ft Polk, LA Sept 15, 1969. Entered WO flight training at Mineral Wells, TX in February 1970; graduated from Flight School and appointed WO1 on Nov 16, 1970.

First assignment as WO was at Ft Hood, TX with the 181st Assault Helicopter Co as UH-1H helicopter pilot. Assigned to 7/1st Cav in Vinh Long Vietnam from July 1971-March 1972. Reassigned to Ft Hood. Has had various positions with numerous attack helicopter (COBRA) units.

Graduated from USA Aviation Safety Officers Crs in August 1976. Was an aviation safety officer at troop level at Ft Hood, squadron level in Korea, and brigade and regiment level in Germany. Assigned to HQ V Corps in Frankfurt,

Germany on May 18, 1992, as the WO and aviation officer assignment manager. Qualified in the following aircraft: AH-1S, AH-1Q, AH-1G, OH-58A/C and UH-1H.

Awards include the Bronze Star, Air Medal (13th awd), ARCOM w/2 OLCs, Army Achievement Med, Armed Forces Res Med, Vietnm Svc Rib, SWA Kuwait Lib Med and the Master Aviator Badge.

Education includes BS from American Technological Univ and the WO Senior Crs. Member of VFW and life member of USAWOA.

Married Valerie Norma Flynn of Basingstoke, England.

HARLAND L. VANDERPOOL, CW2, born Feb 15, 1955, HOR Pilot Rock, OR. Joined the service on a delayed entry program April 19, 1973, and entered active duty Aug 6, 1973. Attended basic training at Ft Leonard Wood, MO, August-October 1973; AIT at Ft Jackson, SC from October-December 1973 and Ft Monmouth, NJ from January-July 1974, MOS 26D, ground control approach radar repairman.

Assignments included Coleman Bks, Mannheim, FRG, 1974-76; Ft Sill, OK, 1976-79; Camp Humphreys, Korea, 1979-80; Ft Lewis, WA, 1980-83; Dolan Bks, Schwaibisch Hall, FRG, 1983-85; Ft Hood, TX, 1985-87; WO Entry Crs, APG, MD, October-December 1987; Technical Certification Crs, Ft Gordon, GA, January-May 1988; Ft Riley, KS, 1988-90; Kaiserslautern, FRG, 1991-93; Ft Bragg, NC, 1993-present.

Awards include (5) Army Comm Med, (4) Good Conduct, (2) Nat Def Svc Med, Armed Forces Exped Med and Meritorious Svc Med. Expert on M16, .38, .45 and 9mm. He retired on March 31, 1995.

Married Teresa and has two daughters, Andrea and Megan.

JOSEPH A. VANDERVEST JR., CW4, born March 4, 1939, Ludington, MI. Joined Army Security Agency in November 1956; appointed WO1 (MOS721A), December 1967; and retired as CW4 (MOS290AL) October 1984 after 28 years of service. Spent 24 years overseas in Germany, Vietnam, Thailand and Turkey.

His awards include the Legion of Merit, Meritorious Svc Med, Joint Svc Comm Med, Army Comm Med, Army Achievement Med, Good Conduct Med (3 awds), Nat Def Svc Med, Armed Forces Exped Med, Army Occupation Med (Berlin), Army Svc Med, Overseas Svc Rib (7 awds), Meritorious Unit Citation, Vietnam Svc Med (5 campaign stars), RVN Cross of Gallantry w/palm device, and Vietnam Campaign Med.

Received AA and BS degree from U of Maryland. Life member of VFW, DAV and Sig Corps Regt Assoc and member of AUSA and USAWOA.

Married Janett Van Velzen of Holland and has a son, a daughter and one granddaughter.

MIGUEL H. VANEGAS, CW2, born Sept 4, 1949, Marlin, TX. Entered the TXARNG Sept 1, 1972-May 3, 1973. Basic and AIT training at Ft Ord, CA. May 1973 took Abn Crs at Ft Benning, GA; awarded Parachutist Badge, April 27, 1973. Served with TXARNG, SPT CO, 1st Bn (Abn), 143rd Inf, Marlin, TX, April 1973-Aug 27, 1974.

Enlisted in Regular Army Aug 28, 1974. From September 1974-February 1976 assigned to B Btry, 2nd Bn, 5th ADA, 2nd AD, Ft Hood, TX; February 1976-March 1977 assigned to 45th Trans Co, Korea; April 1977-February 1978 assigned to A Btry 2nd Bn, 52nd ADA, Ft Bliss, TX; February 1978-May 1978 (63C) AIT Ft Knox, KY; May 1978-July 1979 assigned 4th Spt Ctr, 13th COSCOM, Ft Hood, TX.

July 1978-July 1982 assigned to A Btry, 3rd Bn, 71st ADA, Germany; July 1982-April 1987 assigned to HSB 2nd Bn (abn) 2/321st FA (3/319th, Oct 2, 1986) 82nd Abn, Ft Bragg, NC (best time in service). April 1987-September 1987 WOCC (Class 87-6), Co B, 2nd Ord Bn, 61st Ord Bde, USAOC&S, APG, MD; Sept 10, 1987 appointed WO CW1; September 1987-December 1990 assigned to Svc Btry, 6th Bn, 32nd FA, Ft Sill, OK; December 1990-December 1991 assigned HHC 203rd Spt Bn, Germany; December 1991-December 1994 assigned B Co 703rd MSB. MOSs held were 11BP, 63BP, 63 HP, 630A and 915A.

Most memorable experience was as WO in 6th Bn, 32nd FA, Ft Sill, OK. When the battalion commander said to his officers on his first meeting, "Professional soldiers to me are WO, majors and above, captains and lieutenants are learning to be soldiers." .

His awards include the Meritorious Svc Med, Nat Def Svc Med w/star, Army Achievement Med w/2 OLCs, Army Comm Med, (3) Overseas Rib, Good Conduct (3rd) and NCO PDR Awd.

Married Heide Weber of Heilbronn, Germany. Hobbies are fishing, computers and woodwork. Member of the USAWOA.

MELVIN RAYMOND VAN STEENWYK, CWO3,
born July 29, 1950, Sioux Falls, SD. Joined the Trans Corps on Aug 16, 1974; Marine engineering officer 881A2. Military stations include Ft Carson, CO; Wiesbaden, Germany; Ft Eustis, VA; Azores, PO; and Diego Garcia.

Memorable experience was deploying and retrograde from Ahas Tara II and operation Provide Hope.

Awards include EJB, Joint Svc Comm Med, ARCOM, Joint Svc Achievement Med, Army Achievement Med, Good Conduct Med, NCO PDR, Army Svc Rib, Nat Def Svc Med, and Overseas Svc Rib.

Retired from service Aug 31, 1994, with rank CWO-3. Married Ruth (CW3) and has three sons: Thomas (22), Andrew (16), and William (5 months). Maint officer with the 558th Trans Co, Ft Eustis, VA.

RUTH ANN VAN STEENWYK, CW3, born July 8,
1955, Madison, SD. Joined the Trans Corps as Marine engineering officer 881AZ March 3, 1978. Military stations include Frankfurt, Germany; Ft Davis, Panama; Azores, Portugal; and Ft Eustis, VA.

Her most memorable experience was sailing from Panama to Virginia on the LCU-1677, USAV *Brandywine*.

Awards include Army Svc Rib, Nat Def Svc Med, Army Achievement Med, Meritorious Svc Med, Joint Svc Comm, Army Comm Med and Joint Svc Achievement Med. Her current rank is CW3.

Married CW3 Melvin VanSteenwyk and they have one son, William. She is an instructor/writer at USATSCH, Ft Eustis, VA.

MARK E. VARNEY, CW2, born March 29, 1957,
Concord, NH. Began military career in US Army on July 22, 1975, at Ft Jackson, SC with basic training. Attended AIT at Ft Jackson, SC for MOS 63B. Held various positions up through motor sergeant, attaining the rank of SSG.

On June 25, 1986, appointed WO, WO1, as light systems maintenance tech assigned to 123rd Sig Bn, 1st Armd Div, Ansbach, Germany. Transferred to HQ, 1st Armd Div to become the assistant division maintenance officer on June 26, 1989. July 1, 1990, transferred to become the chief of inspections for the division inspector general's office.

Deployed to SWA Dec 27, 1990, and returned on May 1, 1991. Transferred to the combat aviation brigade of the 1st Armd Div to become the brigade maintenance officer.

His awards include the Bronze Star, Meritorious Svc Med, Army Comm Med w/2 OLCs, Army Achievement Med w/4 OLCs, Army Good Conduct Med w/3 knots, Nat Def Svc Med, SWA Svc Med, Kuwait Lib Med, Humanitarian Svc Med, NCO PDR w/#2, Army Svc Rib and Overseas Svc Rib w/#3.

Married Karin Woelzlein of Ansbach, Germany; has one daughter, Diana. Life member of USAWOA and European Region vice president from 1991-1994.

JOEL STEWARD VINSANT, CW4, born March 13,
1938, Whitesburg, KY. Entered the US Army July 3, 1956; basic at Ft Hood, TX; AIT at APG and USNEOD School, Indianhead, MD.

Served with EOD Units in CONUS, Far East and Europe. Commissioned Dec 3, 1966, in Ord Corps as ammunition tech and served as chief, Conv Ammo Br USAMMCS, RSA, Ala, Vietnam during the 1968 Tet Offensive and with a number of DS/GS ammo units in CONUS, Far East and Europe.

Awards/Medals: Silver Star, Bronze Star, Legion of Merit, Meritorious Svc Med w/2 OLCs, Army Comm Med and numerous service and campaign medals. He retired in April 1980.

Married Alice Marie Burkheimer of Ohio. Currently employed as Dep Dir, Chattanooga/Hamilton County Emergency Services and owner of Cornucopia Coin Exchange.

JOEL J. VOISINE, MW4, born July 30, 1951, Ft Kent,
ME. Entered the US Army Dec 22, 1970, attended basic training at Ft Polk, LA and flight training at Ft Wolters, TX and Ft Rucker, AL. Served as UH-1 pilot with the 82nd Avn Co, Ft Bragg, NC and the 117th Avn Co, Korea.

Attended the UH-1 Instructor Pilot Crs and served in that capacity in the 9th Avn Bn, Ft Lewis, WA. Received training and certification as instrument flight examiner and served with the 2nd Armor Div, Germany, and as operations officer for SHAPE flight detachment. Prior to

his present assignment he was platoon leader for the Blackhawk instructor pilot course and served in the aviation proponent office for a short period of time.

Awards include the Defense Meritorious Svc Med, Meritorious Svc Med w/2 OLCs, Army Comm Med and numerous service and unit medals.

Currently the Chief, Leader Development Branch, WO Div, PERSCOM. Member of Army Avn Assoc of America, TROA and USAWOA. Served as vice president, Aviation Center WOA Chapter.

Married Gloria (Kim) Dubois also of Ft Kent, ME and has two children, Josh and Nicole.

JOHN T. WADE, CW4, born Oct 6, 1936, Columbia,
TN. Enlisted in TNARNG May 3, 1954, with the 30th Inf Div Band. Served as euphonium and trombone player, section leader, drum major, brass group leader and enlisted band leader. Unit was redesignated as 30th Armd Div Band in 1955 and as 129th Army Band in 1972. Appointed CW2 from MSG on March 20, 1970. Promoted to CW4 April 22, 1982; MOS 420C, Bandmaster; SQI instructor and instruction methods developer; and ASI master fitness trainer.

Awarded the Meritorious Svc Med w/OLC, Army Comm Med w/3 OLCs, Army Achievement Med, AF Achievement Med, Army Res Component Achievement Med w/4 OLCs, Nat Def Svc Med, Armed Forces Res Med w/2 HG, Army Svc Rib, Army Res Component OCONUS Trng Rib w/number 2, Expert Marksmanship Badge w/pistol and rifle, Dist Svc Med, Comm Rib w/2 OLCs, Recruiting Merit Rib w/OLC, Individual Achievement Rib, Svc Rib w/SLC, Volunteer Rib, Recruiting and Retention Unit Commendation w/OLC, Governor's Unit Comm, Governor's Dist Unit Comm w/3 OLCs, ARNG Master Recruiter Badge, AG Staff Badge, Theodore Roosevelt Medal and Order of Horatio Gates Bronze Med.

Graduated with BS and MA degrees from George Peabody College of Vanderbilt Univ with 55 post MA semester hours in music, administration and supervision. Retired from Metropolitan Nashville-Davidson County Public Schools in 1982 after 25 years of service. Currently teaches music and band at Davidson Academy, Nashville, TN.

Wade married Jane Wjlliams and has two sons. Hobbies are camping, canoeing, hiking and volunteer work with Boy Scouts of America. Member of USAWOA, NGA ROA, Music Educators National Conference, National Education Assn, Phi Mu Alpha Sinfonia and National Band Assoc.

LARRY KENNETH WAGGONER, CW4, born Aug
20, 1940, White Cloud, KS. Joined Army June 6, 1958, and served at several Nike Ajax/Hercules ADA sites in CONUS and Korea. Began Flight School in 1966 (WORWAC 66-15). Assigned to 3rd Sqdn, 17th Air Cav, Ft Knox, KY, November 1966. Deployed with C Trp to Dian, RVN, November 1967. In-country training with D Trp, 3rd Sqdn, 4th Cav at Cu Chi; returned to scout platoon, later gun platoon C/3/17; redeployed to Tay Ninh; July 1968 infused to 128th AHC at Phu Loi where he served until October 1968.

Inter-theater transfer to Fairbanks, AK to fly CH21s for 18 months; back to CONUS for Fixed Wing Flight School and OV-1 qualification; RVN (Jungle Survival School, Philippines en route), January 1971, assigned with HQ, 7th Sqdn, 17th Air Cav, Qui Nhon; later Lane AHP. July 1971 assigned to 173rd Surveillance Airplane Co (OV-1), Tui Hua until November 1971, unit was stood down, he reassigned to Ft Rucker, AL.

Completed Instrument Flight Examiner School, U-8 qualification, WO Intermediate Career Crs, and one year bootstrap to complete education in business administration. Assigned as chief of standards (OV-1 and UH-1), Ft Huachuca, AZ, 1974-1977. Transferred May 1977 to Stuttgart, Germany as instructor pilot with Det 1, 330th ASA "Quicklook" Co and 73rd MI Co (OV-1).

Returned to Ft Leavenworth, KS for retirement in July 1980, culminating 22 years of active service. Awards include Legion of Merit, Dist Flying Cross, Bronze Star, Purple Heart, Meritorious Svc Med, Air Med (36 D), Army Comm Med (2nd awd), Good Conduct Med (3rd awd), and numerous service medals. September 1989, awarded the Red Feather by Red Feather Society on the Iowa, Sac and Fox Indian Reservation in White Cloud, KS.

Married Gloria in White Cloud, KS August 1959 and has three children and five grandchildren. Today owns and operates Lindsay Water Conditioning, White Cloud, KS and St Joseph, MO.

THEODORE ALVAREZ WALKER, CW3, born
June 8, 1954, Decatur, IL. Enlisted with Ord Corps Jan 31, 1974. Military education consists of Armor/Cavalry Maint Tech WO Adv Crs (outstanding graduate); WO Candidate Crs; Supervisors Diagnostic (SD) Courses, SD 315D/C M2A1 Bradley fighting vehicle and the M1A1 Abrams Tank/Airborne School; Air Assault School; Jungle Warfare School.

He was last WO to serve with F Co, 40th Armor, USArmy Berlin Bde, Berlin, Germany during days of Berlin Wall. Assigned to HHC, 2nd Bn, 29th Inf Regt, Ft Benning, GA; was responsible for his unit winning the award as the best intermediate category maint facility in TRADOC for fiscal years 1992 and 1993.

Walker was hand-picked to serve with HHC, 4th Bn,

325th Inf Regt (Abn Cbt team), Vicenza, Italy, the Army's only Abn Bn in Europe. He served over 20 years in the maintenance field; he demonstrated in-depth technical training and leadership experience as maintenance tech at both company and battalion levels; experience as service school instructor/writer; armor/cavalry maint tech; light systems maint tech; and automotive tech.

His most memorable experience was the fall of the Berlin Wall.

Awarded Meritorious Svc Med (5), Army Comm Med (2), Army Achievement Med (5), Good Conduct (3) and Dist Svc Med (2).

Married and has one daughter; currently residing at Ft Benning, GA.

EDWARD LEE WALLS, CW4, born Sept 28, 1936, Roberts, MD, and raised in Centreville, MD. Graduate of U of Maryland with BS degree in business and management. Entered the US Army in July 1954 and retired in February 1984. Completed basic training at Ft Gordon, GA and served in 83rd, 815th, 76th, 75th and 2nd Engr Bns. Also served in infantry; final tour of duty was with MILPERCEN's WO Div from January 1981-February 1984. Completed all levels of WO training.

Awards include Cbt Inf Badge, Expert Inf Badge, Vietnamese Cross of Gallantry w/palm, Overseas Svc Bars (5), Legion of Merit, Bronze Star w/2 OLCs, Army Comm Med w/4 OLCs, Meritorious Unit Comm, Good Conduct Med, Nat Def Svc Med w/OLC, Vietnam Svc Med, Armed Forces Exped Med, Armed Forces Res Med, NCO PDR, Overseas Svc Rib (2) and RVN Campaign Med.

Married Lois McGuire and resides in Centreville, MD. Plays five string banjo and leads the "Bay Country Gentlemen" playing bluegrass and country music in a four state area.

EDDIE J. WASHINGTON, CW3, born April 3, 1941, Little Rock, AR. Entered US Army July 19, 1962, taking basic training at Ft Leonard Wood, MO and AIT at Ft Devens, MA. Spent his entire career in Army MI and served with the US Army Security Agency/Intelligence and Security Command in Germany, Turkey and CONUS. Performed as electronic warfare supervisor and instructor before being appointed WO1, MOS 983A, emanations analysis tech, Feb 27, 1975. As WO he performed in projects HIPPODROME, TENCAP and TACSIM before retiring in 1984 with 22 years of service.

Earned his BA degree in 1976; BS degree in 1977; and MS degree in 1981. Awards include the Nat Def Svc Med and the Army Res Component w/2 OLCs.

Married the former Mary Moses of Baltimore, MD and has two children, Edward and Eric. Since retirement has been a program manager at Veda Inc, a defense contractor.

EMMETT WAYNE, CW2, born May 9, 1959, Louisville, KY. Entered the US Army June 23, 1977, at Ft Jackson, SC. Served as personnel specialist and computer programmer with various units in Germany, Kentucky and Kansas, reaching the rank of SFC while serving with the 194th Armd Bde at Ft Knox, KY. Attended WO training at Ft Rucker, AL, and Ft Gordon, GA; appointed WO1 data processing tech on June 2, 1989. Served as team chief of the 334th Trans Det in Yokohama, Japan until June 1992. Currently serving as data processing tech for the 101st Abn Div (Air Assault), Ft Campbell, KY.

Awarded the Meritorious Svc Med w/OLC, Joint Svc Comm Med, Air Assault Badge and numerous other commendation, achievement and service medals.

Married the former Sheila Sullivan of Rock Island, IL; they have two children, Jennifer and Bradley. He is a member of the WOA, Assoc of the US Army and the 101st Assoc.

JOHN H. WEATHERFORD, CWO2, born Nov 14, 1928, Latta, SC. Joined USN from February-June 1945. Enlisted in RA July 24, 1947, taking basic and leadership training at Ft Jackson, SC. Served as MP, Provost Marshal's Office, GHQ, Tokyo, Japan, 1948-50; MP 8210th MP POW Co, handling prisoners directly from Korea front line, 1951.

Graduated from US Army Adj Gen's Corps School, Ft Benjamin Harrison, IN, 1953; served as personnel sergeant, Sig Corps Gp HQ, Ft Gordon, GA, 1952-1955; personnel sergeant, Arty Bn, Camp Drake, Japan, 1956-58; personnel sergeant, Sig Corps HQ, Ft. Gordon, GA, 1959-62; Arty Bn, Munich, Germany, 1963-66; promoted to master sergeant E-8, 1966; appointed WO in 1966 while assigned to US Army Recruiting Cmd, Ft Monroe, VA; personnel officer, Arty Bn, Ft Stewart, GA, 1966-67; personnel officer, Hawk Msl Bn, Chunchon, Korea, 1968; staff duty officer on night that USS *Pueblo* was captured by North Korea; personnel officer, Special Trps, 4th US Army, Ft Sam Houston, TX, 1969 until retirement in 1970 (23 years of continuous service).

Awarded WWII Victory Med, Army Comm Med w/ OLC, Army of Occupation (Japan), Good Conduct, Korea Svc Med w/10 Campaign Stars, Korea Pres Unit Cit, Nat Def Svc Med and the UN Svc Med.

Attended St Mary's Univ, San Antonio, TX, 1970-73. Employment following military service included banking and finance in Dallas, TX with Heller Financial Corp; MBank; Foothill Capital Corp; retired as vice-president, First City Bank, Dallas, TX, February 1993. Member of Chas Anderson Masonic Lodge 1413, 32nd° Scottish Rite Bodies, and Alzafar Shrine, San Antonio, TX; lifetime member of TROA; charter member of VFW, Harlem, GA and member National Society of Public Accountants.

Married Marjorie Castle of San Antonio, TX; has four children from a previous marriage and five grandchildren. Hobbies include golfing and hunting.

CHARLES E. WEEKLEY, WO1, born April 26, 1911, Stewartsville, OH. Enlisted in Sig Corps Aug 3, 1929; served 10 years at Sig School, Ft Monmouth, NJ; received civil service appointment to the Government Printing Office, Washington, DC, September 1939.

Re-enlisted with Sig Corps Feb 3, 1942; promoted to sergeant February 23; promoted to first sergeant Co D, 14th Sig Svc Regt April 20. Appointed WOJG Sept 13, 1943; assigned to the 221st Sig Depot Co as personnel officer; served in ETO; hospitalized December 1944-February 1946.

Retired for disability in February 1946. Awards include EAME w/2 Battle Stars, Good Conduct Med, American Campaign Med and WWII Victory Med.

Retired from civil service in 1953; life member of TROA and DAV; member of WOA. Selected for biographical history by bicentennial edition of *Outstanding Americans* in 1976 and received a plaque.

Married Emma and has three children: Donna Molloy, husband Douglas; Holly Waisner, husband Doyal; Jeffrey, wife Helen; four grandchildren and three great-grandchildren.

DAVID P. WELSH, CW5, born Dec 17, 1939, Brookline, MA. Entered US Army Jan 14, 1957, as PV1. Appointed WO1 April 23, 1965. Assignments were chief, administration, officer, chief Army Reserve; adjutant, Army Res Spt Ctr, Arlington, VA; PBO, 483rd Engr Bn, Ft Rodman, MA; Food Service Advisor, 329th Engr Gp, Brockton, MA; Log officer, Office, Deputy Chief-of-Staff for Logistics DA; recruiting area commander, later operations officer, 94th ARCOM, Hanscom, AFB, MA; and MILPO, later real property officer, 399th CA Gp, Danbury, CT. Completed WO Sr Crs, February 1981; Master WO Crs, March 1991; promoted to CW5, Nov 18, 1992. Currently USAR WO program manager in the Office, Chief Army Res.

Awards include Meritorious Svc Med, Army Comm Med w/OLC, Humanitarian Svc Med, Army Comm Med w/ OLC, Army Achievement Med, Armed Forces Res Med w/ 2nd HG, Army Res Component Achievement Med w/OLC, Nat Def Svc Med w/BS, Good Conduct, Army Staff Identification Badge and Army Superior Unit Awd.

Past-president of the USAWOA, served as national president from 1988-90 and 1990-92. Awarded the Lifetime Trustee Award.

Married Kathleen "Kay" Pelletier of Westborough, MA; they have four children and seven grandchildren.

GERALD J. WENTWORTH, CW2, born Nov 7, 1954, Mt Pleasant, MI. Entered US Army April 12, 1977, taking basic training and cobet at Ft Jackson, SC and AIT at Redstone Arsenal, AL as a 27E tow/dragon weapon system repairman, graduating as an honor graduate and was retained as instructor.

Assigned to 725th Maint Bn, Schofield Barracks, HI, 1980-1985; returned to RSA, AL and assigned to Land CBT Development Div, 1985-1990; attended the NOC Advance Crs and promoted to SFC/E-7, 1987; applied for LCMS rep tech, WO and attended WOCS in 1990 at Ft Rucker, AL and technical training at RSA, AL.

After appointment to WO1, he was assigned to 2nd Armor Div (FWD) in Garlstedt, Germany. January 1991, deployed to SWA for Desert Storm and Desert Shield. Upon deactivating the 2nd Armd Div in 1992, he moved to his present assignment at the 563rd Ord Co, Pirmasens, Germany. Scheduled to PCS in August 1995.

Awards include the Army Comm Med w/5 OLCs, Meritorious Unit Cit, Good Conduct (4), Nat Def Rib, SWA Svc Med, SWA Bronze Star (2), and the Kuwati Lib Med.

Served two terms as president of the USAWOA Rheinlandpfalz Silver Chapter 0102 and was elected President of European Region #1 of the USAWOA in June 1994. Married Maryann Dekorne of Philadelphia, PA and has three children: Donielle, Gerald II and Jennifer and one grandchild, Tony Jr.

WAYNE E. WEST, CW5, born Dec 25, 1938, Ticonderoga, NY. Enlisted in US Army Sept 13, 1957. Served as enlisted soldier, general supply tech, accountable officer, CMD supply tech and staff policy officer in various assignments in the States, RVN, Korea, Germany and Ft. Knox, KY.

Attended Supply Officer Mgmt Crs, 1971; Management Practices Crs, 1972; WO Sr Crs, 1977; Master WO Trng, 1989; BA degree in business from McKendree College, Lebanon, IL, 1983.

Most memorable experience was the inactivation of ne 56th FA (infantry treaty) and realizing that his service in ne Armed Forces had, in fact, given freedom a chance.

Awards include Legion of Merit, Bronze Star, Meritoious Svc Med W/5 OLCs, Army Comm Med w/5 OLCs, Army Achievement Med w/2 OLCs, Good Conduct (2nd wd), Nat Def Svc Med (2), Vietnam Svc Med (3), Armed Forces Exped Med, Army Svc Rib, Overseas Svc Rib (8), ROK Pres Unit Cit and Vietnam Campaign Med.

Married Imagean Isaacs and has seven children and 13 grandchildren. Member of Caleb Butler Masonic Lodge, Radcliff, KY Lions Club, USAWOA and TROA. He is working in HQS USAREUR/7A, ODCSLOG as supply policy officer.

DANNY O. WHITE, CW3, born Dec 3, 1949, Lenoir, NC. Entered US Army May 26, 1969, taking basic training at Ft Bragg, NC and AIT at Ft Eustis, VA. Served as helicopter repairman, crew chief and door gunner with the 11th Avn (GS), 1st Cav Div, RVN until discharge. In June 1976 he joined the NCNG, then returned to active duty in November 1977. Received AIT at Ft Jackson, SC as supply man. While enlisted, he served on battalion staff, supply sergeant, division supply inspector and AIT instructor. Appointed to WO in December 1984 and served as POMCUS site supply tech, G4 supply tech and POMCUS site supply and property book officer.

Awards include Meritorious Svc Med, Air Med, Army Comm Med w/4 OLCs and several service and campaign medals.

Married Josephine Battaglia of Syracuse, NY; they have four children. Member of the USAWOA and past-president of the Limberg USAWOA Chapter. Currently assigned to the 16th CEC in Belgium.

DAVID L. WHITE, CW5, QM, born July 27, 1942, Emmett, ID. Joined the US Army on July 29, 1963. He was the first food service tech to be promoted to CW5. Assignments include food service officer for Evac Hosp and large dining facility in Vietnam; food advisor for two infantry divisions plus a COSCOM and the USAREUR Theater.

He has been a school director and instructor in food service schools. Served five tours in Germany; two tours in RVN, TET 68 RVN; one tour in Korea; Ft Lee (twice); Ft Carson; Ft Hood; and Ft Lewis.

Memorable experiences include combat conditions in RVN and travel throughout the world on TDY.

Awards include the Bronze Star, Meritorious Svc Med (3), Army Res Component Med (4), Good Conduct and several service ribbons.

Attended the Sr WO Crs and Master WO Crs plus several job related courses. Holds an associate and baccalaureate degree in management.

Married and has two sons, one who is an artillery officer. He enjoys all outdoor activities and is looking forward to a nice retirement, probably somewhere in the Rocky Mountains.

HOWARD W. WHITTINGTON, WO1, born July 2, 1948, Eugene, Lane, OR. Joined USAR February 1969, taking basic at Ft Lewis, AIT 68G at Ft Eustis. Stations included Hunter AAF; 63B at Camp Parks, CA; WOCS at Camp McCoy; WOBC, APG, MD. His MOS was 915A. He participated in Vietnam from November 1970 to February 1972.

Awards include the Bronze Star, Army Res Component Med (3) and Army Achievement Med.

Married and has three children and three grandchildren. He is senior mechanic on a 500-acre combination nursery, stock and raspberry farm. Member of USAR Unit 364th CA Bde, Portland, OR.

ROGER W. WILF, CW4, born June 30, 1942, West Palm Beach, FL. Entered the US Army, September 1960. Upon completion of basic training at Ft Jackson, SC, he was assigned to the 50th Abn Sig Bn, Ft Bragg, NC. He graduated from 82nd Abn School in February 1961; trained at Special Warfare Center, Ft Bragg; assigned to Germany, 1962; then to the 2nd Inf Div, Ft Benning, 1963. Attended school at Ft Belvoir, VA, 1964; attended special training at Ft Lewis, WA, 1965, and was first assigned to Team #23, MACV, Qui Nhon, Vietnam. Assigned to the 69th Sig Bn, Than San Nuht, 1966; relocated, 1967, to Germany and in 1968 reassigned to Vung Tau, Vietnam. Promoted to SFC August 1968. Received honorable discharge in 1968.

Re-entered the US Army in January 1971 as SSG and assigned to instructor duty, Georgia Inst of Technology, Atlanta, GA; appointed WO1, May 5, 1973, assigned to Korea. Additional assignments were Ft Stuart, GA, 1977; Heilbronn, Germany, 1979; 25th Inf Div, Hawaii, 1982; 51st Sig Bn, Germany, 1986 with ultimate assignment as chief maint tech, 93rd Sig Bde, and assisted that brigade for movement to Desert Storm.

Retired in January 1991. Awards include Legion of Merit, Meritorious Svc Med w/2 OLCs, Joint Svc Comm, Army Comm w/2 OLCs, Army Achievement Med w/OLC, Nat Def Svc Med w/star device; Armed Forces Exped Med, Good Conduct Med w/2 knots, Vietnam Svc Med w/7 Campaign Stars, NCO PDR, Overseas Svc Bars (5), RVN Cross of Gallantry, Parachutist Badge, Mechanic Badge, Driver Badge, and Expert with several weapons.

Military schools include Airborne, Ranger, NCO Academy, 3rd Armor Div, Precise Power Generation 52nd, Inf Opns 11F, WO Advanced Mechanical Maint, WO Senior Crs. Graduated from Pikes Peak CC with AS Automotive and U of Maryland with AA.

Joined the USAWOA in 1974, Seoul, Korea; Ft Stuart Chapter, 1978; life member #106; ER Historian, 1981; president, Heilbronn Chapter, 1982; president, Stuttgart Silver Chapter, 1989. High point of his career was administering the oath of office and commissioning his son, 2LT John A Wilf, upon his graduation from FSU, 1989.

Affiliations include F&AM, 32nd°, Shriners, Rotary International, AUSA and the 25th Div Assoc.

Married Lynn T. who is a DOD Civ with PWC, Pearl Harbor, HI. They have two sons, Raymond G., who is employed as DOD Civ with the Dept of the Navy, Pearl Harbor, HI; and John A., 1LT, USAR, and employed by Palm Beach County, FL. Wilf and his wife reside in Mililani, HI and are the owners of Professional Home Inspections Co, a service company supporting the real estate industry.

LEONARD L. WILFONG, CW2, born Oct 23, 1927, Harrison County, WV. Graduated Weston HS, Weston, WV,1945. Drafted in US Army at Camp Atterbury, IN. Completed basic training and assigned to USAAC, 25th Auto EQ Mech (014), attended Tech School at Gieger Field, WA.

Participated in occupation of Japan, 5th AF, Tachakawa, Japan, and destroyed Japanese combat equip and recovered Army equip combat damaged at Iwo Jima, Okinawa and Korea. Completed Wheel and Track Mechanic School at Philippines Ord School, Manila, Philippines. Assigned to USAF SAC as heavy const equip repairman (47150), Westover AFB, MA; completed assignments overseas in Greenland, Morocco, Spain, Germany, England and Labrador. Most of stateside duty was at 8th AF, Westover AFB, MA. Assigned additional duty as manager SAC Aero Clubs at Westover and Torrejon, Spain for eight years. Last AF assignment was at DM AFB, (SAC) Tucson, AZ as NCOIC of Titon II Msl Spt Equip.

Direct commission as WO1 621A was approved Sept 28, 1967; attended WO orientation at Ft Belvoir, VA and Ft Sill, OK; assigned to the 93rd Engr Bn, B Co, Vietnam as maint officer; assigned to D Btry, S&F Bn, Sch Bde, USAADS, Ft Bliss, TX, as instructor for eng EQ supporting safeguard ABM system in February 1969. Elected to retire June 1972.

Moved to Tucson, AZ, completed Airframe and Power Plant School at Cochise College, Douglas, AZ, 1973. Accepted employment with Empire Machine Co, the caterpillar dealer for Arizona and Sonora, Mexico as heavy diesel mechanic. Served as supervisor of the Service Dept, Rental Dept and Trans Dept before retiring in November 1986.

Awards include the Bronze Star, Army Comm Med, WWII Victory Med, Army Occupation Med-Japan, Good Conduct (Army and USAF), Nat Def Svc Med, Vietnam Svc Med, RVN Campaign Svc Med w/device, Asiatic-Pacific Theater, Meritorious Unit Cit and diplomas from many service schools.

Married Aurea and has five daughters. Hobbies are flying, deep-sea fishing and boating.

DONALD E. WILGUS, CW4, born Jan 2, 1926, Seattle, WA. Joined the US Army 741B AGC on Oct 1, 1945. Stationed in Europe, Vietnam, Korea, Okinawa, Thailand and Japan.

Memorable experience was the opportunity to meet some mighty fine people.

Awards include WWII Victory Med, Occupation Med, Vietnam Svc Med, Meritorious Svc Med w/OLC and Comm Med with clusters. Retired April 30, 1980, with the rank of CW4.

Divorced, he has three sons and seven grandchildren. He is fully retired and enjoying it.

BILL K. WILLIAMS, CWO, USA, born Aug 28, 1918. Enlisted on June 18, 1938. His service as a WO was due to taking a two day written exam while stationed at Camp Blanding, FL in March 1942. On May 15, 1942 he received word that his name was on the list from the War Dept and that he was to be appointed WOJG. He was very proud to get the appointment.

He and his wife had been married just one year and three days when the news came. On Feb 27, 1943, while on duty with the Finance Dept at Camp Murphy, FL, they were blessed with their first son. Two days later he was promoted to CWO. He and his family had a few more months together until he was shipped to the Far East Cmd.

While in the Philippines he was stationed with the 174th Fin Disbursing Station at San Fernando La Union in 1945. While in the Korean War, he was sent to Okinawa and was in the 176th FDS. He volunteered while in Okinawa to lead a Boy Scout Troop; they started with 25 boys and a year later, when he was ordered home, there was over 100.

Separated from the service in March 1948 as a CWO. Later he re-enlisted as a master sergeant, served a while then was given a direct commission and retired as a 1st lieutenant on June 30, 1960. He had 21 years in the service.

Spent a great deal of free time serving the Boy Scouts, coaching baseball, football, basketball, as well as played on Army and city teams. He now participates in senior games.

He has three sons, 12 grandchildren and one great-grandson.

CARL L. WILLIAMS, CW3, born May 31, 1939, Manhattan, NY. Began military career in 1954 by attending high school aboard the New York City School Ship, *John W. Brown,* for Maritime Trade. Graduated in 1957 and entered NYARNG, Btry C, 1st How Bn, 369th Arty. Attended WO basic training courses and appointed WO1 Aug 18, 1978, assigned to the 1569th Trans Co as maint tech. While with the 1569th, he took several security, NBC and supply courses, attended WO Advanced Crs at APG, MD in 1985 and 1986. Selected to head part of the 1569th Co in 1989 for overseas duty in Turkey. In 1990 his entire battalion was deployed for SWA (Operation Desert Storm) for eight months.

Awards include the Meritorious Svc Med, Army Achievement Med, SWA Svc Med, Nat Def Svc Med, Armed Forces Res Med w/HG, Army Res Overseas Trng Rib w/#4, Lib of Kuwait Svc Med and State Long and Faithful Svc Med, four years through 35 years.

Married Linda Williams and has three sons: Nathaniel, Joseph and Pierre. Resides in The Bronx, NY and is presently a commercial technical representative with Consolidated Edison of New York with 35 years of service.

JAMES EDWARD WILSON JR, CW4, born Dec 15, 1949, Bartow, FL. Member of QM WO Corps and joined the US Army on May 8, 1969. Military education includes the WO Sr Crs, Log Mgmt Development Crs, WO Advanced Crs, Supply Mgmt Officers Crs, Army Depot Operations Mgmt Crs, DS4 Crs, and SAILS Mgmt Crs. Civilian education includes an MS degree in systems management with the University of Southern California, bachelor of computer science, information systems management degree with the U of Maryland, an associate in liberal arts degree with St Leo College of Florida, and an associate of arts in business administration with Central Texas College.

Served three assignments in Germany; one in Greece; one in Korea; one in South West Asia; one in Ft Hood, TX; two in Ft Stewart, GA; and one in Ft Benning, GA.

His most memorable experience was being selected and appointed as WO.

Awards include Bronze Star during the Gulf War in South West Asia; US Army Meritorious Svc Medals (3), US Army Comm Medals (3), Army Achievement (2), US Army Good Conduct (2), Nat Def Svc Med (2), SWA Bronze Stars (3), NCO PDR, Overseas Ribbons (4) and SWA Kuwaiti Lib Med.

Married a beautiful Greek lady, Vrysiis Kalligery, and has a 24-year-old son, James Shannon. Currently assigned to the 19th Materiel Mgmt Ctr, 3rd Corps Support Cmd in Wiesbaden, Germany, has assignment orders for Ft Hood, TX and is in the primary zone for promotion to CW5.

MICHAEL D. WILSON, CW3, born July 26, 1945, West Union, IA and raised in Elgin, IA. Graduated from Valley Community School District. Began his military career in the USAR, 289th Ord Co, Waterloo, IA on Aug 29, 1965. Entered basic training, September 1966, at Ft Leonard Wood, MO and AIT at APG, MD, December 1965. In 1968 transferred to 1st Plt, Co A, 389th in Decorah, IA. In late 1968, unit was redesignated Co 389th Engr Bn.

Held various positions up through motor sergeant with rank of SFC. On June 21, 1980, appointed WO1 and served as motor officer until September 1983. Entered AGR status in September 1983 as engineer equip repair tech for HHC 389th Engr Bn. Currently assigned as auto support maint tech for 372nd Engr Gp.

Awards include Meritorious Svc Med w/2 OLC, Army Comm Med, Army Achievement Med w/4 OLCs, Army Res Component Achievement Med (6th Awd), Nat Def Svc Med, Humanitarian Svc Med w/#2, Army Svc Rib, Army Res Component Overseas Trng Rib w/#5, Expert Badge M16, Mechanics Badge W, T, Drivers Badge W, T. Member of ROA.

JAMES J. YATES, CW4, born April 29, 1923, Durham, NC. Graduated from Durham HS Jan 22, 1942; drafted into US Army Jan 29, 1942, Ft Bragg, NC; assigned to 439th Engr Depot Co. Basic training at Camp Swift, TX and AIT on the desert at Needles, CA, serving as a company clerk. Served overseas in New Guinea, Philippines and Japan. Discharged as tech 4th grade in 1946. Entered Duke University and graduated in 1950 with AB degree in business administration.

Entered the USAR, September 1948, as corporal; shortly after graduation, moved to Charlotte and joined the 386th Engr Gp (CONS) and advanced through the ranks of sergeant major. Appointed WO on March 3, 1954; advanced to CWO on March 22, 1970; served in assignments with the 363rd QM Bn, 812th Trans Bn and the 3285th USAR School. Retired on April 29, 1980.

Awards include the Victory Med, APT Campaign w/2 Bronze Svc Stars, Philippine Lib w/Bronze Star, Am Theater Med, Good Conduct, AF Res Med and AFRM Device (10 years) and other campaign medals and ribbons.

Life member of ROA, past-master of Masonic Fraternity, past-patron of Eastern Star. Employed by Mecklenburg County as tax auditor II. Single and resides in Charlotte, NC.

JOHN F. ZIMMERMAN, CW5, born Jan 20, 1943, Tampa, FL. Entered USA June 24, 1960, at Ft Jackson, SC. Served as clerk and infantry operations specialist with HQ V Corps, Germany until discharged in June 1963. He was administrative supply tech for the GAARNG until recalled to active duty as a supply WO in 1967.

From 1968-72, he served as S4 and property book officer with the 13th Cbt Engr Bn, Korea; 3/38th SGT Msl Arty Bn, Ft Sill, OK; 815th Const Engr Bn, Vietnam; and 4th Msl Cmd, Korea. From 1973-77, he designed and developed the initial automated standard property book system (SPBS) for the Army while assigned to USA Log Ctr, Ft Lee, VA. From 1977-82 he was the international supply officer for HQ Central Army Gp (NATO) in Germany and the senior auditor for industrial plant equipment with Field Cmd, Def Nuclear Agency in Albuquerque, NM.

In 1982 selected to serve as first CWO of QM Corps. Between 1986-92, he served two tours in Korea as the consolidated supply officer, HQ Combined Field Army (ROK/US), and as senior combat service support WO proponent with the USA Log Ctr at Ft Lee. In 1992 selected to serve as CWO of the QM Corps, a position he currently holds.

Has BS in vocational education and MA in contract management/procurement and international finance. Is graduate of first Master WO Crs (1988) and among the first promoted to the grade of CW5.

Awards include the Legion of Merit, Bronze Star, Def Meritorious Svc Med w/OLC, Meritorious Svc Med w/3 OLCs, Army Comm Med w/2 OLCs, Army Achievement Med w/OLC, AF Achievement Med, Good Conduct Med, plus numerous service medals.

Married Nancy Cochran and has two children. Member of the USAWOA, USA Assoc of QM, Loyal Order of Moose and the American Legion.

Late Submissions

EDWARD COLE (CW4) (RET), born June 7, 1936, in Findley, OH, and raised in Litchfield, MI. Entered US Army November 1955; appointed WO February 1968 as engineer equipment repairman and was medically retired November 1988.

Assignments: Ft. Carson, CO; WOC 97th Sig Bn, Germany; Ft Knox, KY; 568th Engr Bn (const), Ft Wolters, TX; 317th Engr Bn (cbt) Germany (two tours); 1st Engr Bn (cbt) RVN; 249th Engr Bn (constr) Germany; 14th Engr Bn (cbt) RVN; 548th Engr Bn (constr) Ft Jackson, SC; 130th Engr Bn (S-4) Germany; TACOM (project manager) M-60 Tank, Warren, MI; director training development power generation, Ft Belvoir, VA; MILPERCEN; Engr Proponent Office, Ft Belvoir, VA; WOEC, Ft Belvoir, VA; WOAC, Ft Belvoir, VA; WOAC APG, MD; WOSC Ft Rucker, AL.

The most challenging assignment in his career was as a career manager in the WO Div. He was impressed by the attitude and professionalism of the civilians and military personnel assigned to MILPERSEN.

One cannot comprehend the pressure and responsibility that is put on the career manager until one is in that position. The most rewarding aspect of the job is when you can meet all the military requirements, needs of the family and desires of the individual soldier.

One part of the assignment he enjoyed was the opportunity to visit the soldier and his family in the field while giving the MILPERSEN briefing and counseling soldiers on their career development and assignments. One very important part of the assignment at MILPERSEN was attending our candidate courses and briefing our newly selected warrant officers on career progression and assignment policy; plus discussing their responsibilities as officers an their transition from the enlisted to the officer ranks; relaying to them his personal trials and errors during his first year as a new warrant.

He was fortunate during his assignment to WOD of having the opportunity to participate in the Total WO Study and incorporation of the WOC courses. He was more involved in the TWOS after leaving the WOD as he was assigned to the Engineer Proponent Office at Ft Belvoir, VA. This assignment involved grading the warrant officer positions in the active and reserve components and the need for more education.

The one thing he will always cherish about the assignment at MILPERSEN was having the opportunity to meet so many outstanding professional soldiers and their families.

ALECK Q. FLETCHER, CW4, USA, RET, born Nov. 18, 1939, in Cowen, WV. Entered the USCG in 1958 upon graduation from Cowen High School, Cowen, WV. Discharged from the USCG July 1962 and enlisted in the US Army June 1963. Served as an enlisted member until December 1968 when he received an appointment as a WO1 in the Corps of Engineers as an engineer equipment repair technician. During his tenure as a warrant officer, he served in several unique assignments which included two tours in Vietnam, the US Army Engr School, Germany, WO Div as an assignment officer in the Weapons and Utilities Branch and as the liaison officer for the 9th Inf Div, Office of the Deputy Chief of Staff Operations and Plans, The Pentagon, Washington, DC.

Retired from active service Oct 1, 1984. Awards include the Legion of Merit, Bronze Star w/OLC, Meritorious Svc Med w/OLC, Army Comm Med w/2 OLCs, Good Conduct and four Svc Bars. He holds a degree in automotive technology issued by Northern Virginia Community College, Alexandria, VA. He completed the WOSC and all branch related courses while on active duty.

Residing in Northern Virginia, he is a military marketing consultant with Caswell International Corp., Minneapolis, MN. Married to Charlotte Tapp and they have a son, serving as a first sergeant, on active duty.

WILLIAM M. HELM, CW4, USA, RET, born Jan. 29, 1944, in San Francisco, CA and raised in Bend, OR. Entered the military on Dec. 19, 1961, at Fort Ord. From July 1962 to June 1970 he served in a wide variety of positions and units world-wide including test psychologist, finance specialist, and personnel management specialist ultimately being promoted to SFC while assigned to the 1st Cav Div in Vietnam. In 1964 he met and married Jacqueline Bjork. Upon his return from Vietnam he was appointed a WO one with an initial assignment to Ft Riley as a personnel technician. His subsequent assignments included the 8th Field Station Vietnam, APG, and the 1st Inf Div in Germany.

During 1982 he attended the WOSC at Ft Rucker. Upon graduation he was reassigned to the position of personnel actions officer in the WO Div until July 1985 when he was reassigned to Ft Huachuca. He held various positions ultimately serving as the assistant director for military personnel. He was selected for master warrant at the time of his retirement in January 1990.

Awards include the Meritorious Svc Med w/2 OLCs, Air Medal, Bronze Star w/OLC, ARCOM w/5 OLCs, AAM, Good Conduct, Meritorious and Valorous Unit Awards.

Residing in Arizona, he is a computer systems engineer

with Data Systems & Technology working for Information Systems Engineering Command to install computer networks at Army installations worldwide. His civilian education includes a major in management with a minor in computer science.

DON HESS, CW4, RET, born June 7, 1932, in Johnstown, PA, where he resided and attended school until being drafted in the Army in January 1953.

After basic and advanced training he served in numerous personnel assignments including the Armed Forces Spec Wpns Project and the Office of the Joint Chiefs of Staff in Washington, DC.

He was appointed as a warrant officer in September 1961 and served in personnel assignments in Germany with the 16th Sig Bn and in Vietnam with the 36th Engr Bn as well as assignments as post personnel officer, Ft McNair, WA,

DC; personnel officer, MDW; Army Personnel Officer, Def Atomic Sup Agency, Washington, DC; and administrative officer for the spec asst for the Modern Volunteer Army, Office Chief of Staff, Army.

In September 1973 he was assigned to the White House Communications Agency as adjutant/personnel officer responsible for procurement and management of all military personnel assigned to WHCA to include pay, promotion, awards, reassignment, separation and retirement. Also responsible for publication and distribution of all administrative directives within the agency.

Upon his retirement in 1975 he began full-time employment with the USAWOA which he founded in 1972. He holds the position of executive vice president and also serves as the secretary to the The Military Coalition, a consortium of associations representing the entire military community in legislative matters. As executive vice-president he is charged with managing the national office, editing and publishing a monthly magazine, lobbying on Capitol Hill for military benefits and maintaining a professional relationship with the Dept. of the Army staff to ensure that the interests of the WO Corps are considered in policies affecting the officer corps. As secretary of the military coalition, he is responsible for preparation of monthly minutes which record the numerous actions of the coalition. Also visits members of Congress and their staff to inform them of the position of USAWOA members on pending legislation affecting the military community.

He was selected as the first honorary WO of the Adjutant Corps Regimental Association and was the third recipient of the Horatio Gates Gold Medal. His duties included briefing WO classes and performing ceremonial duties on behalf of the regiment.

His community activities include: 23 years as a member of the Exchange Club of Capitol Hill, a service club which meets weekly in the nation's capitol for breakfast, listening to government and industry speakers on areas of national interest and interaction with other association/government members of the club. Served as past president (1985) and currently serving as program chairman and newsletter editor.

A 15 year member of the Optimist Club, Reston, VA, a service club dedicated to community involvement. Served as past president (1986) and currently serving on the board of directors.

A 30 year member of the Oakton Church of the Brethren, serving in numerous leadership positions such as chairman of the board, church school teacher, special committees, i.e. pastoral search committee, Homeless Shelter Committee, Deacon Committee. A member of the Mid-Atlantic District Ministry Commission serving as chair of the Ministry Consultation Committee (11 years) involved in assessing pastor-congregational relationships for the 75 churches within the District. Served on the denominational Veterans for Peace Committee to improve dialogue between military veterans and conscientious objectors.

Ft. Drum, NY. The Virginia M. Holcombe Spouse of the Year award was presented to Anne M. Rollinson for her service to the Mannheim, Germany community. The award was announced at the 1990 Annual Meeting and presented to Anne by former European President Dave Adams at Ft. Drum .

Fort Myer, VA. CW3 Albert Bamsch is presented the 1990 USAWOA Warrant Officer of the Year award by LTG Reno, Army DCSPER during the 1990 Annual Meeting.

Fort Rucker, AL. The staff and faculty of the Warrant Officer Career Center (WOCC) in January 1995. The WOCC was established on 1 October 1992 under the U.S. Army Training and Doctrine Command (TRADOC), Fort Monroe, VA with specific command and control of warrant officer candidate and other warrant officer training. The primary mission of the WOCC is to be the executive agent for warrant officer career development.

A

CW3	GEORGE V AARON
WO1	JACQUELINE AARON
CW4	MARK ABERNATHY
CW3	ROBERT ABOD
CW2	EDWARD ABRAHAM
CW4	ARTHUR A ABRAHAMSON
CW2	EDGARDO D ACADEMIA
CW4	EFRAIN ACEVEDO
CW3	ANTHONY L ACOSTA
CW3	LOUIS A ACOSTA
CW3	ALFRED J ACUNTO
WO1	ERIC THOMAS ADAIR
CW4	MICHEAL S ADAIR
CW3	DAVID C ADAMS
WO1	EDDIE W ADAMS
CW2	GLEN E ADAMS
CW3	LAURENCE C ADAMS
CW3	LEROY ADAMS
CW3	CHARLES ADAMS,JR
CW4	BENTON L ADCOCK
CW2	ELIZABETH A ADCOCK
CW2	DENNIS L ADDISON
CW2	DAVID J ADDLEY
CW5	THOMAS L ADKINS
CW2	PERRY N ADKISON
CW2	JERRY J AERTS
CW2	DOUGLAS S AGEE
CW2	BETTY J AGNEW
WO1	JOSE M AGOSTO
CW2	PAUL AGUAYO
WO1	DANA J AHL
CW3	DENNIS A AHRENS
CW3	WILLIAM W AHRENS
CW5	STEPHEN C AKERS
WO1	WANDA J AKERS
WO1	JAMES N AKERS,III
WO1	DAVID J ALBAUGH
WO1	ROGER R ALCENDOR
CW2	JOSE ALEJANDRO
CW4	BILLY E ALEXANDER
CW3	DANNY N ALEXANDER
WO1	DON ALEXANDER
CW4	ALFRED C ALEXANDER,JR
CW3	ANN F ALFAR
CW3	SALVATORE ALGOZZINO
CW2	KELI M ALGREN
CW2	CARLTON A ALLEN
CW2	HERBERT B ALLEN
CW2	HERBERT D ALLEN
CW2	JERRY A ALLEN
CW4	JOHN W ALLEN
CW2	MICHAEL J ALLEN
WO1	ROBERT H ALLEN
WO1	SHARRON D ALLEN
CW2	WILLIAM J ALLEN
MAJ	CYRIL ROLLING ALLEN,III
CW4	JAMES E ALLEN,JR
WO1	RUTH ALLEYNE
CW2	CLAY G ALLISON
CW4	JOHN B ALLNATT
CW4	DON ALSBROOKS
CW4	DAVID R ALSOP
CW2	RICHARD A ALSTON
CW3	RAFAEL ALVAREZ
CW2	RICKIE JAMES AMERICA
CW3	BRIAN G AMES
CW2	TROY R AMIE
WO1	MICHELLE A AMSDEN
CW3	AUSTIN W ANDERSON
CW3	CARL S ANDERSON
CW4	CARL V G ANDERSON
CW4	CHARLES ANDERSON
CW2	CLARK E ANDERSON
CW2	CURTIS J ANDERSON
CW2	EDWIN L ANDERSON
CW3	ERVIN H ANDERSON
CW2	KEITH E ANDERSON
CW2	MARCELLOS E ANDERSON
WO1	RICHARD E ANDER-SON
CW2	STEVEN L ANDERSON
CW5	SPENCER ANDRESS
MR	BRUCE ANDREWS
CW5	RICHARD F ANDREWS
CW3	WILLIAM B ANDREWS
CW4	PAUL E ANGELO
CW5	CHARLES ANGLE
CW3	GEORGE C ANKENBRANDT,JR
WO1	BILLIE T ANKESHEILN,JR
WO1	CHARLES K ANSELMO,JR
CW4	WAYNE H ANSPACH
WO1	DANIEL J ANTONSON
CW4	JOSEPH L ANUSZEWSKI
CW2	JOHN S ANZULIS
CW2	ALBERTO A ARAUZ,JR
CW2	JOSEPH ARMATA
CW2	THOMAS R ARMBRUSTER,SR
WO1	HAROLD G ARMENTA
CW5	GARY ARMENTROUT
CW3	ANTONIO S ARMIJO
CW3	DONALD J ARMITAGE
CW4	BILL L ARMOUR
CW3	THEODORE W ARMOUR
CW2	BRETT J ARMSTRONG
WO1	SAMUEL E ARNN,II
CW3	PATTI S ARNOLD
CW2	ROBIN M ARNOLD
CW3	STAN M ARNOLD
CW3	DONALD LEE ARNS
WO1	JEFFREY F ARNTZ
CW4	JACKIE L ARRINGTON
CW2	WILLIAM ARROTT,JR
CW2	SANTIAGO ARROYO-BERMUDEZ
CW2	ANTONIO ARROYO-PAGAN
CW5	PEDRO A ARROYO-ROSA
CW2	MICHAEL J ARSENEAU
WO1	GEORGE M ARTHURS
CW2	JoANN A ASERCION
CW2	WILLIAM G ASHBAUGH
WO1	TIMOTHY S ASHCOM
WO1	VON R ASHCRAFT
CW3	DONALD L ASHENFELTER,JR
CW2	MICHAEL D ASHFORD
WO1	ALI R ASHOURI
WO1	LORENA A ATCHISON
CW4	MICHAEL J ATHEY
CW3	FRANKLIN R ATKINS
CW5	CURTIS ATKINS,JR
WO1	ROBERT C ATKINSON
CW2	FRED R ATKINSON,JR
CW2	DAVID L ATTARD
CW4	WILLIAM D AUBUCHON
CW3	MELVIN R AUCOIN
CW2	JERRY E AULT
CW3	DALE G AUSBORN
CW3	CURLEY A AVANT,JR
CW4	MARK S AVEY
WO1	JEFFREY G AVIS
CW3	SALLY L AYER
CW4	FRED D AYERS
CW2	RICHARD B AYERS
CW4	ROBERT L AYERS
CW3	ALFREDO AYUSO

B

CW2	BRUCE D BABBS
CW3	ROBERT BACHAND
WO1	DANIEL BADE
MR	STANLEY M BAHMURSKI
WO1	KAREN L BAHRE
MW4	HEROS H (MIKE) BAILES
WO1	BURL S BAILEY
CW4	DONALD A BAILEY
CW3	JAMES O BAINES
CW4	VINCENT A BAIOCCHETTI
CW3	DARYL G BAKER
CW2	GRANDYON W BAKER
CW3	HELENE A BAKER
CW3	KEITH M BAKER
CW4	LEE E BAKER
WO1	PHILIP D BAKER
CW3	WILLIAM B BAKER
CW3	LEO R BALDONADO
CW2	DAVID C BALDWIN
CW2	JOE BALDWIN
WO1	KEVIN L BALDWIN
CW4	ROBERT E BALDWIN
CW4	THOMAS E BALDWIN
CW2	TINA Y BALL
CW2	ROBERT W BALL,SR
CW3	JOHN H BALLARD
CW3	RON BALLARD
WO1	ROSA M BALLARD
CW2	MICHAEL S BALLBACK
CW4	ARTHUR H BALLIS
CW2	JAMES E BALOGH
CW4	CHARLES J BALZER
CW4	ALBERT W BAMSCH,JR
CW4	DANNY L BANE
WO1	BRADLEY M BANISTER
CW5	JIM BANKSTON
WO1	CLINTON M BANNER
CW3	MICHAEL E BANYACKI
CW2	CHARLES A BARAN
WO1	LELA M BARBEE
WO1	CARL B BARBER
CW4	DARRELL L BARBER,SR
CW4	HOYT F BARBOUR
WO1	TERRY R BARBRE
CW2	MARIO S BARCENILLA
WO1	SEAN P BARCOE
CW2	GARY A BAREFOOT
WO1	CHRISTINA B BARGER
CW2	DANNY J BARGER
CW2	STEVEN H BARGER
CW2	JAMES M BARKER
WO1	JOSEPHINE BARKER
CW3	RON BARLOON
CW2	DANNY G BARLOW
CW4	JESSE A BARLOW
WO1	DENNIS K BARNES
WO1	LUE B BARNES
CW2	MICHAEL L BARNES
CW2	PAUL T BARNES
CW3	ROGER P BARNES
CW3	SARAH P BARNES
CW2	GERALD W BARNETT
WO1	EDWARD M BARNHART
CW3	GUY H BARNHART
CW4	CHARLES F BARR
CW3	ALEXANDER F BARRESI
CW4	DOUGLAS L BARRETT
CW3	WILLIAM J BARRONS,II
CW4	WILLIAM J BARRY
CW2	CHRISTOPHER R BARTIN
CW4	MICHAEL T BARTIN
CW5	ROBERT L BARTLETT
WO1	GLEN S BARTO
CW2	PATRICIA ANN BARTON
CW4	G EDWIN BARTON,JR
CW3	PETER W BASKER
WO1	DEBRA K BASS
CW3	JOHN B BASSILI
WO1	RONALD ALLEN BATE
CW2	JAMES G BATEMAN
CW4	WILLARD W BATIEN
CW4	WILLIE J BATTLE
WO1	RONALD W BAUER
CW4	EDWIN F BAUER,JR
CW2	JAMES A BAUMBACH
CW2	WILLIAM B BAUMBACH
CW3	RAYMOND BAUTISTA
CW4	EDWARD R BAWIEC
CW4	GEORGE A BAXLEY
CW3	JOSEPH K BAYS
WO1	SONY BAZILE
WO1	CYNTHIA M BEAIRD
CW4	HAROLD G BEALE
CW4	ROBERT S BEAMON
CW3	HOPE L BEAN
WO1	KEITH O BEAN
LTC	ROBERT A BEAN,JR
CW4	KENNETH W BEARD
CW4	LARRY L BEARD
WO1	THERESE BEATTY
CW3	DENNIS J BEAUPRE
WO1	MICHAEL D BEAUREGARD
CW4	EDWARD J BEBAN
CW4	JOHNNIE H BECERRA
CW3	MARVIN W BECK
CW2	NOLAN G BECK
CW3	DAVID F BECKER
CW2	JERRY J BECKER
CW3	MARK K BECKLEY
WO1	PETER BECOLA
CW5	ROGER BECTON
CW2	ROBERT W BEDIENT
CW2	HOWARD J BEECHER
CW2	SUSAN L BELANGER
CW4	EDWIN L BELGARD
CW2	BRIAN L BELL
CW2	CURTIS BELL
CW2	CURTIS W BELL
WO1	DAVID M BELL
CW4	LELAND A BELL
CW2	LESLIE D BELL
CW5	RAYMOND A BELL
CW3	RALPH J BELLINI
CW3	MARK J BELSKY
CW3	LUIS M BELTRAN
CW2	BRIAN J BENAK
CW3	MARK A BENDE
CW2	BRUCE B BENDER
CW2	R WESLEY BENDER
CW4	THOMAS W BENDER,JR
WO1	CHRISTOPHER J BENEAT
CW4	HOLMES D BENGE
CW2	DANIEL P BENKE
CW5	BRADLEY R BENNETT
CW2	DARRYL N BENNETT
CW2	MAX C BENNETT
WO1	RANDOLPH N BENNETT
CW2	AUSTIN A BENOIT
CW2	BRENT J BENSON
MR	DONALD A BENSON
CW3	RAYMOND C BENSON
CW3	BARTON K BENSON,JR
WO1	WILLIAM BENTLER
CW3	ALTON M BENTLEY
WO1	MICHAEL D BENTON
WO1	KARINA BENTSH
CW4	LOUIS BERECZ
CW5	DALE M BERG
CW3	JAMES R BERG
CW2	JACK BERGER
CW2	DANIEL S BERGERON
CW2	JOHN R BERING
CW4	MICHAEL J BERKERY
CW3	ROBERT A BERNAL
CW3	PETER J BERNARDI
CW2	ROBERT G BERNHARDT
CW4	ARTHUR W BERNIER,JR
CW3	KENNETH J BERNSTEIN

CW2	ROBERT P BERRA
CW4	WILLIAM BERRIMAN
WO1	CESAR BERRIOS-MAYSONET
CW2	JAMES INGRAM BERRY
CW4	JAMES R BERRY
WO1	RICHARD E BERRY,II
CW3	DAVID J BEST
CW4	DONALD E BEST
CW3	RICHARD J BEST
CW2	STANLEY P BIELAWSKI
CW5	DONALD J BIERE
WO1	DWAYNE R BIERLY
CW2	TIMOTHY E BIGLER
CW2	WALTER T BIGLEY
CW2	ISAAC BILLIE
CW3	TYRONE BILLINGSLEY
CW3	ROBERT P BILLINGTON
CW4	ANTHONY J BILLITTIER,III
WO1	MARSHA BILLODEAUX
WO1	CEDRIC BILLS
CW2	ERIC S BINGER
CW2	CLIFFORD H BINKLEY
WO1	NANCY L BINKOWSKI
WO1	RONALD P BINKOWSKI
CW4	JOHN O BIRCHMAN
CW4	GERALD D BIRD
WO1	RALPH P BIRD
CW4	JOHN L BIRKNER
WO1	ROBERT D BIRKS
CW2	JAMES R BIRNBAUM
WO1	TIM N BISBEE
WO1	MARK E BISHOP,III
CW3	BETSY L BISSETTE
CW3	LARRY N BIVENS
WO1	CHARLES A BLACK
CW2	FRANK M BLACK
WO1	RICHARD A BLACK
CW2	ROBERT BLACK
CW3	DONALD LEE BLACKMON
CW4	ANTHONY O BLADES
CW3	LAVERN C BLADO
WO1	YVETTE S BLAKE
CW5	WILLIAM H BLAMEY
CW2	JOHN J BLANC,JR
CW2	DAWN M BLANCHARD
CW4	ROBERT W BLANCHARD
CW2	CESAR A BLANCO
CW3	ROY L BLAND
CW3	EDWARD C BLANKSCHEN
CW2	DAVID L BLAZEK
CW4	DONALD W BLAZEK
CW2	ROBERT L BLEVENS
CW3	BOBBY E BLEVINS
CW2	GEAMS B BLEVINS
WO1	CLIFFORD BLIZZARD
CW3	RONALD R BLOOD
CW4	HOLLOWITH BLUE
CW3	CHARLES E BLUNK
WO1	THOMAS BOASTON,JR
CW2	ROBERT L BOATMAN
WO1	VINCENT E BOAZ
CW3	RICHARD E BOEHNLEIN
CW3	HARRY L BOGARD
CW2	TIM BOGARDUS
WO1	CHARLES H BOGGESS
CW4	LARRY BOGGS
CW3	SEONGOK C BOHANNAN
CW2	TIMOTHY BOHLER
CW2	PETER N BOHN,II
WO1	JIMMIE E BOILES
WO1	MARK P BOLLA
CW5	BERT A BOLLAR
CW4	THOMAS A BOLLS
CW2	DENNIS J BOLTE
WO1	ROBERT M BOLTON
WO1	DONALD R BONDS
CW3	CHARLES R BONDURANT
CW4	GORDON E BONHAM
CW2	DANIEL BONILLA
WO1	WILFRIDE R BONILLA-WARD
WO1	LAWRENCE K BONKOSKI
CW4	CLIF BONNER
WO1	SCOTT D BONNER
CW2	BRYAN D BOOKER
CW4	ALONZA BOONE
CW2	CLARENCE E BOONE
CW3	GERALD L BOORTZ
CW2	HAROLD A BOOS
CW2	ROBERT W BOOS,II
CW3	GLENN D BOOTH
CW2	JAMES R BOOTH
CW3	ROBERT D BORDEN
WO1	BRIAN L BORER
CW3	ALBERTO BORRERO
CW4	RICHARD C BOSS
CW3	CLINT F BOSWELL
CW4	GARY DAVID BOSWORTH
WO1	STUART J BOTHWELL
CW2	MIKE BOTKIN
CW2	R MATTHEW BOTNEN
CW5	KENNETH E BOUCHARD
CW3	DAVID C BOUCHER
CW2	JOANNE M BOUCHER
CW2	TODD M BOUDREAU
CW4	D C BOULANGER
CW3	GERALDINE BOUR GEOIS
WO1	EDWARD M BOURNE
CW4	DAVID L A BOUSE
WO1	FRANK J BOWDEN
CW4	GARY D BOWDEN
CW2	EDWIN L BOWE
CW4	STEVEN L BOWEN
CW3	HARRY E BOWEN,SR
CW4	HENRY E BOWER,JR
CW4	CHRISTOPHER L BOWERS
CW3	VERNON F BOWERS
WO1	NICO L BOWERSOCK
CW2	MARK A BOWES
CW4	ROBERT BOWLES,JR
CW3	WADE L BOWLIN
WO1	RONALD D BOWMAN
CW2	TAMMI BOWMAN
CW2	TIMOTHY D BOWMAN
WO1	HERMAN S BOWSER
CW2	WILLIAM T BOYD
CW4	DAVID A BOYER
WO1	MICHAEL W BOYER
CW2	ROBERT A BOYKINS
CW2	SHEARRIN BOZEMAN
CW3	CARLO BRACCI
CW4	THOMAS D BRADFORD
CW3	BENNIE BRADLEY
CW4	RONALD L BRADLEY,SR
CW3	WILLIAM T BRADSHAW
WO1	DUNCAN BRADY
CW2	JONATHAN P F BRALEY
CW3	GARY D BRAMAN
CW2	JAMES A BRAME,JR
CW4	JACK R BRAMMER
CW2	DONALD J BRANCATO,JR
WO1	SHAWN K BRANCH
CW2	DANNIE L BRANDES
CW4	THOMAS BRANDLI
CW5	THOMAS F BRANDT
CW3	WAYNE L BRANN
CW4	GARY W BRASHEAR,SR
CW2	REBECCA S BRASHEARS
CW3	ARMAND C BRASSEUR
CW4	KENNETH A BRASWELL
CW4	ALAN N BRATTER
CW4	DONALD T BRAUN
CW4	ROBERT L BRAUN, SR
CW2	RICHARD BRAY
WO1	WALLACE F BRAYN,JR
WO1	DALE E BRECKON
CW4	DONALD L BREEDEN
CW3	KENNETH M BREEDEN
CW3	CARL E BREEDING
CW3	GEORGE L BRENENSTAHL
CW3	GARLAND S BREWER
CW5	RUSSELL G BREWER
CW3	ROD L BRICK
WO1	KEITH M BRIDGEFORTH
WO1	GORDON N BRIDGEWATER,JR
CW2	EARL D BRIGGS
CW4	JOHN E BRIGGS
CW3	DAVID EARL BRIGHT
CW3	ROBERT D BRIGHT
WO1	JOHN B BRINDLE
WO1	JAMES J BRINNER
CW3	JOHN D BRINSON
CW3	DAIVD E BRISTOL
CW4	BRIAN D BROADWAY
CW3	ROBERT F BROCKINGTON
CW4	JAMES L BRODERICK
WO1	KENNETH G BRODHEAD,JR
CW3	CHARLES H BROGDEN
CW2	ELZA V BROKAW,SR
CW2	MICHAEL L BROOKINS
CW3	BRUCE RICHARD BROOKS
CW2	DANIEL S BROOKS
WO1	RAYMOND A BROOKS
CW3	RICHARD BROSTROM
CW2	BRADLEY W BROTH-ERS
CW2	ARTHUR L BROWN
WO1	CHRISTOPHER L BROWN
CW5	CLIFFORD L BROWN
WO1	CLIFFORD L BROWN
CW4	CONRAD L BROWN
CW2	DAVID ELLIOTT BROWN
WO1	DERIC K BROWN
CW2	DONALD B BROWN
CW2	EDDIE C BROWN
WO1	GARY P BROWN
CW2	GREGG BROWN
CW4	HENRY C BROWN
WO1	IRA D BROWN
CW4	JACK A BROWN
CW4	JACK L BROWN
CW2	JEFFREY S BROWN
CW4	JOHN L BROWN
CW3	JOHN P BROWN
CW3	JOSEPH C BROWN
CW4	KIRK W BROWN
CW2	LAWRENCE E BROWN
WO1	MARY E BROWN
WO1	MORGAN B BROWN
CW4	ROBERT BROWN
CW4	ROBERT A BROWN
CW4	ROBERT G BROWN
CW2	SABRINA F BROWN
WO1	SIMONETTA L BROWN
CW3	STEPHEN E BROWN
CW2	TEMPLE H BROWN
CW3	TRAVIS W BROWN
CW2	WARREN E BROWN
CW2	SILAS BROWN,JR
CW4	WILLIE M BROWN,JR
CW3	JAMES W BROWN,SR
CW3	JOHN A BROWNE
CW3	DAVID V BROWNEWELL
CW3	ROBERT J BROWNLIFE
CW2	MARK A BROXTERMAN
CW2	RALPH J BRUCE,JR
CW2	DENNIS B BRUNS
CW3	ROBERT C BRUNS
CW2	WILLAIM L BRUNT
CW4	LEE D BRUSH
CW4	DANIEL BRYAN
CW2	JOE D BRYANT
CW2	RICHARD E BRYANT
CW2	TIMOTHY L BRYANT
CW3	WAYNE W BRYANT
CW4	BRUCE E BRYANT,SR
WO1	PHILIP E BRYSON
CW4	BRUCE E BUBAR
CW3	JAMES P BUCCELLATO
CW3	RONALD E BUCHER
WO1	BRIAN L BUCHTA
MW4	DALE K BUCK
CW3	EDWARD M BUCK
CW4	HENRY W BUCK
CW3	STANLEY J BUCK
CW3	BRADFORD D BUCKLEY
WO1	ROBERT A BUDERUS
WO1	WINSTON R BUDRAM
CW4	ROBERT E BUFFUM
WO1	ROBERTO BUITRAGO
CW4	TIMOTHY P BULICK
CWO	STERLING E BUNCE
CW3	JAMES E BUNDGAARD
CW2	JOHN F BUNTEN
CW4	BONI (BUTCH) M BUONI
CW4	GEORGE F BURANDT
CW5	LAWRENCE R BURBANK
WO1	MICHAEL E BURCH
CW2	MICHAEL L BURDEN
CW4	ROBERT G BURGE
CW2	RONALD L BURGE
CW4	RONALD E BURGESS
CW4	TIMOTHY A BURGESS
CW4	JOSEPH BURGESS,JR
CW3	WILLIAM R BURHANS
WO1	JEFFERY D BURKE
WO1	JOHN A BURKE
WO1	FRANCIS J BURKE,JR
WO1	TRACEY L BURKE,SR
CW3	ROBERT A BURKHARDT
CW4	JOSEPH BURKHARDT,JR
CW3	MICHEAL S BURKHOLDER
CW4	CARL M BURNETT
CW5	PETER R M BURNETT
LTC	TOM BURNETT
WO1	JAMES L BURNHAM
CW2	ANOR B BURNSIDE
CW4	FREDERICK M BURR
WO1	WILLIAM F BURR,JR
WO1	STEVEN N BURRELL
CW2	STEVEN L BURRILL
CW3	CHARLES M BURRIS,SR.
CW3	M WAYNE BURTON
CW3	HERMAN O BURTON,JR
CW3	ROBERT W BUSBY
CW3	THOMAS C BUTCHER
CW2	BRYAN LEE BUTLER
CW2	CHARLES D BUTLER
CW2	DOUGLAS C BUTLER
WO1	RODERICK E BUTLER
CW2	STEPHEN A BUTTERFIELD
WO1	CHAD M BUTTERS
CW2	GORDON S BUTTERS
CW4	FRANCIS R BYE
CW2	CHARLES E BYERS
WO1	HARRY L BYRD
WO1	MARTIN R BYRNES

C

WO1	ISRAEL R CABALLERO
CW3	INOCENCIO D CACHO,JR
CW4	ANTHONY L CALABRESE
CW4	EUGENE R CALABRO, SR
CW2	JOHN A CALBICK
WO1	JEANNETTE M CALDERON
CW2	GIL E RIOS CALERO
CW4	RAYMOND W 'ROCKY' CALHOUN
WO1	SHANNON R CALHOUN
CW3	JAMES P CALLAHAN
CW2	RANDALL M CALLAHAN
CW3	KEVIN J CALLAWAY
WO1	GARY CALLISTER
CW2	RICHARD K CALNON

CW5	WILLIAM J CALVERT
CW3	JOHN W CAMERON
CW4	MAURICE E CAMMACK
CW2	BRIAN E CAMPBELL
CW4	DAVID A CAMPBELL
WO1	JEFFERY EUGENE CAMPBELL
CW2	JOHN W CAMPBELL
CW2	KARL L CAMPBELL
WO1	KEVIN W CAMPBELL
CW3	MICHAEL R CAMPBELL
WO1	NEAL A CAMPBELL
CW2	ROBERT H CAMPBELL
CW2	ROGER N CAMPBELL
CW4	STEVEN H CAMPBELL
CW2	VINCENT RONALD CAMPBELL
CW4	WILLIAM L CAMPBELL
CW2	GEORGE E CAMPBELL,JR
CW2	KAREN D CAMPER
CW4	RAYMOND J CANFIELD
WO1	STEVEN G CANGIANO
CW4	ROBERT A CANN
WO1	WALTER 'JERRY' CANNON
CW3	THOMAS F CANNON,JR
CW2	DERWIN CANTRELL
WO1	ERNEST E CANTRELL
WO1	CLIFFORD CANTY
CW3	ROY E CAPELLE,JR
CW2	QUINTIN CAPLE
CW2	DAVID M CAPUTO
CW4	MATTHEW P CAPUTO
CW2	REYNALDO CARABALLO
CW5	TROY WAYNE CARBAUGH
CW2	JOANN CARDWELL
CW2	JACK F CARDWELL,JR
CW4	DOUGLAS F CARLBERG
CW2	CRAIG L CARLSON
CW2	GILBERT CARLSON
CW4	JOHN D CARLSON
WO1	KATHLEEN E CARLSON
WO1	EDWARD F CARMAN,III
CW3	WILLIE E CARMICHAEL
CW4	JOHN R CARNELL
CW4	CARL R CARNES,JR
CW4	PETER CARNESALE
CW4	ROBERT L CARNEVALE
CW2	RONALD E CARNS
CW2	DONALD E CAROLINE
WO1	DAVID M CARPENTER
CW4	JIMMY E CARPENTER
CW3	LINDA R CARPENTER
WO1	AARON J CARR
WO1	GWENDOLYN G CARR
CW3	JAMES M CARR
CW2	ROBERT D CARR
CW4	RODOLFO CARR
COL	JESUS 'JESS' CARRANZA,JR
MAJ	LUIS CARRERAS
WO1	BARRY CARRINGTON
CW4	DAVID M CARROLL
CW4	JACKIE C CARROLL
CW3	LESLIE M CARROLL
CW2	MICHAEL T CARSON
CW3	STEPHEN W CARSTENSEN
WO1	ANDREW F CARTER
WO1	HILBERT D CARTER
CW3	MARVIN E CARTER
CW3	MARY CARTER
WO1	MICHAEL E CARTER
CW2	ROBERT A CARTER
CW2	ROBERT N CARTER
WO1	WENDALL A CARTER
CW4	WILLIAM L CARTER
CW4	WILLIAM A CARTER,JR
CW5	GERALD D CARTIER
CW4	HENRY T CARTMELL
CW4	EBER D CARVALHO
WO1	BRIAN H CARVER
WO1	MITCHELL K CARVER,JR
CW4	RICHARD L CASE
WO1	VINCENT G CASHO
CW3	EDWARD J CASSELL
CW2	ROBERT A CASTEEL
CW4	LESLIE J CASTER,JR
CW4	JAMES CASTILLO
WO1	JUAN-EDWIN O CASTILLO
CW3	BENEDICT T CASTRIOTA
CW4	FERNANDO CASTRO
CW2	ORLANDO F CASTRO
WO1	PAUL CASTRO
CW4	THOMAS P CATAPANO
WO1	TIMOTHY W CATER
CW4	BRIAN W CATES
WO1	KEVIN D CATTRAN
CW5	CHARLES COLTON CAULK
CW4	WAYNE E CAVALIER
CW3	LOUIS P CAVROS,JR
CW4	DOUGLAS A CAYWOOD
CW3	FREDERICK J CAZZOLA
WO1	THERESA A CECCHETTI
CW2	THOMAS W CERNY
WO1	SUSAN A CERVANTES
CW2	NELSON D CEZAR
CW5	E A CHACON
CW3	MICHAEL A CHALMERS
CW2	RANDALL J CHALUPKA
CW2	WAYNE L CHAMBERS
CW3	MICHAEL G CHAMBLESS
CW2	TODD J CHAMPAGNE
WO1	LENNOX A CHANCE
CW3	RICHARD J CHANDIK
CW2	CHRISTIAN J CHANDLER
WO1	THOMAS B CHANEY
CW4	THOMAS M CHANEY
CW3	EDMUND J CHAPIN
CW4	RICHARD L CHAPMAN
CW2	PENNY CHARLES
CW3	GUY R CHARLTON
CW2	CHARLES HENRY CHARLTON,JR
CW4	JAMES F CHATT
CW2	BARBARA J CHAUVEY
CW2	DEE DEE S CHAVERS
CW2	JANICE CHAVIS
CW3	LYLE E 'CHAD' CHEADLE
CW2	JEAN M CHEGASH
CW2	BERNARD F CHESMAN
CW2	BRENDA L CHESTNUT
CW4	DANIEL T L CHEU
CW2	BRADLEY C CHILDRESS
CW2	ROSS A CHILDS
CW2	FARRELL J CHILES
CW3	THOMAS E CHILTON
CW4	JOHN W CHIZMAR
CW2	BRIAN L CHMIELEWSKI
CW2	DAVID Y CHOI
WO1	SIMON CHOI
WO1	JINOK CHONG
CW4	FRANCIS G CHRISTENSEN
CW2	MIKE M CHRISTENSEN
CW4	DUDLEY F CHRISTIAN
CW4	RICHARD E CHRISTIAN
CW3	RICHARD G CHRISTIANSEN
CW4	DENNIS L CHRISTMAN
CW5	WILBUR A CHRISTOPHER
CW4	THOMAS W CHUDIK
CW3	ALLAN L CHURCH
CW3	JAMES R (RICK) CHURCH
CW3	WILLIAM A CHURCH
WO1	ROMAN I CHYLA
CW2	AKIRA I CIBULKA
CW4	JOSEPH M CICARELL
WO1	RON CINGLE
CW3	RONALD C CIRCLE
CW3	FREDERICK R CLAASSEN
CW3	DOUGLAS R CLABAUGH
CW3	JOHN MICHAEL CLANCY
WO1	AUDRA A CLAPP
CW2	CHARLES K CLARK
WO1	EDWARD W CLARK
CW4	PATRICK LEE CLARK
CW3	PAUL A CLARK
WO1	RICHARD D CLARK
CW2	RICHARD J CLARK
CW2	ROBERT L CLARK
CW4	ROBERT RAY CLARK
CW3	SCOTT W CLARK
CW4	DANIEL E CLARK,III
CW3	CHARLES L CLARK,JR
CW3	EARL E CLARK,JR
CW2	THOMAS E CLARK,JR
CW3	TOMMIE L CLARK,JR
CW4	CLEOPHUS J CLARK,SR
CW3	PAUL H CLARKE
CW3	CATHY A CLAUSEN
CW4	TED A CLAUSSEN
CW3	JOSEPH T CLAY
CW2	LINDA S CLAYBURN
CW3	CHARLES E CLAYTON
CW4	PATRICK J CLEARY
CW4	RICHARD J CLEARY
WO1	BENARDE P CLERX
CW4	JOHN J CLEVER
CW4	JOE B CLIFFORD
CW2	RODGER A CLIFFORD
CW3	CHARLES F CLIFT
CW2	DAVID D CLINE
CW4	ROBERT J CLINTON
CW3	WILLIAM K CLOUGH
CW3	RANDY J CLOUGH,SR
WO1	WILLIAM F CLOWERS,SR
CW2	PATRICK J COAKLEY
CW3	DANIEL D COATES
CW3	GLEN H COATS
CW3	JACK E COCHENSPARGER
CW3	TEDD COCKER
CW4	DEWEY A COCUZZOLI
CW2	BRIAN C COFFEY
CW2	CRAIG O COFFMAN
CW3	TED EDWARD COHAN
CW4	DANIEL C COKER,JR
CW3	THOMAS R COLAIZY
WO1	DEBRA MASAYO COLE
CW3	JAMES C COLE
CW3	JOHN R COLE
CW4	BENNY V COLECCHI
CW4	BOBBIE WAYNE COLEMAN
CPT	JAMES E COLEMAN
CW4	MURPHY COLEMAN
CW2	RIAL D COLEMAN
CW4	GORDON D COLIS
WO1	PAMELA J COLLIER
CW2	PATRICIA M COLLIER
CW2	DEBORAH M COLLINS
WO1	EDGAR A COLLINS
CW4	JEROME E COLLINS
WO1	MARY K COLLINS
WO1	WILLIAM SCOTT COLLINS
CW3	ROBERT E COLMAN
CW4	DONNA D COLON
CPT	JUDITH E COLVER
WO1	MICHAEL F COLVIN
WO1	RON J COLVIN
CW2	RONALD R COMBS
CW2	GREGORY L COMMONS
CW3	JOHN S CONCEPCION
CW3	DAVID E CONDIT
CW3	WENDALL CONDON
CW3	JAMES W CONLIN
WO1	GEORGE A CONNER
CW3	THOMAS CONNER
CW3	DENNIS J CONWAY
CW4	ELMER COOK
CW3	LONNIE C COOK
WO1	TIMOTHY W COOK
WO1	RONALD DUANE COOKS
CW3	WILLIAM C COOLER
CW4	RICHARD R COOMBE
CW3	CHARLES L COOPER
CW4	ROBERT N COOPER
WO1	DAVID B COPE
CW3	LANCE ME COPE
CW3	DONALD V COPELAND
MW4	DALE GENE COPLEY
CW2	JAMES P CORBETT
CW2	ROBERT M CORDELL
CW4	ROMAN CORES-ORTIZ
WO1	WANDA CORIS
CW2	JOHN J CORKHILL
CW4	RICKY H CORNELIUS
CW3	RONALD U CORNISH
CW2	LESLIE ERROL CORNWALL
CW2	JOSEPH A CORREA
CW2	RICHARD P CORRENTE
WO1	ROBERT P COSTELLO
CW3	VICTOR A COTE
WO1	RITA FAYE COTHRON
WO1	RAY D COTMAN
WO1	DARLENE COTNER
CW2	MICHAEL M COTTER
CW3	JERRY R COUCH
WO1	WILLIAM R COUCH
CW4	MICHAEL W COURSON
CW4	CHARLES W COURTNEY
CW4	DONALD L COURTNEY
CW3	LENNIE V COUSINS
CW4	JAMES N COWART
CW3	ALFRED E COX
CW3	DWIGHT L COX
WO1	GREGORY D COX
CW4	LARRY M COX
CW3	ROBERT E COX,JR
WO1	JUDY COX-GRAVES
CW2	SAMUEL L COXSON
CW2	MICHAEL B COY
CW2	JOHN J COYLE,II
CW2	GRANT S COYOUR
CW3	JESSE C COZART
CW3	JOHN L CRABB
CW4	LOWELL T CRACE
CW3	THOMAS R CRAIG
CW4	WENDELL R CRAIG
CW2	BRUCE L CRAIL
CW4	LEONARD R CRAIN
MW4	JACK L CRAMER
COL	RICHARD W CRAMPTON
WO1	SHAWN CRANDALL
CW2	ANDREW C CRANFORD
WO1	VIKKI J CRAVENS
CW2	JOHN CRAWFORD,III
CW2	JOHN T CRERAR
WO1	ALLEN W CREWS
CW4	MACK H CRIDDELL
CW2	ROBERT 'SCOTT' CRIDER
CW2	L LAINE CROCKER
WO1	JOHN W CROCKETT
CW4	HENRY J P CROES
CW2	T J CRONIN
CW3	JOHN E CROSBY
CW4	GORDON V CROSS
CW2	RALPH H CROSS,IV
CW3	JOHN R CROUSE
CW4	JAMES D CROW
CW4	HENRY A CROWDER
MW4	JAMES D CROWLEY
CW2	STUART ALAN CROWN
CW2	JOHN N CROWSON
CW3	KENNETH P CROWSON
CW4	JOHN W CRUSE
CW2	ELISA R CRUZ
CW2	THOMAS J CRUZ
CW3	JOSE R CRUZ-BERNIER
CW2	ROBERT ALLARD CUDDEBACK
CW2	AARON E CULVER

CW3	DONALD D CULVER	CW3	SUMNER 'SKIP' J DAVIS	CW4	WILLIE M DICKENS	CW3	PAUL DUBUQUE
CW2	DANNY A CUMBEE	CW3	WALKER E DAVIS,JR	CW2	CHARLES P DICKER	WO1	STEPHEN F DUDKA,JR
CW3	CHARLES CUMMINGS	CW4	JAMES E DAWKINS	CW3	DENNIS J DICKINSON	CW3	DAVID L DUENAS
WO1	CHRISTOPHER P CUMMINGS	CW3	RONALD D DAWSON	CW3	ROBERT L DICKON	CW2	JOEL DUENEZ
CW2	KEVIN R CUMMINGS	CW3	HAROLD J DAY	CW4	RICHARD E DICKSON	CW2	ERIC D DUERR
CW4	ROBERTA SPIKES CUMMINGS	CW3	J T DAY	CW2	VIRGINIA A DIEHL	MR	JOHN E DUFFANY
CW4	GEORGE A CUNEY	CW3	KENNETH W DAY	CW3	DALE E DIEHLL,SR	CW2	JOHN D DUFFEY
CW2	EDWARD J CUNNINGHAM	CW2	ROOSEVELT DAYMON	CW5	WALTER E DIETZ	CW2	JACK W DUFRIN
WO1	KENNETH A CUNNINGHAM	CW3	CAREY D DEACHIN	WO1	MARYAN B DIFFIE	CW2	WILLIAM V DUFRIN
CW5	DOUGLAS CUNZEMAN	CW4	HAROLD L DEAL	CW4	NICK DiGIROLAMO	CW3	MICHAEL P DUGGAN
CW3	THOMAS CURRAN	CW2	DAVID G DEAN	CW4	VINCENT D DiJOSEPH	CW4	AUBREY D DUGGER
CW4	HARVEY L CURRY	CW2	PAUL M DEAN	CW4	GEORGE D DILL	CW2	JEFFREY R DUGLE
WO1	KEVIN T CURRY	CW4	WALLACE R DEAN	CW2	LONNY W DILL	CW2	JOHN M DUKE
CW3	RICHARD L CURTIS	CW4	LEON A DEAN,SR	CW5	LLOYD S DILLARD	CW2	RALPH J DUKE
CW5	SUZANNE E CURTIS	CW2	FRANK DeANGELIS	CW2	CLARENCE A DILLMAN	CW2	MICHAEL M DULAK
CW4	THOMAS C CURTIS	CW3	GABRIEL D DEAS	CW3	SCOTT M DILLON	CW3	DAVID R DULL
CW3	WARREN A CURTIS	CW2	DAVID D DEASON	CW3	THOMAS J DITTMAN	CW5	DONALD C DULL
CW4	WILLIAM R CURTIS	WO1	CHRISTOPHER C DeBACA	CW5	MICHAEL A DIVITTIRIO	WO1	ROBERT W DUNAWAY
CW4	ROBERT H CURTIS,JR	WO1	J P DEBOURBON	CW3	EDWIN E DIXON	CW3	ALFONZA DUNBAR
CW2	JOHN CUTLER	CW3	PATRICIA A DECKARD	CW3	NATHAN D DIXON	CW5	DAVID L DUNCAN
CW3	RALPH W CWIEKA	WO1	RAYMOND E DEEDON	CW5	JOHN C DIXON,III	CW3	KELLY R DUNCAN
CW3	ANDREW J CZECHOWSKI	WO1	TONY RAY DEESE	CW4	DWIGHT J DOANE	CW2	TRUDY A DUNCAN
CW4	LAWRENCE J CZOSNEK	WO1	WILSON P DEFIESTA	WO1	STEPHEN G DOBBIN	CW3	GREGORY M DUNFIELD
CW2	MARY TERESA CZUHAJEWSKI	CW2	TROY A DeGOLYER	CW4	RICHARD A DOBBINS	WO1	LESLIE R DUNHAM
		SFC	BEVERLEY ANN DeGRATIA	CW2	JULIA DOCKERY-SKINNER	CW4	CHARLES E DUNN
	D	WO1	EDDY DEGUERRE	CPT	JACK DOCKTOR	CW2	DANIEL F DUNN
CW4	PLACIDUS D'AGRELLA	CW4	PHILIP A DeHENNIS	CW2	TONY DODSON	CW3	MICHAEL DUNN
CW5	MICHAEL D'ANTONIO	CW2	D D DEHNEL	CW3	CHRISTOPHER J DOERSAM	CW2	MARK L DUPLESSIE
CW2	ALDO COSMO D'EREDITA	CW4	THOMAS J DELANEY	CW4	LAWRENCE D DOGGETT	WO1	MICHAEL G DUPRE
CW3	STEPHEN F DACEY	CW3	GERRY R L DELAQUIS	CW3	RICHARD D DOHMEN	CW5	DENNIS E DURA
CW2	ARTHUR G DAHL,IV	WO1	CARLOS R DeLEON	CW4	WILLIAM C DOLCE	WO1	TRAVIS L DURBIN
CW2	THOMAS E DAILEY	CW3	HERMAN L DELK	CW3	WILLIAM T DOLLARD,II	MW4	JOSEPH L DURBIN,JR
WO1	JOHN O DAINES	WO1	PAT DELLA-FERRA	WO1	TERESA A DOMEIER	CW2	CHARLES W DURHAM
CW3	DONALD S DAISLEY	CW4	CHARLES C DELMURO	CWO	JERRY DONAGHY	CW2	JO A DURM
WO1	WILLIAM B DALGARN	CW3	JESSIE J DELOACH	WO1	JAMES D DONALDSON	WO1	JAMES C DURRSCHMIDT
CW3	VINCENT F DALLMIER	CW3	ALEXANDER P DELOREY	CW2	JAMES L DONALDSON	WO1	KENNETH F DUSTIN
CW3	JAMES D DALY	WO1	ABRAHAM S DELOSSANTOS	CW2	MARGARET A DONALDSON	CW2	WAYNE DUTSON
CW4	FRANK A DAMIANO	WO1	RODNEY F DEMARRE	CW3	DARREN F DONICA	CW3	STEVE D DUTY
CW2	GARY DAMON	CW3	DONALD J DEMCHAK	CW2	FRANCIS A DONOVAN	WO1	DANIEL L DUVAL
CW2	JOHN D DANDRIDGE	WO1	ERICH DEMEL	SFC	MARCUS K DOO	CW2	LOUIS L DuVERNAY
CW3	ROBERT B DANDRIDGE	CW3	NOEL A DEMERS	CW3	DAVID W DOODY	CW5	FRANK H DYER,SR
CW2	NEVIN PAUL DANIEL	CW2	JAMES K DEMPSTER	CW2	JAMES G DOOLEY	WO1	PAUL S DZIEGIELEWSKI
CW4	JERRY R DANIELS	CW2	GILBERT DENCHE	CW2	KENNETH J DOOLEY		
CW3	RICHARD DANIELS,JR	WO1	DOMINIC D DENIRO	WO1	MATTHEW J DOORLEY		**E**
CW4	GEORGE DANKO	CW4	JOHN F DENNER	CW2	ROBIN ANN DORAN	CW4	JAMES R EAKINS
WO1	PAUL R DANNAR	CW5	DONALD W DENNIS	WO1	CHRISTIAN F DORE	WO1	MICHAEL G EARHART
CW4	DAVID C DANNELLY	CW2	MICHAEL D DENNIS	CW5	JAMES J DORNHOEFER,JR	CW3	RICHARD C EASINGWOOD
CW4	WILLIAM T DARNELL	CW3	THOMAS S DENNIS	CW4	ALAN L DOROTHY	CW3	ABRAHAM B EASTER,SR
CW2	JOSEPH M DaROSA	CW4	ROBERT E DENNISON	CW3	KLAUS D DORRSTEIN	CW4	MICHAEL E EASTMAN
CW2	SPENCER DASE	WO1	WINFRED G DENSON	CW4	CYRIL H 'BOB' DORSK	WO1	NORMAN P EBERLY
CW2	TEDDY C DATUIN	CW3	MORRIS S DePAUW	WO1	DOUGLAS T DOSLAND	CW4	GEORGE W EBY
CW5	TROY A DAUGHERTY	CW4	JOHN B DERDEN	CW3	ARDIE A DOSS	WO1	CARMELO ECHEVARRIA
CW4	ROY E DAUGHTRY	CW2	BRUCE A DERKSEN	CW2	THOMAS R DOSTIE	CW2	THEODORE M ECKMANN
CW4	TOMMY W DAUGHTRY	CW3	DEBRA K DeROSIER	CW4	ROBERT L DOTOLO	WO1	JOHN C ECKROAT
CW2	MATTHEW M DAVENPORT	WO1	KEITH A DERRICK	CW4	JAMES S DOTY	CW5	ANTONIO B ECLAVEA
CW3	CLINTON L DAVID	CW3	GARY D DESHAZER	CW4	JAMES A DOUGAN	CW4	JAMES R EDENS
CW3	RONALD W DAVIE	CW4	DONALD G DESJARDINS	CW5	JOHN R DOUGHERTY	WO1	DAVID W EDGAR
CW4	DANIEL J DAVIES	CW4	ANGUS B DESVEAUX	CW3	RICHARD B DOUGHERTY	CW4	DOUGLAS C EDGELL
CW3	GERALD A DAVIES	CW5	LOREN D DETHLEFS	CW2	ALLEN V DOUGLAS	WO1	DOUGLAS E EDGINGTON
CW3	LINDA DAVIES	WO1	KENNETH C DETTBARN	CW4	HUGH W DOUGLAS	CW4	ROBERT E EDINGER
CW3	MARK A DAVIES	CW4	ALLAN O DETTMANN	CW4	CHARLES R DOWD	CW2	EARL E EDKIN
CW4	ALTON L DAVIS	WO1	ADAM J DeVALLE	CW4	STEVEN L DOWDY	WO1	CARLOS A EDMONDSON
CW3	BRUCE A DAVIS	WO1	ROMY R deVENECIA	CW3	CHARLES R DOWDY,JR	CW3	JOSEPH R EDSTROM
CW4	CAMERON E DAVIS	WO1	DANIEL D DeVENY	CW4	H. FINLEY DOWNES	CW4	FORREST A EDWARD
CW3	DAVID F DAVIS	CW4	RONALD J DeVILLERS	WO1	GREGORY M DOWNING	CW2	DAVID B EDWARDS
CW3	DAVID O DAVIS	CW3	ROBERT E DeVORE,JR			CW2	GENE L EDWARDS
CW4	DOUGLAS T DAVIS	SGT	CURTIS A DeVRIES	CW5	ARTHUR J DOYLE	WO1	GEORGE L EDWARDS
CW4	GERALD D DAVIS	MAJ	JON C DEVRIES	CW4	CHARLES J DOYLE	CW4	JAMES A EDWARDS
CW5	J W 'BUTCH' DAVIS	WO1	JIM T DEW, JR	CW2	MARK A DOYLE	WO1	JAMES T EDWARDS
CW2	JAMES F DAVIS	CW3	CARL W DeWITT	CW2	STEVEN E DOYLE	CW3	MICHAEL S EDWARDS
CPT	JIMMY D DAVIS	CW5	JERRY L DEWITT	CW3	THOMAS S DRAKE	CW3	WALTER L EDWARDS
CW3	JOHN A DAVIS	CW4	ROGER G DeWITZ	CW2	KEITH A DREAS	CW2	WAYNE R EDWARDS
WO1	KENNETH DAVIS	CW4	DAVID DEWS,JR	CW2	MARSHA A DREIER	WO1	WILLIE M EDWARDS
CW3	MICHAEL DAVIS	CW3	LARONALD W DEWS,SR	CW4	FRANCIS H DRISCOLL	CW4	ALBERT S EGGERTON
CW3	PEGGY J DAVIS	CW2	GEORGE M DIAS	WO1	JO ANN DRISCOLL	CW4	RONNIE D EGNEW
CW2	ROBERT E DAVIS	CW4	JOSEPH DIAZ	CW5	JOSEPH E DRISCOLL	CW2	RONALD L EHMANN
CW2	ROGER W DAVIS	CW2	LOUIS P DIAZ	CW3	DENNIS DRIVER	CW2	DOUGLAS E EHRLE
WO1	ROY W DAVIS	CW2	LUIS R DIAZ	CW4	RICHARD A DROPIK	CW2	BURTON E EICHEL,III
		WO1	GEORGE E DICK	CW3	MARK L DROUIN		
		CW3	MICHAEL A DICK	WO1	LEANNE R DROZD		
		WO1	CHRISTOPHER M DICKENS	CW5	JOSEPH D DUARTE		
				CW3	GEORGE J DuBOIS		

SEE Pg 80 - WM. F. FERGUSON,

CW4	BETHEL L EILAND
CW4	CARL R EISEMANN
CW5	GARY J EISENBRAUN
CW3	PAUL A EISHEN,JR
CW2	MARK A EITREIM
WO1	LARRY T EL-AMIN
CW2	CLAUDE ELAM
CW3	THOMAS B ELDER
WO1	WALTER J ELDER
CW4	JAMES W ELDRED
CW3	LEROY E ELFMANN
CW4	ROBERT F ELIAS
WO1	CHRISTOPHER D ELICKER
CW2	JOHN S ELKINGTON
CW2	CHRIS E ELKINS
CW4	DALE W ELLENBARGER
WO1	GERALD A ELLIOTT
CW2	LYNDA G ELLIOTT
CW3	GEORGE R ELLIOTT,JR
CW3	BOB ELLIS
CW2	LARRY D ELLIS
CW4	LAWRENCE E ELLIS
CW4	RAYFORD ELLIS
CW5	STEWART L ELLIS,JR
CW2	GREGORY A ELLISON
CW2	MARTIN G ELLISON
WO1	CARTER J ELMORE
WO1	KELLEYE S ELMORE
CW4	TED R ELSNER
WO1	MICHAEL J ELWOOD,JR
CW3	ARCHIE L EMANUEL
WO1	DAVID J EMEOTT
CW4	BARRY B EMERY
CW3	ERNEST A EMIG
CW2	DAVID L EMORY
WO1	DAN Y ENG
CW2	DAVID H ENGELSKIRCHEN,JR
CW4	DANIEL R ENGLAND
WO1	DAVID A ENGLAND
WO1	DOUGLAS J ENGLER
CW3	DANNY W ENGLUND
MW4	NEWELL M ENOS
CW3	LEWIS W EOFF
CW3	LASZLO EOSZE
CW3	RICHARD E EPPLER
CW4	HILMER ERICKSON
CW2	MARTHA ERVIN
CW3	HECTOR J ESCALONA
CW2	THOMAS F ESPOSITO
WO1	MOHAMED G ESSA
CW3	RICHARD F ESTERON
CW3	ARNOLD M ESTES
WO1	FERNANDO M ESTRELLA
CW2	ALBERT J ETELMAN
CW4	ANDREAS ETZEL
CW4	JAMES P EURY
CW2	GERALD A EVANS
CW3	JACK EVANS
CW4	JOHN M EVANS
CW3	RICHARD H EVANS
WO1	RONALD J EVANS
CW4	WILLIAM H EVANS
WO1	KENNETH J EVANS, JR
CW4	WILLIAM J EVANS,JR
WO1	TODD F EVERETT
CW2	FREDERIC H EVERLY
CW2	SAM H EWALD
CW3	FREDERICK D EXLEY
WO1	BRIAN K EZELL
WO1	RODNEY J EZELLE

F

CW3	JEFFREY T FACKLER
CW3	RODNEY G FAGAN
CW4	GEORGE G FAIRFAX
WO1	NORMAN FALCHER
WO1	RONALD L FALDE
CW4	DARRYL E FALLIS
CW4	DANIEL A FALLS
CW2	CELESTINO FALSO
CW3	LUTHER W FARNSWORTH
CW4	RICHARD A FARRANT
CW3	SUZAN R FARRELL
CW3	NANCY A FARRINGTON
CW4	BARRY D FARRIS
CW2	BRIAN R FASCI
CW3	PAUL E FAUBERT
CW2	ROLAND H FAUCHER
CW2	ALLEN J FAUST
WO1	JASON A FAUTH
CW2	ARNOLD A FAZIO
MW4	JOHN J FEDERICO,JR
WO1	TRACY L FEDOR
CW4	RICHARD R FEGREUS,JR
CW2	DAVID B FEIL
CW3	MILTON A FELIBERTY
CW2	THOMAS FENNESSY,JR
CW4	KEITH A FENRICH
CW2	DANIEL C FENTZKE
	COREY J FERGUSON
CW2	ROBERT E FERGUSON,JR
	EDWIN M FERNANDEZ,SR
CW3	FRANK FERRAIVOLO
CW2	JIMMY FERRER
CW4	THOMAS E FETCHET
CW2	DOUGLAS C FIALA
CW3	BOBBY H FIELDS
WO1	ROBERT E FIELDS
CW2	RODNEY L FIELDS
CW3	STEVEN M FIELDS
WO1	JESSE P FIELDS,JR
CW4	JERRY A FIGURES
CW3	EDWARD M FILKINS
CW2	VLADIMIR FILZOW
WO1	DAVID F FINCH
CW3	KENNETH I FINCH
WO1	ADAM L FINDLEY
CW3	JERRY S FINK
CW4	MICHAEL E FINK
CW2	ANTHONY V FINO,JR
WO1	JAIME E FIORENTINI
CW4	CHARLES A FISHER
CW3	DANIEL J FISHER
CW2	KIMBERLY A FISHER
CW5	MICHAEL A FISHER
CW5	DAVID C FISHER,JR
CW4	EDWARD R FITTING
CW2	GEORGE T FITZGERALD
CW5	MARY C FITZGERALD
WO1	MICHAEL R FITZSIMMONS
CW2	DAVID FIVECOAT
CW3	RANDY L FIZER
CW3	STANLEY M FLACK
CW4	BILLY K FLANAGAN
CW4	JAMES P FLANAGAN
CW2	ROBERT A FLAUGH
CW3	GERRY E FLEMING
CW4	WILLIAM T FLEMING
WO1	DENNIS N FLEMING,JR
CW2	ROBERT L FLEN
CW2	ARTHUR J FLINN
CW3	LONNIE JASPER FLONNORY
CW3	BRODIE J FLOOD
CW3	CURTIS L FLOOD
WO1	DEREK W FLOOD
CW3	FRANK FLORES
CW3	JOSEPH W FLORIANO
CW3	BURL B FLOYD
CW3	STEPHEN R FLOYD
CPT	WILLIAM J FLYNN,III
WO1	JOHN F FOBISH
CW5	DANIEL N FOE
CW5	GENE R FOERSTER
CPT	ROBERT E FOGEL
CW3	BARBARA S FOGERLUND
CW2	BARRY P FOLEY
CWO	BILLY J FOLEY
CW4	THOMAS G FOLGATE
CW3	DONNA LEA FOLI
CW5	LESTER O FOLTZ,JR
CW3	EDWARD L FORD
CW4	LARRY D FORD
CW2	LEROY E FORD
CW2	MELVIN B FORD
CW4	RICHARD L FORD
CW4	ROBERT I FORD
MW4	DAVID H FORD,SR
CW4	GLENN A FORDYCE
CW4	RONALD E FORRER
CW2	JERRY C FORREST
CW4	LARRY FORRESTER
CW4	DON E FORSHEE
CW4	DAVID C FORTIES
CW3	THOMAS H FORTUNE
CW3	BRADFORD C FOSTER
CW2	JEROME FOSTER
WO1	KEVIN M FOSTER
CW3	ROY D FOSTER
CW2	PAUL E FOSTER,JR
CW4	CHARLES T FOUTS
2LT	BRYAN E FOWLER
CW2	WILLIAM FOWLER
CW3	DEAN C FOX
CW4	ROBERT A FOX
CW3	PATRICK J FOXEN
CW4	JON G FOZARD
MR	UDO FRAMME
CW4	ALLAN D FRANCIS
CW4	PATRICK D FRANCIS
WO1	SUZETTE M FRANCISCO
CW3	JOHN A FRANK
CW3	HARRY J FRANKLIN
CW2	JAMES E FRANKLIN
CW3	KENNETH R FRANKLIN
CW4	REGINALD A FRANKLIN
CW2	STEVEN A FRANKLIN
CW4	WILLIAM W FRANKLIN
CW3	ROBERT A FRANZ
CW3	ROBERT B FRANZ
CW4	FRANCIS J FRANZE
WO1	JAMES T FRASER
CW2	LARRAN FRASIER
CW4	EDWARD J FRAZER
CW4	TOMMY J FRAZIER,JR
CW2	TIMOTHY D FRED
WO1	FRANK C FREDERICK
WO1	DALE K FREE,II
WO1	BARBARA S FREEMAN
CW4	BERNARD E FREEMAN
CW3	CHARLES T FREEMAN
WO1	JOHN P FREEMAN
WO1	RICHARD D FREEMAN
CW4	RICHARD P FREESLAND
CW5	ROBERT W FREITAG,II
CW4	ARTHUR A FRENZEL
WO1	F LOUIS FRERE
CW2	CRAIG A FRERICHS
CW3	RICHARD FRERICHS
CW4	LYNN A FREUND
WO1	JERRY D FREW
CW5	JOSEF W H FREY
CW2	LYLE J FRIDLUND
CW5	MICHAEL L FRIED
CW2	MICHAEL D FRIEDBERG
CW2	RICHARD C FRIEDBERG
WO1	YOLANDA T FRIENDLY
CW4	DONALD T FRIERSON
CW4	PHILLIP Q FRISKO
CW3	RAYMOND G FRISON
CW4	BILL FROST
WO1	MARCELL FROST
CW3	JEFFREY W FROUDE
CW3	GUSTAVE R FRUAUFF
CW3	GREGORY FUCHS
CW2	GARY L FUGATE
CW4	REGINALD K FUJIMOTO
CW3	REGINALD A FUKUSHIMA
CW3	RICK L FULGIUM
CW2	BRIAN R FULLER
CW2	KELLY G FULLER
WO1	PATRICK L FULLER
CW4	ROBERT J FULLER
CW3	MICHAEL R FUNK
CW2	VICTOR L FURCHES
CW4	ROBERT W FUREIGH
CW3	MICHAEL A FURTNEY

G

CW2	PETER F GABER
CW4	MARIO GABRIEL,JR
CW4	RICHARD GADARIAN
CW2	GARY G GAFFNER
CW5	PHILIP M GAFFNEY
CW4	JAMES THOMAS GAGEN,JR
	GEORGE S GAGNON
CW4	HOMER D GAINES
CW4	WALTER S GAINEY,JR
CW2	TIMOTHY F GALECKI
CW2	HENRY C GALETSCHKY
	WILLIAM J GALLAGHER
CW3	GILBERT G GALLENTINE
	RONALD G GALLOWAY
CW5	SAMUEL P GALLOWAY
CW3	JIMMY N GALPIN
CW4	ROBERT L GAMBERT
CW3	ROBERT J GAMBINO
CW4	WILLIAM H GAMBLE
CW2	OTTO GAMBREL,JR
CW3	EDDIE GANCERES
CW3	ROBERT W GANT
CW2	JON W GANUES
CW2	JAY E GARBUS
CW4	FERNANDO GARCIA
	GERALD GARCIA
CW2	RICHARD L GARDNER
CW5	BRUCE P GARDNER,JR
CW4	DONALD E GARLIN,JR
CW2	WILBUR L GARLING
CW4	DONALD R GARLOW
CW4	SALVATORE GAROFALO
CW3	MICHAEL W GARRETT
CW4	ROBERT E GARRISON
CW3	LeROY E GARRISON,JR
CW4	JAMES H GARST
CW4	WILLIAM R GARTMAN
CW3	HAROLD W GARWOOD
CW3	PETE R GARZA
CW2	WILLIAM H GASAWAY
CW3	BILLIE R GASTON
CW3	DAVID M GASTON
CW2	MICHAEL E GASTON
CW5	ROBERT E GATES
CW4	VON E GATES
WO1	JOSEPH GATHERS
CW3	PIERRE F GAUDET
WO1	ERIC J GAUDETTE
CW2	GEORGE R GAUKEL
CW3	ROBERT M GAVER
CW4	VIRGINIA M GAVIN
WO1	MICHAEL D GAY
CW4	RICHARD V GBURZYNSKI
MR	HEINRICH GEBAUER
WO1	FOWOOD M GEBHART, III
CW3	WINFRIED W GEIER
CW2	ROLLY S GELHAUS
CW3	JOEL GELLER
CW3	EDWARD J GELSONE
CW3	ROBERT SCOTT GENAILLE
CW3	PAUL E GENEREUX
CW3	SALVATORE J GENUALDI
CW2	DEAN E GEORGE
CW3	LARRY R GEORGE
CW3	MICHAEL D GERACE
CW2	JOHN E GERKIN
WO1	FRANK R GERLACK
CW2	PAUL GERMAIN
CW4	WILLIAM M GERO
CW4	RODNEY O GERSON
CW3	JOSEPH F GERVAIS
CW3	GLENN L GESTEWITZ
CW2	DAVID RAY GETZ
CW4	FRANK T GEYSEN,JR

CW3	L SCOTT GIACOBBE
CW3	BILL L GIBBS
CW2	JOHN M GIBBY
MR	ARTHUR EARL GIBSON
CW2	EDSON G GIBSON
CW5	LEO G GIBSON
WO1	CHRISTOPHER N GIDULA
CW4	RUTH L GIEBEL
MW4	ROBERT (BOB) P GIFFIN
CW2	GREGORY GIGLIOTTI
CW4	VINCENT J GIGLIOTTI
CW2	RONALD GILCHRIST
CW4	MONROE GILDERSLEEVE,JR
CW2	LARRY GILES
CW2	LEROY GILES
CW4	JAMES GILFONE
CW3	JOSEPH C GILL
CW2	TANYA J GILLCREST
WO1	DAVID GILLESPIE
CW2	DAVID C GILLESPIE
CW2	THOMAS H GILLESPIE
CW3	JAMES M GILLHOUSE
WO1	CHARLENE V GILLIAM
CW3	THOMAS H GILLIGAN
CW3	RICHARD S GILLOGLY
CW3	GREGORY M GILMAN
CW5	KENNETH E GILMAN
CW2	SEAN F GILPIN
CW4	WILLIAM A GILSTRAP
CW4	MATTHEW GINALICK,JR
CW3	GARY L GINN
CW3	VINCENT A GIOVANIELLO
CW4	DAVID E GIVENS
CW2	JIMMY GIVENS
CW5	DOUGLAS W GJERTSON
CW3	CHARLES R GLASS
CW4	HAROLD GLASS,JR
CW4	DENNIS F GLASSER
CW3	LEONARD B GLASSER
WO1	ANTHONY G GLAUDE
CW2	JOHNNIE A GLEAVES
CWO	WILLIAM R GLEICHAUF
WO1	RICKY T GLENN
CW2	VICKI C GLOCK
CW4	ROBERT O GLODICH
CW3	RONALD GLOTZER
WO1	MICHELLE L GLUBKA
WO1	EDWIN W GLUNT
CW4	DANIEL GNALL
SGT	GREGORY L GOBER
CW2	RICKY C GODBOLT
CW2	DALE C GODDARD
WO1	KIPP C GODING
WO1	MICHAEL R GODWIN
CW4	STEVEN C GOETZ
CW3	SANDRA L GOFF
CW4	WILLIAM S GOFORTH,JR
CW3	THOMAS F GOGGIN
CW2	DONALD M GOIN
CW3	RICHARD GOINS
CW2	FRED G GOLD
CW3	JERRY A GOLDEN
CW4	JACK GOLDMAN
WO1	RODNEY C GOLDMAN
CW2	JOSEPH A GOLDSMITH
CW2	STEPHEN A GOMES
CW4	GEORGE K GONSALVES
CW5	ROLANDO GONZALES
CW4	SANTIAGO GONZALES
CW3	RICHARD G GONZALES,II
CW4	JOSEPH GONZALEZ,III
WO1	CRUZ GONZALEZ,JR
CW3	RAFAEL A GONZALEZ-ARROYO
CW2	ALLEN P GOODMAN
CW2	GEORGE C GOODMAN,JR
CW4	CALVIN L GOODRICH
CW3	WALTER E GOODRICH
CW3	ROSANNE J GOODSTEIN
CW3	TIMOTHY R GOODWIN
CW3	JOSEPH GOONAN
CW2	EMERALDINE M GORDON
CW2	JAMES D GORDON
CW3	TEX M GORDON
CW3	FRANK GORDON,JR
WO1	WILLIAM C GORDY
CW2	ADAM F GORE
WO1	BRYAN K GORE
CW3	JOHN J GORMAN
COL	RONALD E GORNTO
CW2	DAVID H GORTON
CW2	DAVE GOSINSKI
CW2	ANDREW F GOSSELIN
CW2	BEN GOTTFRIED
CW4	RICHARD GOTZ
CW4	JAMES M GOULD
CW3	THOMAS E GOULD
CW3	GREGORY A GOUTY
CW4	DARRELL P GRAF
CW2	ROGER A GRAF
CW2	GEORGE C GRAHAM
CW4	JAMES C GRAHAM
CW4	JOSEPH M GRAHAM
CW3	MICHAEL L GRAHAM
CW3	MANUEL A GRANADO
CW2	ERIC K GRANT
CW3	HENRY GRANT
CW2	STEPHEN M GRANT
WO1	THOMAS L GRANTMAN
CW4	GEORGE C GRATCHEN
CW2	RICHARD A GRAVES
CW4	CLOISE D GRAVES,JR
CW4	DOUGLAS G GRAY
CW4	JIMMIE C GRAY
WO1	MATHEW C GRAY
CW3	CHARLES L GREELEY
WO1	ANGEL GREEN
CW3	CHARLES GREEN
CW3	ERNEST GREEN
WO1	JEFFERY J GREEN
CW3	JOHNNY L GREEN
CW4	LEAMON L GREEN
CW3	SHEILA L GREEN
CW2	THOMAS S GREEN
CW4	THOMAS W GREEN
WO1	LEE D GREEN,SR
MAJ	WARREN O GREENE
CW4	J T GREENHAW
CW2	JAMES L GREER
WO1	DONALD M GREER,III
ILT	STEVEN C GREGG
WO1	GILBERTO E GRENALD
WO1	MICHAEL P GRENIER
CW3	GENE L GRESSLEY
CW5	THOMAS G GRICE
CW2	WENDY Y GRICE
CW3	THOMAS A GRIER
CW3	MICHAEL W GRIFFIN
CW4	NOEL R GRIFFIN
CW2	ROBERT L GRIFFIN
CW4	ROGER M GRIFFIN
WO1	HAROLD W GRIFFIN,III
CW3	CHARLES E GRIFFITHS,SR
WO1	MICHAEL D GRIGG
CW4	KENNETH I GRIGGS
CW3	GORDON L GRIMES
CW3	WILLIAM A GRIMES
CW2	DAVID SCOTT GRIMM
WO1	MARIO T GRINER
CW2	WARREN R GROFF,JR
CW4	LANCE S GROMME
CW2	MARK A GROSS
CW2	MICHAEL W GROSSKOPF
CW4	JOHN H GROTE
CW2	KATHLEEN GROTE
CW2	ARRON A GROTTOLO
CW5	LAWRENCE D GROUT
WO1	CURTIS LEE GROVER
CW4	PAUL GROVES
CW4	WILLIAM W GRUBB
CW4	LAWRENCE C GRUBER
CW2	ALAN L GRUEL
CW5	ROBERT P GRUVER
CW4	JAY G GRUWELL
CW2	SALVADOR GUARDIOLA
CW3	ALBERT R GUENSCH
CW4	WAYNE S GUFFY,JR
CW3	HENRY J GUIETTE,JR
CW4	JAY M GUILD
CW5	BERT R GUILLORY,JR
CW4	DONALD M GUIMOND
CW2	MANUEL C GUIZAR
WO1	FRED W GULDBRANDSEN
CW2	CHARLES R GULLY
CW4	DON S GUNNING
WO1	CRYSTAL GUNTHER
CW5	RAYMOND T GUSTAFSON,II
CW2	PAUL A GUTEKUNST
CW2	DAVID D GUTIERRES
CW2	JOSEPH F GUTIERREZ
CW2	WILLIE F GUY
CW3	JAMES J GUYRE
CW2	EDMUND E GUZMAN
CW3	LUIS GUZMAN
CW2	AARON S GWIN

H

CW2	MARK A HAAS
CW4	CALVIN C HABERER
CW4	WILLIAM J HABERMAN
CW3	PAUL M HABHAB
WO1	MARIANNE L HACKNEY
CW3	WILLIAM D HADDIX
WO1	JAMES A HADDOCK,III
CW2	GLENN D HADLEY
CW4	GORDON D HAFEMAN
CW2	RICHARD L HAGAN
CW2	THOMAS HAGNEY
CW2	WILLIAM C HAGUE
WO1	DEBORAH L HAHNENKAMP
CW4	HOWARD C HAIDER
CW2	ROBERT L HAILEY,JR
CW3	FANNY J HAINE
CW2	ROBERT O HAINES
CW3	RICHARD J HAINES,JR
CW3	KATHRYN M HAISLAR
CW4	JOHN L HAKKER
CW4	MIKE G HALBY
CW4	EUGENE S HALE
CW3	MATTHEW J HALE
WO1	RONALD A HALE
CW2	CHRISTINE D HALEY
WO1	ELMER HALL
CW3	FREDERICK A HALL
CW4	JAMES L HALL
CW2	JESSE E HALL
CW4	JOSEPH R HALL
CW5	KEITH V HALL
CW2	KIRK D HALL
CW4	REGINALD G HALL
WO1	TOMMY H HALL
CW4	EDWARD ROBERT HALL,JR
CW2	WAYNE HALLAM
CW3	EDMOND E HALLMARK
CW2	CURTIS L HALLMARK,JR
CW2	CARL K HALLSTROM
CW2	RONNIE K HALSELL
CW3	MARLIN B HALSTEAD
CW2	PAUL D HALVORSON
CW3	WILLIAM J HAMELIN,JR
CW4	BERNARD HAMILTON
CW2	CHRISTOPHER A HAMILTON
CW3	JAMES E HAMILTON
CW4	JAMES M HAMILTON
CW3	LOWELL D HAMILTON
CW2	REGINALD L HAMILTON
CW2	ROBERT L HAMILTON
CW2	WAYNE DREW HAMILTON
CW4	WILLIAM M HAMILTON
CW3	CHARLES W HAMILTON,III
WO1	MICHAEL C HAMLIN
CW4	ARTHUR E HAMMAR
WO1	BRIAN C HAMMER
CW2	DONALD D HAMMOND
CW2	JOSEPH A HAMMONDS
CW2	HERMAN HAMPP
CW3	JERRY M HANCHETT
CW3	BILLY J HANCOCK
CW5	DUANE L HANECKOW
CW3	MARY A HANLEY
WO1	JAMES K HANNER
CW2	ROBERT E HANSEL
CW4	DALE E HANSEN
WO1	KAREN L HANSEN
CW5	RANDALL S HANSEN
CW3	MICHAEL HANSOM
CW4	MICHAEL F HARBIN
CW4	ADRIAN G HARD
CW2	HUGH HUNT HARDCASTLE,III
CW2	ROBERT E HARDEE
CW3	JOSEPH L HARDESTY
CW4	JOHN E HARDIMAN
CW2	JOHN E HARDING
CW4	ROGER L HARDMAN
CW3	WILLIAM H HARDY
WO1	CAREY HARGETT,JR
CW3	OWEN N HARNED,JR
WO1	RODNEY W HARP
CW3	ALBERT L HARPER
CW4	BETTY HARPER
WO1	JOLLY HARPER
CW3	KEVIN L HARPER
CW3	STEVEN L HARPER
CW3	TIMOTHY W HARPER
CW2	WILLIAM H HARPER,JR
WO1	TERRANCE K HARR
CW2	NEIL R HARRINGTON
CW2	DOUGLAS L HARRIS
CW4	FRANK HARRIS
CW3	FRED D HARRIS
WO1	JARROD T HARRIS
CW2	JULIUS HARRIS
WO1	KATHLEEN A HARRIS
CW4	ROBERT A HARRIS
WO1	RODNEY A HARRIS
WO1	TODD A HARRIS
CW4	WILLIAM E HARRIS
CW4	WILLIAM T HARRIS
CW2	EDWIN D HARRISON
CW3	ROBERT C HARRISON
CW5	WILLIAM J HARRISON
CW4	JOHN L HARRISON,SR
CW3	TROY R HARROLD
CW2	MARCUS A HART
CW3	ROBERT E HART
CWO	WILLIAM S HART
WO1	CARLTON T HART,JR
CW2	DERRY S HARTLEY
WO1	SAMUEL J HARTMAN
WO1	ROBERT P HARTSFIELD
WO1	JERRY L HARTSOCK
CW4	ROBIN HARVARD
CW2	RONNIE HARVELL
CW2	DONALD HARVEY
WO1	MONIQUE HARVEY
CW4	NEIL E HARVEY
CW3	HERBERT T HARWELL,JR
WO1	INTISAR HASAAN-REED
CW4	JERRY K HASHIMURA
WO1	DAVID B HASKINS
CW2	BRYAN HASLETT
WO1	GEORGE B HASSMAN
WO1	KEITH D HASTEDT
CW4	DAVID B HASTING
CW3	DAVID L HASTINGS
WO1	WILLIAM J HASTINGS
CW3	RICK HATFIELD
CW5	RICHARD W HATHAWAY
WO1	REGINALD H HATHORN,III
CW2	BOBBY L HATTER
CW3	SAM HAUGABOOK,JR
CW4	WILLIAM L HAUGER

CW2	PIERRE HAURE,II
WO1	JEFFREY A HAVELOCK
CW3	JOHN R HAVERTY
WO1	BARRY L HAWK
WO1	KENNETH R HAWKINS
CW2	DAMON HAWKINS,JR
WO1	GREGORY T HAWLEY
CW4	EARL F HAWN
CW3	FRED L HAWN,JR
CW3	GERALD G HAWORTH
CW4	MARTIN F HAYDEN
WO1	STANFORD T HAYDEN
MAJ	MAXWELL L HAYDON
CW2	MICHAEL J HAYDUK
CW3	HERB HAYES
CW2	M D HAYES
WO1	SANDRA HAYES
CW3	ALLEN J HAYES,SR
CW3	ROBERT C HAYNES
CW2	NIDSA D HAYS
CW3	HENRY G HAYS,JR
CW3	EDWARD HAYWARD
CW3	WILLIAM R HAYWES,JR
CW3	THEODORE W HAZEN
CW3	LOUISE M HEAD
CW3	TIMOTHY L HEAD
CW2	CLIFFORD A HEADLEY
CW4	ARTIE A HEAPE
WO1	RICHARD G HEATH
CW2	ROGER G HEATH,SR
CW4	ALEX O HEATON
CW2	HAROLD E HEAVNER
WO1	JAMES E HECK
CW4	JERRY A HECK
CW4	ROBERT M HECKER
WO1	MICHAEL H HECKMAN
CW4	BERNARD C HEDGE
CW3	GEORGE M HEDRICK
CW4	PAUL D HEGGOOD
CW2	JACK L HEIDENESCHER
WO1	ROBERT J HEIDMAN
CW3	RANDY A HEIDT
CW4	EDWIN E HEIDTKE
CW2	DOUGLAS A HEIMBACK
CW5	CLARENCE L HEINER
CW3	JOSEPH M HEISER
CW2	JEFFREY L HELD
WO1	ROGER L HELM
CW2	BRIAN A HELMS
WO1	DOUGLAS W HELMS
CW5	DAVID E HELTON
CW4	RICHARD M HEMINGSON
CW2	LOWELL J HEMMELGARN
CW4	JOHNNY P HEMMINGWAY
CW2	DONALD HEMRIC
CW3	CHRISTOPHER J HENDERSON
CW3	EDDIE HENDERSON
CW3	FLOYD D HENDERSON
CW2	MARBRY L HENDERSON
CW2	RICKY A HENDERSON
CW4	SAMUEL W HENDERSON
CW2	STEFAN A HENDERSON
CW4	CHARLES E HENDRICKS
CW2	DONALD R HENDRICKSON
WO1	MICHAEL P HENDRICKSON
WO1	MICHAEL S HENDRICKSON
CW5	KENNETH J HENDRIX
CW4	WILLIAM A HENDRY,III
CW4	THOMAS J HENNEN
CW3	DENNIS J HENNING
CW2	DAVID E HENRIKSEN
CW2	LESLIE S HENRY
CW4	ROBERT F HENRY
WO1	RONNIE DEWAYNE HENRY
CW3	WILLIAM E HENRY
CW3	WILLIAM R HENRY,JR
CW4	RICHARD T HENSELEN
CW2	JAMES D HENSLEY
MR	PETER G HENSLEY
CW2	JEFFREY D HENTON
CW4	ROBERT P HERKA
CW4	LARRY HERLIHY
CW3	STUART G HERMAN
CW4	EFRAIN HERNANDEZ
CW3	PABLO HERRERA
CW5	RONALD A HERRING
WO1	LINDA HERRINGTON
WO1	KENT D HERSMAN
CW3	MICHAEL S HERZBERG
CW4	CARL L HESS
CW4	DONALD E HESS
CW4	ELERY H HESS
CW5	GERALD L HESS
WO1	ROBERT HESS
CW3	DOUGLAS C HETTLER
CW4	PETE B HEWITT
CW3	PHILIP C HEWITT
CW2	CHARLES LLOYD HEYDT
CW3	LAWRENCE E HICKERSON
WO1	JAMES HICKS
CW2	WILLIAM B HICKS
CW3	WILLIAM L HICKS
CW2	RAYMOND A HICKS,JR
WO1	HEATH A HIELSBERG
WO1	MICHAEL R HIERONIMCZAK
CW2	CLINT J HILBERT
CW5	DELBERT L HILL
WO1	ERIC S HILL
WO1	ERIN R HILL
CW3	KENNETH B N HILL
CW2	MARVIN E HILL
CW4	LEROY HILL,JR
CW3	HAROLD W HILLIS
CW3	JOHN A HILLYER
CW3	VON R HIMELRIGHT
CW2	JOHN M HIMES
CW3	LESLIE M HINDS
CW2	ROCELIA A HINDS
CW4	YOUNG HINES
CW2	BRYAN J HINKEL
CW2	JOHN F HINKLE
WO1	JAMES F HIRT
CW3	PAUL C HIRTZ
CW3	THOMAS J HITCHCOCK, II
CW2	JAY D HIZER
WO1	ROMEO M HIZON
CW3	SHAWN J HOBAN
CW3	JEFFREY L HODGE
CW2	FRED L HODGES,JR
CW4	JOE E HODGES,JR
WO1	RICHARD R HODKINSON
CW4	ROBERT K HODSON
CW3	DAVID J HOFER
WO1	HERMAN L HOFFMAN
CW2	JERRY D HOFFMAN
WO1	LORI R HOFFMAN
CW3	RICHARD D HOGLE
CW4	DONALD E HOGLUND
CW4	FRANK G HOGUE
CW2	JAMES HOGUE
CW3	EARL C HOKANSON
CW2	DEAN H HOKREIN
WO1	ROBERT D HOLBROOK
CW2	JAMES M HOLDER
WO1	FRANCIS J HOLLAND
CW4	GEORGE L HOLLAND
CW3	JAMES D HOLLAWAY
CW4	EUGENE L HOLMAN,JR
CW2	ELIZABETH L HOLMES
MW4	ROBERT OTIS HOLMES
CW2	CHRISTOPHER L HOLT
WO1	JAMES K HOLTZ
CW4	ROBERT A HOLYBEE
CW4	FELIX H HONDZINSKI
CW2	RANDY W HONE
CW2	JAMES O HOOD
CW2	JOSEPH H HOOD
CW2	RITA A HOOD
CW3	LARRY F HOOGSTRAAT
CW4	CLAUDE L HOOPER
CW4	MARY L HOOTMAN
CW4	NORMAN HOOVER
CW2	EDUARDO ANTONIO HOPE
WO1	DAVID B HOPKINS
WO1	MICHAEL J HOPKINS
CW2	GAIL D HOPPE
CW3	LeROY F HORAN,JR
CW2	WALTER I HORLICK
WO1	DAVID R HORN
WO1	ROBERT J HORNBEAK
WO1	TERRY L HORNER
CW2	TODD J HORNESS
CW2	KIM HORTON
CW2	CRAIG S HORVATH
CW3	DONALD M HOSKINS
WO1	ELMER HOSKINS
CW2	MELINDA Y HOSLEY
CW3	AMALIE B HOSSELRODE
CW3	TIMOTHY R HOUCK
CW2	GARY K HOULEHAN
CW3	FREDERICK H HOUSEL
CW2	LENNIE J HOUSTON,III
CW2	MARTIEN G H HOUTKOOPER
CW3	CHARLES E HOVER,JR
CW3	DAVID J HOWARD
CW3	DERRAL L HOWARD
CW4	JACOB M HOWARD
CW3	LESLIE E HOWARD
CW3	RICHARD L HOWARD
CW4	RON HOWARD
WO1	MARK A HOWDESHELL
WO1	HAROLD K HOWE
CW2	ANNE M HOWELL
CW4	DENNIS HOWELL
CW4	JOE L HOWELL
CW4	MICHAEL D HOWELL
CW5	WILLIAM G HOWELL,SR
CW2	JAMES W HOWERTON
WO1	VALERIE A HOWLEY
CW3	WILLIAM D HOY
WO1	RUSSELL S HOYER,JR
CW2	KEITH M HOYLE
CW2	ROBERT J HRDLICKA
CW5	JOHN A HRUBIK
CW2	ROGER W HUBA
WO1	SHERRY HUBBARD
CW2	JEFFREY W HUBER
MRS	ELKE HUBERS
CW3	HERMAN J HUCK
CW3	MATT HUCKFELDT
CW3	JOSE G HUERTANUNEZ
MAJ	PATRICK D HUFF
CW3	ROBERT L HUFFMAN
WO1	ODIE HUFFMAN,JR
WO1	DOUGLAS W HUGGINS
CW2	ROWMELL HUGHES
CW2	STEVE A HUGHES
CW2	TIMOTHY O HUGHES
CW4	WINSTON B HUGHES
CW3	JOHN W HUGHES,JR
CW2	JOHN J HUILMAN
CW3	JIMMY P HULL
CW4	ROBERT M HULL
WO1	STEPHANIE S HUMES
WO1	DANIEL R HUMESTON
WO1	BARRY L HUMRICH
CW2	WILLIAM C HUNGER,JR
WO1	DAVID J HUNT
CW2	MICHAEL J HUNT
CW4	HOWARD B HUNT,JR
WO1	ANGELA M HUNTER
WO1	GUY K HUNTER,II
CW2	JAMES G HUNTLEY,III
CW2	PATRICK I HURD
CW4	GERALD D HURLBERT
CW2	DONNY HURLEY
CW3	CHRISTIAN L HURST
CW2	JONATHAN E HURST
CW2	KATHLEEN HURST
WO1	CASSANDRA J HURT
WO1	OLIVER J HURT
WO1	KEVIN J HUSKEY
WO1	JEFFREY L HUSTON
WO1	ROBERT S HUTCHESON
CW4	ROBERT L HUTCHINSON,JR
CW2	JOHN W HUTCHISON
CW5	MICHAEL J HUTSON
CW2	WILLIAM R HUYCKE
CW2	MARTIN J HYDE
CW3	JAMES D HYSLIP
CW3	NOEL E HYSTEN,II

I

CW3	VITO J IACONO
CW3	WILLIAM F IANNONE
WO1	JAMES WILSON JOLLY III
CW2	STEPHEN C IKEDA
CW2	MARK W ILG
CW3	CARLYLE B INGLE,JR
CW4	RICHARD A INGLES
CW2	JEROME A INGRAM
CW2	WILLIAM L INGRAM
CW4	WILLIAM D INMAN
CW2	ROBERT W INSCORE,JR
CW2	BRUCE K IRWIN
CW5	EARLE C IRWIN
SFC	LEVI ISAAC
CW2	REBECCA B ISAAC
CW4	JON A ISEMINGER
CW2	MARK B IVEY
WO1	RICHARD IVEY

J

WO1	ARLAND W JACKSON
CW2	BERRYL E JACKSON
WO1	CRAIG JACKSON
CW2	DARRELL L JACKSON
CW3	FORREST A JACKSON
CW3	GINA A JACKSON
CW3	HARVEY J JACKSON
CW4	JAMES A JACKSON
CW4	JAMES L JACKSON
CW2	KEVIN N JACKSON
WO1	MICHAEL A JACKSON
CW3	MICHAEL P JACKSON
CW2	RAYMOND E JACKSON
WO1	RUDOLPH V JACKSON
CW2	WILLIAM T JACKSON
CW2	HARRY JACKSON,JR
CW4	JEFFERY L JACKSON,JR
WO1	QUITMAN D JACKSON,JR
CW4	DONALD E JACKSON,SR
CW4	REGINALD JACOBS
CW3	ROBERT H JACOBS,JR
CW4	JOHN A JACOT
WO1	PATRICK M JACQUET
WO1	DUANE A JAHNER
CW4	DAVID W JAMES
CW3	RONALD J JAMES
CW3	TOMMY L JAMES
CW2	VERNON J JAMES
CW5	WILLIAM I JAMES,JR
CW2	LARRY J JAMISON
WO1	CHRISTOPHER T JANIS
CW4	DANIEL A JARNER
CW3	WILLIAM JARVIS
CW2	REGINALD C JASPER
CW2	JOSEPH S JAWORSKI
CW2	GERARD D JEAN
WO1	RICHARD A JEFFERSON
WO1	ROGER E JEFFERSON
CW4	HOWARD C JENKINS
CW2	JAMES H JENKINS
WO1	JERRY JENKINS
CW4	SUZANNE JENKINS
CW4	TOM JENKINS
SFC	ALAN I JENKS
CW3	CLINTON S JENNINGS
CW2	DARWIN L JENSEN
CW3	JERRY F JENSEN

CW4	MARVIN G JENSEN
CW2	JAMES C JESSEN
WO1	ROSEMARY JETER
CW4	ROGER M JETT
CW2	RONNY C JEWELL
WO1	ANGELA A JEWETT
CW3	JOSEPH L JIMENEZ
MW4	DENNIS M JINKS
WO1	CLYDE E JOHANNES
CW2	HANS-ACHIM H JOHN
CW3	ROBERT E JOHN
CW2	ABDULLAH M JOHNSON
CW4	ANSEL PIKE JOHNSON
CW3	BARENT 'BARRIE' JOHNSON
CW3	BRUCE M JOHNSON
CW5	CARL H JOHNSON
CW2	CAROL A JOHNSON
WO1	CHARLES JOHNSON
CW3	CHARLES E JOHNSON
CW5	CLIFTON V JOHNSON
WO1	CYNTHIA R JOHNSON
WO1	DANNY R JOHNSON
CW2	DAVID J JOHNSON
CW2	DERICK S JOHNSON
WO1	DOROTHEA JOHNSON
WO1	GARY L JOHNSON
CW3	GEORGE ELLES JOHNSON
CW2	GRANT H JOHNSON
CW4	JAMES M JOHNSON
CW4	JAN M JOHNSON
WO1	JEFFERY W JOHNSON
CW2	JEFFREY D JOHNSON
CW2	JERRY D JOHNSON
CW2	JOHN F JOHNSON
CW2	JOSEPH J JOHNSON
CW3	JULIUS E JOHNSON
WO1	KEVIN J JOHNSON
WO1	MICHAEL J JOHNSON
CW3	NEIL W JOHNSON
CW5	RALPH JOHNSON
CW3	RAYMOND J JOHNSON
CW2	RENA L JOHNSON
CW3	ROBERT JOHNSON
CW4	ROBERT F JOHNSON
CW3	ROY JOHNSON
CW2	SARA M JOHNSON
CW4	THURMOND JOHNSON
CW2	TIMOTHY O JOHNSON
CW2	TOM L JOHNSON
CW4	URBAN R JOHNSON
WO1	VINCENT H JOHNSON
CW3	WADE JOHNSON
CW3	WANDA JOHNSON
CW4	WARNER L JOHNSON
CW4	WILLIAM R JOHNSON
CW2	WILLIE J JOHNSON
WO1	JAMES R JOHNSON,JR
WO1	JOSEPH E JOHNSON,JR
CW2	CHRISTOPHER R JOHNSTON
CW3	DAVID A JOHNSTON
CW4	FLETCHER S JOHNSTON
CW3	JOHN M JOHNSTON
CW2	ROBERT G JOHNSTON
WO1	THOMAS G JOHNSTON
CW4	WARREN T JOHNSTON
WO1	ALVIN F JONES
CW4	CURTIS C JONES
CW4	DAVID C JONES
CW4	DEBRA L JONES
CW2	DONALD E JONES
CW2	GILBERT JONES
WO1	GREGORY JONES
CW2	JAMES W JONES
CW4	JOHN RICHARD JONES
WO1	JOSEPH R JONES
CW2	KEVIN D JONES
WO1	KEVIN J JONES
CW2	MARK E JONES
CW2	MARK W JONES
WO1	MATTHEW ALAN JONES
CW2	MORRISON G JONES
CW3	RANDY JONES
CW2	RAYMOND S JONES
CW3	RICHARD R JONES
CW3	ROBERT W JONES
CW2	RODERICK A JONES
WO1	RODNEY JONES
WO1	SHARON L JONES
CW3	STANLEY A JONES
WO1	THAD A JONES
CW2	VICTORIA JONES
CW2	WILLIAM H JONES
CW3	WILLIAM L JONES
WO1	WILLIE A JONES
CW4	WILLIE E JONES
CW2	HOSEA JONES,JR
CW2	CHERYL A JONES-STRONG
CW2	ARTHUR T JORDAN
CW4	ELLIS EDWARD JORDAN
WO1	GERALD R JORDAN
CW2	KEITH P JORDAN
WO1	KEVIN W JORDAN
CW3	RALF JORDAN
CW2	ERIC J JORGENSEN
CW4	JACK D JORY
CW4	FRANK F JOSHUA
CW4	DONALD R JOYCE
CW4	EDWARD J NYBERG, JR
CW3	DAVID L JUBA
CW4	PATRICK O JUDD
CW3	RICHARD D JULER
CW4	JUNIUS H JULIEN
WO1	PIERRE R JULIEN

K

WO1	THOMAS P KABERLINE
CW4	RAPHAEL R KABLISKA
CW4	DANIEL E KADIN
WO1	THOMAS L KAISER,JR
CW3	ROBERT B KAIZAR
WO1	EDWARD O KALBACH
CW3	JAMES R KALE
CWO	GEORGE H KALLSTROM
CW5	PETER R KALOGRIS
CW3	MICHAEL A KAMINSKI
MR	JAMES A KANE
CW4	BERNARD M KAPLAN
CW4	FRED KAPLAN
CW4	SEAN L KARAMATH
WO1	DENNIS S KARAMBELAS
CW4	FERDINARD A KARBOWSKI
CW3	DENNIS J KARCZEWSKI
CW2	STEFANOS KARIOTIS
CW4	DANIEL S KASPRZYK
CW2	JERALD J KASSEL,II
CW4	WILLIAM N KASSON
CW3	MARVIN G KASTAMA
WO1	DAVID L KASTEN
CWO	RONALD T KATRENICK
CW4	JEFFREY A KAUFMAN
CW2	EDMOND W KEARNEY
CW4	JOHN V KEATING
CW2	JOHN B KEAVENEY
WO1	FRANK KEEHAN
CW3	KENNETH R KEEN
CW4	LEO KEENAN
WO1	ELIZABETH ANN KEENE
WO1	ROBERT W KEENE
WO1	JERRY P KEENEY
CW3	JOHNIE M KEETER,SR
CW4	JACOB D KEGRIS
CW3	CATHERINE A KEHOE
CW4	JAMES E KEIRSTEAD
CW3	STACY T KEITH
CW3	DENNIS H K KEKONA
CW2	DAN KELCH
CW4	NELSON W KELINSKE
WO1	PHILLIP B KELLEHER
WO1	ROBERT P KELLENBERGER
WO1	JOHN G KELLER
CW3	WILLIAM J KELLER
CW4	CLAY E KELLEY
CW2	DONALD E KELLEY
CW2	DONALD WAYNE KELLEY
CW3	MICHAEL J KELLEY
CW4	STEVEN D KELLEY
CW2	TONY B KELLUM
CW2	ALFRED L KELLY
CW2	KAREN S KELLY
CW2	RUTH N KELLY
CW3	EDWARD A KELLY,JR
WO1	MARK D KELSEY
CW3	DAVID J KEMPER
WO1	KARL F KENDALL
CW2	JERRY L KENDLE
CW2	ROY A KENDRICK
CW3	DAVID R KENNEDY
CW4	GEORGE H KENNEDY
CW4	GORDON R KENNEDY
CW4	RAY L KENNEDY
CW2	SALLY KENNEDY
CW4	THOMAS H KENNEDY,III
CW3	MICHAEL P KENNY
CW3	JOHN H KENT
CW4	ALAN P KENYON
CW4	WAYNE L KERN
CW5	HAROLD E KERNAHAN
CW3	DAVID KESEL
WO1	KURTIS D KETCHUM
CW4	FREDRICK KETZ
CW2	DAVID J KEYMANN
CW4	LAURENCE L KICKER
CW2	DOROTHY J KIDD
CW3	JAMES L KIDDER
CW3	FREDERICK L KIEHL
CW4	ROBERT L KIEMLE
CW4	ART KIERAN
CW3	JOSEPH G KIHL
WO1	KAREN E KILBURN
CWO	FRANK E KILBY
CW3	STEVEN T KILDE
CW4	MICHAEL P KILLIAN
CW4	ARTHUR F KILPATRICK
CW3	HARRY G KILPATRICK
WO1	PAUL H KIM
CW2	WENDY L KIMBLEY
CW2	JACK L KIME
WO1	DARREN J KING
CW3	DOUGLAS KING
CW2	JAMES S KING
WO1	JEFFREY THOMAS KING
CW2	JOHNNIE H KING
WO1	LORETTA KING
WO1	MELINDA S KING
WO1	MICHAEL KING
CW3	MORTON F KING
CW4	PAUL W KING
CW4	RICHARD P KING
CW2	ROSA L KING
CW3	WALTER C KING
CW4	WAYNE C KING
CW3	WILLIAM A KING
WO1	CAROLYN KING-JACKSON
CW4	JAMES KINGSMILL
CW3	KENNETH C KINLOUGH
WO1	GARY KINNEY
WO1	SCOTT A KINNEY
CW4	WILLIAM KINSELLA
CW4	JACK R KINSEY
CW2	RANDALL KINSEY
CW4	CHARLES L KIRBY,JR
CW3	RANDY M KIRGISS
CW3	TIM KIRKLAND
CW3	JESSIE H KIRKLAND,II
CWO	JIMMIE J KIRKLEY
WO1	MATTHEW KIRKPATRICK
WO1	RICHARD F KISER,III
CW5	STEPHEN T KISS
CW4	HADLEY F KITTREDGE,SR
CW2	MICHAEL G KITTS
CW2	DAVID A KLAAHSEN
CW2	TERRY A KLASSEN
LTC	ROBERT LUCIEN KLEIN
CW4	WILLIAM M KLEIN
CW2	JEROME T KLEIN,JR
CW2	JOHN R KLEVEN
WO1	DOYLE KLINE
CW2	ERIC KLINE
CW3	HERBERT E KLING
CW5	DALE L KLINKEFUS
CW5	GERALD E KLINKEFUS
CW3	GARY S KLIVANS
CW4	CARLYN J KLOMP
CW4	HANS J KLOSSNER
CW4	JAMES D KLUCK
CW4	GLENN F KLUTTZ
MR	PETER M KNAPP
CW4	EDWARD KNEAFSEY
CW4	THOMAS I KNEDLER
CW2	STEVEN J KNIERIM
CW2	MICHAEL K KNIGGE
WO1	MARK C KNIGHT
CW4	WILLIAM H KNOPF
CW2	CHRISTINE M KNOTT
CW2	DOUGLAS H KNOX
WO1	DAVID M KNUDSON
CW4	ROBERT T KNUDSON
CW4	GORDON G KOCH
CW4	EDWARD J KOCIK
WO1	RONALD W KOEHN
CW4	GERALD J KOEPPEN
CW4	STEVE N KOHN
CW3	EVA KOLLER
CW4	EDWARD J KOLOSKI
CW3	EDWARD B KOLOSVARY
WO1	SEAN JAMES KONECCI
CW4	IGNATIUS J KONING
CW3	MARSHALL KONO
CW2	JAMES F KONZAL
CW2	WAYNE M KOSKI
WO1	CURT A KOSKO
CW3	NICK KOSTELECKY
CW2	GEORGE C KOSUT
CW3	JAMES P KOUSOULAS
CW2	BRYAN R KOUTH
WO1	ROBERT W KOVEN
CW3	MATTHEW C KOZATEK
CW2	JOHATHAN P KOZIOL
WO1	DELIA M KRAMER
CW4	GARY M KRAMER
CW2	SCOTT T KRAMER
CW3	SAMUEL W KRATZER
CW2	RICHARD L KRAUSE
WO1	CHRISTOPHER M KRAWCZYK
CW3	DAVID JAMES KRIENS,SR
CW3	WESLEY C KROHN
WO1	CAROLYN A KROOT
CW2	JOHN E KROPF
MW4	OTTO L KRUEGER
CWO	PAUL M KRUEGER
CW2	LARRY JOHN KRUG
CW2	NIKOLAS B KUBLI
CW4	LEROY L KUCZYNSKI
CW3	ANGELA E KUEBAUGH
WO1	KEVIN D KUHN
CW4	JAMES E KUIPERS
CW4	WILLIAM C KULOVITZ
CW2	JAMES J KUNTZ
WO1	DAVID K KURODA
CW3	MELVIN KUROWSKI
CW2	CHRIS S KURZ
WO1	PETER P KUTLEIS
WO1	KAREN L KYLLONEN

L

CW3	EUGENE M LABOWSKIE
CW4	MICHAEL F LACKIE
CW4	LAWRENCE E LaDOUCEUR
WO1	MELANIE A LADRA
CW5	EDMOND A LAFANTASIE
CW2	RONALD L LAFFERTY

WO1	LARRY L LAHVIC
WO1	JEFFERY A LAIRD
CW2	BRUCE A LALIBERTE
CW3	MARIO J LaMAESTRA,JR
CW4	DONALD K LAMB
CW2	ETTA L LAMB
WO1	JOHN A LAMBRECHT
CW2	ROBERT K LAMPHEAR
CW2	PAUL M LAMSON
CW2	EDWARD B LANCE
CW2	KENNETH L LANE
CW3	THOMAS O LANE
CW2	VERNON E LANE
CW4	RONNIE D LANGLEY
CW3	WALTER LEE LANHAM
CW3	GARY D LANIER
CW4	THOMAS L LANNING
WO1	MARY KELSEY LAPOSTA
CW2	ANTONIO F LaROSA
CW3	STEVEN F LAROSA
CW4	BRUCE H LARSON
WO1	MARK LAWRENCE LARSON
CW3	RICKIE L LARSON
CW2	ROSANNE M LARSON
CW2	RUSSELL LARSON
CW4	JEFFERY K LASHBROOK
CW2	RAY T LaSTRAPE,SR
CW3	RUSSELL H LAUDERMILCH
CW3	RICHARD J LAURO
CW2	GREGORY M LAUSIN
CW2	STEPHEN M LaVELLE
CW4	ROBERT J LAVIN
CW3	HARRY K B LAW
CW4	RICHARD S LAW
SFC	MICHAEL G LAWLER
CW3	DONALD E LAWRENCE
CW2	JERRY L LAWSON
CW3	MARY H T LAWSON
CW3	KENDALL GENE LAWTON
WO1	LORI LYNN LAYNE
WO1	TERESITA P LAZARO
CW3	JAMES D LEACH
CW2	CONSTANTE M LEAL
CW2	DANIEL F LEARY,JR
CW2	RODNEY W LEAS
CW4	LEONARD L LEATHERMAN
CW4	GABRIEL A LeBLANC
WO1	ROBERT L LeBLANC
CW3	THOMAS E LeBLANC,JR
CW2	EDGARDO LEBRON
CW2	ARTHUR M LECLAIR,JR
WO1	RICHARD J LEDBETTER
WO1	DENNIS R LEE
CW2	JEFFERSON W LEE
CW4	ROBERT D LEE
CW4	ROBERT E LEE
CW5	ROY S LEE
CW2	WALTER R LEE
CW3	BILLY R LEEDY
WO1	EDWARD LEFERINK
CW3	LIONEL E LEFLER
CW2	LEONARD LEGER
CW3	JAMES E LEGGETT
CW3	JAMES W B LEGGITT
CW4	ROSCOE D LEGGS,JR
CW2	MARK L LEHTIMAKI
WO1	MICHAEL LEICHLITER
CW2	STEPHEN M LeMAY
CW3	CARYNN B LeMIEUX
CW2	ALFRED A LEMKE
CW2	GARY S LEMOINE
CW3	CHARLES W LEMONS
CW4	JAMES A LEMONS
CW3	LAWRENCE N LENTZ
CW3	MIGUEL A LEON
CW3	VICTOR J LEON
WO1	ROY M LEON-GUERRERO
CW3	JAMES A LEONARD
CW4	FRANCIS A LEONE,SR
WO1	DARREN L W LESTER
WO1	WILLIAM T LESTER
WO1	GERALD LEVERICH
CW3	CLARENCE LEVY,JR
CW3	GARY L LEWIS
WO1	LAYNE LEWIS
WO1	MARVA D LEWIS
WO1	MICHAEL W LEWIS
WO1	RICHARD L LEWIS
CW3	ROBERT F LEWIS
CW4	THOMAS E LEWIS
WO1	WILLIAM D LEWIS
CW3	WILLIAM T LEWIS
CW4	LEROY G LEWISTON
CW4	PAUL LIBERA
CW2	MARTIN J LICKTEIG
	BUDDY L LIGGENSTOFFER
WO1	JEREMY T LIGHT
	CHARLES W LIGHTFOOT,JR
WO1	ALMERICK C LIM
WO1	HOOI K LIM
CW2	FAUSTINO V LIM,JR
CW2	GERALD H LIMBACH
CW4	WALTER F LINDEMANN
	CHARLES J LINDERMAN
LTC	PHILIP W LINDLEY
CW3	LES C LINDNER
CW5	J LINDSAY
WO1	BELYNDA LINDSEY
CW3	STEVEN W LINDSEY
CW4	FRED LINDSLEY
CW2	DAVID J LINDSTEDT,JR
WO1	CRAIG M LINGHOR
CW2	JAYNE E LINGO
CW2	JAMES C LINK
CW3	RICHARD D LINK
CW2	WAYNE LIPHAM
CW2	JOHN L LIPNICKY
CW4	IRA MARK LIPSON
WO1	RICHARD D LITLE
CW2	MARK E LITTLE
CW2	PEGGY J LITTLE
WO1	DAVID W LITTNER
CW3	JOSEPH A LIVINGSTONE
	LEO LLERENA
CW2	PAUL A LOACH
CW4	STEVEN M LOCASCIO
CW2	JOHN W LOCKETT,JR
CW3	JOEL L LOCKHART
WO1	JAMES F LOCKLEAR
CW3	PETER E LODERMEIER
MSG	STEPHEN M LODGE
WO1	M F LOFFREDO
CW4	JAMES D LOGAN
CW3	JOSEPH J LOGAN,JR
CW3	WALTER J LOHEIDE
CW2	RORY M LOHMAN
CW3	STEPHEN M LOMAGO
WO1	JOSEPH V LONG
CW4	LINDA M LONG
CW2	MICHAEL J LONG
CW4	RANDALL G LONG
CW4	ROBERT W LONG
WO1	THOMAS D LONG
CW2	TIMOTHY A LONG
WO1	KYLE D LONGCRIER
WO1	DAVID J LONGSTAFF
WO1	PATRICK A LONGTIN
CW2	DANIEL J LOOMIS
WO1	HAROLD LOONEY
CW4	ELISEO T LOPEZ
CW2	PETER LOPEZ
CW2	STEPHANIE A LOPEZ
WO1	DENNY LORD
COL	RICHARD F LOREN
CW4	DOUGLAS A LORENZ
CW2	DANIEL L LOSCHEIDER
CW3	RICHARD J LoTEMPIO
CW4	G F LOTT
CW3	DAVID A LOUNSBURY
CW4	MARK E LOUTTIT
CW2	DUDLEY F LOVE
CW3	JERRY W LOVE
CW3	GERALD W LOVE,JR
CW2	ROBERT E LOVE,JR
CW3	MICHAEL J LOVELY
CW3	WADE H LOVORN,III
WO1	BRYAN R LOWE
CW4	KESTER H LOWE
CW2	RICHARD E LOWE
CW4	DANIEL W LOWERY,SR
CW2	DAVID K LOWES
CW2	JOHN J LOWES
CW4	EDWIN L LOWREY
CW2	JAMES F LOZINSKI
CW4	BOBBY LUCAS
CW4	BRADIE L LUCAS
CW2	PHILLIP A LUCERO
WO1	DOUGLAS E LUCIUS
CW5	JOHN E LUCIUS
CW2	GILBERT L LUCKEL
CW4	JOSEPH S LUDOVICI
WO1	SHAWN LUEDERS
CW4	JONATHAN H LUELLEN
CW4	CRAIG H LUFKIN
CW4	WALTER E LUFT
CW4	JOHN M LUKE
CW5	MICHAEL R LUKES
WO1	FRANK A LUMLEY
WO1	WILLIAM LUNDELIUS
CW5	HOWARD LUNDIN
CW2	THOMAS D LUNN
CW3	RICHARD P LURIE
CW4	BERNARD R LUSK
CW4	JAMES T LUTTRELL,JR
CW2	HANS L LUTZ
CW3	RAYMOND M LUTZ
CW2	RONALD F LUX
CW4	JOSEPH A LYLE
CW4	BRIAN E LYNCH
CW3	HUGH L LYNCH
CW5	JOHN (JACK) F LYNCH
CW2	MATHEW G LYNN
CW2	JULIA L LYONS
CW2	WARREN C LYONS

M

CW3	ROBERT M MACARTNEY
WO1	PAUL A MacDONALD
WO1	JAMES C MacDOUGALL
CW2	SCOTT A MACE
WO1	GREGORY MACK
CW3	DANIEL J MacLAUGHLIN
CW3	PATRICK A MacPHERSON
CW3	LARRY E MACY
CW4	DAVID S MADDEN
CW4	MICHAEL MADDEN
CW2	FELIPE B MADRID
CW2	JOHN P MADRID
WO1	JESUS R MADRIGAL
WO1	PETER H MADSEN
CW2	ANTHONY J MAFNAS
CW2	STEVE MAGLISCEAU
CW2	GRIMUR MAGNUSSON
CW4	GARY L MAGOWAN
CW4	HUGH J MAGUIRE
CW3	JAMES A MAHANEY
CW4	JOHN R MAHON
CW3	CHARLES R MAHONEY
CW2	ROBERT F MAIER
CW2	VOYT B MAIK
CW4	ANDREW C MAJOR,JR
CW3	MICHAEL B MALASKY
CW2	BYRON K MALBROUGH,SR
CW2	EDUARDO MALDONADO
CW3	EFREN G MALDONADO
CW4	LaROY W MALIN
WO1	ROBERT A MALINOWSKI
WO1	SHAWN M.MALINOWSKI
CW4	EDDIE E MALLARD
WO1	VANESSA A MALONE
CW3	TIM I MALOTT
CW4	CHRISTOPHER M MANDIC
CW3	JAMES B MANESS,III
CW4	EDWARD J MANGANO
	PRAIMNAUTH MANGAR
CW4	JAMES E MANLEY
WO1	LORRAINE MANN
CW5	LEON A MANN,JR
CW2	DEAN L MANSFIELD
CW2	CESAR B MANUEL
CW2	JAMES P MANZO
CW2	MARK R MANZO
CW2	VERNAE MARCH
CW2	RONALD W MARCUS
CW4	EDWARD G MARFUT
CW2	EDWARD R MARGENTINO
	DAVID S MARI
WO1	RICHARD K MARIANI
CW4	JOSEPH F MARINAK
CW4	JOHN J MARINI
CW4	MARK S MARINI,SR
CWO	DANIEL A MARINIELLO
CW4	GODFREY B MARK
CW4	JOHN W MARKER
CW2	HOMER M MARKEY,JR
CW4	RICHARD C MARKLE
CW4	RICHARD J MARKOWSKY
CW3	THOMAS G MARLETT,JR
WO1	JOHN S MARLOW
CW2	SHARON K MARLOW
CW3	LAWRENCE F MARONEY
CW2	JOSE L MARQUEZ
CW3	PABLO MARQUEZ-CRUZ
WO1	JOSE H MARRERO
CW2	JUAN A MARRERO
CW2	ARTHUR MARSHALL
CW3	GEORGE MARSHALL
WO1	NATHANIEL D MARSHALL
WO1	CHRISTINE A MARTELL
CW4	JAMES B MARTELL
CW2	CANDIS R MARTIN
CW3	CARL R MARTIN
WO1	DANIEL J MARTIN
CW3	EDWARD N MARTIN
CW4	FRANCIS E MARTIN
CW3	GERALD R MARTIN
CW4	JOHN E MARTIN
CW2	JOHN R MARTIN
CW4	LEE V E MARTIN
CW3	MARTY J MARTIN
CW3	PERRY MARTINDALE
WO1	CHRISTOPHER MARTINEZ
WO1	ERNESTO MARTINEZ
WO1	LUIS E MARTINEZ
CW4	MICHAEL P MARTINEZ
CW3	PEDRO MARTINEZ
CW4	ROBERT H MARTINEZ
MW4	RUBIN MARTINEZ
WO1	VANESSA PAIGE-MARTINEZ
CW2	DIXIE MARTINI
MR	THOR MARTINSEN
WO1	CARMEN F MARTUCCI
CW2	GARY L MARVEL
CW3	GREGORY SCOTT MARVEL
CWO	STEVEN A MASCARI
CW3	JAMES W MASON
CW3	LARRY G MASON
CW5	LESTER K MASON,JR
CW5	ROBERT A MASON,JR
CW4	EMANUEL MASSARELLA
CW2	MARK P MATA
CW3	BILL MATCHETTE
CW4	HENRY B MATHEWS
CW2	JACK D MATHEWS
CW4	RONNIE R MATHEWS
CW2	RODNEY J MATHEWSON
CW4	BRIAN P MATHY
CW3	BRENDA B MATTHEWS
CW4	GERALD B MATTHEWS

WO1	JOHN F MATTHEWS	CW4	GEORGE ROBERT McGEE	CW2	ALEXANDER MENDALOFF,III	CW2	WILLIE F MITCHELL
CW3	LINDA S MATTHEWS	WO1	MICHAEL P McGEEVER	CW3	GEORGE E MENDEZ-MERCADO	CW4	ROBERT E MIX
CW4	RAYMOND J MATUS	MRS	HELEN McGILLICUDDY	WO1	WAYNE M MENSEN	CW2	THOMAS HOWARD MIX
CW3	GEORGE E MAULDIN	CW5	ROBERT P McGINNIS	WO1	MICHAEL MERAY	WO1	EDWARD E MIZE
CW3	ROY J MAULT	WO1	TIMOTHY P McGINTY	CW4	REX C MERCIER	CW4	PHILIP G MIZZELL
CW2	DALE K MAUPIN	CW3	MARY E McGOFF	WO1	BRENDA Y MEREDITH	CW3	KENNETH L MOAN
WO1	CRAIG A MAURER	CW2	DAVID R McGOUGH	WO1	CARLOS A MERINO	CW2	RODNEY LEE MOATS
CW3	J ANDRE MAURICE	WO1	RICHARD C McGOWAN	CW3	RAYMOND MERLOCK,JR	CW2	DENNIS W MOEN
WO1	PAUL D MAUS	CW2	ROSLYN A B McGRUDER	CW3	JAMES H MERO	CW2	HELAINE MOESNER
CW4	DANIEL H MAUSS	CW5	ARBIE V McINNIS	WO1	JOSEPH C METZGER,II	CW3	RODNEY R MOESNER
CW2	ANDY G MAXFIELD	CW2	MAXIE N McINNIS	CW2	ROBERT W MEYERHOFF	CW2	ALLEN J MOHR
WO1	DAVID M MAXSON	MAJ	DAVID L McINTIRE	COL	JERRY F MEYERS	CW3	SHAPOUR MOINIAN
CW4	HERCULES MAXWELL	CW3	MERIDA McINTOSH		JOHN C MEYERS	WO1	JOSE V MOLANO
CW5	THOMAS L MAXWELL	CW2	PAUL L McINTOSH	WO1	MARKHAM A MICHEL	CW3	RANDY P MOLITOR
CW3	LAURENCE M MAY	CW2	KENNEDY R McIVER	CW2	HELMUT MICHITSCH	CW4	MICHAEL J MOLNAR
WO1	NORMAN G MAY	CW3	TOMMY D McKAY	WO1	ISAAC MIDDLETON	CW2	MICHAEL F MONAGHAN
WO1	RICK MAY	CW4	BENNY R McKEE	CW5	WILLIAM MIDDLETON,JR	CW4	RICHARD R MONROE
CW2	ROBERT G MAY,JR	CW4	DAVID E McKEE	CW2	SAMUEL N MIHALIK	WO1	ALVIN L L MONROE,I
CW4	WILLIAM H MAY,JR	CW3	RALPH H McKEE	CW3	E J MIKESKA,JR	CW2	ALFREDO MONTALVO
WO1	KRISTINA D MAYBIN	WO1	ELIZABETH A McKEEVER	WO1	JESSE H MILES	CW4	ALBERT R MONTESI
CW4	SAUL MAYENS	CW2	RODERICK L McKELLAR	WO1	BENNY R MILLER	CW2	CHARLES S MONTGOMERY
CW5	RUDOLF S MAYER	CW2	MICHAEL A McKENNY	CW4	CHARLES A MILLER	CW3	NASH D MONTGOMERY
CW2	GARY MAYERS	CW2	EARL McKENZIE	CW2	CHARLEY LEE MILLER	CW4	NICHOLAS W MONTGOMERY
CW3	BETTY C MAYES	WO1	KEVIN S McKENZIE	CW3	CHRISTOPHER C MILLER	CW3	SCOTT D MONTGOMERY
CW5	JOHN C MAYNE,JR	CW3	ROBERT W McKEOWN	WO1	CRAIG A MILLER	CW2	PHILLIPS C MONTGOMERY,JR
WO1	EDDIE A MAYNER	CW2	MICHAEL J MCKINLEY	CW4	DALE A MILLER	CW5	RUFUS N MONTGOMERY,SR
CW3	FRANCISCO J MAYORAL	WO1	JEFFREY G McKINNEY	CW3	DONALD R MILLER	CW2	ARNOLDO J MONTIEL
CW2	RUSSELL D MAYORAL	WO1	KEVIN McKINNEY	CW2	DOUGLAS S MILLER	CW2	MARCIA J MOODY
CW2	PAUL W MAYS	CW3	BLAINE J McKIVISON	CW2	GARRY A MILLER	CW2	STEPHEN M MOODY
CW2	THOMAS MAYS	WO1	CHRISTINE MYRA McKOON	WO1	GUY K MILLER	CW4	JAMES C MOONEY,JR
CW2	ANTHONY MAZZA	CW4	THOMAS P MCLAUGHLIN	LTC	JAMES L C MILLER	CW3	ARCELIA M MOORE
CW3	DAVID A MAZZACONE		VICTOR M McLAUGHLIN	CW4	JIMMY F MILLER	CW3	ARCHIE C MOORE
WO1	DAVID T MAZZUCHELLI	CW3	JOHN D MCLEAN	CW4	JOHN P MILLER	CW4	CURTIS A MOORE
CW3	JOSEPH A MAZZUCHELLI	CW3	ROBERT N McLEAN	CW3	JOSEPH MILLER	CW4	DONALD R MOORE
WO1	TARA L McADOO	CW2	DANIEL T McLEISH	CW3	KENNETH W MILLER	CW2	EDWARD A MOORE
CW3	JOHN S McAULEY	CW3	GEORGE K McLELLAN	CW2	KEVIN W MILLER	WO1	GENE A MOORE
W01	JEFFREY M McBRIDE	CW2	HEYWARD O McLENDON	WO1	PAUL A MILLER	CW3	HARRY R MOORE
WO1	TODD T McCAFFERTY	CW2	RONALD L McLENDON	CW2	RICKEY L MILLER	CW3	JEFF L MOORE
CW2	JAMES E McCALEB	WO1	TINA M McLENDON	WO1	ROBERT J MILLER	WO1	JEFFREY L MOORE
CW3	WILLIAM D MCCALLUM	WO1	NEILL MCLEOD	CW3	ROGER L MILLER	CW3	JOHN B MOORE
CW2	JOHN C McCANDLESS	CW4	JAMES G MCMAHON	WO1	ROGER NEIL MILLER	CW3	KEITH A MOORE
CW2	MIKE J McCANN	CW2	PATRICK J McMAHON	CW3	WAYNE A MILLER	CW2	KEVIN M MOORE
CW4	WILLIAM H McCOLLISTER	WO1	GEORGE E McMAKIN,III	WO1	WAYNE S MILLER	WO1	MARK B MOORE
WO1	JAMES R MCCOLLUM	CW4	JERRY L McMILLEN	CW4	WENDALL E MILLER	CW2	MICHAEL B MOORE
WO1	WEST H McCOLLUM	CW3	RONALD H McMILLIAN	CW3	WILLIAM W MILLER	WO1	RONALD S MOORE
CW4	RUSSELL V McCONNELL	CW4	MICHAEL A McMULLEN	CW4	WILLIAM W MILLER	CW4	EARL F MOORE,JR
CW5	DENNIS X McCORMACK	CW2	ROBERT P McMULLIN	CW4	WILLOUGHBY G MILLER	CW4	ROBERT MOORE,JR
WO1	PATRICK M McCORMICK	CW4	ROOSEVELT P McMURREN	CW4	S W KENT MILLER,III	CW2	ERNEST A MOORE,SR
WO1	CATHERINE E McCOY		LARRY D McNABB	CW4	DONALD F MILLER,JR	CW2	ANTHONY F MOOREHEAD
CW3	RUTH M McCOY	CW2	JEROME McNAIR	CW2	DAVID E MILLIGAN	CW4	MICHAEL T MOOREHEAD
CW4	JOHN P McCRAVEY	CW3	DENNIS C McNECE	CW3	DAVID L MILLIGAN	WO1	LUIS R MORA
CW4	GEORGE E McCREA	CW3	BESSIE McNULTY	CW2	EDITH JANE MILLIGAN	CW3	ANGEL D MORALES
CW4	DONALD A McCUISH	CW2	JAMES T McPHAIL	CW5	BERNARD W MILLOY	CW3	HOMER L MORAN
WO1	DONALD H McCULLOUGH	CW3	KEVIN W McPHERSON	CW4	BILLY L MILLS	WO1	JOHN MORAN
CW2	TOMMY S McCULLOUGH	CW2	STEPHEN MCPHERSON	CW4	CHARLES L MILLS	WO1	DAVID J MORAVEC
CW3	STEVEN K McCULLUM	CW2	JOHN E McPOLAND	CW2	JAMES MILLS	WO1	CHARLES JOHN MORESHEAD
CW3	HARRY C McCURDY	CW5	JAMES A McQUAIG	CW2	JOHNNY A MILSAP	CW3	GORDON L MOREY,JR
CW2	BRADY McDANIEL	CW3	DARRYL W McRAE	CW2	JOHN STEPHEN MILUCKY	CW4	EULYS H MORGAN
WO1	JEFFREY McDANIEL	CW2	DONALD S McRAE	WO1	BERNARD MILYO, JR	CW3	GREGORY P MORGAN
WO1	DANIEL W McDERMOTT	WO1	DORIS M McRAE	CW3	WAYNE MINARDI	WO1	JEFF J MORGAN
CW4	PETER J MCDERMOTT	CW2	JERRY A McREE	WO1	CHERYL B MINICK	WO1	TIMOTHY L MORGAN
WO1	CURTIS R McDONALD	CW4	VIRGIL T McVICKER	WO1	MITCHELL G MINNAERT	CW3	WILLIAM BRYAN MORGAN
CW4	EDWARD R McDONALD	CW2	JOHN D McWATERS	CW3	JEWEL BOYCE MINTZ	WO1	CHARLES A MORITZ
CW3	JERRY L MCDONALD	CW4	MICHAEL McWILLIAMS	CW2	JOSE R MIRAMONTES	MAJ	SHERRY MORREY-AUGSBURGER
CW3	JOHN C McDUFFEY	CW2	LYNN E MEAD	WO1	EARNEST L MITCHEL,JR	CW2	ROBERT L MORRILL
CW3	LANCE V McELHINEY	CW3	DAVID E MEADE	CW4	CHARLES F MITCHELL	CW3	CHESTER H MORRIS
CW5	LEE RAY McELROY	WO1	GLENN R MEADOWS	CW2	CHRISTOPHER MITCHELL	CW3	DONALD L MORRIS
CW4	PATRICK M McELROY	WO1	SHAWN E MEASE	CW2	DAVID S MITCHELL	CW4	JIMMIE C MORRIS
CW4	JOHN J McEWEN	CW2	JOSEPH E MECKEL	CW3	DEAN D MITCHELL	CW3	JOYCE E MORRIS
WO1	RONNIE W McFADDEN	CW4	ALBERT R MEDEIROS	CW2	DENNIS N MITCHELL	WO1	LEE R MORRIS
CW4	DONALD R McFARLAND	CW3	PATRICK J MEEHAN	CW3	ENRICO L MITCHELL	CW3	STEVEN A MORRIS
CW4	JESSIE McFARLAND	CW4	FRANKLIN D MEEKS	CW3	JOHN J MITCHELL	CW2	ELISHA MORRIS,III
WO1	TIMOTHY P McFARLAND	CW3	DAVID H MELCHERT	CW3	LESTER R MITCHELL	CW2	HOLLIS A MORRIS,JR
CW2	TOMMY L McFARLAND	CW4	WAYNE A MELESKY	CW3	MICKLE C MITCHELL	CW4	DONALD E MORRISON
WO1	ROBERT J McGALLIARD,JR	CW4	THEODORE R MELINE	CW3	ROBERT A MITCHELL	CW3	EDGAR MORRISON,JR
CW3	JAMES M McGARRY	WO1	JAMES S MELTON	CW2	ROY A MITCHELL	CW4	DAVID ARTHUR MORTON
		WO1	JOHN D MELVIN	CW4	THOMAS L MITCHELL		
		CW2	SALVADOR MENA				

CW3	GEORGE B MORTON
CW3	GEORGE E MORTON
CW3	JOHN M MOSKAL
CW3	VICTOR E MOSLEY
CW3	JANE B MOSLOW
WO1	CHARLES J MOSS
CW2	JEFF MOSS
CW3	TIMOTHY L MOUL
WO1	BRUCE M MOULTON
WO1	NANCY A MOULTON
CW4	DUANE M MOYER
CW2	JOSEPH E MOYERS
WO1	DAVID A MOZDEN
CW2	JAMES L MUCKLEROY
CW2	CARL L MUELLER
WO1	DAVID L MULDOWNEY
CW3	WILLIAM D MULKINS
CW4	EDDIE D MULL
CW3	LAWRENCE A MULL,JR
WO1	DEREK MULLER
CW4	CHARLES W MULLINS
CW5	WILLIAM C MULLINS
CW3	JOSEPH I MUNDIS
CW3	SOPHIA P MUNDIS
CW3	WILLIAM N MUNDY,JR
CW2	JUAN A MUNOZ
CW2	GILBERTO MUNOZ-COLON
CW4	ROY W MURDOCK
WO1	RICHARD H MURDOCK,JR
CW3	NELDA JANE MURPHY
CW5	STEVEN J MURPHY
CW4	THOMAS J MURPHY
WO1	TRACY D MURPHY
CW5	WILLIAM R MURPHY
CW2	EDWIN MURPHY,III
CW3	CLINTON J MURPHY,JR
CW4	RAYMOND J MURPHY,JR
CW4	AURELIA V MURRAY
CW4	EUGENE L MURRAY
CW2	NOEL M MURRAY
WO1	PETER R MURRAY
WO1	ERIS MURRAY,JR
CW3	GRAHAM MURRAY,JR
CW2	HERMAN G MURRAY,JR
CW3	HICKEY J MURRAY,JR
CW2	WARREN S MURRAY,JR
CW5	FRANK MURTAGH
WO1	JERIEL L MUSIC
WO1	DAVID A MYERS
CW4	JAMES MYERS
CW4	MICHAEL J MYERS
CW2	RICHARD MYERS
CW3	EDWARD P MYLOTTE
CW3	DAVID J MYRAND

N

CW4	DALE R NAGAN
COL	ALFRED J NAIGLE
CW2	JOHN F NAILOR
WO1	STEVEN D NALEY
CW2	KENNETH M NANCE
CW3	STEPHAN T NAREWSKI,SR
CW3	RANDALL L NARMI
CW2	JAMES J NAUGHTON
CW4	RAMON NAVARRO
CW3	MARVIN A NEAL
WO1	GERALD E NEATHERLIN
WO1	LANCE W NEECE
CW2	TIMOTHY R NEFF
CW4	ROBERT NEGLIA
CW4	JAMES L NEILSEN
WO1	JOHN L NEININGER
CW4	MARTIN J NEISES
CW2	WALTER S NELLENBACH
CW2	HINTON S NELMS
CW2	DAVID W NELSON
CW2	EUGENE C NELSON
CW4	HUEY R NELSON
CW2	JERRY NELSON
CW2	PETER A NELSON
WO1	RON NELSON
CW3	VAUGHN E NELSON
CW3	WILLIAM H NELSON
CW3	WILLIE J NELSON
WO1	JOHN C NELUMS
CW4	LASZLO NEMETH
WO1	DARRYL L NESBITT
CW4	DONALD NESHEIM
WO1	KENNETH E NEU
WO1	WILLIAM M NEUENDORF
CW2	TIMOTHY G NEWELL
CW3	CARL D NEWHART
WO1	CURTIS L NEWKIRK
WO1	JEFFERSON S NEWMAN
CW3	RONALD H NEWMAN
CW5	LARRY W NEWSOM
CW4	GENE A NEWTON
CW4	SANDRA K NEWTON
LTC	CHARLES B NEWTON,JR
MW4	EDWARD C NEY
CW2	DAT T NGUYEN
WO1	LIONEL A NICHOLAS
CW2	GREGORY R NICHOLS
CW4	VINCENT J NICHOLS
WO1	JAMES D NICKENS
CW3	THOMAS N NICKLES
CW3	GEORGE J NIEBLER
CW2	WAYNE D NIEHUS
CW4	CHARLES NIELSEN
WO1	CYNTHIA L NIELSEN
WO1	RHONDA L NIELSEN
CW3	JULIA L NIELSON
CW5	RANDY L NIELSON
CW4	ROLF E NIELSON
WO1	KATHRYN M NIEMASIK
WO1	MICHELE NIESEN
CW3	TIMOTHY J NIESEN
CW2	RONALD E NILES
WO1	LISA A NINER
CW3	GARY NISKER
WO1	ALAN D NIX
CW3	CECIL NIXON,JR
CW4	WALTER J NIZGORSKI
CW4	RAY M NOBLE
WO1	KIMBERLY R NOE
CW2	WINSTON NOEL
CW4	STEPHEN M NOON
CW2	HERMAN M NORDBRUCH
WO1	ERIC D NORDBY
CW5	FRED NORMAN
CW3	NELSON W NORMAN
CW2	TODD C NORRGARD
CW4	JUKKA P NORRI
CW4	DAVE K NORRIS
CW4	GEORGE D NORRIS
CW4	JAMES H NORWOOD
CW2	EDWARD E NOSBAUM
WO1	DALE E NOVAK
CW3	THOMAS V NOVAK
CW2	GARY P NOVIS
CW4	JAMES A NOWLAN
WO1	TAMARA JEAN NUDING
WO1	MARIANO NUNEZ-VELAZQUEZ
WO1	DANIEL NUNN
CW2	PETER J NUNNERY
CW2	DAVID NUSS

O

WO1	MICHAEL O'BRIEN
CW4	KEVIN J O'CONNELL
CW2	SHAWN C O'CONNELL
CW4	DENNIS G O'CONNOR
CW3	JERRY G O'CONNOR
CW4	DONALD D O'CONNOR,JR
CW4	PATRICK F O'CONNORS
CW4	ROBERT C O'DAY
CW3	HUGH H O'DONNELL
CW2	PATRICK A O'DONNELL
CW2	RONALD R O'DONNELL
CPT	PATRICK H O'HARA,III
CW3	DAVID H O'MALLEY
CW4	PETER E O'MALLEY
CW2	DAVID E O'NEIL
CW3	JOHN S O'NEILL
CW2	DANIEL J O'RAHILLY
CW4	FOSTER OATES,JR
CW4	STANLEY J OBLAWSKI,JR
CW2	ANGEL L OCASIO
CW2	MARIO D OCHOA
WO1	GBOLAHAN M ODELE
CW4	JAMES T ODOM
CW3	JANET L OETKER
WO1	CARMEN OFFICER
CW3	MARTY W OGBURN
CW4	RODERICK M OGG
CW4	ROD OGLE
CW4	SAM OHMACHT
CW5	BRUCE W OHNESORGE
CW4	VINCENT R OLACH
WO1	ERNEST S OLDAKOWSKI
CW5	WILLIAM CURT OLDROYD
CW3	RUTH OLINGER
CW5	ROBERT E OLIVE,IV
CW4	GREGORY C OLIVER
CW2	RAMON OLIVO
CW2	TIMOTHY P OLSEN
CW4	DANIEL J OLSON
CW5	DONN D OLSON
CW3	GAIL D OLSON
CW4	GARY C OLSON
CW4	KENNETH D OLSON
CW3	KENNETH W OLSON
CW4	LYLE D OLSON
CW2	MICHAEL A OLSON
CW3	MICHAEL L OLSON
CW2	RONALD L OLSON
WO1	STEVEN C OLSON
CW4	WILLIAM K OLSON
CW2	RUSSELL C OLSON,JR
CW4	JOHN STANLEY OLSON,SR
CW2	JEFFREY J OOSTING
CW3	BERNADETTE A OPP
CW2	BRIAN A ORLOSKY
CW4	DANIEL W ORMSBY
WO1	THOMAS F OROHO
CW2	LUIS F ORTEGA
WO1	PAUL J ORTHEL
WO1	JIMMY J ORTIZ
WO1	JOSE L ORTIZ
WO1	SINFORIANO ORTIZ-BERDECIA
CW3	CHARLES E ORTT,SR
CW2	JOHN R OSHIRO
WO1	EUNICE OSKIN
CW4	JAMES C OSTRANDER
CW2	WILLIAM OSTROWSKI,JR
CW3	MICHAEL J OSZMAN
CW4	LEONARD D OTT
WO1	CHARLES D OTT,JR
CW4	CLARENCE F OTT,JR
CW4	JAMES T OTTEN
CW4	JAMES O OTTERNESS
CW4	RONALD E OTTOSON
CW4	BRENDA J OUTMAN
WO1	CURTIS T OVERTON
WO1	ANTHONY J OVERWAY
CW3	JAMES A OWENBY
WO1	CHAD R OWENS
CW4	EDGAR L OWENS
CW4	IDA B OWENS
WO1	ROBERT M OWENS
CW2	JOHN THOMAS OWENS,II

P

CW4	JACK W PACE
CW3	JOHN E PACE
CW2	MICHAEL PACE
CW3	VICTOR M PADILLA
WO1	HONESTO DEL CARMEN PADLAN
CW3	THOMAS G PAGANO
WO1	ALISA PAGE
CW2	STEVEN W PAGE
CW2	FOREST PAIGE
CW2	RODNEY L PAIS
CW3	REYNALDA EBARLE PAL-LAYA
WO1	EDWIN R PALAGAR
CW4	CARLOS PALMA
CW3	CHRISTINE PALMER
CW2	DOUGLAS A PALMER
CW4	DUANE V PALMER
CW2	GLENN A PALMER
WO1	KEVIN K PALMER
MW4	RANDY C PALMER
WO1	STEVEN E PALMER
CPT	STEVEN R PALMER
CW2	DOUGLAS ANDREW PALMQUIST
WO1	KENNETH J PANDOLFI
CW4	WILLARD W 'BILL' PANGBORN
CW3	ANDREW J PANISH
CW2	LARRY W PANTHER
WO1	DAVID M PAOLUCCI
CW3	ARISTOTEL J PAPATREFON
CWO	GEORGE T PAPPAS
CW4	MICHAEL A PAPPAS
CW3	ROBERT E PAQUETTE
CW3	GARY W PAQUIN
CW4	EDGAR J PARISH
WO1	TERRY W PARISHER,JR
CW4	ROBERT H PARK
CW4	CHARLIE R PARKER
CW4	DANIEL C PARKER
CWO	DOUGLAS P PARKER
WO1	JOEY W PARKER
CW3	JOHN B PARKER
CW3	JULIOUS PARKER
CWO	JUNIUS U PARKER
WO1	RONALD PARKER
CW4	GEORGE L PARKS
CW3	RUTH PARKS
CW3	RALPH COY PARKS,JR
CW4	JAMES I PARNELL
CW4	JOSEPH R PARRA
CW5	JOHN M PARRY
CW2	JAMES A PARSON
CW4	RICHARD J PARSONS
WO1	EDWIN G PARUBRUB
CW3	THOMAS C PASCH
CW2	MICHAEL W PASSMORE
WO1	CHARLES G PATILLO
CW3	HAROLD D PATRICK
CW2	RONNIE L PATRICK,SR
WO1	JEFFERY O PATRIGNANI
CW4	GEORGE R PATT
CW2	MALCOLM W PATTERSON
CW3	PATRICK A PATTERSON
CW3	THOMAS L PATTERSON
WO1	SAMUEL C PATTON
CW2	CHARLES L PAUL
CW4	HARLOW W PAUL
CW4	HARRY L PAUL
WO1	MICHAEL J PAUL
WO1	JOSEPH B PAUL,JR
CW2	JOHN C PAULACHAK
CW2	DAVID J PAULEY
CW3	STANFORD W PAULEY
WO1	DANIEL JAY PAULSON
CW3	NICHOLAS D PAUSTIAN
CW3	HOWARD F PAVLAT
CW4	STEPHEN J PAWLICK
CW3	DONALD T PAXTON
CW2	CONNIE M PAYETTE
WO1	BLISS A PAYNE
CW4	DONALD R PAYNE
CW2	TIMOTHY A PAYNE
CW3	RAY E PAYTON
CW2	DAVID L PEARCE,JR
CW4	BRUCE R PEARSON

WO1	DAVID L PEARSON
CW4	JOE F PEARSON
CW4	ROGER J PECHACEK
CW4	WILLIAM R PEEBLES,JR
CW3	VAUGHN R PEERMAN
WO1	ALBERT A PEFLEY,JR
WO1	JEREL D PEHL
CW2	MICHELE D PELLECCHIA
CW2	JOHN H PELLETIER
CW3	JOHN M PELOSE
CW4	DAVID L PELSOR
CW2	JAMES W PEMBER
CW2	CAROL A PEMBERTON
CW4	ALFRED PENA
WO1	EDGARDO A PENALOER
CW3	JAMES C PENDLETON
CW4	JUNIUS PENN
CW3	HELEN J PENNINGTON
MG	JAMES C PENNINGTON
CW5	TOMMY T PENROSE
CW2	BRADLEY R PEPPER
CW4	GEORGE E PEREIRA
WO1	MARGARITA D PEREIRA
CW2	EMILIO G PEREZ
CW2	FERDINAND PEREZ
WO1	TONIA R PEREZ
WO1	SANDRA PERILLARD
WO1	TIMOTHY J PERKINS
CW5	JIMMIE G PERNELL
CW2	RICHARD A PERRETTA
WO1	KYLE PERRIER
CW3	EUGENE L PERRINO,SR
CW4	BOBBY RAY PERRY
CW4	FRIZZELL S PERRY
CW4	GEORGE J PERRY
CW3	JESSICA M PERRY
CW3	PAUL G PERRY
CW2	RICHARD G PERRY
CW4	VINCENT W PERRY
WO1	WILLIAM G PERRY
WO1	WILLIAM R PERRY
CW4	JUSTIN PERRY,JR
WO1	HARRY L PERSHAD
CW3	DAVID M PERUZZI
CW3	RONALD W PETERMAN
WO1	DONALD W PETERS
WO1	DONNELL D PETERS
CW4	JAMES K PETERS
CW2	JEFFREY T PETERS
CW2	MARIA A PETERS
CW3	MARVIN W PETERS
MW4	HENNING PETERSEN
CW2	JOHN MATTHIAS PETERSEN
CW2	ARTHUR F PETERSON
CW4	BRIAN L PETERSON
CW2	DAVID M PETERSON
CW5	JOHN L PETERSON
CW4	KEVIN G PETERSON
WO1	ROBERT J PETERSON
CW5	ROBERT M PETERSON
CW3	WILLIAM J PETRAK
CW4	PHILLIP C PETRIE
CW3	BILLY D PETTY
CW3	RONALD G PETTY
CW2	PETE PEZZOTTI
CW4	DONALD G PFEIFFER
CW2	MARK A PFENNING
CW2	JOHN PFLASTERER
CW2	DOUGLAS L PHELPS
CW4	ARTHUR F PHILLIPS
CW4	CHARLES A PHILLIPS
CW5	DENNIS J PHILLIPS
CW4	JOHN F PHILLIPS
CW3	KENNETH R PHILLIPS
CW3	LOU PHILLIPS
WO1	MARK S PHILLIPS
CW4	OSCAR L PHILLIPS
CW2	PETER R PHILLIPS
CW4	ROBERT D PHIPPS
CW4	THOMAS A PIATTI
CW5	LISLE F PICKARD
WO1	RICHARD PICKARD
CW3	DAVID G PICKERING
CW5	DONALD D PIERCE
CW3	FRANKLIN R PIERCE
CW2	JAMES L PIERCE
CW4	JAMES T PIERCE
CW2	PAUL PIERCE
WO1	RONALD W PIERCE
CW2	WILLIAM D PIERCE
CW3	WILLIAM M PIERSON,III
CW3	JOHN A PIERSON,JR
WO1	WILKIE X PIETRI
CW3	WILLIE CHARLES PIGGEE
CW3	DEAN PILARINOS
WO1	SCOTT K PILINGTON
WO1	STEVEN K PILKINGTON
CW4	VINCENT N PINAULT
CW2	CARLOS M PINEDA
WO1	ANTONIO A PINEIRO
CW3	JACK C PINES
CW4	OSCAR L PINKSTON
CW4	RONALD D PIOTROWSKI
CW3	DENNIS M PIPKIN
CW3	GEORGE F PITTENGER
CW2	ROBBIE T PITTS
CW3	WILLIAM E PITTS
WO1	ROBERT C PITTS III
CW2	REGAN G PLATH
CW4	JEFFREY M PLATT
CW4	JUAN C PLAZA
WO1	RUSSELL D PLEWE
WO1	AMY L POE
CW4	RENZIE M POE,JR
CW2	XAVIER L POINDEXTER
WO1	TIMOTHY C POLLARD
CW2	TERRY B POLWORT
CW3	KENNETH F POND
CW3	PHILLIP G PONEY
CW4	FORREST M POOLE
CW4	EDWARD POOS
CW5	DARRELL C POPE
CW2	PONSUK P POPUN
CW2	JAMES R PORTER
CW4	JESSE J PORTER
CW3	PHILLIP R PORTER
CW2	THOMAS F PORTER
CW3	TIMOTHY A PORTER
CW3	LLOYD E PORTER,JR
CW4	JOHNNY L POSTLEWAITE
WO1	DEBBIE L POTTER
CW4	LEROY D POTTER
CW2	JAMES D POTTS
CW3	THOMAS W POULOS
CW4	CHARLES R POULTON
CW4	EVA I POWELL
CW4	HERMAN PAUL POWELL,JR
CW2	GARY L POWER
WO1	DAVID S POWERS
CW2	ROBERT E POWERS
CW3	MITCHELL P PRADIA
CW4	HARVEY D PRENDEVILLE,JR
	DONN M PRESTON
	WILLIAM R PRESTON
CW2	CHRISTOPHER A PRICE
CW2	GARY N PRICE
CW3	JOHN D PRIMAVERA
CW4	LARRY L PRINE
CW3	JUDITH PRINGLE
CW4	CHARLES S PRITCHARD,JR
MW4	STEVEN V PROCTOR
CW2	DONN R PROVEN
CW4	RHEA R PRUETT
CW3	RAY PRUSINSKI
CW4	WALTER M PRZYBYL
CW2	ROBERT S PTASZEK
CW3	VINCENT W PUCHER
CW5	STEVE S PUE
CW5	JOHN S PUKAJLO
WO1	H ANDREW PULLENS
CW3	PATRICIA J PURCELL
CW4	NORMAN D PURDY
CW4	WALTER S PURKOSKI
CW2	JOHN J PURPURO
CW3	ROLLIE E PURVIS
CW4	VAL E PUZULIS
CW2	DAVID A PUZZUOLI
CW3	TINA PUZZUOLI

Q

CW2	HAROLD D QUARLES,JR
CW4	ALLEN E QUINLAN
WO1	KENNETH J QUINLAN,III
CW4	JOHN J QUINN
CW2	RAYMOND A QUINO-NES
WO1	JUAN CARLOS QUINTANA
WO1	ROEHL M QUISMUNDO

R

WO1	MELISSA L RADER
CW4	LINWOOD E RADFORD
CW2	ALEXANDER J RAHAL
CW4	MICHAEL RAHM
CW3	RANDY W RAINVILLE
CW2	DARRELL L RAKESTRAW
CW2	GEORGE F RALPH,JR
CW2	ROBERT D RALYEA
CW2	JOE N RAMBO
CW3	VALENTIN RAMIREZ,JR
CW2	ARTURO RAMOS
CW2	FEIX RAMOS
CW4	GREGORY P RAMOS
WO1	JEFFERY RAMSEY
CW5	WILLIAM H RAMSEY
CW2	MICHAEL S RANDALL
CW2	THOMAS E RANDALL
CW2	ZINA RANDOLPH
CW3	HOWARD G RAPPOLD
CW4	BILLY L RASBURY
WO1	MITCHELL L RATCLIFF
CW2	MICHAEL RATHGE
CW4	DAVID A RATLIFF
CW5	GARVIN RATLIFF
WO1	STEPHEN V RAUCH
CW4	MARK L RAWL
CW2	RENETTE F RAWLINS
CW2	BRENT R RAY
WO1	JOSEPH B RAY
CW4	LESLIE L RAYBURN
CW4	WILLIAM W REAVES,JR
CW3	GERALD R RECELLA
NA	ARMY RECRUITING
WO1	DENNIS D REDDEN
CW2	GEORGE E REDER,II
CW2	GARY D REDFIELD
CW3	DAVID E REECE
CW2	JULIA A REECE
CW4	BENJAMIN A REED
CW4	DOROTHY ANN REED
CW3	EDDIE R REED
CW3	JAMES F REED
CW3	ROBERT REED
CW2	ROBERT W REED
WO1	SAMANTHA L REED
CW2	GLEN E REESE
CW3	KENNETH W REESE
CW3	DONALD W REESMAN, SR
CW3	ALICE V REID
CW2	DENNIS E REID
CW5	JOHN W REID
CW4	WILLIAM S REID
CW2	VICKIE F REID-LONG
CW2	THOMAS E REISER
CW2	ANN M REITZER-SMITH
CW4	EDWIN J REMALEY
CW3	JAMES REMSBURG,JR
CW3	RICHARD J RENAUD
CW5	PATRICK A RENEHAN
MW4	MIKE RENFROE
CW4	DENNIS E RENKEN
CW3	VERONICA JEAN RENKEN
CW3	DALE L RENNINGER
CW5	GEORGE T RENO
WO1	ELOISE RENTERIA
CW3	MICHAEL J REPKO
WO1	DAVID B REPPERT
CW3	STEVEN D RESEL
CW5	ROBERT A REUTER
CW5	JAMES E REVELS
WO1	GLENN K REYNOLDS
CW4	JOHN R REYNOLDS
CW3	MICHAEL P REYNOLDS
CW3	H G RHEIN
CW2	BERT L RHOADES
CW5	R G 'ROCK' RHOADES
CW4	WILLIAM F RHODE
CW4	BILLY S RHODES
WO1	ROBERT B RHODES
CW2	ALBERT L RHONE
WO1	RICHARD LEE RHONE
CW3	TIM RHYNE,SR
WO1	BARRY E RIBBLE
CW2	JAMES E RICE
CW2	JAMES L RICE
CW4	JAY R RICE
CW3	KATHLEEN M RICE
CW3	JOHN D RICH,JR
CW4	JOSEPH G RICHARD
CW4	PAUL B RICHARD
CW2	BRETT A RICHARDS
CWO	JAMES C RICHARDS
CW2	WALTER L RICHARDS
CW4	EDWARDS N RICHARDSON
CW3	GARY D RICHARDSON
CW4	JULIUS RICHARDSON
WO1	LINDA D RICHARDSON-SMITH
CW2	PENNY G RICHENBERG
WO1	RANDELL RICHMOND
WO1	WILDIE E RICHTER,JR
CW4	ALLAN E RICKARD
CW4	HAROLD E RICKARDS,JR
CW2	DARRELL J RICKER
CW3	CLARENCE RICKS
CW2	WALLACE RICKS
WO1	STEVEN M RICKWA
WO1	EDDIE I RICORD
CW5	LYNN D RIDLEY
CW4	ARLIE J RIEFER
CW3	YVETTE RIEHLE
WO1	RONALD L RIES
CW4	JOHN E C RIGBYMETH
WO1	BRYANT W RIGGEAL
WO1	WILLIAM G RIGGS
CW3	WILLIAM A RIGHTER
CW3	GARY F RILEY
WO1	GEOFFREY J RINEBERG
CW4	HARREL G RINEHART
WO1	TIMOTHY P RINEHART
WO1	MICHAEL D RINGLE
CW2	ERIC E RINGS
CW3	GILBERT U RIOS
CW3	DONALD R RIPKA
CW2	MICHAEL W RISHER, III
CW3	KATHLEEN W RITCHIE
CW3	JIMMY L RITTENHOUSE
CW4	RONALD RITTER,JR
CW2	REINALDO RIVERA
CW2	WILMER RIVERA
CW2	OVIDIO RIVERA-BAEZ
CW3	DIONISIO RIVERA-LUGO
WO1	FREDY RIVERA-SANTOS
CW4	JAMES D ROBBINS
WO1	JEFFREY A ROBBINS
CW3	JIMMIE D ROBBINS
MAJ	DONALD W ROBERTS
CW5	FLOYD W ROBERTS
CW4	WILLIAM J ROBERTS
WO1	PATRICK M ROBERTSON
WO1	FRANK J ROBICHAU,JR
CW2	CHRIS ROBINSON
CW2	DEIRDRE ROBINSON
CW4	DONALD ROBINSON

CW3	JAMES H ROBINSON
WO1	JIMMY R ROBINSON
WO1	JOHN A ROBINSON
WO1	RICHARD E ROBINSON
CW3	RICHARD G ROBINSON
WO1	ROBERT D ROBINSON
CW5	RUSSEL N ROBINSON
WO1	TIMOTHY M ROBINSON
CW4	WILLIAM C ROBINSON
CW3	WOODIE L ROBINSON
CW2	JOHN R ROBISON
CW2	DAVID ROBLING
WO1	DONALD R ROBSON
CW3	DAVID A ROCCO
CW2	E DAVID ROCHA
CW3	ALAN D RODDY
WO1	PETER S RODERICK
WO1	DANIEL C RODGERS
CW4	JOSEPH R RODRIGUES
CW2	JOHN RODRIGUES,III
WO1	TAMARA K RODRIGUEZ
WO1	JORGE L RODRIGUEZ,JR
WO1	MIGUEL RODRIGUEZ-GIST
CW4	RAFAEL RODRIGUEZ-MARTINEZ
WO1	EDWIN RODRIQUEZ-PAZO
CW2	ROBERT R ROEBUCK
WO1	WILLIAM J ROELL
CW4	EDWARD A ROGALEWICZ
CW2	ANDREW D ROGERS
WO1	ERVIN L ROGERS
CW2	JAMES R ROGERS
CW3	RICHARD ROGERS
CW3	TED L ROGERS
CW4	GUIDO H ROHDE
CW3	JOHN ROHRBECK
CW4	JAMES A ROHRER
CW4	ADAM G F ROHRHUBER
WO1	BRIAN P ROKUSEK
CW2	GERALD W ROLLER
CW2	KENNETH R ROLLINS
CW3	GEORGE ROLLINSON
CW3	DEVIN C ROLLIS
CW2	ANTONIETTA M ROMAN
CW3	EDGARDO ROMAN-GONZALEZ
CW4	JOSEPH P ROMANO
WO1	RANDALL A ROMENS
CW2	FRED ROMONOWSKI
CW3	DONALD L ROOP
CW2	MARK A ROORDA
CW4	DANIEL J ROOSE
WO1	JESTINE G ROPER
CW4	BENNIE ROSALER
CW3	DAVID ROSARIO
CW3	ANTHONY J ROSE
CW5	DAVID J ROSE
CW3	ROBERT B ROSE
CW4	RUSSELL A ROSE
CW3	ELIAS ROSEN
WO1	SHIRLEY M ROSENCUTTER
WO1	WILLARD S ROSENER
CW2	ANTONIN H ROSENKRANZ
CW4	JOSEPH P ROSETO
CW2	BERT W ROSS
CW5	DELORS ROSS
WO1	RANDALL W ROSS
CW2	WILLIAM R ROSS
CW3	WILLIAM P ROSSER
CW3	DENNIS F ROTENBERRY
CW3	ANTHONY B ROTTI
CW5	KENNETH E ROUGEOU
CW4	JAMES F ROUHAN
CW4	RONALD L ROUSSEL
CW4	ROB R ROUTH
CW4	GARY D ROWE
CW2	JOHN P ROWE
CW5	RODNEY H ROWE
WO1	LEE A ROWLAND
CW4	MAX D ROWLETT
CW2	RODERICK A ROWLEY
CW2	ALTON P ROYER
WO1	GWENDOLYN ROYSTER
CW2	LEVI A ROYSTER
CW3	JOYCE I ROZELLE
WO1	TIMOTHY D RUARK
CW4	WALTER C RUCKER
CW4	GREGORY P RUESTOW
WO1	JOE RUETER
WO1	MICHAEL W RUMSEY
CW2	DANIEL J RUPP
CW2	DONALD A RUPPRECHT
CW2	MACK B RUSHING
CW3	RANDALL M RUSHING
CW2	GEORGE E RUSSELL
CW3	GREG RUSSELL
CW2	KARL K RUSSELL
CW4	KENNETH RUSSELL
CW3	MARVIN H RUSSELL
CW4	STEWART RUSSELL
CW4	JOHN G RUSSELL,JR
CW2	JILL G RUSSO-DOWNEY
CW2	JERRY D RUST
WO1	DERALD J RUTHERFORD
CW2	DOC RUTHERFORD
CW3	WILLIAM H RUTHERFORD III
CW3	ROBERT D RUTLEDGE
CW3	ALAN F RUZICKA
CW2	DANIELLE M RYAN
CW3	JOHN D RYAN
CW3	LYNN M RYAN
WO1	STEVEN M RYAN
CW2	RICHARD J RYAN,JR

S

CW2	DIRK J SAAR
CW3	WALTER D SABEY
WO1	STEPHEN J SACAYAN
CW3	MICHAEL J SACIA
CW3	MARVIN G SACK
CW3	ALBERT B SACKWITZ
WO1	ROSAURO H SACRO
MW4	MITCHELL SADDLER
CW3	RICHARD N SADDLER
CW2	GARY M SADGER
WO1	BEHZAD SADIQ
WO1	BARNEY A SADLER
	JORDAN SAGE
WO1	MELVIN L SAGE-EL
CW2	CHRISTOPHER A SAINDON
	GLENN A SAINT-PAEN
CW4	ANTHONY H SAKANIWA
CW3	PHIL R SALAS
CW4	TERRY A SALAZAR
CW3	GABRIEL T SALIBA
CW2	JEFFREY C SALLEE
CW2	JON A SALLOT,JR
CW2	TIMOTHY F SAMP
CW2	THEODORE A SAMTER
CW4	MARK SAMUELSON
CW2	JIMMY R SANCHEZ
CW2	JOE A SANCHEZ
WO1	MARIA G SANCHEZESPINOZA
	GEORGE SANCLAIR
WO1	GREG L SANDEN
WO1	AMENDA C SANDERS
WO1	PHILLIP O SANDERS
CW3	THOMAS T SANDERS
	THOMAS W SANDERS
WO1	THURRELL CLARKE SANDERS
CW4	MICHAEL B SANDLER
CW2	JOSEPH G SANDRA
CW2	DARRELL G SANDSTROM
CW4	EARL JOHN SANDSTROM
CW4	SCOTT R SANETEL
CW4	CLAUD M SANFORD
WO1	MARK S SANFORD
CW2	JUAN B SANTANA
WO1	GERALDO SANTIAGO
WO1	NORBERTO SANTIAGO
CW2	BETTYJO SANTIBANEZ
CW4	JOSE A SANTINI
CW4	JOSEPH G SANTINI
CW3	PEDRO C SANTOS
CW3	RAFAEL A SANTOS
CW2	RAMON A SANTOS-AYALA
	KENT T SAPP
CW2	PAULINE SAPP
CW2	IVAN SARAC
CW4	RENALDO SARDANOPOLI
	PAUL A SASCHUK
WO1	GLEN A SASEK
CW3	ROSALEE A SATKOWIAK
CW3	WARREN J SATRE
CW4	BERNARD L SATTERFIELD
CW2	GREGG W SAUCIER
CW4	RICHARD A SAUER
CW3	RICHARD A SAUNDERS
CW5	WILLIAM D SAUNDERS
WO1	LYNWOOD T SAVILLE
CW2	SHERRY H SAVIO
CW3	RONALD P SAVOY
CW4	RICHARD G SAYLOR
CW3	PAUL J SCAFFIDI
CW4	RICHARD A SCALFANI
CW5	RICHARD M SCALZO,SR
CW3	DENISE A SCARBORO
CW2	BRADY J SCHAFER
CW3	MICHAEL J SCHAFFER
CW3	JAMES T SCHALLA,JR
CW3	DAVID L SCHALLER
CW4	ROBERT L SCHALLER
CW4	ALBERT V SCHARTNER
CW2	MICHAEL A SCHEEL
CW2	PAULA A SCHERER
CW2	STEPHEN P SCHERER,JR
CW5	JOHN T SCHEY,JR
WO1	ROBERT R SCHICK
WO1	WILLIAM D SCHILLINGER
CW2	KENNETH M SCHIRMER
CW4	DOROTHY T SCHLEGEL
CW2	SHAWN P SCHLOESSER
CW2	ROGER M SCHLOSSER
CW3	ARTHUR L SCHMID
CW2	NORBERT L SCHMIDT
CW4	PAM A SCHMIDT
CW3	STEVEN L SCHMIDT
CW2	LARRY M SCHMITT
	PATRICIA A SCHMITT
CW2	GREGORY D SCHMITZ
CW4	DALE F SCHNABEL
WO1	QILLIAM J SCHNABEL
CWO	WILLIAM H SCHNAKENBURG
WO1	ROGER SCHNETZEL
CW4	JAMES C SCHOENE
CW4	WALTER R SCHOENEMAN
WO1	CRAIG A SCHOLLE
CW2	OTTO F SCHOLZ,JR
MR	HEINZ SCHOTT
WO1	RANDY L SCHRIVER
CW3	ALBERT A SCHUBERT,JR
CW3	CHARLES A SCHUE,JR
CW4	ROBERT A SCHULTE
WO1	DON E SCHULTZ
CW3	EDWARD M SCHULTZ
WO1	JACK A SCHULTZ
CW3	KURT A SCHULTZ
CW5	KENNETH LOUIS SCHUMANN
WO1	KLAUS P SCHUMANN
CW3	RICHARD B SCHURKUS
CW5	MERLYN D SCHUSTER
CW3	JAMES M SCHWANKE
CW3	LINDA SCHWARTZ
CW2	JOHN A SCHWARTZ,III
WO1	STEPHEN T SCHWETZ
CW2	MICHAEL E SCHWIND
WO1	JOLIANA C SCIPIO
CW3	BOBBY H SCOTT
CW3	BRADLEY J SCOTT
CW3	DANIEL G SCOTT
CW2	HAL LARRY SCOTT
CW2	PORTER C SCOTT
CW2	RICKY SCOTT
CW4	ROBERT DONAT SCOTT
CW3	JOHN A SCOTT,II
CW4	LONNIE B SCOTT,III
WO1	ROGER B SCOTT,III
CW3	WELLESLEY E SCOTT,JR
CW4	THOMAS J SCUTTI
CW2	JAMES C SEACOTT
CW4	NOEL C SEALE
CW3	ERNEST W SEARCY
CW2	GABINO SEDA
CW2	KATHY J C SEEDERS
WO1	KEDRA A SEGLER
WO1	DAVID SEIDEL
CW2	JOHN L SEITZ
CW3	RONALD C SEITZ
CW4	WILLIAM W SELF
CW5	THOMAS L SELFRIDGE
CW3	LARRY L SELLARS
CW3	JACOB F SELLERS,JR
CW4	CHARLES W SELVIDGE
CW3	STEPHEN P SENIUK
CW3	SCOTT G SEPTRICK
CW3	TERRY P SERFACE
WO1	DAVID L SEWELL
CW2	ERWIN J SEYDLER,JR
CW3	JAMES A SHADDOX
CW2	RANDELL J SHAFER
CW2	LEONARD B SHAFER, JR
WO1	RIZWAN ALI SHAH
CW3	ALBERT SHAMAEL
WO1	LAURIE J SHAMBLIN
CW5	LARRY SHARON
CW2	CORINNE C SHARP
CW4	JAMES A SHAW
WO1	KEVIN J SHAW
MW4	ROBERT B SHAW
WO1	RANDY SHAWN
CW4	LANGAN E SHEA
WO1	ROCHELLE SHEHI-MARTELL
CW3	JAMES T SHEIMO
CW3	MICHAEL E SHELDON
CW3	HAROLD S SHELDT
CW4	MARKHAM J SHELLEY
CW3	GEORGE E SHELTON
CW2	JOHN JOSEPH SHELTON
CW2	HARRY B SHELVOCK
CW4	DENNIS B SHEPARD
WO1	GLENN A SHEPARD
CW4	JOHN J SHEPARD
CW3	MARK L SHEPARD
CW3	PAULETTE A SHEPHERD
CW2	DORRICE SHEPHERD,JR
WO1	DAVID P SHEPPARD
CW2	MATTHEW A SHERIDAN
WO1	THELMA M SHERIDAN
CW2	ROBERT M SHERMAN
CW2	GERALD R SHERRILL
WO1	BARRY J SHERWOOD
CW4	FRED L SHINBUR
CW3	RICHARD L SHIPP
CW4	JAMES L SHIRELEY
CW4	JERRY D SHIRLEY
CW3	DANIEL K SHISHIDO
CW5	ROBERT L SHOFFNER
CW4	FRANKLIN J SHOLEDICE,SR

CW4	ORLO G SHOOP
CW2	NEVILLE S SHORTER
WO1	DEBORAH A SHOWERS
CW2	CHRIS A SHRONTZ
CW4	LAWRENCE L SHUE
WO1	ROGER E SHUFORD
CW4	GORDON E SHULTS
CW3	RICHARD P SHULTZ
CW2	STEPHEN F SHULTZ
CW3	EDWARD M SHUMATE
CW2	MARY A SIBRAVA
CW4	LAWRENCE F SICHERI
CW4	JOSEPH W SICKINGER
CW4	ANDREW E SICKLER
WO1	VIRGINIA SIDBERRY
CW4	JIM SIEBOLD
CW4	EUGENE C SIEGFRIED
WO1	GLENN P SIEGRIST
CW3	MARCIA E SIERRA
CW2	CRAIG T SIETING
CW3	ROGER L SIFFORD
WO1	MARK A SILBERMAN
CW3	ROY A SILFIES
CW4	WAYNE H SILK
CW2	DANIEL E SIMMONS
WO1	FRED B SIMMONS
CW2	JESSIE F SIMMONS
WO1	KEITH ALLAN SIMMONS
CW4	PAUL L SIMMONS
CW2	BRUCE LAWRENCE SIMON
CW3	EDWARD H SIMONDS
CW4	JOAN B SIMONDS
CW3	BRYAN D SIMPSON
CW3	SANDRA K SIMPSON
MW4	JOHN E SIMS
CW3	JOHN T SINCAVAGE
CW3	THOMAS J SINCLAIR
WO1	LISTON SINGLETARY,III
CW3	HENRY L SINGLETON
CW4	FARRELL L SINK,JR
CW2	DENNIS F SINNING
CW4	JAMES A SIRMANS
CW2	MIKYONG SIRMANS
CW3	JOHN D SISARIO
CW4	JOHN D SISSELL
CW3	DAVID M SIUDZINSKI
WO1	STEVEN SKAAR
WO1	TROY H SKAGGS
CW2	MICHAEL L SKELLY
CW4	JOHN I SKELTON
WO1	MICHAEL A SKINNER
CW2	RAYMOND L SKINNER
CW4	TIMOTHY B SKINNER
CW5	MYERS SKINNER,JR
CW4	M E 'LISA' SKIOLD-HANLIN
CW3	RICHARD C SKRINE,SR
CW4	ANDREW SKUNTZ
CW4	THADDEUS J SKURA
CW3	R DAVID SLADE
CW3	DAVID S SLAUGHTER
CW3	THADDEUS C SLAWINSKI
CW3	JOSEPH H SLEDGE
WO1	PAUL H SLEEPER
CW4	RAYMOND L SLEMER
WO1	RHONDA LYNN SLOAN
CW3	ALFRED W SLOVENZ
CW2	LUKE SMALLEY
CW2	EARNEST L SMILEY
WO1	ALLAN G SMITH
CW5	CHARLES KEITH SMITH
WO1	CRAIG A SMITH
CW2	DARRELL E SMITH
CW2	DAVID C SMITH
WO1	DEBBIE L SMITH
CW3	DONALD LEE SMITH
CW3	DONNA N SMITH
CW3	ERIC A SMITH
CW4	GARY L SMITH
CW4	GERALD G SMITH
CW4	HOWARD I SMITH
CW4	JACK L SMITH
CW3	JAMES RANDY SMITH
CW4	JEFFREY D SMITH
CW3	JEFFREY J SMITH
CW2	KENNETH M SMITH
WO1	LARRY D SMITH
WO1	LARRY E SMITH
WO1	LICHIA M DAVIS- SMITH
CW2	LILA R SMITH
WO1	LORIN SMITH
CW3	MARK G SMITH
WO1	MARK L SMITH
CW2	MERRELL A SMITH
CW3	MERRILL L SMITH
CW2	MICHAEL E SMITH
CW4	MICHAEL HUNTLEY SMITH
CW3	MICHAEL J SMITH
CW4	MICHAEL R SMITH
CW4	MICHAEL Z SMITH
WO1	RACHEL M SMITH
CW4	RALPH W SMITH
CW5	RAYMOND L SMITH
CW3	RICKIE A SMITH
CW4	ROBERT L SMITH
CW4	RONALD W SMITH
WO1	RUSSELL P SMITH
CW3	SAMUEL SMITH
CW4	STEPHEN J SMITH
CW4	THOMAS R SMITH
WO1	THOMAS RAY SMITH
WO1	TIMONTHY M SMITH
WO1	TONY M SMITH
CW3	TRACY E SMITH
CW4	VERNON D SMITH
CW3	WARREN L SMITH
WO1	WAYNE C SMITH
WO1	HARRIS S SMITH,II
CW3	ALFRED N C SMITH,III
CW2	DANIEL M SMITH,JR
CW4	ROBERT C SMITH,JR
CW3	ROBERT R SMITH,JR
CW4	THOMAS H SMITH,SR
CW2	PAUL R SMULIAN
MW4	CONSTANCE J SNAVELY
CW2	MARTY R SNEED
CW4	ERIC L SNOW
CW4	KENNETH R SNYDER
CW4	WILLIAM R SNYDER
CW4	DONALD D SNYDER,JR
CW5	HARRY S SOBJACK
CW2	CRAIG L SODERBERG
CW2	CALVIN A SOLOMON
WO1	JEFFREY BRET SOLOMON
CW2	HAROLD W SONNIER
CW2	DAVE SOOKBIRSINGH
CW3	SOONDAR K SOOKDEO
CW3	GUY A SOPER
CW2	CHRISTOPHER SORENSEN
WO1	STEVE SORENSEN
WO1	TRINA L SORRELL
CW2	ISRAEL SOTO
WO1	JUAN I SOTO
CW4	JOHN CHARLES SOULE
CW4	DOUGLAS C SOUSA
CW5	GRANT L SOUTH
WO1	BEVERLY A SOWELL
CW4	CHARLES J SOWLES,JR
WO1	REGINA G SPAETH
CW4	EDWARD B SPALDING
CW3	ROBERT L SPANN,III
CW2	FRANK D SPANNRAFT
CW4	H WILLIAM SPARKS
CW2	KENNETH R SPARKS
CW2	MICHAEL R SPARKS
CW4	ROBERT M SPARKS
WO1	THOMAS D SPARKS
CW4	CHARLES J SPECK
CW3	ROBERT P SPEE
CW4	ANGELO SPELIOS
CW3	JAMES P SPELLER
CW2	JEAN SPENCER
CW2	JOSEPH R SPENCER
CW3	JAMES F SPIERS,JR
CW4	MICHAEL J SPIRO
CW3	PATRICK E SPROUL
MW4	DAVID M SPURGEON
CW4	MAURICE D SQUIRES
CW4	JESSE E STACY,JR
WO1	WILLIAM J STAKES,JR
WO1	ENITA D STALEY
CW2	MICHAEL G STALEY
CW4	WILLIAM A STALLSMITH
WO1	FRANK STAMEY
CW4	DAVID L STAMM
CW4	PHILLIP M STAMM
CW4	FREELON F STANBERRY
CW4	DAVID T STANDISH
WO1	LAURA R STANDLEY
CW4	EDWARD W STANHOPE
WO1	JAMES N STAPLEFORD
CW4	LAWRENCE E STARBUCK
CW4	GLENN L STARK
CW2	DAVID P STARK,JR
CW4	WILLIE E STARNES
WO1	KENNETH W STATON
CW3	WILLIAM C STATON
CW4	JOHN D STAVNESLI
WO1	JAMIE G StDENNIS
CW4	FRANK A STEELE
WO1	JENNIFER D STEELE
CW4	ROBERT J STEELE,II
CW3	KERRY C STEERE
CW4	DENNIS W STEFFEN
CW3	ANTHONY J STEFKO
WO1	JOHN L STEGALL
WO1	WENDY M STEGALL
CW3	DONALD M STEIN
CW4	JOSEPH B STEIN
CW4	ANN F STEINKELLNER
CW4	DUANE M STENSRUD
CW3	BARBARA J STEPHENS
CW2	BARRY M STEPHENS
MW4	JESSE L STEPHENS
CW5	JOSEPH A STEPHENS
CW3	MICHAEL T STEPHENS
CW4	ORVIL JOE STEPHENS
CW4	EDMUND C STEPHENSON,JR
CW4	ROBERT M STERRETT
CW4	DANIEL E STEVENS
CW5	GLENN W STEVENS
CW2	JEFFREY T STEVENS
CW3	JOSEPH M STEVENS
CW3	JUNIUS B STEVENS
CW4	ROBERT O STEVENS
CW2	SCOTT P STEVENS
CW4	JOHN M STEVENSON
CW2	BRUCE A STEWART
CW3	DAVID N STEWART
CW2	DEREK K B STEWART
CW3	JOHN F STEWART
CW3	JOHNNY R STEWART
CW3	MARK A STEWART
CW2	MICHAEL D STEWART
CW2	NAOMI J H STEWART
CW2	ROY R STEWART
CW2	TIMOTHY M STEWART
CW4	WALLACE W STEWART
CW3	NORMAN C STEWART,JR
CW5	DONALD E J StGERMAIN
CW3	LOUIS T STIBBARD
WO1	TIMOTHY M STIFF
CW2	DAVID S STINE
CW3	DAWN R STIRLING-SMITH
WO1	RICARDO P STITH
WO1	JAMES R StJUNIORS
CW2	JAMES L STOCKFORD
CW4	CHARLES D STODDARD
CW3	MANFRED STOEKLEN
WO1	STEVEN J STOIBER
WO1	MARK STOKAN
CW3	DIANE PENNY STOKER
CW4	CHARLES F STOLL
CW3	MARY E STOLTZ
CW3	WAYNE C STOLTZ
CW3	DAVID J STONE
CW4	DONALD M STONE
CW3	JAMES I STONE
CW4	ROBERT A STONECIPHER
CW3	DAVID L STONEKING
CW4	WILLIAM H STONESIFER
WO1	ROBERT S STOPAR
CW4	RICHARD L STORIE
CW5	THOMAS A STORY
CW4	WARREN A STOWELL
WO1	KEITH N StPETER
CW4	VAN B STRAHAN,JR
WO1	PAUL D STRAKA
WO1	GLORIA D STREET
CW4	JAMES D STRICKLAND
WO1	VICTORIA A STROM
WO1	ANTHONY B STRONG
CW3	CURTIS STRONG
WO1	LARRY D STRONG
CW2	ROY M STRONG
CW3	DALE E STROUD
CW2	WILLIAM J STROUT
CW3	JAMES N STRUDER
CW3	MICHAEL G STRUSKI
CW4	THOMAS T STRVCK
CW2	TOMMY STUBBLEFIELD
CW3	JOSEPH D STUBBS,JR
CW2	NORMAN A STUCKEY
CW3	WILLIAM M STUDIVANT
WO1	THERRILL L STUFFLEBEEM
WO1	PAUL C STULTZ
CW2	MICHAEL L STURTEVANT
CW3	MORRIS T SUDDETH
CW4	ROBERT L SUDDUTH
WO1	JAMES R SULKANEN
CW3	ALEXANDER E SULLIVAN
CW4	LAWRENCE C SUMMERS
CW2	JEFFREY A SUMNERS
CW2	KENNETH M SUMNERS,JR
WO1	MICHEAL SUMODI
WO1	TREPHYA D SUMPTER
CW3	BENNIE S SUMPTER,SR
	FELIX J SURIS
	MORTON SUSSMAN
	THOMAS G SUTTERFIELD
CW4	CHARLES A SUTTLES
WO1	MARK L SUTTON
	JOSEPH M SVOBODA
	ROBERT M SWADISH
	RICHARD L SWANSON
WO1	TYSON SWANSON
CW4	PETER V SWANZ
CW3	RICHARD L SWARENS
CW3	SHARON T MAYO SWARTWORTH
WO1	DAVID SWATSKY
CW4	HAROLD D SWEARENGIN
WO1	BERNARD R SWEENEY
CW2	DONNHUGH A SWEENEY
CW3	HOWARD J SWEET
WO1	DENNIS R SWEET,JR
CW3	JOHN C SWEETING
CW2	TIMOTHY S SWEITZER
CW2	KEITH E SWENSON
CW4	MICHAEL J SWENSON
WO1	CHARLES R SWINEHART
CW3	ROGER A SWINFORD
CW4	FRANCIS A SZVERRA

T

CW2	TIMOTHY J TAAFFE
CW3	HAROLD A TABERNER
CW3	TIMOTHY E TAETS
CW2	FAYE E TAGEANT
CW3	BRUCE T TAIJI
CW3	ROLAND F TAITANO
CW2	FRANK J TALBOT

CW3	LOUIS J TALBOT
WO1	GREGORY A TALBOTT
WO1	RANDALL P TALLEY
CWO	JOHN M TALLO,II
CW2	ROBERT E TALMADGE
CW3	MICHAEL TANNENBAUM
CW3	JAMES L TANNER
CW3	JERRY H TANNHAUSER
CW2	EDMUND TANNINI
CW4	RICHARD L TARBOX,SR
CW3	ALLAN S TARDIFF
CW2	SHAWN J TARDY
CW4	CHARLES R TARR
CW2	JULIUS M TARR
CW2	ALVIN L TASWELL
WO1	ALEXANDER TAYLOR
CW3	CANDACE L TAYLOR
CW3	DALE C TAYLOR
CW4	DANIEL L W TAYLOR
CW4	DEWEY M TAYLOR
CW2	EARL TAYLOR
CW5	EDWIN B TAYLOR
CW4	FREDERICK J TAYLOR
WO1	JAMES R TAYLOR
CW4	JERRY E TAYLOR
CW3	JOHN F TAYLOR
CW4	JOHN V TAYLOR
CW2	JOY D D TAYLOR
WO1	MICHAEL H TAYLOR
CW3	NORRIS H TAYLOR
CW4	P DAVID TAYLOR
CW4	RICHARD W TAYLOR
CW2	ROBERT L TAYLOR
WO1	SHANNON M TAYLOR
CW4	THOMAS E TAYLOR
CW2	THOMAS RAY TAYLOR
CW3	WILLIAM A TAYLOR
CW2	BOOKER M TAYLOR,JR
CW2	CHARLES A TEACHEY
CW2	JOY Y TEAGLE
CW5	ROBERT C TEBBETTS
CW2	MICHAEL A TEELON
CW4	KENT L TEEPLES
CW5	BRADLEY D TEITELBAUM
CW2	JOSE E TEJEDA
CW3	CHARLES H TEMPLE
CW2	CHARLES R TEMPLETON
CW4	RICHARD E TENNEY
CW2	LEVI A TERBIO
CW2	HARRY TERIBURY
CW3	EDWARD J TERIFAY,SR
CW4	WILLIAM E TERRELL
CW3	MICHAEL H TETHER
CW4	ELMER J TEW
WO1	PRINCIDO TEXIDOR
CW2	HAROLD A THACKER
CW3	HELEN A THAXTON
WO1	ERICK G THEK
WO1	FREDERICK E THEOBALD
CW2	RAYMOND P THERRIAULT
CW3	RICHARD R THETFORD
CW2	CARL A THOMAS
CW4	JAMES RUTHERFORD THOMAS
CW3	JOHN R THOMAS
WO1	PATRICK J THOMAS
CW5	RODNEY M THOMAS
CW2	RUTH A THOMAS
WO1	VINCENT THOMAS
CW5	WILLIAM K THOMAS
CW3	WILLIE J THOMAS
CW4	EARNEST THOMAS,JR
CW3	ARTHUR E THOMPKINS
CW3	GEORGE N THOMPSON
CW3	GRANT THOMPSON
CW3	JAMES E THOMPSON
CW2	LYNDA C THOMPSON
CW2	PATRICK M THOMPSON
CW2	PHILIP G THOMPSON
CW4	ROBERT H THOMPSON
CW3	TOMMIE N THOMPSON
CW3	JOSEPH A THORNBURG
CW2	JAMES E THORNE
CW3	KATHLEEN THORNTON-HIRSCH
WO1	TONEY THREATT
CW4	ROBERT THURMAN
CW2	ROBERT J THURSTON,JR
CW5	LLOYD N THYEN
CW3	BERNARD E TIBBETTS
CW4	JOHNNIE TIDWELL
WO1	MARK C TIEMAN
CW4	MICHAEL B TIGGES
CW3	JORGE TIJERINA
CW4	PAUL J TILLEY
WO1	ROBERT P TILLISCH
WO1	JOANN M TIMM
CW3	JOHN A TIMM
CW3	STEPHEN A TIMMONS
CW4	JIMMY W TINER
WO1	RICHARD F TINGLEY
WO1	GUY L TIRK
WO1	FREDERICK R TOBISCH
CW4	TERRY W TODD
WO1	JAMES TOEPKE
CW3	JAMES TOLBERT
CW3	ROY TOLBERT
CW3	ROY A TOLLE
CW3	JOE G TOLSON
CW2	JOHN J TOMANIO,JR
CW2	MICHAEL GLENN TOMES
WO1	MARK A TOMEUCCI
CW3	GLENN W TOMLINSON
WO1	HECTOR A TOMLINSON
CW2	MARY D TOMPKINS
CW3	JOHN H TOOLEY
WO1	ROBERT B TOOMBS
WO1	DAVID A TOOMEY
WO1	ISRAEL C TORO
CW2	CARLOS C TORRES
WO1	ELIVD A TORRES
WO1	WILFREDO GONZALEZ TORRES
WO1	ANTOLIN TORRES,JR
CW3	MICHAEL E TOTER
CW3	ERNEST TOUMPAS
CW3	JAMES M TOWNSEND
CW3	JOHN F TOWRY
CW3	LARRY K TRACHT
CW4	WILLIAM J TRAINER
CW4	THOMAS P TRAINOR,III
WO1	JOSEPH C TRANFAGLIA,JR
CW2	JEFFREY J TRAPP
CW3	RICHARD L TREADWAY
CW4	WILLIAM M TREAT
CW5	ROBERT W TRETTER
WO1	DALE L TREXLER
WO1	WILLIAM J TRIPP
CW3	RONDEL H TRITT
CW3	STEVEN J TRONNES
CW2	ROBERT A TRONTI
CW4	STEPHEN J TROTTER
WO1	DAVID E TROUTMAN
CW5	LAWRENCE G TRUEAX
CW3	LAMAR TRUSSELL
CW2	KIRK R TSCHIDA
WO1	SANCHAI T TUBTIM
CW3	EDRYCE N TUCKER
WO1	GERALD E TUCKER
CW2	NERO J TUCKER
CW3	ROBERT M TUCKER
WO1	BRUCE TUDMANN
WO1	CARRIE E TUNING
CW4	VICENTE R TUR-ROJAS
CW5	DAVID A TURLEY
CW3	STEPHEN C TURLEY
CW3	MICHAEL R TURNER
CW4	RALPH TURNER
CW3	KEN TUTHILL
CW2	DANIEL C TUTTLE
CW3	ROY D TUTTLE
WO1	KRISTIN TVEDT
CW3	MARK L TWIGG
CW4	FRED V TWITTY
CW4	WILLIAM L TWOHIG
CW3	ASHLEY S TYLER
	ALEX TYMS,SR

U

CW5	GLENN S UCHIYAMA
WO1	HEIDI UDWARY
CW4	MAYNARD M UHLIG
CW3	DONALD E UMLAUF
CW4	RONALD L UNDERHILL,JR
	FREDDIE L UNDERWOOD
CW2	RUSSELL A UNDERWOOD
CW4	SMITH D UNDERWOOD,JR
CW4	GEROLD J UNRUH
WO1	SAUL URDIALES
CW3	DONALD L URISTA
WO1	RONALD P URSO
CW2	WILLIAM W USRY
WO1	DAVID R UTTER

V

CW3	ROBERT M VACHON
CW2	TOMMY J VADEN
CW2	DANNY W VALE
WO1	ANDRES ELIAS VALENZUELA
CW4	ROY A VALIANT
CW2	DENNISSE VALLELLANES
CW3	DAVID L VanAGTMAEL
CW4	ANTHONY VanALSTINE
CW2	JAMES F VANAS
CW3	GERALD L VANCE
CW5	LARRY W VanCLEVE
CW3	RICHARD A VANDERMOLEN
WO1	DIRK C VANDERNEYDEN
CW2	HARLAND L VANDERPOOL
CW4	JOSEPH A VANDERVEST,JR
CW4	LEROY J VanDOREN
CW4	LENNY VanDORP
WO1	RYAN G VanDYCK
CW2	MIGUEL H VANEGAS
CW5	BEN A VanETTEN
CW5	NATHAN B VanKEUREN
CW3	MELVIN R VANSTEENWYK
CW2	RUTH A VanSTEENWYK
CW2	DEBORAH J VARGA
CW2	PAUL J VARIAN
CW3	MARK E VARNEY
CW2	MANUEL D VASQUEZ
WO1	RUBEN VASQUEZ
CW2	PAUL J VASTA
CW4	RAYMOND A VAUGHAN
CW3	WILLIAM G VAUJIN
CW5	WILLIAM F VAWTER
CW4	WILLIAM VAZQUEZ-ARADAS
CW4	RAFAEL VEGA
CW4	JOSEPH V VEIGA,JR
CW2	SCOTT A VELAZQUEZ
WO1	ELLIOTT J VELEZ
CW2	ANTHONY B VENEY
CW3	VINCENT VENTORINO
CW4	WILLIAM H VERNOR
WO1	GARY F VERNUM
WO1	LUIS ANTONIO VIERA
CW3	PEDRO N VIERA
CW2	TIMOTHY S VIEREGGE
CW2	ROBERT M VIERS
CW2	JOSE A VILLEGAS
CW4	ATELANO VILLON
WO1	KELLY A VINAL
CW5	GEORGE F VINCENT
WO1	JAY W VINCENT
CW4	JOEL S VINSANT
CW2	LEODINDO DS VIRAY
WO1	MEAGHAN VOGEL
CW4	ROBERT C VOGES
CW5	RALEIGH L VOIGHT,JR
CW5	JOEL J VOISINE
CW2	ERIC G VonBOSSE
WO1	ROBIN M VOZAR
CW3	MICHAEL J VOZEL
CW4	TIMOTHY J VREEMAN
CW4	JOSEPH A VUMBICO

W

WO1	ALAN K WADDELL
CW2	ANTHONY T WADE
CW4	EARL WADE
WO1	GEORGE M WADE
CW5	JOHN T WADE
CW2	WILLIAM J WAGGENER
CW2	BETTY G WAGNER-MALLARD
WO1	RICHARD N WAHL
CW4	ROBERT J WAHL
CW3	GORDON W WAHLGREN
CW4	ROBERT WAHLUND
CW3	HARVEY C WAIT
WO1	DARWIN E WAKEFIELD,JR
CW2	RONALD WALCZAK
CW4	LARRY E WALDRON
CW4	DENNIS M WALES
CW2	BERNICE L WALKER
CW3	DAVID B WALKER
CW4	DONALD G WALKER
CW2	FREDERICK L WALKER
CW2	GAREY D WALKER
CW3	GENE WALKER
CW3	JAMIE L WALKER
CW3	JOHN C WALKER
CW2	JOHNNY L WALKER
WO1	NATHANIEL L WALKER
CW4	OSCAR L WALKER
WO1	SHIRLEY A WALKER
CW4	THEODORE A WALKER
WO1	TONY L WALKER
CW4	WAYNE K WALKER
WO1	WILLIAM D WALKER
WO1	WILLIAM K WALKER
CW2	JEFFERY S WALLACE
CW3	JOHN D WALLACE
CW2	TYMAN M WALLACE
CW2	BARBARA J WALSH
CW4	BRYAN M WALSH
CW3	WILLIAM F WALSH
CW3	AMOS WALSTON,JR
CW2	CLARE L WALTERS
CW4	GERALD A WALTERS
CW4	JOHNNIE L WALTERS
CW3	JOHNNIE LEE WALTERS
CW4	MARVIN M WALTERS
CW4	KENNETH H WALTON
CW3	ERIC L WALTZ
CW4	DAVID C WARD
CW2	DAVID T WARD
CW2	MICHAEL L WARD
CW3	OWEN S WARGO
CW3	ROBERT H WARKENTIN
CW3	BRENT C WARNOCK
WO1	VIRGINIA L WARRELL
CW3	LARRY D WARREN
CW3	ROBERT L WARREN
CW4	HOWARD L WARRINGTON,JR
WO1	ALOIS J WARZECHA
CW3	HOMER H WASHINGTON
CW3	GORDON E WATANABE
WO1	JAMES T WATKINS
CW2	MICHAEL L WATKINS
CW3	STEPHEN E WATKINS
WO1	CLINTON K WATSON
CW3	KENNETH WATSON
CW3	KENT THOMAS WATSON

CW2	RHONDA F WATSON
CW2	DAVID D WATTS
CW3	GABRIEL WATTS
CW2	JOHN A WATTS
CW2	EMMETT WAYNE
CW4	KALMATH G WEATHERFORD
WO1	LYNN A WEATHERSPOON
CW2	CAROLYN B WEAVER
CW2	ROBERT C WEAVER
CW4	WILLIAM L WEAVER
CW4	CHARLES C WEBB
WO1	CHARLES EDWARD WEBB
CW4	EDWARD C WEBB
CW2	MICHAEL WEBB
WO1	RANDY A WEBB
CW3	ALONZO M WEBBER
CW3	KIRK D WEBBER
CW4	MAJOR E WEBER
CW2	SUSAN M WEBSTER
WO1	CHARLES E WEEKLEY
CW4	L E WEIDELL
CW2	MICHAEL D WEIGART
CW2	FRED K WEIGEL
CW4	CHRISTIAN J WEINHOLTZ,JR
CW3	WAYNE J WEIS
WO1	CHARLES J WEISS
CW3	MICHAEL E WEIST
CW2	JOSEPH M WELCH
CW4	MAYNARD L WELCH
WO1	ROBERT S WELCH
CW2	SEAN H WELCH
WO1	KARLA M WELDING
CW3	MARTIN H WELDON
WO1	BILL R WELKER
CW2	ROGER L WELLES
CW3	JAMES B WELLING
CW4	HARRY M WELLS
CW4	JIM WELLS
CW3	MARY K WELLS
WO1	MICHAEL J WELLS
WO1	WILLIAM STEWART WELLS
CW3	DAVID WELLS,JR
CW5	DAVID P WELSH
CW5	DONALD R WELSH
CW4	ROBERT K WELTON
CW2	STEVEN R WENSMAN
CW2	GERALD J WENTWORTH
CW2	PAUL W WERE
WO1	JENNIFER J WERNER
WO1	MICHAEL WERNER
CW4	PAUL D WESSELER
CW3	DANIEL S WEST
CW3	ROBERT J WEST
CW5	WAYNE E WEST
CW3	JAMES T WESTBERRY
WO1	JOHN A WESTBROOK
CW2	ALI L WESTBY
CW3	FEDERICO D WESTERN
CW2	BOYD WESTFALL
CW2	WALLACE J WESTFALL
CW2	BOBBIE C WESTWICK
WO1	NANCY R WEX
WO1	REATA M WEYRICH
CW2	JOHN A WHALEN
CW4	RONALD J WHALEN
CW5	ROBERT J WHATLEY
CW4	CHARLES WHEELER
WO1	DONALD P WHEELER
WO1	NANCY L WHETSTONE
CW3	EDWARD V WHITAKER
CW2	ALTON L WHITE
CW3	DANNY O WHITE
CW5	DAVID L WHITE
CW2	DAVID LEE WHITE
CW3	DEVON WHITE
CW2	DOUGLAS A WHITE
CW4	EDMUND M WHITE
CW5	FRANK E WHITE
CW3	JAMES T WHITE
CW3	KENNETH E WHITE
CW2	LEONARD H WHITE

CW3	ROBERT C WHITE
CW4	ROBERT F WHITE
WO1	RODNEY A WHITE
CW3	WILLIAM S WHITE
CW3	PRESTON WHITE,JR
CW4	WILLIAM G WHITE,JR
CW2	STEVE A WHITECOTTON
CW2	TROY M WHITEHEAD
CW3	MICHAEL A WHITELEY
WO1	TIMOTHY E WHITFIELD
CW3	BOB WHITFORD
CW4	JOHN R WHITLOW
CW4	DOUGLAS WHITMIRE
CW4	JOHN G WHITTIER
CW3	MARK W WHITTINGTON
WO1	KEITH R WHITTLE
MW4	DONALD W WIDMAN
CW3	STEVEN M WIDMER
CW4	DARRELL WIEBESICK
CW2	JUDY E WIECHERT
WO1	MICHAEL A WIECHERT
CW4	JOHN H WIEDERECHT
CW2	ALBERT R WIGGINS
CW3	JAMES WIGGINS
CW4	CHARLES WIGGLESWORTH
CW2	CURTIS L WILCOX,JR
CW2	RICHARD L WILDER
CW4	KEVIN L WILDMAN
CW4	ROGER W WILF
CW2	LEONARD L WILFONG
CW4	DONALD E WILGUS
CW4	THOMAS D WILHARBER
CW2	WILLIE WILKES
MW4	WILLIAM A WILKINS
CW3	DANIEL WILKINSON
CW4	LARRY J WILLETTE
CW4	MARY E WILLIAMEE
WO1	ANDRE Q WILLIAMS
CW3	ANTHONY R WILLIAMS
CW4	DAVID E WILLIAMS
CW4	DAVID L WILLIAMS
CW2	DAVIE R WILLIAMS
CW4	DENNIS R WILLIAMS
CW2	ERNEST L WILLIAMS
WO1	GARY L WILLIAMS
CW2	JIMMY R WILLIAMS
CW5	JOHN H WILLIAMS
WO1	KEITH L WILLIAMS
CW2	LYLE D WILLIAMS
WO1	MICHAEL M WILLIAMS
CW3	PAUL L WILLIAMS
CW5	RICHARD L WILLIAMS
WO1	SHAY WILLIAMS
CW3	ZACKARY R WILLIAMS
WO1	EDDIE WILLIAMS,III
CW4	WILLIAM W WILLIAMS,IV
	ARTHUR WILLIAMS,JR
WO1	JOHN F WILLIAMS,JR
CW3	LEON WILLIAMS,JR
CW2	LEWIS WILLIAMS,JR
WO1	JOE F WILLIAMS,SR
CW5	NATHANIEL W WILLIAMSON
CW4	SUSAN P WILLIG
CW3	JOHN M WILLINGHAM
CW4	B SCOTT WILSON
CW3	CHRISTOPHER P WILSON
WO1	JAMES ELBERT WILSON
CW3	JAMES M WILSON
WO1	JOHN ARNOLD WILSON
WO1	LEWIS S WILSON
WO1	MELODY L WILSON
CW3	MICHAEL D WILSON
CW4	PAUL R WILSON
CW5	ROBERT E WILSON
WO1	SAMMY WILSON
CW2	TERRY M WILSON
CW3	WILLIAM D WILSON
CW3	GEORGE L WILSON,JR
CW2	WILLIAM E WILTFONG

WO1	JOE WILTZ
CW3	WARREN D WILVERT
WO1	BENITA AUDREY WIMBERLY
CW3	KENT WINGFIELD
WO1	DOUGLAS R WINQUIST
CW4	NAILOR R WINSTON,JR
CW4	HENRY M WINTER,JR
CW4	WILLIAM F WINTERS
CW2	PHYLLIS A WINTON
WO1	DALE A WIPPLER
CW3	CURTIS F WISNIEWSKI
CW4	R BRYAN WITHERS
CPT	CHARLES E WITTGES
CW4	KENNETH WITTMAN
CW2	THEODOR WITZEL
CW4	HERBERT WOBITO
CW5	MATTHEW A WOJDAK,JR
CW3	MONTE LEE WOLD
CW5	MELVIN E WOLFF
CW4	GEORGE R WOLTMAN
CW3	RANDY WONDERLICH
CW3	DWIGHT L WONGUS
WO1	CHRISTOPHER D WOOD
WO1	FREDERICK G WOOD
CW3	WILLIAM A WOOD
WO1	WILLIAM R WOOD
CW2	GRADY L WOOD,JR
CW2	CHARLES D WOODARD
CW3	STEPHEN M WOODBURN
CW4	FREDRICK C WOODLAND,JR
CW2	SYLVESTER L WOODLEY
CW3	GARY T WOODRICK
CW5	DONALD W WOODRUFF
CW2	BOBBY L WOODS
CW4	JAMES C WOODS
WO1	JESSE J WOODS
CW3	JOHN R WOODS
CW4	ROGER J WOODS
CW4	THOMAS R WOODS
MW4	WILBUR L WOODS
CW2	JAMES L WOODWARD
WO1	JAMES A WOOF
CW3	J D WOOLARD
CW3	TOM B WOOLERY
CW2	CHARLES K WOOLLEY
CW2	HAROLD G WORKMAN
CW4	KERRI L WORKMAN
CW3	JOHN L WORLING
WO1	DEDDRICK J WORTHY
CW3	STEVEN J WORTLEY
CW4	GEORGE M WRAY
CW4	SAMUEL W WRAY
CW4	BRIAN K WREDE
CW5	RICHARD E WREDE
CW3	CHARLES L WRIGHT
CW3	JAMES H WRIGHT
WO1	JASON K WRIGHT
CW4	JOHN DAVID WRIGHT
CW3	KENNETH R WRIGHT
CW4	WILLIAM D WRIGHT
CW4	WILLIAM R WRIGHT
CW5	BENJAMIN WRIGHT,JR
CW2	NATHAN C WRISTON
CW4	ROBERT J WURM
WO1	ALAN C WYATT
CW4	RICHARD W WYCKOFF
CW2	MARK K WYKOFF
CW4	MICHAEL C WYMAN
CW3	ROGER B WYNN
CW3	JAMES J WYNNE

Y

CW3	ROBERT T YANDALL
CW4	RALPH M YANDLE
CW2	DOROTHY J YARDE
WO1	NORMAN RUSSELL YARDE
CW2	DAVID YATES
WO1	GEORGE D YATES
W01	JAMES L YATES

CW4	EDWARD A YATSKO
CW4	ARLESTER YEAGER
CW3	JUDITH D YEATMAN
WO1	JONATHAN O YERBY
1LT	MICHAEL A YERKIC
WO1	CHONG K YIM
CW2	MORRIS L YOCKEY
CW4	CHARLES W YORK
WO1	MATTHEW J YOUNG
CW3	OTIS J YOUNG
CW3	RICHARD N YOUNG
CW3	ROBERT A YOUNG
CW4	STUART YOUNG
CW5	WILLIAM F YOUNG
CW3	JACK D YOUNGS
CW2	JAY L YOURA
CW4	PAUL J YOVIENE
CW2	ADRIAN YUNSON

Z

CW4	RAYMOND H ZACHOW
CW4	MICHAEL A ZAGYVA
CW3	MICHAEL E ZANTOW
WO1	DAVID ZARRELLA
WO1	JOHN C ZAUN
CW4	RICHARD F ZAWALSKI
WO1	MIGUEL A ZAYAS
CW4	JAMES M ZEITLER
WO1	GLENN J ZEMANEK
CW4	EDMUND E ZIELINSKI
CW3	JOSEPH J ZIELINSKI
CW5	JOHN F ZIMMERMAN
WO1	SCOTT J ZINDA
CW2	GREGORY J ZINK
CW3	JOHN S ZIOLKOWSKI,JR
CW4	BUTCH ZIRPOLO
CW4	EDWARD W ZLOTKOWSKI
LTC	DAMIAN J ZOLIK
CW2	STEVEN M ZURICK

Index

The roster and the individual biographies were not included in this index since they appear in alphabetical order in their respective sections.

143

Ft. Rucker, AL. MW4 David Helton (center) is promoted to CW5 by MG Dave Robinson, Commanding General, Aviation Center; BG Robert Goodbarry, Deputy CG; and Mrs. Betty Helton on October 1, 1992 before 500 newly appointed warrant officers and invited guests in an impressive appointment and promotion ceremony.